T0314242

The Deportation Express

AMERICAN CROSSROADS

Edited by Earl Lewis, George Lipsitz, George Sánchez, Dana Takagi, Laura Briggs, and Nikhil Pal Singh

The Deportation Express

A HISTORY OF AMERICA THROUGH FORCED REMOVAL

Ethan Blue

UNIVERSITY OF CALIFORNIA PRESS

University of California Press
Oakland, California

© 2021 by Ethan Blue

Library of Congress Cataloging-in-Publication Data
Names: Blue, Ethan, author.
Title: The deportation express : a history of America through forced removal
    / Ethan Blue.
Other titles: American crossroads ; 61. Description: Oakland, California :
    University of California Press, [2021] | Series: American crossroads ; 61 |
    Includes bibliographical references and index.
Identifiers: LCCN 2020058518 | ISBN 9780520304444 (cloth) |
    ISBN 9780520973107 (epub)
Subjects: LCSH: Deportation—United States—History. | Imprisonment—
    United States—History. | Immigrants—United States—Social conditions.
Classification: LCC JV6483.B59 2021 | DDC 364.6/8—dc23
LC record available at https://lccn.loc.gov/2020058518

Manufactured in the United States of America

30   29   28   27   26   25   24   23   22   21
10   9   8   7   6   5   4   3   2   1

*The publisher and the University of California Press
Foundation gratefully acknowledge the generous support of the
Peter Booth Wiley Endowment Fund in History.*

CONTENTS

ILLUSTRATIONS

FIGURES

MAPS

ACKNOWLEDGMENTS

Most of this book was written on unceded and sovereign Wahdjuk Nyoongar boodja, where I have lived since 2005. Before that, I was raised on Coast Miwok land. I have benefited from being a settler/invader twice over, at least. My own travel from the United States to Australia for work was difficult. I missed friends and family, my children were (and are) distant from their grandparents, and it's hard to get back to US archives and scholarly communities. But mine can only count among the most privileged migrations in the world.

I arrived in Perth as a married, cisgender, straight white man, whose migration was sponsored by a prestigious employer. The Australian government judged my health to be adequate, and my criminal record—after a misstep when the FBI said my fingerprints were "unclassifiable"—was clean enough that I arrived with enormously elusive permanent resident status in a nation deeply structured by settler colonial violence and anti-immigrant animus. I am grateful to my friends, comrades, aunties, and uncles in and around the First Nations Deaths in Custody Watch Committee for helping me to better understand what it means to struggle for justice in this land and beyond. I have been particularly grateful for the opportunity to learn from and to walk together with Uncle Ben Cuimermarre Taylor AM, Auntie Helen Corbett, Auntie Carolyn Kelly-Lewis, Auntie Carol Roe, Anne Annear, Paul Kaplan, and the late Marc Newhouse.

Friends, colleagues, and students gave invaluable feedback on papers, chapter drafts, in classes, and just in passing. Some are still at the University of Western Australia, while others have moved on. Thanks to Milda Whitaker, Richard Small, Michelle Tucson, and Traci Taylor, without whom the university and the School of Arts could not function. Thanks too to Clarissa

Ball, David Barrie, Harry Blagg, Andrew Broertjes, Sue Broomhall, Fausto Butta, Phil Chilton, Ann Curthoys, Ned Curthoys, Sarah Collins, Rob Cover, Tanya Dalziell, John Docker, Kirk Essary, Giuseppe Finaldi, Farida Fozdar, Rahul Gariola, Andrea Gaynor, Sam Han, Tauel Harper, Nick Harney, Tony Hughes D'Aeth, Shino Konishi, John Kinder, Michael Levine, Alexandra Ludewig, Jane Lydon, Jeremy Martens, Shalmalee Palekar, Lorenzo Polizotto, Nadia Rhook, David Savat, Bill Taylor, Kati Tonkin, Jacqueline Van Gent, Richard Vokes, and Brenda Walker. Gordon Flake at the Perth-US Asia Center has been a solid advocate since his arrival in Perth. Lauren Caterson, Amy Pracilio, and Vanessa Sofoulis provided wonderful research assistance. A University of Western Australia research grant, teaching relief, and study leave provided crucial time and space for thinking, reading, and writing. The Australian Academy for the Humanities is waging a valiant struggle to support the humanities and education in Australia, and it also supported this project at a very early stage with a Traveling Fellowship.

Further afield, and thanks to those travels, I've benefited from support and conversations that are too many to mention. I was fortunate to be a research fellow at the University of Michigan's Eisenberg Institute for Historical Studies, whose participants demonstrated a remarkable model of university life. Thanks to Ron Suny, Karen Auerbach, Kevin Gaines, Matt Lassiter, Gregory Parker, Ronen Steinberg, Alexandra Minna Stern, Penny M. Von Eschen, and Steven Ward. Stephen Berrey heard the earliest musings and read the full manuscript at a late stage and deserves special note.

I was also lucky to spend a sabbatical at Stanford University's Center for Spatial and Textual Analysis. Zephyr Frank, Celena Allen, Nicholas Bausch, Matt Bryant, Richard White, Gabriel Wolfstein, and Erik Steiner were gracious hosts while I absorbed as much as I could about spatial history. Kimberly Krebs, Gabriela Levikow, Fangzhou Liu, and Yesid Castro poured over documents, helped build spatio-temporal databases, and offered ways to think through how to visualize them.

Dedicated archivists helped the project immensely. Zack Wilske and Marian Smith, historians at US Citizenship and Immigration Services, were generous with their knowledge of the Department of Labor and Immigration records, and Bill Creech shared more of the same on the ground at the National Archives in Washington, DC. Anna Kaplan and Robb Hill helped with research at the National Archives when I could not be there myself. Cara Moore, an archivist at the National Archives and Records Administration–Saint Louis branch, offered outstanding support from afar. Kate Hutchins and Julie Herrada guided me through the riches at the Joseph A. Labadie Collection at the University of Michigan. Thanks also to Marje Schuetze-Coburn and Joy Kim at the University of Southern California East Asian Library's Henry DeYoung Collection, Mary Wallace at Wayne State University's Walter P. Reuther Library, Simon Elliott with University of California at Los Angeles Charles E. Young Library Special Collections, Scott Sandberg at Indiana University Northwest's Calumet Regional Archives, Carlos Cortez at the University of Texas at San Antonio, and Daniel Hartwig and Tim Noakes at Stanford University Library Special Collections. And while I was in Washington, DC, Steven Galpern and Patti Simon provided wonderful friendship and accommodation.

The distance between Perth and most other venues means that conversations at conferences, with editors and collaborators, have been all the more precious. Many thanks to Thomas Adams, Norwood Andrews, Luis Alvarez, Benjamin Balthasar, Brian Benhken, Rachel Ida Buff, Robert Chase, Suchetana Chattopadhyay, Ben Chappell, Frances Clarke, Clare Corbould, Leon Fink, Mark Finnane, Neil Foley, Ruth Wilson Gilmore, Gareth Griffiths, Sarah Gleason-White, Tanya Golash-Boza, Cindy Hahamovitch, Christina Heatherton, Charles Heller, David Hernández, Kelly Lytle Hernández, Madeline Hsu, Moon-Ho Jung, Andy Kaladelfos, Daniel Kanstroom, Marilyn Lake, Julian Lim, Jenna Loyd, Ann McGrath, Mike McDonnell, Karl Hagstom Miller, Klaus Neumann, Phillip Mead, Mae Ngai, Naomi Paik, Sharon Pickering, Andonis Piperogolou, Lorenzo Pezzani, Jean Pfaelzer, Samuel K. Roberts, Gilberto Rosas, Chantel Rodriguez, Scott Saul, Micol Seigel, Tyrone R. Simpson, Nayan Shah, Yorick Smaal, Gregory Smithers, Patrick Timmons, Andrew Urban, Lea VanderVelde, William Walters, Leanne Weber, Shane White, Daniel Widener, Elliott Young, and Kenyon Zimmer.

Staff and readers at the University of California Press have been wonderful in shepherding an ungainly project to completion. Thanks to Niels Hooper, Madison Wetzell, Laura Briggs, George Lipsitz, Torrie Hester, Rachel Buff (again), the unnamed readers, and particularly to Megan Pugh for wonderful editorial help and Bill Nelson for his maps.

My deepest thanks go to my family. Griff and Mary and the greater Garwoods are an inspiration. Patty Blue-Garni and Don Garni, Adam and Jenny Blue and Alisa Garni and Frank Weyher: thank you all. This book is dedicated to Zadie and Amaya, and to Shae Garwood, with love, wherever our travels take us.

Introduction

A WHITE BUS PACKED with men, women, and children departs from a private detention center. There are bars across the bus windows. The passengers are in chains. Eventually the bus stops at a small airfield, one among the recent proliferation of Immigration and Customs Enforcement deportation hubs that include Alexandria, Louisiana; San Antonio, Texas; and Mesa, Arizona. Often wearing whatever they were arrested in, the deportees, hobbled by shackles, climb down from the bus. Older children with school backpacks reach toward their parents, younger ones drowse in their parents' arms, crowded by the straps of purses and duffel bags. Red mesh sacks, what counts as luggage for many, slouch beside the tattered suitcases of those who had time to gather their things.

Private guards from the detention center and federal officials in dark windbreakers shepherd the families across the tarmac and to the rolling staircase to a Boeing 737, provided by Swift Airlines or another private contractor. They remove the prisoners' leg irons—there is nowhere to run on an airplane—and gather them for the next busload. As has already happened again and again in their jails, guards pat down the deportees' pockets and look into their mouths, one last bodily indignity to endure on American soil. In 2016 the United States deported more than 110,000 people on chartered flights, and 6,100 more on commercial airlines.[1] In the twenty-first century—an age of mass migration, mass deportation, and mass incarceration—flying "ICE Air" has become an American journey—as American, perhaps, as apple pie in a prison mess hall.

Aboard the plane, a mix of fear, anxiety, and nerves. Seatbelts are fastened beneath shackled hands and compete for space with waist chains. Many of the passengers have never flown before. Others were shuttled between a dizzying number of detention centers, where they were locked for long periods. The blue fabric seats, the white-pebbled plastic trays, crowd close. Suffice to say, there is no first-class cabin on ICE Air. Economy, after all, is the point. ICE flight attendants spray cloying air freshener into the plane, thin cover for the underlying odor of bodies and long-unwashed clothes. Passengers have at best limited access to the toilet on a journey that can last from a few hours to half a day, depending on the number of stops the plane makes. Through the engine's incessant whine, beyond airsickness or turbulence to come, the deportees pass the time, planning how to survive the coming months and if or how to return to the United States, where they can try to make a life again. They get a meal in a cardboard box. It can't be easy to eat.

Officials laud the efficiency and speed of removal aboard the planes, framing their collaborations with private contractors like Swift Air as a dynamic and welcome innovation. Acting Director of ICE Matt Albence, aware of widespread protests over grim conditions in immigrant detention and removal, quipped about how much deportees enjoy the amenities: "They're smiling!... This is probably better than some of the commercial airlines I fly on." Television crews don't film deportees' faces. Any smiles, perhaps at the thought of reunion with family and friends from whom they have long been apart, must be tempered by worries about how they'll make ends meet. They left their homes in Guatemala, El Salvador, Ecuador, or elsewhere, because life had been too dangerous, or too wracked by poverty, to survive. In addition to the brute fact of forced removal, one man reported that guards deliberately "tried to make us feel bad." And even when guards are friendly, it's clear enough to all that this airplane is a mobile prison. No one doubts that there is a can of mace just behind the sprayed potpourri.[2]

Flash back a century ago, and you could encounter a similar scene. Rather than boarding an airplane, the group of deportees would have been forced onto a reconfigured Pullman tourist train car, administered by the Immigration Bureau and the Department of Labor. Today's ICE Air 737s are slightly aging but certainly serviceable for the advanced infrastructure of global air travel. A century ago, the Pullman cars had seen some miles, but they were sturdy too. They had been designed in 1907 and introduced for service in 1910. The train's steel frames were a safety improvement on wooden carriages of an earlier era, and featured electrical light and a low-pressure vapor heat system. By

1917, Pullman cars advertised "innumerable hidden mechanisms" designed to make travel more comfortable. An individual car contained "nearly a mile of laminated copper wire, over a half mile of pipes," as well as a dizzying number of switches, circuit boards, dynamos, motors, ventilators, push-buttons, "and other apparatuses."[3] Enthusiasts of the day could marvel at the train's feats of mechanical and electrical engineering, and ordinary passengers on Pullman cars enjoyed the comforts appropriate to the tickets that their budgets—or race, given Jim Crow regulations—allowed.[4]

Pullman train cars were wonders of modern technological development, and after 1914 they were updated for deportation traffic with bars across the windows. Deportation trains were prison cars. Like ICE airplanes, once the doors were shut and the wheels turning, the trains were closed vessels, conveniently suited to forced travel. Guards and matrons—hard men and stern women from the immigration bureau, or on loan from the Southern Pacific Railroad or another train company—were stationed at each end of the carriage and walked up and down the aisles, prepared if they thought any of the deportees got out of hand.[5]

One trip in 1920 had around forty deportees aboard, gathered from state hospitals, prisons, or jails. In Portland, Oregon, immigration agents brought aboard a Turkish man, whom the trip's doctor described as a "weazened [sic] dark skinned little fellow of about a hundred pounds...well dressed in a black suit and panama hat" who was being deported "because he had been a procurer." Another was a Spaniard, convicted of violating the White Slavery Act. Three Germans were also added to the train. It was in the wake of the First World War, and one young man had been at Alcatraz, presumably a prisoner of war. The two older German men had been in asylums in Oregon and Washington. Another was an Italian convicted of bootlegging.[6] In Pendleton, Oregon, an insane Italian man was brought aboard, and in Omaha, Nebraska, additional deportees included insane Bulgarian and Canadian men.[7] In Chicago, immigration agents brought aboard five more deportees, including a "middle aged Italian with long black moustache and wild flashing eyes full of resentment." He was being deported along with his four-year-old son, "who was likewise wide eyed with wonder at being placed in such surroundings." There was also a "blank faced Finn," a "dull countenanced Swede," and an anarchist, for whom the guards showed particular disdain.[8]

Newspapers of the day covered deportation traffic, much as the occasional story runs about ICE Air today, but some of the richest descriptions come from novelist Theodore Irwin, who recounted a deportation journey in his 1935 book *Strange Passage*. In the book's opening scene, Paul, an artist and the male protagonist, describes the smell of the train: "The disinfectant in the air—these men from the county jails seem to breathe it out. The smell from our bodies—we haven't bathed in a long time. The foodstaleness—from the stuff some have taken along. The scent of five-and-ten powder on the women. The baby. The burned coal. The lavatories, open-doored." Paul imagines how he would paint the scene: "I would have to find new colors, all of them muddied with a dung-brown smear."[9] The astringent cut of disinfectant, a result of the medical controls to which they had been subject and dangers of bacteriological contagion. That the passage ends with a sense of shit—smeared, no less—reveals much about not just the reality of closely packed bodies but also how people facing deportation in this earlier era were perceived. The novel's opening passages conclude by describing the train as a living, convulsing beast, consuming and vomiting undesirable aliens:

> At Spokane, at Whitefish, at Glacier Park, at other key cities over the long journey, aliens were being swallowed up; the Deportation Special was gorging itself. To the exit gate of the nation, and the train would spew out what it had swallowed along the way. Then, out with you, go back where you came from, you dago, you hunky, you scoovy, you mick, you sheenie, you limey. Get out and stay out.[10]

Between 1914 and the Second World War, the Immigration Bureau's reconfigured prison railroad cars made constant circuits around the nation, gathering so-called "undesirable aliens"—disdained for their poverty, political radicalism, criminal conviction, or insanity, perceptions compounded by maligned national and ethnoracial difference—and conveyed them to ports and borders for exile overseas. The trains were the culmination of a century's worth of immigration law, materialized in the steel of its rail networks and force of its engines, expanded in its complex links of public administrative bureaucracies and private corporate power. It was complex network—or, put another way, a politico-technical assemblage—that conjoined a host of security-oriented laws, agencies, and techniques, and enabled and extended the will and desire for an expansive understanding of national protection.[11]

The trains were mobile, carceral spaces, and their history reveals the deportees' journey as a process through which national territory, political sovereignty, and community—three defining features of modern nation-hood—were created and contested.[12] Previous deportation procedures had been violent, expensive, and relatively ad hoc.[13] But the use of the railroad—perhaps the exemplary technology of industrial modernity—facilitated the mass expulsion of the undesirable. The material capacity to deport large numbers of people—or at least to make a deportation credible threat—powerfully affected those who remained. Indeed, thanks to the train, American nativists' long-standing fantasies of immigrant exclusion and mass deportation finally appeared within reach. ICE Air is just the latest manifestation of the impetus behind the American deportation trains. This book tells the story of those trains, and of some of the people who were forced aboard them.

Along with the mounting number of restrictive immigration laws in the late nineteenth and early twentieth century, deportation was a governmental attempt to regulate the periods' unprecedented forces of global mass migration—some twenty-six million migrants arrived in the United States between 1870 and 1920—but also a means of trying to control the flows of commodities and capital, including labor, in a rapidly globalizing, racially structured economy.[14] Compared with the twenty-first-century standards, the numbers of people officially expelled in the first part of the twentieth century were small, climbing from 1,630 in 1893 to 4,741 in 1914. Official removals dipped during the First World War, and annual reports documented the more than 4,500 people with approved deportation warrants between 1915 and 1919 who could not be officially removed due to limits on oceanic travel.[15]

But expulsions from the interior accelerated in the first half of the 1920s (from 2,765 in 1920 to 9,495 in 1925) and climbed to 18,142 in 1931.[16] The numbers that the immigration bureau generated are sketchy, however, and inconsistently account for those deported under Chinese exclusion law rather than ordinary immigration law, for people who were turned back at ports of entry, and for people who were coerced into "voluntarily" removal and whose numbers were never recorded. Between 1914 and 1931, nearly 130,000 people were deported from the nation's interior to beyond its hardening borders, with the numbers climbing steadily.[17] According to the Department of Homeland Security, in the age of rail-based removal—roughly from 1914 through 1945—some 939,456 people were either "removed" or "returned" from the United States.[18]

Yet significance of rail as a means of mass removal exceeded the numbers of people expelled in any given year, because it offered anti-immigrant officials a system with the flexibility to expand or contract in response to its political or economic desires. In the century since the trains' deployment, deportation has grown into a massive regime and flashpoint of contemporary global racial political economics.[19] Removal rates skyrocketed under the Clinton, Bush, and Obama administrations—this has been a bipartisan effort undertaken by Democrats and Republicans alike—and in 2013 alone, 434,015 people were expelled. Recent Department of Homeland Security documents report more than fifty-six million "returns" and "removals" from the United States between 1892 and 2018.[20] Donald Trump and his supporters saw this as far too few, and as a result, built a far more punitive system on their predecessors' foundation.[21]

Then, as now, people who were deported from the United States were typically poorly educated and working class. They were, in the most literal sense, the United States' most marginalized peoples. Among them were the mad and the criminal; the destitute and the disabled; people who were criminalized for the location of their birth, and the passage of racist and restrictive laws, or for the beliefs they held. Underlying deportation was a persistent logic of eugenics: a notion that states should control the reproduction of their biological populations, and that "unfit," "defective," "degenerate" people should not be permitted to exist. That included people of color. Eugenicists like Lothrop Stoddard portrayed immigrants as a flood, an invasion, or as in the title his best-selling 1921 book, a "rising tide of color." Each "wave" threatened to drown an imagined American national past of racial purity and imperil the country's future. In an article called "Scum from the Melting Pot," Edwin E. Grant, a former California state senator and president of the California State Law Enforcement League, was forthright about the eugenic benefits of mass deportation. "Systematic deportation," he praised, "eugenically cleanses America of a vicious element." Grant believed the United States shone upon the world as city on a hill and that the benefits of forced removal would trickle down to the darker corners of the globe. "The moral effect upon their native countries makes deportation of offenders," he continued, "in an international sense, doubly worthwhile."[22] Harry Laughlin, of the Eugenics Records Office, echoed the sentiment in his "expert" testimony before Congress in 1928, calling deportation the "last line of defense against contamination of the American family stocks by alien hereditary degeneracy."[23]

Not everyone endorsed such outright scientific racism, but even committed liberals could embrace racist and eugenic logic when it came to forced removal. "Deportation laws are, of course, necessary," wrote reformer Ruben

Oppenheimer in 1931. "No other penalty than deportation will protect the United States from being inundated by defective, diseased, delinquent, and incorrigible persons. No other penalty will adequately discourage border jumpers or stowaways or the industry of smuggling undesirable aliens at our borders."[24] The belief in the American nation as coherent and sovereign, the insistence on the inviolability of its territory, and the desire to control the future of its population, of who might contribute to its wealth and benefit from its resources—these were ideas shared by liberals and conservatives alike.

The deportation regime described throughout this book took shape in a period when the United States was climbing to a position of global prominence, and it coincided with the accelerated integration of a modern, global, racially stratified, and industrially dominated economic world system.[25] Some explanations for America's rise celebrate an ethereal American exceptionalism, the nation's godliness and genius and capacity for democracy. Other explanations are more persuasive. In the second half of the nineteenth century, the United States had absorbed the vast wealth generated through the centuries of the anti-Black chattel slavery that fueled the US economy and reinvested it into its massive and expanding productive apparatus. That apparatus was peopled by the global working classes who had themselves been displaced from their homes in the Atlantic and Pacific worlds by the forces of imperialism, or through local variations on the global theme of industrial disruption. By the turn of the twentieth century, the United States had wrested military and political control of the western half of the continent from Native Americans and occupying Mexican colonial societies and was fully engaged in luring fresh workers from around the globe to extract wealth from the land. The United States was, structurally speaking, transforming from a relative semiperiphery to a core, if not the core, of the global economy.

Across the planet, railroads were at the center of colonial and economic accumulation. Within North America the transcontinental railroad has stood among the master symbols of the United States' social and industrial progress, and for good reason. The railroads were literal as well as metaphorical engines of US political, territorial, and economic expansion, accompanied by a boosterism that has led scholars and enthusiasts to echo grandiose claims about the "epic tale" of American railroads.[26] Testimony before the 1887 Congress's Pacific Railway Commission gave a partial list of why the transcontinental railroads should be built, but foremost among them were its military and economic potential. Rail lines would "furnish a cheaper and more rapid means of transportation for mail, troops and munitions of war," which might finally "end the Indian wars." Military capacities of rail infrastructure would also help the United States fend off rival or "foreign" imperial claims on the continent. And perhaps most important, the transcontinental rail would have inestimable economic benefits, speeding "the development of the resources of the vast and then unpeopled territory between the Missouri and Sacramento Rivers."[27]

Railroad corporations did this and more. Facilitated by the US military and paid for by US taxes and major financial institutions' investments, railroads accelerated the dispossession of Indigenous peoples from their lands. They did so in many and diverse ways, but perhaps most simply by delivering brute numbers of migrants from across the planet deep into the continent, whose sheer volume wreaked catastrophic harm on Indigenous worlds. Occupation of the land made conquest, previously only notional, into a harsh reality. In the same stroke the railroads knit together the continent's material resources and linked formerly peripheral regions of the global economy under the auspices of US-led free trade.[28] The rail system was recognized as integral to industrial development and the United States' so-called Manifest Destiny to overtake the continent. But in what has become a recurrent motif of American history, the people who actually built the lines were reviled as racial threats to law and order and American citizenship.[29] Moreover, their work was dangerous, highly coercive, and poorly paid. Irish workers displaced by famine and English colonialism were central to building transport infrastructure in the mid-nineteenth century Eastern Seaboard and northern-central states; Chinese workers in the Pacific states and Mountain West did similar work under terrible conditions in the second half of the century.

In the post–Civil War South, Black workers, criminalized through the convict lease system, were forced under the lash to build the infrastructure that sped the regional transition from slavery to industrializing capitalism and deeper integration in world markets. After the 1882 Exclusion Act dammed the legal flow of Chinese workers, eastern and southern Europeans filled the gaps in the lowest echelons of US midwestern and central states' railroad labor, while smaller but still significant numbers of Japanese and then Mexican workers built and maintained the increasingly dense rail networks traversing the North American West and southwestern borderlands from the

1880s through the Mexican Revolution. By the time of the First World War and the 1917 Immigration Act, when poor workers from eastern and southern Europe could no longer cross the Atlantic, Mexican track workers traveled further from the southwestern borderlands and into the Midwest, the northern central states, and the mid-Atlantic and East Coast.[30] By 1916 more than 250,000 miles of rail traversed the United States. Exploited and racialized workers were not incidental to the building of American wealth and railroads; they were at its heart.

Railroads have loomed equally large in US popular culture. Under the heading "Westward The Star of Empire Takes Its Way," a June 1871 issue of *California Mail Bag* shows a locomotive charging through the Sierra Nevada mountains, scattering crudely drawn Indians and wildlife from its path.[31] With greater acuity and loftier ambitions, John Gast's *American Progress* (1872) depicts the rail as a key component in the expansion of white civilization, driving out Indigenous peoples and bison—an expression of the Manifest Destiny of enlightened American Christendom and a progression of frontier to farms, towns, and cities.[32] And entering the era that concerns us here, John Ford's 1924 silent film *The Iron Horse* brought the story to America's movie theaters. In Ford's telling, visionary surveyors, intrepid explorers, and a multiethnic crew of workers battled corrupt businessmen, hostile Indians, and the land itself to build the transcontinental road. By expanding west, they symbolically reunited a north and south riven by Civil War, and realized America's proclaimed world-historical mission of westward expansion.

In Ford's film, white, American-born men directed the Union Pacific works coming from the east, while their female counterparts served either as gentle tamers of the masculine frontier or as devious seductresses. The white Americans were aided by Irish men as sidekicks and comic relief, lower on the white racial scale but still useful. The Irish also helped to challenge Italian workers—lower still among the Europeans—when the Italians threatened to go on strike. Chinese workers, too, labored for the Central Pacific in California's mountains, though by the time Ford's film was made, the Chinese had been prohibited from coming to the United States for more than forty years. Still, the film's idea of American whiteness—variegated as it was into the hierarchy of Anglo-American, Irish, and Italians—was usefully defined against three foils: the Chinese, as racially undesirable and legally prohibited migrants; the Indians, whom the white settlers forced from the land; and African Americans, whose enslaved labor built the United States and Atlantic world economy, but who, once emancipated, were entirely absent from Ford's American epic.[33]

Ford's story was compelling and the film was popular, not least because it narrated the building of the railroads as a project in which immigrant classes contributed to this self-consciously American project. The film fit within a liberal vision of the United States as a nation of immigrants, as a melting pot and land of opportunity, of which many Americans have long been proud. Nevertheless, migrant denizens and travelers who could not or would not adhere to the eugenic contours of settler citizenship risked capture, arrest, and expulsion as undesirable aliens, often along the very tracks that Ford's celebrated immigrants helped build.[34] Large-scale deportation, whose legal precepts were increasingly materializable in the early twentieth century thanks to new federal capacities for coordinated capture and removal, operated in tandem with incarceration as a means of racial, spatial, and behavioral governance.[35] Deportation asserted sovereignty over national territories by regulating community membership through the partitioning of citizenship, undesirable alienage, and criminality.

The deportation assemblage made "undesirability" appear as an individual person's failures, even as that person was part of a group identified by its supposed racial or national characteristics: their personal disabilities, their bad choices, their immorality, and so forth.[36] It was generally conjoined by any number of particular racializing processes; the supposed atavism of being an Irish man, which was taken to be distinct from French women's particular immorality, as distinct from the deviance that racial scientists understood characterized South Asian men or that lay behind putative Chinese docility. Yet looking at the deportation train as part of an expanding system, or what some have called an integrated assemblage, allows us to see this key facet of structured and spatialized inequalities through the networked relationships among the multiply dispossessed as they were located in an increasingly interconnected economic world system. That system had long been shaped by racial hierarchies. Some were primarily anti-Black, in the traditions of chattel slavery, segregation, ghettoization, and, in years since, the capacious forms of mass incarceration. Others were anti-Indigenous, such as settler-colonial policies of forced removal, extermination, and forced assimilation in boarding schools. Here, anti-immigrant nativisms were reinvigorated and targeted the foreign-born through its networks of capture and removal.[37]

This book is guided by a few major concepts. The first, and largest, is racial capitalism.[38] By this, I mean a global political and economic system dating from at least the fifteenth century based on capitalist relations among people (whose sorting into racialized groups enables exploitation and mitigates against working-class solidarities), and between businesses and the more-than-human world, in which the search for profit trumps all other values. Racial capitalism is an analytic term to make sense of what has become a global system, but this isn't to say the system is everywhere the same. Far from it. The specific details of particular places matter, just as the varying and mutable processes of racial marking and ethnic differentiation are central to its creation, sustenance, and operation. Because racial capitalism concerns the reproduction of wealth, the reproduction of racialized groups, and the reproduction of workers over time, it is also invested in ideas and worries about social and biological reproduction. This is one reason why gender—imaginings and practices of differently gendered bodies, identities, and desires, put in hierarchal relations—is a key feature in the reproduction of racial capitalist systems over time.

Scale matters, too. The material consequences of place offer the people who live and work in different regions, countries, and even neighborhoods within regions and countries, very different opportunities, crises, and dangers. Place-making also validates and indeed, actively constructs, racial identities and hierarchies. Those who live in the centers of capital and benefit from the privileges of whiteness tend to have better living conditions and more opportunities than those who live in its peripheries, and, with European economic expansion from the fifteenth century on, the centers—by and large, Europe and the United States in this period—and the peripheries relate, more or less directly, to the histories of European imperial expansion and colonization across the globe. They map, too, onto the imagined human racial geographies and civilizational discourse of the late nineteenth century, in which notions of whiteness were located in northern and western Europe and the United States, along with the hazier, not-quite-white identities of southern and eastern Europeans, while the multiple forms of racial denigration were placed across Africa, Asia, and Latin America. Again, scale matters, and the spaces of racial capitalism's enactment—and moreover its partial regulation by states—demands that we analytically zoom in and pan out (from the micro- to the meso- and macro- levels), from bodily to the architectural, from neighborhoods to cities, nations, regions, and the borders imposed between them.[39] Racial capitalism may be a large concept, but it stakes room for people's individual and collective actions. Indeed, the decision for people to migrate is a principal factor in how they address spatialized racial and political-economic inequalities.

A second major concept is settler colonialism. This describes a process in which settlers (or, put another way, invaders) find a land that is new to them and claim it as their own by attempting to eliminate or absorb Indigenous peoples and then replacing the population with the people they think are most appropriate to build a new, durable and, they hope, permanent version of their older society. The United States, Australia, Canada, and New Zealand are prime examples of settler-colonial societies in the Anglophone world. Settler colonialism is different than extractive colonialism. Where settler colonies generally seek to replace Indigenous populations with their own, extractive colonies seek to control preexisting political systems and populations, while syphoning wealth and political power into their own coffers (think of the British in India).[40] A century ago, much like today, economic changes and human migration across borders made American settler communities anxious and prompted strident assertions of national sovereignty.[41] There was deep irony. The US government had little compunction about disregarding Indigenous sovereignties, deeming Native Americans as legal aliens and, through warfare, fraud, and force, displacing and removing Indigenous peoples from the lands and confining them in reservations.[42]

But in its immigration and deportation policy, the United States—a settler nation embedded within a racial-capitalist world system—was attempting to both stabilize its territorial borders and determine who, among all the people set into motion by that system, would be permitted to arrive and remain in the land it claimed.[43] Immigration control and the deportation apparatus was thus a second-order process of settler colonialism, regulating who might be permitted as a settler and eventually, perhaps, a full citizen, and restricting or expelling the rest.[44] Race—or rather, racism—was a central determinant of a person's ability to travel. In a 1915 essay, W.E.B. Du Bois, the towering Black American intellectual and critic who had already identified the color line as the problem of the twentieth century *within* the United States, saw it playing out globally:

> [A] white man is privileged to go to any land where advantage beckons and behave as he pleases; the black or colored man is being more and more confined to those parts of the world where life for climatic, historical, economic, and political reasons is most difficult to live and most easily dominated by Europe for Europe's gain.[45]

Du Bois referred to the global partitioning of imperial metropoles and colonized lands, but it applied as a color line of enclosures and exclusions built of walls and topped with barbed wire, which targeted Chinese workers and then generations of racialized and otherwise disdained migrants, limiting their arrival into the United States.

A third concept is biopolitics. The term sounds complicated and, in many scholars' hands, it is. But here, I mean it to describe a modern mode of governance in which the US state used police and welfare institutions to regulate its population en masse, and to determine the physical, biological, and behavioral characteristics of its desired citizenry.[46] This, in turn, would shape who would and would not be able to have children within America's borders and thus propagate the country's population into the future. Gender, particularly as it intersects with race and other forms of perceived differences, becomes central. Biopolitics, whose key concern is the governmental control of life, is conceptually counterposed to more violently foundational forms of rule and racial domination, which others call "necropolitics" and which makes freer use of murderous force. (The Nazis offer the most familiar, but hardly the only, example. Nazi policies to improve the health, well-being, comfort, and reproduction of the so-called Aryan race can be seen as firmly biopolitical, while the highly bureaucratized genocide of the Jews, Roma, queer folks, people with disabilities, and communists, among the others the Nazis hated—inspired by their racial-colonial aspirations—can define necropolitics).[47]

Modern governments draw on both biopolitics and necropolitics: sometimes in tandem, depending on the target population; sometimes emphasizing one over the other in the interests of efficacy. Because the United States is a settler-colonial society, it was (and remains) deeply invested in controlling the specific qualities of who can—and cannot—become a settler. Over its history the United States has drawn on a full spectrum of biopolitical and necropolitical mechanisms and institutions to offer support to its citizens, secure the capitalist economy, and to dominate or eliminate those they saw as unfit or as "undesirable aliens"—people who hailed, not coincidentally, from across the colonized world, or the peripheries of the global racial economy. At many stages in the American past, from dispossessing Indigenous peoples, to replacing them with European settlers, to expelling the so-called unwanted, the railroads have been central to America's domestic empire and to the American nation itself. The Nazis, of course, also used deportation trains. But the US deportation regime refined these techniques, with parallel goals but a different result, and they did so a generation before the Nazis.

The American deportation regime flourished in the early twentieth century because, in perverse but important ways, it was understood to satisfy modern, positive, and beneficial aspects of US governance. It was integral to the complex ways in which the ideas and practice of modern citizenship would be bolstered and enforced.[48] In the late nineteenth and early twentieth century, many Americans turned toward government for protection from the vicissitudes of an unpredictable world. For many, big industries were the face of that unpredictability. In cities and towns, industrialized assembly lines crushed the bargaining power that skilled workers once cherished. If workers organized, they could be replaced by machines operated by new migrants— often Black Americans or noncitizens formerly excluded from the labor aristocracy. At the same time, industrialization made many work harder, faster, and at someone else's direction. Farmers, sharecroppers, or migrant workers saw the fruits of their labor thrust into global markets and suffered the fluctuations of commodity prices, and their own prospects varied accordingly. At the heights of the economy, smaller firms were driven out of business or engulfed by massive, vertically integrated corporate trusts, whose middle managers drove production and whose bosses wielded tremendous power with friends in government.

Still, elected officials were forced to respond to voters, and as ordinary white citizens and liberal elites argued for governmental regulations of the free market, politicians and bureaucrats responded with slow steps toward social welfare.[49] Since the advent of welfare, its managers have sorted its recipients into the so-called deserving and the undeserving poor. From almshouses and workhouses to asylums, charities and social welfare institutions, public and private organizations offered benevolent (if patronizing) support to those who fell on hard times, or, for whatever reason, were poorly suited to industrializing capitalist production. In the tradition of the English poor laws, welfare was also to be allocated by location and belonging. Benefits were always calibrated by race, sex, class and political power, into those citizens who were to be varyingly pitied or entitled to social welfare.[50]

But the modern state developed harsher options for those who were deemed to be undeserving, such as the mad, the criminal, or those who rejected wage labor or the state's claimed monopoly on violence. Prisons anchored the harsh, violent, and more explicitly racialized end of the modern disciplinary carceral-welfare spectrum. As a generation of research into the US carceral state has shown, it grew across the late nineteenth and twentieth century, arriving, at the turn of the twenty-first century, at the largest prison system that the world has ever known. At the level of intents and ideals (though hardly in actual practice) carceral institutions were geared toward the recuperation of errant citizens through the temporary withdrawal of citizenship rights and meant to help manage the nation's population across time. The institutions partitioned those who undermined or fit poorly within national citizenship projects into facilities ostensibly tailored to their specific shortcoming (hospitals for the physically ill; jails for the recalcitrant or violent; asylums for those with mental illness or cognitive differences).

In the case that the mad might be coaxed to rationality, the thief or pauper taught to love labor, and the prostitute returned to her wifely homebound duties, each might be redeemed and their citizenship restored. The citizens that each of these various institutions sought were supposed to be radically self-sufficient, independent, autonomous, able to vote in an election without suasion, and capable of wage labor. They would not need support from external agencies or collectivities—save perhaps for the male-led nuclear families of which they were part. As self-regulating, able-bodied, self-contained individuals, of sound mind, and within male-led families, proper and sanctioned citizens would help to reproduce the nation into the future.[51]

Some scholars have suggested that the American welfare state arose as "a means of organizing mutual aid among strangers," but the coincidence of the deportation regime's emergence alongside that of the proto-welfare/carceral state reveals who was considered too much a stranger to merit aid.[52] The deportation apparatus helped to systematically differentiate between the "beneficiaries" of the national carceral/welfare systems and those noncitizens who would be shunted beyond it. The deportation system that emerged in the late nineteenth century and matured with the deportation train in the early twentieth century, then, was coterminous with the rising demands of a modern US penal-welfare state. Carceral and social welfare systems existed on a spectrum from which noncitizens would be excluded. Indeed, under modern carceral-welfare states the social safety net, such as it was, became a web, ever more widely cast and finely spun, not just to discipline and correct citizens but to ensnare and deport noncitizens.[53] Rather than a correctional or disciplinary apparatus, deportation offered abjection, elimination, and spatial removal—permanent banishment rather than temporary, calibrated, if still painful, incarceration.

Still, until the deportation system took shape with the train at its center, most of these institutions remained relatively isolated from each other. Administrators attended to their own administrative and geographic jurisdiction, based on expertise in their own category of malefactor. There was little reason for the director of a municipal almshouse to be in touch with the director of the state prison, and even less call for interaction with federal authorities, to say nothing of connections made between municipalities or among institutions in different states. Deportation trains engendered new and more durable connections among these different carceral-welfare institutions. The deportation assemblage helped to generate a more cohesive carceral state as a means of labor and political control that particularly targeted people of color and immigrants.

The deportation regime flourished in the early twentieth century because it made efficient use of new technologies—and particularly new means to ensnare people in its webs, to communicate across departments and regions, and to send the people it arrested across vast distances.[54] Put somewhat more abstractly, the deportation regime grew because it drew on and contributed to governmental systems of logistics and infrastructures. These, in turn, helped the deportation state develop new capacities for *capture* and for *flow*.[55] The origins and consequences deportation's logistics and infrastructure shed light on the evolution of legal and material practices of defining, regulating, and physically controlling US and global populations. Military theorists and geographers have recently argued that logistics—the techniques of moving supplies and people—came to lead rather than follow military strategies.[56] In a similar way, we can see how the infrastructures of removal enabled, and in some respects led, the modern deportation state. At the same time that the deportation state insisted that its citizens be self-sufficient, autonomous, and rely on no one or nothing, it developed and entrenched its own densely networked systems of governmental interconnection, relationality, and interdependence.

And so a century ago, local officials in county jails or in public and private mental hospitals began to liaise with their counterparts at the state prisons and asylums, who in turn corresponded with the federal immigration authorities about the so-called undesirable aliens in their midst. Thanks to the telegraph, they could communicate with near instantaneous speed. Telegraph cables, pulsing with electricity and information, punctured the barrier that regional or even continental distance once posed. At the same time, government agents developed cozy business partnerships with colleagues at private detention centers and railroad and shipping firms to hold and then deport the unwanted. This new, more sophisticated government infrastructure enabled the deportation regime to identify, track, and then remove unprecedented numbers of people. In the process, deportation became a key driver in the making of a coherent, interconnected, modern American *carceral* state. It happened, we might say, on two axes: vertically, the carceral state began to cohere with new and tighter connections across municipal, state, and federal levels of government. But it also undertook a process of horizontal integration across regional and geographic space as well as across different categories of institutions. The deportation regime was increasingly complex, even messy, and it never achieved the eugenicists' dream of complete national purification. But even with its many gaps and failures, it was increasingly, and sometimes terrifyingly, effective.

The Deportation Express examines the history of US deportation by following a composite Deportation Special train journey as it wound its way through these dense networks and across the country. Most histories tell a linear story of change over time, but I think the deportation train, and the assemblage of which it was a part, is better served by a form—like the rail network itself—that is simultaneously globalized and indelibly local, giving attention to multiple routes and journeys, with knots and braids, intersections and loose ends, overlaps, side-trips, and unexpected detours.[57] The path we follow and the stops we make are more or less typical of the era. Eastbound journeys usually gathered people who originally hailed from across Europe and the Atlantic world and delivered them to the Eastern Seaboard for transatlantic shipment to Europe. Westbound trips typically collected people from across the United States' continental or transpacific colonial domains—from Mexico, China, India, the Philippines, or, after 1917, the so-called Asiatic Barred Zone, origins that largely (if not uniformly) were understood to make one racially unassimilable.

To learn about the lives of the people forced aboard the deportation train, I have reconstructed the passenger lists from some of the trains' earliest itineraries and selected the stories from among them that seem to speak to the most important issues in understanding the history of US deportation.[58] Unlike the great or infamous men about whom history has traditionally been written, these people are not especially remarkable—other than in perhaps a

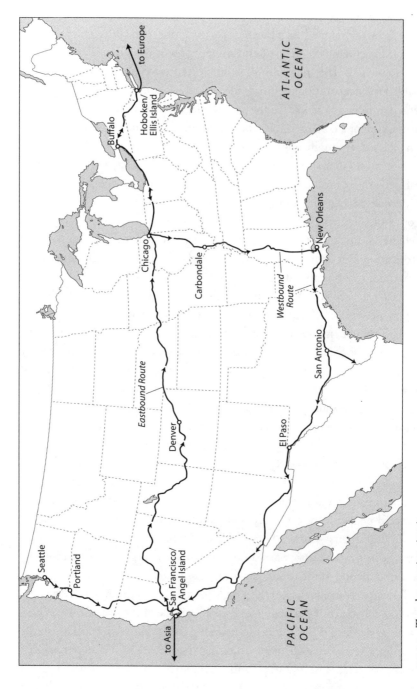

MAP I. The deportation circuit.

romantic sense, to which I hold fast, that everyone is, in their own manner, extraordinary. Other researchers might have chosen other passengers and other stops on the train, and a different set of itineraries would have yielded a very different kind of analysis. Since 1892, there have been more than fifty-six million American deportation stories to tell. There are more every day. But in focusing on the long journeys of those who traversed the world only to become ensnared in America's carceral state, the book insists that their lives were not reducible to the deportation regime. The deportation train played a cruelly important role in their lives, but it was not the only or the most important part. Human actors, making complex decisions in circumstances beyond their control—are the drivers of this story. Indeed, migrants' inventiveness—in departing the lands where they were born, and evading or accommodating one or multiple border policing regimes, are what forced state reactions and stoked nativists' fears.

Migrants' stories, dreams, and desires deserve to be taken seriously, even when sources are scant. In his song "Deportee (Plane Wreck at Los Gatos)," the folk singer Woody Guthrie mourned the twenty-eight Mexican women and men killed when the airplane on which they were being deported—the updated version of the deportation train—crashed. Newspapers reported on the pilot and crew but said little of the women and men forced aboard: "You won't have a name / When you ride the big airplane / All they will call you / Will be, deportees," Guthrie lamented, and their namelessness made for one more intolerable erasure—first their bodies, in deportation; then their lives, in the crash; and finally their names and memories, in the news.[59] In the same way, it is important to understand the complex lives of people who faced incarceration and forced removal, their braveries and fears, their strengths and failings, and their generosities as they confronted forces much larger than themselves—revolution, war, the structural violence of poverty, the impositions of racial and gendered dominance—but all lived intimately and at the intersection of personal and collective traumas of the families and communities around them. The book is animated by a belief that their "small" stories offer expansive vistas and deep insight into the structures of the past. Not just as a narrative device, but because individual people have a sense, more or less complete, of the worlds they inhabit. They can only rarely change those worlds to suit their needs, but they think things through, make decisions and act on them, doing the best they can with the tools at hand, or whatever they can devise.

To this end, *The Deportation Express* is a counterintuitive contribution to the field of global history, told through the experiences of a system whose explicit intent was to partition and segregate the planet's population by race, by physical and cognitive ability, by specific notions of morality (and especially sexual morality), and political sensibility. At the same time, by focusing on global migrant stories, their understandings and contributions to diasporic politics, the book seeks to at least partially decenter the US national and its political systems, even as it, by circumstance and necessity, centers on the machinery of that segregation and differentiation. It is, then, a history about global divisions, in which the US nation-state was working very hard to assert its dominance.[60]

Throughout the book we pass through migrants' home villages and meet the families they left behind, travel with them to the immigrant ghettos they built, the jobs where they struggled to earn a living, the taverns and coffeehouse where they spent what little money or leisure time they had, and the homes and tenements where they fought and loved and, in some cases, died. We visit multiple asylums, military camps, state prisons, county hospitals, city jails, and charitable homes for wayward women, pass by vigilante groups who attacked them, and attend the interrogations and hearings where they were declared unwelcome. And we board, with them, the deportation train.

The deportation train made for a complicated social space. It was a hybrid of the poorhouse, the prison, the hospital, and the asylum, and moreover, it was on wheels. It was as racially diverse as any city in the country and more diverse than many.[61] The deportation train confined many of those deemed contemptible or pathetic—the procurer and the prostitute, the pauper and the lunatic, the anarchist and the disabled worker, and the Chinese laborer, racially ineligible for citizenship. The trains gathered together people marked by multiple and intersecting forms of difference, as objects of pity, danger, or disgust—dozens of features rendered them "undesirable" and the conceptual opposite to the virtuous citizen.[62] When the state worked with private transportation firms to run deportation trains, and the globe-spanning networks of which it was a part, they helped to define the inside and the outside of the nation. It limned the qualities of belonging, and institutionalized the strategies and technologies of otherness, of literal alienation. By materially and administratively linking the United States' continental welfare-carceral archipelago, and serving as a closed conduit for moving abjected peoples from interior disciplinary spaces to the beyond its increasingly fortified borders, the deportation train was an engine in the production of American being and American citizenship.[63]

This returns us to people brought together by the deportation train. In most cases, the people forced to ride it had little to do with one another prior to boarding. They lived in different cities, spoke different languages, came from different lands, faced different existential struggles and joys. Nevertheless, for a few uncomfortable days, they all sat together. An Italian smuggler might sit across the aisle from an Irish woman deemed mad; a Punjabi Sikh itinerant laborer across from a French prostitute; an impoverished English woman and her son behind a recently widowed Korean woman and her daughter; a Chinese merchant accused of pandering in front of a Mexican man, injured at work. Their stories scarcely pose a comprehensive representation of US deportation but offer rather an itinerary of moments, nodes, stops, and eruptions—as well as interruptions.[64]

Untangling the deportees' histories offers insight into the worlds they inhabited over their lives, throughout and beyond the United States; the accidents that brought them into the deportation regime, and then aboard the train. Together, their entangled stories give a much larger perspective on the global walls and networks of early twentieth-century world, and the United States' response as an anxious country, trying to control the land, the resources, and the people it claimed. Complex forces set in motion by global political economies linked disparate parts of the planet. Migrants responded to the forces that dispossessed them of their livelihoods and made hopeful decisions imagining where their families might make new lives, or how they might make money before returning to invigorate their old ones. Conditions in Punjab were radically different from those in Sicily, different still from Liverpool or Guandong, and different again from Matamoros or Kobe. The paths that travelers laid from their homes and way-stations toward the United States were also radically different. When they made their way across the planet, they reconfigured the conditions of possibility for themselves and their communities and forced gatekeeper nations like the United States to grow or to reveal their limits of their democratic promise.[65]

But, for a moment here, a lifetime there, they converged in Pittsburgh, in Gary, in Portland, in San Antonio. For the unfortunate ones whose circumstances brought them into the deportation regime, they came together aboard the deportation trains. Theirs are the stories of those marginalized and exiled from America, their journeys through its settler-carceral institutions, eliminated through the infrastructural networks that bound the United States together and in turn pulled the world apart.

PART ONE

Building the Deportation State

THE US SYSTEM OF FORCED EXPULSION was not born fully formed. It started small and was built piece by piece. Transcontinental deportation required unprecedented legal, administrative, material government infrastructures. It required workers—career employees and bureaucrats—to develop and administer those systems. Agents built the means to identify and imprison those whom they disdained and move them across vast distances cheaply and according to the law. In the process, they connected a host of carceral institutions: prisons and jails, hospitals and asylums, workhouses and welfare offices, and detention centers of all sorts. They joined forces with huge private railroad firms and linked multiple levels of government—from the municipal to state, federal, and international. It was a contentious process, even among the clerks and bureaucrats, but their efforts made this branch of the American state into the juggernaut it has since become.

ONE

Planning the Journey

IN JANUARY 1914 THE IMMIGRATION AGENT Henry Weiss said good-bye to his wife and four children, approached the Seattle railroad yards, and heaved his bags aboard the nation's first Deportation Special. Weiss was in charge of the journey. His job was to collect the deportees from where they had been locked up and deliver them to the proper locations and agents who would take charge of the deportees' international removal. Along the way, Weiss would keep track of their paperwork and bags, make sure they were fed and reasonably healthy, and guard them so that no one could escape. He spent the rest of his working life on these trains, and his career helped consolidate a nationally integrated, globe-spanning deportation regime.

Until deportation trains began their steady circuits around the United States, the federal government had yet to develop a smooth system to remove unwanted immigrants from within the nation's borders. Congress had passed a series of increasingly restrictive immigration acts in the late nineteenth century—the Chinese Exclusion Act and the Immigration Act of 1882, the Foran Act of 1886, the Geary Act of 1892, along with others in 1903, 1907, and more to come in 1917, 1921, and 1924—but the government had largely focused its energies on policing ports of entry. For much of the nineteenth century, where deportation was concerned, states and localities held sway more than the federal government did. Funds were too scarce and distances too great for a national deportation regime to take shape. And there was simply no official guidance to specify how, for example, an Italian woman convicted of prostitution in Nevada could be shipped to New York and forced to travel across the Atlantic, or for how a Chinese man without papers in Chicago could be sent to California's Angel Island to await deportation. Some immigrants were transferred by US marshals, and others, by immigration agents.[1] Deportation still happened, but it tended to be locally administered and expensive. It was also frequently violent and typically ad hoc. The first decades of formal exclusion were characterized by widespread state uncertainty, administrative confusion, and questions about who would pay for removal.[2]

But as the years went on, federal bureaucrats worked hard to build a deportation regime that could make American nativist fantasies a reality. The railway was central to their success. It enabled them to compress continental distance and, by grouping so-called undesirable people together in barred train cars, to speed the pace and lessen the costs of removal. The trains certainly increased in number: eleven transcontinental trains ran between April 1914 and February 1916, nine in 1921, and nineteen in 1931.[3] The National Commission on Law Observance and Enforcement reported more than ninety thousand people were deported between 1921 and 1931, with an additional ninety-five thousand coerced to "voluntarily depart" between 1925 and 1931, tamping down the numbers recorded.[4]

Officials had weighed the possibilities of coordinating deportation journeys as early as 1905, and there were further discussions in 1910, 1911, and 1912.[5] After some trial runs organized by local governments, the Bureau of Immigration began partnering with private rail firms in 1914 to set up a nation-spanning deportation circuit. They partnered with local affiliates, some legally authorized, others less so, to sweep through asylums, hospitals, and prisons in search of immigrants deemed unfit for residence in the United States. They experimented with train car design to balance cost with surveillance and control capabilities. They hired a guard corps authorized and equipped to use physical force to detain deportees. And they centralized power over removal from regional immigration stations to the central offices in Washington, DC, a shift in governance that legitimated mass expulsion as a federal priority, centralized governmental responsibility, and helped weave a tighter, nationwide network to capture and expel so-called undesirable aliens.

The federal agency responsible for immigration control, and eventually forced removal, had gone through several iterations. In 1903 the Bureau of Immigration had been transferred from the Treasury Department to the Department of Labor and Commerce. Under the Treasury Department, migrants had been regulated, awkwardly, as either permitted or contraband goods, but under Labor and Commerce, immigrants were understood as sources of labor who needed to be managed accordingly. Just three years later, however, the office was renamed the Bureau of Immigration and Naturalization, reflecting administrative goals to assimilate some immigrants and to exclude others. By 1913 these priorities proved sufficiently incompatible that the Bureau of Naturalization became an altogether separate entity from the Bureau of Immigration, although both bureaus remained within the newly created Department of Labor.[6] As the name changes suggest, the government's efforts to control migration and manage and arrange deportation were always a work in progress, reflecting shifting policy priorities and tensions. Regardless of the name it took, the deportation regime was a deeply embedded and increasingly important part of the American carceral state, linked to prisons, hospitals, workhouses, and asylums. Beyond the name changes and overarching administrative structures, new technologies offered state agents novel means of identifying and caging so-called undesirable people and of handling their expulsion. In other words, the deportation state drew on and developed new methods of capture, control, and flow.

But it wasn't just some vague abstraction called "the state" that developed efficiencies in deportation infrastructure. People did. The state—a complex amalgam of ideas, bureaucracies, personnel, buildings, and forces—was nothing without its employees. Opinions on those employees varied widely. Most, perhaps, saw immigration agents, and immigration agents likely saw themselves, as professional protectors of a sovereign but besieged land. Others, like Mary Roberts Coolidge, a critic of Chinese exclusion laws, reported that many immigrant inspectors were characterized by little more than "ignorance, prejudice, untrustworthiness and incompetence."[7] Whether agents approached their jobs with zealous dedication, dispassionate professionalism, or workaday indifference, immigration agents conjured the deportation state into existence. They transformed the words of deportation law into policy and—by applying brain, ink, muscle, and steel—set policy into practice. Their sweat and ideas put the technology to work and made it hum. In turn, deportation agents gave new definition to the immigration regime, and thus to the carceral state, and to the qualities of the people it counted as deportable aliens or worthy citizens.[8]

Henry Weiss entered the immigration bureaucracy in November 1903, when he applied to work as a translator at the Immigration Bureau. Born in Constantinople in January 1866, he grew up speaking German at home with his family, among the Germans promoting trade and colonial expansion across the Ottoman Empire and broader Middle East.[9] His was a cos-mopolitan upbringing in that cosmopolitan city: in addition to German, Weiss learned to speak French, Spanish, Italian, and English, and acquired a more-than-passing familiarity with Syrian, Hebrew, and Portuguese. He left Constantinople and made his way to San Francisco, where the twenty-four-year-old landed in 1890. He likely met his future wife there. They soon moved to New York City, where the first of their children was born and in 1896, Weiss was naturalized as a US citizen. After a stint as a proofreader, he worked for Cook's Tourist Agency, which helped middle-class travelers navigate the railway system and the globe for pleasure. Later, he worked for the US Government Printing Office.[10]

When Weiss took a competitive language and civil service exam to apply for the translator job with the Immigration Bureau, he passed with high scores across multiple languages. In December 1903 he swore an oath of office to enforce immigration laws and defend the Constitution. The oath mentioned the $1,200 salary he would earn, but as it paid homage to God and Notary as witness, and to the state and nation, the oath ritually linked Weiss's belief system and subjectivities to the state. The money mattered but for Weiss, an immigrant himself, it was more than just a job. It was a crucial form of upward mobility—a powerful assertion of American belonging. He was one of many first- or second-generation immigrants who dedicated their professional lives to immigration control. The United States, as a multicultural, settler-colonial nation, hired people of different ethnoracial groups to serve as immigration agents, offering a bargain by which people drawn from the peripheries of America's imperial and economic networks could secure their own families' freedoms by circumscribing others'.[11] At Angel Island, Ellis Island, and along the nation's borders, recent Chinese, Italian, and other immigrants or their children were tasked with regulating their erstwhile compatriots' entry, exclusion, or as in Weiss's case, removal. Fiorello La Guardia might be taken as an example of a child of immigrants who lobbied on immigrants' behalf—even while working at Ellis Island—but others took more restrictionist turns.[12]

As a new member of the immigration bureaucracy, Weiss had little control over his professional fate. His superiors gave him about a week to move his family across the country, to Seattle, Washington.[13] They had to pay for their own relocation, which came to about a third of Weiss's annual salary. Just two months later, they were transferred to Port Townsend, Washington. As Weiss's superiors described it, Port Townsend was a vital and hectic post for Pacific trade and travel, "where all incoming alien seamen are now being manifested" and which required "a constant demand for [Weiss's] services."[14] His hours were long and difficult, and he was a hard worker. In order to interview incoming seamen, a category of traveler regulated by its own subset of immigration law, Weiss had to row a small boat through Port Townsend's often rough weather, boarding and departing anchored ships from a swinging rope ladder. One stormy day, he was sure he'd been injured at work, with an abdominal rupture—perhaps a hernia—but he continued his labors.[15] Though his official job was as an interpreter, he also mastered new record-keeping and statistical methods, and by March 1904 he was Port Townsend's acting immigrant inspector. The elevated title and responsibilities did not increase his salary, but his direct supervisors lauded his work. Inspector Estell, to whom he reported, rated Weiss as "one of the most valuable employees in this district."[16] Weiss applied for a promotion and had Estell's support, but it was denied for unclear reasons.[17]

In correspondence, Weiss appears to have been frustrated that the Immigration Bureau failed to recognize his value. Perhaps he was stymied because he was working on a far periphery of the bureaucracy, or perhaps because he was an immigrant himself. Coworkers with fewer skills and responsibilities were paid more, and it grated.[18] He applied for a transfer out of Port Townsend, which the Seattle inspector in charge, John H. Sargent, opposed "unless an equally good interpreter can be assigned to take his place." Given Weiss's remarkable language skills, that was unlikely. Weiss solicited Congressman Julius Kahn's support, but the secretary of commerce and labor wrote "there is no official reason why his request should be favorably considered."[19] Weiss's efforts eventually bore fruit. In October 1908 he was transferred to the Seattle office. The larger city better suited his family and was the launching ground for a new level of professional success.[20] His break came in 1912, after the commissioner of the Portland office requested that Weiss be detailed to his station so that he might tour Oregon's insane asylums in search of deportable aliens. "Inspector Weiss, by virtue of his linguistic ability and general experience in this character of work," the commissioner wrote, "is more highly qualified to conduct such an inquiry than is any employee connected with this station. In fact, there is no one in this office who has all the necessary qualifications for such an investigation."[21]

This kind of mission—sifting through disciplinary, carceral, and welfare institutions—became central to the deportation regime, providing an administrative conduit between disparate municipal, state, and federal disciplinary institutions and the national deportation network.[22] More recent and more theoretically inclined scholars have referred to what they call a "surveillant assemblage" that tracks migrants across a range of spheres to better control them. Surveillance and communication were key here, too, as the regime sought to gather, circulate, and coordinate more information about who might be deported.[23] A few years earlier, immigration officials simply hadn't known how many noncitizens were on relief or locked in charitable, penal, and reformatory institutions, and, in 1898, sent surveys to those institutions' administrators. In 1904 they found nearly ten thousand immigrants locked in state prisons and county or city jails.[24]

Equally important were the means through which information about potentially deportable people could be communicated. The Immigration Bureau's formal powers of arrest and deportation required warrants signed by the secretary of labor, who was based in Washington, DC. Local inspectors felt hamstrung by how long this could take, and immigration authorities seized on telegraphy as a new technology to speed information across vast distances and thus increase efficiencies in capturing people. Telegraphic warrants folded telegraphy into a state apparatus of capture and gave local agents the ability to act quickly while meeting legal obligations. Guidelines suggested that the telegraphic warrant should be requested sparingly, "only in case of necessity" or "when some substantial interest of the government would thereby be served."[25] DC-based supervisors were concerned that local officers would become overzealous without guidance from superiors in Washington. By 1908, however, telegraphic warrants were increasingly perfunctory and offered inspectors administrative cover to proceed in their investigations without substantive oversight. Immigration law codified the procedure in 1917 but still required two warrants—one for arrest, and one for deportation—to be signed by the secretary of labor.[26] There was no small amount of abuse, as people were arrested and held for days or longer on weak evidence—sometimes with warrants requested well after their detention.[27]

Procedurally, after warrants had been issued for deportation, administrative gears turned to process the person's removal. The Central Office of the Immigration Bureau would begin its own communication with foreign authorities. After all, deportation involved foreign governments and acquiring passports, which was usually the purview of the State Department. Yet the Department of Labor maintained what one official called "informal arrangements" with foreign legations and embassies in Washington to arrange passports. The State Department, for its part, also gave "informal approval" to being sidestepped.[28] Nevertheless, securing passports could be difficult. Few countries were particularly excited about receiving a new public charge in the form of someone whom the United States had deemed mad, disabled, ill, politically radical, likely to succumb to penury, or a convicted felon. As of 1920, the English, German, Swiss, Romanian, Swedish, Norwegian, and Yugoslav authorities required extensive "documentary evidence" on each case before they would issue a passport. Moreover, the Germans, Swedes, and Romanians insisted that anyone who had been outside of their country for ten years lost their citizenship. If someone, in the breadth of their travels, had arrived in the United States two years earlier, but had left Sweden twelve years before, they had become essentially stateless. Immigration authorities feared that some who fell into this category might become a permanent charge, and they came to live in a deportable legal limbo.[29]

Still, US inspectors thought there was far too little internal investigation. Legislative directive for federal immigration agents to more systematically scrutinize prisons and related institutions came with the 1907 Immigration Act. It built on much longer provisions to prevent the arrival of paupers as likely public charges. Indeed, even prior to nationhood, the Massachusetts Bay Colony set the colonial precedent in the mid-1600s by legally prohibiting the arrival of indigent immigrants, but until the 1890s there were few provisions to specify the means of capturing (or paying for the removal of) so-called public charges.[30] The 1907 act tasked federal immigration agents to conduct periodic sweeps of the "penal, reformatory, and charitable institutions"—both public and private—in their districts to find people who might be deported.[31] Each regional station would lead its own investigation, and federal officials hoped that the connections officers made with state and local penal, medical, and welfare officers would form a net to capture the undesirable. The tighter the net was woven, the more effective filter it would be, but it required a lot of work and was not always successful.

Federal agents began visiting those institutions in person in 1908—the personal touch was more effective than a survey—and many left standing requests with institutional administrators that they be notified of the arrival of any noncitizens. The sweeps were successful "for a short while." But as the commissioner-general of immigration would later complain, these institutions' weak memories (worsened by turnover in their politically appointed staff) limited the likelihood of their contacting the Immigration Bureau. Moreover, and particularly in the urban Northeast, some locally elected officials were beholden to migrant communities and were loath to be overly active about removing potential constituents.[32] As a result, "the practice of reporting new cases soon fell into disuse," and, despite similar requirements written into the 1917 Immigration Act, the commissioner reported that there were too few visits to public institutions between 1908 and 1923.[33]

But in 1912, Agent Weiss was one of the stalwart agents bucking that trend. He found twelve people to be removed immediately from Oregon's asylums, and a dozen more who bore further investigation.[34] His superiors in Washington, DC, were sufficiently impressed that they soon assigned him to travel with an Austrian deportee from the Western State Hospital for the Insane in Fort Steilacoom, Washington, to Ellis Island, in New York City. Staff at Ellis Island would hold other deportees until Weiss arrived, so that he could oversee their removal aboard Hamburg American and North German Line steamers.[35] If his mission in Oregon's asylums had been to identify and arrest people who might be expelled, he was now tasked with refining how to move deportees great distances. Structurally speaking, his job shifted from building an apparatus of capture to conducting an apparatus of flow. To that end, the acting commissioner-general directed Weiss

> to furnish a complete daily report respecting the condition of the aliens during the progress of the ocean voyage, this report to show in what portion of the ship said aliens were carried; if under restraint, the nature thereof; the sanitary measures employed; amount of supervision recorded, and by whom, and the condition of general health. He will also furnish any other information that he may be able to gather concerning the general systems employed by the transportation companies in taking care of these persons while in their custody.[36]

Weiss's mission had two purposes. First, the bureau could assess whether the quality of care that deportees received accorded with US sensibilities of decent treatment. (Given the repugnant conditions in most US asylums, the bar would have been relatively low.) Second, and more important, Weiss would learn from private shipping firms' experience in forced removal. It would help the bureau build up the professional, administrative, and logistical knowledge it needed to develop the federal deportation infrastructure.

When Weiss was filing his report, there was considerable discussion about how to structure deportation efforts at both local and national levels, and some western states were already experimenting with deportation parties. In 1910, for example, the acting secretary of immigration, Benjamin S. Cable, complained about drastic delays in deporting the insane noncitizens held at California's Napa State Hospital. As public charges, these immigrants cost the state money and therefore, Cable reasoned, should be immediately deported. But as Daniel J. Keefe, the Washington, DC–based commissioner-general, related to Cable, the costs of administering each deportation were quite high, involving visits to state hospitals, transit fare, food arrangements, staff salary and time, and so on. Accordingly, the San Francisco office proposed that they would deport the insane by the carload rather than singly.[37] Cable's background in the railway industry likely contributed to his embrace of deportation via the rails: his father had been the president of the Chicago, Rock Island, and Pacific Railway Company—better known as the Rock Island Lines—and Cable had been an attorney there for a decade. The company would soon profit from deportation traffic.[38]

Washington State officials followed suit, chartering a Pullman car from Seattle to New York to rid themselves of ten noncitizens in 1913. Most were Italian or Greek, convicted initially for petty larceny or minor assault, but nonetheless deemed, according to one newspaper, "a menace to American civilization." The Department of Labor supplied the chief guard, but the Seattle deputy sheriff, John Cudihee, commanded the party. Cudihee was already experienced with forced mobility. After he had become a deputy chief US marshal in Alaska during its 1897 gold rush, one of his jobs was to convey prisoners to California's San Quentin State Prison. Cudihee told a reporter that innovative methods of removal would help Seattle cope with what he called "the Japanese situation" and the southeastern European migrants who "ought never to be allowd [sic] to come into the country."[39]

There were other local and regional experiments in group removal by rail, and occasional journeys forcing Chinese migrants from the Eastern Seaboard to the Pacific Coast for removal.[40] But little coalesced at the federal level until late 1913, when the Los Angeles–based immigrant inspector Richard H. Taylor submitted a report to the DC Immigration Bureau on how to cut costs by centralizing and systematizing administrative procedures. Taylor was a dogged investigator who had relocated to Los Angeles as part of his work. A former naval cadet and once a much-trusted bodyguard to Theodore Roosevelt, Taylor had been detailed from the US Secret Service to investigate misconduct in the federal government and extend civil service reform, professionalizing and modernizing its ranks. He joined the Immigration

Bureau in 1907 to ferret out collusion in Chinese smuggling, but his interests ranged further.[41]

When Taylor turned to deportation traffic, he found common cause with other Progressive Era managers who thought government itself would benefit from a healthy dose of economic rationalism. The costs associated with deportation had been steadily rising for a decade, largely because migrants were traveling further from their points of entry, and lengthier return trips cost more.[42] Because of rising costs, Taylor wrote, deportation journeys needed "to be properly regulated." He recommended combining eastbound parties from Seattle, Portland, and San Francisco. Compiling the numbers of agents and attendants, their Pullman fees, railroad fare, and per diem expenses, Taylor examined the costs of seventeen separate eastbound journeys from Seattle, San Francisco, and Portland in 1912 and 1913. He found that in total, 143 people were deported at a cost of $17,781.22. Had the trips been combined, he wrote, "a saving of $10,310.99 would have been effected, less the two days' subsistence" required by lengthening the journey.[43]

For railroad firms a government contract to ship deportees promised lucrative and stable income, and when Taylor approached them, they were ready to cooperate. Passenger agents were logistical experts, but they were also salesmen, and they promised the bureau fine customer service. The Nickel Plate's John Y. Calahan verged on obsequiousness, pledging to Taylor that he would be "pleased to co-operate with your department" and offer "any assistance which may be required." He promised that a Nickel Plate representative would be "at the disposal of the Inspector in charge...without expense."[44] Calahan maintained a chummy rapport when he tried to upsell Nickel Plate services to the Immigration Bureau, closing typed letters with a handwritten "personal regards" for Inspector Taylor and others.[45]

Taylor decided that Southern Pacific's offer was the best, and their logistical recommendations most useful. It was no surprise. The Southern Pacific was among the world's largest transport firms. By 1916 it had absorbed nearly two hundred predecessor companies; its more than fifteen thousand miles of rail lines linked urban streetcar networks to rural farmlands, and partner firms extended from coast to coast and deep into Mexico; its steamship affiliates traversed the Atlantic and Pacific Oceans.[46] And so, with the Immigration Bureau's request in hand, the Southern Pacific proposed to

handle all deports in a tourist kitchen car; originating the parties in Seattle and collecting the aliens in Portland and San Francisco and then East either via Ogden, Omaha and Chicago, which would enable deports from Salt Lake City, Denver, Chicago, and other intermediate points being attached thereto, with only the additional expense of transporting them to the main line points through which the car would pass.[47]

They would partner with the Nickel Plate and the Lackawanna in the east to complete the journey from Chicago to Hoboken: John Calahan's glad-handing wasn't for nothing. The combined trip would make more stops over a longer and more convoluted route than a straight journey from a single West Coast city to New York, but Taylor believed that the savings on labor offset additional costs for subsistence. Southern Pacific also offered material and human capital, including a "cook, waiter and porter," along with meals at the rate of seventy-five cents per traveler.

Although the railroad company would provide key staff, ultimate responsibility for the trip was shifting toward the Immigration Bureau's Washington, DC, office. It marked a change from how staffing had worked before, when regionally based immigration officers had been in charge and, in Taylor's view, abused the position by using the eastbound trips as paid vacations. Officers from regional stations were in the habit of hiring friends or their wives, Taylor reported, and twelve of the trips he surveyed included matrons or attendants who appeared to be related to the agent in charge. On occasion officers took further advantage of the system by overstaffing the trips. Taylor pointed to one instance when "an officer in charge and four attendants accompanying five aliens, at a cost of over $1100," which he thought was highly inefficient. "I am afraid it will be necessary for the Bureau to make it plain to some of the officials in charge that deportation trips are not pleasure jobs."[48]

Taylor proposed a test run for the new system beginning on January 12, 1914, in which a train with six deportees would leave Seattle and gather ten more in San Francisco before heading east.[49] Where staffing was concerned, he wrote, "three attendants, and a matron when there are female aliens, would be sufficient" to administer a deportation train, "especially in view of the fact that there are 4 railroad employees in the car" who might be called upon in an emergency. In Taylor's plan the inspector in charge and one attendant would be on duty during the day, and two attendants on duty at night. Inspector Weiss, based in Seattle, was put in charge of the party. The train left Los Angeles on January 15, with twenty-four "deports" loaded in a tourist kitchen car. Their names were not recorded in available records, but they included three Mexican nationals who would be offloaded at Tucson and sent across the border at Nogales, Mexico. Two of them were originally supposed to cross the border in El Paso, but it was cheaper to deport them through Nogales, and Taylor, not particularly concerned with whatever might befall them or the difficulties destitute new arrivals would cause Mexican border communities, recommended continuing to do so in the future.

A few problems arose when the train reached Hoboken about a week later, and Ellis Island staff made recommendations for fine-tuning the system. The train's deportation officers needed to inform Ellis Island staff of their arrival times, numbers, and medical needs well in advance. They could not just assume that Ellis Island ferries would always be available to meet deportation parties at Hoboken. Moreover, Ellis Island's psychopathic ward lacked the capacity to house large numbers of "violent insane" inmates who arrived with little warning. They might be locked at the Combes Sanitarium in Queens, at a rate of $5 per capita per day plus transport charges, and officials soon signed a contract with the sanitarium to outsource detaining the mad. Baggage needed to be labeled better, too, to avoid delays or inconvenience.[50]

Weiss was more positive about the trip. He told Taylor that the train's staffing had been "entirely satisfactory and that the number of attendants was sufficient."[51] The San Francisco office had insisted that a physician join the party—a $210 expense that Taylor found extraneous—but the physician hadn't been a good fit, for some reason "unable or unwilling" to perform his duties.[52] Taylor suggested that in the future the department should avoid a doctor altogether and find guards with policing and medical expertise: "good able-bodied attendants such as peace officers and hospital employees who are familiar with the character of work." Taylor recommended that the inspector in charge of the party specifically choose a matron, guards, and attendants to his liking, since they would be working so closely together.[53]

With the first eastbound journey completed, Taylor began planning a second. Southern Pacific again supplied the route and scheduling, and Tacoma-based inspector Charles Keagy, rather than Henry Weiss, would take charge.[54] According to the Seattle commissioner, Henry White, the carriage was "the best one that has ever left this district with deportees," in "first class condition, being newly painted and varnished and thoroughly overhauled." Unlike the car Weiss had accompanied the month before, this one had bars across the windows, which White described as "a great relief to the officer in charge of the party as well as the accompanying attendants."[55] Taylor was determined to use it efficiently. The train would depart Seattle on February 19, picking up more deportees in San Francisco. "Should a large number join the party at either Kansas City or Chicago," Taylor instructed Seattle's agents, "double them up in the berths in order to convey as large a number as possible."[56]

From Taylor's perspective, packing people inside the train car was cheap, efficient, and for those reasons, an obvious priority. But it also provoked backlash among guards, who were less concerned about cutting costs than they were about maintaining order and discipline on the trains. Samuel Backus, of the Angel Island Station, told the Immigration Bureau that the train left Seattle on February 19, 1914, with one deportation officer, four attendants, and sixteen deportees on board. Thirteen more deportees would be added in San Francisco, two in Los Angeles, and seven in Denver—forty-three people in all. Yet the car "contains only thirteen sections, twenty six berth[s] available for our use." Moreover, the party included "men, women, and children, black and white, in same [sic], immoral, convicts, diseased and respectable public charges." Packing them into a single car was neither feasible nor good policy. Indeed, it undermined ideas of racial segregation, as well as the general disciplinary principles, attendant in medicine and in the growing field of the New Penology, that recommended different classes of people be separated— the dangerous apart from the merely destitute, the sick from the healthy, and so on—as a means of liberal and progressive social management. In addition, agents from Denver, Chicago, and El Paso had complained about the situation to Backus and sought his guidance, but given what he called an "absence of advice and instructions" from his superiors in DC, Backus was as bewildered by this new systemic innovation as anyone. Seeking clarification, he asked his superiors: "Is there any centralization of authority over arrangement and if so where[?]"[57]

When Inspector Keagy returned to Seattle after the February trip, he expressed concerns of his own. Deporting large numbers of mad deportees via the meandering southern route, he thought, was a bad idea, because it took so much longer. "These aliens, owing to the lack of exercise, became very restless and it was difficult to handle them without considerable physical restraint." He had little trouble for the first four or five days, but "after that time they were very difficult to manage, their appetites were not so good, their bowels became inactive, they became disturbed mentally, were extremely nervous, and some of them were more or less ill, due...to the length of the trip."[58] Seattle Inspector Sargent proposed having two routes from the West Coast, one departing Seattle and one departing San Francisco, and though it might cost "a trifle more, better results will be achieved."[59] But this ran against the cost savings that Taylor's combined plan promised and was dismissed.

To answer regional staff's concerns and clarify logistical matters, the Bureau of Immigration issued a circular to offices across the country on March 6, 1914. It outlined chains of command and included guidelines for appointing attendants, setting routes, and labeling deportees' baggage.[60] The circular noted that deportation infrastructure was a dynamic and improvable system and invited advice from the rank-and-file.[61] It also described the extent of the responsibilities that regional offices maintained in planning, staffing, and paying for deportation parties that originated in their regions. The San Francisco office was to notify "the officers in charge at El Paso, Denver, Helena, St. Louis, Chicago, etc., as to the schedule and routing of the party." Officers in intermediate cities, such as Denver, Helena, and Minneapolis, would inform officers in the larger hub cities of Chicago and Saint Louis about the number and timing of deportees who might be arriving to board the central train. At any point, the circular explained, "the officers in charge *who add the aliens to the party* will secure the necessary railway tickets through to the destination, delivering such transportation to the person in charge of the party."[62]

Telegraphy, as an increasingly important and virtually instantaneous communication technology early in the century, featured prominently in the emergent deportation system outlined in this memo. Sending stations were required to record the names of the "aliens composing the party, which of them are insane and the names of those who are violently insane and require restraint," and to telegraph this information "at least 24 hours in advance" so "that sufficient time is allowed for mustering deportees and making arrangement for their delivery at the time and place appointed." The bureau would use code words in telegraphic communication to condense information, cutting communication costs and increasing efficiency.[63] Telegraphic warrants enabled the systems of capture, and here telegraphy facilitated information to manage travel: the rail lines and telegraph cables braided together.

Information was also to be conveyed to the seaports of deportation, with full information about the number of deportees, their surnames, and their mental status—especially for the insane and the violently insane, who officials thought required restraint. The same memo listed a series of code words to be used in deportation proceedings, also in the interest of telegraphic economy and cost savings: "Devolution" meant that a party of aliens would be delivered on a certain date, and on a certain train. "Dauphine" indicated that a party contained a number of insane aliens. "Desperado" indicated "violent cases requiring restraining." And, with surprisingly appropriate melancholy, the code "Despondent" denoted the remainder of the party.[64] Scholars of Nazi Germany have pointed out how that regime, also keenly interested in grim efficiencies in population control, embraced the telegraphic codes' instrumentalization and obfuscation, compressing language for maximum efficiency.[65]

Coordination would be key to the trains' success but to obtain "the highest efficiency…at minimum cost," the bureau strove to limit the number of guards and attendants.[66] Anticipating pushback, the circular affirmed that the "Bureau will insist upon full cooperation by all officers concerned." Moreover, "officers in charge at all stations shall promptly report to the Bureau regarding any failure of other officers to observe the foregoing instructions, so that appropriate corrective measures may be taken as needed."[67] Regional inspectors in charge and commissioners of immigration were not reassured. Shortly after the circular was sent, Samuel Backus, at Angel Island, received many confused inquiries from other offices about upcoming deportation parties. He complained to the commissioner-general of immigration, Anthony Caminetti, that

> this office is in possession of no information whatever as to what is contemplated in this direction and is therefore unable to give the information required. Will the Bureau please advise us what arrangements are being made for the forwarding of another party to New York, when it is to start, where it is to originate, what route it will take, and to whom we shall look for information regarding the detailed arrangements?[68]

What's more, Backus wrote, under the new directive to limit staffing, his office had lost the opportunity to select attendants, which had previously been a useful incentive, a way of "rewarding with a trip to the East those who have rendered the Service valuable assistance."[69]

Seattle's commissioner, Henry White, underscored Backus's final point. He wrote Commissioner-General Caminetti to "personally protest" the increased centralization of staffing power in the DC-based bureau, particularly under Henry Weiss, whom White thought was too inexperienced and would likely just hire his own friends as attendants. White insisted that he had always chosen well-qualified guards and attendants and that these appointments helped him secure the support of labor organizations as well as the police and sheriff's office. Doling out appointments was more than a job perk. Keeping trade unions close expanded the bureau's capacity to surveil potentially radical organizations, but also the Chinese and Sikh migrant workers whom exclusionist unions had long reviled. Offering unions and police paid trips as guards and attendants meant that they would be "more friendly to our service…and able to assist us." Without that power, White and other district commissioners would "have nothing whatever to offer anyone and thus secure cooperation in their work."[70]

The Minneapolis inspector in charge echoed White's concerns, surmising that if Minneapolis officials were no longer able to help select train attendants, "it is likely we will receive less cooperation from the city and state officials than in the past."[71] In other words, regional officers argued that giving paid trips to their friends outside the bureau helped to expand and consolidate the means of policing, capturing, imprisoning, and removing so-called undesirable aliens, and members of civil society served as an important, if informal, element of the localized carceral state. Regional commissioners believed that administrative centralization would undermine their powers to regulate immigration through local networks. "The Bureau's control [is now] to such an extent," White wrote, "that there is no patronage or discretionary power lodged in the Commissioners of the different Districts." Without it, they were less able to do their jobs.[72]

As the struggle between locally directed and DC-imposed power was playing out, the machinery for removal kept turning. In late March, Samuel Backus was arranging an upcoming deportation party that would be the first full circuit, from West to East and back again. It would depart Seattle around April 2, pass through San Francisco on the Southern Pacific line to El Paso, and "thence El Paso and Southwestern on Rock Island to Chicago Nickelplate [sic] to Buffalo and West Shore to New York."[73] On the return trip the train would bring Chinese and other passengers from the Eastern Seaboard to the West for removal, eliminating the need for the bureau to pay for agents' empty-handed return travel. Henry Weiss was placed in charge of the journey.[74]

Backus remained concerned about conditions aboard the train. Given that there would likely be thirty-one people departing San Francisco and Seattle, with two dropped off in San Diego and a handful more in New Orleans, he recommended using two train cars. "I am reluctant in parties of this sort to crowd into one car, insane people, immoral people, diseased people, and respectable but unfortunate women and children," he explained. Using two cars "proved very satisfactory with the last party except that it entails a considerable care upon the deporting officer, and it is the view of this office that he should be furnished with sufficient attendants to cover all the watching necessary, and leave him free to have general supervision of the party and attend to details properly incumbent upon him." To that end, Backus suggested hiring "one deportation officer, one or perhaps two female hospital attendants, and at least six guards," with staffing provided more or less equally between the Seattle and San Francisco offices.[75]

At first, Backus's request was denied. "Use but one car," was the terse response from the acting commissioner-general, F. H. Larned, "and reduce number of attendants accordingly."[76] Larned thus continued the experiment of how many deportees could be packed into a single train, and how few guards or attendants used to control them before the system broke. Racism meant that deporting Chinese people allowed for particular economic efficiencies, it seems. Field officers were instructed to book one berth for each two Chinese deportees, because "a considerable saving may be effected in this way."[77] A week after Backus's initial request, however, Larned begrudgingly told the Chicago office that an additional eastbound car might be added if it became entirely necessary.[78] Nevertheless, Larned grilled Chicago's inspector in charge, Prentis, about his decision to add the car and additional attendants, and demanded a "detailed statement" of explanation.[79] Prentis, for his part, was more than willing to make the case. Understaffed trains, he argued, were dangerous trains.[80]

In justifying his decision, Prentis recounted that Henry Weiss had sent him a telegram the day before the train was to arrive, complaining that the thirty-four deportees in his car were a "bad crowd" and that Prentis should "secure sufficient and good attendants for [his] party."[81] Prentis would add twenty-seven more people in Chicago, with eight more scheduled at Fostoria, one from Cleveland, and three more at Buffalo. "From our experience in handling deportation parties," Prentis reflected, "this party was undermanned rather than over-manned." Moreover, Prentis reported that Weiss had informed him of "one violent insane who, at times, called for the attention of his entire force." Four additional mad deportees, three of whom had been classified as "violent insane" by asylum authorities, would come aboard in Chicago and need constant attention.[82] Prentis lauded cost savings but still, he wrote, "in addition to the question of economy, the question of safety should...be taken into consideration." Safety required at least six attendants.

"If any disturbance should occur enroute [*sic*], such as the outbreak of a violently insane, or if a break for liberty should be made by several of the aliens at once, the three attendants on guard would have extreme difficulty to control the party." Guards needed to be posted by the doors at each end of the carriage, and male and female attendants available to watch as deportees used the toilet. "One female deportee did escape through the window of the toilet while being conveyed with a Chicago deportation party," he reminded them.[83] Balancing economy and security in the deportation machine was hard work. Choosing the right people, organizing the right systems, and selecting the right equipment was important.

On April 22, 1914, Commissioner Caminetti appointed Henry Weiss the first chief deportation officer. It was a considerable promotion, with new responsibilities. Weiss would take charge of both the day-to-day running and administration of "all deportation parties from Pacific Coast points" that needed conveying to the Eastern Seaboard. His duties would include "selection of attendants, with special reference to their fitness to perform the work expected of them, the supervision of feeding accommodations, the internal discipline of parties, etc.,—in fact, the complete supervision of these deportation movements in all essential particulars."[84] And while the March circular had indicated that a West Coast supervisor would administer the national records of determining who would be deported from each region and substation, Weiss's appointment came with news that this planning, too, would be centralized in Washington, DC. Using a system developed by DC-based inspector Roger O'Donnell, the DC bureau would keep records of deportation warrants and "order the party forward."[85] Once the higher-ranking clerks and officers in DC determined the deportees who were ready for removal, Weiss would receive a telegram and begin arranging the deportation party to move ahead.[86]

Taking an oath of office on June 5, 1914, Weiss advanced, perhaps belatedly, two pay grades. The new position required being away from his wife and four children. The personal sacrifice was evidently worthwhile to Weiss, and at age forty-eight, the Turkish-born, naturalized citizen began riding the trains nearly continuously. As a multilingual immigrant turned immigrant inspector, he would be able to communicate with many of the people forced aboard the train and under his control. And as the nation's first chief deportation agent, he would enable the machinery of removal to run with newfound efficiencies.

Over the next few years, as train-board agents and managers tried to balance "economy" with "safety," they agreed that the cars should be designed for optimal control. Until 1916 the Southern Pacific typically provided the Immigration Bureau with tourist cars for its eastbound journeys, in which people of European descent were conveyed across the country to Ellis Island, and "prison cars" for the westbound parties, which contained more explicitly racialized peoples from Mexico and across the Pacific world.[87] Tourist cars were updated versions of the mid-nineteenth-century emigrant cars intended for working-class and middle-class customers; more comfortable than the earlier generation, but a far cry from the domestic opulence that wealthier travelers might find on Pullman's range of sleepers, parlor cars, libraries, and dining cars.[88] The "prison cars," which had screens and bars across the windows and open-plan architecture to enable maximal surveillance, were almost certainly repurposed from having carried Chinese "Coolie" laborers in earlier decades.[89] The architectural differences counterposed the supposed pathos of European unfortunates with the so-called Yellow Peril of Asian menace. Yet as hysteria over European saboteurs, anarchists, and communists grew through the First World War, Red Scare, and Palmer Raids, the lines between the dangerous and the pathetic blurred. Simpler and safer, most managers thus preferred to use the prison cars. They never knew when the pathetic might rise to become a threat.

Within the train cars, agents organized deportees according to their perceived level of danger. Open-plan design could make that difficult, though, and permitted what some critics saw as too much mingling among deportees. After all, many were wont to move about the carriage, and simply assigning someone a seat hardly meant they would stay there.[90] The bureau experimented with a different model of train car that would allow them to partition deportees in what prison designers would have recognized as a cellular model. Commissioner-General Caminetti led the bureau's effort to lease the Pullman car *Lorenzo* and modify it according to carceral specifications. The *Lorenzo* had nine rooms—two parlors and seven staterooms, all lit by electricity—and one toilet.[91] Each stateroom probably accommodated up to four people. A two-feet-two-inches-wide aisle ran the length of the train, on the port side of the car for half, crossing over, and along the starboard side for the other.[92] The *Lorenzo* made its first round-trip circuit in May through June 1919.

Leo Russell, who would replace Henry Weiss as deportation agent and

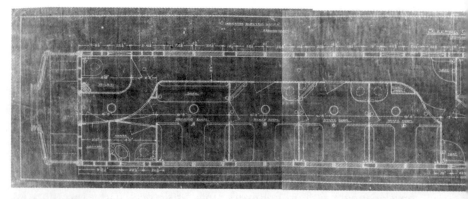

FIGURE 1. Blueprint of the Pullman train car *Lorenzo*, ca. 1918. Its staterooms were intended to mimic a prison or hospital's cellular design. *Source:* RG 85, Entry 9, 54645/325, National Archives and Records Administration, Washington, DC.

chief of the Transportation Bureau within the Immigration Bureau, oversaw the trip and wrote Caminetti to share his appraisal of the *Lorenzo*. The staterooms, he thought, were an improvement over the open-plan system. Like prison cells or hospital wards, he could use staterooms to separate deportees by sex, class, hygiene, ailment, or potential of disruption. But overall, the car needed to be hardened to prevent escape. "When it comes to putting anarchists and criminals in these places," he wrote, "the compartment must be so secure that it will be practically impossible for one of these men to get out." He proposed solutions for what he saw as an abundance of carceral shortcomings. The compartment doors were "entirely too small" and afforded "limited surveillance." When the bunks were down, it was "practically impossible to see a man in the lower berth next to the window." Russell recommended the viewing ports be enlarged. The locks Pullman provided were "soft bronze which could be sawed through with a penknife" and should be replaced with case-hardened locks. Moreover, all the fittings should be attached with rivets rather than removable screws; the windows needed to be modified to only open six inches; and Pullman would need to install steel bars across the transoms.[93] As Russell oversaw these changes, he helped set a template for the criminalization of so-called undesirable aliens. Planning for the state's worst-case scenario became the norm.

But the higher-ups soon decided that, where *Lorenzo* was concerned, liberal precepts of classification and carceral segregation were simply too costly. Budgetary concerns, driven by an anticipated appropriations shortfall, prompted the bureau to end its lease of *Lorenzo* on September 30, 1919.[94]

The cheaper prison cars, they decided, were good enough, and the open-floor plan would be the norm. In coming years, private transport firms, hoping to entice new contracts and profit from deportation traffic, would add technical modifications to the carriages—elevated guards' seats for better surveillance, more bars on the windows, a window on the toilet door, in case a guard wanted to look inside.[95] Agents still tried to distinguish between the dangerous and the pathetic, and reiterated spatial distinctions concerning notions of security, sex, and gender.

By the time Leo Russell was suggesting improvements to the *Lorenzo,* he had been ascending the ranks in the Immigration Bureau for more than a decade. Russell was born in Washington, DC, in 1884. His father worked as a printing officer and stenographer for the government, and Leo and his brother would both follow their father into government service. Russell attended two years of high school and the Temple Shorthand School, learning a writing technology designed for efficient transfer of knowledge that would help him in government or other kinds of administrative work.[96] He first worked for the Navy as a messenger boy, and later, a stenographer and copyist.[97] In late 1906, Russell began work as a copyist and clerk in the secretary's Office of the Immigration Bureau and worked his way up pay grades, acquiring new responsibilities and earning excellent efficiency ratings. According to a 1909 supervisor's report, Russell's job involved arranging "correspondence topically in proper files and assist[ing] in preparing name index therefrom. Work requires accuracy and some familiarity with subject-matter."[98]

At first glance, indexing and filing mail seems mundane to the point of

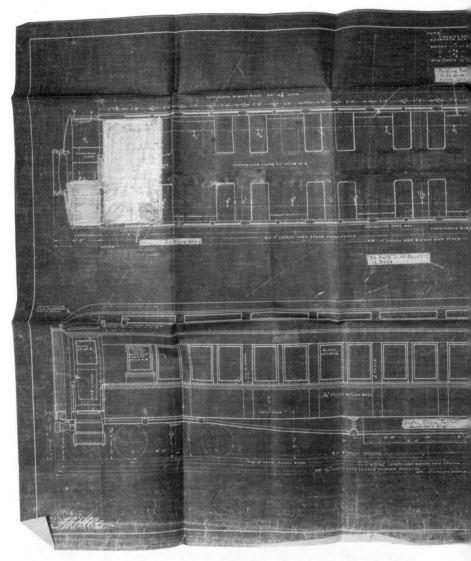

FIGURE 2. Proposed modifications to an open-plan deportation carriage, ca. 1934. *Source:* RG 85, Entry 9, 56193/283, National Archives and Records Administration, Washington, DC.

insignificance. But it is crucial to the creation and maintenance of any large organizational system. Correspondence clerks like Russell helped create the institutional memory indispensable to establishing and maintaining the state's knowledge infrastructures and communicative networks. A decade earlier, Terrence Powderly, the commissioner of immigration, had worked to

expand administrative reform across the country, and Frank Sargent, who replaced Powderly as commissioner-general in 1902, continued the move for administrative sophistication, with a focus on network building, including personal visits to immigration stations around the country, improving channels of communication, and demanding more systematic recordkeeping.[99]

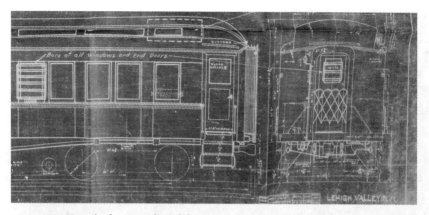

FIGURE 3. Detail of proposed modifications to an open-plan deportation carriage, ca. 1934. *Source:* RG 85, Entry 9, 56193/283, National Archives and Records Administration, Washington, DC.

Leo Russell was one of the clerks who answered the call. The systems he developed strengthened bureaucracies and connected governmental departments and facilitated their interactions with citizens, applicants, and nongovernmental agencies. His was an informational network at the heart of what legal historian William Novak, following Michael Mann, has called infrastructural power.[100]

Russell soon took on a supervisory role extending the correspondence filing system, and by 1911 he oversaw seven other clerks.[101] That same year, Russell was told to report to Portland, Oregon, to convey three men from Oregon to the Atlantic seaboard for deportation.[102] It was his first time working as a short-term deportation officer, but it was far from the last. He made another trip as a deportation officer to Cleveland in November 1912, and again to Norfolk, Virginia, in 1915, when he would accompany an insane seaman to New York.[103] The following year, Russell was assigned to transport a group of deportees from Seattle to New York.[104] He soon took over as deportation agent, supervising more than a dozen people and overseeing eastbound and westbound deportation journeys. At the same time, he was also chief of the Mail and Files Division.[105] When World War I began, Russell, like a great many Immigration Bureau investigators, was transferred to the war effort. He joined the Bureau of Naval Intelligence—his wartime work demonstrating circulation between ostensibly distinct military and civilian fields.[106] Records do not precisely reveal how his talents applied to Naval Intelligence, or if his specialist knowledge of infrastructures contributed to overseas warfighting or domestic counterinsurgency, but we do know he helped to improve its recordkeeping.[107] Indeed, the director of Naval Intelligence stressed that Russell's help in "revis[ing] our filing and index system" was "a vital part" of their wartime mission.[108]

After the war, Russell retuned to the Immigration Bureau with new titles and experience. He remained in charge of Mail and Filing but also was the official chief of the Transportation Bureau, which involved planning and administering deportation parties. He lobbied for more money for his department. "Immigration to the United States has been of the lowest type," he wrote, "and it is presumed that many of these aliens will become public charges."[109] He celebrated his department's success in having eliminated the unwelcome who had accumulated during the war, but further noted that there had not been an entire "cleaning out of all institutions . . . for ten years."[110] There was more work to be done.

Russell never wavered from the bureau's ongoing mission to expel so-called undesirable aliens, and for the rest of his career he worked in a variety of positions to increase efficiency across the deportation regime. That included remaking the organizational system at the Chicago office, which he oversaw in 1922 when its acting inspector in charge was absent and, as inspector in charge of the Transportation and Deportation Division in 1924, ensuring that transoceanic deportations were "accomplished in the most economical and efficient manner."[111] When he was promoted to assistant to the commissioner-general later that year, he oversaw sixty people across multiple bureau divisions: Correspondence; Transportation and Deportation; Mail and Files; and Information.[112] The responsibilities varied, but what united them was Russell's expertise in logistical planning and coordinating flows of information and people. He retired in July 1925, for reasons that are unclear, at the age of forty-one.[113] That same year, 9,495 people were deported from the interior on warrant proceedings, a substantial number of the nearly 35,000 people removed.[114] Five years later, Leo Russell died.[115] From 1917 until the year Russell stepped down, 185,228 people were officially removed from the United States.[116]

Russell's work, both in DC and on assignment at regional offices and on prison train cars, helped solidify and expand the deportation regime. He was a talented bureaucrat, highly skilled in developing systems to organize, access, and communicate institutional knowledge. The indexing of knowledge from correspondence—communication within and between growing, complex, and disparate government departments across the continent—was at the core of modern state systems. But the systems still required people to translate knowledge into force, ride the trains, control unwilling passengers, smooth snags, diminish friction, and generally maintain the system. Edwin M. Kline became the best known among them.

Kline would assume many of Russell's duties aboard the Deportation Special, and indeed, Russell and Kline's careers overlapped. In 1920, when Russell served as notary witnessing Kline's oath of office, the young clerk seemed fairly unremarkable.[117] But by 1946, when Kline retired, his name had become synonymous with deportation parties, which he oversaw from his Washington, DC office. Like Russell, Kline was born in Washington, DC, in 1876, and had some early general and technical education, but he attended neither high school nor university. And like Russell—but unlike Henry Weiss—Kline's pedigree as a native-born white man was largely unquestioned. Still, Kline foundered until 1898, when the twenty-two-year-old landed an entry-level job as printer's helper at the Treasury Department.[118] Kline was too old to be eligible for the position, but his father, who was a clerk in the Treasury Department, had successfully pushed to get him the apprenticeship.[119] It was not an uncontroversial decision. Some noted the bureaucratic irregularities—they were too politic to call it nepotism—from which the younger Kline benefited.[120] He gained incremental promotions, shifting between bureaus and departments, including the Department of Commerce and Labor and the US Coast and Geodetic Survey (USCGS).[121] Supervisors' reports were solid but, as had been the case with Henry Weiss, Kline's salary remained stable. Unlike Weiss, Kline found other ways to get ahead. In 1909 his uncle contacted his senator to lobby on his nephew's behalf, who in turn suggested that Kline be promoted. He was.[122]

Kline returned to the USCGS but sought work outside the agency.[123] His USCGS supervisor went to remarkable lengths to find Kline a job—elsewhere.[124] Few agencies were interested, and those with vacancies explained that Kline was unqualified. The Bureau of Corporations commissioner was unimpressed, calling Kline "hardly . . . the type of man for a clerical position."[125] The Census Bureau did have an opening, but Kline would need to take the civil service examination. When he did, he scored 62.85, well short of the required 70. Once more, one of Kline's senior administrator allies threw his weight behind the application, firmly but officiously quoting precedent and a 1907 executive order that gave the Census Bureau commissioner discretion to waive applicant examination scores. It is hard to know what, if anything, took place behind the letters, but Kline retook the civil service exam. This time, he passed—with what might strike some as the frankly suspicious score of 70.05.[126] In May 1914, Kline began work for the Bureau of the Census.[127] He appears to have done this with reasonable success but earned the enmity of at least one colleague. Michael F. Mullen, whom Kline supervised, accused Kline of anti-Catholic bigotry, flagrant abuses of power, exploiting the labor of the people he supervised, and accepting bribes from those he interviewed. The same colleague accused Kline of being secretly Jewish.[128]

In 1916, Kline applied for a promotion at the Census Bureau. His supervisor did not support the promotion, but it still went ahead. Mere weeks later, Kline took a junior clerk position in the Immigration Bureau. His managers at the Census Bureau might not have advocated for his promotion, but they absolutely supported his transfer to Immigration.[129] Kline's timing for the transfer was good; indeed, he arrived shortly after Anthony Caminetti's appointment as commissioner-general of immigration, who began an entrenchment of revanchist hires.[130] The bureau was hiring more "old stock" Americans, and high-ranking officials were skeptical about newer immigrants' capacity for what they thought was genuine Americanism.[131]

As an agent and an enforcer of the newly centralized system, Kline fit the bill. He had fewer of the regional or local allegiances that seemed to grow in cities like Seattle, San Francisco, or Chicago, and which had concerned centralizing reformers like Richard Taylor. Kline was also different than agents based in the Southwest, whose roots and allegiances tended to sit deeper in borderland soil—and violence—than his own East Coast origins. Instead, Kline's loyalties were to the networks of Washington, DC, even as DC extended its reach into more distant domains. His race and manhood, along with his family ties, seemed to confer a sense of entitlement, and it underwrote his professional success: white male mediocrity, if born in the right time and place, begat upward mobility.

Kline was forty years old when he started at the Department of Labor. He transferred to the New York City office, where he worked in cooperation with the New York City Public Employment Bureau. Despite indications that his career was built on nepotism, Kline evaluated migrants' opportunities for work based on merit, directed them to employers, and kept detailed records in their cases.[132] Supervisors said he was good at this, and Kline was soon promoted from junior clerk to clerk.[133] The First World War proved a boon to his career. In December 1917 he took temporary leave to join the War Emergency Employment Service, where his experience linking people with vacant jobs stood him in good stead. He was promoted to senior examiner at the Washington, DC, branch, and then federal director of the US Employment Service in September 1918.[134] At least from a financial perspective, Kline must have been sad to see the war's end: returning to the Immigration Service in late 1919 as a junior clerk in the Baltimore office, he earned less than he had during the war.[135]

Kline began a steady rise in the Immigration Bureau. He was appointed to deporting officer in February 1920, promoted to clerk in late 1920.[136] Working under Leo Russell, and increasingly central to deportation parties, Kline found his calling. The same year, Dr. Leo L. Stanley, the San Quentin–based physician who occasionally provided medical services aboard the deportation trains, described Kline as "a man of the highest integrity and capabilities . . . thoroughly competent and qualified to handle the class of people who come under his care."[137] In 1924, Kline was promoted to principal clerk (deporting officer), in charge of conducting deportation parties, and a year later, to immigrant inspector.[138] He developed an understanding of the practices, the risks and opportunities of the work, and the frontline sensibility attributed to prison guards and police about how to read their subjects' desperation, dangerousness, or quiescence. Kline continued to lead the deportation parties through the 1930s. He was promoted accordingly. Word spread. Indeed, a trainload of deportees became known within the administration as a "Kline Party."[139]

In the coming decades, federal Kline parties aimed to be as regular as clockwork, based in administrative liberalism and under the auspices of federal law. After DC-based clerks combed through records of the nation's prisons, hospitals, and asylums for likely people to expel, the trains ran every five or six weeks, taking about a month apiece to complete their journeys.[140] But other nativist efforts—unofficial deportations and "repatriations"—ran on a different, if overlapping, time.[141] Despite the regularity of the national deportation regime that Taylor, Weiss, Russell, and Kline helped build, at moments of crisis, nativists and exclusionists returned to more openly racist, spasmodic, illiberal forms of removal.

Mexican Americans and Mexican migrants were long familiar with the hazy border between white legal and extralegal violence. Indeed, after the conquest of Mexican lands in the US–Mexico War (1846–1848), periodic spasms of anti-Mexican mob violence surged, particularly around the California Gold Rush in the 1850s, during fears of Mexican border banditry in the 1870s, and in the midst of the Mexican Revolution in the 1910s.[142] The Texas Rangers had never shied from bloody violence against Mexicans in any of those periods, but US Border Patrol, formed in 1924, coupled brute force with more subtle spatial controls and regulations to control Mexican migrants and Mexican American workers' lives.[143]

Extralegal violence was never absent, but by the 1930s it was augmented by forced removal. With the high unemployment of the Great Depression, nativists accused Mexican workers of stealing white Americans' jobs and welfare, and wanted to drive them out. In 1931 local and county officials in Los Angeles announced impending raids on Mexican American barrios and neighborhoods, joining local sheriffs and police with federal authorities to sweep through Angeleno communities. The La Placita raid in Los Angeles was the best known of many similar events that swept the country's Mexican communities, its site chosen to stoke terror among nonwhite residents. Four hundred people were rounded up in the square for interrogation, with thirty ethnic Mexicans, five Chinese, and one Japanese resident held for further investigation.[144] Elsewhere, Mexican communities in Mississippi, Indiana, and Texas were threatened with violence unless they boarded trains or packed up their cars and "voluntarily" left.[145] The subsequent exodus from around the nation—Seattle to Pittsburgh and all points South—was enabled by a patchwork of state, municipal, and private concerns, from state welfare offices to religious charities and transport companies offering reduced fares. Together, they revealed a continuous extralegality in the collusion among white civil society, businesses, and state actors.[146] As a result, as two historians put it, "small barrios virtually disappeared," and busy colonias "took on the eerie look of abandoned ghost towns."[147]

The 1931 deportations were a white racist social movement sparked by economic crisis, demanding anti-Mexican ethnic cleansing, driven by a white civil society mobilized by the Depression, and are best understood as a spasmodic form of locally driven (if geographically extensive) expulsion. In contrast, the Kline parties were a more mundane form of "good governance." They sublimated at least some of that white desire for catharsis through expulsion within the rule of law.[148] And they signaled the administrative state's persistence, all the more durable because of its banal institutionalization, thanks to the grinding, quotidian, clockwork practice overseen by the

DC Immigration Bureau. After all, liberals stood on firm ground when they charged the spasmodic raids and removals as unbecoming of a liberal democracy.[149] The violent spasms and the banal procedural forms of removal have never been entirely exclusive; they reflect tensions between different tactics of national control.

When the Second World War began, the trains Kline used to expel so-called undesirable aliens from the nation's interior to beyond its borders reversed their journey and served instead the cause of Japanese and other "enemy alien" internment (forced removal, internal relocation, and incarceration). Overseas removals slowed during the war years, and Mexican migrants were once again welcomed as vital wartime workers. But aboard the Deportation Special, Kline carried so-called enemy aliens deep into the national interior, to concentration camps that were far from both co-ethnic communities and strategically vulnerable ports and borders.[150] With the war's end, Kline was lauded for having "conducted in a most efficient manner the deportation parties of the Service as well as enemy alien train movements," and he received another raise and promotion, to inspector in charge at the Baltimore office.[151] In 1946, Edwin Kline, then seventy years old, retired.[152] From 1925, when Kline assumed control of the trains, to his retirement in 1946, the United States recorded 427,751 people officially removed—a number that did not include the anti-Mexican deportation drives.[153] When Kline left the Immigration Bureau, he was feted by colleagues, admired for his longevity, and renowned for never having lost a deportee. The attorney general thanked Kline for his "outstanding record of achievement...of which the entire Department can well be proud."[154]

Others, including members of immigrant communities torn asunder by Kline's trips on the Deportation Special, saw him in a harsher light. In 1940 journalist Willis Thornton rode a deportation train from Cleveland to New York for a week and reported, as the headline of his story in the *Milwaukee Journal* read, "Kline's Deportation Party Is a Grim Affair for Aliens." The train Thornton rode was relatively modest, with fifty-nine deportees aboard four cars: two tourist coaches, one standard Pullman, and a diner. Some of Kline's largest trains, Thornton noted, were made up of many as twenty-two cars and carried six hundred or more deportees. A few of the people Thornton spoke to had committed crimes, a few were seamen who came ashore without papers, and a few had volunteered to return to their homelands. Many "told a similar story of failure . . . in which initial success had been followed by disaster—they had been cheated, their savings stolen, their little store burned, their strong arms weakened by age." Along with a "decent young Welshman" and his American-born son, Thornton described a "weatherbeaten old Bulgarian" who kissed his daughter before boarding the train. "Just before the door banged shut his gnarled fingers gestured an uncertain good-by to his daughter and to America[,] the America those hands, so warped and knotty, had helped to build." Between 1930 and January 1940, Thornton reported, "there have been 126,763 such deportees."[155]

Thornton's article inverted the classic American immigrant narrative of arrival and incorporation, becoming instead a story of confinement and expulsion. The train they rode, and the infrastructure of which it was part, was, like Thornton's America, built by many hands. The US deportation regime was built through an evolving, dynamic combination of people, of procedures, of material objects. It took shape through the imbrication of governmental actions with the capital investment and expertise of large-scale transportation firms. Still, well before Thornton's article came out, the commissioner-general of immigration found cause for celebration. The hard work he and his agents put in was paying off. "The deportation work of the bureau has been systematized and coordinated," he reported, "resulting in a marked degree of efficiency and economy." He boasted that the bureau was well on the way to creating "practically a perfect system" for deportation.[156]

Increasingly centralized in Washington, DC, with close partnerships with the private sector, the deportation apparatus mobilized the unmatched power of the US federal government to extend the settler-colonial dream of seizing the land and controlling who got to be a settler—and who didn't. Its national investigative and carceral network promised to police migrants' behavior and lock up anyone who didn't fit: the mad, the disabled, the politically radical, the uneducated or illiterate, people whose sexual moralities or practices challenged the norm, or those whose conditions of economic precarity meant they might become a public charge. It also captured migrants who were deemed racially ineligible to citizenship but who had made their way to the country nonetheless.

Taken by its own measures, of course, the system remained far from perfect. There was never enough money to remove as many people as officials wanted, paperwork got lost, people resisted their removal or escaped, and for-

FIGURE 4. Deportation train cars, 1934. The otherwise stark surface is marked only by the remnant pattern of a liquid—perhaps a drink, perhaps vomit—spilled through the bars of the speeding train. *Source:* "Around the World 1934," Leo L. Stanley Papers, Box 2, Vol. 1, SC070, Stanford University Library Special Collections.

eign governments could refuse to accept the people the United States wanted to offload. Internal reports revealed the inevitable flaws and uneven reporting or coordination among the United States' vast network of prisons, jails, and hospitals.[157] But every time officials identified weak points, it was part of the project of what they envisioned as a perfectible, globe-spanning, deportation infrastructure.

Still, the train rolled on and gathered its passengers along the way.

PART TWO

———————

Eastbound

AS THE DEPORTATION TRAIN SWEPT from West to East, it largely contained women, men, and children who had come to the United States from across Europe and the North Atlantic world. They followed the paths laid by friends and relatives before them, from their long-established communities to their new cities, jobs, and homes. But no matter where in Europe they were from, and no matter how so-called racial scientists classified their ancestry, whiteness would have remained a provisional, tenuous status, fully afforded only to the most fortunate among the native-born. Any misadventure might land these travelers in a jail or a hospital, institutions intended to retrain a fractious, mobile, or unproductive working class, which, given the effective discipline and self-discipline these institutions were meant to impart, might signal racial and national assimilability of immigrant whiteness.

Europeans who refused disciplinary instruction would be expelled to save the nation's limited welfare money for those deemed more deserving and less biologically or politically disruptive. A brush with the carceral/welfare state threatened to dash the hopes by which immigrants might shed their ethnic identity for untrammeled whiteness, with the fuller belonging it entailed: the ability to control their lives, to work, to have children, and perhaps to own land in America's settler-colonial society. As W.E.B. Du Bois proclaimed, this was the goal and the basis of American whiteness: "'But what on earth is whiteness that one should so desire it?' Then always, somehow, some way, I am given to understand that whiteness is the ownership of the earth forever and ever, Amen!"[1]

We now turn to the stories of a handful of Europeans deemed incapable or undeserving of owning American property, and whose children would be denied the same, and found themselves aboard the Deportation Special.

MAP 2. Eastbound route.

TWO

Seattle

FOR MUCH OF THE NINETEENTH CENTURY the boundary between
the United States and Canada—stretching from British Columbia and
Washington State in the West to New Brunswick and Maine in the East,
and traversing the Great Lakes—was little more than a shifting line on a
map. Those maps held power, to be sure: they disregarded First Nations peoples' sovereignties, guided property claims, and evolved, as the United States
and British or Canadian governments negotiated respective territories. But
on the ground there was little to proclaim that *this* side of a patch of forest
was the United States, or *that* side of an otherwise open prairie was Canada
in any ways that really mattered. The people who lived in the communities
across the borderlands crossed back and forth as a matter of little concern.
But as US exclusion acts radically cut Chinese legal entry at Angel Island,
migrants increasingly tried to enter the United States through Canada, and
by the turn of the twentieth century, Canadian and US officials dedicated
more resources to guarding the northern borderlands. The efforts generally
ignored whiter and well-to-do travelers, but they crested and swelled against
particular people—Chinese laborers, Sikh migrants, and anticapitalist as
well as anticolonial radicals of all sorts. In 1914, Commissioner Caminetti
bemoaned the small numbers of agents "specially assigned to the herculean
task of guarding these frontiers" but also mythologized their prowess, their
"ingenuity, ability, and bravery...for it must be remembered that danger is...
ever present in this work."[1]

Immigration and customs officials transformed what was once a haphazard border into a more complex, if hardly airtight, policing system.
Checkpoints popped up, and officers demanded papers. Special agents liaised
with transportation companies, county sheriffs, and private citizens to gather

intelligence. They built new facilities or repurposed old ones to lock up any-one who ran afoul of the new laws. This patchy but accumulating network of agents made the United States–Canadian border, once notional, into a harsh reality.[2] Despite new laws, migrants continued to traverse the borderlands and forced the state to develop and refine processes of capture, investigation, detention, and removal, which led to new rounds of evasion, resistance, and escape. These struggles, as they took shape in the northwestern borderlands, deserve our attention before we board the deportation train itself.

On the morning of June 2, 1914, Immigrant Inspector Horwitz did a favor for his colleagues at customs. Customs was short-staffed—one of their agents was on leave and another was ill—and Horwitz filled in. That morning, a mechanic at the Northern Pacific rail yard just south of the border in Sumas, Washington, saw what he thought were some suspicious-looking men. He didn't say what exactly made them suspicious, but they were waiting near some stacked lumber at the Northern Pacific yards. The mechanic called, and Horwitz came to investigate.[3] Horwitz found three men sitting in a refrig-erator car attached to a Seattle-bound train. As an acting customs agent, he demanded that they follow him to the station so he could search them for contraband. Lest anyone question the legality of Horwitz's search, Horwitz had been granted considerable police powers by the Treasury Department

> to stop, search, and examine any vehicle, beast or person, and to board any boat, sloop or launch, on which or whom he may suspect there is merchandise unlawfully introduced into the United States. If such goods be found he is empowered to seize the vehicle, beast and all packages, and arrest the person or persons in possession of the same.[4]

Using the pretext that he was searching for illegal substances, Horwitz saw that one man had pouches of tobacco from Canada, and two had Canadian-brand matches. They had no contraband, but based on the contents of their pockets and the place where they sat—a freight yard rather than a passenger terminal—Horwitz accused the men of unlawfully entering the country: *they* were the contraband.[5]

According to Horwitz, the men got a little surly. They "objected when I took the tobacco away from them, and stoutly maintained that they were coming from Seattle and had never been in Canada." He commanded them to the station, but they "balked at every few steps," moving slowly or else simply starting wander away. Horwitz kicked one man, although it wasn't much of a kick, he insisted, "more in the nature of a shove." The man did not take it well. Horwitz looked away but "turned around just in time to see [one] throw something at me." It was a pint bottle of whiskey, which cut Horwitz's cheek. Two of the men fled south along the railroad tracks, with Horwitz in pursuit. The one who did not run, Liborio Nanna, was arrested. The others escaped.[6]

Two hours later, inspectors caught one of the men near Nooksack, about seven miles south of Sumas along the rail tracks. He gave his name as Chini Rossi and told the inspectors he had been working for a farmer north of Nooksack for about two years. He had never been to Sumas, and moreover he said that he was Austrian, not Italian.[7] Nevertheless, Horwitz identified this man as the one who had hit him with the bottle. Three other men claimed to witness the event, including a car inspector and a freight conductor—they worked for Northern Pacific, not the US government—as well as an undertaker.[8] Rossi was taken into custody, and two months later, in July 1914, was convicted of assault on Inspector Horwitz at the US district court. Rossi was sentenced to six months of hard labor at the King County Jail.[9]

Shortly thereafter, immigration officials worked to have Rossi deported. They considered having him expelled to Canada—which might be cheap and quick—but determined that he would simply try to sneak across the border again.[10] Deportation to Italy was costlier but ultimately an effective way to expel Rossi beyond the still porous northern borderlands. The captured man spoke little English, so Henry Weiss, the multilingual immigration and deportation agent, conducted the deportation hearing in Italian. Though the accused had given different names, he now went by the name Dominico di Stefano. He said that he had been born in 1890, in Colle De Macine, in the piedmont province of Chieti, Italy. Chieti had undergone dramatic changes in the years since di Stefano's birth. The region's economy, long based on small-scale wheat and sheep production, had been devastated by the transport revolution and global markets in American wheat and Australian wool. Regional communities had seen dramatic population growth, and the increasingly fatal combination of more people and fewer opportunities for local livelihoods drove Italian peasant migration toward the coast and then overseas.[11]

Dominico di Stefano was among the 2.5 million Italians who left for North America, and returned, and left Italy again, between 1906 and 1915.[12] Though geographically midway on the Adriatic Coast, Weiss designated di Stefano as *southern* Italian, a marking thick with that land's own ethnoracial disdain, but which spoke more to rural poverty than strict geography. He had been a general laborer, leaving his home in 1907 for Naples and New York in June of that year. As historian Carlo Levi has related, in the steerage holds of transatlantic ships, Italian peasants brought with them stories of New York as "an earthly paradise" and a land of riches. Levi's treatment also portrayed how evasive spiritual and material fulfillment could be in the United States: "It is so sacred as to be untouchable; a man can only gaze at it even when he is there on the spot, with no hope of attainment."[13] This would ring true to di Stefano. He lived in "an Italian colony on Morris Avenue near the Bronx" and pieced together odd jobs around New York City. He returned home to Colle De Macine in June 1912, married, and had a daughter. He then returned to the United States in April 1913, working his way back and forth across the border, and across the continent, mostly in construction. When jobs dried up in Vancouver, di Stefano headed back to the United States with some friends, as they'd done before, skipping the closer but more tightly patrolled crossing at Blaine, Washington, and trying their luck near Sumas.

Weiss was particularly interested in the detail of how di Stefano made his way across the border. "We took the electric car and paid 25c each," di Stefano explained. "I think we went to New Westminster but I am not sure. We then took a train and paid $1.05; we changed again and paid 40c. (Fare from New Westminster to Sumas is $1.75 [, noted the inspector]), and we got off at some station, I don't know the names and we walked for about two hours until we came to Sumas where we got into a freight car to go wherever the train went so we could look for work." The men had not presented themselves to immigration authorities for inspection, because none were around as they entered. As Weiss turned the interrogation to the events at the rail yard, di Stefano was resolute that he had not thrown the bottle. "I saw the other fellow hit the officer with a bottle," he said, "I was scared…so I ran away." In his summary of the hearing, Weiss characterized di Stefano as "of the usual Southern Italian laboring type and made a decidedly unfavorable impression." He compounded the ethnic slurs with a recommendation that di Stefano be deported.[14]

Four and a half months after di Stefano's arrest and reentry into the United States, his deportation warrant was issued on the grounds of being "Likely to become a Public Charge" (LPC) as well as entry without inspection. Curiously, assault on an immigration officer—which might be taken as committing a crime of moral turpitude shortly after entry—was not among the charges.[15] Definitions of LPC were remarkably capacious and allowed

LPC to rank among the most common grounds on which people were deported—even if, as was the case here, they had been arrested on other matters.[16] In 1914, 2,447 immigrants were deported for having become public charges or were retroactively determined to have been LPC. In the mid-1910s some 60 percent of deportations were on LPC grounds.[17]

It isn't clear what conditions di Stefano faced in the King County Jail, or the kind of hard labor he did there. The jailers may have treated as him as white and elevated him above Indigenous or Asian inmates. Or—perhaps in addition—he may have been disdained as a dangerous foreigner who had assaulted a state agent, which may have increased his standing among the inmates.[18] After seven-and-a-half months of incarceration, officers brought di Stefano to the train station. A week later, he was aboard the SS *Athinai*, bound from Ellis Island to Naples and eventually to his wife and daughter, to a return to a region in economic decline and the maw of European war. In their search for steady work, di Stefano and his companions used subterfuge, deceit, and aliases, and ultimately violence to escape and evade the emergent border enforcement regime's patchwork system.

They had been doing the same for years, but the border control network had tightened. And if it might catch travelers near the borders of European whiteness—for southern Italians were hardly considered fully white—it was harder still for South Asian and Chinese migrants. Those who tried to enter the United States despite accumulating prohibitions on their arrival—especially and increasingly South Asian Sikhs—needed to travel complex routes into and through the United States and employed similar tactics to enter, work, and survive in cities, nations, and even empires that despised them but still demanded their labor.

. . .

Dominic di Stefano was caught because he was in a suspicious transport hub and drew inspectors' suspicions. Had he been in a train station rather than a rail yard, he would have drawn less attention, because white men could be expected in public places like that. Not so for people of color. An immigration inspector in eastern Washington boasted that no "Hindu...could be in Coleville 24 hours without this office being advised," followed by immediate interrogation.[19]

Three months into di Stefano's sentence in the King County Jail, Surup Singh, Attar Singh, Channan Singh, and Lall Singh were traversing the

Puget Sound's complex waterways near Orcas Island. They were looking for work, too.[20] The intricate waterways and islands teemed with shipping, passenger, fishing, and other traffic, and led immigrant inspector John Sargent to call the "district one of the most difficult in the United States to guard against the surreptitious entry of unlawful aliens."[21] Orcas Island had long been part of the First Nation Lummi peoples' homelands and waterways, and a village whose name, recorded not long after these men's arrest, was Hut-at-Chl.[22] The Lummi were near neighbors of the S'Klallam and Samish, all of whom had, since 1788, met, contested, confronted, and intermingled with a welter of Euro-American explorers, aspirational conquerors, and migrants, and survived the repercussions of each.[23]

The detail of the Sikh men's capture isn't recorded in any documents. One said they were caught after getting off of the ferry to Bellingham; other references indicated that they were captured on Orcas Island itself. In any case, officials quickly locked the nine men in the immigrant Detention House in Blaine. The men testified that they were traveling from the United States to Vancouver, a statement that somewhat confounded immigration officials and impeded their removal. But Bishin Singh and Pakar Singh, who had separately been captured and imprisoned in Blaine's detention center, swore that they saw the men in New Westminster, Canada, shortly before their arrest.[24] The nine were transferred from Blaine to Seattle's larger detention center. There they faced lengthier interrogations that tried to map their lives, document their illegality, and justify their deportation.

Although Surup Singh, Attar Singh, Channan Singh, Lall Singh, and their five companions hailed from different points across the Punjab district of India, they had only recently come to know each other. Across the Pacific Northwest in the early years of the century, small groups of Sikh men commonly gathered under the direction of a straw boss, who spoke a bit more English than the others and facilitated their jobs and journeys. They might travel together for a short time, forming a sort of loose, temporary, diasporic Sikh community-in-motion. Their collective experiences—of global mobility, labor, detention and interrogation, and opposition—sheds light into the complex nature of Sikh and South Asian community formation in struggle with the emergent national border policing regime. Sikh migrants' experience in North America reflected how different people developed and applied strategies for responding to imperial global racial capitalism.

Most Sikh migrants in North America focused their attention on the conditions of their labor and the communities they might build, regardless of the inconvenient and degrading barrier that the Canada–United States border imposed. Many flagrantly disregarded the emergent white nations' borders, but they were not political radicals. Nevertheless, in their travels across the subcontinent, through British imperial ports of the Far East and across the Pacific Coast of North America, they crossed paths with Sikh and Indian men and women who were in fact revolutionaries. These anticolonial insurgents sought to overthrow British domination in South Asia and white rule in North America, using the relative freedom of the Pacific Coast and border-crossing to shake off pursuers and mount attacks on the British empire and Canadian and US white supremacy. Migrant revolutionaries identified global forces of oppression and confronted them directly. Others in the US-Canada borderlands certainly transgressed geopolitical relations but without seeking to upend them.[25]

Sikh and broader Punjabi migration grew in tandem with the nineteenth-century British empire. The East India Company formally annexed Punjab in 1849, thereby embroiling Punjabis and Punjabi Sikhs within Britain's globe-spanning regime. Sikh travel and diaspora was comprised through "interwoven, overlapping, but occasionally independent sets of webs."[26] The first were built by the British empire's political, economic, and military demands for moving labor, capital, and soldiers across the planet to meet the needs of "merchants, missionaries, and administrators." The commercial, political, and administrative networks linked Punjab to the rest of British India and then to the rest of the empire from South Asia to Australia, Africa, and the Americas. Punjabi migrants laced the second web, comprised of kinship structures and religious institutions and networks, into the imperial labor markets of the first.[27]

An earlier generation of Punjabi Sikhs had traveled throughout the British empire as imperial soldiers and police; British officers imagined Sikhs as a manly and martial race that had demonstrated its loyalty to the Raj after the 1857 Indian mutiny. They laid paths that some, after retirement from the military, or others, seeking work, would follow—across Burma to Malaya, from Hong Kong and Singapore to Thailand, the Dutch East Indies, the Philippines, and soon, beyond.[28] Sikh soldiers returned from the 1897 Queen Victoria Jubilee saw opportunities in British Columbia, and Sikh migrants began to arrive in North America in 1904, with numbers growing to around two thousand Sikh laborers in 1906.[29] They had been encouraged by the

Canadian Pacific Railway as replacements for the steerage traffic lost in the wake of mounting Chinese head taxes exacted by the Canadian government, as well as by agricultural capitalists who foresaw Sikh workers replacing the dwindling numbers of Chinese and Japanese low-wage workers in the wake of exclusion.[30]

The first migrants, sending remittances home, led the way for more. They began to establish local institutions to serve local and far-flung communities. These included temples and sites of worship, from Stockton, California to Vancouver, British Columbia, as well as newspapers that circulated information about opportunities and travails, including anticolonial and nationalist messages.[31] They also faced increasingly virulent racist reaction across the Pacific Coast. By 1906 white nationalists in Canada and the United States fixated on Sikh arrival as a source of contagion and pollution, much in the vein of Chinese exclusion. They were harassed, badgered, driven out of town, even as other Canadians sought to employ them in large numbers in lumber mills. Whites rioted in Bellingham and Everett, Washington, and in Vancouver in 1907, attempting to drive so-called Hindus from their midst. Extralegal violence coupled with legislative action. In 1908, having met with success in passing Chinese migrant head taxes, Canada levied a $200 head tax on Sikh travelers. It also passed the continuous passage law, which prohibited the arrival of any migrant whose journey was not a single voyage. Because there was no continuous steamship travel from Calcutta to the North American Pacific Coast, all South Asian migrants became ineligible to enter. The logic behind continuous journey restriction was stretched but still accorded to imperial legal principles. Canada, as a commonwealth nation, had been unable to restrict the travel of South Asian British subjects without disrupting the stability of the British Raj. Canadians took a page from the South African and Australian restrictionist playbook (who had learned it, in turn, from processes of disenfranchising African Americans in the US South) and developed colorblind language that accomplished much the same end.[32]

At the turn of the century, many South Asian intellectuals and radicals chafed at the impositions of British rule in India as well as white supremacy and oppression in North America. Taraknath Das had been a leader in a secret revolutionary nationalist organization in Bengal in 1905–1906 before moving to Canada. He opened a school for Sikhs at Millside in New Westminster, a popular area for Sikh migrants, and lectured on politics and revolution. He later moved to Seattle.[33] His and aligned anti-imperial movements, including the Ghadr Movement, which grew in the San Francisco Bay Area in 1913, found room to breathe in North America and intended to ignite violent and intellectual revolution in India. Although the newspaper *Ghadr* was particularly targeted toward ridding India of the British, as the newspaper traveled through the workers' quarters, union halls, and temples of the Pacific Coast, its lessons would come to apply in those domains too.[34]

Revolutionary insight sharpened when South Asian radicals connected with domestic radical working-class movements. In March 1914, Har Dyal, a writer, activist, philosopher, and Stanford lecturer, was arrested and ordered deported on charges of advocating sedition against the British empire and being a foreign anarchist. He was also involved in the San Francisco Radical club, whose membership reportedly included "Socialists, revolutionists and members of the Industrial Workers of the World."[35] Dyal was arrested after giving a lecture at the Industrial Workers Hall in San Francisco. He discussed British rule in India, but another speaker on the bill gave what one newspaper called a "radical lecture on the 'problem of the unemployed.'" Dyal was released on bail but transferred under "special guard" to Angel Island as more than two hundred supporters looked on.[36]

In March 1914, Gurdit Singh chartered the *Komagata Maru* from a small Japanese shipping concern, Shinyei Kisen Goshi Kaisa. Gurdit Singh had been born into a small farming family in Sirhali. Rejected from military service and largely self-educated, he traveled to Malaya in the footsteps of his father and a brother. He learned Chinese and Malay in Taiping and started a handful of successful businesses in dairy and cattle provisioning, rubber, and railroads. He also became a nationalist critic of British rule. "The main purpose of every Sikh," Singh proclaimed, "was to fight for independence."[37]

Gurdit Singh saw economic as well as political opportunity in transporting Sikh workers to Canada on the *Komagata Maru*. The ship's arrival in North America would pit Canada's restrictive immigration law against Britain's desire to quell political dissent among South Asians across the empire. As Singh explained to an American reporter in Shanghai: "If we are admitted [to Canada]" he said, "we will know that the Canadian government is just. If we are deported we will sue the government and if we cannot obtain redress we will go back and take up the matter with the Indian government."[38] A nation should be able to protect the well-being of its subjects overseas, he reasoned, and allowing Indians to be denied entry to Canada due to an unjust law would shame India's government. The ship departed Hong Kong in early April 1914.[39] It gathered more Sikh travelers en route, reaching nearly four hundred passengers. In Moji, Singh and his Japanese hosts discussed the possibilities of Indian independence as well as potential partnerships among the Japanese, Chinese, and Indians of ridding Asia of European control—a possibility given credence by the Russo-Japanese war of 1905.[40]

After its lengthy voyage across the Pacific, the *Komagata Maru* finally anchored near Vancouver in late May. Most of the passengers were denied landing and forced to remain on the ship.[41] While the courts saw a protracted legal battle, public debate stirred white exclusionary movements up and down the coast, and a host of South Asians came together to support the new arrivals. In order to keep an eye on the anticolonial movements, a British special agent named William Hopkinson organized a network of South Asian informants and counterinsurgents along the North American West Coast and liaised with imperial police forces—from Ottawa to London and Calcutta—to infiltrate and disrupt radical movements.[42] Hopkinson and his allies waged covert battles up and down the coast against the *Komagata Maru* travelers' supporters.[43] The migrants lost their legal case and the government affirmed Canada's right to exclude the travelers, but the struggle was being fought on multiple fronts. Four Sikhs had crossed from Canada into the United States and were caught returning with pistols and ammunition. They had been in touch with anticolonial radicals in Seattle and San Francisco, and officials were convinced that the weapons were intended for the *Komagata Maru*.[44]

After the *Komagata Maru*'s departure, officials from each nation aimed to establish, in some legislators' words, tighter "border patrol from the Cascades to the coast" and suppress what they saw as the "serious and menacing aspect" of South Asian migration.[45] Moreover, when the First World War began in August 1914, immigration officers successfully lobbied for greater funding to police the Canadian border for Axis infiltrators and South Asian anticolonial revolutionaries, workers, and other radicals.[46] Leaders of the Ghadr Party and revolutionary movements suspected that the war would weaken British rule in India, and planned to return to South Asia and struggle closer to home.[47] In early September, radicals killed two Sikh informants who had been involved Hopkinson's surveillance networks. In retaliation, Bela Singh, one of Hopkinson's principal agents, shot and killed a member and the president of Vancouver's Sikh Kalhsa Diwan Society. The violence continued.[48] In October, Mewa Singh, the priest of the Sikh Kalhsa Diwan Society's gurdwara, shot and killed Hopkinson before he could give testimony to exculpate Bela Singh at the murder trial. Mewa Singh had been among the men arrested bringing revolvers into Canada from the United States, and investigators were confident he was part of a larger plot.[49]

This was the political context in which Lall Singh, Sundar Singh, Salig Ram, and their fellows were captured on Orcas Island. Sikh and South Asian laborers and revolutionaries had been moving back and forth across the ill-defined, but increasingly policed, US-Canada borderlands. Some confronted the violence of imperialism head-on. Lall Singh, Sundar Singh, Salig Ram were aware of the Ghadr movement, but there is little evidence that they were active partisans. Instead, they were caught in the more quotidian struggle over their place within imperial networks and global racial capitalism.

The deportation hearings that the men faced—the first, a preliminary examination, and the second, a more formal hearing—were fundamentally different from the kind of entry proceedings and interrogations conducted at Ellis Island, Angel Island, or other formal points of entry.[50] Entry processes were designed to screen suitable from unsuitable migrants, searching for signs of undesirability. At Ellis Island inspectors rolled back European migrants' eyelids with buttonhooks, and if someone had a limp, they struggled to mask it from inspectors, and hoped they answered the litany of questions correctly in order to gain entry. It was harder still at Angel Island, where inspectors typically presumed that Asian arrivals ought to be turned back and devised labyrinthine questions to snare the Chinese travelers they presumed to be trying to cheat the Chinese exclusion acts by pretending to be merchants or students, rather than laborers, or else to be related to Chinese legally residing in the United States and therefore eligible to enter.

Deportation interrogations followed a different script, because people facing deportation were already inside the country. They were fraught dramas, often conducted in a hospital, jail, or a prison visiting room, and they took the form of a criminal trial.[51] Migrants might speak little or no English, and an interpreter might speak a different dialect or have their own interests rather than migrants' interests—or even the law—at heart.[52] Migrants were frequently bullied and harassed, badgered and asked leading questions that sought new and additional charges of deportability. In addition to reviewing whatever charges may have been brought before them, a major part of deportation hearings consisted of transcribing, in exquisite detail, the routes that migrants had traveled to, and then within, the United States, what Herman R. Landon, chief of the Exclusion and Expulsion Division, called the migrant's "personal history data." Much of this included spatial information and the migrant's life story.

Calls to transcribe personal histories were codified in 1940, but the practice had been in place for many years. Spatial questions included the person's place of birth, including the nearest city of importance, as well as the province and country. It also included the most recent city of residence in their birth country; their most recent foreign residence; and the country from which they entered the United States. Questions included the names, addresses, and citizenship status of the migrant's nearest relatives overseas as well as the names, addresses, and citizenship statuses of family within the United States. So too did agents demand the dates, places, and manner of entry into the United States as well as verification of the manner and place of entry.[53] The information was a scarcely neutral means of ascertaining geographic fact. Indeed, this spatial information helped to construct or contradict a spatial narrative that would adhere or depart from the immigrant inspectors' sense of plausibility and more pointedly verifiability of modes of permissible travel and entry. Spatial storytelling was a key site of struggle around border formation and could flag the difference between sanctioned or criminalized travel.[54]

Officials accused the nine Sikh men of trying to take advantage of the region's unguarded waterways to sneak into the United States without inspection. They were arrested and detained at the Seattle Detention House, where they were interrogated multiple times. Investigators focused on matters of geography and labor—especially potential impoverishment and susceptibility of becoming a public charge. The men told stories about labor—the hard work they did, and where they did it—but they also told of community support in the face of racial violence, exploitation, and deceit, even as they tried to subvert the hearings themselves.

The men explained that they all arrived in the United States some years earlier; they named the ships on which they had traveled and, as best they could, the dates on which they had arrived and the litany of the places where they had worked. The men were interviewed one at a time, with all nine in the room together. This made it relatively easy for the interrogator to ask questions from one man to the next and check their stories against each other. It was quick and relatively straightforward, but the men could hear each other's testimony, attempt to influence each other, and shape their responses accordingly. On multiple occasions during Chandan Singh's interrogation, for example, Suren Singh tried to whisper things to him about time spent in Stockton, California. The men were scolded but still tried to subvert the interrogation.[55]

They also told investigators that they were on their way to Canada for work when they were detained. The journey they described was just one part of the globe-spanning networks they wove. Their travels began in their respective Punjabi villages, continued along the Grand Trunk Road to Calcutta, and dispersed across Far Eastern networks before gathering in the Pacific Northwest. Twenty-eight-year-old Salag Ram, from Taldihari village in the Punjab's Patiola district, told investigators that he departed from home in 1910 and traveled from Punjab to Calcutta. He spent about a year in Manila before arriving in Seattle in late November 1911 and then traveling to San Francisco. Government agents verified the information he gave about his travels. Ram worked for a number of different farmers across California over the next few years, but did not provide much detail, other than that he traveled north to Seattle on September 14, intending to go north to Vancouver to visit "people from my own districts" who lived there. Chandan Singh, whom Ram said he met in Seattle, helped arrange a boat and local captain to take them through the waterways to Canada.[56]

Chandan Singh was interrogated next. At thirty-six years old, Chandan Singh was older than the rest. He was 5'11" and 190 pounds, with a full beard and long hair.[57] He had left Durd, in the Patiola district of Punjab some sixteen or seventeen years earlier. His travels took him from Punjab to Burma, Shanghai and then San Francisco on the *SS Mongolia* in June 1909. As he explained it, he worked on a railroad in Oakland for six months, then in Astoria, Oregon, for Hammond Lumber; then to Vancouver, Washington, for the Dubose Mill and the Monarch Mill; then back again to Astoria and the Hammond Mill, and on "some railroad." He left Astoria around September 10 for Canada.[58] He met the others there, he said, and the soon met the white man who promised to ferry them across the border.

When Sundar Singh was interrogated the first time, the twenty-six-year-old told the investigator that he had been born in Burggil village, Nacha [sic] district, Punjab. In 1909 he traveled from Punjab to Hong Kong, and from there to San Francisco, landing in March or April 1909. He spent three months picking oranges and plums near Oroville, California, and about a year doing railroad work on the Western Pacific near Portola. He worked in Tracey, California, for about six months and eventually walked to Marysville,

California (about 110 miles), working from farm to farm on the way. He spent about a year on a farm two miles outside of Marysville, picking sugar beets. The inspector was especially curious about the farm near Marysville.

Q: Which way [was the farm] from Marysville?

A: I don't know which way....

Q: Is Marysville in the mountains, or on the plains?

A: Plains.

Q: How far away are the hills?

A: Very far.

Q: Is there any river or water there?

A: No.

Q: No river?

A: Yes, a small rivulet, a small river.

Q: How many?

A: I don't know how many.

Q: Is [Marysville] on the railroad?

A: There is no railroad there. I was working on the farm, didn't see any railroad.[59]

It may have been difficult for Singh to parse the examiners' intended scale: did he mean a river on the farm, or in the town? The inspector tried to trip him up with what seemed to be personal knowledge of the town, bolstered by a bird's-eye view of the city: "There are three railroads running through Marysville and the town is situated at the junction of two rivers.... You couldn't go anyplace without going through the town." Singh responded that yes, there was a railroad, but it was far away from the farm where he worked and that he never went into the city. The 1907 race riot in Bellingham was a very real memory, and possibility of another outbreak always loomed. Threats, racial abuse, and confrontation were common. A Sikh man familiar with the area explained that he "used to go to Marysville every Saturday.... One day a drunk ghora [white man] came out of a bar and motioned to me saying 'Come here slave!' He came close to me and I hit him and got away fast."[60]

Sundar Singh might reasonably choose to avoid that possibility. Nevertheless, he went on to pick grapes in Fresno for two weeks before traveling to Seattle around September 13, 1914. The inspector challenged Singh's chronology, linking space, time, and labor into a coherent narrative: "You say you have been here only five years, yet you have only accounted for three years." Singh responded as best he could but failed to convince the inspector: "I have been walking around, working from place to place; I don't remember the exact dates." Inconsistencies in the spatial narratives and travel stories heightened inspectors' skepticism. The interrogators also tested the men's stories against each other. Even though they heard what the others said, it was hard to remain consistent, as the interrogation drilled for ever-finer detail. Chandan Singh was asked how, where, and when the men met.

Q: Who did you meet first?

A: Attar Singh; he came from Portland with me; then met Santa Singh and Sundar Singh.[61]

They split up while Attar Singh and Chandan Singh made arrangements with the man who promised to ferry them across the border. There was further interrogation about how they met and then connected with the man with the boat. The questions moved back and forth in terms of time, narrative, and location. The investigator pursued one line of questioning about how they met the white man, then asked when Chandan first met Salag Ram. Chandan said he met Salag Ram for the first time "at the station in the evening," although he didn't remember the date. This contradicted Salag Ram's earlier testimony, which was that they had met at 6:00 in the morning and that they left for Canada that night. The inspector pressed the point: "Suppose Salag Ram says he met you in the morning and that [you] all went down to the boat together, is he a liar?" Chandan Singh was stuck, not knowing if he was being tricked or not. "I don't know," he replied.[62]

The search for decent work was the foundation of Sikh mobility across the Pacific Northwest. But the men also suggested some political rational for their movement. Chandan Singh wanted to go to Canada to because "some people were wounded in the Sheik [sic] temple; [he] wanted to see those people."[63] Attar Singh explained that he "heard there was some disturbance in Canada and wanted to go there.... [O]ne of my people is dead and another is detained," and he "wanted to see those people."[64] According to Sundar Singh, "The priest was the leader of the community and was shot dead and I wanted to investigate."[65] The event they described was related to the *Komagata Maru* incident, when police informant Bela Singh shot the Vancouver gurdwara priest in the aftermath of the *Komagata Maru*'s departure. "There was trouble in the Sheik [*sic*] temple," Santa Singh reported, and he "wanted to see what happened; some people were murdered; there was a riot." The inspector asked for more detail, so Santa Singh said that "Harnan Singh was dead; he was my friend"; Santa Singh "wanted to see who murdered him and what happened."[66]

It is difficult to know where these men sat on the spectrum of South Asian and Sikh diasporic politics, and if their dead or detained friends favored its revolutionary or the counterinsurgent factions. If Santa Singh's friend Harnan Singh was also occasionally known in Seattle newspapers as *Herman* Singh, he was one of the police informers recently killed by insurgents.[67] This would suggest, though hardly definitively, allegiance with the more conservative elements of the Sikh diaspora. But the truth of their politics, whatever they may have been, soon became even more difficult to assess. There are no records of what exactly happened in the Seattle Detention House in the week between their first and second interrogations, but at the second round of questioning, the men now claimed that they were captured entering the United States from Canada. The men's motivation for travel was still very much tied up in the search for work. But it is also possible that they left New Westminster and Vancouver because of intra-Sikh revolutionary and counterinsurgent violence. Either way, once evidence of their undocumented entry came to US immigrant inspectors' attention, and on the premise that, as working-class Sikhs they were likely to become public charges, the warrants for their deportation were signed.[68]

Removal was now a matter of governmental logistics. It was no guarantee of success.

On the evening on November 28, 1914, the nine men were at the Seattle Detention House, along with sixty other immigrant prisoners. They had been locked up for around two months. The guard whose shift began at 3:45 p.m. did a head count just before dinner, a routine typical to carceral institutions. Dinner was served between 4:00 and 5:00 in the afternoon. At 5:00 p.m. the prisoners were locked in the main hall upstairs. According to the senior watchman, Thomas Latham, the hall had been "very much crowded of late, a constant moving back and forth, jostling and pushing one another." It was also noisy, especially between dinner and lights-out at 10:00 p.m. A prisoner had to "holler very loud...to make himself heard" over the din.

The combination of noise and overcrowding made it "very difficult," Latham complained, "for hall watchmen to observe all movements."[69]

Louis H. Engels was on duty from 4:00 p.m. until midnight as the second floor's front watchman. His responsibilities included answering the phone, punching the clock every twenty minutes, and inspecting the rooms at irregular intervals. November 28 had been particularly busy. He was helping to coordinate "two separate deportation parties," complex logistical work that he said "occupied a great part of [his] time." Moreover, someone had jammed a shredded a towel into a toilet in Room 9, which Engels begrudgingly removed—so that "the Hindoos could use the toilet." The toilet room and the bathroom flooded at around 8:00 p.m., and he had to mop up the water from each.[70] Latham, suspicious that the toilet might "be a ruse to draw his attention," concentrated on a big, unbarred window in the front of the hall. For the few previous nights, Latham recalled, "the Hindus in room 4 [had] got quite ugly even to the point of mutiny." The prisoners objected to the guards coming in throughout the night and turning on the lights to check on them. They had "strung the globes up high and turned them off in the room so I could not snap [them] on in the hall," Latham reported. As a result, he "had to go in the darkened room, climb up on the bunks, to turn one on" to see into the room. The men also stymied Latham's efforts at surveillance by insisting on closing the door to their room. They would "complain of [a] draft," if he tried to keep it open. Latham kept watch through a small window in the door, but someone had pasted an official notice on the window, which blocked the view.[71]

The night eventually settled into a quieter routine. Engels mopped the water. Latham watched the window that concerned him. They peeked into the hall and the bunkrooms as best they could. Yet when an incoming watchman did his midnight headcount—the one about which prisoners complained as disturbing their sleep—he realized that Surup Singh, Attar Singh, Salig Ram, and Lall Singh were missing. Latham thought they must be hiding in the building, because he had been unusually cautious looking for escaping inmates. But they soon found a small hole in the wire netting inside Room 4's window. Engels had caught two white detainees trying to escape through the same gap and reported it months earlier, but it had not been fixed.[72] Six-foot-long horizontal iron bars stretched across the window's exterior—daunting enough, but in fact they were made of "soft iron," Latham reported, and "easily sprung" because there were no fastenings between them. Latham didn't think that anyone could squeeze through, but saw that the window's lower sash had been torn out—it was only attached with small nails—and was loosely in place. An inspector found footprints and a ten-foot strip of black cloth below the window, which they concluded the men had used to lower themselves from the second story window. At 12:30 on the morning of November 29, 1914, they called for help and distributed photos of the escaped men to police in Washington and Oregon.[73] The bars on the window were reinforced a few days later.[74]

After planning and enacting their escape, Surup Singh, Attar Singh, Salig Ram, and Lall Singh split up, likely believing they would attract less attention individually than together. Salig Ram was recaptured and returned to detention a week later. Surup Singh traveled east and, in the midst of a storm, came to the farm of a civil engineer named D. B. Skinner in Bellevue. Skinner offered Singh shelter, and Singh worked on Skinner's ranch for the next week.[75] The Immigration Bureau soon received an anonymous tip that a "strange Hindu" was working on Skinner's farm. Senior watchman Leroy B. Smith was sent to investigate. The man who escaped from the Detention House wore a long beard, long hair, and a turban. But the one working on the farm was clean-shaven, had short hair, and sported a western-style hat rather than a turban. Smith "closely compared the physical marks of the alien" to those listed in his record and was convinced that they were the same person. The man eventually admitted that he had recently escaped from the detention house.[76]

According to Skinner, Surup Singh was "an efficient, willing, and intelligent worker, and so likable a chap that I have become interested in his case." Skinner thought Singh was "entirely capable of caring for himself without expense to the community" and was willing to pay a $500 bond as surety against his becoming a public charge.[77] Skinner's informal employment and support of the fugitive, and as well as his formal advocacy on Surup Singh's behalf, mirrored the patchwork system of anti-immigrant movement and capture—the anonymous call to authorities, for example—that overlay the Pacific Coast borderlands. Despite Skinner's support, Singh was returned to detention. Surup Singh cut his hair and beard and nearly escaped. Lall Singh left no trace of how he evaded capture, and authorities were never sure if the man they arrested—in 1933, also named Lall Singh—was the same as the man in these records.[78] In any case, Attar Singh was more successful still. He was never caught.

On January 8, 1915, Inspector Weiss took charge of Salig Ram, Surup Singh, Suren Singh, Santa Singh, along with Mal Singh and Lashman Singh, and delivered them from Seattle to San Francisco. It was decided that they did not need a special train and so traveled on a steamship instead down the Pacific Coast, a side trip within the deportation state's networked infrastructure. The men would soon arrive at Angel Island to await removal across the Pacific.[79] His job done, Weiss quickly returned from the Bay Area to his home in Seattle. A few days later, on January 15, Mewa Singh was hanged for the killing of Inspector Hopkinson.[80] It was the latest in more than two-dozen killings in the North American front of global anticolonial struggle that swirled around the *Komagata Maru*.[81] Salig Ram and Surup Singh's deportation was not violent in any straightforward manner, but as with the revolutionary and counterinsurgent killings, it traversed the borderlands of racial capitalism and the three imperial nations. More violence awaited them when they landed in Calcutta and through their journeys to Punjab. But that is the subject of another chapter.

Weiss had little time to rest, get clean clothes, or see his family before heading off for another work trip. Indeed, on the day of Mewa Singh's execution, Weiss heaved his bags on to the Deportation Special and checked the paperwork on his prisoners. Dominic di Stefano, whom he had interrogated months earlier, was among them. They were soon wending their way across the continent, toward Ellis Island, the Atlantic, and Europe, beyond.[82]

But now, before turning east, we travel south, with the Deportation Special into Oregon. As the train left Seattle's outskirts, it rolled by smaller cities like Tacoma, leaving Poverty Bay behind and to the west, Mount Rainier—known as Takhoma to the long-standing Indigenous inhabitants—loomed, exerting a kind of gravity even shrouded in clouds, to the east.

According to Theodore Irwin, passengers on the Deportation Special sat cramped amid the "creaking and straining of the antiquated tourist-type pullmans, built for endurance rather than comfort. The tooting of the train-whistle at every grade crossing. The clickety-click of the wheels in their ears. The slam-bang of the couplings. The sounds of escaping steam."[83] Soon passengers would have caught glimpses of tidy fields and orchards, of thickly

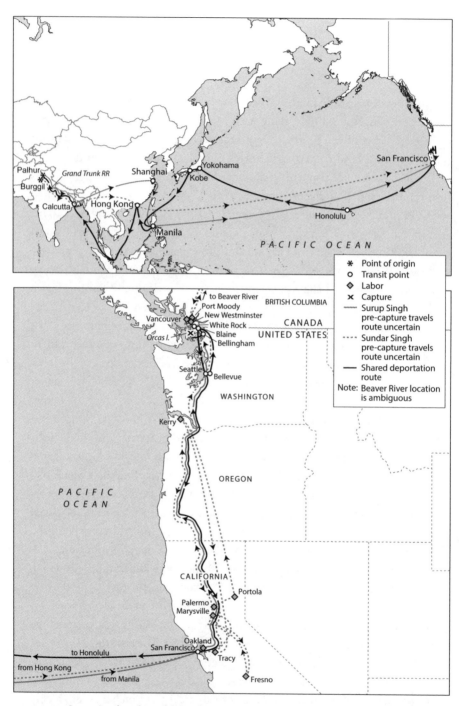

MAP 3. Surup Singh and Sundar Singh's routes.

wooded hillsides and others, ravaged by clearcutting—Sundar Singh, who had worked in timber, would know them well. Beyond the barred windows, railcars tightly packed with logs or finished timber, huffed their way from sites of extraction and refining to shipping depots. It was a settler and extractive colonial dynamic. Speculators and railroad companies saw latent value in the forest, and they paid newcomer workers meager wages to hack down the old growth trees. Where once they had been integral to forest ecologies, the felled trees were reduced to timber, salable commodities integrated into global markets, and further damaging the existing Indigenous human and more-than-human worlds.[84]

The railroads themselves were agents of massive deforestation. Between 1870 and 1900 railroads consumed nearly a quarter of all timber in the United States. In 1890 railroads bought some seventy-three million ties for new track or to repair decaying ones, and by 1927 the railroads spent more on timber than anything other than fuel, and again, consumed a fourth of timber from the United States, cutting down trees and forest far faster than it could replenish itself.[85] But the forest fed the economy, and that was what mattered most to the region's elite. Other than a brief period during the First World War, the lumber industry provided around half of all manufacturing jobs in the Pacific Northwest between 1889 and 1929.[86] Men found work but also friendship and intimacy in those labor camps, and Astoria beckoned as one temporary home and a community. Portland, the deportation train's next destination, was another, larger still.

THREE

Portland

AS THE DEPORTATION SPECIAL approached Portland, it furthered the national project of defining and regulating a particular kind of sexual morality, and of the intimacies that took shape not only in remote timber camps but also in the region's cities and towns.[1] Indeed, the passengers it took on board helped demonstrate how the new deportation regime focused as much on policing sex as it did on efforts to control workers, and it sometimes did both in the same person. Since the 1875 Page Act, Chinese women had been lambasted as likely prostitutes and their entry to the nation radically restricted, in large measure because restrictionists feared that Chinese women would lure white men into their clutches, placing otherwise virtuous white families in peril.[2]

In the following decades, governmental efforts to regulate and investigate immigrants' sexual lives interwove with notions of racial danger, biological degeneracy, and physical and mental debility. Sex workers were also to be deported as of 1891, and the 1907 act approved deportation for those guilty of "immorality" or prostitution within three years following their entry.[3] The biomedical investigative practices, along with regulation and enforcement mechanisms, spoke to capacious fears around morality and sexuality, of what kinds of men and women, with which behaviors, desires, and practices, would be permitted in the country and which would be denied. In the process, ideas of proper sexual practices were written into immigration law and enforced through the deportation train. In his 1914 *Annual Report*, Commissioner-General Caminetti proudly pointed to increased deportations over the past year, but hastened to point out that the bureau was barely "'scratching…the surface' so far as the sexually immoral classes are concerned."[4]

As the hub of the regional commercial economy, Portland thrived in the first decades of the century. Middle-class clerks, small producers, and managers looked after the city and region's commerce. Portland also became a way station for a multiethnic, transient, male community of timber workers, whose labor transformed the region's historical ecological abundance into the commodities that the middle classes traded. People came from far and wide to the Rose City, seeking the comforts of home and better prospects than the places they had left. Protestants and northern Europeans made up most of its population, but recent arrivals were more diverse. Germaine Monet was one among them. She had lived in Portland since 1914, but in June 1919 she was brought aboard the Deportation Special. The details of the twenty-nine-year-old woman's travels are bit hazy, but we can discern certain key elements from her life's path.

Much as Portland's population was growing and its economy modernizing, women's place in Portland's workforce grew too, from 14 percent in 1900 to 24 percent in 1924. Women tended to do low-wage labor, like making clothing, doing domestic work, agricultural processing, or taking on boarders. Smaller numbers entered Portland's pink-collar clerical world.[5] In Portland, as elsewhere, growing numbers of women in the urban workforce and outside of the home prompted fears about women's place in society. Social conservatives sounded dire warnings about the threat that working women posed to morality, the patriarchal family, and even national well-being. Meanwhile, middle-class women challenged the notion of a separate women's sphere. They demanded public authority on the day's most pressing issues: poverty, suffrage, temperance, immigration, child welfare, public health, birth control, the dangers of urbanization, and access to education, just some among them. Many of their concerns came together when they turned toward prostitution.[6]

Few figures gave rise to as much public sentiment in the first decades of the century as did the so-called white slave. In the literature of the day, which drew on and expressed a moral panic about white slavery, the white slave was a young white woman whose inattentive parents did not understand the dangerous allures of her working, unsupervised life in the city. Unhappy with poor wages, and drawn in by immigrant pimps and procurers' promises of easy money, gullible young women were forced into sexual servitude. According to B. S. Steadwell, president of the American Purity Foundation, the white slave trade was voracious, requiring sixty thousand new girls each year. Per Steadwell's remarkable (and unverified) statistics, most of these young women died within five years.[7] In keeping with the opinion of social hygiene advocates, prostitution did not just threaten these young white girls, but all of society. Ellis D. Bruller, Washington State's commissioner of immigration, lamented that prostitution was "an ever-present evil which will require ceaseless attention in order to prevent the undermining of the social fabric." He continued: "There is possibly no other evil...so far reaching or so deadly in its ultimate results, and consequently there is no other evil which requires such constant vigilance."[8] Between 1916 and 1931 some 6,603 people were deported from the interior of the United States for their involvement in sex work.[9]

The white slavery panic seized the nation, and drove the 1911 Dillingham Commission's investigation into the conditions of international migration and sex trades. Progressive Era reformers, social hygienists, and social purity activists pitied sex workers as innocent victims but also blamed them for succumbing to immoral cravings.[10] Perhaps unsurprisingly, white women were more likely figured as innocent victims of the sex industries, while women of color or recent immigrants were portrayed as immoral offenders.[11] Between 1903 and the First World War, prostitution became the second most common category justifying deportation.[12]

Portland's sex industries concentrated in the city's historical Chinatown and edged into the area known as the North End. Nearly 60 percent of the North End's ward resident population was foreign-born, African American, or had one or both parents born overseas, giving it the highest concentration of immigrants in the city.[13] Its concentration of taverns, bars, theaters, and cheap rooming houses made it especially attractive to unattached men passing through the city. A 1907 article in the *Oregonian* described the throngs of working men "who so densely...pack the sidewalks...that one could hardly elbow his way through the throng.... Poolrooms and saloons are crowded until closing time, 1 a.m., and are quickly filled again at the opening of the morning."[14] Those who knew where to look could find opium dens, shooting galleries, prize-fighting rings, massage parlors, and obscene picture shows. These sights and experiences of picaresque and working-class consumption were the scourge of respectable Portland.[15] When a writer outlined the risks of disease that "started in the poorer quarters of the city [but] may spread to the prosperous portions and endanger the lives of its residents," he may as well have referred to the inhabitants and their activities, rather than the germs they supposedly carried.[16] The city's leaders understood the North End as a vice-ridden and racialized space. Not unlike the efforts to control national borders, the North End's migrants were taken as a biological risk to the stable, respectable community.

Germaine Monet was working as a prostitute when, on November 12, 1914, Portland police arrested her and brought her to the Portland City Jail.[17] The police contacted the Immigration Bureau, and two days later, after submitting a telegraphic warrant for her arrest, inspectors arrived at the jail to conduct an initial hearing and determine Monet's legal status.[18] Immigration hearings like these were notoriously one-sided affairs; inspectors harassed and badgered the accused in hopes of provoking some sort of self-incriminating statement. A few years later, the liberal critic William Van Vleck would indict the hearing process as an administrative "quasi-criminal" procedure devised "with a maximum of powers in the administrative officers, a minimum of checks and safeguards against error and prejudice, and with certainty, care, and due deliberation sacrificed to the desire for speed."[19] This was absolutely true. The passage appended to the end of Monet's hearing, like countless others—that it took place "without duress or coercion on the part of the officer," rings as if it protests too much—deserves to be read with skepticism.[20]

Nevertheless, deportation hearings were complex performative events. Investigating agents performed the state, with its suite of interrogating powers, coercions, and rationalities. So-called undesirable immigrants played limited, if important roles, as they responded in a give-and-take to the investigating agents. The relationship was, of course, deeply asymmetrical, but some were better prepared than others. In Monet's case, officers solicited Monet's admission of prostitution, the act that so incensed Portland's anti-vice operatives. She responded accordingly, but she was playing them too. Perhaps in her experience as a sex worker, she had learned how to give the customer what he wanted while still maintaining a limited degree of control.[21] In any event, in her hearing, Monet was unrepentant about her trade. She dispelled any sense that she was a "white slave" and explained that she and Charles Ern, her husband, pimp, and partner of some years, rented a hotel room from a French woman named Jennie, above a French restaurant on Fifth Street, where Monet worked and had been arrested.[22] That was only the most recent of her places of work.

Monet explained that she had been born in Brussels, Belgium, in January

1886. She moved to Montreal, Canada, in the summer of 1911. She was vague on some details, and this raised the inspector's suspicion. That said, he was not overly concerned, because Monet had already admitted to working as a prostitute, which assured her deportability. Nevertheless, from the summer of 1911 until 1913 she worked at a laundry on Hotel de Ville Street near St. Catherine and Cadieux Streets, and though they had not officially married, began living with Charles Ern "as man and wife." They moved to Vancouver, British Columbia, near the docks. She worked as a prostitute in the summer of 1913 but found other ways to make ends meet for the rest of the time. In mid-October 1914, Monet explained, she and Ern came to Portland. Although information about her transatlantic voyage was uncertain, the detail of her train trip from Vancouver seemed real enough. En route, she said, an immigration inspector spoke to Ern but ignored her, and she was generally excluded from the conversation. She slept while the men talked. Monet peppered detail throughout, including that she and Ern had gotten married in Vancouver, Washington, because they thought it would be safer for her if she were married, especially because he was an American citizen. Claiming US citizenship through marriage seemed not to trouble the inspector, and he did not seek clarification as to whether he might risk deporting a US citizen. Instead, he asked where she would want to be deported to. Montreal was her first choice. When asked where in Belgium she would want to be removed to, she said it did not matter, since she had no family there— but she would "prefer to be sent to the nearest place to France."[23]

The inspectors proceeded with Monet's deportation warrant to Belgium. The warrant listed a host of offenses: having "committed a felony or misdemeanor or other crime of moral turpitude prior to her entry" and, moreover, that she was a prostitute at the time of her entry; had entered the United States to be a prostitute (or for other immoral purposes); had been found residing in a house of prostitution; had entered the country without inspection; and had submitted false documents.[24] Each of these justified her expulsion under existing law; together, however, they made for an ironclad case. Monet was released from jail shortly thereafter, in order to be "detained" at the Home of the Sisters of the Good Shepherd, a Catholic organization within a self-described heroic Purity Movement to save fallen women.[25] Immigration officials commonly sent women arrested on prostitution charges to such institutions to save costs, though the Sisters still charged the government $5 per week for Monet's detention.[26] The Sisters Home was a Catholic variation on already existing women's carceral facilities, but its religious orientations perhaps harkened closer to the longer and religious past of the penitentiary than did the early twentieth-century prison.

Monet's move from the Portland Jail, a municipal carceral facility, to a charitable (but still coercive) institution demonstrated the multiple modes and forms of immigrant detention and complexities of the early US deportation infrastructure. Much as the US deportation regime relied on private firms like Southern Pacific or the Great Northern railroad, the Sisters of the Good Shepherd demonstrated how public control interlocked with corporate or charitable systems.[27] Though the government sent Monet to the Sisters to cut government costs, the Sisters Home, like other charitable-coercive facilities, had its own religious, moral, pedagogical, and gender-specific pedagogy in proper womanhood. The Sisters commonly drew on domestic and religious metaphors in their nomenclature of *missions* and *homes*. In truth, this hardly distinguished them from many Progressive Era women prisons, which drew on similarly homey metaphors of "cottages" rather than prisons. Evidence is limited, but we might presume that charitable institutions, like jails and prisons, were racially segregated.[28] The historian Ruth Rosen found that rehabilitation programs in rescue homes in Portland, Oregon—and possibly the Sisters of the Good Shepherd where Monet found herself—included almost exactly the race, class, and gender training in explicitly punitive women's carceral facilities. Such instruction as there was typically included sewing, scrubbing, and preparation for a life of waged or marital domestic servitude: precisely the kind of drudgery that many sex workers hoped to avoid. Nevertheless, prison matrons and reform home managers alike believed "that proper training in feminine domesticity was an essential precondition for redemption."[29]

Whatever conditions Monet found in the Sisters Home, immigration officials continued to deliberate on her case. Clerks determined that deporting her to Belgium would be impossible. War had broken out in Europe; Belgium was in Axis territory, on the far side of the trenches and the Western Front, so officials could not arrange her travel. Moreover, although passenger ships (and deportation traffic) still made the transatlantic voyage, it was a risky affair. By December 1914 officials decided that Monet could be released from the Sisters' custody. She should pay a bond if she could afford it, or—demonstrating a level of trust and largesse—she would be released on her own recognizance if she could not.[30] Sources are silent about Germaine Monet's experience for the next five years, after the Sisters Home and resumed life during the war. Perhaps she settled into a more mainstream domestic life, as did many who transitioned out of sex work, or perhaps she returned to her trade but managed to avoid detection. Nevertheless, by February 1919, and as deportation traffic resumed with the war's end, Monet received word that she would be deported to Belgium.[31]

Monet met with immigration agents soon thereafter. When she did, she confessed that she had deceived them. Her real name, she explained, was Germaine Rigolout. She was not from Belgium but rather was from Besançon, France, where both of her parents still lived and where she had French citizenship. She had claimed to be from Belgium because of the war. "I thought that if I said I was a Belgian," she explained, "I would not have to go back. I came to this country right after the war was declared." She clarified that she had tried to come to the United States in 1911 but, as a woman traveling alone, had been detained at Ellis Island for two weeks before being debarred. On the 1914 journey she said that she traveled to Brussels, where she met with a French man named Gabriel (whose surname she refused to divulge), and they fled immediately after the war began to avoid the fighting. Their journey was more or less as she had suggested earlier, with a few variations.[32]

Immigration inspectors were furious. Portland's Inspector Bonham fumed that she lied "for the purpose of defeating, or at least delaying, deportation, assuming and in this instance correctly, that if she claimed to be a subject of Belgium she would not be returned thereto during the war." Moreover, she remained unrepentant and would still give little information to the investigators about the name of her supposed procurer. "She consistently refused, telling the ridiculous story that she never knew his last name, notwithstanding that she lived with him in France, joined him in Belgium, and traveled with him…to England and…Canada, and finally with his connivance entered the United States where they were together up to about the time of her arrest." Germaine said that she was reformed and wanted to stay in the United States, but Bonham was entirely unswayed. In return for her unwillingness to identify the man for whom she had worked as a prostitute, or as a spouse—for whatever reasons—the immigration inspector would deny her leniency, support, or advocacy. This withdrew any potential pitiable status as victim of white slavery and affirmed her status as a social threat to American sexual morality.[33] Soon enough, she received her French passport under the name Germaine Rigolout, and her travel was arranged.

Thanks to Germaine Rigolout's ability to give men enough of what they wanted, she was able to claim something for herself. Fooling the deportation

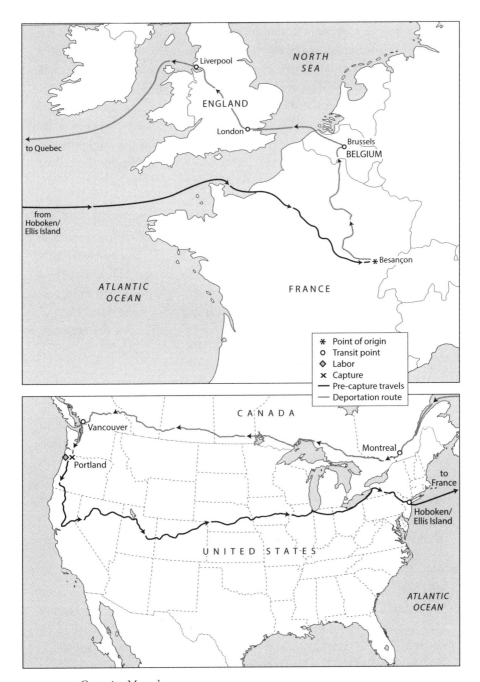

Liverpool

NORTH SEA

ENGLAND

London

to Quebec

Brussels

BELGIUM

from Hoboken/ Ellis Island

* Besançon

ATLANTIC OCEAN

FRANCE

* Point of origin
o Transit point
◇ Labor
× Capture
— Pre-capture travels
— Deportation route

CANADA

Vancouver

Montreal

Portland

to France

Hoboken/ Ellis Island

UNITED STATES

ATLANTIC OCEAN

MAP 4. Germaine Monet's route.

regime with a false identity and birthplace allowed her to remain in the United States for five years, escaping the industrial carnage and war that devastated Europe—and avoiding the fate of the ten thousand French civilians sent to work in German camps, or the French women forced into hard agricultural labor on the Axis's behalf, and accused, ironically, of being "fallen women" themselves.[34] Others who boarded the deportation were not so lucky. Some earlier passengers were deported back into the war itself; others, like Frank Abbott, would fight in the war before coming to the United States, only to be returned to a devastated postwar world.

In late August 1919, Frank Abbott boarded the Deportation Special in Pendleton, Oregon. Abbott was being removed because he was retroactively determined to have been likely to become a public charge (LPC), one of 1,155 such cases that year. But he was also among the eighty deported in 1919 on the grounds of being "mentally or physically defective at the time of entry." The real reason, hidden behind the LPC and accusations of defectiveness, was that he had approached male youth for sex at the Walla Walla YMCA and subsequently been locked up.[35]

Abbott, a twenty-one-year-old Englishman and Great War veteran, had spent the previous six months in jail in Walla Walla, Washington. The lanky young man, 6'5" tall, had been never been in the best of health, and time behind bars had taken an additional toll.[36] Despite having been incarcerated for six months, he was never charged with a criminal offense. But the deportation regime's evidentiary rules were supple enough to enable Abbott's expulsion. His experience also reveals something of transient and sedentary male youth sexual cultures in the Pacific Northwest, the evolution of middle-class attacks on same-sex sex, the symbolic protection of white male children as future national leaders, how queerness articulated with disability, and how men with same-sex desire were treated by their families. Definitions of "normal" white American masculinity and citizenship, along with ideas around the age of consent, were being produced and negotiated, while foreignness and queerness were linked with disability and pollution.[37] Deportation offered a federal system to affirm such differences in citizenship and alienage. As a Walla Walla county prosecutor proclaimed: "We don't want them and we won't have them" in this country.[38]

Known as the Garden City, Walla Walla was a prosperous and rapidly growing farming community in southeastern Washington State. The town's promotional literature boasted its tree-lined streets and that visitors would find "more fine homes in proportion to size than any city in the state."[39] Boosters were less open about the state prison in their town, built in 1886, but it played its part, and no few noncitizen inmates made their way aboard the Deportation Special too.[40] Frank Abbott's family numbered among the immigrants who contributed to Walla Walla's growth. Born in Hanover Square, England, in December 1897, he and his father, Charles Abbott, arrived in New York in December 1918.[41] They were to meet Frank's mother, Isabella, and his sister, Eileen, in Walla Walla. Isabella's brother, James Taylor, ran a successful restaurant there and laid the path from England that his sister's family would follow.

Many, perhaps most, of the people who found themselves within the reaches of the US deportation regime had been displaced from their natal lands by the forces of global racial capitalism or imperialism. Frank Abbott's family had been more the agents than the victims of each, but now, in the aftermath of the Great War—when those imperial powers turned on themselves—they had fallen on hard times. Frank's mother was born in India in 1869. Her father, a general in the Second Bombay light cavalry, died shortly after her birth. She returned to London, where she was educated by private governesses and eventually came to move in rarified circles, hosting Ladies' Club events at her home. She met her future husband when he attended a meeting. Charles was an actor, and charming.[42] He came to visit frequently, and Isabella's friends soon talked her into marrying him, lest rumors begin about the propriety of their relationship. As Isabella later related, as Charles's career stalled and he turned to drink, he became abusive and terrorized the family with threats, tantrums, and brutal violence.[43] One evening, Isabella refused sex with her husband, who became incensed. Frank, then a teenager, insisted on staying with her through the night. His mother owned a revolver, which Frank held all night. He was prepared to shoot his father, "not to kill but to maim," his mother later insisted.[44]

This was young Frank's home life. His mother regretted that could not provide him a private education and he seemed ill suited for public schools but eventually found his footing at a boarding school overseas. He began learning about engines and automobiles, and put those skills to use when the war began.[45] Frank became a driver and mechanic in military and civilian service roles, and he served in France in 1916. Frank was discharged after an unspecified confrontation with a noncommissioned officer but then entered the infantry. Awkward and physically uncoordinated (he had grown seven inches very quickly), he chafed against infantry life. Military physicians eventually pronounced him "mentally unfit," and shortly after the war ended, his family left postwar London for better chances, they hoped, in Walla Walla.[46]

Frank and Charles traveled together from England to the United States in late 1918, arriving in Walla Walla in December that year. Frank found a job at a bicycle repair shop.[47] His father drummed up work as an entertainer and wrote and directed farcical plays for local audiences.[48] Father and son lived together for about three weeks, until Frank moved to the YMCA.[49] Between the repair shop and at the YMCA, Frank found a community of young men and boys to be better company than his drunk and abusive father. YMCAs had become important cultural and social institutions in the Pacific Northwest, much as they had across the nation. In addition to inexpensive food and lodging, Abbott might have taken part in its moral education and physical exercise programs, designed to address middle-class fears of the supposed underdevelopment of young white men.[50]

The patterns of young male sociability suited Frank and reminded him of the best parts of his time in the military and at boarding schools. E. R. Liggett, who owned the bicycle shop where Frank worked, explained that it was common for young men to "monkey around the shop," which included joking, wrestling, and other tomfoolery.[51] The YMCA was similar; a place where young men and boys gathered for homosocial banter. According to fourteen-year-old Edwin Smith, telling "dirty stories" was common among his friends.[52] Smith and Abbott became friendly at the YMCA, and on one occasion Abbott invited Smith to his room to play checkers. The older, worldly Abbott told Smith stories in the midst of the games. He also proposed that they play a kind of strip checkers—and measure their penises against each other. Abbott explained to Smith what oral sex was and offered it to him. Smith, uncomfortable with the proposition, declined.[53] In the ensuing investigation, an inspector asked, "Was [sic] you afraid of him?" Smith said he was. But he also said that Abbott never tried to force him but had tried to "coax" him into sex. Abbott might have overpowered him if he had wanted to, Smith said, but Abbott "just took hold of my hand and then let it go. That is all."[54] Smith went home and told his father.

The elder Smith confronted Fred Applegate, secretary of the YMCA, and contacted A. J. Gillis, county deputy prosecuting attorney in Walla Walla, demanding that he arrest Abbott for sodomy. Washington legislators recently expanded legal definitions of sodomy to include oral sex, making it punishable with a ten-year prison sentence.[55] Gillis explained that conviction was unlikely because there had only been the "proposal to commit the crime" and not "the act of forcing it." Nevertheless, Gillis called Frank Abbott into his office, and Frank admitted to the entirety of the event.[56] Applegate kicked Abbott out of the YMCA, and because he seemed "particularly helpless," Applegate said, he gave Abbott five dollars, lest he become a public charge.[57] Abbott now faced the choice of life on the street or returning to his abusive father. Authorities discussed simply forcing Abbott out of town, but Gillis decided that "a young man of [Abbott's] proclivities ought not to be allowed to be at large." Knowing that immigration law's evidentiary standards were looser than the criminal law's, Gillis contacted Walla Walla's Immigration Inspector Feris.[58] Abbott wouldn't need to choose between the streets or his father, after all. Instead, he was locked in the Walla Walla county jail.

On February 12, Frank Abbott was arrested for "the attempt of malpractice of a young boy at the Y.M.C.A."[59] Sexual intimacy among men and male youth was relatively common in the Northwest's transient working-class cultures, if somewhat less so in middle-class spaces.[60] The relationships could involve elements of economic exchange, intimacy and support, but also coercion and force. Abbott's case involved neither economic exchange, force, nor in fact any physical sexual act. Nevertheless, immigrant inspectors leveled a swarm of charges against Abbott. They charged him with sexual immorality and threatening to become an economic burden on the state. Most important, however, was that his sexuality posed a threat of sexual contagion.[61] In prosecuting his case for removal, immigration agents rhetorically conjoined metaphors of psychopathy and degeneracy, bolstered by physical pathologization. By propositioning Smith, they reasoned, Abbott was undermining the future economic well-being and erotic foundations of the nation.

Walla Walla was primed for a scandal. Antigay fervor had swept the region a few years earlier, and Walla Walla's YMCA was the site of a local sex panic. Despite middle-class concerns about working-class migrants' sexualities, the earlier scandal centered on middle-class white men.[62] A highly reputable Walla Walla church trustee and newspaper editor named John Gibson confessed to engaging in sodomy with fifteen- to eighteen-year-old youths at the YMCA. Gibson begged forgiveness and was sentenced to the nearby state prison. Community members soon forgave him, and the Walla Walla *Bulletin* suggested the town should "endeavor to forget this case."[63] Nevertheless, residents would keep a keen eye on the YMCA. Middle class and elites in the Pacific Northwest were at pains to save white male youth from the multiple dangers that modernity seemed to pose, and particularly its erotic, urban worlds. They feared that young people would be forever tainted, and their corruption would inevitably lead to broader social degeneration.[64] In nearby Portland newspapers ran dozens of headlines proclaiming "A Plea for the Boys," "Habits of American Youth," and "Who Is Responsible for the Boys," and surely found readers in Walla Walla. Boy Scout and YMCA movements proliferated in response, with reformers taking special interest in the sexual lives of male youths.[65]

Inspector Feris tried to learn what exactly happened at the YMCA but also to develop a fuller sense of Abbott and the young man's world. He interviewed Abbott, his family, and multiple members of the Walla Walla community. In addition to determining how and when Abbott might be deported, officials tried to identify the origins of his transgressions. As the historian Margot Canaday has argued, the medico-scientific knowledge of homosexuality and the modern state developed in and through each other, and the investigation delved deep into Abbott's life, his character, and indeed his body. Medical science pathologized same-sex sexual desire—and particularly its manifestation toward youth (itself a liminal category also in the midst of historical contest)—as a kind of physical defect and mental disability.[66] Abbott was remarkably forthcoming and deeply desired to understand how and why he felt the way he did. He admitted to masturbating at different times in his life and explained that had never been with any women. Abbott learned of oral sex when he was ten or eleven years old, at school in England, he explained, but said it had "died down with some of the boys at school naturally."[67] At the time, fellatio among working-class men in the Pacific Northwest was rare, and though middle-class men who increasingly embraced homosexual identities practiced it, in Abbott's case, it was an import from his British schooling.[68]

Abbott was confused and conflicted about Smith's age, he said, as well as the basis of his own sexual desires. The confusion was perhaps unsurprising, given that the very notion of male age of sexual consent and appropriate sexual activity—and with whom—was in the midst of historical change.[69] Yet Inspector Feris had no doubts: he repeated that Smith was "just a boy," and that Abbott was twenty-one years old. "You would ruin this boy's life for just a little pleasure," Feris accused, "what kind of a man are you?" Abbott wasn't sure of the answer. "It is astonishing to everyone else and to myself," he replied.[70] Abbott, apparently filled with self-loathing, said he was "disgusted with the causes, the motives and the results of the whole affair."[71] He thought it was a continuation of the passing phase that had started as a youngster, and attested that this episode had passed as quickly. In 1912, John Gibson's allies in Walla Walla believed that he was not "constitutionally homosexual," but rather, that a nervous breakdown led to a temporary sexual lapse.[72] Two prominent Walla Walla physicians examined Frank Abbott. One speculated that if the "defects grew from some physical cause," Abbott "might be cured." But if there were mental causes, the case would be "exceedingly difficult and practically hopeless." It would be hard to know, because in the physician's experience, "the victims of this practice were such ungodly liars" that nothing they said could be believed.[73]

While words might deceive, the body might give direct evidence. The second physician therefore performed a physical examination and determined that Abbott had a "masturbator's prostrate [*sic*]." One wonders if the investigation involved a rectal exam and the degrees to which the examination could constitute digital rape. Nevertheless, the doctor determined that Abbott was "addicted to other offenses than the one he had solicited"—oral sex—and presumably this meant sodomy. Together, the physicians concluded that Frank was "a pervert and a degenerate and that there was no real hope for a cure." Abbott sought clarification about what exactly a masturbator's prostate was and queried if it were "a physical disability"—seeking, perhaps, a medical cure. The prosecutor was not a physician but opined that the "cure must come from the mental side rather than the physical side."[74] Debate over the causes of Abbott's desire, as a mental ailment or of glandular and thus hormonal etiology, would scarcely be clarified here.[75] The inchoate opinion congealed in the catch-all category of *degeneracy*, a capacious eugenic designation that could be made to explain racial difference, class hierarchy, sexual variations, and mental disability.[76] No medical, legal, or psychological expert could command full knowledge, though each would stake a claim.

As a result of the investigation, the inspector determined that Frank Abbott was "a degenerate and according to doctors, if he should succeed in doing this act of using his mouth on a boy, it might ruin the boy for life by getting him started into doing something that he would be unable to stop." The sex Abbott proposed with Smith was understood as a degenerative disease, a contagion that traveled across bodies and through time, sinister pleasure that endangered the future of white national manhood. Being "unable to stop" similarly drew on medico-moral language of addiction, a feared erosion of self-restraint and self-denial necessary to manly comportment.[77] According to Walla Walla prosecutor A. J. Gillis, it was "an abuse of our Immigration laws to allow a young man" like Abbott "coming here from a foreign country to become a citizen." The idea of Abbott's arrival and potentially queer citizenship appalled Gillis, who feared Abbott "would make the worst [citizen] if he is allowed to become a citizen at all."[78]

The inspector determined Abbott was "mentally and physically weak" and a "homo-sexual pervert," both of which had been the case prior to his arrival in the United States. He also reckoned that Abbott suffered from "constitutional, psychopathic inferiority" at the time of entrance, that he was a "degenerate" and "probably incurable." He was also considered physically defective at the time of entry, and inspectors predicted that "it is only a question of a short time until he would become a permanent charge on the state."[79] In May 1919 the Immigration Bureau issued a warrant for Abbott's deportation.[80] It was determined that the steamship company that brought him to the United States should have identified these ailments and that they would be made to pay for his removal.[81] Until then, he remained at the Walla Walla county jail. Others proposed sterilization of so-called sexual deviants as a eugenic fix for transgressions and elimination of supposed heritability into the future. There is no indication that this was undertaken in Abbott's case; spatial elimination through deportation was adequate.[82]

Isabella Abbott was distraught. Despite the doctors' diagnoses, she was sure his father's abuse was the source of her son's ills.

> [H]ad this boy received different treatment from his father during the short time he has been in America, he would never have been in trouble....His father...has ever worked against him and has done his very best to prevent me from knowing where my son was or what has been done or let me see him....I am feeling quite sure that all the faults and weakness and vice that are in the son are inherited from the father and the father's parents.[83]

Despite her best efforts, however, Mrs. Abbott undercut her son's case in key points. When she indicated that her husband was to blame and suggested that his family had a tradition of failures, she offered ammunition to eugenic arguments for her son's removal. Mention of her son's so-called abnormal development (by which she apparently meant his interest in same-sex sex) did the same. Moreover, her demonstration of maternal care posed an impossible bind. She might be accused of "Momism," a belief that too much of a mother's love prevented young men from reaching full manhood.[84]

Nevertheless, Isabella continued to beg the federal government to permit her son to remain. In a May letter she pitted a notion of familial care against that of the state. If deportation was based in some regard on the English Poor Laws' notion of a natal municipality looking after a public charge within a sense of *jus solis* citizenship, Isabella Abbott's case was based on maternal care and the domestic home. It was a smaller circle of caregiving. Moreover, English citizenship made no sense for her son; its welfare state may have done something, but there was no *family as such* to stand behind it. "If he is deported back to England," she wrote:

> he is practically lost...because his home is now here. I have come here to settle, and where I am, there is my son's home, and by deporting him he leaves his home and is cast adrift practically in a foreign land....[H]e is perfectly capable of earning his own living and...I have been urgently longing for him to be free to come and help here in the restaurant.[85]

Her brother, with whom she ran the restaurant, would look after Frank as if "he were his own son."[86] She used every argument she could muster: that he was sorry and that he was cured; that his months in jail were punishment enough; that his military service merited consideration; that she and his sister needed him as much as he needed his family. When the US government offered little hope, she wrote to the British consul in hopes of their support.[87] She was willing for them all to move to Canada if it would prevent their separation.[88]

Isabella Abbott's pleading came to naught. There was never any evidence of sexual contact beyond suggestions, but Frank Abbott had admitted to desires that signaled a danger to the national future. Medical opinion drew on a eugenic theory of sexual degeneracy to substantiate the calls for his removal, even though he would have no family to care for him in England. Moreover, his abusive father remained very much at large, while his mother, sister, and uncle strove mightily to look after him. Abbott was taken aboard the Deportation Special; the young men and the sexual morality of Walla Walla were understood to be safer. The difference between Abbott and John Gibson's case, a few years earlier, was stark. Both claimed to repent for their transgressions, but Gibson was elite and, in Walla Walla's Reverend Brooks's words, a "worthy and capable citizen."[89] Abbott was deemed neither physically capable nor a citizen. He lacked any support beyond his mother.

And so Abbott boarded the Deportation Special. The ungainly and uncertain twenty-one-year-old veteran, wounded by family and by circumstance, had been understood as a danger in and of himself. Deeply conflicted over his desires, he quite possibly agreed with the diagnosis. He rode east on a Union Pacific and CN&W lines and joined the Nickel Plate and DL&W lines toward Hoboken. Though he spent six months imprisoned in the Walla Walla jail, he would spend just two nights at Ellis Island. On August 30, 1919, he was loaded aboard the *SS Baltic*, bound for England. Frank Abbott would surely be better off apart from his father. But without his mother, sister, or uncle, he could hardly call London home.

As the train traversed the rugged mountains between Oregon and California, it skirted lands haunted by the history of American racial cleansing. In 1906, before either Germaine Rigolout or Frank Abbott passed through, a mob of white men forced Chinese cannery workers—legal residents and skilled laborers—from Port Kenyon and Eureka to a place known to the settlers as "Indian Island." The cannery workers spent a week there before being forced onto steamships bound for Portland and San Francisco. And the Chinese workers were likely as unaware of that place's history as Germaine Rigolout, Dominic di Stefano, or Henry Weiss would have been. Because sixty years before the train passed, Wiyot Indian women were holding a women's religious ceremony on the island, with their children among them. There were no men. A settler militia unit, known as the Hydesville Volunteers, converged on them and killed as many as they could. The military drove 450 Indians out of the region, with no recompense for lost land or lives.[90] The precedent for mass removal was well and truly set. But now, focused on the expulsion of undesirable immigrants, as the train rolled south, the history of Indigenous removal was hidden from the deportation train's windows.

The next stop was the Sea Gull Spur in Oakland, California, on the San Francisco Bay. From the Oakland train station, if you looked east, across the hills, and over the rail lines, the rest of the continent beckoned. If you turned west, you might see San Francisco's fabled skyline, its hills descending to the Golden Gate and the wide Pacific beyond. At the mouth of the Bay stood the Presidio, a fort built by Spanish conquistadores and seized when the United States conquered northern Mexico, becoming the headquarters for US Pacific military operations in the nineteenth century. You might imagine the city's storied wealth and mansions, its Chinatown, Mission District, and Little Italy, its monuments to American commodities, extraction, and ties to world markets. Gold, wheat, timber, and more flowed through the Golden

Gate more quickly than the tides, and further—along steamship routes that spanned the globe. But people could not move so freely. Alcatraz Island rose from the Bay, still a military facility, but which would become the famed federal penitentiary in 1934. Angel Island was nearby and stood between the Pacific and North American abundance. Its detention center, opened in 1910, was the first place many Pacific world travelers would see as they arrived in the United States. For others, Asian and non-Asian alike, it was the last land they would know before they were expelled.

———

FOUR

San Francisco

DR. LEO STANLEY MADE HIS WAY from San Quentin Village, the picturesque neighborhood adjoining the State Penitentiary where he worked, and into San Francisco, the metropolis built on hemispheric networks of mining, finance, and migration. San Francisco's waterfront teemed with the frantic physical jostle of everyday urban trade; dockworkers hoisting boxes, sacks, and nets of goods while other stevedores hoped for the call for work; ferries and boats sliding in and out of their berths; the briny Bay air mingling with oily engine smoke, animal and human wastes; streets abuzz with their mix of automobiles, cable cars, and horse-drawn carriages, foot traffic swirling in and throughout the city; occasional beggars causing eddies in the movements around themselves, among the Victorian buildings, piers, warehouses, theaters, and saloons.

He might have seen the Pacific Mail Steamship Company's infamous Pier 40 and the rickety detention shed where Chinese migrants were detained and interrogated between the passage of the Chinese Exclusion Act in 1882 and when Angel Island opened in 1910. The hoopla, signage, and architecture from the 1915 Panama-Pacific International Exposition was testimony to the United States' global ambitions as it overshot the continent; its military victories in 1898 and occupation of the Philippines (and as Pearl Harbor overtook San Francisco as the center of US Pacific military operations for the new century). Throughout, San Francisco's tycoons saw endless opportunity in munitions and war-based production, sharing just enough of the wealth—but no more—to quell union protests and keep the multiethnic masses of workers productive. Further south on the Peninsula, the Potrero Hill ironworks provided machinery for deep extractive mining in the North American hinterland—and wealth for its owners.[1]

Leo Stanley was at the start of a working vacation. After dodging taxis, hawkers, and traffic on his way to the Southern Pacific station at Third and Townsend, he bumped into Mrs. Austin in a busy streetcar. They had met before. For most of the year Austin worked as a translator at Angel Island, but today she brought two women from the Stockton State Asylum to the deportation train for removal. Ever the physician, Stanley judged one of the women to be a "melancholiac, for she would not speak, raise her eyes from the floor of the car, or show any signs of intelligence." The other, he said, was "rather alert, taking in all the surroundings, but at the same time making peculiar grimaces."[2] While Stanley and Austin chatted, we can imagine the women's confusion and bewilderment, and indeed melancholy, having been moved from the confines of an asylum to the tumult of the city. For all of its charms, San Francisco had a long history of alienating and controlling those deemed ill, disabled, or who grimaced inappropriately. The city was home to the United States' first "ugly law" ordinance, passed in 1867, and legally prohibited those who were "diseased, maimed, mutilated, or in any way deformed" from "appearing in streets and public places."[3] Unsightly beggars, with physical or mental disabilities, would be hidden away in almshouses or, as in Stanley's day, if they were noncitizens, loaded aboard the Deportation Special.

After arriving at the station, Austin and Stanley found their train, distinguished by the bars on the windows and set aside from the others under the train shed. They soon greeted the arriving members of the deportation staff. This wasn't Stanley's first trip on the Deportation Special, and he was delighted to see many of the guards he'd met on previous deportation journeys.[4] Two of the guards were also inspectors at Angel Island, like Austin, and had also worked the deportation trains. "In fact, much of the personnel of the staff, even including the cooks," Stanley explained, "were the same as before."[5] The six others were private guards for Southern Pacific. The matron for the trip was Miss Sech, a nurse in San Francisco who had served in the First World War.[6]

A Black porter named John, who, unlike Mrs. Austin, Stanley did not dignify by giving a last name, met them as they arrived, and took the women's bags. Stanley explained in his journal that he had fun joking with John and his wife, who had come to see him off. At least Stanley did not call the man "George," as many white patrons were wont to do of Black sleeping car porters. Still, another guard referred to John "Uncle Tom's twin brother." He likely intended to praise John's selfless service—porters labored endlessly

FIGURE 5. Deportation agent Ed Kline and the porter "John" (Leo Stanley provided no last name), 1922. *Source:* "Five Weeks Leave," Leo L. Stanley Papers, Box 1, Vol. 4, SC070, Stanford University Library Special Collections.

on train journeys—but it is hard to know how John might have received the sentiment.[7] And while Stanley was pleased to see John, the feeling may not have been wholly reciprocated. In an extant photo, John offered a stern look to Stanley's camera.

For Stanley, arriving at the train station held a kind of mystery and excitement, even as it gelled with his broader life's work. Stanley was the chief surgeon at San Quentin State Penitentiary, a position he held from 1913 until 1951. There, his practice intermingled medical concern with punishment and exploitative research. He was an avid eugenicist. California's sterilization law was passed in 1909 and refined in 1913. The Golden State, due to its combination of a large transient and multiracial population, its state and philanthropic infrastructure, and "progressive" politics, became a world leader in sterilization. More than twenty thousand Californians were forcibly or "voluntarily" sterilized over the next seven decades. Most took place in mental institutions and asylums—as in Stockton—rather than prisons like Stanley's San Quentin, and in 1940 Stanley lamented that he had only been able to sterilize six hundred. He believed that the country would have been better if he had been permitted to wield his scalpel with a freer hand.[8]

But Stanley was also a keen traveler, pleased that his services were useful for deportation. "In order to give the best care to its charges," he wrote, "the Government has provided that a qualified physician shall accompany each party, to treat any who may become ill on the way, or to provide adequate emergency treatment in case of accidents."[9] As deportation agent Henry Weiss would learn, this was not always the case. Still, in the person of Leo Stanley, the deportation physician could enforce his political and medical vision through the guise of firm, benevolent caregiving. For this reason, playing a guest role as a physician on the Deportation Special—a spatial rather than a surgical elimination of the unfit; their expulsion across borders, rather than across families or generations—suited him perfectly.[10] In these early days of the deportation regime, before much in the way of civil service or professionalization had deeply penetrated government service, Stanley became involved in deportation through a fraternal organization. Indeed, he was attending an Elk's Lodge Christmas "Jinks" in 1919, when an Angel Island immigration official told him he would be the perfect deportation party member and suggested that he submit an application to join in.[11] Stanley did, and the day before the trip, he met the immigration staff at Angel Island to discuss the care that Stanley was expected to provide. An old hand at coercive medicine, he packed a medical bag to last a week.[12]

For students of American immigration, San Francisco is perhaps most famous as home to the largest Chinatown in North America, the center of Chinese migration to the United States after the Gold Rush. A source of both fear and fantasy for white Californians, Chinatown was a place of relative safety but also a gilded ghetto for Chinese and Chinese Americans in an otherwise hostile land. Despite this—or rather because of this—no Chinese would board the eastbound Deportation Special in San Francisco. Many were *offloaded* from westbound deportation trains here, to board steamships to Hong Kong, but the people joining this *eastbound* train were more likely to hail from across the Atlantic world, or else from Mexico, or others who might be expelled along the southern border.

And there were no few immigrant European San Franciscans who fell afoul of the law. Despite the centrality of anti-Chinese racism in the production of American and Californian whiteness, any number of offenses might land European Americans in the mental asylums or carceral facilities, like Stanley's San Quentin, that fed the deportation train. European whiteness held value, to be sure, and particularly when situated against those racialized as Black, Asian, Mexican, or Indigenous. But whiteness was not always and everywhere the same. It could be squandered, lost, or canceled, overshadowed by the taint of madness, radicalism, indigence, or criminality. The "hobo panic" that seized California's southland early in the century made clear that even white men, unencumbered by family or consistent work—but whose migratory, seasonal labor remained crucial to California agriculture and broader political economy—could be subject to considerable state repression, imprisonment, and removal.[13]

Thanks to Leo Stanley's diary, we briefly met two women transferred from the Stockton Asylum to the Deportation Special. In early 1915, Delfina Rosa Andrade made the same trip, from the Stockton Asylum to the deportation train. The seventy-two-year-old woman was being returned, unwillingly, to the village São Bento, on the island of Terceira, the largest of the central group of five islands in the North Atlantic archipelago known as the Azores. The Azores had been a historical meeting ground and resupply point for North Atlantic trade since Portuguese colonization in the fifteenth century. There, a predominantly Portuguese-descended population made its living by farming, fishing, and restocking the ships that stopped by.[14] Agricultural land tenure was organized around perpetual leasehold, in which small farmers leased the land from owners and then passed the lease to their children. As long as they paid the lease, they kept the proceeds or bore the costs of crop sales.[15] As leases passed across generations, available land diminished, prompting, as in many other locales, waves of peasant outmigration. These land pressures, coupled with concern about mandatory Portuguese military service, led young men to seek opportunities elsewhere. In the early nineteenth century, many joined American whaling vessels, traveling extensively before settling in Massachusetts; others, by the middle of the century, made their way to the California goldfields and laid the foundations of chain migration into the Golden State's Central Coast, the East Bay, and the Central Valley. They were part of a remarkable Azorean Portuguese diaspora, in which a quarter of the Azorean population lived and worked in the United States.[16]

Department of Labor documents recorded Andrade's occupation as a housewife but, given the broad integration of Azorean women in family economies, she had likely also been involved in fishing, farming, or both. She bore fourteen children. Three daughters and four sons lived into adulthood, some of whom relocated to California.[17] After Delfina's husband died, she joined her children in Sacramento and the Central Coast regions of California, where the largest numbers of Portuguese (and Azorean) migrants settled in the Golden State.[18] Despite relative success as farmers, Azorean Portuguese migrants in California saw no small nativist disdain. Immigration records listed Andrade's race as "Portuguese"—that is to say, more or less southern European and on the fringes of whiteness.[19] Most Azorean migrants were Catholic, often illiterate, and of a peasant background, and though they hardly suffered the blunt racism that Black or Asian Americans faced, they were restricted from the full benefits of white supremacy. Mark Twain called the people of the Azores "eminently Portuguese—that is to say, it is slow, poor, shiftless, sleepy, and lazy.... The people lie, and cheat the stranger, and are desperately ignorant, and have hardly any reverence for their dead. The latter trait shows how little better they are than the donkeys they eat and sleep with.... The donkeys and the men, women, and children of a family, all eat and sleep in the same room, and are unclean, are ravaged by vermin, and are truly happy."[20]

Delfina Andrade stayed with her children in Central California for a decade, but it appears that by 1906 her mental health began to deteriorate. Azoreans at home in the archipelago and through Californian diaspora generally maintained deep familial connections and stressed the importance of mutual caregiving. Yet as her mental capacities changed, the stresses of her own and her children's new lives in California undercut her family's ability to care for her.[21] In 1906 her children arranged for her to return and live with a son who had remained in the Azores. She became part of the early century cycles of Azorean migration and return. The most lauded among them were those who returned with accumulated wealth, and built new and—relatively speaking—lavish homes in their natal villages.[22] Delfina's story was not as happy. She stayed with her son until, as she later explained, he died. She was distraught, and though she did not contact her children, Delfina returned to the United States in 1913. A Board of Special Inquiry in Providence noted her "senility," but remarkably permitted her to land and travel to Sacramento. She had arrived on an expensive Saloon Class ticket, which she said she had purchased herself, and carried $60.[23] This apparent display of status convinced inspectors that she would not become a public charge.

Although Delfina had at least one son and a niece in Sacramento, she would remain with her family for just six months. Her family noted a change in her behavior, and on December 26, 1913, had her confined in the Stockton State Hospital.[24] According to medical records, her family had had difficulty looking after her. "She was violent and unmanageable," a physician reported. "Her relatives could do nothing with her."[25] Though certain modes of historical analysis suggest a top-down historical transition in which states and physicians orchestrated a "great confinement" of the so-called mad or people with mental disabilities, Delfina's case suggests that this was less a coherent, top-down process of mass confinement, than one in which families, now in the historical context of Californian modernity, were at a loss at what to do with family members who could not or would not adhere to social norms and for whom there was no socially accepted place.

At the same time, many psychiatrists—or alienists, as they were also known—saw a large role for themselves in protecting the nation from the foreign-born people who populated their asylums. There had long been restrictions on the arrival of people deemed unwell. After all, a 1740 act in Delaware tried to prevent the arrival of "lunatiks" who might become public charges, and in the era of eugenics and mass immigration many physicians believed in a biological link between criminality and madness among the so-called degenerate immigrant classes.[26] G. Alder Blumer's 1903 presidential address to the American Medico-Psychological Association was one among many alienists' statements that bemoaned the high numbers of the foreign-born in American asylums, and applauded federal action that made it easier to deport them. In New York, he complained, "the foreign-born populations is only twenty-five percent of the whole, [while] fifty percent of the inmates in State hospitals are of foreign birth."[27] Psychiatrists and asylum superintendents were gratified when the length of time to remove undesirable people was extended to three years in 1903. When their budgets were tight, removing noncitizens helped keep their costs down, and they insisted on the removal of the noncitizen inmates among their wards.[28]

Andrade was diagnosed with Manic Depressive Insanity and spent the next year in Stockton State Hospital. Conditions in mental institutions varied dramatically, but a great many were remarkably overcrowded. Staff were frequently badly paid and poorly trained, and their small numbers relative to the people who were detained meant that the institutions—and the patients—were commonly filthy.[29] In 1912, Edward Kempf, a newly appointed alienist and assistant physician at Indiana's Central Hospital for the Insane reflected: "This indifference to the health of the patients, attendants and physicians is intolerable and a positive criminal neglect."[30] Complaints about the degrees of filth abounded, from urine and fecal matter to food to bodies and bedding, the stench of pungent medicines and unwashed bodies. So too did complaints of brutality, from ostensibly sanctioned (but torturous) therapeutic treatments to unsanctioned beatings by malicious or simply frustrated staff.[31]

Andrade was physically healthy, doctors reported, but she disrupted institutional routines. She tried repeatedly to escape. She destroyed furniture and fixtures. She was convinced that someone was trying to kill her and was confined in a padded room. She expressed her social alienation and psychic dislocation through what a physician called "incessant chatter in Portuguese."[32] She tried to choke herself and refused food but was force-fed through a tube—a violent form of life-saving.[33] Officials at the Stockton Asylum surely wanted this troublesome patient gone. Perhaps her children heeded the advice of these medical experts, or perhaps they saw the state of the facility where she lived. As they had done in 1906, her children, and now grandchildren, agreed that she would be better off returning to São Bento.[34]

Immigration officials issued a deportation warrant for Delfina Rosa Andrade on the bases of insanity and as likely to become a public charge, and in late January 1915, ordered her onto the next eastbound deportation train.[35] Immigration officials would later complain that the war years and closing of the sea lanes "resulted in the accumulation...of in the neighborhood of 3,000 aliens, mostly insane," who were being supported at state expense and would be expelled as quickly as possible when the war ended.[36] But Andrade did not wait that long; she soon departed New York on the *SS Roma*.[37] She was locked in the "women's part" of the ship's hospital, and the surgeon and nurse checked on her "every day." The master and chief surgeon of the *SS*

Roma attested to Andrade's relative well-being on the seven days of her travel, jotting a terse "good" on the line designated for each day.[38] We can hardly know what she felt of the journey. Historian Robert Santos has remarked on the feelings of *saudades,* or a "deep yearning in one's soul for the past," that many diasporic Azoreans felt for their home islands.[39] One might hope that perhaps she felt some fulfillment of this longing. If she did or not, she landed at Angra, just miles from her birthplace, on May 4, 1915. Her daughter, Maria do C. Andrade e Modo, signed documents confirming that she received her mother.[40] While neither her extended American family nor that country's welfare or healthcare apparatus would look after Delfina, her daughter would now do her best with whatever resources she had.

The circuits of capital, commodities, and labor traversed the Atlantic world and North America and across increasingly restricted national borders. Families were stressed, stretched, transformed, and pulled apart by these forces. In Delfina Andrade's case, new conditions of twentieth-century modernity's mobility and the restructuring of extended families in California's political economies, coupled with her inability to conform to dictates of rationality and domestic productivity, led to her institutionalization and forced removal across the continent and Atlantic. Yet the families stretched by distance and frayed by national borders cannot be easily romanticized. The story of James Pepper, loaded aboard the deportation train in San Francisco, makes this all too clear. A miner originally from Longdale, England, Pepper ostensibly affirmed the notion of a coherent patriarchal family when he returned to England from the silver mines of Fairview, Nevada, to bring back his seventeen-year-old daughter, Olive, to live with him in his new home. But theirs was a story in which family was itself a source of violence. Immigration laws claimed to protect the sanctity of white, male-led families as the natural foundation in the reproduction of the settler population, but there is no question that Olive would have been better far away from her father. [41]

It wasn't clear how James Pepper made his way from Fairview, Nevada, to San Francisco, where he was eventually arrested. But the destination wasn't entirely surprising. Today, Fairview is a barely even acknowledged ghost town, situated between the Walker River Paiute Tribe's Reservation and a US Navy installation. But a century ago, the silver and minerals Pepper helped draw from the Northern Paiute and Western Shoshone borderlands pulled the bustling boom town close, financially and symbolically, to San Francisco's centers of commerce. For a white man with some money in his pocket, it would have been an easy trip.[42]

James Pepper left his family in Longdale, England, in 1904, to earn decent money as a Head Timberman at gold and silver mines in Fairview and Fallon, Nevada. His wife died while he was in the United States, and his two children moved in with his sister. In Nevada he began living with Minnie Brundage, who had a teenage daughter from a previous relationship. As an Englishman and a skilled worker, his whiteness and class status appeared secure. His gender and sexual status as a proper man and father were more troubling. In late 1913, Pepper traveled to England and returned to the United States with his daughter, Olive, who was then seventeen years old, but left his younger son in his sister's care. When immigration authorities confronted unaccompanied women at Ellis Island, they offered a patriarchal mix of concern, coercion, and surveillance to ensure that young women would be safe from white slavery or exploitation on their way to their new homes.[43] Because Olive Pepper traveled with her father, authorities assumed all was well.

They were wrong. According to testimony Olive Pepper would later give, her father raped her at a hotel in New York and again on the train from New York to Nevada. Remarkably, though she was newly arrived and lacked an established support network in Fairview, Olive Pepper turned to the people around her for help. She spoke to her de facto stepmother, Minnie Brundage, and reported the attacks to local authorities. Minnie was prepared to believe her. She had reportedly sent her own teenaged daughter back to Germany—the official reason was for her music education, but really, the rumors went, it was to keep her safe from James Pepper.[44] After Olive brought the charges against her father, he was arrested and locked in the county jail. The charges were soon dismissed, because the rapes had happened beyond Nevada state lines, and thus matters of jurisdiction and formalism limited legal options for redress.

James Pepper was jailed while the charges were investigated. But it also seems that he was locked up for his own protection. Indeed, a mob formed and threatened to castrate him. Its members included townspeople from Fairview, but a doctor from Wonder, Nevada, was called to aid in the procedure. Under other circumstances—had Pepper not been white, and the victim not his daughter—the mob might have demanded his release to lynch him or otherwise exact their own summary justice. That didn't happen. Instead, when Pepper was released from jail, he was told to get out of Fairview. He soon left for San Francisco.

Meanwhile, Fairview's citizens raised about $200 on Olive Pepper's behalf. Part of the money went toward a train ticket to New York City—a form of benevolent community removal, perhaps, in contrast to her father's having been warned out. When Olive Pepper arrived in New York, she lodged at the Florence Crittenden Mission Home, a facility to aid so-called fallen women. Like the Sisters of the Good Shephard in Portland, where Germaine Rigolout had been sent after her arrest, the Mission Home was part of the broader network of charitable institution with ties to the deportation regime. Administrators at the Mission Home must have had close ties with agents at Ellis Island, because ten days after she arrived, immigration officials at Ellis Island sought a warrant for Olive Pepper's arrest. They brought her from the Mission Home to Ellis Island, where she was detained and interrogated.

Some women who had fallen into disrepute through the so-called white slave trade were accorded the status of victims, considered worthy of being saved by those who might instruct them in the virtues of Victorian Protestant femininity.[45] Pepper could have been a good candidate. As she explained, and with immigration officials' permission, she hoped to remain in New York and study nursing, a seemingly ideal and appropriately feminine form of labor. She even had some money left over from the citizens of Fairview to help her get started. Yet, as the historian Estelle Freedman has argued, if the ability to level rape charges is a measure of someone's sexual and political sovereignty, and thus a measure of their citizenship, Olive Pepper's proved to be a threshold case.[46] The people of Fairview believed her, but the immigrant inspector who heard Olive's case had little patience for her plans. Instead, the inspector determined "that on account of the criminal tendencies of her father, [she was] a person likely to become a public charge." The LPC designation was, as ever, a malleable accusation and nearly impossible to disprove.[47]

The inspector's recommendation followed a callous eugenic logic, in which the crimes her father committed against her were evidence of her future guilt. Because Olive Pepper was abused by her father rather than entrapped by a stranger, she received none of the benefits of victim status. In such an understanding, Olive was less the victim of family sexual violence than she was an inheritor of her father's criminality. The futurity of her offense was the possibility of receiving public aid—either collecting welfare or serving time in a jail—rather than any kind of intergenerational trauma. For those reasons, Olive was deported from the United States, likely returning to her aunt and younger brother in Longdale.

While Olive's case was being investigated, inspectors went forward with charges against her father. He had fled Fairview but soon was arrested and brought to Angel Island in California. There, he faced questioning about his life in the United States, his relationship with his daughter, and the details of their travels. He flatly denied all wrongdoing. In the face of conflicting testimony and little direct evidence, the immigration inspectors had to make a difficult decision. Commissioner Backus was inclined to dismiss the charges as based on "the worst form of 'hearsay' evidence," although he did acknowledge that judicial standards of evidence did not apply.[48] In contrast, Inspector Lawler believed that there was little motive for a daughter to make false charges against her father and that that because he nearly faced summary justice in Nevada, the accusations were likely true.[49] Commissioner Backus eventually concurred. According to Backus, the threats to James Pepper's life by the citizens of Fairview revealed "a state of popular disapproval and public indignation as would indicate the truth of the charges made by the daughter." James Pepper would be deported too.[50]

Their decision to deport James Pepper sublimated lynch violence through legal territorial removal, and was enabled by the federal government. Here, the traditions of lynch violence were incorporated into the federal deportation regime's ostensibly bloodless forms of spatial control. Still, James Pepper's forced removal displaced, but did not address, the family violence that Olive Pepper survived. James Pepper was loaded aboard the Deportation Special in San Francisco, bound for Ellis Island, and then onto a steamship for Liverpool. From there, however, available records fall silent. Like his daughter, he probably returned to Longdale, and he probably visited his sister. We don't know how Olive might have protected herself when she and her father met again. US immigration officials were not particularly concerned.

Even within the deportation regime, or aboard the train, a young woman like Olive would not have been safe from the men who claimed to work for national protection. Stephanie, a protagonist in *Strange Passage*, was groped by a train guard. As she approached the bathroom, the guard's "hand went out, touched her leg, caressed it briefly. Stephanie jumped. A terrified glance at the guard's eyes and she scuttled back, trembling, a hot sensation stabbing through her stomach." She immediately sat next to a big blond Polish woman, a former prostitute with marcelled hair.

No one apparently had noticed what had happened. But Stephanie was afraid to look up. She felt that the eyes of all the men were fixed on her, all suddenly like the eyes of the guard. This was her first day on the train. At the thought of the night, Stephanie wilted within herself and she gagged to keep back the tears.[51]

Similar cases of sexual abuse within the deportation regime would abound in the century to come.[52]

As the Deportation Special departed the Bay Area, it gathered speed across California's Central Valley. Outside the barred windows, migrants—Mexican nationals but also Filipinos and South Asians like Attar Singh, who had themselves replaced Chinese and Japanese workers denied by exclusion—drew vast wealth in wheat, tomatoes, and citrus from the soil, even if little of that wealth made its way into their wages. Occasionally, at an unforeseen stop in Brawley or El Centro, a carload of produce would be hitched onto their train, linking the rail-based circuits of capital, commodities, and people.[53] As long as the migrant workers bolstered growers' profits and did not protest against poor pay or working conditions, as long as they stayed out of the regime's way, they were safe from the Deportation Special.

The train would spew soot and ash as it climbed the foothills and then Sierra Nevada proper, unpredictable stops and new stations, perhaps adding another locomotive for power.[54] The unfree travelers would endure another headcount on the train, the unfamiliar passengers forced next to them; the jostles, the noise, the smells, as "the odors of ten-day socks and underclothes corked their nostrils."[55] Yet Leo Stanley was enjoying himself. Though passengers like Olive or Stephanie had reason to fear for their safety throughout the night, Leo Stanley awoke refreshed. He waxed poetic on the beauty of the American landscape outside his window, the sun cresting the Sierras and "casting its rays upon the peaceful farms in the floor of the valley."[56] Still, fancying himself sensitive to the vagaries of the human condition, Stanley noted some pathos among his charges. He considered a Mexican woman, dressed in mourning black, with her three young children. Her husband had died, and they were therefore deported as public charges. She was "train sick most of the time... [and] laid curled up in one of the seats." Her four-year-old son, concerned, would occasionally pull aside the mantilla she had over her face to give her a kiss and comfort her.[57] Sad, to be sure, but Stanley wouldn't let that dampen his journey, or his mission to keep the country safe from people like that.

FIVE

Denver

ON THE MORNING OF JULY 12, 1917, Sheriff Harry Wheeler led some twenty-two hundred armed deputies and vigilantes through Bisbee, Arizona, kicking down doors and demanding to know "Are you an American, or are you not?"[1] There was a strike going on. It was peaceful, led by the Industrial Workers of the World (IWW). Bisbee was home to Phelps Dodge, one of the immense, and immensely profitable, mining corporations that turned the Sonora desert into integrated copper-producing borderlands.[2] Bisbee was a company town, but Sheriff Wheeler wasn't any simple Phelps Dodge shill. He had been relatively independent of the executives and managers who looked for any opportunity to crush organized workers. More of a nationalist and patriot than a company man, Wheeler believed that the strike was a German effort to undermine the United States. In the wake of the Zimmerman telegram (which threatened German support for Mexico opening a new front in the world war) and his own long-standing effort to protect the US Southwest from what he saw as a Mexican invasion, Wheeler believed that forcibly removing the IWW and strikers, especially noncitizens, was a means of national defense.[3]

Prior to the door-kicking raids through the town that July morning, many of Wheeler's "deputies" had taken part in a semimilitary organization to defend Bisbee from the Mexican revolution. Some drew from the middling or wealthy ranks of the Citizens Protective League, others were pro-company workers who believed that they were protecting white workingmen from competition with Mexicans and other, especially Slavic, foreigners. They sought to make Bisbee a "white man's camp."[4] So it was that 1,186 "undesirables" were forced out of Bisbee, Arizona, in an incident known as the Bisbee Deportation. The victims were jammed into trains and shipped to

Hermanas, New Mexico, and unloaded in the desert. They were then sent to the US army outpost at Columbus, New Mexico.[5] Despite relentless patriotic proclamations, the Bisbee Deportation was no formal, federally sanctioned event. Indeed, investigators for a Presidential Mediation Committee later called it "wholly illegal" and conducted by a "vigilance committee" with "no authority whatever in law."[6]

A similar dynamic was unfolding far to the north in Butte, Montana, with local attacks on striking workers, particularly against the IWW. Federal administrators and Presidential Mediation Committee members bristled at local authorities' and vigilantes' actions in driving out radicals. Things would run more smoothly if the federal government got rid of immigrant political agitators, especially if there were international connections at play. That was one lesson from the movement against South Asian radicals in the Pacific Northwest. And that's how it played out in Butte. Between 1918 and 1931 the federal government deported more than one thousand people under the antiradical clauses of immigration law, sending a clear message to those who remained.[7]

Denver sat midway between Bisbee and Butte along the edge of the Colorado Rocky Mountains. It was the next stop on the Deportation Special. In the mid-nineteenth century, Denver's boosters relentlessly lobbied for their city's primacy in the Rocky Mountain economy as a transport hub for minerals and agricultural goods. When the Kansas Pacific Railroad arrived from the east in 1870, and the Denver Pacific Railroad connected the city to Union Pacific tracks in Cheyenne, Wyoming, Denver's place was secure. Soon, the Denver and Rio Grande Railroad ran along the base of the Rockies and connected to the southwestern networks. Denver's location as an economic capital for the Rocky Mountain region helped see its ascendance from 1870 through the depression of the 1890s. Falling silver prices hurt, but gold from mines in Cripple Creek saved Colorado's economy and stabilized the national monetary system.[8]

Denver's Union Station was at the heart of those networks.[9] New York industrialist Jay Gould and local businessman Walter Scott Chessman built the station on Seventeenth Street, the so-called "Wall Street of the Rockies," affirming the correlation between circulating material commodities—especially ore and grain—and the more ethereal financial flows. It is hard to know how much of the skyline was visible from the windows of the Deportation

Special as it came into the city, or if passengers could peer through the barred windows, or marvel at the station's vaulting ceilings, grand arched windows, and natural light. Like the financial systems behind Denver's Union Station, the sandstone, rhyolite, and granite from which it was built had been chiseled, hammered, and blasted from the Rocky Mountains, leaving behind a scarred landscape of tailings and scrap. For someone looking down from the gilt windows of the Seventeenth Street banks, it must have been a beautiful building.[10]

The political economy of the Rocky Mountain West in the second half of the nineteenth century—and well into the twentieth—was built on a durable, symbiotic relationship between the expropriation of Indigenous peoples' land, mineral exploration, mining resource extraction, and railroad expansion. Another key element was global migration and labor exploitation. Prospectors—only mildly interested in population settlement but keenly driven by resource extractive colonialism—discovered and developed new mine sites. The most successful gained backing from large corporations (the less successful were supplanted by them) and developed relationships with railroad firms. The communities of miners that settled amid the diggings or who simply passed through on their way to the next job were wracked by struggle between the mine owners' relentless drive for profits and the workers' equally relentless demands for control of their working lives and dignity when they were off the clock. Time and again, owners tried to weaken their workers by hiring people from different migrant ethnic communities, and it often worked. When it didn't, self-proclaimed white workers attempted to limit competition from those they disdained as nonwhite—Chinese, Japanese, Mexican, southern or eastern European. It was a common pattern, interrupted only when the Western Federation of Miners, and later and more forcefully, the IWW swore off racism in favor of global and cross-racial working-class solidarity.

Precious metals like gold from California Sutter's Creek and Colorado's Cripple Creek, and silver from the Colorado's Comstock Lode, facilitated American financial expansion and growth in the currency and speculative circuits of world markets. Base metals—iron from the Mesabi Range, copper from Arizona and Montana and lead from Colorado—allowed the proliferation of rail lines across the continent, which in turn accelerated the flows of commodities from North America's western hinterlands across the planet. By the 1890s copper pulled from Montana and the Arizona/Sonora borderlands allowed new and cheaper forms of communication via telegraph and newly electrified urban and industrial worlds. Burning coal, pulled by hard-working miners from the anthracite regions of Pennsylvania and from Ludlow, Colorado, released the energy to set these commodities and people in motion across integrated but alienating social and economic worlds. Labor struggles in the rural and Mountain West had long been heated and periodically violent and became more so in the early twentieth century. The combination of rapid industrialization and unforgiving labor conditions, the cultures of masculinity and of rapid transience, the multiethnic combinations of recent and longtime immigrant populations and attendant emergences of nationalist conflict, the forms of spatial and physical labor control, and low wages and indebtedness to owners or contractors comprised a volatile mix in which workers were only somewhat less likely than owners to resort to violence.[11]

Joseph Kennedy was 5'8" tall, with dark, deep-set eyes and hair parted over a high forehead, a long nose, and full lips. In a photo from July 1919—a mug shot—a bruise is fading beneath his left eye. He boarded the Deportation Special in Denver. As a member of the Industrial Workers of the World, he was familiar with state surveillance and physical attacks; the bruise was hardly the worst injury he'd borne in the Wobblies' struggle for industrial democracy in Butte, Montana, where he had recently been living.[12] Kennedy was being deported because he was considered a political radical. Since 1903 and in the wake of the McKinley assassination, the United States had refined immigration and deportation codes around political beliefs, and anarchists were painted as the most dangerous of all. So it was that Kennedy's ideas of industrial democracy and workers' rights exceeded the boundaries of permissible political thought, especially during the coercive hyperpatriotism of the First World War. But Joseph Kennedy hadn't always been a radical. Life—and death—as a worker in the Butte copper mines made him into one.[13]

Joe Kennedy was born in April 1885 and raised in Belfast, Ireland, and when he was nine years old, he ran away to live on a small farm outside of Newry, County Down. There, he worked for a farmer named John Kinney. Shortly after his twentieth birthday, Kennedy became one of the fifty-three thousand Irish migrants to the United States in 1905, striving, as he put it, "to better his condition."[14] An uncle who already lived in Helena, Montana, bought young Kennedy's ticket, and he arrived in New York in May 1905 and soon joined his uncle. He was one of the 3.1 million Irish emigrants who trav-

FIGURE 6. Joe Kennedy, 1919. *Source:* RG 85, Entry 9, 54161/74, National Archives and Records Administration, Washington, DC.

eled to the United States between 1856 and 1921, contributing skill and toil to the emergent Atlantic world economic system. They were drawn by the prospect of economic well-being, but also driven by major transformations in the Irish economy, none of which boded well for its peasantry.

Jointly held tenancies and shared rundale farming were sundered, common lands were enclosed, poorer landholders and tenants were evicted as wealthy men known as "strong farmers" gathered property. These farmers in turn consolidated their own political and economic power. Even the tenants who maintained access to land came to rely on passing the land—or rather, access to land, since they did not own it—to their first-born sons, forcing other sons and daughters alike to seek fortunes elsewhere.[15] US- and English-made goods were dumped into Ireland, which led to the deindustrialization of southern Ireland. As one historian succinctly put it, "there were no jobs, no inheritances, no dowries, no access to land, no promise—or even faint hope—of a secure future."[16] Rural workers in other countries might move to cities with industrial foundations within their own borders, but because Ireland had no large cities and little industry, overseas travel was the best among limited options.[17]

And for Irish migrants, Butte, Montana, shone brightly. The city grew in a small alpine basin dotted with mountain grasses and sage. A mountain, the famed "Big Butte," descended from the northern end of the basin toward the valley floor, and its geology and visible surface evidence of mineralization—metal-rich quartz veins; green-blue copper carbonates; rusty brown and black signs of iron, zinc, and manganese—promised vast riches underground and tantalized prospectors.[18] Marcus Daly was one of them. In 1856, Daly left the Ulster County of Cavan for the United States. The fifteen-year-old stayed in New York for five years, lived with a sister in San Francisco, and then worked in Comstock's silver mines in Nevada. He was promoted up the ranks and tasked by his employers with examining the silver prospects in

Butte. He invested in one mine and soon bought another—the Anaconda—which he converted from silver to copper.[19] Daly ascended American social and economic ladders but remained a renowned Irish nationalist and patron-employer of Irish migrants—often to the exclusion of non-Irish workers. Still, his legacy meant that Irish national pride, and the complexities of Irish diasporic politics, ran thick in Butte's streets.

As the mines bore riches, Butte transformed from a collection of shacks to a mining camp and into a bustling city.[20] The intricacy of its social world was mirrored by the labyrinthine tunnels miners dug in search of ore, creating vast interconnected passageways, stopes, and shafts.[21] The expanding urban and subterranean networks were matched—though of course on a much grander scale—by a surface transport infrastructure to move capital (in this case, ore and workers) across the planet. Union Pacific completed its spur connections to Butte in 1881, allowing to move more copper to the market.[22] As copper flowed out—with much of the associated wealth moving through Denver—workers streamed in. Between 1881 and 1908 four different rail lines connected to Butte: travel was cheap, and the extractive cycle continued.[23] As long as the money flowed—and it did, in vast quantities—Butte's Copper Kings would dominate Montana politics.[24]

Butte was home to a sprawling multiethnic community, with Irish and Cornish miners the longest established among the migrants. By 1900 there were twelve thousand first- and second-generation Irish migrants in Butte's Silver Bow county, which made the Irish a quarter of the local population. Irish comprised a higher percentage of Butte's residents than they did in any other city in the country. They were soon joined by Slavs and Italians, Finns, Swedes, Germans, Chinese, Mexicans, and a score more recent arrivals, each of whom gathered among their compatriots in certain neighborhoods. Dublin Gulch had been predominantly Irish but was also home to Slav miners; Meaderville became Butte's Little Italy; Black and Mexican families tended to concentrate in the "Cabbage Patch" neighborhood. Cree, Chippewa, and Metis Indians, displaced by the diggings and little remarked upon by contemporaries, kept a camp on the outskirts of the city.[25]

Joe Kennedy arrived in Butte in 1909, to live among what one novelist called a "tangled mass of smokestacks, gallow-frames, shabby grey buildings, trestles…[and looked] like a gigantic shipwreck."[26] Kennedy came from Belfast and was younger than many of the established Irish copper miners, who tended to hail from Cork. Longer-term Irish were suspicious of the newer arrivals; transients, they feared, who might not fully appreciate the work they had done to establish themselves as Americans. But Kennedy was not one of the bindlestiff itinerants that concerned Butte's elite. His people were in Helena, and once in Butte, he got to know the mines well. As he drolly put it, he "shoveled a while"—in the Bell Mine and the Diamond, the Leonard and, in 1917, the Black Rock.[27]

The money was far better than what Kennedy would have earned in Ireland. Anaconda insisted that its wages were high, but prices in Butte were higher still.[28] Moreover, Butte wages had fallen relative to other locations, even as Anaconda continued to reap huge profits and drove its workers hard and fast.[29] Kennedy explained that if the shift boss demanded that you filled twenty cars and you couldn't make the target, you risked your job. Conditions in the mines were brutal.[30] As Kennedy related, the air in some was so oxygen-poor that "4 or 5 candles would not burn together." They needed extension lights at the Leonard Mine, where he worked in 1910, because a single candle would go out. On the twelve-hundred-foot level, he said "you could not draw your breath from the heat and gas." The suffocating air was compounded by the oppressive heat. One official report called the mines "dangerous places and hot boxes…where lives are snuffed out," a description that certainly fit with Kennedy's experience.[31] Kennedy estimated the temperature in the mines averaged 98 or 100 degrees Fahrenheit, but his guess was lower than some of the measurements—an investigation in one of Butte's deepest mine shafts found air temperatures of 107 degrees, the rock 113 degrees, and the water at 113 degrees, with humidity at 100 percent.[32] Cave-ins were another constant threat. At the Bell Mine, Kennedy worked the twelve-hundred-foot level in five hundred feet of open ground "without a stick of timber" to support the roof.[33] "Working in stope, small man-way into the stope and no timber to protect you [from a cave in]….Any minute [it could] fall on you."[34]

Simply put, mining was deadly. Between May 7, 1914, and December 14, 1920, no fewer than 239 men died in twenty-six different incidents in Butte copper mines. In 1916 alone, 3,084 accidents in Anaconda mines required hospitalization. Forty-one men died between January 3 and June 7, 1917.[35] And none of this accounts for the mundane injuries that stoic men bore in silence, or the slower, grinding assaults on their lungs and bodies that would show no sign for years. In a 1916–19 study, 42 percent of Butte miners examined suffered from phthisis or silicosis, better known as "miners' consumption."[36]

So it was in early 1917, as war raged in Europe, that Montana's immigrant miners experienced their private travails. They were about to get worse. On the evening of June 8, 1917, Joe Kennedy was walking home from a long shift at the Black Rock Mine when he saw smoke spewing from the Speculator Mine shaft. A gang of company gunmen kept crowds back, and he knew little of what happened underground. But it must have been awful.[37] What happened was this. A team had been trying to move an electrical generator from the twenty-six-hundred-foot level to the twenty-four-hundred-foot level in the Granite Mountain shaft of the Speculator Mine. Sixteen hours into the job, and exhausted, they discovered that one of the cables had tangled and coiled around a hoisting rope. A team went to untangle the snag, and disaster struck when one of the miner's carbide lamps touched the cable where lead sheathing had worn away, revealing its oil-impregnated, and thus highly flammable, insulation.[38]

Fire, smoke, and poisonous gas spread quickly across the twenty-four-hundred-foot level. The entire Speculator Mine received its air from the Granite Mountain shaft, and the ventilation system—which was woefully inadequate for providing fresh air under the best of circumstances—now circulated not fresh air but noxious smoke.[39] One reporter said the flames shot from the Speculator shaft like a "mighty geyser," lighting the night sky.[40] Miners desperately fought to escape raging fire, poison gasses, and intense heat.[41] The noise, coupled by the smoke and flames, brought most of Butte into the streets, and many rushed to offer whatever help they could. It was then that Joe Kennedy came by. Miners waged valiant battles to save others from within the inferno. Some succeeded. A young miner named Manus Duggan sacrificed himself to save twenty-five miners. Others failed, and watched their colleagues die. Two trapped station tenders were roasted alive in front of their coworkers. Of the 410 men in the mine that night, 162 died of smoke and gas inhalation.[42]

Many blamed the company. After all, it was hardly surprising that someone might make a mistake after sixteen hours of grueling labor. Some, and particularly older-line conservative Irish workers, combined ethnocentrism with class critique and lambasted the company for using poorly trained, less skilled workers, eastern and southern Europeans among them. Still others pointed to failed safety features. Montana law required that all bulkheads have functioning iron doors so miners could pass through in an emergency. It wasn't the case here. Dead miners were found piled against the bulkheads, their fingers worn to the knuckles as they tried to claw their way to safety.[43] The state's mine inspector would surely have seen that kind of violation and could have done something about it. But according to Joe Kennedy, the mine inspector was in Anaconda Copper's pocket. Since Kennedy started in the mines, he'd never once seen him.[44]

Joe Kennedy was one of thousands of miners, old line and new arrivals, driven into the union movement by the horror of the Speculator disaster, but it was a movement in disarray. The Butte Mine Workers formed late in the last century, and though strong and consistent, the group tended toward conservative positions and had a close relationship with management. But Butte also hosted Local #1 of the radical Western Federation of Miners. In the back-and-forth struggles between Anaconda Copper and the mine workers, the owners had eroded workers' protections. By 1914, and until the Speculator fire, Butte miners lacked strong representation, and the copper kings had successfully repressed the unions through force, cooptation, or intimidation, or by pitting different unions against each other.[45] The unions that existed were more geared toward protecting the older Irish aristocracy of labor from competition with the newest arrivals. For the past few years Anaconda and the other copper companies dictated nearly all working conditions.

Kennedy and others thought that the existing union structure wasn't up to the moment. Instead, they were drawn to the emergent Metal Mine Workers Union (MMWU). At an early meeting, Kennedy volunteered to be its recording secretary. He urged everyone to join up, he said, "to better the conditions for the miners."[46] Three days after the Speculator fire, between ten thousand and twelve thousand workers went on strike.[47] The strike appealed to Butte's mainstream conservative unionists, and they were vital to its strength. But there were also radical currents, tied to global circuits of political struggle. Much as Punjabi Sikh workers on the North American West Coast took part in transpacific anticolonial struggle against British imperialism, Butte's Irish cast their eyes across the Atlantic in developing a radical imagination. Radical Irish workers in Butte particularly looked to the anticapitalist, anticolonial struggles waged under the socialist leadership of James Connolly. They saw English empire and Irish landlord capitalists as the conjoined oppressors of Irish (and other) peoples. "The cause of labor is the cause of Ireland the cause of Ireland is the cause of labor," Connolly argued, "they cannot be dissevered."[48] An important tendency came to Butte through Irish revolutionaries like James Connolly and Jim Larkin, who held meetings and developed ties through the radical Irish diaspora. In 1916, and in the wake of the Easter Rising, Butte's Jim Larkin founded the Pearce-Connolly Irish Independence Club. Though Butte's old guard Irish patriots were put off by its socialism, the club appealed to new masses of Irish workers who had been foresworn by the established elites. The club also made firm connections with the IWW and with the region's radical Finns.[49]

As the MMWU secretary, Kennedy worked closely with organizers from the Industrial Workers of the World.[50] The IWW grew from the radical movements established by the Western Federation of Miners and proved to be one of the most inspirational (and most thoroughly demonized) labor organizations of the early twentieth century. Trade unions commonly tried to protect their members' bargaining positions through ethnoracial exclusion, but the Wobblies renounced racism in their effort to organize workers previously kept out of mainstream unions. Wobblies worked toward immediate improvement in living and laboring conditions, but always had an eye toward when the One Big Union would finally overthrow of the capitalist class. Wobblies generally saw electoral politics as secondary to direct action, but the idea of direct action, and what it meant in practice—be it strike, sabotage, or something else—was loosely defined.[51]

The IWW had been in good shape as war mounted in Europe. Though antimilitarist and antinationalist, the IWW avoided taking a firm stand after war was declared in 1914. Recognizing the difficult political position they would face once the United States became involved, Wobblies preferred to argue that class war was the only war that mattered. Still, their membership grew from around forty thousand in 1916 to more than one hundred thousand in 1917.[52] Wartime hysteria mounted, and unforgiving patriots demanded immigrants' unstinting declarations of allegiance to the United States. Across the country ordinary citizens and voluntary organizations variously beat, bullied, shamed, and even murdered those they thought did not demonstrate their patriotism loudly enough, or with requisite enthusiasm or cheer.[53] Things got harder in Butte after the United States joined the war as a combatant in 1917, when criticism of England, or of Anaconda Copper, was treated as tantamount to treason. Butte's Irish nationalists and militant trade unionists found themselves in a nearly impossible position. The local Robert Emmet Literary Association—which earlier had gone so far as to field armed units in preparation for liberation from the English—effectively went into hibernation for the duration of the war. The Pearce-Connolly Club, however, continued to agitate.[54]

But in the wartime climate of forced patriotism, the copper barons held a stronger hand. They had allies in the federal government, and they were more than willing to use violence, all on their own. Conservatives like Arizona's Senator Harry Ashurst said that the letters "IWW" really stood for "Imperial Wilhelm's Warriors." Cartoons depicted Wobblies alongside spies and draft-dodgers undermining American safety.[55] A wide spectrum of the US press condemned the IWW as damnable enemies, venomous traitors, cancerous growths in need of excision, beasts in need of killing, at the very least seditious agents to be arrested or exiled.[56] J. Edgar Hoover, then cutting his teeth as a young agent at the Justice Department's Alien Enemy Bureau, saw this as a world-historical struggle for an imperiled white civilization. Thanks to these radicals, he wrote, "civilization faces its most terrible menace of danger since the barbarian hordes overran Western Europe and opened the Dark Ages."[57] Much as they had in Bisbee, Arizona, the copper barons wrapped themselves in the flag and declared war on the IWW.[58]

The federal government openly attacked the IWW. In 1917 the War Department authorized army officers to "sternly repress acts committed with seditious intent" and to protect "public utilities" in their localities that they deemed essential to the war effort. The language proved flexible enough to account for local officers' discretion to suppress industrial actions. Commanding officers commonly worked with local authorities and businessmen, and took very seriously their opinions on what constituted seditious intent toward public utilities. At the platoon level, lieutenants and their men would be made available to municipal authorities.[59] The federal government raided IWW outposts from Washington to Montana to Chicago and beyond, breaking up meetings and jailing members.[60] The vast majority were imprisoned on the grounds of *anticipated* lawlessness, rather than for the actual commission of a crime.[61]

Indeed, despite massive efforts, investigators never found any evidence of Wobblies committing criminal acts or accepting funds from German agents. Instead, legal cases concentrated on quotations and citations, often pulled out of context, from IWW newspapers. A Justice Department prosecutor focused on what he called "the seditious and disloyal character and teachings of the organization" which, he believed, "necessarily brought it into conflict with other federal laws."[62] For prosecutors this was adequate, and many judges agreed. In one trial thirty-five Wobblies were sentenced to five-year sentences, thirty-three to ten years, and fifteen to twenty years in prison, on the basis of their ideas alone.[63] Justice Department agent Clay Allen recommended that all Wobblies be jailed for the duration of the war, or if they were noncitizens, that they be deported. Others concurred, believing that if the plan did not accord with the government's legal powers, it was still the right thing to do.[64]

Frank Little arrived in Butte in mid-July 1917. The thirty-eight-year old was a renowned—or notorious—IWW organizer. His claims of Cherokee heritage were likely exaggerated, but he had been raised on Cherokee-allotted land and educated at a Quaker Mission Schools in Oklahoma.[65] When he arrived in Butte, he had a broken leg and one good eye. He was a small man, but he had a loud voice and big ideas. He led strikes across the country, notably in Bisbee, Fresno, and Spokane.[66] Little had organized in lumber camps, oil fields, among migrant harvest workers, and was a vocal advocate of anti-capitalist direct action and sabotage, even in the midst of the US war. He did not mince words, which won him serious enemies. Indeed, he had recently escaped lynching in Michigan.[67]

The day after his arrival, Frank Little spoke before six thousand strikers at an open meeting of the MMWU at the Butte ball park. According to the *Butte Miner*, Little was a "frail man, supporting the weight of his body with the aid of crutches, his face contorted with physical pain and the passion which rocked his body." Little "worked himself into a maniacal fury as he denounced the capitalists of every class and nationality." He did not call for violent revolution but still reportedly "intimated a world-wide revolution of the working classes."[68] Little made it very clear that he had no interest in the world war—he thought it was a battle in which different sets of capitalists merely sent different groups of workers to kill each other—and neither should the workers gathered before him. "Either we're for this capitalistic slaughterfest, or we're against it," he proclaimed. "I'm ready to face a firing squad rather than compromise."[69]

Anaconda Copper, the North Butte Company, as well as agents from the US government sent spies and infiltrators into MMWU and IWW meetings, and infiltrators reported that Little called for direct action. He was a firebrand. He reportedly told the MMWU to increase their militancy. "You fellows are conducting a peaceful strike! Great God! What would Uncle Sam say to the Soldiers he is sending to meet the German Army if they *laid down their arms* and said *we* are conducting a peaceful war!"[70] Little stressed that class struggle was class war; the workers risked their lives when they did not use all the tools at their disposal. Little may have war-based metaphors, but what precisely he meant by this—be it through force of arms, argument, or industrial action and withdrawing labor—was unclear. But the Montana press claimed no doubt about Little's intention. The *Butte Daily Post* called him treasonous, asking "How long Is [Butte] Going To Stand for the Seditious Talk of the I.W.W. Agitator?"[71] Anaconda Copper wanted district attorney Burton Wheeler to arrest and prosecute Little for sedition, but Wheeler found no material basis for the charge. Wheeler's reluctance frustrated Anaconda lawyers, who thought that if government prosecutors in other districts could be creative in their legal prosecutions of the IWW, Wheeler could too.[72] If the law could neither find (nor manufacture) grounds to rid them of Little, Montana's copper kings would find other means.

Little was staying at the Steele Block, a boardinghouse affiliated with Finlander Hall, the meeting house of the radical Finnish Workers Society, which opened its doors to the IWW and the Pearce-Connolly Club. At 3:00 in the morning on August 1, 1917, six masked men parked a large black car outside the building. One stayed with the car while the other five barged in, kicked down the landlady's door, Ms. Nora Byrne, and told her: "We are officers and we want Frank Little." Terrified, she pointed them to his room. They pulled Little from the building, beat him mercilessly, and forced him into the car. They stopped a short while later and tied Little to the bumper and dragged him through the town. Reports were that his kneecaps were torn from his legs.[73] The killers took Frank Little to the Milwaukee Bridge, a railroad trestle just outside of Butte. Apparently, he still clung to life, so they pistol-whipped him some more, before finally hanging him by the neck from the bridge. As his body dangled from a hemp rope, his murders pinned a placard to his tattered remains: "Others take notice, first and last warning, 3-7-77." The numbers were clear to those in the know—it referred to a Montana vigilante organization. A series of letters were somewhat more cryptic: L-D-C-S-S-W-T. The L was circled. Some believed the letters represented the names of other labor activists marked for death, and the circle meant that the "L" for "Little" was finished.[74]

Will Campbell, editor of the Anaconda-owned *Helena Independent* and a member of the vigilante group Montana Council of Defense, celebrated Little's murder. "Good work," he wrote. "Let them continue to hang every I.W.W. in the state.... It sort of quickens the blood in the veins of some of the pioneers of Helena to see the fatal figures in print—3-7-77."[75] Again, the *Helena Independent* opined "that unless the courts and the military authorities take a hand now and end the IWW in the West, there will be more night-

FIGURE 7. Frank Little's funeral, 1917. *Source:* Walter P. Reuther Library, Archives of Labor and Urban Affairs, Wayne State University Digital Collections.

visits, more tugs at the rope, and more IWW tongues will wag for the last time when the noose tightens about the traitors [*sic*] necks." It was unsurprising that Montana's media—much of which was literally owned by the copper industries—would support attacks on the strikers. But even the faraway *Chicago Tribune* justified the lynching and called for more state coercion. "If the mine owners hired [Little's] lynchers they only anticipated what the community would eventually be compelled to do if the law did not act. And the law must act with more power and promptness against such men."[76]

Frank Little's funeral was held on August 5, 1917. Three thousand people marched in the procession, and thousands more watched it pass by. Joe Kennedy was surely among them. He had just become a Wobbly. He later reflected that on the morning of Little's lynching: "I went up to the hall and there was a great crowd of men, women and children crying, and then they called a meeting, and everybody went up, and then they asked everybody to join and then I joined on account of the Frank Little lynching."[77] MMWU leaders were at the head of the march. They carried an American flag—which would have infuriated Little—but which the organizers can only have intended to defuse accusations of un-Americanism. The *Bulletin* called his funeral "a protest against tyranny."[78] The leaders followed the Wobbly imperative, seeing the march as an opportunity not just to mourn but to organize. The MMWU-led strike continued apace for the rest of 1917, protesting against the patently unsafe conditions and inadequate pay.[79] By December 1917 most of the miners returned to work.[80] In any case, at best the 1917 strike yielded mixed results for workers. They won some concessions and new benefits, but—and this was perhaps the most important matter—the MMWU failed to earn union recognition.

Things would get harder still for the left unionists. Because now, the copper kings' forces, already bolstered by vigilantes and not a few company gunmen, were joined by the US military. Indeed, shortly after Frank Little's murder, federal troops came to Butte, ostensibly to keep the peace. They would remain until January 1921. Their task was to restore law and order in the face of vigilantism while protecting utilities against German espionage. Yet they essentially served as open allies to Anaconda Copper.[81] It was perhaps ironic, because the mine owners were the chief purveyors of violence. Indeed, the chairman of the Butte Council for Defense said as much when he proclaimed that "the minute the military here stop detaining men for seditious acts we have got to take it into our own hands and have a mob. And we don't want to start that. I can get a mob up here in twenty-four hours and hang half a dozen men." Similarly, mine owner W. A. Clark claimed not to "believe in lynching or violence of that kind... *unless it is necessary.*"[82] Federal troops succeeded in lessening vigilante violence only by adopting the mine owners' mission of suppressing the radicals themselves. To this end, vigilante and company violence was incorporated into a hybrid governmental and private practice.

Nevertheless, Joe Kennedy and his allies in the IWW and the MMWU continued to struggle for a workers' democracy. Many of the longer-term Butte mine workers invested their futures on American patriotism and reconciling with whatever the copper owners would offer, so the Wobblies who remained committed to industrial democracy faced a lonely and uphill battle. They were reeling from the mass arrests and the imprisonments of the IWW national leadership. Closer to home, the press continued to rail against any challenge to Anaconda's hegemony as an existential threat to the nation, driven by German infiltrators. Moreover, spies and informants paid by copper companies and the US Army infiltrated the IWW and MMWU, reporting on their actions and undermining from within.

But workplace injustice remained, and Joe Kennedy, one of the Wobblies still free to organize, continued the struggle. He became a full-time organizer and secretary for the Butte IWW. As he explained it, his duties included office work, mainly making out cards for members, collecting dues, and when someone wanted to buy a songbook or other IWW literature, providing it.[83] If someone wanted to call that being an agitator, he was okay with it. Kennedy's definition of labor agitation was "trying to bring before the people the truth of how the companies or corporations treat the workers," and struggling "for the betterment of the conditions of the workers."[84] He was resolutely hopeful that once conditions were known to the public that they could scarcely fail to support workers' rights.

The Wobblies' strategy was simple, but it placed undeserved faith in American industrialists' and government willingness to recognize workers' rights. It also underestimated the depth of antipathy to so-called anarchist causes. Wobblies believed that they could challenge the industrial order by mobilizing in key wartime industries—copper, agriculture, and lumber—in hopes that the federal government would be willing to support their demands rather than risk industrial slowdowns. They wagered that industrialists, already making good money from accelerated wartime production, would be willing to concede benefits.[85] Kennedy and his comrades did not fully grasp the mine owners' intransigence; indeed, one owner proclaimed that he would rather destroy his own mine than permit the IWW to organize there. They were similarly stymied by how deeply America's compulsory hyperpatriotism had cowed or compelled the general public.

While the local but collective traumas of the Speculator disaster and of Frank Little's lynching strengthened Kennedy's commitment to economic justice, a larger number of Americans seemed to be engaged in a wholly different, and fully nationalistic, debate. The Wobblies consistently affirmed a focus on working conditions, but their attackers staunchly ignored the issue of economic justice and turned every conversation toward sedition and nationalism. The nationalists' drumbeat of war drowned out any voices for industrial democracy. Despite the Montana press's hyperbole around the Wobblies, attorney Burton Wheeler remarked on how remarkably peaceful the Butte protests were. He reported to the attorney general that the strikes were "conducted in a manner heretofore unheard of in mining regions," with neither violence nor lawlessness nor threats of sabotage.[86]

According to some scholars, Kennedy and his fellow travelers' undertaking in 1918 was essentially a fool's errand. But it is hard to know what else he might have done. The IWW's strongest and most experienced leaders, like Bill Haywood, were locked up, and the ones who remained—like Joe Kennedy—may have been more easily led astray by the spies who had infiltrated the union. Perhaps, like the Robert Emmet Literary Association society did, Kennedy and the IWW could have folded up shop for the duration of the war, waiting until conditions were more amenable. It might have been easier and saved him trouble. But it did not seem to fit his character. Kennedy continued to work for the IWW, which earned him ongoing harassment from local police. In March 1918 he was having a beer in a saloon when the chief of police arrested him for "disturbance," jailed him for ten days, and fined him $20. He was arrested and held for eight days for "being an IWW" in August 1918. While those were both ostensibly legal matters conducted by legally recognized police officers, Kennedy was eventually drawn into the deportation regime in the lengthy aftermath of raids by not just local police, but by a wider range of federal, municipal, civilian, military, and paramilitary vigilante groups.

Raids on the IWW offices in August and September 1918 involved police and soldiers as well as Anaconda's hired gunmen. Kennedy testified that a special agent from the Department of Justice nominally led the raid but Ed Morissey, the chief of detectives, and John Berkin, associated with the County Council of Defense and "known as a gunman" for Anaconda Copper, also took part. After the raid, gunmen forced Kennedy into a car, recalling Frank Little's fatal experience. But while Little had been beaten and murdered, raiders brought Kennedy back into the hall, where they searched his clothes and rifled through his office. Afterward, he was locked in the city jail. Kennedy and other miners continued to organize after his release, and on the morning of September 13, miners walked off the job site to protest a wage cut. Between two hundred and three hundred workers were gathered in Finlander Hall when it was raided, an unknown number of whom were stabbed by soldiers. As with the August raid, Kennedy later explained, many who took part were company gunmen.[87] After the September raid some forty miners were booked as being "held for [the] Council of Defense," although the legal basis under which this vigilante group could imprison people is unclear.[88]

It is hard to know with certainty, but at least one historian familiar with Department of Justice records argues that September 1918 IWW strikes were precipitated by agents provocateurs and infiltrators from Anaconda Copper and US army intelligence. If this is the case, Joe Kennedy and his comrades may have been tricked into an unwinnable strike by agents planted among them.[89] It would have made for an astounding case of entrapment. If the argument for repressing the Wobblies was that they undermined wartime production, here was a situation in which—according to a later report—US Army operatives "were guilty of a strike against the Army which the Army very dutifully crushed."[90] Army spies fed the rumor of a general strike and of wartime danger to the US Army, which then believed that there was a military threat to copper production.[91] In these circumstances the US Army—already closely aligned with Anaconda Copper, took further action against the IWW. Major Omar Bradley led the US Army's involvement and partnership with the local police and Anaconda gunmen. A later chronicler called it "an unfair, unrestrained, vicious…veritable reign of terror." Even other government officers—no friends of the IWW—spoke out against the raids and brutal tactics.[92]

Kennedy was released after the September raids and arrest. But in February 1919, during another strike, he was arrested for deportation. Immigration agents now took part, and based on their selective readings of Marx, Lenin, and Trotsky, among others, charged Kennedy with membership in an organization advocating the forcible overthrow of the government.[93] But his lawyers successfully argued that the relevant legislation was passed after his August and September 1918 arrests and thus constituted ex post facto charges. Prosecutors changed their line of attack and charged Kennedy with advocating the unlawful destruction of property. They had no evidence, other than the lyrics to IWW songbooks stored in the union hall.

In his defense, Kennedy and his lawyers returned to the theme of industrial democracy and the need to protect working people from the dangers of the mines. His interrogators steadfastly refused to acknowledge this line of reasoning. Instead, they hammered the themes of sabotage, of nationalism, of the overthrow of the government. As in Wobbly trials elsewhere, debate hinged on the definition of "sabotage." It was made more complicated because the term was not defined in the 1918 immigration statute. When investigators asked Kennedy what he meant by "sabotage," he followed Elizabeth Gurly Flynn and defined it as the withdrawal of labor in the interest of safety. "Suppose I am working in the mine and the shift boss tells me to get in and drill when there is 30 or 40 feet of open ground, and tells me to drill and blast at noon-time, then I believe in laying down [tools] until the ground is timbered up."[94] His answer may have been designed to avoid prosecution but suggested that such sabotage was not terribly radical at all.[95]

Nevertheless, when no criminal charges could be levied against Kennedy, the prosecutors turned, as they did against other noncitizens, to immigration law, which was much more amenable to prosecutorial discretion. And even when immigration law didn't allow for expulsion on charges of anarchism, they had other means available—the commissioner-general was pleased to report that an unspecified number of suspected anarchists were deported on charges other than anarchism in 1919.[96] Ninety-two people were ordered deported as anarchists in 1919, and although fifty-five still awaited removal, Kennedy would be among them the thirty-seven expelled.[97] Kennedy's arrest warrant was signed in February 1919, and the deportation warrant was signed on May Day, 1919.[98] In mid-June 1919 he was loaded aboard an eastbound deportation train, along with fellow Wobblies and other so-called undesirables. It is unclear whether or not the train crossed the bridge from which Frank Little was hanged. When Kennedy landed at Ellis Island, he was among hundreds of radicals facing expulsion.[99]

Radicals on the deportation trains could continue to cause trouble. One train, dubbed "the Red Special," left Seattle in February 1919, with forty-seven passengers, mostly associated with the IWW or the Union of Russian Workers who had been involved in a general strike throughout the Pacific Northwest. The *Times* maligned the deportees aboard as a "motley company of I.W.W. troublemakers, bearded labor fanatics, and red flag supporters." Apparently one thousand Wobblies waited for the train in Butte, in hopes of either freeing their fellows or at least lining the tracks to show solidarity, but the train's planners rerouted the trip through Helena to bypass Butte and avoid the protests.[100]

At times, radical deportees jeered and harangued the train guards throughout the journey. One of the guards complained that it "went against my grain, as well as every guard aboard the train, to handle them without force, as they were very insulting at times." It bears note that physical violence would have been unnecessary and likely counterproductive aboard the moving train. Another guard said that they would be better served with gags rather than handcuffs—a statement that held a grain of truth, given that most were expelled for their political beliefs rather than for actively championing violent action. Still, they kept each other's spirits up in the midst of the journey. "They sing foreign songs for hours," a guard complained. "Some of 'em wake up in the night to do it."[101]

Still, Kennedy's work was scarcely done. At Ellis Island radicals continued to organize among themselves.[102] And though Butte's copper kings may have been rid of him, he would eventually land in the ferment of Belfast, a site in the Irish War of Independence from Britain, where the memory of James Connolly's Easter Rising remained within a torrent of guerilla warfare, nationalist uprising and brutal repression, anti-Catholic Loyalist movements and antiworker expulsions.[103] Butte was just one site of a global network of insurgencies and counterinsurgencies where Joe Kennedy might agitate against capitalist imperialism and exploitation. There were more to choose from. It is unclear what Kennedy did on his return to Ireland, or where he might have gone to continue the IWW's struggle. British police would do their best to keep an eye on him.[104] State agents reported that back in the UK, he was in touch with "leading extremists," likely among revolutionary the Irish nationalists with whom he and his comrades had contact in Butte.[105] The Americans would keep watch too, in case he tried to return.

In a curious way, Kennedy's deportation as a political radical was a victory for the emergence of American liberalism's durable, supple, and repressive power. He wasn't lynched, and neither was he part of a mass expulsion.[106] Indeed, Commissioner Caminetti, though hardly liberal himself, stressed "the *tenderness* with which the law acts" against anarchists. "Deportation is not punishment for a crime," he insisted. The anarchist is "merely removed from one field of activity to another, where he [*sic*] may continue his work."[107] Though Kennedy's removal engaged the coercive power of the state and employers to expel those they disdained—and to repress political action—he was one of the only Wobblies deported from the Butte raids. Historian William Preston saw Butte as a location where federal immigration officials exercised particular restraint.[108] Department of Immigration officials in Butte were, in Preston's estimation, political moderates who understood that many of Butte's IWW members had been framed, that there was widespread local corruption, and that there was no evidence that Wobblies were involved in anything illegal.[109]

Nevertheless, the Butte raids were unquestionably part of a repressive process that transformed the IWW from a militant labor organization into a legal defense fund.[110] The Immigration Bureau, the Department of Labor, and the US military learned a new lesson too. Nationalists came to understand they could use deportation, or the threat of removal, as a primary weapon in its arsenal against foreign-born radicals. They could purify political society, crush migrants' supposedly divided loyalties, and enforce migrants' compliance with increasingly narrow definitions of permissible

thought. During the First World War, deportation became, in one scholars' words, the nation's "absolute weapon against the foreign-born radical."[111]

Yet as Joe Kennedy's legal battles were taking their toll, others foreswore
the Wobblies' peaceable revolutionary direct action. Incendiary language
had gotten the Wobblies nowhere but sent to prison or on a ship overseas. In
late April 1919 unknown radicals sent explosives to the mayor of Seattle, Ole
Hanson, who had earlier violently suppressed a strike in the city. A former
Georgia senator received a package the following day, and a large number
of explosives were found in the New York post office and other post offices
around the country, awaiting delivery. There were riots on May Day.[112]

Attorney general A. Mitchell Palmer and J. Edgar Hoover's Justice
Department led the government's response. Palmer authorized sweeping
antiradical raids in late 1919 and early 1920, arresting thousands and order-
ing warrants for their deportation.[113] Eventually, many American liberals
would decry Hoover and Palmer's raids as woeful overreaction that undermined civil liberties and American democracy. Louis Post, acting secretary
of labor, wrote a book calling the raids a "Deportation Delirium" unsuited
to American justice. Post was no radical. Rather, he understood the use and
the necessity of following proper procedure. Cooler-headed liberals would
be more effective anticommunists, better defenders, he believed, of the borders of American thought. In practice, of course, leftists would continue to
confront both liberal anticommunists and their reactionary, bare-knuckled
partners. Still, increasingly, radicals who challenged the bounds of permitted political thought or the questioned capitalism's untrammeled rule would
no longer necessarily face the violence of lynching, or even the terror of having vigilantes kick down their doors. Slower but relentless governmental
procedures would continue, though it was hardly as *tender* as the commissioner general seemed to think. The lynch mob's claim of right to kill was
absorbed within the federal government's legal power to expel. Leftists like
Joe Kennedy did not necessarily need to die, but they could not live in the
United States.

SIX

Chicago

AS THE TRAIN LEFT DENVER and crossed the great plains, vast expanses of wheat would blur beyond the windows, the train would rock and lurch, the unfree passengers would hear the relentless pattern of its rattle, its vibrations resounding through their bodies. In the summer, heat would bake, and in winter, the chill windows would draw the warmth from their bodies as time and miles passed. Eventually, smaller agricultural communities would give way to larger ones. Towns and populations gathered more densely the closer the train got to that great center of American commerce, Chicago. In his diaries Leo Stanley, the San Quentin physician, remarked on the congestion of houses and families, the tenement housing, and that he could see into the homes of working people; he particularly remarked on Black families and others doing their washing or otherwise engaged in the banality of daily life. The air had been clear in the Iowa farmlands, Stanley said, but the sky darkened with smoke from factories as they neared Chicago.[1]

Chicago's skyline bespoke opportunity and danger. As Upton Sinclair, one of turn-of-the-century Chicago's most influential storytellers, recounted: "The line of buildings stood clear cut and black against the sky; here and there out of the mass rose the great chimneys, with the river of smoke streaming away to the end of the world. It was a study in colors now, this smoke; in the sunset light it was black and brown and gray and purple. All the sordid suggestions of the place were gone—in twilight it was a vision of power."[2] The Windy City was the beating heart of the United States' Midwestern economy, and the hub and transfer point through which American capitalism cycled: the masses of wheat and grain just outside the train's windows made a journey that was similar to their own. So did the livestock—cattle, pigs—soon to be dismembered at slaughterhouses that were themselves models of economic efficiency. Material goods were converted to commodities, abstracted by Chicago's markets into exchange values and into capital itself. American farmers removed native grasses and planted wheat to sell, their cows and horses displaced bison, and new settlers had by the 1910s done their best to remove the Plains peoples who had lived there before them.[3] Chicago's businessmen had as voracious an appetite for immigrant workers as they did for pigs, lumber, cattle, and grain, because the migrants' labor would transform the pigs and the lumber into their profits. The 2.5 million immigrants who came between 1880 and 1920 made Chicago the nation's second most populous and second wealthiest city.[4]

For the deportation agents aboard the train, Chicago meant work. The sheer scale of the city's migrant population, and its location as a continental hub, meant it was also a busy point for the deportation regime, and new prison cars would be added to the Deportation Special. They would take on passengers from across metropolitan Chicago but also from nearby feeder routes from Saint Louis, Kansas City, Omaha, Fort Wayne among them, as well as from Joliet or Leavenworth or any number of nearby prisons. Stanley described that on one journey, two new carriages were added in the Windy City; one was filled with people from around Chicago, the other came all the way from El Paso.[5] Novelist Theodore Irwin described how in Chicago the "Deportation Special was growing like a triumphal snake-dance," extending and distending itself as it consumed more passengers, writhing its way across the land.[6]

On a journey that Stanley described, the many others cars and locomotive they'd traveled with from California had been broken up. Passengers and commodities in other cars were decoupled and directed elsewhere in the not quite chaotic circulation of goods and people through the metropole. Their car crossed the "maze of railroad tracks" to the LaSalle Street station, where they changed onto the C.C.C. & St. Louis road and waited for the engine that would carry them east. Stanley didn't need to worry about how their carriages would navigate the tangle of lines that sprawled across Chicago, because Henry Weiss or another of the deportation agents, aided by friends at Southern Pacific or Nickel Plate, took care of the complex logistics to smooth the transcontinental journey. Instead, Stanley added color and narrative tension to his journals, indicating the sense of boredom, and of unease, that stasis in Chicago provoked for he and other deportation staff. "Not a breath of air was stirring," he wrote, and "engine smoke hung heavy" in the already bad humidity.[7]

The guards' job was made harder still because of the Chicago station's immigrant social networks. The density of migrant lives in the Chicago station "necessitated close vigilance on our part," Stanley said, "to see that there were no escapes."[8] The station became an interface between the Windy City's metropolitan worlds and the deportation regime's attempted closed circulatory system. Indeed, at points like this the deportation network was not hermetically sealed, and a large number of newly loaded peoples' families came to say goodbye to their loved ones. Some entered the cars to spend a few last minutes with their exiled kin. Stanley had little sympathy and saw security threats; the systemic porousness and trains' general disarray gave a moment in which the prisonlike atmosphere in which he was most comfortable was overwhelmed by those over whom he had no control.

Spiros Olebos, twenty-two years old and born in a Greek Peloponnesian village called Sondena, boarded the Deportation Special in January 1915. Spiros's older brother, Gust, might have come to the station to see him off, fulfilling his obligation to look after the family's honor and well-being. Spiros's wife, a US citizen named Mary, could not bid him farewell. She had recently been arrested, and had just begun a five-year sentence at the Indiana State Penitentiary.[9] Stanley, an educated man and something of a racial scientist, would likely have ascribed to the opinion voiced by sociologist Henry Pratt Fairchild, who thought that the Greek "race" was "much inclined to be indolent, egotistical, vain and superficial," characterized by a "universality of the habit of lying."[10] Regardless of these broad racist typologies, Stanley would assuredly have looked at Spiros Olebos with contempt, for Olebos would be counted among the procurers, pimps, and others involved in the so-called white slave trade. At least twenty-seven hundred people would be deported on similar grounds over the next decade and a half.[11] To that end, Stanley, like his colleagues, would have understood the deportation regime as protecting against a cruel market in women's bodies, and in helping to guarantee the American gendered and racial order, ensuring that only proper families would remain and grow in the country.

Gust Olebos, who was deeply invested in the politics of Greek-American respectability, might have agreed. Spiros and Gust were two among the vast number of Greek migrants to the United States. The 1910 US Census listed 101,285 Greek residents, and a decade later, more than 228,000. Drawn by labor and kin networks from home villages to sites of industrial labor, more than 90 percent of them were men. Most made homes in Chicago and the urban industrializing Northeast and Midwest. Smaller but still substantial numbers of Greek migrants lived and worked in the mountain or urban West or San Francisco.[12] The country's largest Greek neighborhood was in Chicago's Near West Side.[13] When Spiros landed in New York in 1911, he listed an address on Blue Island Street—one edge of Chicago's "Greek Delta"—as his destination. Spiros traveled a well-trod path. While by no means typical, his journey offers insight into the Greek diaspora in the Americas, traversing global political economic currents from the borderlands of the Ottoman and British empires and into the industrial vortex of the United States' imperial ascent. Spiros Olebos, like many, navigated complexly gendered familial relationships, the dense racial and economic hierarchies of urban life, and confrontation with some of the most powerful corporations on earth.

Greeks had traveled for centuries across the Mediterranean and the Levant.[14] As subjects of the Ottoman Empire, Greeks were drawn into its trade networks and toward the centers of political power.[15] British and western European capital penetration of Ottoman territories in the early nineteenth century destabilized Ottoman economies and enabled Greek nationalists to claim independence from Ottoman rule. Western great powers supported the move, but nonetheless systematically underdeveloped Greek and broader Balkan economies and undercut local industrial growth. By the second half of the century, western European capital invested heavily in regional infrastructure, extending markets in Thessaly's cereal production, while a railway from Patras to Kalavita drew Peloponnesian supplies of grain, cotton, wool, and dried fruits—particularly currants—into western European markets. Across the region, rail developed cosmopolitan networks of migrants, merchants, laborers, and traders.[16]

This had complex consequences for the residents of the Peloponnesian hinterland, such as Spiros Olebos and his kin. Mountain-dwelling villagers commonly lived in multifamily, patrilocal households, under the eye of a single patriarch. Most were subsistence farmers who grew food and tended animals for themselves but also, and increasingly, cultivated olives, currants, and figs to sell.[17] But especially currants. After a phylloxera blight devastated French vineyards in the 1880s, France bought around half of Greece's currant crops, which boomed as the region's principal export. There was cash to be had, and many destroyed their olive trees to make room for the more lucrative crop. But France reestablished production in the 1890s, increased their domestic yield, and passed new legislation to stop Greek imports. Russia, a secondary market, did the same. This led to a glut in the currants market, and in 1895 the crisis of overproduction led to massive underemployment and more or less directly prompted outmigration to the United States.[18]

So it was that in 1893, Spiros Olebos was born into a declining regional economy that was dependent upon and tied ever more tightly into the boom-bust cycle of global markets. Peloponnesian farmers often owned their own land (unlike their tenant farmer counterparts in Thessaly), but, as was common throughout rural villages the world over—and as we have already seen in Italy, the Azores, and Ireland—issues of inheritance across generations and dowry-giving split landholdings into ever-smaller parcels. Younger sons felt the pressure to seek their fortunes elsewhere.[19] Between 1890 and 1912 one-fourth of males between the ages of fifteen and forty-five left the greater Greek region to seek work overseas. Most went to the United States.[20]

In 1911, Spiros Olebos said goodbye to his family and friends, and his father, George, who may have served as patriarch of the extended family. Two years earlier, his brother Gust made a similar journey and had been doing well enough in the United States to inspire Spiros's travels. It would have been an auspicious moment as the nineteen-year-old Spiros took this step, staking out his own independent manhood, buoyed by distant kin networks but now unencumbered by paternal oversight.[21] He likely took the Kalavita rail line to Patras, where hotels were crowded with emigrants seeking out tickets, and warehouses were filled with goods for trade. In 1907 more than twenty-one thousand Greeks left through the Peloponnesian ports of Patras, Kalamata, and Zante for New York. Many others made their way to the United States by more circuitous routes, via Italy, England, or France. In Patras, Spiros would have crossed paths with Greeks from villages distant from his own but also with Turks, Armenians, Albanians, and Macedonians and others from throughout the Levant. They too followed in friends' and relatives' paths. The remittances sent back and the stories they heard from returning travelers offered plenty of incentive—Greek migrants sent between $4 million and $5 million home in 1905.[22] And if that weren't enough, US-based industries advertised opportunities across southern and eastern Europe, trying to draw eager workers to labor for low wages. US Steel, which just opened up its massive works at Gary, Indiana, was one of them.[23]

It was to Gary, and the massive US Steel works, that Spiros Olebos would travel. After landing in New York, he made his way to meet his brothers, Gust and Jim. Spiros was nineteen years old, 5'1" tall, and healthy—he had passed physicals in Patras and in New York—and was hearty from a life of farm labor.[24] In this he was similar to huge numbers of his fellow diasporic

Greeks and other southern and eastern European migrants to the industrial Midwest. Many Greek migrants became street vendors, bootblacks, restauranteurs, or small business owners. But the largest proportion, around 20 percent, labored in factories and on railroad construction.[25] Spiros would be among them, doing hard, heavy, and poorly paid labor. If Patras had bustled with migrants and traders, Chicago in 1911 must have been dazzling. With a population of nearly 2.2 million in 1910 (not including the outlying areas), the city was clogged with factories and tenements, smoke and slaughterhouses; its welter of wealthy and impoverished residents teemed in streets and alleys, saloons and pubs.[26] He quickly traveled, however, to nearby Gary, Indiana. Chicago grew because it became the epicenter of the North American West's diverse and expansive trade networks. Gary, Indiana, was built by US Steel alone.

Founded in 1901, US Steel brought together 213 previously uncoordinated manufacturing and transport firms, and became perhaps the most powerful corporation that the world had ever known.[27] US Steel emerged from the ruthless competition, and eventual collaboration, between some of the most powerful names and industries in American history: Carnegie, Morgan, Frick, Gould, and more—titans of steel and iron, oil and transportation, finance, speculation, and banking. They consolidated a brutal set of industries into a behemoth, the United States' first billion-dollar corporation.[28] As an early analyst summarized, US Steel was a "fully integrated industrial empire, from raw material to finished products. It controlled its own iron ore and coal, its own railroads and steamships; it made pig iron and crude steel; and it shaped its steel into finished products to go into railroads and ships, bridges and skyscrapers, tin cans and pipe lines, wire fences and cannon. It was estimated at the time that it had absolute control over the destiny of a population almost as large as that of Maryland and Nebraska."[29] It catapulted the United States to global economic dominance. US Steel was responsible for nearly half of the nation's iron and some three-fifths of the nation's steel. Due in large measure to US Steel's vertically integrated control and the vast resources it commanded, when the First World War began, the United States accounted for two-fifths of all world steel production.[30]

US Steel's goals quickly outpaced its existing capacity, and in 1905 the firm bought nine thousand acres of land at the southern shore of Lake Michigan for a massive new facility. Thirty miles southwest of Chicago, the new plant would be well placed to receive lake freighters with iron ore and limestone from Minnesota and Michigan. The region's dense rail networks would speed coal from Appalachia. Lake Michigan and the Calumet River provided abundant water for production and for dumping waste. Finished steel could move via rail to nearby Chicago, for the girders and structure for countless new buildings that shot into the sky. Workers like Spiros Olebos, who followed kin from around the planet to the Windy City, could make their way to the new factories opening up.[31] The city, named after US Steel's CEO Elbert H. Gary, was incorporated in 1906.[32]

The Gary Works became the foundation of US Steel's boundless ambitions. The industry publication *Gary Works Circle* called the new plant "the eighth wonder of the world."[33] Construction workers removed twelve million cubic yards of sand before they laid the foundation, which used two million cubic yards of concrete. The railroad yard could hold up to fifteen thousand cars; its mile-long, twenty-five-foot deep harbor would accommodate huge iron ore boats as they delivered raw materials to the plant.[34] The Gary Works also signaled a radical reshaping of the earth to suit US Steel's productive desires and the purposes of capital—leveling dunes and dredging the lake, filling in the Lake's shoreline; redirecting, narrowing, and straightening the Calumet River.[35] The rails that US Steel produced for the railroads allowed, in direct fashion, the transcontinental consolidation of the US economy and an expansion of settler domination of Indigenous lands and territories, and access to the material abundance they contained.[36] By the end of its first year, the Gary plant's 6,800 workers had produced 570,000 tons of steel. The plant accelerated production and drew high profits. By 1920 it housed 12 blast furnaces, 838 coke ovens, 45 open-hearth furnaces, two 25-ton converters, a rail mill, a billet mill, a slabbing mill, a dozen merchant mills and many more specialized mills, plus a dozen mechanical shops, covering 300,000 square feet, to keep the machinery humming.[37]

Gust and Jim Olebos lived together in Gary, but Spiros would not live with them.[38] Still, for the older two, it made sense to stick together in the new country. In part, adult brothers sharing a roof partially replicated the familiar patrilocal model of living and patriarchy they had known in Sondena. It also offered a kind of safety in numbers; Greek migrants in the United States saw their share of racist violence from police and mobs. Intellectual racists like Henry Pratt Fairchild thought that Greeks were predisposed toward crime and feared that the US legal system would be overrun by Greek immigrants and, over generations, their US-born children.[39] While that sort of opinion came from Yale-educated researchers, street-level mobs brought their own versions of anti-Greek gendered racism. Armed and masked men drove a group of Greek laborers from Mountain View, Idaho, and similar stories abounded. The most infamous incident took place in February 1909, when a policeman in South Omaha, Nebraska, confronted a Greek man as he spoke with a woman alleged to be a prostitute. The Greek man shot and killed the policeman. Some five hundred South Omaha residents signed an open letter that drew on classic and emergent invective of white masculinist rule, accusing that Greek men had "attacked our women, insulted pedestrians... [and] openly maintained gambling dens and other forms of viciousness."[40]

Residents drew up plans for what was effectively ethnic cleansing through mass deportation, to "rid the city of undesirable Greeks and thereby remove the menacing conditions that threaten the very life and welfare of South Omaha."[41] A mob tore through the city's Greek neighborhoods with police and municipal authorities' tacit or explicit approval, destroying nearly $250,000 worth of property and driving twelve hundred Greek denizens from the city. Others who "appeared" Greek, regardless of their ethnoracial identity or their place of birth, bore the mob's wrath.[42] A later investigation suggested that the policeman who provoked the inciting incident had himself been drunk and had no actual grounds for accosting the Greek man.[43]

In the face of this kind of ethnoracial disdain and violence, many Greek immigrants—like Black Americans similarly accused by white racists of immorality and lasciviousness—came to espouse a politics of respectability.[44] The mobs in South Omaha had claimed to target *undesirable* Greeks, so perhaps some Greek migrants, through hard work and rectitude, might prove themselves to be *desirable* migrants. They proudly proclaimed an upright virtuousness, with strong emphasis on schooling, religiosity, church attendance, and membership in fraternal organizations.[45] It was part of a broader Greek diasporic politics in settler colonies that drew on Anglophone philhellenism as a counterweight to anti-Greek ethnoracial derision.[46]

Greek American advocates of respectability politics implored younger men to avoid coffee shops as a bad influence and urged them to attend night school instead. The better class of coffee shop owners might be lauded by Greek community leaders, but more working-class establishments were impugned for shaming the community by allowing space for unsavory behavior—gambling and meeting disreputable women. By the time of the forced Americanism of the First World War, many Greek Americans lobbied hard that they should loudly proclaim their conformity and Americanism, buy war bonds en masse, and enlist in the US Army.[47] These were matters of pride and honor—even survival—for the Greek communities of Gary. But for Spiros Olebos, for his wife, Mary, and for Spiros's older brother, Gust, they were also intensely personal. Those personal politics of respectability bore tragic consequences.

Spiros did not live with Gust or Jim, and if his brothers thought Spiros's domestic arrangements were unconventional, his work life in Gary would have been familiar enough. Spiros started as a laborer on the Elgin, Joliet, and Eastern Railway, a US Steel subsidiary. Soon, Spiros said, "They dispatched me to the tinplate company."[48] If it was a promotion, it still paid poorly. That was no accident. Steel barons had spent decades refining techniques to break down their workers' control of the labor processes, to command them more and pay them less. They had been largely successful. Efforts at de-skilling and ethnic stratification pitted US Steel's workers against each other, separated craft worker unionists from nonunion laborers, and made them replaceable if they protested.[49]

Labor in the steel industries had been animated by struggle between and among workers well before Spiros Olebos and his brothers were born, with "native-born whites" or else northern Europeans or Englishmen high among the ranks in US steel mills. By the 1890s they were joined in substantial numbers by African Americans and eastern and southern Europeans.[50] Constant streams of migrants came to Gary looking for work. Immigrants in peasant clothes and carrying meager bundles reportedly came on every train arriving into Gary.[51] Once hired, Poles were reputed to predominate in the rolling mills, Austrians in the blast furnaces, and Italians, joined in increasing numbers by Mexican men, on the railroads.[52] Tin plate workers like Spiros were among the lowest paid in the industry. In 1912, even better-paid workers, toiling seven days per week, struggled to support a family. Men in Midwestern blast furnaces averaged $11.15 for a week's labor. Men in Bessemer converter departments earned $12.10; blooming mills workers took home $12.13; plate mill workers $11.04; rail mill workers $12.07; sheet mill workers, $10.72; and workers in tin plate mills—like Spiros—earned just $10.37 each week.[53] Even then, work in the steel industries was as susceptible to the market as the price of Greek currants. As one early documenter recorded, "One year the steel worker was a man favored above all others of his class, the next [year], he was getting his meals on charity from the 'soup houses.'"[54]

FIGURE 8. Tin sheet work at the American Sheet and Tin Plate Company, Gary, Indiana, 1921. *Source:* Calumet Regional Archives, Indiana University Northwest, Gary, Indiana.

In the midst of such massive industry, and under accelerated production, the forces and the heat and the vast scale, it should come as no surprise that steel work was notoriously dangerous, scarcely better than the copper mines in Butte. The Chicago *Daily Tribune* reported on the more than four hundred dead and two thousand injured steel workers in 1906 alone. There were stories of men buried in molten slag or forced to sign away compensation claims while incapacitated and in overwhelming pain.[55] The Gary Works promised to improve safety measures and launched a Safety Commission, which along with other US Steel subsidiaries produced annual reports that lauded their own policies. In 1911, US Steel began a Voluntary Accident Relief Plan to give financial relief to workers injured on the job or support to their widows.[56]

Under the premise of controlling all aspects of production, US Steel sought to direct its workers' living arrangements when they were off the clock. To that end, it founded the Gary Land Company, a subsidiary firm to plan the city and provide for its workers.[57] The town was set on a grid that ignored all local geographic features, with Fifth Street and the plant as its northern edge and Ninth Street, which ran along the Wabash tracks, the southern boundary. Broadway, the principal north-south thoroughfare and retail strip that bisected the company-sponsored area, led directly to the plant gates. The 1908 Gary Land Company census counted dozens of nationalities in residence, but ethnic and class differences soon stratified the US Steel-developed neighborhoods, just as they did at the Works. The census listed 250 African Americans, who, though presumably among the construction and transport workers from the American South, were differentiated from presumptively white people listed simply as *American* in the census.[58] Some 70 percent of Gary's resident were immigrants or the children of immigrants.[59] In 1910 the 218 Greek-born Gary residents were the sixth most populous group born outside of the United States, following Austrians (2,228), 1,979 Hungarians, 1,086 Russians, 639 Italians, and 526 Germans. Many others hailed from England, Canada, Ireland, Sweden, Norway, France, and beyond.[60]

Kirkland was one of Gary's more desirable neighborhoods, and it attracted better-paid, US-born workers. Another neighborhood was known as "Hunkyville." Its buildings were designed to house laborers with families, but they soon filled with single immigrant men who could scarcely afford more than a bed. In 1909 one report found 428 people living in thirty-eight of the neighborhood's dwellings, many of them sleeping in shifts. The *Gary Daily* maligned Hunkyville "a cesspool of lawless men." In 1911 the neighborhood was cleared out through a mass eviction. The homes were destroyed, and houses for middle-class managers built in their place.[61] Evicted tenants had little choice but to move to "The Patch," an immigrant slum and mostly Black ghetto south of the Gary Land Company's subdivision, split off from Gary's respectable neighborhoods by the Wabash Line railroad tracks. The Patch was bordered by Broadway to the east, Madison to the west, and between Tenth and Fifteenth Streets, to the north and south. It hosted more than two hundred saloons and was home to Gary's African American residents, its recent immigrants, and its unskilled laborers.[62] Spiros Olebos would be among them.

The Patch sported tarpaper shacks, few or ill-enforced building codes, and exorbitant rents for overcrowded and dilapidated lodging. According to one researcher, mosquitoes bred in the marshy land, "and the pestilential outhouses, unpaved alleys, damp cellars, and overcrowded dwellings were breeding grounds for typhoid, malaria, and tuberculosis."[63] Gary police chief Joseph Martin called the Patch "hell on wheels," and the city's wealthier residents abhorred the gambling, drinking, solicitation of prostitutes, and fighting that took place when new immigrant and Black steelworkers were off the clock.[64] The city's elite publicly distanced themselves from what went on in the Patch. But the fact of the matter was that they were responsible for it. Indeed, Gary's wealthier set profited from the Patch's ethnoracial geography, the regional housing shortage, and proximity to the plant. After the Gary Works plans were announced, real estate speculators bought lots in the unincorporated lands on the other side of the Wabash line, south of the mill's planned community, leading to a real estate boom.[65]

Speculative investors in Gary's real estate were the city's earliest slum lords. They built flimsy houses and, because of the high demand, charged exorbitant rents—often more than what would be charged in the company's subdivision on the "better" side of the tracks.[66] Realtors in 1912 estimated that between twenty-five hundred and four thousand workers had to live outside Gary due to inadequate housing supplies.[67] Shacks, one hundred feet long and eighteen feet deep, were divided into two-room apartments, with internal rooms just nine square feet. To make ends meet, many families had to take multiple boarders in their tiny two-room apartments. Shared privies and pumps sat in the tight, muddy laneways between the shacks. Residents had little choice but to trudge through the sewage and waste.[68]

If domestic spaces were too cramped for easy socializing, it was easier to talk, drink, meet friends or make new ones in the public multiethnic bustle of the Patch. Saloons and shops were most pronounced male spaces, while women more commonly gathered in front of butchers and groceries to catch up with their neighbors and others with whom they shared a common language.[69] Streets teemed with thousands of men walking from their homes in the Patch along Broadway to the plant's main gates or back, speaking their native tongues, wending their way among pushcarts and peddlers, stopping at a saloon or coffeeshop, eager to rest and relax before the next day's work.[70]

Broadway and Whiskey Row gave rise to a remarkable world of overlapping multiethnic spaces, and as he passed through them, Spiros Olebos would have surely been drawn toward Greek-owned markets, and especially to Greek coffeehouses. Coffeeshops appealed to younger, single men like Olebos because they offered more fun and excitement than the churches, schools, or stodgier coethnic fraternal societies they might join. Young Greek men, tired from a day's labor, could meet with others in similar positions and relax before returning to cramped boardinghouses or living quarters.[71] Spiros already lived away from his brothers, but furthered the distance by carousing through the Patch. Gust and Jim had become well-respected members of Gary's Greek community, a group that found its seedier coffeehouses and saloons distasteful. An investigator referred to Gust and Jim Olebos as "hard working respectable people" well-known among Gary's upwardly mobile Greek American community.[72] Gust and Jim did not approve of Spiros's behavior.

It was likely in one of the Patch's coffeeshops, saloons, or poolrooms, that Spiros Olebos met Mary Jura.[73] Mary had been born in West Virginia, was a US citizen, and was a year or two older than Spiros. Mary's parents, Valentine and Katie Jura, lived in Iowa. Mary had, for a time, worked as a prostitute, and perhaps this was how they met. In any case, Mary's working past did not much bother Spiros. They grew close, and though most Greek men in the United States married within the Greek community, marrying beyond it wasn't particularly rare. Mary's family lineage is unclear, but Spiros and Mary were married by a Romanian priest in early 1914.[74] For a time they lived in an apartment in the Adams Hotel, just off the Patch's Whiskey Row.[75]

Under other circumstances, and given the traditions of family life in Sondena, Gust and Jim might have hoped that Spiros and Mary would live with them, that it would be a return of the prodigal brother, now with a wife, to the patriarchal fold. But the newlyweds' decision to find their own housing may have been a matter of circumstances; perhaps the brothers' home was already crowded with other tenants. Familial conflicts and matters of honor also played a role. Indeed, Spiros may not have even told his brothers about the marriage.[76] According to one investigator, the older brothers would "never have consented to [Spiros] marrying a prostitute."[77] Gust, for his part, later said that the marriage "was a disgrace." It dishonored the family, but his hands were tied, he said. "I could not help it."[78]

With Spiros and Mary recently wed, and possibly imagining starting a family of their own, Spiros approached masculine ambitions of shedding youthful manhood and growing into the patriarchal status that marriage promised. By the early twentieth century, in Greek law and practice, the male-led nuclear family was slowly displacing the older model based on a single patriarch who oversaw the honor and status of the multiple patrilocal families who lived together in their rural village homes. Now, in Gary, this broader transition was realized when Spiros and Mary distanced themselves from Spiros's brothers' oversight—especially Gust, who assumed the local role of paterfamilias.

Spiros and Mary agreed that she would stop sex work, and indeed all labor outside the home. For Mary, the decision meant giving up difficult if lucrative work under unpredictable conditions and embracing dominant notions of domestic respectability. With Mary at home, Spiros would accrue the honor and prestige that her domestic labor would offer as well as the promise of children, who would similarly, he surely hoped, honor their father. Some Greek men saw it as a disgrace for their wives—or even sisters—to work outside the home, because they thought it meant they lacked the fortitude to provide for their family.[79] Of course many women did work outside the home, and Greek men could scarcely control their wives' lives and bodies so thoroughly as to meet their patriarchal ideals.[80] For whatever tangle of personal reasons—the tension between nuclear household and the multifamily patriarchies, revised in Gary with his older brother as patriarch; Mary's checkered working past—Spiros did not initially tell Gust about his marriage to Mary. Familial disapproval can be powerful, but forces greater still undermined Spiros and Mary's marriage. In 1913 and 1914, just as Spiros and Mary were wed, the steel industry hit an economic downturn. Layoffs were widespread.[81]

Times were tough for the newlyweds, and Spiros could only find occasional work. But worse disaster struck when Spiros injured his foot in an accident at the tin plate factory. Starting in July 1914, "I did not work for practically a month.... My foot was hurting so."[82] Spiros, of course, was hardly alone among the steel industry's casualties. He stayed at the US Steel hospital—part of its efforts at welfare capitalism—and was released about a week later.[83] But US Steel's compassion was suffused with condemnation. Despite its embrace of welfare capitalism, managers blamed workers for their supposed carelessness in getting injured. And because US Steel prized efficiency above all else, it would have been unlikely to hire Spiros back with a disability.[84] Hunger and eviction loomed. And so in late 1914 he was out of work. He was physically disabled, injured, and in pain. He was unable to provide for his family. Any one of these physical or economic factors would have contributed to a kind of masculine crisis; together, they posed a profound challenge to his aspirations of patriarchal manhood. Spiros and Mary still had to eat and to pay the exorbitant rents that the Patch's slumlords demanded.

Facing hard choices on how to make ends meet, Spiros and Mary took different paths. Spiros had previously spurned his brothers by striking out on his own, but now turned to them for help. He borrowed money from Gust but also from grocery store owners—really, from whomever he could. Spiros's community-based borrowing was in part underwritten by a fund of social capital based on a sense of respectability and the belief that he would repay—or put another way, honor—the debts. It would have required Gust's sanction and involved Gust's status too. Mary, like Spiros, returned to what she had known before. Rather than drawing on family or community lending, she returned to the underground economy of sex work. Her experience was hardly uncommon; many women did the same after their family's primary breadwinner was injured.[85]

But once again, circumstances far beyond their control intervened. Gary's elites had recently decided that one way to instill order amid the economic tumult was to crack down on vice, especially alcohol and prostitution. Police partnered with the federal Bureau of Investigation to raid and shutter the Patch's saloons. In earlier years the same police had been just as likely to get a cut from the Patch's underground economies, or else in the political battles among bosses for control of the city.[86] And the police were never shy about using violence to control Gary's newer immigrant population. When some sought redress after a policeman murdered a Hungarian, one politician reportedly claimed that it was a "disgrace for an officer to be arrested for killing a 'Hunky.'" This politician, at least, seemed to believe police should be able to kill immigrants with impunity.[87]

Soon rumors began to circulate through Gary's Greek community that Mary Olebos was working again. Word got back to Gust and Spiros. "I seen my wife begin to do those things and I could not stand it any longer," Spiros said. He had been unconcerned with Mary's career when they first met. But now, when he was both physically and economically vulnerable and reliant on his brothers' largesse, he said it enraged him. He reported with no shame that he physically beat her—likely a cruel effort to recoup his fragile sense of masculine control through family violence. He then "left the hotel" where they lived, he said, "and I had her arrested."[88] Yet if Spiros thought that this break with his wife would put him in better stead with his brother and with Gary's respectable Greek community, he was wrong. Because for unclear reasons, Gust had Spiros arrested. Perhaps Gust believed that where he could no longer assert fraternal control, Gary's police might help set his brother straight. This wasn't uncommon, either. By the 1920s many families sought the police's help to restore what they saw as proper order to their households.

Parents contacted state agents to control daughters who either experimented with illicit sexuality or found their own partners rather than consenting to their parents' choice. It was an effort for families to use the state to reassert patriarchy in the intergenerational reproduction of desired families, which accorded with state agents' sensibilities of the proper heteropatriarchal order too.[89]

But as Gust Olebos's behavior suggests, people could also try to use the state to help enforce older, multifamily patriarchal lineages rather than just nuclear families, and control the behavior of subordinate male family members. When Gust had Spiros arrested, he likely did so because Spiros threatened to bring shame to their extended family and undermine family honor. Gust, as an older male sibling, drew on the force of the state to shore up not parental authority but a conservative form of extended family patriarchy. Spiros was convinced Gust had him arrested because, as he said, "I went with that woman."[90] Gust may have been well-intentioned, but nevertheless he clearly misunderstood the nature of the US state, and how the deportation regime intersected with forces of class, gender, and ethnoracial control. In the midst of the white slavery panic and the Gary vice raids, Gust scarcely foresaw that his brother would become a casualty. Once Spiros was snared in the Gary's policing bureaucracy, powerful institutional forces pulled him deeper into the carceral state.

Immigration Inspector Roak, who was ordinarily stationed in Chicago, came to Gary when he learned that the Gary police were holding Spiros on prostitution-related charges. Roak asked around their neighborhood, and tracked Mary down at an apartment in the Patch. Bolstered by the extensive policing powers that antivice work offered, Roak entered the apartment. He found Mary plying her trade in one room, with another couple in the next room over. Roak came to believe that Mary was an irredeemable prostitute. Under interrogation, Mary told Roak that her relationship with Spiros had been good for a few months, but it fell apart after his injury. "We had nothing to eat and no place to sleep." As a result, she said, Spiros "beat me up and told me to go out and make a living." She earned $60 to $70 per week—nearly six times what Spiros had made in the tin plate plant. When she told the inspector that she "gave it all to him," she provided precisely the information that Roak needed to ensure Spiros's deportation, based on 1907 and 1910 immigration law, as an immigrant involved in the sex trade.[91]

But two days later, Mary sent a handwritten letter to immigration officials, as she said, "confessing the truth." In it, Mary implored officials to "please release Spiros, for he is not guilty of the crime." Spiros was a "good fellow," she said, and "he was working every day and never alowed [*sic*] me to do any hustling he always wanted me to quit. but I started my self.... [Spiros] was out of work[,] like many." He found occasional jobs but "they laid him of[f] because he cut his toe and for two weeks he did not work so family he had nothing to live of[f]." She continued,

I offered him help and of course he could not starve he took my proposition[,] he did not start me hustling. I was in that life years before I met him if you wish you may look up the record I served to [*sic*] sentences in the bridewell in Chicago for prostitution and huseld [*sic*] in Chicago in Hotel Wabash and in Gary before I met him and the money I made in Gary with the time I was with him I forced him to that life he was forced by me to live that life he has a good record he is a hard working man but now when there aint work for any of them he cant make the company give him work. if you look up that record about me in Chicago look for the name Mary Stonoff and you will find it the lie I told against him was I wanted to get even with him for arresting me for bigamy. so now I realized the fault I done him so I will confess the truth it is true he lived with me but he never forced me to live that life I lived that life on my own acord [*sic*]. I am here and if you wish to hear this statement from me you may send for me and I will tell all.[92]

Confronting this contradictory testimony, we are forced to wonder: which of these statements represented Mary's truer voice? The one prompted by Roak's interrogation, or the letter written from home? It is difficult to say. Perhaps Inspector Roak presented Mary with an opportunity to bear witness to a violent husband, who had coerced her into selling her body. Perhaps she saw immigration officials presenting an opportunity to save herself from abuse.

But perhaps the interrogation was less free than that. Perhaps the interrogation was one in which Roak cajoled Mary, and threatened her with imprisonment for prostitution unless she incriminated Spiros, and over the course of which, officials drew from her the testimony necessary to secure Olebos's deportation, and to build a case against others in Gary's vice industries. No stranger to dealing with the police, Mary would have likely understood that offering Inspector Roak a narrative in which he could be the manly savior of an innocent woman was a safer path to avoiding her own arrest. Perhaps the letter she wrote two days later, and which testified to Olebos's relative decency, was the truer document. Perhaps, when she said Spiros was a good man, and that she had volunteered to resume working as a prostitute, this was a truer indication of her choices. Perhaps, given the limited economic opportunities Mary and Spiros faced, she chose returning to sex work as a kind of small-proprietorship, in relatively equal partnership with her husband. A far from ideal option, given that she had quit hustling when they married, but the best option available under confined choices.

The truth of Spiros and Mary's relationship is elusive, as are the degrees of coercion, of collaboration, and in the depths and vortices of their care or animosity for one another, the dynamics and intimate asymmetries of power, and the multiple and competing forms of patriarchal control. It is far easier to compartmentalize the complexities of sex work, and of family violence and abuse, into Manichean purities of victim and oppressor. But the contradictions between Mary's testimony and her letter suggest that the truth, or truths, were more complex: that family violence could intermingle abuse and affection, support with pain. It is possible that Spiros did not want Mary to continue her work, because it undermined his sense of manhood and what he imagined as his ownership of her sexuality. It is also possible that because of his disability and unemployment, that they needed the income her sex work provided, that he resented her for that and expressed it through violence. Mary, too, may have resented the need to do this labor, alternatively normalizing and destigmatizing its moralized baggage and alternatively being traumatized by the experience. The realities surely layered these many meanings, as did the political economic structures that forced Mary and Spiros into this situation and led her back to a life that they both hoped she might leave behind.

Regardless of whether Mary was understood as a victim of violence or perpetrator of sex work, once she was within the carceral state's reach, things spiraled out of their control. In the course of the investigation, it came to light that Mary had previously been married, and though separated, was never divorced. Judges who convicted women of bigamy or adultery commonly had them returned to their husbands: state agents saw the patriarchal home as the best institution to restore the nation's intimate social order.[93] But Spiros was facing deportation, and with neither a respectable home or husband to discipline her, the judge sentenced Mary to five years at the Indiana State Penitentiary at Michigan City. It is unclear what became of her at the prison, or beyond.

As Spiros tried to prevent his removal, his brother Gust also offered support. They hired a lawyer with deep ties to Gary's Greek community. Their defense painted Mary as a manipulative seductress who had led the gullible otherwise hard-working Spiros astray. He admitted that he knew she had once been a sex worker, but "I married her under the promise that she would be a good woman."[94] And once he learned that she turned to sex work, he said, "I tried to get rid of her." But Mary carried a gun, and said she would kill him if he tried to leave her. There were never any witnesses to her threats, but Spiros testified that "she would put the gun at my head and say she would write her name in my head with the gun."[95] Throughout all of the questioning led by his lawyer, Spiros held that he never knowingly received money earned from her prostitution. Instead, he borrowed money from across the Greek community, especially from his brother.

If it is true that Gust had always disapproved of Mary and Spiros's relationship, Gust could now make Mary into the villain. The dominant white slavery narrative held that immigrant men ensnared and coerced white American girls into sex work. At the same time, the actual consequences of antivice and antiprostitution policing criminalized and vilified sex workers, and commonly portrayed them as irredeemably fallen women, temptresses and scourges of respectable society. Spiros's defense capitalized on the narrative of the dangerous woman. It also inverted the story of the immigrant coercing the white American girl. Spiros's lawyer's closing statement offered that "this woman was a prostitute and the evidence shows that she induced him by threats to stay with her even after he discovered that she was a prostitute. Those [sic] kind of women are well acquainted with the art of inducement in inducing men to stay with them. The record shows that she was a bigamist and that she is serving a sentence. I believe that under such evidence a man should not be deported."[96]

It did not work. Inspector Roak did not care whether or not Olebos knew that the money Mary brought home came from sex work. Chicago's Inspector Prentis was somewhat sympathetic to Spiros, even as he maligned Mary. He thought Spiros Olebos appeared to have "behaved himself properly and earned his living at legitimate employment until…he married a prostitute." But it didn't matter. According to Prentis, the "evidence was conclusive": Olebos had shared in her earnings, and he therefore merited deportation.[97] Gary's police initially hoped that Spiros might have been part of a major vice ring, but he was a small fish indeed.[98]

We cannot know what someone like Dr. Leo Stanley might have read in Spiros Olebos's face, if he watched him board the train in the Chicago station. He would likely have fixated on his dark hair and features, and if he saw his deportation warrant, he may have painted Spiros Olebos as a procurer exploiting and endangering white women. Stanley would not have seen the depth of family strain Spiros Olebos had borne—and caused—all of which was exacerbated by the vagaries in steel and housing markets, the price of Greek currants, the costs of love and sex, or the weight of family honor. Stanley would not have thought about how an injury at work, and the lack of workers' protections, set a cascade of crises to befall the Olebos family. Or that the rails that they would soon ride were indelibly bound with the labor, the sweat, the suffering, and the blood of men like Spiros Olebos. Nor would Stanley have seen how the women whose caregiving labor—be it paid sex work, or unwaged domestic labor, or childrearing—was an intimate manifestation of that larger world system.

And so the Deportation Special sped past the smokestacks of US Steel's Gary Works, perhaps over tracks that Spiros had laid in his first job there. But on they went, along the Great Lakes. The network of rail lines grew denser as they traveled east. If Leo Stanley's records were right, they left Chicago on the Nickel Plate lines at 8:35 p.m. It would be a long night and day until their next stop, when they arrived at Buffalo, New York, at 3:50 p.m., the afternoon of the next day.[99]

SEVEN

Buffalo

THE TRAIN LEFT CHICAGO and headed east toward Buffalo. "Towns passed by more frequently now," wrote Theodore Irwin, "Through the misty rain, they could see Lake Erie, the smoking factories, the ships tied up."[1] Leo Stanley described the mix of factories and small farms across northern Indiana and then skirting the lake shore. Railroad traffic was more congested. The New York Central Railroad ran four tracks parallel to the Nickel Plate; Stanley counted one freight train with 130 cars, laden with coal, pulled by immense locomotives. Many headed east, others west; the westbound ones heavy with coal were likely on their way to the furnaces in Chicago and Gary they had just left behind. At Cleveland their train passed across a high trestle, and for those whose eyes and minds wandered, as did Stanley's, they could see workers and stevedores loading and unloading coal and ore from whaleback boats, and a "heavy cloud of smoke from the factory chimneys overhung the city."[2]

Soon, as Irwin reflected, "Buffalo crept up on them, and the aliens who were being deported via Canada got their baggage ready. The Englishman, the Spanish dancer and the hunchbacked boy"—supporting characters in Irwin's novel—"briefly said good-bye. The others watched them march out of sight of the station."[3] Deportation to Canada, understood to be another "white" country, thick with its own histories of settler invasion and racial exclusion, is a lesser known aspect of US deportation history, but it was common early in the deportation regime.[4] The deportation of people with disabilities, including children, like Irwin's fictional hunchbacked boy, was common too.

The early century welfare state was a hodgepodge of locally based programs, with little federal involvement or regional integration, and its adherents were keen to adjudicate between the reputable and disreputable poor, between those considered worthy of relief, and the dissolute but sturdy beggars on whom it would be wasted. Understandings of race and behavior were central to this debate, with social workers and charities seeing as people of color as dissolute and likely to become dependent, while those whom they understood as white were more deserving of help.[5] But in the era of the deportation trains and a more thoroughly integrated carceral-welfare apparatus, and with scientific racism coinciding with and mobilizing immigration controls, if a presumptively white noncitizen with a disability ran afoul of this welfare state, they risked removal too. Put another way, when migrant status and disability intersected with presumptive whiteness, the privilege of whiteness, and its pathways to citizenship, could be lost. Assumed to be incapable of labor, maligned as defective, and disdained as likely public charges, people with disabilities, and their families, suffered from forced removal.[6]

Minnie Lester and her young son John boarded the Deportation Special in Buffalo. Minnie had been born in Birmingham, in the heart of the English midlands, in 1885. Birmingham had been in an extended economic depression since 1873, which only abated a decade after Minnie's birth.[7] Still, Birmingham saw relatively little industrial strife, and a US-based writer esteemed Birmingham as "the best governed city in the world."[8] Economically and geographically driven problems with sewage disposal and access to clean water led to varying mortality rates, with this or that neighborhood gaining a reputation as pestilential "black spot" districts.[9] Municipal medical and health officers documented neighborhoods with "narrow streets, houses without back doors or windows" and "the impossibility in many instances of providing sufficient privy accommodation."[10] Government soon claimed the ability to acquire and demolish houses in "insanitary areas" and rebuild in their place.[11] The city made great gains in lessening the high mortality rates and became a source of considerable municipal pride.[12]

Minnie married and took her new husband's name, becoming Minnie Lester. They had a son in 1912, whom they named John, after her father. We do not know where precisely Minnie lived with her husband and son, if was one of the "black spots" or the more respectable neighborhoods. But a year after their son's birth, her husband died of typhoid fever.[13] Clearly, efforts to provide clean water fell short. A year later, Minnie, twenty-nine, and John, three, traveled to the United States, where they planned join Minnie's two brothers and make a new start in Rochester, New York. Her brother Frederick Felton paid for their tickets. Minnie and John arrived at Ellis Island in April 1914. As nativist attacks against southern and eastern Europeans mounted around the turn of the century, English migrants still came in large numbers. Minnie and John were two among the nearly 270,000 who traveled from England, Scotland, and Wales to the United States between 1911 and 1914.[14] Entry documents record Minnie as being 5'3" tall, with a dark complexion, brown hair, and grey eyes. And despite Minnie's presumptive whiteness as an English woman, immigrant agents sought signs of physical weakness, illness, or disability. Indeed, one officer though that Minnie's left eye was "defective," but that concerned the inspector less than the fact that she was a single mother, traveling without a man.

When arriving at Ellis Island, being female—and particularly a single woman—was a kind of impairment. Immigrant inspectors looked askance at women traveling without men. Single women, they thought, were likely prostitutes, come to the United States to ply their trade, seduce upright men, and wreak havoc on otherwise moral American families. Even if they weren't prostitutes, inspectors believed that women without male protectors were more likely be lured into the sex industry by white slavers. Or, barring that, if they were not attached to a male breadwinner, they were understood as more likely to become public charges.[15] Officers, of course, were little concerned about the inequity of women being paid adequate wages on which to live, or how this fundamentally limited women's capacity to enjoy recognition as full members of society.[16] They presumed that men would earn a wage substantial enough to support a family—a family wage—and that women had little need to earn for themselves. And they believed that a single mother, who would presumably be dedicated to looking after her child, was even more likely to become a public charge.

This was why Minnie and the three-year-old John were locked up on Ellis Island upon arrival—wards of the state rather than wards of a patriarch— until one of Minnie's brothers came to "claim" her. Had he not, they would have been debarred and returned to England. Women's proper social roles, in immigrant agents' eyes, were to care for the home and their children—in other words, to do reproductive labor—rather than being able or entitled to decent earnings from work outside the home.

Once released from detention on Ellis Island, Minnie, John, and her brother traveled to Rochester, New York, the Flower City. Rochester grew by the Genesee River, along earth rich from sedimentary deposits and that fed into Lake Ontario. The river took its name from the Haudenosaunee—the Mohawk, Cayuga, Onondaga, Oneida, Seneca, and Tuscarora Peoples—whose principle villages were twenty miles to the southeast of what would become the city, and, for generations before European arrival, made ample use of the river and waterways for food, travel, and as conduits through their worlds.[17]

The river carved three substantial cataracts through dolomite and limestone strata, the power of which, beyond their beauty, struck European explorers and fur traders as an ideal site for water-powered milling. After 1788, American settlers began to build mills and, through a combination of trickery and force, to deny Haudenosaunee peoples access to the river, the falls, the mills, or their lands.[18] By the first decades of the nineteenth century, Rochester thrived as a milling depot and transit point on route for western colonization. When the Erie Canal was finished, Rochester's population grew with its economic power.[19] In 1860 nearly 40 percent of its residents had been born overseas, with the largest number hailing from Ireland, Germany, and then followed by Great Britain and Canada.[20] By 1890, Rochester was home to some forty thousand foreign-born residents. More than half were German or eastern European, and the proportion of British and Irish among the foreign-born declined. By 1890, recent immigrants and their children made up some 70 percent of Rochester's population.[21] Mutual aid and religious associations formed to help their respective country-people, be they Italian, Polish, Irish, German, Protestant, Catholic, or Jewish. The African Zion Methodist Church and a Douglass Union League provided support for African Americans. Not to be outdone, older residents and nativists formed the Sons and the Daughters of the American Revolution.[22]

Ray Stannard Baker in 1910 called Rochester "one of the brightest, busiest and most attractive cities in this country." He lauded the city leaders' spirit of community self-improvement as well as their commitment to social uplift.[23] The population continued to increase, from 89,000 in 1880 to 218,000 in 1910.[24] Rochester was increasingly cosmopolitan, with a welter of languages spoken in the downtown streets and throughout its more ethnically coherent neighborhoods.[25] In the first decade of the century those born in Germany or in Great Britain were still the largest immigrant groups, the children of multiple immigrant diasporas intermingled with the US-born in processes of second-generation acculturation. Many had already been naturalized, and more would do so in the immediate future, to safeguard their belonging against the era's mounting nativism.[26]

Minnie Lester needed to find paid work. As a widow and mother, she may have lacked a partner, but she was hardly alone in facing dire economic straits; losing a husband and breadwinner forced many women into the workforce.[27] Minnie soon worked as a housecleaner and doing washing, labor that meshed with gendered notions of women's proper activities. Though socially devalued and often disrespected, it was the kind of work necessary for people, society, and the economy to reproduce itself over time. According to historian Laura Briggs, this labor, which can be understood as the labor of social reproduction, involves "not only having and raising children but also feeding people; caring for the sick, the elderly, and those who cannot work; creating safety and shelter; building community and kin relationships; and attending to people's psychic and spiritual wellbeing."[28]

Domestic labor was among the country's worst-paid fields, and between 1910 and 1920, between one-third and a quarter of employed women in the United States worked in a form of domestic labor.[29] Terrible rates of pay and poor conditions led to turnover, and anyone who could leave, did. Whenever possible, they entered the better-paid and more prestigious ranks of salespeople, factory workers, or in transportation, professional service, or clerical work.[30] Investigators were surprised to learn that a great many women chose to be sex workers, as dangerous as it might be, rather than endure the poverty, drudgery, disrespect, and ill-treatment as domestic workers. Germaine Rigolout and Mary Olebos might have told them the same. Live-in domestic laborers commonly earned as little as $3 per week (an abysmal wage justified on the grounds that they needn't pay rent elsewhere) and commonly faced sexual harassment from employers.[31] Recent immigrants and Black women tended to be the ones largely restricted to domestic work, the product and consequence of stigmatization. Economists calculated that a single person needed $8 per week as a living wage. But single mothers tended to earn less than half of that, between $2 and $4 per week.[32] A vast number of US domestic servants were Irish women, but working-class English immigrants were among them too.[33] Minnie Lester made ends meet, but just barely.

Minnie was doing reproductive labor for other peoples' families: her washing and cleaning in other peoples' homes enabled the reproduction of their households. But working in someone else's home meant that Minnie Lester was unable to do that work in her own home and with her own son, John. She enrolled John at the Rochester Industrial School, an institution whose mission was for the "care of children of working mothers."[34] The school opened in 1858 and was modeled on the industrial workhouse popularized through the English Poor Laws.[35] As a site of early industrialization and a passageway to the industrializing West, Rochester saw a large number of orphaned children, and the Industrial School was one of a host of poor-relief institutions—part charity, part prison—to arise in Rochester in the mid-nineteenth century.[36] The mix of benevolence and control came through in its moralizing rebuke of impoverished parents: The school's mission was

> to gather…vagrant and destitute children, who from the poverty or vice of their parents, are unable to attend the public schools, and who gather a precarious livelihood by begging or pilfering, to give them means of moral and religious duty, to instruct them in the elements of learning and in different branches of industry, and enable them to obtain an honest and honorable support, and to become special members of society.[37]

The school provided indigent children with food, clothing, education, and perhaps most pointedly, vocational instruction. Boys would learn basic trades work—presumably by doing it—and the school's principal, Ida Bernard, remarked in 1890 on the need for better trained girls to work in people's homes. "How many people have not been tried with incompetent servants, who even when told and shown the proper manner of doing things still persist in their own way by force of habit?…[W]e must work with these girls while they are still young."[38] Bernard's was an implicit attack on immigrant domestic workers—like Minnie—as surly and troublesome.[39] And though vocational training was crucial to the future citizen, the school's 1917 *Annual Report* noted the goal of moral instruction: "to awaken in the child a moral sense which will distinguish between good and evil and an ambition to make of himself [*sic*] a self-respecting member of society."[40]

Minnie usually picked John up from the school around 2:00 or 3:00 in the afternoon, when she got off of work. It cut into the amount of time she might be earning money, but at least she was able to spend a bit more time with her son. Yet by November the staff at the Industrial School refused to look after John, and moreover, their treatment seemed cruel. "They said he was too much trouble," Minnie explained. "Twice they had him tied up when I went for him." He could be a difficult child, she lamented; he spoke little and needed help going to the bathroom. Had John been easier to care for, or had he fit into more commonplace categories of physical and cognitive ability, things might have gone differently. Instead, it appears that John had what would today be called a cognitive disability, and was perhaps epileptic, so the school refused him. Yet John showed signs of improvement, and Minnie was hopeful, because John's fits were fewer and further between. He hadn't had one in months.[41]

Families with children who did not fit within increasingly stringent definitions of normalcy—and these generally accorded to their anticipated capacities for labor in an industrial or domestic economy—had fewer resources available to draw on. Many turned to family for this kind of help. Indeed, in previous generations family members with divergent bodies or mental capacities found valued locations within a spectrum of opportunities to contribute productive (or reproductive labor) in the domestic sphere. But Minnie's brothers were stretched thin, and if they were married—sources are silent on this—their spouses couldn't help.[42] With the Industrial School's doors closed, Minnie might have looked into the other schools, asylums, and institutions in the region to look after John. Turn-of-the-century New York State was thick with orphanages, asylums, training schools, and institutions for the "feebleminded" and so-called "idiots." Yet these involved long-standing family separation and generally required that a parent relinquish control of their child to the institution. Because inmates were understood by hereditarians as permanent burdens on society, residents were increasingly confined for the rest of their lives.[43] Many impoverished and widowed mothers like Minnie were compelled by circumstance to place their children in institutions, but Minnie worked hard to prevent that from happening.[44]

Orphanages, asylums, and related institutions tended to be frightening, harsh, and unforgiving. Beyond moralizing instruction or industrial training, they also posed real threats to children's lives. At the turn of the century, it wasn't unheard of for an institution to have a mortality rate of 97 percent for children under three years old—right around John Lester's age.[45] And so Minnie Lester left John with a neighborhood woman named Mrs. Keegan while she was at work, even though it cost money. She did everything she could to keep John close at hand. Minnie eventually turned to local government for support. In late November 1914 she applied to T. J. Bridges, Rochester's superintendent for the poor, for relief to help pay for John's caregiving so she could continue to work.[46] Laws providing mothers' pensions were first passed in Illinois in 1911, with twenty more states following suit by 1913, and more than forty states had similar laws by 1926. The pensions were intended to give widows generous cash grants to allow them to look after their children.[47] Minnie began receiving $2 per week, which she used to pay Mrs. Keegan. Minnie acknowledged the hard work that Mrs. Keegan did for she and John, gratefully remarking that "Mrs. Keegan earns her $2. a week."[48]

But the aid proved a concrete risk. The process was uneven across the country, but welfare agencies began to ensnare noncitizen adults when they took their children to receive state care.[49]

Superintendent Bridges gave Minnie $2 with one hand, but took away much more with the other. He reported them to the immigration bureau and called for their expulsion. Minnie had mistaken the idea of state or county welfare for a broad interest and concern for humanity and well-being. This was not the case. The amount of money actually provided for mothers' pensions was far outpaced by the need, and pension payments were often restricted to women that social workers thought were ideal American mothers. Although the pensions were initially passed without citizenship requirement, by 1913 strong nativist currents mobilized against noncitizen mothers receiving aid.[50]

Indeed, Minnie Lester learned that Rochester's welfare system, particularly as allocated through the person of T. J. Bridges, was less concerned for her and John's well-being than he was in dividing and allocating among peoples, and particularly in denying support, such as it was, for people like Minnie and John Lester. The process was far from uniform across the nation and was subject to wide vagaries of local politics and personalities, along with racial presuppositions and regional differences: European migrants in the urban Northeast were far more likely to have the support of social workers and local officials than were Mexican migrants in the Southwest, who were more likely to be reported to federal immigration authorities for removal.[51] Still, Bridges reported to federal immigration authorities that Minnie and John Lester were destitute public charges and should be deported. Rochester's immigration inspector Isaac Martin responded to Bridges's call and had Minnie and John arrested.

During their hearing and in his subsequent report, Martin opined that young John was epileptic and, he believed, feebleminded.[52] "Feeblemindedness" was an imprecise and capacious category that subsumed a great many forms of so-called cognitive and mental undesirability. Howard Knox, Ellis Island's chief surgeon from 1912 through 1916, called feeblemindedness a catchall diagnosis, a "sort of waste basket for many forms and degrees of weak-mindedness."[53] It was useful for exclusion precisely because it was so ambiguous, and John Lester's cognitive abilities could be made to fit within its diagnostic bounds. In the hearing, Minnie Lester explained to Inspector Martin that "I would like to stay here, and I think if my boy could have treatment he might get better." She insisted that she needn't be a public charge.

"I can get lots of work," she said, she just needed childcare during for a few hours during the day.[54] Immigration Commissioner Clark conceded that she was might be counted among the so-called worthy poor, but that there was a problem.

> The woman might be self-supporting if she were not burdened with this child. However...the child should have been excluded at time of arrival in New York as an epileptic, and the mother as a natural guardian, and both as likely to become public charges.[55]

John Lester, by virtue of his epilepsy, and his difficulty in caring for himself, was placed among the ranks of those increasingly understood as a social liability rather than as a full human who might contribute to a broad and diverse society. Under the ascendant regime of industrial capitalism, underwritten by the scientific racism and ableism of eugenics, and constrained by the politically limited finances of the welfare state, John Lester's cognitive and physical differences were marked as permanent liabilities and disabilities, forever incompatible with the US state and its goals for social reproduction.[56]

This was the crux of the matter. It wound together notions of gender and labor, of womanhood and motherhood, and also of disability, of social production and the reproduction of labor. A connection between womanhood and motherhood was affirmed, as was the idea that caregiving for a child with an impairment was a burden to be borne by a nuclear family. Had social structures allowed for John's care, Minnie would not herself be impaired, or so profoundly "burdened" by her son. As a single mother, the lack of childcare options for her child, who seemed, in twenty-first-century language, to have special needs, were concretely disabling. Requirements for her to do caregiving labor therefore kept her from the wage labor force. Moreover, the Rochester Industrial School refused to look after a child they deemed feebleminded, which spoke to issues of disabled children's treatment and notions of mental disability. Similarly, women's location in the workforce was commonly understood to center around feeding and caring for male productive workers; reproducing a next generation of worker-citizens, and so forth— rather than productive labor. Steeped as they were in an inherently eugenic national project, immigration officials, county physicians, and welfare officers considered John to be "defective," and that any caregiving or reproductive labor Minnie, Mrs. Keegan, or the Industrial School might extend was a waste of time, energy, and resources.

As a result, the gears of the deportation machine turned, and arrangements were made for Minnie and John's removal. They were not considered an escape risk, so Minnie and John were permitted to stay at their home rather than be locked up in a municipal facility. That would have cost money, after all. Formal guidelines suggested that deportees with disabilities have a medical attendant to aid their removal, but Rochester's county physician certified that John could travel without an attendant, indeed, his mother could "furnish the special care and attention required for the child on the ocean voyage."[57] This rehashed the state's disavowal of caregiving and underscored its reliance on women's labor. And because John was deemed "defective," his care could scarcely even be considered reproductive labor. According to eugenic philosophies, he shouldn't be allowed to grow, exist, or be reproduced at all.

We do not know what took place when Minnie and John said goodbye to Minnie's brothers, who remained in Rochester, what they might have said to their nephew, or what young John might have felt at the center of this struggle. They were transferred from Rochester to Buffalo and boarded the Deportation Special. Minnie and John would spend another four days detained at Ellis Island. On January 23, 1915, they were loaded aboard the *SS Transylvania*. Transatlantic journeys often took around nine days, which would put them in Liverpool in early February, and at Minnie's parent's home on Portchester Street in Birmingham perhaps a day later.

Angelina Fererra Piazza and her husband, Salvatore Piazza, were not far behind Minnie and John Lester, on the deportation line from Rochester to Buffalo, and then to New York's Ellis Island. Like Minnie and John, they were deported as LPC (likely to become a public charge), due to a disability that predated their arrival in the United States. Yet their experience demonstrated the ways in which disability is not an intrinsically physical condition, but rather, how disability is produced in social and political-economic circumstances.

Angelina and Salvatore were born in the Sicilian province of Caltanisetta; she, in Barrafranca, and he, a few miles to the north, across a low valley, in Mazzarino. Angelina was 5'3" tall, with a rosy complexion, chestnut hair, in good health, and two years older than Salvatore. Salvatore was 5'5" tall, pale, with chestnut hair. They were married around 1905, when both were in their early twenties. In 1910, in what was likely a decision they made together, Salvatore traveled to Boston for work, one among hundreds of thousands of

Sicilian men who temporarily left behind a wife to make money overseas.[58] Unlike the majority of Sicilians and other southern Italians, Salvatore was a skilled artisan and shoemaker rather than a peasant farmer, and Angelina was literate and able to avoid wage work—focusing instead on laboring in their home. Italian women had worked for wages in the late nineteenth century, but rates of wage work for Italian women fell alongside industrialization, and so while it wasn't uncommon for Angelina to not work while Salvatore was overseas, it may have meant she relied on family for sustenance beyond Salvatore's remittances.[59] He lived in Boston from 1910 through 1911, and returned to be with Angelina. In January 1913 the couple traveled to New York, arriving with $40, bound for Rochester.[60] They passed through the battery of inspections at Ellis Island with little trouble.

By 1914 plenty of Sicilians specifically and southern Italians more generally made the Flower City home.[61] Between 1880 and 1900 a handful of established families served as a base for increasing numbers of single and itinerant Italian men. Most did heavy labor in construction, a handful began working in agriculture, and a smaller number became merchants or artisans scattered through urban Rochester.[62] Italian women also began to arrive in larger numbers after 1910.[63] Italians tended to live in Rochester's economically depressed and undesirable neighborhoods.[64] In addition to ethnic ghettoization, Rochester's Italians were subject to both police oversight as well as neglect. While the Rochester police commonly left Italians to settle their own disputes, the newspapers and the city elite called for investigations into prostitution, crime, drunkenness, poor parenting, juvenile delinquency, and more.[65] Still, the Rochester Police Department hired its first Italian translator in 1905, and its first Italian American policeman two years later. Each took part in a state effort to control this immigrant community.[66] Anti-Italian policing culminated in a series of police raids in Italian neighborhoods early in the century, on the pretense of crime control, maintaining the social order, and cracking down on organized crime.[67]

Salvatore and Angelina were drawn to Rochester because it had been a center of the shoe-making industry since the mid-nineteenth century. In the 1860s artisan shoemakers in Rochester had used knives, awls, hammers, and waxed thread to hand-make shoes and boots, and an industry coalesced around their work.[68] By the 1880s industries were centralizing and concentrating, with larger owners concentrating workers in larger factories, exacting greater surveillance and control. Shoe workers organized in the 1870s and 1880s and met occasional success in alliance with the Knights of Labor, but intransigent employers formed a Shoe Manufacturers Association and in the 1890s locked out striking workers.[69] It was part of a steady assault on shoemakers' wages and independence. Factory owners introduced new machinery that allowed them to fire skilled workers and hire newcomers for cheap, thereby increasing profits.[70] Edgar Reed, a shoemaking magnate and lifetime officer in the Shoe Manufacturers Association, marveled at the "bewildering processes by the aid of machinery," which accelerated profits and production. He estimated that in 1920 one-fifth of Rochester's residents were employed shoe- and boot-making.[71] This hardly meant they were well-paid. It is entirely possible the Salvatore and Angelina were pressed to leave Caltanisetta because his work there was undercut by cheaper US-made shoes.

But Salvatore could not find a decent job. "I thought I could get work here at my trade," he lamented, "but I could not get any work." Workers less apt than he filled the factory walls, and someone like Reed had little need for a skilled worker when the machines' bewildering processes made skilled workers superfluous. Still, he and Angelina needed to eat and pay the landlord. He found occasional work in construction and in heavy labor. "I worked for about four months last year with a pick and shovel for different people," which was grueling and difficult. But it was all that Rochester's political economy allowed him, as a non-English-speaking migrant of the so-called "Italian race." As he bemoaned, "that is all the work I have been able to do."[72] It was doubly painful, because some years earlier, Salvatore had developed tears in his abdominal wall known as inguinal hernias. He managed their discomfort with by wearing a truss, a sort of compression bandage that served to reinforce the tears in his abdominal wall.[73] It could be uncomfortable, but it was adequate. The hernia, supported by the truss, never stopped him from working as a shoemaker, and he had never needed to go to the hospital.[74]

Angelina also began to work. Women's labor outside the home was generally looked down on in Sicily, but Angelina got a job in a cannery. As Angelina put it, "we…lived on that and what we could get from our friends and others."[75] By November 1914 they had sold everything that they could part with and could no longer ask friends for help. The weather wasn't getting any warmer. Much as Minnie Lester had done, they approached the Monroe County poor department for support. It was a fateful move. Four days later, T. J. Bridges, the same superintendent of the poor who reported Minnie and John Lester to the Immigration Department, informed Inspector Isaac Martin that Salvatore and Angelina Piazza should be deported. Apparently

Bridges did not think that the Immigration Bureau was moving quickly enough, because in January he contacted them again.[76]

Salvatore and Angelina were drawn into the deportation regime at the intersection of the welfare and health-care systems: the first step in their ensnarement had been to seek public support; the next step was through Salvatore's medicalization. A county physician named L. W. Howk inspected Salvatore's body and diagnosed his ailment as a double inguinal hernia, of which Salvatore had been aware for some time. In his report Howk said that Salvatore's hernia had prevented him from working for the past twelve years.[77] This was not true, but it was a convenient story for the Immigration Bureau. It expressed what disability studies scholars call a "medical model" of disability, in which disability is understood as a physical or corporeal failing and departure from the normal and ostensibly proper bodies.

This was the difference that disability studies scholars identify between an *impairment* and a *disability*. An impairment is a kind of physical, bodily difference from the norm. Yet an impairment only becomes a disability in specific social or political-economic contexts, when society demands that all bodies are required to perform certain activities in order to earn a wage, to move through social space, or to be recognized as fully human and take part in social, political, and economic life. T. J. Bridges, superintendent of the poor, reiterated the idea of Salvatore's hernia-as-disability as the basis for his and Angelina's removal. According to Bridges, Salvatore was "at the time of his entry to this country...suffering from disabilities which prevented him earning a livelihood, and made him liable to become a public charge."[78] This was not accurate. He successfully passed medical inspection at Ellis Island and was able to lug his bags, to climb or descend stairs under the close scrutiny of physicians attentive to minor variances in gait or posture. Had physicians detected an impairment, they would have marked his coat with a chalk "K" for further and more invasive inspection.[79]

Similarly, in the deportation hearing, Inspector Martin insisted on asking about Salvatore's "sickness" and when it began. Salvatore's answer to both charges pushed back at the deportation regime's medical model of disability. He had had the hernia since before coming to the United States, but it had never been an issue. "I worked at shoemaking there and it did not bother me." Salvatore's hernias had never been an impediment shoemaking in Caltanisetta, which required practiced technique and fine motor skills but did not require heavy lifting or activities that would stress his abdominal wall. Rather, Salvatore explained that it was only "the kind of work that I had to do here made it worse." In other words, the manual labor he was forced to do in Rochester transformed a physical *impairment*, which hadn't been terribly onerous, into a *disability*, and one for which he and his wife were deported.[80] "If I could have gotten work at my trade," he said, the hernia would not "have bothered me so much."

Angelina, for her part, reiterated their position and understood that Rochester's ethnoracial political economy, woefully impacted by the mechanization of shoemaking, had disabled her husband. Angelina affirmed that hard labor in Rochester worsened his impairment. Her husband was "not very sick" in Italy, Angelina said. He had "the same trouble that he has now, [but] it would not be so bad if he could have only gotten lighter work" in Rochester.[81] The disability he bore by late 1914 was not the result of his hernia. The global political economy of shoemaking, and of life in southern Italy, and of the demands of heavy labor in Rochester—issues well beyond Salvatore's body—had disabled him.

Thus it was that the immigration regime retroactively misapprehended Salvatore's bodily impairment as an intrinsic, inherent defect, a disability, at the time of his entry. Immigration agents argued that Salvatore should have been excluded on LPC grounds—as having been likely to become a public charge at the time of entry. But as a shoemaker, and at the time of entry, he was not in fact disabled. He only "became disabled" in Rochester, when, thanks to the industrialization of the shoe industry, he couldn't find work in his trade. The deportation regime understood being *disabled* as a noun and as a state of being. While a disability-as-state-of-being might be "fixable" through medical intervention (the Rochester physician said as much, but offered no options for hernia repair), it would have been more accurate to think about Salvatore's *dis-ablement* as a *verb*: a process through which the politics of labor made his bodily characteristics untenable for economic—and thus political and social—citizenship. In other words, and across global scales, he was *dis-abled*. Sicily's place in a global economy made his travel to a center of the US shoemaking industry appear to be the best option. Mechanization unmade his trade. Rochester's political economy *dis-abled* him. Being forced into heavy labor caused him pain and suffering, and eventually led him and Angelina to seek the support of friends, likely Italian mutual aid or religious societies, and eventually the state they hoped might lend a hand.

But this was not to be. T. J. Bridges was on a mission to restrict limited social welfare support to US citizens. Even though European migrants in the Northeast fared far better than Mexican migrants in the Southwest, the politics of ability and disability tainted even those who could plausibly make claims toward whiteness and approach the belonging of citizenship. People with disabilities were treated as a burden to be shed—even to Rochester's much vaunted good government advocates, of whom the Flower City boasted many.[82] In that sense, "good government" was only for those citizens understood to deserve it. Perhaps the efficient identification, capture, and expulsion of so-called undesirables from the body politic was an expression of "good government," and liberal nationalist exclusion, because it promised more efficiencies for the citizens who remained.

Angelina and Salvatore posed no immediate threat to the city, as officials understood it. Like Minnie and John Lester, they were more on the "pathetic" than the "dangerous" end of the spectrum of deportable peoples. They were released without needing to post bail and permitted to stay at their home on Cliff Street. At this point they were prepared to return to Caltanisetta. Salvatore said he was "willing to be returned. I can't make a living here."[83] Angelina agreed. "We both want to go back to Italy," she said, "we have nothing but our clothes, and no money."[84] Caltanisetta would at least offer the support and proximity of family. Officers filed a deportation warrant on March 22, 1915, which was followed by a telegram urging rushed action, since a deportation mainline train would soon pass nearby, and an Italy-bound steamer was due to depart New York three days later.[85]

Despite Salvatore's impairment, Rochester's county physician attested that the couple did not need a medical attendant.[86] Their few belongings were light enough that they could manage. Immigrant Inspector Rowe traveled from the Buffalo office to Rochester and took Salvatore and Angelina Piazza, along with three other Italians slated for removal, into custody. He brought them from Rochester to Buffalo, where they met five more people facing removal. They rolled out of Buffalo on Lackawanna train Number 10 at 6:30 in the evening. The next stop would be the DL&W station at Hoboken, New Jersey, and a special Immigration Bureau ferry to Ellis Island.

EIGHT

Ellis Island

BY THE TIME THE DEPORTATION SPECIAL made the last leg of its east-bound journey, many of its passengers had been aboard for days. Germaine Rigolout, Frank Abbott, James Pepper, and Delfina Andrade had seen the sun set over the Pacific Ocean some nine days earlier, and now saw it rise over the Atlantic. Along with the newer passengers boarded en route, the passengers, forced together while being cast out, inhabited a transitory and precarious world. The deportation agents assigned carriages and bunks, but many managed to choose their seatmates, sometimes by language or ethnicity, as when two mad Italians sat together, one of whom suffered from "persecutory insanity" but quite generously looked after the other, who could scarcely feed or clean himself.[1] Others grouped themselves through a kind of convict affinity. Four had been in prison together and played cards to pass time. Guards considered dividing them into different parts of the car, thereby keeping them apart and lessening the chance to scheme. "But as they made no false moves," Leo Stanley reported, "we decided to let them ride as they were."[2]

The women facing removal seemed to keep to themselves, especially if they were looking after children. The children, according Stanley, who for a eugenicist could be quite romantic about childhood innocence, just wanted to play and frolic. He told many anecdotes about young deportees and shared his concern for their futures. According to Stanley, Dennis, the adopted child of a woman he called Mrs. Smith, played in the train "with the few toys...entirely oblivious to the heartaches and complications from which he had passed."[3] Disorderly deportees, like the Bulgarian "Happy Hooligan," could cause problems, potentially imparting friction into the deportation regime. "Hooligan" bothered other unfree passengers and destroyed the tattered clothing he wore. But because he never reached the point of disrupting the forward progress of travel, guards had "considerable fun watching the other prisoners battle with him." A man named Carl, "who was younger and strong, had several tussles with him, and several times it was necessary to pull Carl off, for fear he would hurt the poor lunatic."[4] In Erie a young Italian man was brought aboard. For much of the rest of the journey, he and Carl unabashedly planned how they would get back to the United States.[5]

As they approached New York, tensions mounted. Increasingly congested cities outside the barred windows made the unfree passengers anxious. Billboards advertising American dreams were more frequent too. "The aliens fidgeted, stretched and paraded the aisle," Theodore Irwin wrote, and they "tried a hundred ways to shorten the day." The closer they got to the end of the line, the worse it got. "The last evening before arrival stretched out like an elastic—so drawn out and taut, every minute you thought it might snap in two. The long grind across the continent, the lack of exercise and clean air, had whipped up nerves, shortened tempers." Projecting one person's interior thought at the end of the overland trip, Irwin wrote: "Soon we'll be saying goodbye to this stinking train, it's worse than a jail, it keeps shaking the guts out of you." Elsewhere, he wrote of their sense of filth and injury, each "acutely aware of their stiff bodies, their sooty faces." One complained: "We had to sit up in a parlor car for five nights on the train. I feel so broken up, when I sneeze my bones rattle."[6]

The anxiety of the journey and uncertainty of what lay ahead could prove too much. In *Strange Passage* an aging miner named Kracevich grew despondent after a work-related injury left him disabled and a public charge, subject to removal. "Kracevich was crippled, penniless, 58 years old and no longer knew anyone in Lithuania.... There is nothing for us where we are going, we might as well die."[7] Kracevich later killed himself. Here, as elsewhere, Irwin's fiction matched real life. It seems that Leung Kai Main, a well-connected New York merchant facing pandering charges and deportation on arrival in San Francisco, tried to escape from the train. It is hard to know if Leung sought release through suicide or simply tried to free himself from the moving train and met an accidental and grisly end. Officers from the Nickel Plate Railroad found Leung's body by the tracks in Sandusky, Ohio. The deportation agent Leo Russell would later report that "every safeguard possible was tried to prevent the escape of this man." He continued:

I do not think he had any idea in getting safely away but am of the opinion that he committed suicide rather than face prosecution....I wish to state again that I sincerely deplore this incident but inasmuch as the car was not entirely safeguarded against escapes I cannot blame anyone for the incident as I had men as attendants who had handled aliens for years. I will take up in a separate communication recommendations for fixing the car to prevent any possible chance of aliens escaping.[8]

Wholly ignoring the despair wrought by carceral control and forced expulsion, Russell offered the classic modernist's solution to the dual problems of suicide and escape: an architectural/technological fix to the car itself.

In the final hours of one eastbound journey, Stanley, unencumbered by worries, enjoyed a light breakfast and mused over the misty skyline. The deportation agent would have been busier, making sure that all of the paperwork and files were in order, that the baggage was tagged and prepared for smooth transfer.[9] In the earliest years there had been considerable difficulty handing the unwilling passengers over from the Deportation Special's custody to the Ellis Island staff.[10] But by the First World War, many of the logistical issues had been identified and resolved. Ellis Island's agents would have received a telegraph well in advance of the train's arrival and prepared for the transfer from the station to Ellis Island. Moreover, for the deportees who had come this far, passports, tickets, visas, and other travel documents were largely sorted out, smoothing the impediments that the other countries demanded before accepting those whom the United States had rejected.[11]

The Delaware, Lackawanna, and Western (DL&W) station at Hoboken was a center of passenger travel freight transfer. The busy Beaux Arts–style depot sported a 225-foot tall, red-brick clock tower, electric lighting made its "Lackawanna" lettering and clock faces visible from far and wide.[12] Built in 1907, near the height of migrant arrivals into New York, an early bureau report described that the station was perfectly laid out for deportation: a major selling point for contracting with DL&W for deportation traffic. The DL&W station

has exceptional facilities for handling aliens upon arrival in Hoboken, as it owns its own depot and has a large and commodious waiting room reserved for the exclusive use of the Government a short distance from the slip where the Ellis Island barge usually awaits the party and transfers can be accomplished without delay or danger of escape.[13]

The Immigrant Building had access to both a ferry pier and to the rail lines, which would allow immigrants smoother lines of travel with less interaction with ordinary, workaday commuters and travelers in its two main terminals. For deportation traffic this meant less interference and smoother lines of travel.[14]

Still, carceral order reigned, and controls would be exercised. When they arrived at Hoboken, deportation agents lined the prisoners in pairs on the platform. Agents from the Ellis Island Deportation Squad along with two uniformed policemen arrived to guard them. They feared gaps between the train and the ferry. The man Leo Stanley called Hooligan, who was mentally unstable, had torn away his clothes at the station in Buffalo, and officials wrapped him in a sheet so that fewer people would see his nakedness. Another man had no coat, but wore only a sleeveless sweater. Deportees traveled in whatever clothing they had—which was often insufficient for New York, let alone the weather they might find on the overseas journey, or where they would land. Stanley remarked that "Tony the Italian...endeavored to hang back a little" and seemed to be gauging his chance to run.[15] There was none. Supposedly dangerous deportees, such as a Swede that Stanley said had killed a policeman, would remain in manacles. Others could be handcuffed to each other. Those who were too unwell to walk might be carried on a litter. Despite the generalized alienation, there were moments of mutual support, as when an unnamed male deportee helped a single mother and her child with their hamper.[16]

Police, immigration officials, and the train's guards—again, a mix of local, federal, and private police forces—marched them to the barge that would take them across the Hudson to Ellis Island. The Ellis Island barges were mostly used to shuttle newly arrived migrants from their transatlantic steamers to Ellis Island for inspection but were equally suited to the removal journey. They could hold hundreds or even thousands of passengers. As one traveler had it, passengers

> were afraid and obviously dreading the events of the next few hours...each family huddled over its trunks and boxes, suitcases or bundles....[S]ome with their pitiful, paltry personal belongings, all they had in the world, tied up in old blue or red bandannas, which they clutched anxiously as they peered over the rail toward the tiny island.[17]

Guards split the deportees into four groups, one at each corner of the main cabin, for easier surveillance and control.[18] As close as they were to shore, officials feared that the desperate might try to escape. Some passengers rumored that guards wore bathing suits in case deportees tried to swim to freedom.[19]

The Lenni Lenape peoples had long known it as Gull Island. Early Dutch and English settlers called it Oyster Island, but by the early nineteenth century, when pirates were executed there, it went by the moniker Gibbet Island. Samuel Ellis bought the island in the eighteenth century and sold it to New York State in 1808, though his name stuck. The federal government used Ellis Island as a fort and munitions store, but repurposed it for immigrant processing in 1890 to replace the outdated Castle Garden facilities. A fire destroyed much of the building in 1897, but the facility was rebuilt with architecture meant to impress: tall red brick, steel-framed buildings, flashed with white trim and punctuated by four tall copper towers. Eagles and shields adorned arching windows. The facility housed the Great Hall, but also offices, dormitories, detention facilities, a hospital, a morgue, a ferry house, laundry and carpentry facilities, and a mental ward.[20]

Most of the deportation special's passengers had been here before, of course. More than fourteen million people came through Ellis Island between 1892 and 1924; around 71 percent of arrivals into the United States over those years.[21] They had survived its harrowing sorting and sifting regime. As one observer wrote in 1906: "Let no one believe that landing on the shores of 'The land of the free and the home of the brave' is a pleasant experience. It is a hard, harsh fact, surrounded by the grinding machinery or the law, which sifts, picks, and chooses; admitting the fit and excluding the weak and helpless."[22] With similar fortitude, they would survive their time here again. Ellis Island had borne multiple names, but by the First World War, for many it was called "The Island of Tears."[23]

As the barge approached the island's seawall, it passed through waters that Harry Curran, who worked there in 1923, said were "thickly tainted with sewage."[24] When their boat landed at Ellis Island, they were forced quickly onshore. As Irwin told it:

Burdened with baggage, their course lined by guards, two strings of aliens emerged from the barge, marched along the path to the entrance.... The sick, some on stretchers, others leaning heavily friendly shoulders, came out first. A strait-jacketed [*sic*] lunatic was driven ashore in a wheelbarrow. An alien who had twice before escaped from the Island walked off manacled to a guard. Women and children marched out white-faced and frightened, crossed the lawn, disappeared into the building.[25]

Stanley, his part of the journey done, grew oddly sentimental. As he watched them file onto the island, Stanley "caught sight of, and received the last glimpse of Mrs. Smith, little Dennis, and the poor demented Italian lady, with her lovable baby."[26] The Italian woman thanked Mrs. Austin, the matron, for the kindnesses she had been shown on the trip. Mrs. Smith was "too deeply affected by her own sorrow" to say goodbye but also reportedly asked the matron "to convey her gratitude to us for the few attentions we had shown her and her boy."[27]

It would have been among the rare kindness as they entered the fully carceral wings and ritual spaces of Ellis Island. While Henry Weiss or another deportation agent transferred their files to Ellis Island's teams of clerks, the deportees came under the charge of the Ellis Island Deporting Division, a group of carceral specialists. Its day shift and night shift were in charge of custodial control, while the deporting squad oversaw transfer from detention on the island to steamers for removal.[28] The deportees' bags and jackets were affixed with new colored tags—blue in 1912 but green by the 1930s.[29] In either case, the tags were an administrative feature meant to systematically mark the unfit among Ellis Island's transient, imprisoned population. One immigrant inspector and interpreter from 1907 explained the tagging system:

> To make things run fairly smoothly in that mixed crowd of poor, bewildered immigrants, we would tag them with numbers... after they had been landed from the barges and taken into the building. ... [T]hey were lined up, a motely [*sic*] crowd in colorful costumes, all ill at ease and wondering what was about to happen to them.[30]

Emanuel Steen explained what it felt like to be tagged:

> Immigration officials slammed a tag on you with your name, address, country of origin, etc. Everybody was tagged. ... They took your papers and they tagged you. They checked your bag. Then they pushed you and they'd point. because they didn't know if you spoke English or not.[31]

Ida Mouradjian, an Armenian woman who arrived in 1922, said that she and others

> were pushed around.... [The staff] were a bunch of patronage job holders, who were ignorant. What's more, they didn't have hearts, they didn't have minds, they had no education. They were very crude. Many were foreigners who delighted in the fact that they could lord over the new entries, the new immigrants.... [T]hey acted the way small people become because they had a little power. They pushed everybody around, actually, literally pushed.[32]

One guard, after being asked why he was so rough with migrants on the barges, said, "Oh, I'm driving these animals back.... You've got to be rough with this bunch. I get so sick of these dirty bums coming over here to this country."[33] Guards treated new and ostensibly innocent migrants this way, and we can hardly expect that guards were more accommodating to those whose colored tags showed that had been definitively scorned.

After their paperwork was processed, they were directed—or more likely, pushed and shoved—into the island's various locked wards. US prison administrators had largely embraced the ideas of spatial segregation and classification in the early twentieth century, and Ellis Island was no different. Commissioner William Williams, who sought ever-more sophisticated systems for controlling immigration at Ellis Island—and especially preventing the arrival of what he called the "backwards races"—insisted that men were to be segregated from women and children, the putatively criminal or immoral segregated from the others. Williams supported the idea that wealthier detainees should be separated from their inferiors. Williams wished that they might further segregate deportees by race or nationality, but there was not adequate space.[34] Nevertheless, Black detainees complained of persistent discrimination and of worse treatment than even those disdained Europeans subject to removal.[35]

Families were separated; Salvatore and Angelina Piazza might have been able to see each other at mealtimes. Minnie Lester and her son John would have been sent to the general holding room for women and children; Germaine Rigolout, as a prostitute, to another. Men suspected to be dangerous—James Pepper, Spiros Olebos, Joe Kennedy—would be sent to Room 204. Salvatore Piazza, whose hernias rendered him merely pathetic rather than dangerous, would be sent to Room 222. Delfina Andrade or others deemed mad would be sent to the psychopathic ward, which, after 1922, was permanently locked, with wire mesh across grimy windows. Men in the psychopathic ward had nowhere to sit, but women like Delfina might be permitted a rocking chair to pass the time. Some might get to spend a few hours on the screened porch, but they were just as likely to be tied to their beds or locked in isolation.[36]

As they settled into the dormitories, they would have appraised their new neighbors and bunkmates. Many kept to themselves. Barbara Barondess, detained in 1921, recalled that people didn't much speak "because everybody was so full of their own fright."[37] They would also surely be taken aback at the stench and filth. "It was almost impossible to provide strict sanitation," one inspector recalled of the detention facilities for new arrivals. "With so many people packed together under such conditions, it was naturally impossible for them to keep clean, for the clean ones were pressed against aliens infected with vermin, and it was not long before all were contaminated." Two years later, Commissioner Williams said, in periods of overcrowding "the conditions are indescribably bad. The toilet facilities too, are inadequate and the ventilating system is incapable of carrying off the foul air."[38] Louis Adamic was afraid of getting sick, because he "had heard that several hundred sick immigrants were quarantined on the island."[39] The buildings were filled with rats and mice, and beds teemed with bedbugs. A recently arrived Russian Jewish man complained in 1909 that he and others were "packed into a room where there is space for two hundred people, but they have crammed in about a thousand. They don't let us out into the yard for a little fresh air. We lie about on the floor in the spittle and filth."[40] This created a bitter irony. As one former employee wrote: "There were bedbugs, but no beds." Instead, they slept in cages with little more than a blanket. "I have seen many jails, some pretty bad," he wrote, "but I never saw a jail as bad as the dormitories at Ellis Island."[41]

A *New York Times* journalist commented on the jail-like nature of the immigration station, so at odds to its image as a golden door to America: "guards are armed, doors are locked, and windows barred." He explained that officials tried to keep the prisonlike feeling from arriving migrants, who were kept separate from the deportees.[42] Less care was taken for those bound for removal. Commentators remarked on the welter of languages and voices echoing off Ellis Island's walls and doors. When one looked closer, the walls were literal palimpsests of migrant voices. Indeed, many passed long hours writing their names on walls and columns, drawing portraits, tracing their hands, or passing messages to compatriots in dozens of languages. Some wrote in graphite pencil, others in the blue chalk or crayon that physicians used to mark "defects" on their bodies. Images of steaming ships, with Greek flags, and waiving passengers signaling either arrival or departure from Ellis Island, either in celebration or sadness. Nearby, written in Greek, remained the fragment: "Out of the 15 Greeks they turned back…Oh…And…my mother's." Their messages, lamentations, drawings, and tracings left what one scholar has called a kind of "sympathetic magic…the name on the wall a simulacrum for the person who had been excluded." Graffiti often was written in small hand, near beds and bunks, occasionally on the steel detention or inquiry room doors—portals controlling movement, entry and exit, within a prison that did the same on a global scale. Officials replastered and painted over the walls and doors, but traces bore through and were written over again by new generations.[43]

The trains needed to run on schedule, but at Ellis Island time had a way of expanding. This was deeply frustrating for those being expelled, but also for officials. Indeed, evidence suggests that officials wanted to have deportees on the island for as short as possible and preferred that they spend the lengthy periods when their paperwork was being processed in dispersed regional and municipal detention centers rather than having them accumulate in a single choke point like Ellis Island or Angel Island.[44] Large numbers of people in a symbolically resonant site like Ellis Island was bad for the government's public relations and attracted the attention of immigrant aid societies. Lengthy stays on the island would also allow political deportees to organize with advocate groups, hire lawyers, and file habeas corpus writs.[45] Common deportees (criminals, the mad, the impoverished) had fewer legal channels and fewer advocates to shape the time of removal to their desires. For this reason it appears that the majority of deportees, in 1919 at least, spent relatively little time at Ellis Island. Salvatore and Angelina Piazza were loaded aboard the SS Patria, bound for Palermo, the same day they arrived in New York.[46] Joe Kennedy, Hannah Sullivan, and John and Minnie Lester were locked in Ellis Island for a few days—unlovely days, to be sure—before being loaded aboard a transatlantic steamer.[47]

Jake Hirsch, who had ridden the train east, was not so lucky. Immigration officials knew that he was simply to be held in the criminals' room at Ellis Island, and that it might take some time for diplomatic arrangements and his transport to Romania to be finalized. Hirsch, having done three years at San Quentin and five months in Texas, knew something about surviving imprisonment. Yet he found the indeterminate wait deeply frustrating. In a

FIGURE 9. "Holding pen for deportees in good weather," Ellis Island, 1902. *Source:* Library of Congress.

letter to the secretary of labor he asked: "What you have transferred me to Ellis Island for, to starve to dead? and be dog't around by those poor Ignoran Guards? Now if I'm to be Deported I wish you would do that at once, has I dont wish to starve by inches in this dirty hole of a place.... Now if you dont want to send me back, then order my release at once." He was exasperated by the months he had been imprisoned. "I dont want any more Monkey business, order my Deportation at once, if not order my release at once."[48] He spent another two weeks in the barred room for criminal deportees before being loaded aboard *SS Jacona*, Romania-bound.

Waiting times at Ellis Island could vary dramatically. In the context of the Great Depression, evidence suggests that few nations willingly received deportees with criminal records or who were likely to need public support. Mexico seemed an exception in its early support for the those netted in the mass deportation drives of 1931.[49] Similarly, it is possible that municipalities were less willing to pay the upkeep for federal detainees in the midst of declining revenues, which could have pushed more deportees toward the federal holding centers. Anarchists and other radicals seemed the most likely to languish, but during the Depression it seemed that many would stay at Ellis Island for a long time. People facing lengthy, uncertain periods of detention protested against the conditions of their keeping. People housed in Room 203 at Ellis Island in 1920 demanded an end to their lengthy incarceration, or at the very least, better food while they waited. Pushed further still, some waged hunger strikes to demand better treatment.[50] Again, the indeterminacy proved maddening.

Characters in Irwin's *Strange Passage* described feelings apparent among many actual deportees, and its thick description evoked the stultifying feel of imprisonment. Room 204, for criminal deportees, "with its plank benches, heavily screened windows, few tables and racks, its barrack-like air, was plainly a disappointment to those who felt that they had completed their prison terms."[51] They, like Jake Hirsch, may have been hard characters, but the looseness of time was infuriating. "It wasn't so much the idea of being cooped up that bothered them," Irwin wrote; "each had spent at least a year in prison in much less comfort, with inferior room and board. But when would they being kicked out? Would the old country take them back? Was there a stretch in the pen waiting for them back home? All this uncertainty made them uneasy, sullen."[52] It also heightened the likelihood of escape attempts, and many showed real creativity in subverting the facilities that held them. A report in 1920 said some were known to smuggle in knives— dangerous on their own—but also capable of being made into a file to saw through bars, or be cut and twisted into a key to force locks.[53]

Another reason that officials wanted people out was that radical deportees could, and did, use their time at Ellis Island for political organization.[54] Walter Baer, who faced deportation for his association with communists in Oregon, spent six grueling months at Ellis Island. A defense committee and public campaign stymied his removal, but he was forever unsure of his fate. Baer maintained a lively correspondence with his allies at the American Committee for the Protection of the Foreign Born (ACPFB). His letters showed camaraderie, melancholy, and remarkable resilience. Some letters were marked with "Ellis Island" and the room number as the address from which he wrote, but more often he looked for comedic variations on his forced domicile, calling it "The Rat Hole," "Le Bastille," "The Hell Hole," or simply "Here."[55]

Baer worked on behalf of other prisoners, making connections between them and the ACPFB. Even Ellis Island could become a space to organize. In one letter he told how he'd given the ACPFB's contact information to a young "dark skin girl" who had been at Ellis Island for the prior two months to seek their support.[56] Angelo Herndon, the Black radical activist, also came to visit Baer. The details of their conversation are lost, but the ACPFB issued a press release about their visit, which publicized the ascendant threat of contemporary racial and ethnic violence. "What the lynch rope and the chian [*sic*] gang is to the Negro," Herndon argued in the press release, "the deportation terror is to the foreign born." All of it took its toll, and Baer could get gloomy too. "I want to go home," he wrote."[57] As ever, he used humor, colloquialisms, and dialectical renditions of popular speech to buoy his spirits in the face of profound and literally maddening alienation of detention. "All of us are 'being patient,' but soon it will be 'patients.'"[58]

Despite humor or other coping mechanisms, anxiety was worsened among them at Ellis Island because people were deported often. Each day, an officer called out the list of deportees for removal. According to Irwin, they had little notice of when it would actually happen. The immigration station maintained a regular institutional schedule of mealtimes, but any consolation that predictability might offer was contorted by the threat of removal. As Irwin told it:

> Eyes focused on the batch of cards in the guard's hand, ears strained to catch the next name called, the men sat stiff with tenseness. This was the climax to the long process of deportation, the final farewell summons. Arrest. Preliminary hearing. Final hearing. Deportation order. Board of Review. Passport.... The long tedium of waiting for the complex machine to get into gear, pick them up and hoist them out.[59]

But this climax, this sense of removal's finality, could be indefinitely delayed.

In an introspective passage, after the tumult of a roll call and as the men left the room, Paul, Irwin's male protagonist, reflected that "the unremitting monotony descended upon the men again and they were thrown back to their newspapers, their knitting, their talk."[60] Paul longed for the precarious monotony to simply end.

> I wish it were over, he told himself. The days are so long, they never seem to end, and I may be here for months. Day after day.... Breakfast. Detention. Lawn. Detention. Lunch. Detention.... Up to dormitories. Lights out at ten.... On and on until they yell at me, Get your baggage![61]

As with the train's journey, Irwin's characters described the anxiety's physical manifestation in their bodies. Stephanie, the female protagonist, felt time to be uncertain and transitory, both minutely structured and a bottomless, shifting abyss that engulfed her to the point of despair.

> It seemed to Stephanie that she was always waiting. Waiting for the mail, to bring her letters or the letters that the bulletin board said she would receive. Waiting for breakfast in the morning.... Waiting for the visiting hour.... Waiting for lunch.... Waiting for the order to board a departing ship.... It was not at all like the deportation train, she remembered.... But here at the Island it was as if you were swimming along with no shore in sight, until you got so tired that you almost wished you could give up and drown.[62]

Paul, her love interest, was similarly driven mad by the uncertainty. It physically sickened him but also rendered him speechless. "Paul shook his head and turned away. He did not feel like talking. The entire business of departure had given him a nausea."[63] Stephanie evinced similar physical symptoms, and a similar speechlessness. Again, Irwin stressed the physical effects of uncertain waiting: "You lose your tongue here, you don't live in your own body."[64]

Irwin's novel clearly featured considerable speculation, but the anxiety was at least corroborated by the *New York Times* reporter who compared Ellis Island—unfavorably—to a prison. "In a jail there are no surprise dismissals; at the end of one's sentence there await familiar surroundings. Here at any moment may come news of papers in order at last, or passports received after weeks, and sometimes months, of waiting." Then a voyage to the "'old' but often totally unfamiliar country."[65] Temporal uncertainty meant constant anxiousness at when one would be forcibly removed. For those whose citizenship was circumscribed by criminal conviction, release from prison meant return to a reasonably familiar place. But for noncitizens, deportation meant removal to a land surely different than the one once left. Even if conditions in the "old country" hadn't changed terribly, the migrant certainly had. The literature of exile is thick with reflections on the impossibility of returning to the home the traveler once knew.[66] But once their names were called, return they must.

Still, for some, the gears turned quickly at Ellis Island, and they barely had time to get situated, much less grow numbed to the duration of their imprisonment. Spiros Olebos, Angelina and Salvatore Piazza, and Minnie and John Lester spent hours or days at Ellis Island before their names were called. Their few belongings were gathered along with their passports, now stamped DEPORTED. They would be loaded about the barges or ferries on which they had first arrived in the United States, but their journey was now reversed. Where they had debarked the Atlantic steamship and boarded a ferry for entry processing at Ellis Island, now they had been processed, detained, and were being released under the control of the steamship firm, for transatlantic removal. They boarded the flat-bottomed ferries, crossed the Hudson, and were loaded aboard the steamships that would bring them across the cold North Atlantic. We cannot know what most thought, but Theodore Irwin's characters reflected and looked backward, "watching the Manhattan skyline, the Statue of Liberty, the Island, all they could think of was, There's the end of the ride. The end of America to them, the beginning of their banishment to homelands."[67] They were placed on board a few hours before departure, but for ships that left early in the morning, they might be placed aboard the night before. They were checked again before the ship left.[68]

Their passage, of course, was the cheapest steerage. The US government would pay the minimum possible, and shipping firms, resentful for being held financially liable for their human cargo, would do no better. On occasion, those deemed mad would be placed in the ships' hospital or another closed cabin, for closer control and surveillance. As it was aboard the train, spatial containment of potentially disruptive passengers would lessen friction in the system. As they knew too well from their previous journeys, conditions in steerage were unlovely at best. Steerage was typically divided into three compartments—men alone, women alone, and families.[69] Edward Steiner reported in 1906 that

> steerage never changes, neither in location nor in its furnishings. It lies over the stirring screws, sleeps to the staccato of trembling steel railings and hawsers. Narrow, steep and slippery stairways lead to it. Crowds everywhere, ill smelling bunks, uninviting washrooms—this is steerage. The odors of scattered orange peelings, tobacco, garlic and disinfectants meeting but not blending. No lounge or chairs for comfort, and a continual blend of tongues—this is steerage.[70]

A 1910 congressional report noted that "filth and stench...added to inadequate means of ventilation....In many instances, persons, after recovering from seasickness continue to lie in their berths of stupor."[71] Toilets were "filthy and difficult of use and were apparently not cleaned at all the first few days....everything was dirty, sticky, and disagreeable."[72] Food was unpalatable too, ladled by staff out of huge pots into sloshing pails. Bigger and stronger pushed weaker passengers from the line.[73] One passenger in 1912 recalled the heavy weather on her journey: "It was so rough! Oh God, it was so rough. I didn't see a thing. A lot of the time you just lay in bed when you don't feel so good.... Oh the waves!! ... I thought the ship would turn over."[74] Another, from 1915, said: "When boat sail I am downstairs in boat. Many, many people down there, very crowded. Everybody was sick. I am so sick I cry and cry, I think I die."[75]

Most unfree passengers simply did their best and left few records of their time aboard steamships. Others, however, particularly political deportees, used the ship as an opportunity for political organization and kept records of their journey and agitation.[76] Ray Carlson, a Swedish lumber worker who had been living and working in Spokane, Washington, did just that. He had been targeted for removal because of his political activism. After more than fifty days in the Spokane county jail (including time in the dark hole for protesting jail conditions), Carlson was separated from his wife and US-born child—who was diabetic—and sent across the country to Ellis Island. Writing from aboard the *SS Roosevelt*, Carlson described how he and seven other workers (he insisted that they were workers, rather than deportees) were taken from Ellis Island by ten guards. They were loaded aboard the *SS Roosevelt*, hidden from sight "under the darkness of the Back of the pier." Aboard the ship they were locked in the "Ladies Rest Room under Heavy guard" for the next four and a half hours. The ship sailed at noon, but they were kept inside this space until the ship was well under way. In addition to the spatial containment, guards likely intended a gendered- and abject-inflected slight in locking them in the women's bathroom.[77]

At 2:30 the men were released and allowed to eat. "The Flunkies started to handel us like a grup of Pigs," giving them dirty forks and spoons. Carlson complained to the steward that he had seen one of the deportation agents point him out to other sailors. Carlson boasted to him "that if there was a mutiny on the Ship it would be my credit." But the steward didn't want a fight, and said he and the others would get anything they needed. On top of that, it seemed that many passengers were sympathetic to the radicals, and he reported "some good little" conversations with the sailors on the ship. "The CP is known to evry body and all speaks to me about communism + my own case + the struggle in general." The ship was dirty, he said, and it felt like a cattle boat. The crew was often drunk and lacked expenses. One sailor jumped ship as they traveled, and many complained about the low wages they received, and the long hours and hard work. By the end of the voyage, Carlson had distributed all of his reading materials among the ship's crew and passengers. In fact, he recommended to comrades still in the United States that future deportees should bring more propaganda material than he had. For some, even the deportation voyage could be a site for politicization.[78]

Still, the practicalities of forced travel impeded on Ray Carlson's life and his political work. The United States Line lost his baggage, and he was unsure how to get their help in locating them. His tickets were also purchased in error. His tickets went to Gotenburg rather than to his father's home. Neither had administrators arranged proper passage through Germany. Despite this, he made his way, without baggage, to Notviken, on the northern shore of the Gulf of Bothnia, near the Finnish border. There, Carlson continued correspondence with his US-based comrades, discussed their shared political struggles and, most pointedly, what he needed to do to be reunited with his wife and young son.[79]

PART THREE

Westbound

THE EASTBOUND DEPORTATION SPECIAL disgorged its passengers at Hoboken, New Jersey. The system of which it was a part had helped to filter the US denizen populations who had traversed the Atlantic world and entered the dynamic and relentlessly growing core of the global economy. It was an ingenious machine for making white Americans. European American alienage might be understood as a status, and a form of difference, that held potential for assimilability into whiteness. Yet those forced aboard the eastbound train demonstrated the notions and attributes that eugenicists and nativists, liberal and conservative alike, deemed undesirable—supposed immorality, disability, madness, political radicalism, illness, or unwanted ethnic difference, among others. The system worked to terrorize those immigrants who remained into submission, since most of them would have heard stories of the unlucky who were sent, unwillingly, to whence they had come.

The machine contributed to the ideas of luck, of deservingness, and—by expelling the supposedly undeserving and dangerous, of a sense of eventual belonging that would develop, by the middle third of the century—a sense of consolidating whiteness. Late in the century, that scarred sense of European migrant survival through travail at Ellis Island and beyond, coupled with whiteness and its associated entitlements, would lead to resurgent white ethnic family narratives with profound if complexly anti-immigrant and anti-Black politics.[1] Having finished the sweep from west to east, the vessel was primed to begin its return journey.

The Deportation Special rolled west. Now it would target people from across the Pacific world, the lands the United States had seized or would dominate through war, conquest, and as the benefits of empire. As the train traveled from the Atlantic Coast, it gathered the Mexican women and men,

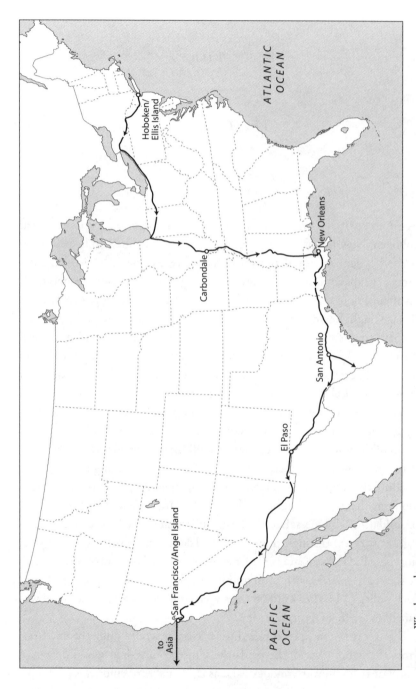

MAP 5. Westbound route.

the Chinese migrants, displaced by the forces of empire and commerce who had made temporary homes on the Eastern Seaboard or in the Midwest; the Japanese or Korean travelers who, despite the legal and material borders raised against their arrival, sought to trade their work and sweat for freedom and fortune in America.

If nativists saw white European ethnicities as a kind of assimilable difference, they understood migrants from America's colonial spheres as more fully racialized and therefore permanently unassimilable. Unwelcome for a host of reasons, these migrants would be forced aboard the train and carried west. Rather than the classic narrative of arrival and incorporation, theirs was a journey of confinement and expulsion.

NINE

Carbondale

AS THE DEPORTATION SPECIAL ARRIVED in Carbondale, the Illinois Central Railroad's station and Town Square passenger terminal came into view. It was a red-brick, one-story building, built in 1903, its windows trimmed in white. A waist-high rail set a scrubby grass square off from the platform and boarding area. Steeply pitched black slate shingled the roof, with the name CARBONDALE proudly announcing itself in white.[1]

Two Mexican families waited inside, beneath beaded tongue-and-groove wood-carved ceilings, with wooden floors that creaked beneath their feet. Light filtered through the double-hung sash windows and glass transoms above the doors.[2] The families had just come from Saint Joseph, Missouri, on a feeder route deportation journey to join the westbound mainline deportation train in Carbondale. Brothers Yndalecio and Genero Huerto, each in their late twenties, would have likely sat together, with the older Genero keeping an eye on his sibling. Fifty-year-old Gumeciendo Vallejo and his wife, Concepcíon Ranjel, looked after their three children but were also accompanied by the two teenage young men who were part of their kin network.[3] The station had separate waiting rooms for women and men, so perhaps, if their guards were feeling vindictive, the families were split up. If so, it would have been only the latest way in which the very idea of family was distorted, stressed, and reconstituted by the US border and the shifting politics of gender and labor, across a range of carceral, economic, and domestic spaces.[4] The families struggled to maintain themselves in the face of poverty, transnational displacement, and racism, and reassert new meanings of home in the industrial Midwest.

Since the nineteenth century, US colonization and capital penetration has transformed lives across Mexico and the recently conquered Mexican north, and prompted Mexicans to respond through a new diaspora north. Their travels and returns, encumbered by the increasingly policed US-Mexico border, have led to radical reformation of what family meant for ethnic Mexican communities. And though the border was more stridently regulated, this chapter (along with chapter 12) demonstrates two different elements of the US-Mexico border/interior-policing-deportation-regime. The first is the more familiar notion of the border as a hard barrier, as vertical wall and razor wire, replete with armed guards, and intended to be impervious to human movement. The second is more geographically amorphous and understands border policing and deportation as an extended regulatory infrastructure.

The experiences of the Huerto and Vallejo families demonstrate the border's second, more biopolitical dimensions of selective porosity. The interior policing and deportation regime could permit selected people tenuous admission, but on the condition of deportability when they or their work was no longer deemed politically or economically necessary, or for any host of noncompliant behaviors. Both the Huerto and Vallejo families had worked, at various times, for the railroads, which saw huge demand for labor during the Great War and special legislative provision for wartime rail workers. But once the war was over, they were no longer welcome. The experience of precarity here came through the destabilization and assaults on the many meanings for family. The harder border is explored in chapter 12.

Carbondale station was designed by Francis T. Bacon, an Illinois Central staff architect, who built similar depots in Champaign, Springfield, and Decatur.[5] The city of Carbondale, like the depot in which they waited, was founded for the profits of railroad firms and speculators, its location decided upon less because of auspicious natural geographical features or preexisting settlement patterns—as had been the case in Rochester—but as a result of how land speculation had the capacity to create worlds from maps and plans based far away. Carbondale was midway between two other preplanned sites in southern Illinois: stations at Makanda and DeSoto, and between the Murphysboro and Marion county seats.[6] And so in 1850, when the federal government offered a land grant on favorable terms, a consortium of speculators from the Illinois Central Railroad acquired the land cheap, anticipating selling it for much more once the town was built and rail lines connected it to extended markets. The founders, looking forward to the day when they might exploit nearby coal deposits, named the newly confected town Carbondale.[7]

The story of Carbondale's rail and mining corporations is a nearly biblical list of the begats and mergers of capitalist consolidation. The first train arrived in 1854, and soon coal mining underscored the new town's name. After the Civil War, coal drew migrants from across the Atlantic as well as emancipated African Americans from the South.[8] In the 1880s, Carbondale turned toward coke and flour milling, feeding both industrialization and the agricultural transformation.[9] By the turn of the twentieth century, the Illinois Central had taken control of the region's rail traffic.[10] In 1905 around thirty passenger and fifty freight trains moved in and out of Carbondale each day. During the First World War, freight increased while passenger traffic declined, but with the war's end, passengers rejoined the shipments of coal, fruit, and vegetables.[11] Carbondale's census figures suggest that locals in 1910 would have been surprised to encounter any Mexicans inside the waiting room.[12] But by the First World War the numbers of Mexican migrants and workers increased across the Midwest. Mexican women and children worked near the pedestrian entrances to the train stations, perhaps selling tamales or other foods, while Mexican men did maintenance along the tracks. Even as Carbondale residents could enjoy food Mexican women prepared and depended on hard-working Mexican male trackworkers for their safety, they likely would have seen overblown stories about Mexican criminality in the newspapers and noticed the small Mexican communities that grew by the region's railyards.

Saint Joseph, Missouri—across the Ozark Mountains and grassy plains from Carbondale, and which the Vallejo family and the Huerto brothers had most recently called home—also owed much of its history to the rails and trading networks. In 1843, Joseph Robidoux founded a trading post on the banks of the Missouri River in what First Nations peoples had called the Blacksnake Hills, had the area platted, and, having envisioned new spatial coordinates for the territory, felt similarly entitled to name it Saint Joseph. In 1846 it became the seat of Buchanan County.[13] Fourteen years later, in thick of the US political crisis of southern slaveowner secession and looming civil war, Saint Joseph became the easternmost station of the Pony Express.[14] This icon of US informational infrastructure, based on the technology of brutalized horses and riders, enabled fast communication for US westward expansion, Indigenous dispossession, and resource extraction—from Saint Joseph to the California goldfields, only recently conquered from Mexico.

Missouri saw massive political and economic transformation in the second half of the nineteenth century. "Our forests are waiting for the saw mill; our prairies lying waste when they should be covered by herds of cattle and sheep; our splendid water power is running to waste as it did a thousand years ago," one Missouri booster declared. "What is now wanted to develop these latent sources of wealth is the completion of the Southwest Pacific Railroad, so as to give us an outlet to market, and place us in communication with the rest of mankind."[15] There were 925 miles of track in 1866, 2,000 miles in 1870, and by 1909 there were 8,000 miles of track in Missouri.[16] Railroads and the industries that followed in their wake, unleashed by integration with the market, led to the timber industry's massive deforestation of the Ozarks, ever-deepening coal mines, as well as quick population growth in the cities where rail lines came together and industries grew to process raw materials.[17]

The railroads provoked some of the Missouri's most heated political struggles, with powerful tensions between self-proclaimed ordinary Missourians and the massive railroad capitalists. Jesse James's outlaw gang won acclaim and notoriety because they brazenly stole from the railroad companies who only somewhat less brazenly robbed Missourians of their public bonds.[18] In 1877 a massive strike by railroad workers—Black and white, US born and immigrant—tried to reform the relationship not just between railroad workers and their employers but also to determine whether the law would work on behalf of the wealthiest corporations or on behalf of the people.[19] Missouri governors continued to battle with the railroads in the first decade of the twentieth century, and many Missourians believed that railroads, which set freight rates, bore heavy responsibility for the high costs of nearly everything.[20] By 1910, Missouri's governor championed growth as a panacea to ills through a regulated but very much capitalist political economy. He was particularly interested in infrastructural and transport acceleration as a means of economic growth and rekindled partnership with railroad firms.[21] The Rock Island Line and the other railroad companies did well from the bargain and hired Mexican workers, like the Huerto brothers and the Vallejo family, in increasing numbers. The Mexican track workers, more commonly known as *traqueros,* used the lines to enter the Midwest's industrial economy.

Mexican migration into the United States grew in the shadow of the US-Mexico War (1846–48) and then through the additional lands taken under the Gadsden Purchase, when the United States conquered the northern third of Mexico's national territory. Despite gaining formal recognition as citizens, US conquest effectively made ethnic Mexicans into a subordinated and racially dominated people, foreigners in the lands where they had lived—from Northern California to South Texas—for generations. Enclosure movements and land centralization in northern and central

Mexico drove newer groups of Mexicans into Mexican cities but also into mines, railroad camps, and agriculture across the northern frontier region. After the 1882 Chinese Exclusion Act and 1907 anti-Japanese Gentleman's Agreement radically restricted these previously racialized and hyperexploitable workers from Asia, Mexican migrants began doing much of the most important (but worst paid) labor across Texas, New Mexico, Arizona, and California. They traveled with the seasons, fueling the radical expansion of what journalist Carey McWilliams called "factories in the fields" across California and the broader Southwest.[22]

The vast majority of ethnic Mexicans in the US lived and worked in the borderland states, but Mexicans had been traveling to what would become the US Midwest since the 1860s. They worked as vaqueros managing the herds of cattle brought from the Texas borderlands to Kansas City, memorialized in "El Corrido do Kainsis" (the Ballad of Kansas), which championed the skill and valor of Mexican men bringing cows to market, the dangers of their work, and the worry of being far from loved ones.[23] Early travelers tended to hail from the border states, but migrants to the Midwest in the first decades of the twentieth century, like the Huerto brothers and the Vallejos, were more likely to have been born farther away, in Jalisco, Michoacán, Guanajuato, San Luis Potosí, and Zacatecas—the states of Mexico's central plateau.[24]

In 1907, when Genero Huerto was fifteen years old, he left home to work in the United States.[25] The Huertos were from Huaniqueo, in Michoacán. His parents, Locadio Huerto and Virginia Cega, were farmers. Genero was born around 1892, and Yndalecio was born two or three years later.[26] An economic depression hit the central plateau the year that Genero left, and inflation made basic subsistence unmanageable. Between 1876 and 1910 real income for most Mexicans declined by 57 percent. The cost of maize doubled, and beans and chili climbed by half again as much.[27] The Mexican population grew by around one-third between 1880 and 1910. Land policy under Porfirio Díaz concentrated farmland in fewer people's hands, which increased productivity but forced untold numbers from village-based subsistence farming into the wage labor market.[28] Whatever personal reasons may have motivated the Genero Huerto decision to leave home, deep structural forces compelled him too.

Genero Huerto joined the untold legions of men from across the planet who, over the previous century, had built the United States transport infrastructure.[29] Their labor was vital to the very notion of industrial progress and the so-called Manifest Destiny of the United States to overtake the continent, but the men themselves were largely reviled as racial threats to good order and American citizenship.[30] As the United States was drawn into the First World War, the rail firms' reliance on *traqueros* increased. As industrial production ramped up, and as men were drawn from the workforce into the military, just about anyone who could leave poorly paid and difficult track maintenance did. The US military alone drained around four million people from the workforce. Europeans had traditionally filled out the bottom of the US industrial labor market, but the war limited transatlantic travel, and the literacy component of the newly passed 1917 Immigration Act similarly cut the poorest Europeans' arrival by about half; indeed the number of immigrants who arrived in the United States in 1918 was about half what it had been in 1914.[31]

Meanwhile, Mexican laborers, who had to cross a desert but not an ocean, remained available. And though the 1917 act also initially limited illiterate Mexican workers' arrival—legal immigration dropped from fifty-six thousand in 1916 to thirty-one hundred in 1917, and the $6.00 head tax did not help—a special proviso of the act permitted entry for vital wartime workers. Exemptions initially focused on agricultural laborers but added workers in mining and railroads, thus Mexican workers traveled deeper into the United States.[32] Recognizing the importance of Mexican track workers, one Rock Island engineer declared: "The Mexican is the 'power behind the pick and the shovel' in the Southwest and the West and his influence is advancing gradually toward Mississippi country."[33]

It was no great surprise that whenever they could, many Mexicans sought work outside of Mexico and beyond the US-Mexico borderlands. Conditions in the industrial Midwest were superior to anything they found in Texas, where employers thought their lives were cheap and their labor was paid even less. As historian David Montejano put it, in Texas "horsewhipping, chains, armed guards, near-starvation diets, to name a few of the props involved, portray the more brutal side of labor coercion. Vagrancy laws, local pass systems, and labor taxes point to a more institutionalized dimension."[34] The Midwest was no utopia, but it was far better than the violence that loomed in places closer to the border, and many determined that if they could stay, they would.[35] And so when Genero Huerto heard about jobs for single young men like himself, to work for the train lines in the Midwest, he took off. Most of his countrymen would travel through El Paso—in 1907 and 1908 six El Paso companies recruited nearly 16,500 Mexican workers to work for midwestern railroads—but Genero's journey took him through Laredo.[36]

Even for workers who might be permitted to cross at legal ports of entry, it was an arduous process. By 1917, US immigration authorities undertook a dehumanizing inspection regime that treated migrants of color as filthy, louse-ridden, and polluted. In El Paso, US public health officials, in collusion with immigration agents, operated one of many quarantine plants at the El Paso side of the Santa Fe Street bridge. Working-class Mexicans, passing through for the day or on a longer journey, were stripped naked and paraded before inspectors while their baggage was fumigated. Men and boys were likely to have their heads shaved, and women's hair was doused with a mix of kerosene and vinegar. More were sprayed with a chemical cocktail that included, among other ingredients, kerosene and later, DDT.[37] Although much of the practice in 1917 was aimed at disinfecting so-called polluted Mexican laborers as disease carriers, taken as a whole, they comprised an invasive process that many saw as a kind of bodily desecration. All this was in addition to the battery of legal questions designed to regulate their entry and accord with the administrative and documentary edifice that would record their travels.[38]

Rail companies sought out young and inexperienced "greenhorns" they could pay less than experienced workers. Moreover, they often preferred these *solos* or *solteros* because men with families expected to receive wages high enough to support their position as the breadwinner.[39] And while being a young single man might provide its own adventures, after two years away from home, Genero Huerto returned to Huaniqueo "to see my family," he later explained.[40] The decision was not unusual. Many Mexican migrant workers, like many Europeans and Asian migrants, planned to go to the United States temporarily, earning enough to return home, perhaps buying land, a shop, or improving their extended family's life. Huerto returned to Huaniqueo with enough money to sustain his family for the next few years, but by September 1914 he decided to cross back into the United States. He traveled to Nuevo Laredo and one afternoon walked across a footbridge to the Texas side of the city. He later said that no immigration agents were there to interview him, so he simply kept walking into the United States.[41]

Genero spent about a month in Fort Worth before traveling to Parsons, Kansas, and arriving in Kansas City in November 1914.[42] The Mexican population in Kansas City, Missouri, was substantial enough by 1916 that the city boasted its own Spanish-language newspaper, *La Cosmopolita*, and the Mexican government maintained a consulate there.[43] Genero was one of 366 Mexican *traqueros* in the Santa Fe's Kansas City division in 1915.

Mexican men like Huerto were in the process of replacing southern and eastern Europeans and becoming the region's largest ethnic group among track workers.[44] The trajectory was similar elsewhere. One estimate held that Mexicans made up between 60 percent and 90 percent of track workers in the West, with the numbers climbing among eastern firms too.[45] Beginning in November 1915, he worked in Keokuk, Iowa, for the Santa Fe but left for Hutchinson, Kansas—presumably with the promise of better wages or working conditions—to work for the Missouri Pacific when the spring and summer maintenance season got under way.[46]

The *traqueros'* work was hard, gang labor. Theirs was a largely male world, thanks to employers' efforts to hire single men. They were also often set apart from typically white, native-born, and better paid laborers: the yardmasters, roadmasters, superintendents, station agents, inspectors, machinists, mechanics, breakmen, carmen, firemen, and section foremen. Mexican *traqueros* might aspire to these positions, but racial status, coupled with a privileging of citizenship and denigration of alienage—especially after the war began—confined most to the bottom of railroad hierarchies; beneath even many Black American rail workers, who themselves saw little but scorn or worse from white workers and bosses.[47] Track work involved construction and repair and maintenance-of-way, and was the most physically difficult and worst-paying work in railroad industries. *Traqueros* shoveled endless quantities of rock. They dug ditches. They filled ditches. They graded road beds. They loaded ties into cars, pulled spikes from rotten ties, dug out the rotten ones to replace the new ones, and hammered them in place. They pulled weeds and cut branches. They adjusted the gauge of the rails when they flexed; they raised or lowered the ties as the roadbed settled or bucked.[48] They were expected to work in heat and cold, day or night—whenever the network needed repair.[49] Moreover, track work was dangerous. Trackmen were injured and killed more often than any other category of rail-based laborer. In 1914 alone, some 398 people were killed and 6,768 people were injured in railroad related accidents in Missouri. Dismemberment was more common than death, with fingers crushed and hands smashed under misplaced or mistimed hammers; limbs broken when a load of ties shifted. This is nothing to say of the muscles sprained, the ligaments or cartilage torn, or the generally sore muscles and strain of repetitive but awkward heavy lifting.[50]

It isn't clear whether or not Yndalecio Huerto ever worked with his older brother as a *traquero*, but track workers developed strong visions of kin and family. One railroad official noted that *traqueros* commonly "travel in pairs, trios, or groups, consisting of relatives, neighbors, or compadres. The different members of these groups will stick together through thick and thin, right or wrong." Bosses would do well to remember who was associated with whom, because if a boss was hard on one of them, it would be "followed by demonstrations from his friends."[51] Rail firms took advantage of the family networks too, by encouraging workers to spread word about their work, to send for male family, friends, and relatives. The Rock Island Line printed flyers in Spanish for their workers to deliver in their home villages at the end of a season. When they did, they bypassed labor agents who might demand a fee for their services and drew on Mexican kin and community networks to expand their labor pool and stimulate new workers for the next summer's maintenance season.[52] Track workers' poor pay and harsh working and living conditions meant that when better options beckoned, workers left.[53] Genero Huerto, who sometimes also went by the name Pete, found better opportunities. His new name indicated, perhaps, a kind of acculturation, upward mobility, and strategic accommodation to US language and labor regimes. In any case, by January 1917 he had left the Missouri Pacific Railroad and moved to Saint Joseph, Missouri. He began working for the Morris Packing House.[54]

Meat-packing was closely related to rail economies. The development of refrigerated railroad cars led directly to a massive increase in midwestern beef and pork industries, as well as the expansion of slaughterhouses where immigrant workers killed, dismembered, and processed the animals into packaged consumer goods. The industry was huge. Some four thousand people worked at the Kansas City P. D. Armour slaughterhouses in 1901, producing $50 million of meat products annually.[55] It was vital to Saint Joseph, which became the nation's fifth largest livestock market. Boosters noted that the city housed three of the "most modern packing house[s] in the world," and the industry contributed near half of the city's annual business.[56] Huerto soon joined in the Packingtown communities taking shape across the region—Oklahoma City, Kansas City, Omaha, and Topeka—and word spread among *traquero* networks when positions opened up.[57]

Saint Joseph was across the Missouri River from Kansas, and despite being across a state boundary, was part of a coherent economic region for track workers and Mexican laborers. In 1910, Saint Joseph was Missouri's third largest city, after Saint Louis and Kansas City.[58] Saint Joseph, like Kansas City and Saint Louis, was more racially diverse than surrounding rural areas.

Mexicans in Saint Joseph, as in much of the Midwest, lived and worked among a broad population of African Americans and recent immigrants from eastern and southern Europe.[59] Missouri was not as freighted with the same history of Mexican conquest and anti-Mexican racism as the border-land states were, and in some respects Mexicans who arrived in Saint Joseph were understood as one among other immigrant groups. Similarly, on the national stage Mexicans were not listed as a distinct racial group in US censuses until 1930, but were until then commonly listed as white or as foreign-born whites.[60]

In the first decades of the century, Saint Joseph's population was a predominantly US-born and white, but with significant nonwhite and immigrant populations. People as listed US-born whites (of US-born and foreign or mixed-birth parents) comprised 84 percent of Saint Joseph's population in 1910 and slightly more (86.3 percent) in 1920. Percentages of foreign-born whites dropped from 10 percent to 8.2 percent, likely due to the Great War's interruption and new limits on European travel imposed by the 1917 Immigration Act. At the same time, and as part of the overall Great Migration out of the rural South and into industrializing cities, Saint Joseph's Black population grew from 5 percent to 5.4 percent, while the numbers of Indians, Chinese, and Japanese remained very small, at less than 1 percent.[61] Even as the overall percentage of its foreign-born residents dropped, the numbers of ethnic Mexicans in Saint Joseph and Buchanan County grew. There had been 137 Mexicans recorded in the 1900 Missouri census, but those numbers grew to 1,573 in 1910, and 3,222 in 1920.[62] The 93 people of Mexican descent in Buchanan County in 1910 meant their population was close to the numbers of French, Danes, and Scots in the city, but far fewer than the Germans, Russians, or Irish who dominated the immigrant populations and made its industries hum.[63] In 1910, Saint Joseph reported 84 ethnic Mexicans in residence, far fewer than the 179 reported in Saint Louis and the 233 in Kansas City.[64] But by 1920, Saint Joseph was home to some 452 ethnic Mexicans. That gave Saint Joseph the state's second largest ethnic Mexican community—behind the 1,797 listed in Kansas City but ahead of Saint Louis's 429.[65]

Saint Joseph—like Kansas City, Chicago, and Detroit in the industrializing Midwest—had an ethnoracially stratified labor market. Much as they did in Gary and Chicago, Saint Joseph's captains of industry sowed ethnic and racial antagonisms among the city's workers and brought in new workers to undercut the older ones. When established workers, often slightly older immigrants with tenuous white racial status, protested for better conditions, industrialists brought in Black workers from rural areas, traditionally excluded from the industrial labor market, to lower their workers' wages or break their strikes. Because many continued to invest more in their whiteness than in the possibilities of cross-racial class solidarities, the strategy was generally successful. German, English, and Welsh miners and others railed against Black and Chinese workers but also Scandinavians and Italians.[66]

As the newest arrivals into the meat-packing industries, Mexicans were typically relegated to the worst and worst-paying jobs—the hide cellars, freezers, glue houses, sorting fertilizer—and suffering ongoing racism from white foremen. Mexicans were perhaps the "most exploited segment of the packinghouse workforce."[67] Labor historian James R. Barrett described the feel of a meat-packing plant: "Within the plants the atmosphere was dominated by the sight, sound, and smell of death on a monumental scale.... In the midst [of] all this squealing, gears ground; carcasses slammed into one another; cleavers and axes split flesh and bone; and foremen and straw bosses shouted orders in a dozen languages."[68] The pace of production made for dangerous work, and many were injured, and others were killed, in the maelstrom of dismembered bodies.[69] Many of the rooms were freezing cold, which made wielding a razor-sharp knife with numb fingers more difficult and perilous; floors slick with blood and entrails would hardly make it any safer.

Though few Mexicans were able to move up the ranks at the packinghouses, "Pete" Huerto made some headway. Rather than working on the killing floor, dismembering the carcasses, or as a janitor, he was in the dry salt department, packing together layers of meat with salts, to prevent spoilage by drawing water out of the meat and inhibiting bacterial growth.[70] Whatever the details, it surely involved heavy and repetitive labor, hefting massive amounts of salt and slabs of meat in frigid temperatures, thick with the tang of salt dust, blood, and his own and his coworkers' sweat. Huerto lived near his work in Saint Joseph, just across the street from the stockyards. The stockyards, like the railyards, were key to Saint Joseph's racial geography, and the concentration of Mexicans in these industries contributed to the city's already complex geography of race, class, and ethnicity. Mexicans shared spaces with many other immigrant and Black populations.

In 1910 more than two-thirds (60 of 84) of Mexicans in Saint Joseph lived in the Eighth and Ninth Wards, with another two dozen scattered between the Third, Fourth, and Fifth Wards. In 1920, Mexicans in Saint Joseph lived mostly in the Seventh and Ninth Wards (232 and 174, respectively), and just

20 in the Eighth Ward.[71] The Seventh and Ninth Wards were more heavily populated by Black and immigrant populations than the city overall and were remarkably diverse. Though fewer than the number of Black residents, Mexicans were Seventh Ward's largest immigrant population, followed by French, Russian, Irish, and a mix of English, Czech, Hungarians, and Italians. Poles were the Ninth Ward's largest foreign-born group (though still fewer than African Americans), followed by Austrians, and then Mexicans, Hungarians, Germans, and Yugoslavians.[72]

Mexican workers' lives in the industrial Midwest were difficult. "From the outset," historian Juan R. García has written, "loneliness, despair, and deprivation" posed deep challenges.[73] In the rooming houses where many lived—these were the cheapest and therefore most common options—roommates often worked different shifts at the plant and scarcely got to know each other. The kinds of recreation that the men engaged in could both relieve but also replicate their alienation—in pool halls, brothels, and cantinas—where drink flowed and fights might erupt.[74] By early 1919, for Genero "Pete" Huerto the loneliness must have been exacerbated, because he knew that his younger brother, Yndalecio, was somewhere nearby. He might have worked alongside his brother at the packing house; it isn't clear. *Traqueros* and migrant workers did their best to maintain family ties, despite the convolutions imposed by the US border and labor regimes upon them. The Huerto brothers' travails were particularly difficult.

The details of when the younger Huerto brother left Huaniqueo and came to the United States are fuzzy. Some records list his entry into the United States in 1914, others in 1918. It is possible that both were accurate and that he, like his brother, came to the United States, returned home, and reentered the United States again. Yndalecio's entry in 1918 was likely sanctioned thanks to a wartime exemption for railroad workers.[75] When investigators later asked, he said that immigration agents inspected him at Laredo in 1918, and he told them that he "came to work for the Santa Fe"—an apparently satisfactory answer. After entering at Laredo, he shipped to Sommerville, Texas, for a few days, then to Fort Worth, and then McAlester, Oklahoma, where he worked on the Katy railroad. Yndalecio soon landed in Kansas City. From Kansas City he traveled to Grand Island, Nebraska, where he worked in a beet factory for about three months.[76] Later, under interrogation, Yndalecio told investigators that he had traveled with a brother named José, but didn't know where he was.[77] He never mentioned a brother named Genero. There may indeed have been a third Huerto brother, but it is also equally plausible that here, when he was being interrogated, Yndalecio offered a false name to avoid giving investigators any leads in how to track down and capture the real brother.

In late 1918 or early 1919, Yndalecio Huerto was in Atchison, Kansas, on the Missouri River roughly midway between Saint Joseph and Kansas City. He was arrested and detained on unspecified charges. Whatever transpired, anti-Mexican racism peppered regional newspapers and almost certainly set the context for his arrest.[78] Police had long cracked down on the Black and immigrant urban working classes. In 1910 a policeman tried to arrest two Black Missourians for the putative offense of cooking a chicken, and in the resulting struggle, the officer shot a killed a woman bystander. In the summer of that year Kansas City police shot fourteen people, four of whom died. Police violence prompted the governor to complain that the Kansas City police were "truculent and belligerent," and drunk with power. The governor worried that the Kansas City police's "promiscuous practice of shooting people must be vigorously dealt with, or else public sentiment is going to become very justly aroused."[79] Unlike Missouri's governor, the governor of Kansas was uninterested in charges of police violence, or violence against Mexicans. The Mexican ambassador wrote of his profound concern about "the ill will that seems to prevail in the State of Kansas against the Mexicans." In two of the incidents that the ambassador reported, innocent Mexicans had been shot by the police. Still, Kansas's governor called "the relations between the Mexicans and the Kansas people...strikingly satisfactory."[80]

Such was the context of Yndalecio's arrest in Atchison. On January 23, 1919—in the beginning of a strange crossing of state and municipal jurisdictional boundaries that Yndalecio Huerto faced—officers from Atchison, Kansas, delivered Huerto to the police in Kansas City, Missouri, where he was jailed. The Kansas City police contacted Colonel J. C. Greenman, variously deemed a "Humane Officer" and "Special Investigator for the Care of the Insane."[81] Greenman served as a point of contact between the city's police, its workhouse, its metropolitan system for imprisoning those deemed mad or insane, and the immigration authorities.[82] Little in his background as a civil war veteran, real estate speculator, and railroad passenger agent suggest his qualifications for the task.[83] Nevertheless, according to the *Kansas City Journal*, Greenman held "charge of all insanity cases for the police department."[84] Local humanitarians critiqued Greenman's cost-cutting efforts and reported that Greenman seemed "to take a certain pride in keeping down the county's expense."[85]

We cannot know the state of Yndalecio's mental health, but Greenman judged him to be "of unsound mind" and unable to look after himself.[86] European immigrants who met hard times might benefit from the presumed possibility of assimilation, or from urban political machines that advocated on their constituents' behalf, but this was not available for Mexicans in the Midwest.[87] Instead, and eager to rid themselves of a burden, the police contacted Kansas City's Mexican consul. The consul spent about half an hour with Yndalecio at the jail and apparently sought ways to have him repatriated to Mexico, rather than to seek care or welfare in the United States.[88] The immigrant inspector, when he met with Yndalecio, thought that his "appearance and actions indicate that he is mentally deranged," and so justified his deportation.[89] Two days later, Yndalecio was sent to the State Hospital at Saint Joseph. The custodial-welfare and carceral apparatus converged, while the deportation apparatus gathered steam. He would be one of 156 people deported for insanity or "other mental conditions" that year.[90]

The State Hospital where Yndalecio found himself, initially known as "State Lunatic Asylum #2," opened in 1874. It was four stories tall, a massive and imposing Kirkbride building, a cutting-edge fusion of architecture and moral rehabilitative treatment. The founding superintendent explained that the hospital was dedicated "to the noble work of reviving hope in the human heart and dispelling the portentous clouds that penetrate the intellects of minds diseased."[91] While the rhetoric was characteristically high-minded, in the years to come conditions were far worse. The building itself, its architecture once a sign of medical progress, was soon superseded by newer ideas and relegated to the realm of the archaic and outmoded. Despite a fire and repair, the building remained. It was surrounded by grounds that the inmates worked as part of their supposed treatment. As managers saw it, tending to the facility's maintenance had the dual benefit of keeping inmates busy and the institution's operating costs low—matters that would hardly go out of style.[92] The institution was soon overcrowded, and Scott Clark, a curator at the psychiatric museum built on the institution's grounds, remarked that the early hospital served as little more than a "dumping grounds for the various people that society did not want to deal with." Family members were told to drop off their kin with "the clothes they wanted them to be buried in," and that they should consider their loved one as dead. And for good reason. According to Clark, the hospital's cemetery has some two thousand graves.[93]

Nevertheless, immigrant inspectors said Yndalecio would be sent there "for his safekeeping" while they arranged his formal deportation hearing.[94]

The assistant physician at the Hospital diagnosed Yndalecio Huerto with "Mania Depressive insanity [sic]."[95] We do not know what moral or biomedical treatment and control regimes that diagnosis would have called for. Hydrotherapy, which included being tightly bound in cold wet sheets or forcibly submerged in hot water for lengthy periods, was of at best uncertain efficacy. Many who experienced it felt it was nothing less than torture, but investigators dismissed their complaints as delusional, reasoning that asylum inmates were incapable of understanding their own experience.[96] Officials used pharmacological restraints too. One attendant later recalled that they would order "paraldehyde by the barrel. It smelled awful." Another related stories of how attendants lined up all the patients who didn't have jobs to do and dosed them with half a cup of paraldehyde, guaranteeing a quiet night in the wards.[97]

Nor do we know the exact living or working conditions that he faced— the degrees of overcrowding, the palatability of the food, the stench of the toilets; where he might have been assigned within the institution's racial hierarchies, with its White and Negro wards, its more accommodating front wards, for those who were seen as curable, or the back wards, with more elements of chaos, violence, and forced sedation.[98] His spatial position may have been better than those of any African American inmates, given the at least formal census identification of Mexicans as racially white. But this was also a transitional period when Mexicans in the Midwest were becoming re-racialized as an invading, dangerous, and unassimilable racial group, different than white ethnic Europeans, who, in fits and starts, were coming to be understood as assimilable into American racial whiteness. Consuls reported on the poor treatment Mexican inmates received, and it would be surprising if Yndalecio's case were different.

After six weeks in the hospital, Yndalecio faced another deportation hearing. Yndalecio was, understandably, somewhat disoriented. The inspector asked him where he was, and he said he thought it must be a hospital of some sort. He wasn't sure how long he'd been there—the experience of time in institutions is highly convoluted, and its vagaries would have been compounded by whatever pharmacological treatments he received. Nor was he sure how he had arrived, or even exactly why he was there. He felt reasonably well, he said, and some elements of memory seemed sharp. In any case, while the life story he gave to inspectors differed in minor detail from the earlier hearing at the Kansas City police station—he now explained having worked in a Saint Joseph meat-packing house, which he neglected to mention before—the broad strokes of his family in Huaniqueo, a life of migrant labor in midwestern industry and agriculture, remained the same.[99]

There was one fateful difference. After six weeks in the bedlam of the state hospital and when immigration agents told him that he would be deported, Yndalecio finally told investigators that he had a brother nearby. This time, he did not mention anyone named José. Rather, he told investigators about his older brother, Genero, who lived just a few miles away in the packing district, and gave them his address.[100] Agents rushed to arrest Genero "Pete" Huerto and locked him in the Buchanan County jail.[101] Inspectors underscored that Genero's brother was confined at the state hospital "at the expense of this service" and that Genero's case should be "disposed of" with his brother's.[102] Genero had minor brushes with the law in his time in the United States, but none merited removal. Yet when his brother was put into the hospital for madness, Genero was suddenly taken as "likely to become a public charge"— notwithstanding the fact that he had been making a living for the past four-and-a-half years.[103]

And here was one way that the US border and labor regime had distended and contorted the brothers' family. It isn't clear how much the Huerto brothers had lived, worked, or traveled together in the midwestern United States— it was common for brothers to work and travel together as *traqueros* and in packing houses. But it is also possible that each brother followed his own path. At the very least, they were in close enough contact that Yndalecio knew where Genero lived and worked. And yet, while Yndalecio was hospitalized and surely suffering, despite whatever else he was going through, he must have known that contacting Genero would put his brother at risk. Yndalecio must have reached a breaking point. We can speculate that to whatever extent Genero knew of his brother's arrest and hospitalization, he could not visit, for fear of being drawn into the deportation regime. Indeed, there would be strong pressure *not* to visit loved ones who were unwell. Rather than offering support of whatever kind, the welfare-custodial state loomed as a net to capture noncitizens.

From early March until late May 1919, Genero "Pete" Huerto was locked in the Buchanan County jail. The brick building was a drab neighbor to the County Courthouse and its resplendent shining dome, and though less impressive than the State Hospital, the county jail was no easier to leave.[104] We don't know if the brothers could communicate from their jail and

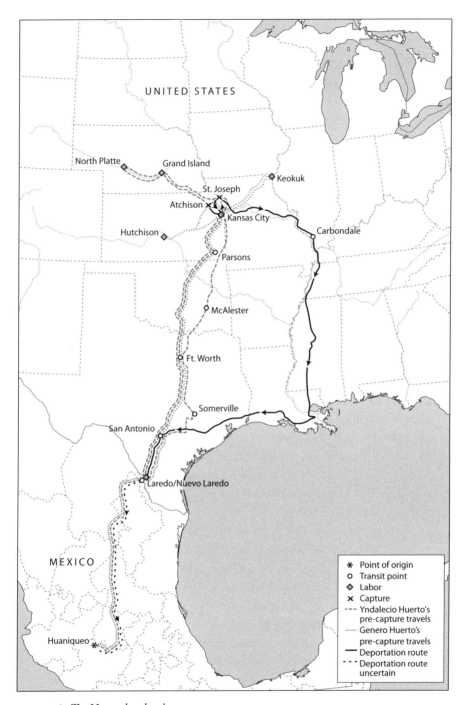

MAP 6. The Huerto brothers' routes.

hospital detention centers, but their illiteracy would have worked against it. Officials surely told each that the other was also being deported. The brothers' reunion could only have been bittersweet. They likely saw each other again on May 26 or 27, as they were drawn into the tributary routes of removal from Saint Joseph, likely through Kansas City, and then to Saint Louis, and Carbondale. They would have met the Vallejo family at the same time, and perhaps this larger kin group, from fifty-year-old Gumiciendo to four-year-old Maria, reminded them of their own family. They might have taken some solace in knowing they would soon see their mother, Virginia Cega, in Huaniqueo. But they would never again see their father. Locadio Huerto had died a year earlier, while his sons were away.[105]

Though the conditions that the Vallejo and Huerto families had faced in Mexico were similar, the border and labor regime that extended into the US Midwest affected the two families differently. Where the Huerto brothers had each left home as relatively young men, the Vallejo family traveled together. Gumiciendo Vallejo was fifty in 1919; Concepción Ranjel was thirty-five years old and married to Gumiciendo, and they had three children: fifteen-year-old José, six-year-old Trinidad, and Maria, who was just four. Yet their kin group was comprised of both more and less than a traditional extended family. Gumiciendo Vallejo's father, Rafael, was likely too old to travel easily and remained in Valtierra. They were joined by José Pérez, who was eighteen, and the similarly-aged brothers Angel and Ramon Ramírez. They hailed from around fifteen miles from Valtierra, but none appear to have been related by blood to the Vallejo family. Still, they all traveled together.[106]

Over the 1910s and into the 1920s, families began to move from Mexico into the United States, following the paths that single men had set. The pressures to leave home pressed across ages and genders—high prices, unavailability of land, the violence of the revolution, and so forth, diffracted through the specificities of race, age, and gender. But a key change was under way in the United States and in the Midwest. Employers at the major railroads, in sugar beet fields, and in the packing houses who once had focused on hiring single men, began hiring men with families. Because just as Genero Huerto had done, unattached male workers quit when better wages beckoned—when crops came ripe, a new section of track needed repair, or a spot at a packing house opened—and they left their former employers shorthanded.[107]

As a result, firms began hiring men with families because they believed that once their families were established, it would be harder to leave.[108] Some managers believed that having a "happy wife" nearby would affirm traditions of Mexican patriarchy (or at least their understanding of such patriarchy) and lead men to work harder, with more attention, and fewer accidents.[109] As a result, loyal men who had developed good relations with their employers could bring their families with them. Given that Gumiciendo was fifty and had almost surely made trips to the United States before, the extended Vallejo family was squarely among this newer wave of Mexican migrants. The firms, of course, were not tied to their workers, and those workers, no matter how loyal, could be dismissed at will.

The Vallejos likely traced the path that Gumiciendo had traveled before, from the central Mexican plateau to Nuevo Laredo. They arrived around March 1, 1918, in time for the summer track season. Gumiciendo explained that when they got to the border, they sent "one of the boys to the office" at the immigration checkpoint to gauge the reception they would receive as they tried to enter. They did not have the money required to pay the head tax, and he was concerned that "the inspectors would not let us cross the bridge."[110] Undeterred, they headed about four miles outside of town. No mounted watchmen—on the lookout for Chinese travelers, but who might take an interest in them—were apparent, so they waded across the Rio Grande and walked into Laredo. They made their way to Fort Worth, where the men worked for the Texas Pacific Railroad, before moving to Saint Joseph in June 1918.[111]

For Gumiciendo and his compatriots, even poorly paid jobs in track work were coveted, and Gumiciendo had a decent position among *traqueros*. The lowest ranks of the *traqueros* were the extra gangs that traveled to wherever the company sent them, and their lives were considered peripatetic even among migrant workers. In contrast, Gumiciendo, whose age suggested long experience and whose family indicated stability, was part of a section gang. They could bring their families with them, and establish more deeply rooted communities. The conditions of life and labor for *traquero* communities revised gendered divisions of labor in urban and industrial contexts. The stricter partitioning of men's industrial labor from women and children's domestic labor expressed new forms of patriarchy in US urban and industrial contexts. In addition to better wages, part of the appeal of industrial work seemed to be the valorization of Mexican industrial manhood and its distance from a feminine domestic sphere.

Gumiciendo Vallejo, his fifteen-year-old son José, Angel Ramírez, and José Pérez were four members of the Rock Island Saint Joseph section gang. Section gangs looked after portions of the track where high traffic demanded constant upkeep.[112] It was endless. In 1909 the Atchison, Topeka, & Santa Fe (AT&SF) used 3,775,937 new ties along 12,908 miles of track. They began using chemically treated ties around this time; durable but noxious and unpleasant to work with. Still, in 1925, workers on the AT&SF replaced nearly two million ties along eighteen thousand miles of track.[113] An inexperienced *traquero* around José Vallejo's age could expect to earn around a dollar for a ten-hour day. Skilled section workers took home more, but even a decade later they made just $35 for two weeks' work, or $840 per year—about $12,000 in 2017 dollars.[114]

At the end of a shift, Gumiciendo and other section gang workers returned to the housing provided to them by the Rock Island lines. Just as Genero Huerto lived in the stockyard and meat-packing district, the Vallejo family lived in the nascent barrio around the Rock Island shops. Rail firms commonly bought land and developed facilities just outside of towns and smaller cities, and Rock Island operated a six-block facility just outside of Iowa City, with a freight depot, stockyard, and passenger depot hugging the rail lines. The Mexican barrio grew as section workers arrived and began to stay. They developed a community immediately next to the rail yards, just hundreds of feet from the lines.[115] As was the case elsewhere in the Midwest, these neighborhoods became the foundation of what would soon become Mexican American communities. We don't know if the Vallejo's neighborhood had its own nickname, but Kansas-based families called their various neighborhoods La Yarda, Los Bottoms, Las Casitas, El Huarache, and La Quemada, among others. Detroit, Chicago, and South Chicago each had multiple communities, some intermixed with poorer Black and immigrant neighborhoods.[116] Some boxcar communities were entirely Mexican; others had a mix of Mexicans, Greeks, Italians, Romanians, Irish, and African Americans.[117] Many families lived in a succession of these communities until they were able to find more permanent housing.[118]

There is no doubt that the section gang families appreciated free housing, but it proved to be the result of a negotiation between workers and the firms. Like the industrial company towns at Pullman and Gary, the rail firms provided housing to cultivate a stable, loyal, and productive workforce.[119] Workers who relied on their employers for their homes, owners believed, were less likely to quit or strike. A writer for the *Rock Island Magazine* believed that giving the workers "free" housing led them to express their gratitude to the company through "strict obedience to the law."[120] It also meant that bosses always knew where the workers were, and the *traqueros* were available at any time of day or night. Indeed, the Rock Island Maintenance and Construction Department's "Rule 80" specified:

> Section men will be expected to board at section houses, where they are provided for that purpose. Where section houses are not provided, or where… the men are excused from boarding at same, the section foreman must… have no difficulty in reaching them if… they are wanted… outside of regular working hours.[121]

Boxcar homes were common, even for families.[122] While single men in extra gangs might sleep in boxcar bunkhouses with a dozen beds, the new reliance on families reconfigured the housing. A partition down the middle of a boxcar meant two families could live in it, though at times four might call a car home. Uninsulated, they were cold in the winter and hot in the summer. On hot days they were "ovens… unbearable, forcing little ones with their mothers to turn out an seek shelter underneath amidst the wheels."[123]

Depending on local conditions, it wasn't uncommon for large and extended families like the Vallejos—a husband and wife, multiple children, and additional young men from nearby village—to share a shanty house rather than a boxcar.[124] Fidel Ybarra, who lived in railroad housing in Emporia, Kansas, recalled that even in the nicer shanty homes, there was "no electricity, no running water," and no insulation "except my mother's wallpaper." Six similar shanties, each home to a dozen people, completed his community. There were two outhouses, one for men and one for women, between them. The company provided old track ties, pieces of boxcars, and torn-down depots, which residents used for cooking or warmth. Many of the ties had been soaked in creosote or other chemicals and gave off noxious fumes when they burned.[125]

Yet the families made the spaces their own, and we can presume that the Vallejos did the same. Mexican migrant families beautified their homes by repurposing materials discarded from production, and added porches, plants, gardens, pets and chickens, and electric light where they could run the wiring.[126] This was as true of the boxcar homes in Missouri as it was for cement plant workers in Colton, California.[127] The longest residents in the boxcar communities lived in the nicest of the boxcars available, while the newer arrivals tended to occupy the least favorable ones.[128] Families furnished their homes with reused materials until they might save enough to buy beds, chairs, or more permanent furniture.[129] Those who could afford them hung family photos on the walls, alongside religious icons brought from Mexico. They used wallpaper to domesticate the industrial surfaces and kept their homes as clean as the circumstances allowed.[130] Children would have brought home trinkets they gathered while playing in the yards or going to and from school. One visitor to a community observed that "the humblest section house or slum *jacal* [thatched hut] built of old piano boxes, has its flowers or potted plants."[131]

All members of *traquero* families were expected to contribute, and they did so in gendered ways. Fathers, sons, and male cousins worked together on the section lines, doing hard industrial labor in the public sphere. For the Vallejos, this was Gumicendo, his son José, Angel Ramírez, and José Pérez. On very rare occasions women worked on track crews, holding the spikes steady with *pinzas* (pincers) while their partners—family members or spouses—hammered the spikes.[132] It was far more common for women like Concepción Ranjel and their daughters to perform the unwaged, family-based work that scholars identify as reproductive rather than productive labor: cooking, gardening, cleaning, mending clothes, and so forth. Moreover, the gardens they kept maintained symbolic and culinary ties with rural Mexican life. Many were proud of how well they grew their chiles, tomatoes, cilantro, and onions, and how their gardens supplemented their diets, improved their families' health, and extended their family income.[133] Younger children might make games from activities like gathering coal fallen from the yards, looking after chickens, or tending their gardens. Families sent their children to school whenever they could, though it appears that neither Trinidad nor Maria had the chance in Saint Joseph.[134]

Women like Concepción often extended these domestic tasks into the public sphere, earning cash by taking in laundry or sewing, or preparing and selling food at nearby train stations or in the downtown districts. Women, girls, and children would also make chorizo in their boxcar communities, buying *tripa* from the meat-packing houses, and filling it with their own blend of ingredients.[135] As was the case for many other young immigrant women, some hired themselves out as domestic workers—doing laundry, cooking and cleaning, and so forth, for middle-class white women.[136] Though sons expected to keep part of the paychecks they earned, daughters were expected to give all of their earning to the family. This could lead to intrafamily tension, especially when daughters felt torn between the worlds of consumerist pleasures and filial respect.[137]

Other women entered the industrial workforce.[138] But they risked the ire of their husbands by upsetting notions of patriarchy that were taking shape in midwestern industrial settings. Many urban Mexican men did not approve of their wives working outside the home and feared the wage labor workplace—doing laundry, working retail, working in restaurants—was a bad influence on their wives and daughters.[139] There is no indication about how, or even if, these dynamics impacted the Vallejo family, or if Gumiciendo would have felt his masculine status undermined if Concepcíon worked outside the home. But some men were dismayed by women's independence, even, or perhaps because, women were so central to the organization and sustenance of their immediate families and their larger communities.[140] Living together in or nearby the railyards led *traqueros* to provide important mutual support in the face of crisis, and women were at the center of this community, when someone got hurt at work, but also in the ordinary routines of life—helping look after children, providing a small loan, sharing food, and so forth, in the face of a crisis, or of racial capitalism's ever-changing demands.[141]

Saint Joseph's *traqueros* were hardly the only ones who affirmed extended kinship and community in the face of political economic insecurity. The social and economic changes driven by capitalism led to a welter of social welfare, fraternal, and similar organizations, and Saint Joseph was home to 128 such groups in 1908. In a multiethnic but white-supremacist society, such groups included trade unions, the Masons and Oddfellows, the Knights of Columbus, and the Ku Klux Klan.[142] The anti-Mexican racism many of these groups espoused was a perverse, if predictable, element of white fictive kinship that coalesced around ideas of Americanness. When Midwesterners protested against the presence of Mexicans, they displaced their own fears of economic exploitation and expendability onto racially subordinated and colonized peoples. It was an extension of the logic that their bosses had developed, pitting ethnically differentiated workers against one another. The long history of anti-Mexican racism in the borderlands was a new arrival in the Midwest.

Saint Joseph residents began to transpose southwestern frontier-themed racisms to the urban Midwest, where it mixed with extant racism and nativism. Beliefs that Mexicans were taking "American" jobs, that they worked for cheap, exacerbated racist preconceptions of Mexican pollution. A resident of Flint, Michigan, said her Mexican neighbors were "terribly dirty and crowded…they're all bad people."[143] Another said: "Some of them are dark, just like the niggers; I wouldn't want to live among them. I want to live among white people."[144] One former boxcar resident recalled being refused service in nearby Cottonwood, Emporia, and Topeka due to anti-Mexican racism.[145] The tentative, incompletely racialized status that Mexicans were afforded in the 1910 and 1920 censuses, to whatever extent it had held among the broader white population, was clearly no more. In the face of the postwar economic slump, some white workers began calling for Mexican workers to "return home." When US Steel imported Mexican workers to break a September 1919 strike in Gary, Indiana, there was serious anti-Mexican backlash.[146] It was part of a postwar shift that led to rounds of removals in the early 1920s.[147]

Midwestern newspapers increasingly represented their Mexican denizens as racial, nation, and biological outsiders. They referred to Mexican communities as consisting of "boxcar palaces" populated by "swarthy sons of the Montezumas," and reported that Mexican migrants were liable to "wreak havoc" on white communities.[148] Newspapers lavished lurid detail about Mexican men's putative violence and criminality, which might overflow the borders and the liminal spaces of boxcars and shanty barrios and into "respectable" white neighborhoods.[149] White communities disdained these emergent Mexican communities as a health risk and a social nuisance, but at the same time, denied Mexicans the ability to live in better housing.[150]

Mexicans in the United States rarely sought government support and generally relied on friends and neighbors in dire straits.[151] But when people faced problems that family or neighbors could not handle, they had little choice but to seek help from social welfare institutions. Most agencies were located in Missouri's larger cities, but some sent representatives out to section gang housing. Because Mexican women were central to the forms of social reproduction and community welfare, they were the main point of contact with welfare institutions, and did everything possible to access whatever resources they could—through church groups, the wealthier women for whom they sometimes worked, via individualized patronage networks if not philanthropic social welfare institutions.[152]

But help from white philanthropists, settlement house workers, and social services came at a cost. It was part of a complex and multidirectional negotiation among US-born white social welfare providers, European immigrants, and ethnic Mexicans, around the meanings of social belonging in the United

States and in the Midwest in particular.[153] Progressive social workers increasingly understood European migrants' poverty, ill health, or inadequate housing as caused by structural, systemic, or environmental causes. But when they met Mexican families in similar straits, they thought Mexican cultural and racial backwardness was to blame.[154] Just as Mexican men were attacked for taking white men's jobs, now Mexican families were attacked for taking an undue share of social welfare. And while the police might focus on Mexican male criminality, social workers lambasted Mexican women for "primitive" standards of domestic hygiene. They chastised Mexican women for keeping "steamy" rooms without adequate ventilation, but did not blame their employers for paying substandard wages or providing substandard housing. The Kansas City Council of Social Agencies suggested that Mexicans displayed "a characteristic lack of initiative and perseverance" as well as "ignorance of proper standards of living." Opining that Mexican women were unable or interested in caring for their children, social workers thought "a trained sympathetic Spanish-speaking housekeeper who would visit, teach and inspire them to make efforts to improve their home life." Indeed, they believed that teaching Mexican women to conform to Anglo standards of domesticity did double duty: it would uplift the next generation of the Mexican race and help transform them into more assimilated Americans, and would make those women into better housekeepers for the white women who hired them.[155]

The records are silent about how the deportation regime set its sights on the Vallejo family. No documents in their file suggest that any had run afoul of the law. There is no letter from the police, a hospital, or other social welfare agency. Nevertheless, immigrant agents issued arrest warrant for Gumiciendo Vallejo, Concepcíon Ranjel, their children José, Trinidad, and Maria, and José Pérez and Angel Ramírez. The warrant listed that they were likely to become public charges and had entered the United States someplace other than a registered checkpoint, but the charges could only be leveled after they were under investigation. There is room for speculation that in the postwar context, with decreased rail traffic and anticipated labor surpluses, that the family was less desirable. The wartime exemption to the 1917 act that permitted rail workers from Mexico lapsed at the end of 1918.[156]

Moreover, in 1920 the commissioner general reported on the formal expulsion of 532 Mexican laborers who been permitted to enter due to the war, but were now "deported as illiterates, etc." But the commissioner reported that more than thirty-three thousand wartime workers were still in the United States, and it is not clear why the Vallejos were singled out from among them.[157] Perhaps Maria or Trinidad had a fever, and Concepcíon brought them to a social welfare agency, which then reported them to authorities. Perhaps the Rock Island line's foremen saw Gumiciendo, who was fifty years old, as too old to merit employment, regardless of whatever stability this patriarch once offered. Without firmer evidence, the broad historical context of postwar anti-Mexican racism, decreased rail traffic, economic slowdown, and white racial fears of "Mexican dependency" will have to suffice. The Vallejo family's experience anticipated the postwar removal drives that saw more than 150,000 Mexicans expelled through a combination of forced and coerced (if officially "voluntary" removals), and dismantled many—but not all—of the Mexican American communities in the region.[158]

As the administrative gears for their removal were turning, the Vallejo family was not locked up. For whatever threat they were taken to pose to the city, the state, or the nation, they were scarcely dangerous enough to merit incarceration alongside Genero Huerto at the county jail. Instead, they were released "on their own recognizance."[159] Immigrant Inspector Long judged that the extended family would not run off. Sixteen-year-old Angel Ramírez and eighteen-year-old José Pérez and were released "to return to employment" and to live at the Rock Island Section House until they were called for removal. So were Concepcíon, Gumiciendo, José, Trinidad, and Maria.[160] Many in similar circumstances were deported empty-handed, but the Vallejos had accumulated some possessions, perhaps materials they had used to beautify their home. "I have some goods here in this car," Gumiciendo told the inspector, "and my family have [sic] clothing that we would like to take with us."[161]

The deportation regime then, like the Rock Island Line, recognized the power and the durability of these extended families. Families like the Vallejos traveled from the Mexican central plateau into the American Midwest and back, using their networks to survive through revolution, war, dislocation, poverty, and adversity. And even as the deportation state recognized their durability, it used the family as a means of control. They would not need to be incarcerated at taxpayer expense. Instead, they would look after each other. They would continue to live in Rock Island housing. They would continue to work for the Rock Island Line, maintaining the tracks and helping the trains run on time. A month and a half after their arrest, on April 19, they met the

UNITED STATES

St. Joseph

Carbondale

Ft. Worth

San Antonio

Laredo/Nuevo Laredo

GULF OF
MEXICO

MEXICO

Salamanca

✳ Point of origin
○ Transit point
◇ Labor
✕ Capture
— Vallejo family travels
━ Deportation route
┄ Deportation route
uncertain

MAP 7. The Vallejo family's route.

Huerto brothers and were loaded aboard the deportation train feeder route, bound for Carbondale and westbound main line removal. There is no doubt that it was better to spend the weeks between their arrest and their deportation together, rather than being spilt apart in detention. But they could hardly have felt very free.

TEN

New Orleans

CHOI SI, ALSO SOMETIMES KNOWN AS ROBERT LEE, was brought aboard the Deportation Special in New Orleans in May 1919. Thanks to mundane administrative errors by the Immigration Bureau's officials—recorded in the paperwork that deportation agent Leo Russel now carried—Choi had been languishing needlessly in a New Orleans jail for the previous three months. New Orleans in particular and Louisiana more broadly, of course, have many things to recommend them to traveler and residents alike, but their prisons and jails are not among them. Since the 1700s, New Orleans's jails were a borderland between enslavement and free-world punishment; the cages were a common ground shared by the ostensibly distinct realms. Captured runaways and enslaved people whose owners wanted them punished had been held there. Even after emancipation, the descendants of enslaved Louisianans, along with far fewer numbers of unruly poor whites, were brutalized in New Orleans's jails and set to hard labor on its chain gangs. The facilities, be they the ones opened at Congo Square in 1832 or on Tulane Avenue in 1895, were not just overcrowded but so putrid that a recent archeological report marveled at the number of rat skeletons unearthed.[1]

Choi initially came to the United States as a student. Sponsored by governments or missionary organizations intent on westernization programs, student status exempted Asian migrants like Choi from race- and class-laden restrictions written into anti-Asian immigration law.[2] The host of Chinese Exclusion laws treated the Chinese as dangerously unassimilable and servile "coolies" who would undercut American workers' wages and undermine the capacities for American democracy, and targeted laborers—the vast majority of people who wanted to come to the United States—but permitted a much smaller number of elites: those merchants, missionaries, and diplomats who were understood as necessary for extending US trade and influence, and maintaining comity in international relations. The student exemption was not based wholly on American largesse; indeed, permitting immigrant students could become a kind of US investment in the future. When a student's status inevitably lapsed, they would return to their home country but remain ostensibly allied to US aims and sensibilities in whatever field they studied. One American educator referred to the education of Chinese students as nothing less than "the intellectual and spiritual domination of its leaders," a hard-nosed statement about what would later be understood as soft power.[3]

But exempted status was precarious, and noncitizen students risked deportation if immigration officials decided that they were really laborers pretending to be students. Immigration agents, overseas, at borders, and within the United States were often skeptical about those whom they believed merely claimed to be students to scheme their way past the exclusion acts' restrictions. A 1906 memo reported that Chinese inspectors frequently found migrants who had been admitted as "refined students and men of wealth" were really workers, and had been found "employed in laundries, restaurants, canneries and mines."[4]

Nevertheless, Choi, like many students, then and since, ran short on funds. He left school in Hastings, Nebraska, and traversed the country for work. He picked crops in California, Colorado, and Nevada; sweated on railroads in Nebraska; in Wisconsin lumber mills and Wyoming coal mines. He worked in meat-packing in Omaha and cooked in "chop suey" houses, cafeterias, private homes, and at state fairs. He rode the rails between cities, which was cheap but risky. Along the way, police in Texas (Shamrock, Amarillo, and El Paso) and later in Council Bluffs, Iowa, locked him up, checked him out, and set him to work. In county jails a so-called "undesirable alien" like Choi crossed paths with the descendants of chattel slaves. This kind of unfree labor was common in Texas—his three arrests there testified to that—which was both a former slave state as well as a migrant borderland, particularly for Mexican travelers. Iowa's police, however, were apparently less likely to rely on temporary unfree migrant and prison labor than their Texan counterparts. The police of Council Bluffs arranged for Choi to be deported rather than to continue itinerant work, or the possibility of returning to his studies.[5]

While he was surely glad to put those experiences behind him, Choi could hardly have been thrilled to board the deportation train. He was traveling to his home province in Korea—likely Hamgyŏng—a historically marginalized region in Korean political culture under the long reign of the Chosŏn dynasty (1392–1910). The discrimination many Korean northerners suffered from the dominant southern *yangban* class partially explained why Protestant missionaries had made considerable headway there, which might give some clue as to why Choi spoke English as well as he did. Moreover, Korea's northern provinces suffered disproportionately from the devastation wrought by the Sino-Japanese and Russo-Japanese wars, which led to outmigration.[6] More concerning than persistent regional differences, however, was that Korea was then under harsh Japanese military occupation. Five years before he was forced aboard the Deportation Special, Choi had struggled to escape from its grasp—traveling covertly to Vladivostok, then London, England; across the Atlantic Ocean to Quebec, and then to Detroit, with a ticket for Hastings, Nebraska.[7] But soon he would board the *Tenyo Maru* of imperial Japan's TKK line, at which point his return to Japanese military rule would have effectively resumed.

Korean immigrants like Choi were driven by the forces of global racial capitalism and their manifestations in processes of Asian colonial modernity, particularly as Meiji Japan sought to claim its own position as a racially superior empire and reap the economic benefits it felt befitting that status. In the late nineteenth century, Koreans were pressed between the great imperial powers of Russia, China, Japan, and by the early twentieth century, the United States and Great Britain, as each vied for prestige and control over regional resources. Many Koreans were torn between allegiance to the culture of the five-hundred-year old Chosŏn dynasty and the allure of hybridized colonial modernity, which adopted but modified overseas influences. As Japan imposed greater imperial control, Koreans asserted an equivalent (if less militarily powerful) national pride and oppositional movements. Koreans in the United States found themselves pressed between these multiple forces, along with the travails of new American experiences of racialization, the economic strife of immigrant student-hood and the need to do low-wage, often transient labor, just to make ends meet. Still, they found ways to survive within diasporic communities that drew on complex political and military strategies to oppose both Japanese imperialism and US state surveillance. Choi and other Koreans in the United States, then, shared a position with South Asians and the American Irish, in that they were squeezed between imperial powers, old and new: Irish nationalists and South Asian radicals rebelled against the British, while diasporic Koreans sought refuge and opportunities against Japan's consolidating imperial regime.

While the *Tenyo Maru* loomed large in Choi's life, sixty years earlier, the

US merchant ship *General Sherman*—iron-clad and carrying cannons—played a key role in the history of US-Korean relations. In 1866 the *General Sherman* steamed up the Taedong River, only to get stuck on a sandbar. It had recently left China with a store of goods and its captain demanded to do business, despite explicit and official prohibitions. The Americans refused to leave. Negotiations stalled, and the *General Sherman* opened fire on the shore. Korean soldiers overwhelmed the vessel, setting it on fire and killing its Chinese, Malay, and US-born seamen as they fled. Five years later, US Marines returned to exact revenge, killing hundreds of Korean soldiers but nonetheless failing to "open" the Hermit Kingdom to US trade.[8] In 1882, Korea and the United States solidified diplomatic relations, but Korea's principal partnerships remained strongest with China, Japan, and Russia. Its location between three feuding empires—China, Japan, and Russia (to say nothing of ascendant American force)—meant that the Koreans were trapped, as an adage had it, like a "shrimp…caught between fighting whales."[9]

In the late nineteenth century, many Koreans admired Japan's growing international prestige. Others were compelled by traditional dynastic allegiance. Korean officials at various moments invited Chinese and Japanese forces to protect or modernize Korean institutions and often played one against another, but by the 1890s the Japanese military and diplomatic corps seized the upper hand.[10] It established foothold for Imperial Japanese control that would consolidate over the next decade. In 1905, Japan declared Korea as a protectorate, and five years later, formally claimed Korean as a colony and began a concerted process of settlement. Japan's military was formidable, but as historian Jun Uchida has put it, Japanese settlers were "compelled to enlist the cooperation of local elites—aristocrats, bureaucrats, entrepreneurs, landlords, religious leaders, and 'pro-Japanese' elements—who shared similar, though not identical, stakes and class interests in the colonial project." Powerful segments of Korean society saw Japanese-led modernization as a route for rapid transformation. Many profited: entrepreneurs and businessmen saw trading opportunities; landlords were permitted to keep their status and collect rent from peasants as long as they maintained order.[11] Japanese settlers sought to replicate Japanese life and ritual—from Shinto shrines to consumer districts; they also built railroads and fostered massive infrastructural development in the interest of colonial modernity and expanding trade.[12]

Even as it relied on an extensive military, "the colonial government worked with local men and women of influence, often taking care not to alienate voices of dissent but instead to coopt them into its ruling structure."[13] Bureaucrats worked closely with an extensive policing apparatus, engaged in ordinary policing activities, but also tax collection, enforcing sanitary regulations, overseeing key industries, and managing infrastructural improvements, among other things. The colonial dynamic was particularly complex, in that police were nearly as likely to be Korean as Japanese.[14] Japanese elite rulers replaced (or co-opted) Korean *yangban* scholar-officials, instituted imperial rule for dynastic central administration, commanded Japanese-driven rather than locally derived economic modernization, and even attempted to replace the Korean language with Japanese.[15]

Despite the depth of Japanese rule and the degrees of accommodation Koreans undertook to absorb Japanese impulses, Korean nationalists continually resisted Japanese occupation, from peaceful demonstrations to assassinations and political violence. Diasporic Koreans were central to this struggle. In 1905 eight thousand Koreans in Hawai'i, the first wave of Korean American migrants, staged a protest against Japanese rule. In 1907 several thousand Korean insurgents rose against Japanese occupiers on the peninsula, but the movement was summarily crushed by the Japanese military.[16] In 1907 and 1908, US-based Koreans attempted to assassinate pro-Japanese Korean officials and killed Durham Stephens, an American who controlled Korean foreign policy on Japan's behalf. Koreans nationalists waged a guerrilla war against the Japanese after 1907, led by demobilized soldiers, intellectuals, and self-directed peasants. Most of the *ŭibyŏng*, or "righteous armies," had fewer than one hundred members, but others had as many as one thousand mobilized troops. They engaged in some fifteen hundred separate clashes with Japanese forces in 1908, but the militias dwindled in the face of Japanese counterinsurgency, and a great many fled Japanese-occupied Korea for Manchuria and places further afield.[17]

The United States and the Chosŏn dynasty formalized their political relationship in 1882, but diplomatic and economic ties remained relatively slight. American influence was stronger through its missionaries, notably the protestants who imagined fertile ground for souls across the Hermit Kingdom but saw the most success in the northern provinces. As missionaries came to Korea from overseas, so too did Koreans begin to travel from the peninsula. They began going to the United States in 1903, when Hawaiian-based sugar planters sought new and cheap supplies of workers. The planters' appeals were most successful in regions where missionaries had established the deepest roots and when the missionaries also advocated on the planters' behalf.

Earlier, the Korean government had discouraged migration, but in 1903 began to see outmigration as a release valve for struggling workers, particularly from the drought-hit and politically peripheral northern provinces.[18]

Many Koreans remained in Hawai'i and established nascent communities, but between 1903 and 1907—when travel to Hawai'i was cut off as linked to the so-called Gentleman's Agreement between the United States and Japan limited migration—harsh conditions and poor pay led more to look to the mainland, where railroad firms, farmers, and a host of employers hired labor contractors to bring Koreans to augment or replace their racialized and exploitable workers. Even though Japan forbade Korean emigration after 1905, small and scattered groups established Korean communities in California agriculture.[19] Soon, others began traveling as migrant workers, building communities in Denver, Seattle, Salt Lake City, and Butte. The largest concentrations of Koreans remained on the West Coast, particularly in Los Angeles and San Francisco.[20] Ten thousand Koreans came to the United States between 1903 and 1924.[21]

While the first waves of Koreans in the United States were workers, between 1910 and 1919 around three hundred Koreans entered the United States as students. Most, it seems, traveled without the permission of the Japanese government. They held no official passports but often carried letters of introduction written by American protestant missionaries. Letters of introduction operated as a kind of Protestant missionary network analogue to the formal regime of identity documentation developed through the Chinese Exclusion laws. Immigration and customs officials complained that the letters were sometimes inconsistently written, and may or may not satisfy formal requirements.[22] But even a badly worded letter was better than nothing. A letter of introduction demonstrated to immigration officials that the bearer had earned a white person's patronage and good opinion, and offered something akin to the legitimating testimony that only white people could offer in US courts, when people of colors' testimony was dismissed as untrustworthy. With or without letters, many Korean students traveled from Shanghai or Manchuria. They faced strict scrutiny at US ports of entry. Choi likely knew this, and even though he claimed that he had his passport stamped, he may have evaded inspection when he crossed from Canada into Detroit.

Chang Yill Lee, who was to be deported along with Choi, was a student who traveled to the United States and faced this scrutiny.[23] Regardless of the conflicts he knew in Korea or on his travels, on entry to the United States,

Chang Yill Lee confronted the everyday US racism that treated Koreans as simply a variant of generally despised Asiatic peoples. Chang Yill Lee arrived at Ellis Island on February 25, 1914. The eighteen-year-old had traveled with an older brother, twenty-nine-year-old Kyring Chas. Lee, an eleven-year-old younger brother, and a nineteen-year-old cousin.[24] Kyring Chas. Lee had already been in the United States for around ten years—placing him among the earliest Korean migrants to the United States. Given the difficulties of life in Korea under Japanese occupation, he promised his relatives that better opportunities awaited them in the United States. The two brothers and younger cousin covertly departed from Japanese-controlled Korea and met Kyring Chas. Lee somewhere in China. They made their way to France, and then from Le Havre to Ellis Island. Kyring Chas. Lee offered evidence of US bank accounts and traveled with $2,406 worth of ginseng, and was quickly admitted as a merchant. But his younger kin faced exclusion and debarment as laborers and as likely public charges.[25]

Kyring Chas. Lee demanded that a board of special inquiry be held to consider his family's case, and drew on the resources of New York's small but tightly-knit Korean community. Together, they argued that his siblings and cousin be admitted as students. Fred K. Song, a brother-in-law, had lived in Brooklyn for ten years and promised to look after the boys and their education.[26] A merchant named Seek Hun Kimm, of the Asiatic Republic Company, also implored the government to let the young Koreans land. He did so on the grounds of human compassion, and by invoking the specter of Japanese cruelty in its occupation of the Korean Peninsula. Seek Hun Kimm conceded that the youngsters did not have passports, but it was nearly impossible to obtain one. "The Japanese government means to stamp out the Korean race by keeping those people under strict surveillance and discomfit any Korean attempts of any Korean to escape from the boundaries of that shattered nation." He continued:

> Should a Korean be so fortunate as to elude the Japanese officers and safely enter another country he becomes a free man. But if he is deported...he will...be subject to inconceivable tortures and maltreatment to be relieved by death only. In the name of humanity and justice I invoke you to have compassion and exert every power within your authority to effect the admittance of these three Korean boys.

The young men would not become public charges, and he assured officials; they would be provided with appropriately gendered caregiving, including a

Korean woman to look after the youngest. Without the bureau's sympathetic and discretionary decision in their favor, he implored, the young men would face "incessant ordeals…by the Japanese whose cruelness and viciousness is beyond human conception."[27]

The special investigation into whether or not the young Koreans should be permitted to land proved to their benefit. It also demonstrated the ethnoracial complexities of Korean American life in the early twentieth century, situated among the better-known (and differently vilified) Chinese and Japanese populations. Helen Bullis, a special inspectress for the bureau who more commonly worked on white slavery cases, reported to her superiors that "there are not more than 15 or 16 Koreans in New York." There had been more, but many moved into the interior of the United States, moved west, or else returned to Korea. Those who remained "form a very close-knit little colony."[28]

Seek Hun Kimm struck Bullis as unreliable.[29] He had previously worked with the Korean Embassy in Washington, DC—likely the delegation developed after diplomatic relations were developed in the 1880s but before Japan took control in 1905—but she did not take this as evidence of trustworthiness. He had no family, and his bachelorhood remained suspect—even though multiple exclusion policies that portrayed all Asian women as prostitutes, and thus ineligible to land, in considerable measure created East Asian bachelor worlds.[30] Moreover, his income was derived from a small business partnership with Chinese New Yorkers, which indicated to her his unreliability. He also moved to different addresses, which struck her as suspicious, but which he explained helped him avoid surveillance by the Japanese. It was not impossible to imagine this, given the fraught state of Korean nationalist resistance to Japanese occupation, but she dismissed it. Bullis gained a much more favorable impression from a missionary named Miss Clark, of Maywood, New Jersey. Clark had run a mission school in New York's Chinatown. Clark told Bullis that as a rule Koreans were "much less vicious than the Chinese, and much more reliable than the Japanese."[31] Bullis also spoke to May Woon Chun, a business partner of Kyring Chas. Lee. May Woon Chun's son was currently attending Hastings College in Nebraska, studying agriculture.[32] Hastings was a Presbyterian college founded in 1882, and it is likely that Protestant missionaries in Korea laid their path toward the school.[33]

Kyring Chas. Lee told Bullis that he intended for his cousin to go to

Hastings College, too, and his eleven-year-old brother would live with a Korean family and attend school in New York. He was not sure if Chang Yill Lee would go into business with him or attend Hastings College as well. Bullis recommended that they ignore anything that Seek Hun Kimm said. But, she opined:

> Miss Clark is an honest, conscientious woman, and if the boys should be admitted to her supervision she could be depended upon to keep track of them and inform this office if anything went wrong, but is not in a position to take any personal or financial responsibility for them. As for the statements of the other Koreans, while they seemed to be made in good faith, they are obviously valueless as a basis for action, unless backed very substantially.[34]

The young Koreans' case presented something of a quandary. Had they been single young women or girls, they would likely have been excluded as likely prostitutes and public charges. But as young men, different hurdles rose and opportunities beckoned. A supplemental memorandum laid out the possible interpretations of the case. Due to the president's proclamation (presumably of 1907, which excluded Koreans and Japanese from entering the United States from Hawai'i), if they were to be considered *laborers*, they should be excluded.[35] But if they were to be considered *students*, they might be permitted to enter the country. The acting commissioner-general opined that there hadn't been any difficulty in similar cases, where the migrants' intentions were good.[36]

But because this was kind of a borderline decision, the acting commissioner-general judged that an appropriate compromise would treat each of the young men as students, but require a $500 bond for each. The bond details stipulated that the young men would (1) attend day school during the regular terms of the school year until March 1918; (2) not work in any jobs that would interfere with their studies; (3) file a written report to immigration authorities verifying their schooling every three months; and (4) never become a public charge.[37] They were thus released from detention at Ellis Island and admitted into national territory. Records are unclear, but eleven-year-old Wana Chin Lee likely lived with the family in Brooklyn. Chang Yill Lee and his cousin, Moon Chun Hung, traveled to Hastings College, in Nebraska, to begin their studies.[38]

Central Nebraska, and Hastings College in particular, are lesser-known havens in Korean American history, eclipsed by the larger communities in Hawai'i or the West Coast.[39] The college was also a center for one among multiple—and often contentious—strands of Korean anticolonial nationalism. The most militarily driven Korean nationalist leader was named Pak Yong-man. Pak was a middle-class political reformer, a former political prisoner, and critic of traditional Confucianism, and later, Japanese occupation.[40] In 1909 he left Korea after the Russo-Japanese War and enrolled in school in Kearney, Nebraska. He majored in political science and minored in military studies at the University of Nebraska and was convinced that Japan could only be driven from Korea through force. He and a handful of other young Korean men were drawn by the Kearney Military Academy and a Cadet Company at the local high school.[41]

Other single men and families followed the path they laid to Kearney, where they might get military training. As the *Kearney Daily Hub* reported in 1909, "a Korean military school" was in session with thirteen students enrolled. Students' military studies included "command in drill, gymnastics...infantry strategy, duties in corps, salutation." They also learned the "Korean mother tongue, Korean history and geography, algebra, arithmetic English grammar and other sciences. The boys also have an opportunity to learn agricultural affairs."[42] In March 1910 the school partnered with Hastings College, about fifty miles distant, and students could find a three-year program at the military school, where ordinary college classes were combined with military tactics and compulsory Bible study.[43] They often worked on farms during the day and did military training and studies in the evenings. Around 150 students attended the school, and 13 graduated.[44] Pak Yong-man left to continue nationalist political work in San Francisco and opened other military academies for diasporic Koreans in Hawai'i and later in China.[45] Other Korean military academies opened elsewhere on the mainland: in Lompoc, California; Kansas City, Kansas; Superior, Wyoming; and eventually, a flight school in Willows, California.[46]

Chang Yill Lee entered this political milieu in Nebraska sometime around April 1914. He stayed at Hastings College until December 1914, but like other students, including Choi Si, he struggled to make ends meet. He departed for California to earn money for his studies, and perhaps to connect with the more extensive Korean diasporic communities and migrant labor networks in the Golden State.[47] He worked "on several farms...close to Sacramento" for about six months, but also attended what he called the "Oriental School" in San Francisco for about three months, possibly the Hung Sa Dan (Young Korean Academy) opened by fellow Korean nationalist Ahn Cha'ng-ho in 1913.[48] He returned to Hastings College in September 1915 and attended school full-time until May 1917.[49] In 1916, while Lee was studying, his younger brother and cousin both returned to Korea, and connections with his older brother seem to have diminished somewhat.[50] By late 1917 the four-year period of his permitted studies were drawing to a close (they would end in March 1918), and immigration agents based out of Omaha returned their attention to him. In October 1917 an immigrant inspector named Coykendall found Chang Yill Lee working in the washroom of Swift's Packing Plant in South Omaha. "He stated that he was forced to leave the Hastings College last spring owing to lack of funds," Coykendall reported, "and that it is his intention to enter the Omaha High School at the beginning of the second semester of this coming winter."[51]

Nevertheless, because Lee had undertaken paid work when he ought to have been studying, the young man was in violation of the bond agreement under which he had been released from Ellis Island. Saint Louis–based inspector James Dunn (who erroneously referred to Chang Yill Lee as Chinese) thought the bond should be forfeited and Lee should be deported.[52] Anthony Caminetti, who penned a new Supplemental Memorandum in the case, highlighted his change of status, which he took to be evidence of longstanding duplicity. Lee had been permitted to enter as a student, Caminetti wrote, but his "subsequent conduct...justifies the presumption that at the time of his admission he was an ordinary Korean laborer and did not belong to the student class."[53] This of course presumed that one cannot move from being a student to a worker and back again. The retrospective change of Lee's status allowed the bureau to argue that he *should* have been excluded on arrival, that he always was and forever would be a laborer. It was a curious denial of the notion of American upward mobility, or the transformative power of education, but it wasn't out of step with the bureau's class restrictions and antipathy to Asian students. A Portland-based inspector opined that, by definition and design, an exempt student "cannot in the nature of things spring from a village pinched by want."[54] Caminetti apparently believed that Koreans required special skepticism.

> The Bureau has noted that when large numbers of Koreans arrive here it is almost invariably claimed that they are of the student or some other exempted class and furthermore that they set up the additional claim that the Japanese Government discourages migration of Koreans and places obstacles to their getting passports.

Caminetti, who wrote the memorandum, recommended that the Immigration Bureau issue a warrant for arrest. It was a questionable determination. Indeed, just days earlier, Kate L. Brown, principal of the Cass School, signed a letter to the bureau, testifying that Chang Yill Lee was a student at her school.[55] Caminetti was dubious and was "inclined to believe that this is a ruse." He would not rescind the warrant.[56]

In the subsequent hearing, Chang Yill Lee showed himself to be a respectable and hardworking young man. He was forthright about his occasional labor while he was a student. He said that he had supported himself and his studies. He had never received charity and had been able to support himself by working before and after school and in the summers. He had done farm work, worked in domestic service, and cleaned bathrooms in packing houses.[57]

His travel to the United States had not been easy. In a written statement, Lee described what would today be nearly refugee status. He said that he had left Korea for China without permission from the Japanese military government, which held Korea under "cruel…bondage." The occupying Japanese government would punish any Koreans who left without the consent of the District Court and governor-general, he explained. "When I leave Korea for going to China, I did not get any permission from Japanese Judge and Japanese Governor-General and secretly arrived to U.S. through China. If will be back, my hopely [sic] young life will uselessly be placed on the penal servitude under selfish Japanese law."[58] He came to the United States with the help of his brother, who had been living in the United States and who (mindful of his audience) had told him "about the beautiful civilization of the U.S. and about the way to learn in the U.S." Though he likely received some military training at Hastings College—training that the militarist tendency of Korean nationalists hoped they might use against Japanese occupiers—he downplayed this in his hearing. Instead, Lee described a focus on "reading, grammar, and American history," and improving his English.[59]

The hearing made a good impression on Inspector Miller. Miller was convinced that Lee had entered the United States to become a student and that he had attended school for nearly the whole time he was in the country.

He impresses me as being honest, sincere and truthful in his answers. Technically this boy has violated some of the provisions through which he gained entry into the United States by working for a few months in California and a few months in Omaha. However, I am satisfied that he entered the United States for the purpose of completing his education and he has indicated… that he wishes to continue his studies here until such time as he has received a college degree. I was informed by his teacher at Cass School that he is studying very hard, making good progress and that he was a *fine manly young fellow.*[60]

Despite the fact that Miller was impressed by Lee's manly respectability, his superior officer, the Saint Louis inspector-in-charge, recommended Lee's deportation.[61]

Lee's remained a borderline case. The inspector who conducted his hearing recommended leniency and for him to remain, while the inspector-in-charge recommended removal. Caminetti seemed to support deportation, but at the same time, he didn't totally overrule Inspector Miller's opinion. Caminetti said that Lee was an "intelligent young Korean [who] regards himself amenable to the immigration act," but that he was in technical violation of the law. There was "reasonable doubt as to whether he entered this country to be a laborer." Because it wasn't a clear case, and because Chang Yill Lee seemed a fine manly young fellow, working hard to get an education—he was studying, after all, and possibly facing Japanese persecution on return to Korea—once again, he was kept on as a borderline case. Caminetti recommended that Lee's deportation be "held in abeyance for one year" and that he would need to file monthly reports with the bureau. He could remain at large, presumably studying, for that time.[62]

By late 1918, Lee had grown unhappy in Omaha and in the United States. He returned to the Immigration Bureau in Omaha and met with Inspector O. B. Holton to get application forms to travel to Korea. He was drawn home for a number of reasons, but first among them was to see his parents. At the same time, American education was losing its appeal, though that too was tinged with the complexities of family and perhaps a younger brother's hurt at being neglected by an older brother. "Although my brother brought me here to succeed, he never care[d] for my educational conditions at all, so I gave up my ambition to succeed in useful education." Lee was confident, however, that his brother would pay for his return ticket to Korea.[63] To the cost-conscious bureau, this was welcome news indeed.[64] Holton, like Inspector Miller before him, had only good things to report about Lee. Lee, he said, was "very punctual in making his reports personally to this office, is exceedingly polite," and convinced Holton that "his sole purpose of coming to this country was for the purpose of education." Lee was also concerned that the

$500 bond on which he had been permitted to enter the country, paid by a kind person, not be sacrificed.[65]

In January 1919 the Immigration Bureau issued Chang Yill Lee's deportation warrant. The reasons offered were first, for violation of the sixth proviso of Section 3 of 1917 Immigration Act, and second, LPC at time of entry.[66] They knew the reasons to be false and believed in his sincere desire for education. But they applied them anyway.

Chang Yill Lee was to be loaded aboard the deportation train, from Omaha to Saint Louis (likely to Carbondale), and then loop south to New Orleans and west to San Francisco.[67] But in early February 1919 he requested a ninety-day stay of removal to earn a bit more money, he said, for the "expenses of my repatriation."[68] The request was granted. But Korean revolutionary politics disrupted his plans to return. On March 1, 1919, Korean progressives, intellectuals, and nationalists staged a nationwide protest against the Japanese. They were inspired in part by US president Woodrow Wilson's recent Fourteen Point declaration of national self-determination, and of the rights of nations to determine their own futures free from imperial interference. As many as one million women and men from across Korea's economic and social spectrum took to the streets. Over the next two months, protestors gathered in more than six hundred events. The uprising was planned to coincide with Versailles conference, demonstrating their hopes for Korean national independence from Japan, and thereby to influence the agenda for the postwar East Asian world order. They hoped that it would appeal to Wilsonian rhetoric about national independence and self-determination.[69]

But the Korean nationalists had misread US interests. American policy in Asia was eclipsed by pressing military, economic and diplomatic matters in Europe and across Latin America. In fact, US policy, such as it was, worked against Korean nationalists' interests. From 1905 through 1919 the American position on Japan's occupation of Korea was guided by a sense of détente, with the United States and the UK treating Japan as a junior imperial partner, each of whom held strategic aspirations to share control of the Pacific world.[70] In 1905, Theodore Roosevelt's diplomatic corps held secret meetings with Japanese leaders. The resulting agreement promised that the United States would accept Japan's occupation of the Korean Peninsula in exchange for Japanese nonaggression toward American control of Hawai'i and the Philippines. This insulated Japan against American critiques over the next decade and beyond.[71] It was, moreover, underscored by US racial thought, which judged the Japanese as a superior race (though hardly meriting the status of whiteness), which might civilize the supposedly backward Koreans.[72]

In a more immediate sense the funeral of Emperor Kojong triggered the protests. It was the largest nationalist demonstration in Korean history. The protests caught Japanese administrators by surprise. The protests were generally peaceful but prompted violent crackdowns by Japanese officials. Japanese settlers and state agents imagined the protests as a virulent and catastrophic attack on innocent workers, businesses, families, and farmers. They called for increased police, military, and gendarme protection. In one case, Japanese soldiers forced protestors into a church and burned it down. Japanese forces recorded 553 people killed and 12,000 arrested, while Korean sources put the number at 7,500 deaths and 45,000 arrests.[73] The protests eventually forced a shift in Japanese colonial policy from military rule to a period of cultural imperialism, but at this stage conditions were very uncertain.[74] Chang Yill Lee had written to his parents in February 1919 but, he told immigration officials, he "did not receive any message from them on account of bloody condition in Korea." He was willing to return, and quickly, but it would be dangerous. "The Japanese official inspection at the Japanese port or Korean port will be the worst obstacle." He continued: "Now whole Korea is under the martial law and Japanese officials severely prohibit the Koreans to go out abroad and to get in Korea to stop the wide spread of revolutionary campaign."[75]

It is unclear how much of the Korean nationalist ferment Lee imbibed at Hastings College. But even if his focus in the United States was indeed on education and professionalization rather than military training—more the Syngman Rhee camp than Pak Yong-man's—his mentions of the "bloody Japanese" occupation speak to his ideological involvement in a Korean diasporic anticolonial nationalism. In an April 1919 letter Lee requested that his removal be delayed, as he hoped to "stay in this country until the end of the bloody condition in Korea." He promised to continue with his "fair and honest behavior," until he could "make [a] safe trip to Korea."[76] Officials were amenable.[77] He might sit out the current deportation train's circuit, but he would most certainly be on the next one.

Except that he wasn't. Sometime between May and July 1919, Chang Yill Lee left Omaha.[78] It is unclear what motivated his change of mind—if he feared the turmoil of Japanese repression or being swept up in the anti-imperial nationalist effort. It is similarly unclear where he might have gone. The West Coast states still had the largest Korean populations and his brother lived in California, so he may have relocated there. He may have tapped into the network of Korean Americans he came to know in Nebraska, which extended to multiple parts of the country.[79] He may have joined with the delegation of Korean intellectuals and nationalists meeting in Philadelphia to lobby Woodrow Wilson and leverage international opinion toward Korean independence.[80] We can only speculate, because immigration officials reported that he had "absconded" from their surveillance.

Choi Si was less fortunate. In 1918, while Chang Yill Lee was trying to balance his work with his study, Choi continued to travel as an itinerant laborer. In September 1918 agents for the Department of Justice arrested him in Council Bluffs, Iowa, just outside of Omaha, for "failure to register"—possibly for military or wartime service. The lawyer appointed to help Choi with the charges instead reported him to the Immigration Bureau for deportation. Still, he was willing to fight for the United States against Germany, "because," he explained, "I like a democratic government."[81] The statement intrinsically opposed Japanese occupation even as he surely hoped to appeal to his interrogators. It did not work. He came to know, even better than before, the underside of America's racial democracy.

Choi was soon locked up, likely in the nearby Pottawattamie County Jail—an odd, and some said haunted, building.[82] At some unspecified point, Choi was sent from Council Bluff to Saint Louis, where he was locked up once more. In December 1918 he complained about the length of time he remained locked up in Saint Louis.[83] The bureau's deportation staff were initially ordered to deliver him to Ellis Island and await the next Korea-bound vessel, but orders changed, and he was to be sent west to California. Yet after he was transferred on the deportation feeder route to New Orleans, the deportation agent brought the wrong orders. As a result, Choi found himself languishing in the New Orleans jail. In all, he was continuously locked in American jails from September 1918 until June 1919. It was only then that the *Tenyo Maru* returned him, after perhaps forty days at sea, to the bloody conditions of Korean uprisings and Japanese imperial rule.

The Deportation Special's trips through New Orleans typically went, more or less, as planned. If bureaucratic errors meant that someone like Choi might languish in jail longer than intended, his suffering was more easily written off than the additional costs of paying for his imprisonment. Officials were more concerned, however, on the occasions when the cheap-

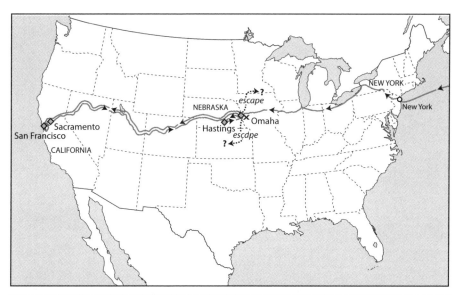
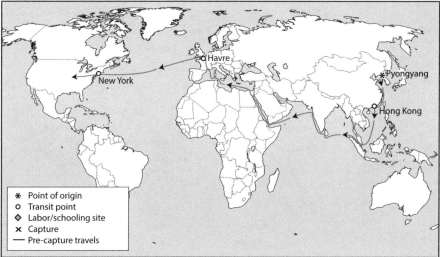

MAP 8. Chang Yill Lee's route.

est itinerary through New Orleans called for a combination of seagoing and train travel, which might lead to interruptions in the flow of travel. Physician Leo Stanley related one trip, when deportees on an eastbound journey were moved from the train car to the Southern Pacific's *SS Comus*. Not unlike the procedure at Ellis Island, the whole of the party was divided into groups for closer surveillance as they were transferred between vessels. Under guard by

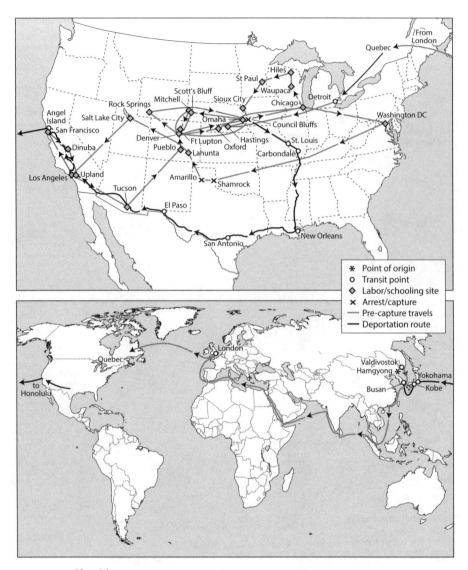

MAP 9. Choi Si's route.

Southern Pacific as well as Immigration Service keepers, the deportees were taken from the train and loaded aboard the ship, ten at a time. The pitiable deportees in the tourist car were transferred first. According to Stanley, a Portuguese family and an insane woman were among those brought across first and led to staterooms. Next, and still in groups of ten, the remaining deportees were unloaded from the prison car, "marched up the gangplank, along the deck, to the forecastle," where they were locked in the steerage-class cabin. Beds were stacked one above the other, and though tightly packed, Stanley judged them "clean and satisfactory."[84]

Administrators for Southern Pacific did not schedule the *Comus* to leave until the following morning. Deportation officials were at the mercy of Southern Pacific's schedule. Even temporary stasis allowed opportunity for deportees to disrupt their expulsion, but in addition to being locked in their cabins, guards stood watch at the top of the companionway and at the foot of the gangplank. The rest of the guards, public and private, would enjoy the evening in New Orleans.[85] But later that night, two men escaped. The steerage cabin, Stanley and the others believed, was an enclosed space, with just one entrance and exit, and he "took it for granted that the place had been properly inspected by the railroad and immigration officials and found secure." But the men had found a thin wooden door between the forecastle and the hold.

According to Stanley, "It was no trick at all for experienced criminals like these two, to get out of such a place." They broke the lock, overpowered the guard on the gangplank, and ran through the warehouse district to the rail yards beyond. The chief steward—a Southern Pacific employee—fired shots at the escaping men, but missed. The guard at the companionway remained oblivious until he heard the shots. Two other guards were sent out to look for the fugitives and notify the New Orleans police. The deportation officer, Edwin Kline, thought that finding them in the midst of the city was hopeless. Rather than disrupting the schedule and spend time and manpower on the search, the *Comus*, and its human cargo, departed the next day.[86]

ELEVEN

San Antonio

AFTER LEAVING LOUISIANA and entering Texas, at some untold point the Deportation Special began to depart from the Deep South and enter the US-Mexico borderlands. As the train left the land of magnolias, cotton, and Jim Crow, porters would begin taking down the Jim Crow signs insisting on anti-Black segregation.[1] The removal of segregation's explicit racial insult was surely welcome, but that hardly meant Black travelers, or porters for that matter, would be thrilled for greater proximity to white passengers. Dr. Leo Stanley noted with some pique that the Porter named John preferred to spend time with Black passengers in the Jim Crow car rather than waiting on Stanley and the deportees.[2] As John took down the signs, Mexican passengers in the midst of expulsion would gather their bags, prepare to get off the train, and willingly or no, cross the border to Mexico.

San Antonio's Sunset Station, where the Deportation Special arrived to disgorge some passengers and collect others, announced the Southern Pacific's attempt to incorporate the grandeur of Spanish past into its brand, implicitly highlighting Spanish racial whiteness and hiding the racial pasts of Mexican and Tejanx Indigeneity.[3] Rounded pediments hailed the nearby Alamo—the master symbol of Texas modernity, as anthropologist Richard Flores has put it—attempting to reconcile the Anglo Americans' understandings of the racial past (and present) with Tejanx peoples' ongoing contests over the new worlds of capitalist transformation.[4] But the US-Mexico border divided far more than US- and Mexican-born populations; it sought to separate the United States from migrants across Asia and the vast the Pacific too.

As it had been at each stop, the railroad was central to San Antonio's history, a symbol of modernity, change, and loss. As one man reminisced, before the Southern Pacific arrived in 1875, San Antonio had been filled with "educated Mexican gentlemen of Spanish blood," living in "ease and splendor." His romantic vision held little room for the exploitative peonage and violence from which the "gentlemen" profited. After the rail arrived, he mourned that "Old San Antonio…of brilliant court and docile peasant was no more."[5] Where the mutual if unequal personal obligations of patronage and peonage once guided relations between "gentlemen" and "peasants," now cold wage-labor contracts did the same, part and parcel of the transformations across the Lone Star State and region. The consolidation of US-based capitalism changed relations between rich and poor, to be sure, but also transformed the landscape, as major fauna shifted from bison to sheep and cattle, as grasslands turned to agribusiness and mountains into mines.[6]

As the train stopped, brothers Genero and Yndalecio Huerto, Gumeciendo Vallejo and Concepcíon Ranjel and their three children, along with Jose Peréz and Angel Ramírez, all of whom had boarded the train in Carbondale, gathered their bags and stepped down onto the platform. San Antonio-based immigration and deportation agents signed off on having received them from the train-based guards. The Huerto brothers and the extended Vallejo family began the next leg of their journey, from the Deportation Special's mainline and into a distributary route, branching from San Antonio to the border at Laredo. The condition of transport from San Antonio to Laredo did not generate many official records, but on May 31, 1919, guards watched them walk across a Laredo footbridge and into Mexico.[7]

It was common practice. Border Patrol officers and immigration officials often dumped Mexican deportees at the border, sometimes near where they claimed to have entered, sometimes wherever it was most convenient.[8] When they arrived in Mexican border towns that they may or may not have known, they had few resources at hand. They were far from friends, family, or the networks that might support them in the midst of such dislocation. Facing grim prospects, many could and did cross back into the United States. Others carried on, by whatever means they might. The ones who stayed had little choice but to make new homes where circumstance forced them, but Mexican border communities and northern cities were ill-prepared to look after new, poor, and unaffiliated arrivals, and often resented them for it. The torments of deportation continued well after Mexican families crossed the border. They were a long way from what could, in any meaningful sense, be called home.[9]

It is unlikely that Luey Mo thought a great deal about political economic transformations, about the paperwork that traded hands, or the complexities of binational border politics when he boarded the Deportation Special in San Antonio, found his seat, and adjusted himself to his fellow passengers. That did not mean he was ignorant of American or Mexican politics. Indeed, he knew too well their most dire consequences. We can only speculate: He may have been recalling the time when he had passed through this very same station a few years earlier, as an unfree laborer and refugee. Or he may have recalled the other times he boarded Southern Pacific's prisonlike train cars, on his initial journey from China into the Americas. Or he may have been more concerned with his visions—of demons or women, of ghosts that chased him still. He was an ordinary man who had experienced remarkable and horrible things.

By interpreting Luey Mo's life, we gain insight into the broader experience of Chinese global travels as well as his specific experience with the structures of gendered white supremacy in Mexico and the United States. He was an ally to US military adventurism in Mexico and a refugee fleeing war, an unfree worker in US military camps and a county jail prisoner, an inmate in an insane asylum and passenger in the deportation state's mobile, carceral regime. In these and more, Luey Mo crossed and subverted the borders of race and nation, of sexuality and madness, of unfreedom and liberation—as they sought to confine him.

Luey Mo was born in Canton, China, around 1888. His parents died when he was young, and he was raised by an uncle. The details of his early life are vague—and many of the statements from which his story is built, taken in San Antonio's Southwestern Insane Asylum, stretched rational coherence.[10] It appears as a young man, Luey Mo was financially secure enough to marry. Though his wife soon died of unspecified causes, they were together long enough to have son, whom they named Kayo Tu. Luey's financial circumstances were such that he chose to leave his son and Canton—he had enough money to afford a steamship ticket but not enough to make a decent living at home—and sought work abroad. There is some indication that he worked in a general merchandise store in Japan after leaving China. Whether that was the case or not, in 1907 or 1908, a twenty-year-old Luey Mo boarded a steamship and crossed the vast Pacific in its dank steerage cabin. Pacific passenger ships divided their accommodation into three classes. In 1916 a TKK ship like the *Nippon Maru*'s first class could cost around $225, "European steerage" cost around $100, and "Asiatic steerage" cost around $50. Asians were expected to travel in Asiatic steerage unless they were very wealthy, and Luey Mo was not. Even the poorest people of European descent would have been expected to avoid Asiatic steerage.[11] Tatsuzō Ishikawa described as passengers descended into the steerage compartments, "they saw five or six carbon lamps in the gigantic room. Along the perimeter of the room were double-decked rows of closely-packed gratings shaped like birdcages. These were our beds. The room was divided into four sections and held 180 to 220 people."[12]

Different ships were fitted with differently configured steerage accommodation, but none were particularly nice. The compartments were always near the engine room or propellers, and thus noisy and wracked by vibrations, or by the bow, and tossed and turned in heavy seas. Some vessels were former cargo ships that turned to passenger traffic when it was more lucrative. As one passenger on a similarly configured ship recalled, "the miserable state of the third class cabins was beyond words. In the hold they had built wooden bunks in two rows like silkworm racks. As my little space was right below the airvent pipe, it was awfully cold when the ocean wind blew through. Not knowing anything else to do, I put my straw hat over the hole."[13] According to Tokuji Hoshino, the physical discomforts of steerage were indistinguishable from more existential suffering; he saw steerage as a kind of liminal punishment; its denizens suffering for some ambiguous offense.

> The rays of light that leaked in from some small, round windows were… weaker than the light of twilight. Inside [the room], the color of the faces of the squirming people were pale and, surrounded by gloom, they half-heartedly endured the difficulties and the inevitable stench.…I felt as though I had committed a crime and had been thrown in prison for life.[14]

The accommodation was poor, and the food was no better. One transpacific passenger in 1907 recalled the "watery and tasteless" soup, with "only two or three small pieces of dried tofu." Moreover, he said, steerage passengers did not eat in the dining room. Instead, "bowls, cups, and dishes were issued to us at the beginning and we kept them throughout the trip, eating in the bunkrooms."[15] On some vessels crew members sold better foods at inflated prices to supplement meager rations, leaving those without money to subsist on whatever fare was provided.[16]

Luey likely traveled on a Pacific Mail steamer. Pacific Mail's fleet included smaller ships and behemoths such as the *Great Republic*, which could carry 250 cabin passengers and 1,200 steerage passengers. But reports stated that some voyages tried to pack 1,400 into steerage, and passengers' health suffered accordingly. Poorer travelers were crowded not just in the steerage cabin but also onto the orlop deck, usually reserved for cargo.[17] Some forty days later, Luey would have landed in San Francisco. Knowing the obstacles that the 1882 Chinese Exclusion Act posed, and ineligible to apply for entry as a student, merchant, or diplomat, he appeared to have few illusions about staying in the United States. Neither did he have connections (or the fraudulent documents) that would allow him to claim he was the child of a US citizen, and legally permit him to enter as a so-called "paper son." After landing in San Francisco, he boarded one of the special barred cars "equipped for Chinese service" operated by private transport firms and took advantage of the transit privileges to cross through the United States to El Paso. In the barred car, Luey and his fellow travelers were held to be legally extraterritorial to the United States, enveloped in the train's jurisdiction, and unable to exert rights claims or social belonging in the nation speeding just beneath their feet. Instead, he was bound for Mexico.

For much of the nineteenth century, Mexican immigration policy had been open, liberal, and remarkably free of Sinophobia, especially compared to the United States, Australia, Canada, and other Pacific world powers. During the Porfirato, Mexican businesses, particularly in the northern borderlands, sought cheap workers from abroad to pull copper from the earth and harvest crops from consolidating agribusiness's fields. Elite Mexicans and their US investor allies thought they might elevate their regional and national status, and immigrant workers would be vital to their aspirations. Chinese workers were crucial to Mexican national capitalist economic development, especially after China and Mexico signed the Treaty of Amity and Commerce in 1899, after which Chinese immigration to Mexico increased.[18]

Many had traveled Luey Mo's path before—indeed, some sixty thousand Chinese migrants ventured into Mexico in the late nineteenth and early twentieth century.[19] Chinese migration to Mexico had been miniscule prior to the US 1882 Exclusion Act, but afterward, roughly from 1882 through 1899, Chinese entrepreneurs bridged labor supplies in China with sites of labor demand and transit points in the United States, Mexico, Cuba, and elsewhere. They cooperated with smugglers, immigration officials on the take, friends in transport industries, and seized and widened legal loopholes.[20] While many of this generation of Chinese migrants sought to covertly enter the United States (estimates ranged around two thousand per year between

1876 and 1911), others remained in northern Mexican and Pacific Coast states—especially Sonora, Chihuahua, and Coahuila—and set down roots, opening stores, and building economies around covert migrant traffic.[21]

A second phase began after China and Mexico signed the Treaty of Amity and Commerce in 1899, as Chinese settlement patterns in Mexico shifted away from the US-focused migrant network in the northern and the Pacific states and toward domestic opportunities deeper in Mexico.[22] Luey Mo's life and travels sat in this latter period. Rather than remaining near the border or trying to double back from Juarez into El Paso, he traveled south to Madera, Coahuila, where he would live for the next eight years. He also spent around a year and a half in Chihuahua City. He likely moved between occasional farming, labor, and perhaps merchant work, depending on the circumstances.[23] Wealthy merchants or skilled tradesmen might bring wives from China or marry into Mexican communities, but laborers like him were less likely to do so.[24] He did, however, occasionally visit sex workers—a matter that would draw scorn from his future American interrogators.[25]

There had been less official anti-Chinese racism in Mexico than there was in the United States or Canada, but nativist Mexican politicians began to follow US patterns. Adopting Sinophobic rhetoric and practice, Mexican public health officials began to insist on denigrating medical inspections of Chinese travelers.[26] Soon, Mexican popular culture, cartoons, and corridos fixated on the idea that wealthy Chinese men might seduce foolish or greedy Mexican women. Chinese men were pictured sometimes as savage beasts, and sometimes as manipulative and oddly queer dandies. These representations contrasted implicitly with a more righteous Mexican manhood, as more deserving protectors (and possessors) of Mexican womanhood.[27] It was a potent mix, more latent than active in the first decade of the century, but worse was soon to come.

The deep inequalities that shot through Mexican society were only getting worse, exacerbated by Díaz's development policies. Real wages for urban and rural workers alike had been falling for more than a decade, and urban workers—from artisans to the least skilled—became increasingly radicalized. The Díaz regime's accelerated pace of rural village land seizure—often in the interests of export-oriented agriculture—prompted agrarian revolt, heightened generations-long antagonisms between peasantry and landowning classes, and reiterated struggles between Indigenous peoples and landed colonists. Moreover, market-driven agribusiness and the decline of locally driven food production led to rising food prices and, in the midst of periodic crop blights, shortages that infuriated hungry masses. Meanwhile, urban intellectuals and provincial elites were increasingly frustrated by the Porfirian regime's inability to address their specific if varied concerns.[28] By 1910 all this and more erupted in the Mexican Revolution, the convoluted and bloody rebellion that would tear through the land for the next decade.

With profound forces and unpredictable violence unleashed, anti-Chinese racism—once largely confined to the symbolic realm—became very real. Revolutionary nationalism equated foreignness with exploitation (not without reason, given US economic incursion across Sonora and beyond). Store-owning Chinese became ready scapegoats and, to no small extent, easier targets than powerful capitalists, landowners, and their governmental allies. Rebels and bandits of whatever political stripe looted Chinese-owned shops, and Chinese in the streets became easy targets for muggers and bandits. The most horrific anti-Chinese violence took place in Torreón, Coahuila. Between six hundred and seven hundred Chinese migrants had established a prosperous community there, operating shops and trading centers, real estate, laundries, market gardens, a bank, and a hotel. When Maderista revolutionaries and civilian mobs took the city in May 1911, they murdered more than three hundred Chinese and Japanese residents.

Stories of atrocity, torture, and butchery abounded. Like the popular cultural forms, attacks in Torreón were racially gendered expressions of economic nationalism. Public speakers before the massacre accused Chinese of harming Mexican women by taking their work, and perhaps implicitly, maligned them as sexual threats, reiterating earlier attacks on Chinese who sought to marry Mexican women.[29] The Torreón massacre only hailed further anti-Chinese violence. By 1919 mobs and rebels murdered 129 Chinese in Mexico City, and 373 in Piedras Negras, Coahuila. Politicians ran campaigns of Chinese vilification, bolstered by legal and extralegal harassment and violence.[30] While Luey Mo escaped the worst of the massacres, he surely saw more than enough, as the revolution tore through Madera and Chihuahua City. He lived through this cataclysmic violence by means we cannot know. It certainly took its toll. Chinese Mexicans sought shelter and survival wherever they might. For Luey Mo and around five hundred other Chinese Mexicans, that support came in the unlikely figure of a US Army General.

John "Black Jack" Pershing had already had a lengthy military career by the time he and Luey Mo crossed paths. Born in Missouri to a prosperous family and trained at West Point, Pershing fought in numerous battles against the Sioux and Apache peoples, and commanded the Tenth Cavalry's African American Buffalo Soldiers, one among the remarkable confluences two of the settler state's fundamentally (though differently) dominated peoples, set against each other.[31] He fought in the Philippines between 1899 and 1903, subduing anticolonial nationalists through US occupation, and securing better control of US trade routes and Pacific bases. He would become an envoy in Japan, serve another tour in the Philippines, and during the First World War become commander in chief of US expeditionary forces.[32]

Still, in 1916 the Great War had yet to draw US troops to Europe. Nevertheless, American leaders were distinctly uneasy about the war's effects on the Mexican border and feared that the Mexican Revolution might provide opportunity for insurgents or Axis powers to destabilize a region that the United States had at best incompletely pacified. When a document known as the Plan de San Diego came to light in 1915—radical even by the standards of the Mexican Revolution—Americans learned of an insurgent vision of Black, Mexican, and Indigenous rebels killing all white men over the age of sixteen and a plan to seize Texas, Colorado, New Mexico, Arizona, and California as liberated territory.[33] US soldiers, Texas Rangers, and self-appointed civilian militia "Home Guards" began to police the border—and terrorize its Mexican and Mexican American residents—more forcefully and more violently.[34]

American fears of Mexican insurgency were realized on March 9, 1916, when Mexican revolutionary Francisco "Pancho" Villa led a raid on Columbus, New Mexico. Villa's goals were many. The raid would be a show of force, a means to secure weapons from poorly defended US armories, and perhaps most pointedly, as a way to terrorize local Anglos and punish the United States for recognizing Venustiano Carranza's constitutionalist government, rather than his own. Early on the morning of March 9, some five hundred Villistas rode into Columbus and set fire to swaths of the town, attempting to seize as much loot as possible. Six hours later, US soldiers from the Thirteenth Cavalry—some of whom were recently returned from counterinsurgency duties in the Philippines—repulsed the raiders. More than one hundred Villistas and seventeen Americans had been killed by the time the Villistas retreated across the border.[35]

Woodrow Wilson called on Pershing to lead a "Punitive Expedition" into Mexico to hunt down and exact revenge on Pancho Villa. The expedition consisted of forty-eight hundred US soldiers and an additional twenty-five hundred Mexican troops, and scoured the Chihuahuan desert. As the search dragged on, Carranza's troops, along with local Mexican populations, grew increasingly resentful of American imperiousness. The expedition's difficulties were exacerbated because Pershing could not rely on local resupply. Carranza's government was reluctant to offer too much support for the Americans, lest he be seen as cozying up to Mexico's exploiters to the north and risk strengthening Villa's image as the true defender of Mexican sovereignty. Carranza's government denied Pershing access to Mexican railroads (many of them built, ironically, by US-friendly capitalist firms in the earlier, more business-friendly Porfirato), and made US resupply and Army Quartermaster duties nearly impossible. Neither did many local Mexicans offer support, because they resented US military presence, feared reprisal from Villistas, or a combination of the two.[36]

But Pershing could, and did, look to Chinese Mexicans like Luey Mo for help. In the midst of the Revolution's rampant anti-Chinese violence, few Chinese appeared drawn to Mexican nationalism or anti-Americanism. Perhaps building on his experience in Philippine counterinsurgency and anti-Indigenous colonial warfare against the Sioux and Apache, and capitalizing on divisions among local populations (be they longer-term residents or recent arrivals), Pershing believed that Chinese guides were less likely than local Chihuahuaenses to provide intelligence to Villista forces, or to be insurgents themselves. As a result, Pershing's venture relied heavily on Chinese merchants, laborers, and guides. Unlike the US Army, Chinese merchants could use rail infrastructure, as well as motor vehicles and mule-drawn wagons, to bring supplies. Indeed, the *New York Times* called the Chinese the "shopkeepers of the army," acknowledging that they had effectively replaced a hamstrung Quartermaster.[37]

Chinese laborers helped set up US tents and dig trenches; Chinese merchants sold US soldiers food, tobacco, and assorted goods; others provided services, from food to laundry; some may have worked among the prostitutes to service the soldiers in the military-administered "sanitary village." For Chinese Mexicans, Luey Mo among them, the American army was a source of ready money in the midst of economic strife. And while the *Times* represented the Chinese as a burden for the US Army—saying that they were "On the Army's hands"—it would have been more accurate to point out that Chinese merchant logistics and supplies carried the army. Still, the relationship was reciprocal. There were credible threats that Villa would continue the anti-Chinese massacres that had taken place across the land. As Chinese merchants and laborers provided Pershing support, the army offered them protection.[38]

Nevertheless, eleven months later, Pershing's mission was a resounding failure. On January 18, 1917, President Wilson recalled Pershing, lest the failures mount and for fear that ongoing US presence might prompt Mexico to ally with Germany, much as the just-decoded Zimmerman Telegram suggested, and open a new front in the war.[39] Rather than demonstrating American power, the expedition enflamed anti-US sentiment and revealed military weakness. Instead of exacting racial revenge and publicly punishing Villa (it was called the *Punitive* Expedition, after all), it lionized him. On February 2, 1917, despite the patriotic bunting that festooned gazeboes in Columbus, New Mexico, to greet the returning expedition, it was far from a success.[40]

More than 2,700 refugees and camp followers—really, in the Chinese case, camp *providers*—entered the United States with the returning expedition. Most were Mexicans fleeing the violence, around 200 were US-born Mormons, and 524 were Chinese.[41] Luey Mo was among them. They were housed at Camp Furlong, a collection of clapboard structures and tents, motor pools and barracks, with an occasional windmill, steeple, or water tower rising above its geometrical grid work, and contrasting with the high and dusty desert's bushes, arroyos, and distant hills.[42] They were kept under armed guard in a makeshift military detention center, replete with a bullpen and stockade for processing.[43]

The US-born Mormons and Mexican refugees apparently entered the United States without great fanfare. Immigration Bureau agents might have impeded the Mormons' return based on antipolygamy statutes written into 1891 and 1907 immigration laws, but apparently chose not to: presumably the Mormons' US-birth and presumptive whiteness overrode any desire among the bureau's staff to prevent their entry, and in any case, antipolygamy legislation of the day primarily targeted Ottoman Muslims rather than these anomalous Protestants.[44] The Mexican refugees, after being subject to medical examination (which likely included spraying with pesticides), were quickly processed and released into broader borderland communities to provide more labor for the wartime economy.[45]

Luey Mo and the five hundred other Chinese refugees were in a more complicated position. After all, Chinese Exclusion had been the ideological foundation of immigration law since 1882, and its precepts of racialized partition and national protection had only grown stronger. According to exclusionists, the threat Chinese refugees posed—to white labor, to wages, to Christianity and national virtue—did not abate just because they fled war across the southern border. Revolution or no, exclusionists saw little reason to allow any Chinese to enter the United States and feared the precedent it might set. Nevertheless, "Black Jack" Pershing and his officer corps insisted that the Chinese refugees be permitted to enter. Despite having no authority to do so—and infuriating US immigration bureaucrats like Anthony Caminetti—Pershing promised them safe harbor in the United States and guaranteed their protection from Villista reprisals.

Pershing, whose background in counterinsurgency may have led him to value local allies, understood that the Chinese had supported him at risk to themselves. He also understood reciprocal paternalistic obligation as more important than the impersonal alienations of contract or law—something an older generation of Texans, or Tejanxs, might have appreciated. Army major John Parker defended the stance. The "honor of the Punitive Expedition and of the United States," Parker maintained, "requires that protection be given to these faithful camp followers." Pershing was paternalistic and frequently condescending to the Chinese—unsurprising, really—but his loyalty for past service was sincere.[46] It also served a convenient military purpose: if the United States broke its promise to locals who supported American occupying forces, would potential allies in future US wars take the same chance?[47] And the long-term cost was not great; Pershing only intended temporary asylum for the refugees. Once the Revolution ended, they might be sent back to Mexico.[48]

For now, however, and under Pershing's protection, Chinese entering the United States received special certificates of identity and legal permission to remain. Luey Mo had entered the United States through Columbus in early February 1917, and in June 1917 he received a Special Certificate of Identity, the document that permitted him to legally remain in accordance with the 1892 Geary Act.[49] Despite having left Mexico, it was unclear the extent to which Luey Mo and his fellows might have been understood as fully residing in the United States. Liminal legal status as "special" noncitizen alien residents led to conditions of unfree labor and drudgery, to legal, political, and economic constraints. The special dispensation and numbered certificates of identity furthered a documentary system of surveillance, but the controls went much further. In fact, Luey Mo and the other Chinese refugees were largely confined to US military bases and other prison-like facilities. Indeed, he would spend the rest of his American life in a succession of partitioned and carceral spaces, until he was finally deported.

Immediately after their arrival, US officials and Chinese diplomats began negotiations to relocate the Chinese refugees from the army camps either to another Mexican state—perhaps Baja California or Sonora—or else be returned to China. The refugees demanded that no action be taken until the Chinese consul arrived from San Francisco.[50] But costs would be high, and no opportunities to relocate the Chinese refugees were clear. In the meantime, the Chinese refugees remained at Camp Furlong in New Mexico. The Chinese legation paid some $180 per day to support them (as well as other refugees in Ciudad Juárez), but the US Department of Labor feared for the precedent it might set in allowing Chinese wartime refugees to enter the country, overriding the exclusion of Chinese laborers.

Having escaped the violence of the Mexican Revolution, Luey Mo and the other Chinese refugees still faced concerted racism and radically circumscribed opportunities in the United States. A handful chose to return to parts of Mexico where there was less anti-Chinese violence, a few more returned to China, and around forty of the refugees were able to demonstrate their merchant status and thus enter the United States in accordance with the Chinese Exclusion Acts' merchant exemptions. Anti-Chinese whites fretted about labor competition from the 472 who remained, and despite their small numbers, laundry owners from Massachusetts to California were worried. A writer from the Missouri Laundry Owners' Association wrote in "emphatic protest to this unlawful suspension of the Chinese Exclusion law." Being magnanimous was not worth the risk, and even if the refugees were allowed to remain, the writer demanded that they be "so segregated" and subject to such scrutiny "that the identity of each individual refugee is not lost or obscured, so that they can be deported from this country at some proper time in the future without a lot of vexatious litigation and expense to our Government."[51]

Officials were happy to make that promise. Louis Post, the secretary of labor, assured that all the Chinese refugees would be kept under full and ongoing surveillance, and returned to Mexico as soon as war abated.[52] Others, however, sought out the refugees precisely because of the low wages they might be paid, and as ostensibly docile and tractable workers. Their prospective employers argued that the wartime political economy led to high labor costs and a shortage of trustworthy workers (which is to say, they deemed ethnic Mexican workers suspect), and the Chinese would be ideally suited in this context.[53] It replayed a persistent tension between those who feared low-paid Chinese workers and those who sought them out as cheap labor.

The military ultimately resolved the contradiction between white desire for Chinese exclusion and the wartime desire for an additional labor source by determining to use the Chinese refugees as unfree workers, contracted exclusively to the US military.[54] The Chinese would be permitted to remain in the United States and they would be compelled to work, but under this arrangement, the theory went, their labor would not affect free white wage workers. (It was similar to the logic that, following early century restrictions on the convict lease system, restricted imprisoned laborers to state-use rather than for-profit industries.[55]) The arrangement apparently satisfied the laundry owners' advocates, and the Chinese consul offered support too. Consul Fong promised to help track down any refugees who left the strict conditions of their employment.[56] At the same time, the military promised that the internees would be paid a "regular and fair wage."[57] Still, if the Chinese workers found better wages elsewhere, they would not have been able to take those jobs. The inability to leave is, of course, the defining feature of unfree labor. Ironically, the restrictionists feared that Chinese laborers might become an unfree "coolie" workforce. In fleeing war and gaining restricted asylum on US military bases, they became just that.

From February until June 6, 1917, Luey Mo and his fellow Chinese refugees lived in the stockade and worked under armed guard at Camp Furlong.[58] It had been the staging area for Pershing's expedition, but as attention turned across the Atlantic rather than the Chihuahuan and Sonoran Deserts, the camp's mission split between guarding the border from Mexican incursion and preparing soldiers for Europe's Western Front. Some eighty of the refugees worked for the Quartermaster Corps. Ten of the Chinese were set to work doing laundry for the 24th Infantry—one of the nation's only African American infantry regiments. The remaining Chinese refugees cleaned the camp, did its maintenance and upkeep, or performed exercises of some sort.[59]

On June 6, 1917, Luey Mo and the remaining refugees were loaded aboard a special ten-car Southern Pacific train, departing from Columbus for San Antonio, Texas. It is a matter of no small historical perversity that members of the Industrial Workers of the World, recently driven out of Bisbee, Arizona, would soon be locked in the barricades the Chinese refugees had just left, and use the facilities they had been tasked with maintaining. Similarly, we might safely surmise that Southern Pacific used its Chinese cars for the refugees' journey, offering a special rate to its military clients, as was a common wartime practice.[60] They arrived at Southern Pacific's Spanish mission–styled station in San Antonio the next afternoon.[61] They were transferred by truck to Camp Wilson, near Fort Sam Houston. At the direction of army engineers and under the hand of a refugee foreman, 350 refugees were immediately set to work clearing the land of cactus, bushes, trees, and preparing the grounds for streets, buildings, and drill areas. They were paid twenty cents per hour and no overtime.[62] Their labor was woven into colonial ecological processes, transforming San Antonio's earth into a military base and training ground. In addition to extending US military infrastructure in the Texas borderlands, the refugees' construction labor, here and elsewhere— at Camp Wilson, Camp Kelly, at Fort Sam Houston—set the conditions of possibility for US overseas warfare and solidified military claims to the Southwest, a region where anxieties about Mexican, Black, and Indigenous uprising persisted.

While many worked at the camps near Columbus and later, San Antonio, others were transferred further afield, across Texas, New Mexico, Louisiana, and Kansas. The Chinese refugees worked in a host of capacities at the military camps. They did hard labor, they did laundry, but also worked in clerical roles, as cooks and blacksmiths and janitors; they did domestic work for officers and their families. They worked as nurses and orderlies in tuberculosis wards and in sanitariums, difficult and at times dangerous work. The social worlds they built in the camps are unclear from the historical record, but historian Edward Briscoe described remarkable esprit de corps and deep Americanization among them.[63]

A major at Fort Leavenworth in Kansas lauded the Chinese refugees' efficiency and bragged about the low wages he could pay them. Others said that they were much better than the white or Black workers they might otherwise need to employ.[64] And having Chinese workers on bases meant that white men—recognized as full martial citizens, while Chinese migrants were not—were available for frontline military duty.[65] A writer from the *San Antonio Express* said the Chinese were hardworking and "painfully polite" to visitors.[66] We might also read the grimace of politeness as more ambivalent: expression of gratitude for asylum from war in Mexico, but also frustration at their confinement and unfree labor. No armed guards patrolled their camps, but the refugees were subject to ongoing surveillance and constantly sus-

十 中 旅 在 式 柒
日 国 館 棉 號 月
字 红   加   拾
會

THE CHINESE ORIENTAL NIGHT
for the Red Cross at the Menger Hotel
JULY 12-1917.

FIGURE 10. "Chinese refugees at Camp Wilson, Fort Sam Houston, Texas," 1917. *Source:* 068-2940, General Photograph Collection, University of Texas at San Antonio.

pected of trying to escape. Confinement must have grated, especially when the work was hard, and conditions could even be deadly. Indeed, ten of the Chinese refugees died while working for the US military.[67] Some did in fact attempt to escape, stowing away on Southern Pacific boxcars passing nearby. Officials began daily head counts of refugees, to make sure none had been successful. Others expressed concern about the pass system the refugees had access to, which allowed them temporary visits to nearby San Antonio.[68] If the refugees needed a pass to travel, they knew that they were far from free.

Luey Mo worked in the Quartermaster Bureau at Camp Furlong, and he rode the Southern Pacific trains to San Antonio in June 1917. The extent of Luey Mo's movement within the US domestic military apparatus over the next year is unclear, but we know that he worked for some time at the Chinese refugee camp at Camp Stanley, Texas.[69] Judging by his actions, he was dissatisfied with the economic and racially gendered bases of American refuge, and chafed under the structures of military camp life and its restrictions on his autonomy. We know this because on August 21, 1918, Luey Mo was arrested for stealing the cash drawer from a store "near Remount #3" in Leon Springs, near Camp Stanley. An officer from Camp Stanley's Military

Police arrested him and delivered him to Tracy Page, the civilian manager in charge of the Chinese refugees. Page had invested a great deal of energy in his patronage of the Chinese refugees, and would later proclaim that they "have been good, loyal, honest servants of the Government, living up to the highest standards of civilization and having a respectful obedience to authority and, above all, a lasting trust in the just principles of our Government."[70] Page likely believed himself to have been betrayed by such ungrateful behavior.

Nine days after Luey Mo's arrest, he was transferred to the San Antonio County Jail, a municipal carceral facility for short-term punishment, or for people who had been arrested but not yet tried.[71] The transfer signaled the shift form one kind of liminality to another—from a refugee with tempered legal standing in the United States (constrained to perform unfree military labor and largely confined to military bases) to an accused criminal facing trial. It is difficult to know where Luey Mo might have been placed in San Antonio's segregated jailhouse. Texas's domestic prison regime was based on the dominant three-way racial division among Black, white, and Mexican inmates. Being Chinese, he did not clearly fit in Texas penality's typical racial scheme, and records are unclear on the matter. However, officers did mention that they thought Luey Mo was "mentally unbalanced." His mental instability destabilized whatever logic the system used, and officers put Luey Mo in a separate cell—probably one ordinarily used for punishment. If the San Antonio jail was like the one in Dallas, deputies probably assigned a prison trustee—larger, stronger, and more violent than other prisoners, but loyal to officers—to control him.[72] It was common elsewhere in the country too. A California State Board of Charities worker wrote in 1916 that

> the mentally ill, while awaiting "trial," are entirely in the hands of the sheriff or his representative, and, except in a few counties, patients are actually detained in jails or in worse places, such as basements, attics, out-houses, isolated shacks, etc. These places in many counties were found to be neglected, unsanitary, even filthy, and in several instances to be fire traps....A favorite custom in jails is to put insane patients in the "misdemeanor tank" to be cared for by such vagrants and petty criminals as happen to be in prison.[73]

In any case, Luey was eventually brought before a county court, and its jury determined him to be insane. After three months in the county jail, he was likely bound and brought to the Southwestern Insane Asylum.[74]

The Southwestern Insane Asylum housed around eighteen hundred peo-

FIGURE 11. Southwestern Insane Asylum, San Antonio, Texas, ca. 1909. *Source:* 083-0672, General Photograph Collection, University of Texas at San Antonio.

ple when Luey arrived. Superintendents ruled their facilities with an absolute hand, submitting only occasionally to whatever modest oversight legislatures might suggest.[75] The Southwestern Insane Asylum was a white-only institution, and the first Black inmates were admitted in 1964.[76] Most other Texas mental institutions were firmly and clearly racially segregated on a Black-white racial axis. Had there been Black inmates, it is possible that even though he was not white, being Chinese might have allowed Luey the dubious benefit of being treated as "not-Black," within Texan traditions of anti-Black racism. But if this was indeed a white-only institution, it seems more likely that being Chinese, and speaking some Spanish, would have led to a firmer and more punitive racialization, perhaps among ethnic Mexican asylum inmates or perhaps with those who shared a similar prognosis. Wherever it was, it was Luey Mo's new home. As before, he could not leave.

The asylum was situated on 640 acres of land. As with similar institutions across the country, inmates' labor kept it running. They grew crops and did other kinds of maintenance, to the extent they were able. Inmates' labor instilled social hierarchy among them. And while the prohibition on Black inmates may have precluded spatial organization into Black and white, the asylum, like most mental institutions, was almost certainly divided into "front" and "back" wards—between the long-term and supposedly hopeless cases, and those whom physicians saw as curable.[77] Attendants were instructed to always be polite to asylum residents. Beating inmates was frowned upon, but some attendants and guards found it necessary or even cathartic. One attendant explained: "When I came here, if someone told me I would be guilty of striking patients, I would have called him crazy himself, but now I take delight in punching the hell out of them."[78]

Moreover, if conditions in the Southwestern Insane Asylum were similar to those at the Austin State Asylum, it was a rank, fetid place. People defecated and urinated in their clothes, especially the aged and senile. Bedding was hopelessly soiled for the same reason and would only have been changed by poorly paid people who, we might imagine, resented the task. Some patients were happy to bathe, others steadfastly refused. Food, excrement, and more festered in cracks between the floorboards. Even after concrete was poured on top, it soon cracked and the stench returned.[79] The reek of paraldehyde, which former New York inmate Mary Jane Ward said had a "musky, fetid, straw smell," would waft through the wards.[80] It is unlikely that whatever treatments and therapeutic discipline he bore—blurring the borders of what physicians saw as care and control—helped him greatly.[81] Doses of heavy metals, including mercury, were used to treat syphilis, but this led to serious complications, including the "loss of teeth, tongue fissures, and hemorrhaging of the bowel."[82] Hydrotherapy, which many recalled as a form of torture more than cure, was commonplace.[83] Forced sterilization was too, and was perhaps likely, given the desires Luey Mo would soon express.

It was standard procedure for new inmates to be interviewed and diagnosed when they entered the asylum. Luey's investigation was quite thorough. He was 5'5" tall, 112 pounds, generally of good physical condition. His body was read for deformities and marks, including scars, signs of injury, vaccination, and so on. His pulse was taken, and his hearing and vision checked, all deemed normal; his tongue was confirmed to be "clean" and "steady." When the alienists watched him walk, they read his gait as steady but his speech as voluble and thick. His appetite was good, his bowels normal. He was sent to Ward H.M. 1, although what that meant in the asylum's spatial regime is unclear. His principal mental symptoms were listed as hallucinations, confusion, eroticism, and faulty judgment.

He reportedly "spoke little Spanish, and less English," and the intake interview at the hospital was conducted in Spanish. The interviewer described him as being incoherent, though confessed it was "difficult to say whether it is for the want of a common language, or from mental confusion." The interpreter described many of these same concerns to the investigator, and this may well bespeak the illness Luey suffered (in which case, the transcript may be fairly accurate). In his "Examining Officer's Statement," Inspector Schafer said Luey appeared composed for part of the examination, but at others became excited. The interpreter told Schafer that Luey "would converse rational[ly] one minute and the next he would talk like a crazy man so that it was very difficult to get his replies."[84] Nevertheless, in the intake interview the physician learned about another racially gendered element that excised him from the privileges of refugee status, and brought him, reviled, into the deportation regime. Whether or not they accord with conceptions of rationality, we are obliged to take Luey Mo's statements seriously.[85]

It is telling that from the interview testimony neither Luey Mo nor the physician were particularly concerned about his alleged theft, or what it might have indicated about his feelings as an unfree, low-wage, military laborer. The physician was more concerned that Luey Mo had been flirting with a white woman—perhaps the cause behind the white doctors' diagnoses of Luey Mo's "eroticism" and "faulty judgment." From the patient history:

Q: Were you in jail in San Antonio?
A: Yes, a long time. With girl. Crazy. Arrested.
Q: Did you write to the American girl?
A: Not here....
Q: Did you write to a girl in Leon Springs?
A: Yes.
Q: Why did you write to her?
A: Because I liked her.
Q: Was she an American or Mexican?
A: Don't know, not Mexican.[86]

According to William Tracy Page, Luey had begun acting strangely a few months earlier, "writing letters to an American girl whom he only knew by sight, and to whose family," Page reported, "he was very obnoxious."[87] Luey Mo's amorous intention toward a white woman was the kind of thing that led Texas whites into murderous collective rage. At the same time, Luey's desire was, perhaps on some level, a response to gendered white supremacy and the forced bachelor cultures of exclusion that so many Chinese faced in the United States, and to a lesser degree, in Mexico.

The interview to this point left the unanswered question of the etiology of Luey Mo's madness, as well as how he responded to confinement—phenomenologically, and what it meant, socially, to the extent that such things can be divined. In the interview, he simply explained that he was sad. When asked why, he explained, "Because I cannot get out."

Q: Why were you sad before coming here?

A: They took me to jail. I couldn't see the girl. (He mixes language so that the interpreter cannot understand.)…

Q: Why do you think you are crazy?

A: Don't know. crazy about girl. was crazy in jail. not crazy now.

Q: What did you do in jail?

A: Girl visited me in jail. devils with saints come in jail. (unintelligent, makes gestures as tho he saw things in the air. says devils here too. woman here gives me milk, devils come over transom at night.)…

Q: Were you crazy in Mexico?…What crazy things did you do in Mexico?

A: Saw cops, devils after me at hotel (describes with gestures).[88]

Luey's gestures, like much else, evade the historical transcript. In his hearing before Immigrant Inspector Schafer, Luey described another of his visions: "Just a little while ago a man and woman got into my room and got to fighting and the woman grabbed the man and squeezed him to death. I tried to stop the fighting and got these bruises on my head that you see." Schafer asked about another vision, about a "devil house" in Japan: "There are all girls there, a man and a child came and said to me to come back to earth, before I was born I was here in this house."[89]

We can only speculate about what Luey Mo's demons and visions meant to him, his fears and terrors, being chased by devils, men in uniform, and others—and which produced physical harm. To what extent did his gestures express the metaphors and symbols of his madness, reflecting his experience of migration across multiple political societies, across unwelcoming and threatening spheres, through racial capitalism, war, asylum, coercion, and detention? Of Mexicans who tolerated him or wanted him dead, of the Americans who protected him, reviled him, imprisoned him, and compelled his labor? His wife's death, his distance from his family, his relationships with sex workers, with other Chinese refugees?

Unsurprisingly, Inspector Schafer did not believe much that Luey said. Physical bruises notwithstanding, devil houses and visions were untrustworthy. Yet Schafer showed remarkable confidence in Luey's ability to say he did not want legal counsel to represent him. He also believed Luey when he said he didn't care where they sent him "as long as I get something to eat." Schafer apparently thought it reasonable enough for Luey to consult with the visions about his removal: "If the images want me to go away it will be alright. I will have to ask them." We cannot know what the spirits felt, but Inspector Schafer recommended that he be deported.[90] The doctors' final diagnosis was that Luey Mo suffered from manic-depressive insanity, of a "depressed type on a defective basis." The initial cause was probably syphilis, and Luey was forthright about having visited brothels for sex. But the alienists judged the immediate cause as the "change of environment and incidents of the Mexican Revolution." The madness of war—revolution against fundamental economic inequality and land distribution as well as the violent racial scapegoating of Chinese migrants—precipitated Luey Mo's madness. Shell shock and trauma were only then being theorized, but the physician believed that the horrors he saw destabilized whatever balance he might have had.[91] Nevertheless, his keepers appeared to be pleased with his behavior. Luey was a "good ward worker [who] keeps to himself a great deal. Is clean and neat in habits." They did find it bothersome that he "persistently ask[ed the] doctor to let him out."[92]

They would release him, but only to be deported to China. Even then, some had misgivings. US officials expressed concern for how the mad were treated in early twentieth-century China, which did not accord with what Americans considered sound treatment. The secretary of state reported, in 1914, that the "Chinese Government...has made no provision for its insane, the treatment of whom at the hands of the people is not conformable to modern practice." For that reason, "it would seem particularly inadvisable from a humanitarian standpoint to deport these undesirable aliens under present circumstances."[93] Nevertheless, humanitarian concerns did not impede Luey Mo's expulsion, and immigration authorities ultimately concurred in the medical officials' diagnosis. Trauma was an explanation, not an excuse, for his behavior, and would not justify his incarceration in the asylum at American taxpayers' expense.

Beyond the signs of madness, Luey had committed two cardinal offenses against American belonging. By stealing money from a store, he implicitly rejected his status as an unfree, low-wage laborer confined to military bases. By flirting with a white woman, he challenged the white male mania for ownership of white women and white women's exalted status as unattain-

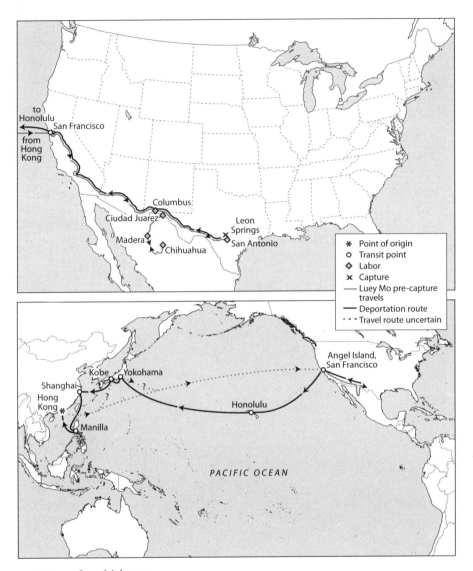

MAP 10. Luey Mo's route.

able emblems of white supremacy. His madness undercut the premises of liberal rationality on which American life was supposedly based. The syphilis, which they suspected led to his madness and they believed he had acquired from prostitutes abroad, similarly underscored what they took to be Luey Mo's sexual immorality. He had entered legally under special refugee status, but he would be deported as a "public charge" from causes that preexisted his arrival and for "entry without inspection"—but not for violation of Chinese Exclusion, because General Pershing, in his patronage, overrode those provisions.[94] The 365 others of "Pershing's Chinese" might have been marginally acceptable to the US polity, given their vital support to a US military adventure, but Luey Mo's transgressions made even Pershing's support untenable.[95]

On February 2, 1920, Luey Mo finally left the asylum and was transferred back to San Antonio, and to the Southern Pacific's faux-Spanish Sunset Station. There, he boarded the Deportation Special and retraced the route he'd traveled a decade earlier, across the Southwest and the Pacific. We do not know whether the demons of war or the ghosts of asylum trailed behind him.

TWELVE

El Paso

THE DEPORTATION SPECIAL ROLLED THROUGH the West Texas borderlands over Southern Pacific Lines from San Antonio to Spofford Junction and toward El Paso. The train came into a city increasingly sundered from its other half, Ciudad Juárez, across the Rio Grande. Passengers might look out one window and see Juárez in the near distance; the border, such as it was, posed no barrier to their vision. Those on the right side of the train might catch a glimpse of Fort Bliss, or signs pointing toward that bastion of militarized border protection. Within the city the railroad tracks made their own smaller-scale border. White communities to the north were increasingly separate from the more diverse communities like Chihuahuaita, south of the tracks, with its mostly Latinx, but also Black, white, and Chinese residents. They tended to work in the nearby smelters and the railyards, and while the city and the industries relied on them as cheap workers, they earned white El Pasoans' disdain.[1]

We have seen this dynamic—in which racialized workers traversed the planet to build industrial infrastructures for empires that built barriers against them—in previous chapters. The three people on whom this chapter focuses—Kondo Johei, Tarashima Tokizo, and Hirakawa Kizo—give insight into a different imperial context, and a harder border, fixed in violence, set against them. Kondo, Tarashima, and Hirakawa show how subordinated peoples built industrial infrastructures across multiple empires and regimes in a racial capitalist system, and when they entered the United States, confronted a border policing regime that tried to regulate the racial composition of its territorial empire. The men were born, by happenstance, into Meiji Japan, whose imperial and economic ambitions thrust them into an industrializing workforce. They chose, among constrained options, emigration to Peru and survived the legacies of racialized labor extraction in a South American nation that was itself an economic colony of grander US and European powers. They departed, and entered the maritime networks of the British empire, maintaining its infrastructural power in slow decline. The men left that world and entered Mexico, which rebelled against, but was inextricably connected to, US-dominated oil, infrastructure, and energy empires. It was a remarkable, ongoing journey. Across all of their travels, their choices, and the things that compelled them, the force that halted their travel—or most profoundly redirected it—was the US-Mexico border. It was an imaginary line, made real through ascendant state power and violence. Their experience was a sign of the times to come.

Until the Southern Pacific Railroad's first train arrived in May 1881, El Paso was overshadowed by Juárez, its more populous and prosperous neighbor. Rail traffic accelerated eastern and western movement, but since the sixteenth century, Spanish conquistadores developed trade and political routes from the capital in Mexico City to New Spain's northernmost reach in Santa Fe, wending among the mountains between the Chihuahua Desert and the upper reaches of the Rio Grande Valley.[2] And for millennia before the Spaniards, the Pueblo, Diné (Navajo), Apache, Comanche, and their ancestors traversed the land: hunting, raiding, trading; cultivating foods, enmities, alliances, and territorial claims among sedentary peoples, and seasonal movements among nomadic ones.[3]

Still, when the Southern Pacific arrived in 1881, El Paso boomed. The city saw massive population growth, skyrocketing real estate prices, and buildings put up as fast as they could be hammered together. Southern Pacific was first among the big lines, but its rails soon linked with the Santa Fe, the Texas & Pacific, the Galveston, Harrisburg & San Antonio, and the Mexican Central Lines. With the rail and telegraph lines—built by some of the world's poorest people but financed by some of the wealthiest—El Paso/Juárez became a central hub between San Francisco, the greater US-Mexico borderlands, Chicago, Saint Louis, New York, Boston, and Mexico City. The networks were extended by the port cities' connections to steamship and ocean lines across the Caribbean, Pacific, and Atlantic worlds.[4] Financiers and speculators, inspired by promises of untold mineral riches through the region, funded the railroads' growth. Huge smelters erupted on both sides of the river, processing ore drawn from throughout the southwestern United States and across northern Mexico.[5] If the winds were right, smoke from El Paso's smelters would have mingled with smoke from the train, as the Deportation Special came into town.

On the border of two nations and yet at the center of a vast network of resource extractive capital, El Paso's population reflected these tensions.[6] And this was one reason why, when the Deportation Special rolled into El Paso, the United States was desperate to solidify the US-Mexico border, transforming the figment of state planners' imaginations from a line on a map into a formidable barrier. The borderlands' capacious connections of human beings and commodities torn from the earth spanned empires and continents. The people who built those networks found their way in and across the imperial and economic networks that sought to dominate the planet's wealth and land. When migrants entered the United States near El Paso, or at least attempted to, they confronted world's most powerful empire's border policing regime. It was an empire on the rise, anxiously trying to regulate the territory, sovereignty, and people it claimed, and separate them from the ones it disdained.[7]

Kondo Johei, Tarashima Tokizo, and Hirakawa Kizo were forced aboard the Deportation Special at El Paso.[8] We do not know where they sat in the train, the looks they might have given or received from the other unfree travelers. Perhaps they sat in the places just vacated by a Mexican family, forced off the train here or a bit earlier, in Spofford Junction, en route to the border crossing at Eagle Pass. We can speculate about how a Korean passenger like Choi Si might have felt about being joined by three men whose country was now brutally occupying his own, but who, given their circumstances, seemed none the richer for it. We can speculate, too, about how they might have felt about being subject to the same ignominious treatment as one of Japan's colonial subjects.

In any event the three men had left Japan years earlier. Kondo Johei, with brown eyes, a pin mole on his cheek and a scar on his forehead, was thirty-six years old when he was loaded aboard the train. He left Japan ten years earlier. Tarashima Tokizo, who had black hair and a scar on the middle finger of his left hand, left Japan in 1913, when he was twenty-six. Hirakawa Kizo, 5'4" tall and who had a "medium dark complexion," literate in Japanese and Spanish and worked as a blacksmith and carpenter, left Japan in 1914, when he was twenty-seven. Hailing from diverse parts of the country, they only came to meet while working as seamen along the shipping lanes and in the ports of Latin America's Pacific Coast and the Caribbean basin.

Much as Chinese laborers displaced by imperialism and capitalist disruption had helped to lay rail infrastructures in the nineteenth-century United States and elsewhere, these Japanese men, displaced by rapid industrialization in southwestern Japan, worked in Latin America, setting up British imperial networks of infrastructure and oil. And like the Chinese, across North and South America, Japanese travelers, migrants, and residents were maligned. California newspaper editor V. S. McClatchy fumed against what he called the "Japanese menace." Japanese migrants, he said, posed economic danger, biological threat, and were racially unsuitable to American citizenship.[9] California senator James D. Phelan based much of his career on anti-Japanese animus, demanding to "Keep America White" and arguing that the Japanese would unmake the United States as a White Man's Country.[10]

The Golden State's governor, William Stephens, less vitriolic than Phelan, described the Japanese as the vanguard of the "teeming millions of the Orient." Stephens insisted he meant no disrespect to the Japanese, who led a "virile, progressive, and aggressive" empire, but felt that Californians believed Japanese were racially unassimilable, either through what he called a "social sense of repugnance" or "insuperable scientific hinderances."[11] In no small way they feared that the Japanese were too good at being settler colonists—yellow peril and model minority, conjoined. Japanese farmers established small but prosperous acreages across California and the Pacific states. They would steal the land that American settler colonists had themselves stolen. Regardless of how offensive American racial politics might be, for many Japanese hunger pressed harder and drove people from their homes.[12]

Japanese emigration policy under the Meiji government underwent significant changes in the second half of the nineteenth century in response to US and European imperialism, and as part of its own imperial ambitions. Indeed, the Meiji government, in power from 1868 until 1911, undertook a crash course in economic modernization to prevent succumbing to imperial domination in the ways that China had. Despite capitulating to unfavorable treaties, the Meiji state nevertheless limited the damage that Western powers inflicted, but at a cost. Rather than suffering transformation from without, Meiji leaders imposed revolution from above. They imported new technologies and subsidized industries with an emphasis on ship-building, weapons development, and other fields that accorded to their imperial aims.[13]

Agricultural modernization had its place too, but uprooted vast numbers of peasants who created new threats of disorder.[14]

Meiji emigration policy satisfied a number of governmental priorities. Many elites believed that the million or so displaced farmers were a Malthusian burden and a social threat, and emigration might serve as a safety valve that would lessen their disruptive presence, provide opportunity for their retraining, and be a source of income as they sent remittances home.[15] Officials hoped migrants would facilitate trade between Japan and their new host countries. And given Japanese colonial desires—in Korea and elsewhere—the migrant/colonists might make inroads for Japanese projects in new lands.[16] Between 1885 and 1924, 200,000 Japanese went to Hawai'i, and 180,000 to the US mainland. They were mostly young men in their twenties or thirties, contracted to labor in agriculture, or, on the mainland, in extractive industries or rail building. Estimates were that around 99 percent had been farmers or peasants, and many, but not all, were second sons, who would not inherit parents' land.[17] Nearly half came from Hiroshima, Okinawa, Kuamoto, and Fukuoka prefectures, all hard-hit by industrialization. Younger men followed the networks their predecessors laid.[18]

Kondo Johei was born in Kobe, Japan, around 1883. We know little of his youth, but it is likely that he, like so many others, was the second or third son of a farming family. He was partially literate in Japanese and in 1909 left home.[19] Tarashima Tokizo, who was to be deported along with Kondo Johei, was a bit younger. He was born in 1889, in Oita Ken, Japan, "not far from Nagasaki," he later explained. Tarashima had worked as a farmer and carpenter, and in 1913 he departed from home as a migrant worker.[20] Hirakawa Kizo, the third of the men, was born around 1889, with his birthplace recorded as Itsu, Kemo county, in Hiroshima prefecture. He worked as a blacksmith, was literate in Japanese, and over the course of his travels, learned to speak and write in Spanish too.[21]

Had the three left Japan a few years earlier, they would likely have gone to the United States. In 1906, fresh after Japan's victory in the Russo-Japanese War and after the United States and Japan negotiated a division of imperial access to Pacific lands (Korea to Japan, Hawai'i and the Philippines to the United States), a conflict, sparked around segregating Japanese from white children in San Francisco schools, escalated from a local to a national and then international incident.[22] This prompted the US government and Meiji diplomats to radically restrict Japanese migration. The turmoil led to two different executive orders in 1907 and culminated in the so-called Gentleman's Agreement, enacted in 1908. Like the Chinese Exclusion Act, it dramatically limited Japanese migration. But unlike the Exclusion Act, restrictions on Japanese mobility under the Gentleman's Agreement would largely be enforced by the Japanese government. Japanese officials would refuse to authorize all but the most prestigious of their citizens to enter the United States. Despite the profound racism leveled against Japan in the US media and popular culture, Meiji diplomats decided that it was in Japan's national interest to maintain comity with the Pacific's ascendant power.[23]

Their decision scarcely diminished the racism that Japanese migrants or their US-born citizen children faced. Indeed, anti-Japanese rhetoric and law only escalated. Much of it bespoke the incipient fears of a settler-colonial nation. In 1913, California passed an Alien Land Law prohibiting land ownership among people deemed racially ineligible for citizenship, and it was soon taken up by a dozen other western and border states. The law did not explicitly name the Japanese, but they were the clear target.[24] Prominent anti-Japanese newspaperman and agitator V. S. McClatchy articulated as clearly as anyone the settler-national anxiety, and perhaps projection, of a fear of being outsettled. In "expert" testimony before Congress, McClatchy fretted that Japanese settlers were "gradually securing control of the soil...[and] control of the markets," and would soon gain "a strangle hold on the economic development of the country itself." He was as keenly aware of how important the control of land could be. Fearful of competition with Japan as a rival settler empire, he quoted a Japanese newspaper from San Francisco. In addition to urging the Japanese to be thrifty and avoid gambling, it urged people to invest in land. "Land is the very life of the Japanese race in California. Land is the foundation of our development." Rather than seeing this—or the rest of the article—as an admirable statement of immigrant respectability, McClatchy took it as evidence of Japanese conspiratorial designs on the land that he and others had claimed as their own racial entitlement.[25] Another anti-Japanese Alien Land Law was passed in 1920.

While the first generation of US-based Japanese Americans focused attention on economic development, farming, and settlement rather than migrant labor after the so-called Gentleman's Agreement, Japanese emigrants, policymakers, and the shippers who profited from their travels were forced to look elsewhere. Canada would soon be closed by the Hayashi-Lemieux Agreement (which tracked closely with the Gentleman's Agreement). Indeed, Japanese migrants who had lived and worked in the US-Canada borderlands regularly crossed back and forth, but after 1909 they were no longer able to do so.[26] But Latin American countries remained open, and Kondo Johei, Tarashima Tokizo, and Hirakawa Kizo answered the call.[27] Before they left, Japanese officials inspected them for disabilities and examined their caste status and professional possibilities, found them unobjectionable, and stamped their passports for Peru.[28]

Like settler capitalists throughout the Americas in the nineteenth century, Peruvian planters sought cheap and tractable workers.[29] Chattel slavery had been abolished in 1854, but Peru, like many other nations, soon began contracting so-called Chinese coolies, some eighty-seven thousand of them, under highly restrictive labor contracts in export-oriented crops like cotton and sugar, but also as domestic servants, on railroads, in mines and guano fields, often replacing or working alongside convict labor forces.[30] But the so-called coolie trade to Peru ended in 1874, and the capitalist classes sought a replacement labor supply. But Peru's criollo elites—of largely European descent—disdained migrants of color. They desperately wanted European migrants to both do their labor and to "whiten" the country, which they felt was weighed down by Indigenous, Black, and now Asian populations. Unable to lure even the most desperate Europeans, elites reluctantly turned toward workers lower in global racial hierarchies: Japanese peasants displaced by capitalist industrialization.[31]

And so in 1898, 790 Japanese contract laborers arrived to work in Peruvian coastal plantations.[32] Conditions were brutal. They suffered corporal punishment, their payments were often withheld or went missing, and living conditions violated the terms of their contracts. Nearly 20 percent of the first arrivals died of disease within four years. On one plantation, just 30 of 226 workers were fit to work after three months. By 1909, 7.6 percent of migrants sent by emigration companies died in the midst of their contracts. Many protested, rebelled, and ran away; 6 percent returned to Japan, and 4 percent left Peru and continued traveling: to the United States, Bolivia, Argentina, and Mexico. Some remained in rural Peru, although many were denied the ability to purchase land. Of those who remained, most relocated to Lima or the nearby port city of Callao.[33]

Regardless of where they stayed, Japanese Peruvians were ghettoized and faced deep racism as well as labor restriction. Peruvian legislators played on racial animosities similar to those taking shape in the United States. The Japanese were denied access to broader Peruvian society and then attacked for refusing to assimilate.[34] Legislators proposed a Japanese Exclusion Act in 1903, and though it failed to pass, the sentiment was clear. Four years later, a Peruvian congressman in said that the Japanese were an "alien race dissimilar in habits, morals, and processes of thought" to real Peruvians. And in a remarkable statement, another Peruvian opined that Japanese were constitutionally geared for hard plantation labor, and they did not need much pay because their standard of living was "as low as that of highland Indians."[35]

This was the Peru that Kondo Johei, Tarashima Tokizo, and Hirakawa Kizo entered: legally open but hardly welcoming. Kondo Johei, who had almost certainly worked in agriculture before, worked on farms in Callao and Lima from 1909 until 1915 and periodically thereafter.[36] Tarashima Tokizo, who had worked as a carpenter in Japan, continued in that trade in Lima. Hirakawa Kizo, whose blacksmithing was a low-status profession in Japan, at least found decent work in Peru.

When whatever labor contracts they had signed were completed, and once they were no longer beholden to local forces, Kondo Johei, Tarashima Tokizo, and Hirakawa Kizo sought better opportunities. Despite ideas about Japanese Peruvian insularity, their ties extended into Callao's maritime networks. Indeed, each of the three transitioned from the relatively geographically stable worlds of Japanese Peru and began to transfer the fruits of their labor upward, from local agricultural capitalists to the bigger masters of the economic world: the European or US-based creditors on whom the Peruvian capitalists relied. US-based interests controlled the country's largest corporations. Italians controlled half of Peru's banking, Germans controlled half of sugar, and Japanese, despite racist impositions, played large roles in retail and cotton production. The British dominated Peruvian railways, mining, agriculture, manufacture, trade, and petroleum.[37]

Kondo, Tarashima, and Hirakawa soon joined Britain's polyglot maritime labor force, drawn from across its colonial domain.[38] It was a vast system, and their particular roles served British imperial maritime infrastructures of communication, and British-owned oil industries across Latin America. Starting in late 1916, Hirakawa "got employment on a cable-laying ship," supporting British telegraphy networks for about a year, "all over the coast of western South America, repairing and laying telegraph cables."[39] Next, he left that job and worked as a seaman on the British steamer *Retriever*. "We traveled all over the coast of Central and South America on that vessel," he said.[40] Kondo Johei also found better opportunities at sea. In 1915 he worked as a fireman and seaman on the British steamer *Azov*, traveling up and down South America's Pacific Coast.[41] Working conditions were difficult for all seamen, but worse for Asians than they were for European or British seamen. Asian workers were commonly contracted on "Lascar" or "Asiatic articles," guaranteeing worse conditions than what their whiter shipmates faced. Firemen, commonly regarded as having among the worst jobs, faced long and filthy hours of shoveling coal into blazing furnaces.[42]

Kondo, Hirakawa, and Tarashima were hardly the only Japanese who manned British-owned vessels during the First World War. Around one thousand Japanese seamen helped their country's ally fill its wartime labor shortage.[43] Following the lead of Meiji predecessors, one wartime Japanese diplomat opined that Japanese seamen would return eventually home, offering "Japanese maritime transportation industries their valuable experiences gained from foreign employment."[44] As much as they might learn, Japanese sailors were justly concerned about violence from British sailors. In 1908, 1911, and 1919, African, West Indian, Chinese and others faced mobs of British seamen who were offended by their presence.[45] The Japanese consul general in Britain, Mr. Yamazaki, warned that Japanese seamen should do their best to avoid being lambasted as a "Japanese Labor problem."[46] Whether or not they were heeding his advice, Kondo, Hirakawa, and Tarashima began to sour on the work, especially the low wages they received.

Just as they had departed poverty in Japan to try their chances in Peru, and as they seized better opportunities in British oil and shipping infrastructures, they escaped from racialized labor on British ships. "I deserted from the ship at Tampico, with a number of other Japanese," Kondo Johei later explained. Hirakawa, too, said he had landed at Tampico late in 1918. Both meant to find work sailing out of Tampico but had trouble signing on to a new ship.[47] And so, for a while, they called Tampico home.

Tampico, on the Caribbean coast of the Gulf of Mexico, was Mexico's most important center of oil refining and shipping, the nexus between Mexico's domestic energy and transport markets and the rest of the global economy.[48] It was a central node of British oil and shipping networks in the Americas. Callao, Peru—from whence Kondo, Tarashima, and Hirakawa departed— was another.[49] The Mexican oil industry started in the 1870s but accelerated dramatically around 1901.[50] Tampico, with its proximity to regional oilfields, a soon-to-be-developed deep water port, and links into the interior via the Mexican Central Railway, became an oil boom town.[51] Capital came from the United States and the UK, but the largest numbers of overseas arrivants were the Chinese who accompanied the American executives and oilmen as cooks, houseboys, and servants.[52] The city's population quadrupled in the eighteen years before Hirakawa, Kondo, and Tarashima landed.[53]

The three men disembarked into a bustling and highly stratified industrial port city. Tampico's richest foreigners, the owners and directors of its heavy industry, occupied the city's best properties, looking down from their elegant neighborhoods on Tampico Hill onto the lesser homes and peoples below.[54] Poorer workers in the lowlands packed into whatever structures they could devise, often along the overcrowded shores of the city's lagoons.[55] As one historian wrote: "Little except the high wages and the expectation to someday move on made up for the unhealthful conditions of living in Tampico's slums."[56] Racial hierarchies structured working and living conditions. Tampico's social geography reflected radical inequality, and as modern as the machinery in the oilfields and refineries may have been, labor relations replicated the coercions of Mexico's feudal *hacendado* system, long designed to control Indigenous agricultural laborers. It was hardly unheard of for bosses to use leg-stocks or draw on local police to help arrest or expel refractory oil industry workers.[57]

US-born and British oil workers were paid the highest wages, with room and board supplied by their companies. They were also segregated from even the highly skilled or educated Mexican-born workers, who resented the foreigners' special privileges—especially in the revolutionary period. Chinese were commonly paid the lowest wages of all: a Chinese kitchen chief, in charge of an important unit, earned the same as a Mexican stable peon, whose work was far less prestigious. At some camps, Chinese workers had their own quarters, separate from the Americans and Brits as well as the Mexican workers.[58]

Tarashima had been a carpenter in Japan and Peru, and found work doing the same in Tampico. Kondo and Hirakawa soon found jobs as firemen in the oil industry. Kondo said he worked for an "American Company," but didn't specify which one. Hirakawa worked for the *Compañía Transcontinental de Petróleo*. Hirakawa's new employer had recently been purchased by Jersey Standard (an offshoot of John D. Rockefeller's megalith Standard Oil and predecessor of Exxon), in that firm's aggressive effort to gain a foothold in the Mexican oil markets.[59] With this change of employment, the men's labor no longer contributed to British imperial networks of transport, telegraphy and oil. They were now part of the extended United States–based networks of oil, energy, and extractive capitalism.

During the revolution Tampico was a difficult place to be a foreigner—not least because the better-paid, and often better-treated, US and European workers and businessmen were renowned for their own racist condescension to Mexican nationals. The city's traditions of trade unionism took an antiforeign cast, and Tampico's workers organized and struck for better conditions, with much animus directed toward racist Americans and their employers.[60] Still, as Luey Mo learned in his own hard journey, many of the ugliest tendencies of revolutionary nationalism targeted the Chinese; it would be surprising if Japanese workers did not suffer the same.[61]

By late 1918, Hirakawa, Kondo, and Tarashima once again decided that better opportunities beckoned. According to Tarashima, Tampico's "wages are low and prices are awfully high."[62] Inflation had driven up the cost of living—which had affected the Huerto brothers as well as the Vallejo family—but rather than raising wages, oil men developed paternalistic welfare-capitalist measures which, given the contours of the era's racial nationalism, tended to exclude Japanese and other non-Mexican workers.[63] Tarashima had heard from Mexicans and Japanese alike that prices were lower and wages higher in the United States, and it only made sense to move. Kondo did not want to stay in Mexico either, where he said there "very few good chances … at present."[64] In January 1919 they ventured from Tampico to Juárez. Hirakawa Kizo bought a map in Chihuahua, which they would use to find their way from Juárez to Las Cruces, New Mexico.[65] The journey from Tampico to Juárez took a few days. As they approached the US border, the stakes of their travel grew more dire. They spent a day or two in Ciudad Juárez and weighed their options. It was no mystery why they decided to avoid trying to cross the border at one of El Paso's sanctioned checkpoints. It simply wouldn't work. The Japanese government had not stamped their passports for US entry, and their government, in collusion with the United States, had effectively criminalized their travel. This was in addition to the insult that El Paso's border delousing stations or the entry taxes posed.

They would need to seek other means of entry. Many Japanese migrants before them hid in water or oil tankers on trains crossing the border. Others tried to cross deeper in the desert, and further, they hoped, from US oversight.[66] All of the choices were risky. They might be forgotten in a train car locked from the outside; they might languish without water, as a Chinese man named Chin Lee did in 1914, in the fetid hold of a ship for five days.[67] They might get lost in the desert, increasingly weaponized by the US state as a means of control.[68] Still, despite the dangers, Kondo Johei, Tarashima Tokizo, and Hirakawa Kizo thought this was better than languishing in poverty in Tampico or shipping out at wages that were not worth their effort.

And so, rather than trying to travel on one of the bridges or river crossings that both connected and divided El Paso/Juárez, Hirakawa, Kondo, and Tarashima walked west. Other migrants hired people familiar with the land to help them cross. Indeed, extensive migrant smuggling networks provided aspiring travelers with detailed maps and directions and sources of support. But these men either did not have the contacts or the resources to access the clandestine networks, which many Chinese travelers, whose longer experiences with legal exclusion, had developed.[69] This may have explained their difficulties. As Tarashima Tokizo explained, they "proceeded quite a distance west"—about ten miles—which they thought was deep enough into the desert that they might safely cross the border. They then "crossed the line" into official US territory. Las Cruces, New Mexico, was about forty miles north of where they entered. It was reputed to have good farming land and a small Japanese population. They did not have any specific contacts among the Japanese farmers, they said, so it was a bit of a gamble—"we were not sure that we would get work."

In any case, Las Cruces would only be a way station. They intended to travel to New York, home of the largest port in United States, and ship out from there.[70] Contrary to the fears of anti-Japanese activists, these men had no interest in settling in the United States, buying land, or starting families. They simply wanted to "ship out from the United States," where seamen might negotiate better contracts. Despite considerable anti-Asian racism in US maritime unions, the 1915 La Folette Act offered seamen solid protections, which they could still use to their advantage.[71] "The wages paid seamen who ship out in other countries are very low...that was the reason for our action."[72] As Kondo explained, he "wanted to come to the United States and earn some money...and ship out again from the United States as a seaman, or fireman."[73] But that was not to be. They had scarcely crossed the border near Strauss, New Mexico, when a mounted watchman patrolling on horseback stopped them.[74] While many of the others aboard the Deportation Special, with whom they would soon sit, had been captured in the interior of the national territory, Kondo, Hirakawa, and Tarashima were arrested at the US border. As such, their capture presaged the militarization of the US-Mexico borderlands.

Kondo, Hirakawa, and Tarashima were not the first, and they were far from the last, to be stopped and arrested by border agents in the midst of a poorly marked desert. Indeed, it was the armed agents who patrolled, and in fact made real, the line across sand, river, and mountain that had been only a figment of US colonizers' cartographic imaginations. The US-Mexico border, only loosely policed after US military conquest in 1848, was by the early twentieth century increasingly fortified.[75] Members of ethnic Mexican communities, be they formally US or Mexican citizens, as well as Indigenous peoples throughout the borderlands, continued to traverse the region in their daily lives, for work, for pleasure, to see family and friends. Even as ranchers and growing numbers of US-based agriculturalists relied on migrant Mexican workers to tend and gather their crops for low wages—particularly after the railroads accelerated commodity and human travel through the region—other Americans, anxious to racially control the population, called for the better control of US territory and definition of the border. Well into the twentieth century the border was a geopolitical fiction. It would be materialized through violence, or by walls and fences, flimsy at first but sturdier later, which would effectively affix violence in space to control movement and territory.[76]

Officer Thomas, the armed and mounted watchman who arrested Hirakawa, Kondo, and Tarashima, was among the people who made the border real. Thomas's mission to transform the imaginary line into a genuine geopolitical barrier was, to be fair, difficult. The border he policed was to be both selectively porous and impervious to movement. He and his colleagues—initially in the Customs Service and later, after 1904, the Bureau of Immigration—were to maintain a nineteen-hundred-mile line between two sovereign nations, pierced by transborder Indigenous peoples' reservations, such as the Yaqui and Tohono O'odham nations. The mounted inspectors' main task was enforcing the 1882 Chinese Exclusion Act by stopping, detaining, interrogating, and deporting Chinese and other peoples who had been prevented from legal entry and resorted to covert measures. After the Gentleman's Agreement, Japanese travelers like Hirakawa, Kondo, and Tarashima, without stamped passports would also be arrested, and after 1917 so would anyone from any part of Asia, illiterate people, or those who breeched a host of new restrictions—including entering without formal inspection.

Yet Thomas and his fellow officers would permit capital and investments, along with the wealthy people in whose names they traveled, to move freely. So too would trucks, trains, and wagonloads of commodities flow unimpeded. Some workers—Mexican track workers, migrant agricultural forces, such as the Huerto and the Vallejos—might be permitted to travel if US business interests demanded them, but their lives would be forever precarious. Immigration as well as customs agents, then, had to decide which people, which trucks, and which trains to inspect, which might impede traffic and raise local ire, and which could pass. They set up checkpoints in the transborder communities at El Paso, Laredo, Nogales, and many more, the towns and cities that served as main points of crossing. Despite federal funding for new guards and checkpoints, official reports lamented that it was never enough: there were "rowboats, carriage roads, pathways and mountain trails, throughout this broad expanse of imaginary line, all passable and all being used for surreptitious entry into the United States."[77] And so agents like Thomas went out on armed, mobile patrols, to police or, in military terms, to project force, further afield from established bases at principal thoroughfares.

The US Border Patrol was created five years after Hirakawa, Kondo, and Tarashima were arrested. It would enforce these laws and conduct sweeps across the region. And while its funding may have been less than its agents desired, the machinery they developed was fearsome. The agency built on the tradition of men like Thomas and, to borrow a term from critical policing scholar Micol Seigel, the "violence work" they performed.[78] Jeff Miller, a former El Paso police chief, was hired as the first mounted Chinese immigration agent "because," as one report had it, "he could ride and shoot."[79] In the final analysis, violence was the truth of the border, the ultimate basis on which sovereign control over national territories and populations would be enforced.

The earliest Border Patrol officers tended to be quite good at that, particularly when it was leveled at Mexican and other communities of color. Nearly a quarter of the first Border Patrol staff had worked in the Chinese mounted patrols, and other early Border Patrol agents had backgrounds in the Texas Rangers or related settler-paramilitary forces renowned for their violence, particularly against ethnic Mexicans, US citizens or not.[80] Indeed, the Rangers were the most storied—or notorious—agents of an expansive borderland formation of settler violence that drew on citizen vigilantes as much as it did on appointed state agents. Indeed, the borderlands were beset by recurrent waves of vigilante murders and anti-Mexican terror, which reached one peak in the 1910s.[81]

Over the next century, Border Patrol agents would devise policy and practice to control migration and commodity travel. Local and regional imperatives differed, and conditions in California were different than in Arizona or Texas, yet increasingly dictated by an assertive federal bureaucracy.[82] They were called upon to decide which migrants might have sanction from the politically connected ranchers and growers whose profits, like much of the US southwestern economy, relied on those exploitable laborers. Moreover, immigration agents developed capacious definitions of where, precisely, the border lay, and expanded the spaces of their own jurisdiction—on occasion, even (if illegally) into Mexico, but also well into the US interior.[83]

In the early years of the century, local deputies and customs agents had devised makeshift solutions to control migrants, local workers, and the circulation of goods through relatively coherent borderland communities. But after 1924 federal agents asserted vast powers to regulate human and material travel, patrolling, arresting, detaining, and deporting peoples. The border only became real when the state developed the material, infrastructural, and violent means to enforce it, and the procedures to determine its variable speeds and qualities.[84] Porousness for precariously sanctioned workers and taxable commodities, imperviousness for those deemed racial or politically inadmissible.

And so, though it was still in the process of formation, on February 19, 1919, when Mounted Watchman Thomas apprehended Kondo Johei, Tarashima Tokizo, and Hirakawa Kizo, they met the hard border, and it became very real indeed. We do not know the means by which Thomas captured them men. We don't know if Thomas drew a pistol or leveled a rifle, if he bound them with ropes or shackles, or if he asked them to accompany him to a nearby detention center, and they went along gently. In any case, they were caught in the US carceral state's border detention regime. Some detained migrants would be imprisoned in private homes or facilities, because entrepreneurial borderlands knew there was good money to be made on caging people, especially if they skimped on provisions. For-profit immigrant detention would continue to grow in the coming years, of course.[85] Despite the trend, Kondo, Tarashima, and Hirakawa were caged at the El Paso County jail.[86]

Once the three were physically detained, the paperwork could begin.

Banal administrative procedure wrote the violence of border enforcement in paper, ink, and electricity rather than in rope, bullets, or blood. It was no less forceful for the change. Immigration officials in El Paso wired applications for arrest warrants to Washington, DC, over telegraph cables similar to the ones that Hirakawa had laid along the Peruvian Coast. Much as the immigrant descendants of Chinese rail road workers would be deported on the Deportation Special (like the *traquero* Vallejo family and the Huerto brothers had been) imperial capitalist technologies they had built were now turned against them. The warrants charged Hirakawa, Kondo, and Tarashima with as many violations as Thomas and agents in the El Paso office could think of: hailing from a country in the Asiatic Exclusion Zone; as likely to become public charges; entering at a nonspecified location; and entering without inspection. And because they were Japanese and therefore subject to the Gentleman's Agreement, inspectors were intent on punishing the men for violating the passport act.[87]

When they arrived at the jail, Hirakawa, Kondo, and Tarashima would have been forced to strip and bathe in the noxious mix of kerosene, vinegar, and gasoline that they had foregone at the Santa Fe Street bridge. Three years earlier, a devastating fire had torn through the jail and killed twenty-seven prisoners, caused by that precise "sanitizing" mixture. There was no specific disaster the day that Hirakawa, Kondo, and Tarashima were caged at the El Paso jail, but the paint, blistered from the intense heat three years earlier, likely remained. If the walls and bars had been painted over, it was probably done with less care than the coverup after the fire, which exonerated the city's Anglo powers but enflamed Mexican resentment.[88] Hirakawa, Kondo, and Tarashima had to contend with the jail's local and immediate power structure, with its staff of city officials, as well as the trustee system, in which clever or brutal prisoners received special privileges while acting as guards and keepers of the rest.[89] The jail would have been run according to West Texas definitions of white hierarchy, though where the Japanese men sat—literally, where they would have bunked among its cells and tiers—in the traditionally white/Black/Mexican segregated structure is unclear. Their Spanish was better than their English, to whatever extent that may have influenced their experience.

The three languished at the jail until April, when they were sent before the US commissioner and grand jury proceedings for violating the passport act.[90] They expressed deep contrition for their actions and told officials that they had learned a valuable lesson about American power. Tarashima Tokizo

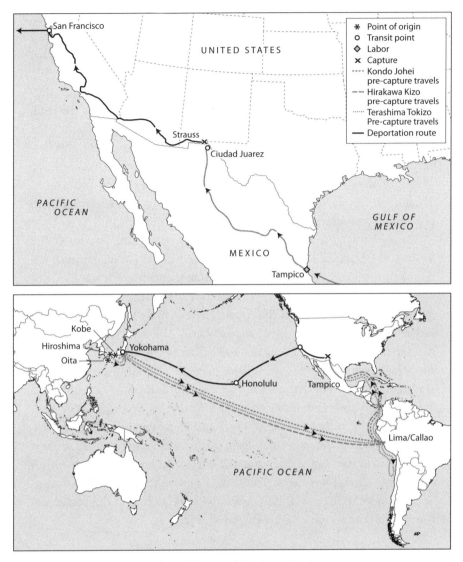

MAP II. Kondo Johei, Tarashima Tokizo, and Hirakawa Kizo's routes.

appealed to the government agents' mercy. "We have done a very bad thing in smuggling into the United States," he said, "and I hope you will be as kind with us as you can."[91] All of the men hoped that they might be simply removed back to Mexico. Tarashima said that he and the others would never dare to enter the United States again. "I have gained through this experience, and I am in no danger of ever trying to enter the United States again." Having attempted to placate the investigators, he expressed his "hope that I can ship out as a sailor in Tampico, Mexico."[92] But that was not to be. Each pled guilty and was sentenced to three months in jail.[93]

In their hearings, they neglected to mention an additional lesson they had also surely learned. Anyone denied the legal ability to cross the land, and whose travel was thereby criminalized, should not attempt to cross the border by themselves. They would do better to hire professionals in the border-crossing clandestine networks, with technical skills and local knowledge of the region's paths and byways. It was too much for amateurs like them. The border, they learned, would produce markets and agents of transgression every bit as professional as the officials who tried to stop them.

And so it was, three months after their arrest, Tarashima Tokizo, Kondo Johei, and Hirakawa Kizo were led from the El Paso jail to the train station. Perhaps it was Officer Thomas who took them; maybe it was someone else. They had traveled much of the breadth of the planet, helping to expand Japanese wealth influence in the Americas. They had suffered but survived racism and exploitation in Peru, a site of Latin American comprador colonial capitalism. They left the relative safe harbor of Japanese Peru and joined the polyglot world of Britain's maritime network, extending the reach while slowing the process of that empire's decline. When prospects dimmed and better options beckoned, they worked for US oil in Mexico, a nation in rebellion against the lure and power of US-dominated capitalism. When conditions deteriorated, they moved on again, to the colossus to the north. But the US-Mexico border, previously a figment of colonial imaginations only then becoming real, stopped them. And now, they were aboard the Deportation Special, under armed guard, moving west with their fellow unfree passengers, toward California and the great Pacific beyond.

THIRTEEN

Angel Island

THE FINAL DETENTION AT ANGEL ISLAND, and then the transfer to
the transpacific voyage, were the last nodes and legs of their globe-spanning
carceral journey. The infrastructure and mechanics of transpacific travel
relied on international collaboration and diplomatic relations between
the United States and the nations on the far sides of the Pacific. They also
required partnerships, sometimes amicable, sometimes less so, between the
nation-states and the private shipping firms who provided the actual steamships for travel. The agents of each nation and each firm treated the deportees
as little more than costly, cumbersome, occasionally disruptive baggage. The
crowded bunks in transpacific steerage were dank and claustrophobic, not
unlike the prisons or asylums many had just left. There was little air or light,
but beyond their portholes lay vast networks and world-historical struggles.
When the people facing removal climbed from fetid holds into the light of
day, and returned to the countries and governments they had left long before,
they often entered new if different carceral states, specific to the needs, fears,
and policing systems of these sites in the world's political economy. The leaders of their homelands understood the new carceral systems—mental institutions, jails, and police regimes—as useful, and also as proof of their own
modernity.

As the train traversed the US-Mexico borderlands toward the Pacific, it
replicated the US journey of westward expansion, colonization and conquest,
following the rails built to convey minerals and goods and the people whose
labor would make the land profitable. For the fifty miles between Yuma,
Arizona, and Calexico, California, the Deportation Special ran on the
Mexican side of the border, where the fastest and most convenient rail lines
lay. The track's primary purpose was to facilitate regional capital circulation,

more so than to affirm national sovereignties. According to Leo Stanley, the train was "considered sealed" while south of the border, although Mexican officials came aboard to keep an eye on things. Stanley, ever the voyeur, marveled at the bright lights and bustle of Mexican saloons, an alluring consumer sin zone for white American men, in contrast to the quieter US side.[1]

The day after they left El Paso, the train gathered four new unfree passengers in Tucson, and arrived a day later in Fresno, in California's Central Valley, to collect more.[2] Police had arrested Frederick Harold Berger for drunkenness and found an IWW card in his pocket. After four months in the Fresno County Jail, immigration officials packed him into the Deportation Special traveling north to San Francisco, where he would await removal.[3] The train rattled northward, through the enormously wealthy agribusiness of California's Central Valley, and past migrant workers and *traqueros'* homes similar to the ones where the Vallejo and Huerto families had lived. As they approached the coast, they more or less joined the Southern Pacific Railroad's Mission Line, retracing the outposts established by Spanish along Alta California, ending in San Francisco's Mission Bay neighborhood.

Long home to Ohlone Costanoan peoples, the rich tidal lowland and its residents faced cataclysmic change as Junípero Serra established the Mission San Francisco de Asís in 1776, which, like its partners to the south, tried to harvest Native souls, land, and unfree labor for God and Spain.[4] It changed again in the wake of Anglo-American arrival and the Gold Rush, when swaths of overland travelers met ships full of hopeful miners from across the Pacific. The Gold Rush saw San Francisco's population multiply by more than twenty-five times, and ships soon crowded the bay's once placid tidewaters.[5]

Sail gave way to steam, and Mission Bay became an industrial and transport hub, particularly after 1870, when the Central Pacific, Southern Pacific, and Western Pacific Railroads won 150 acres in Mission Bay in exchange for constructing a rail terminal.[6] The fifteen tracks would serve the Golden State's commercial future, while the adobe-like stucco finish, tile roof, and mission towers paid symbolic homage to a fantasy Spanish past, and a double erasure of Ohlone peoples.[7] The station's construction for the 1915 Panama-Pacific Exposition, and its use as a transfer point for people facing expulsion, was the infrastructural materialization of a US imperial transhemispheric "Open Door" project. It controlled the flows of people, goods, ideas, and profits in multiple directions: to the south, across the Americas; and

to the west, across and beyond the breadth of the Pacific.[8] Having dominated most of North America, the United States was now trying wrest control of the Pacific from imperial rivals Spain, the Netherlands, England, and
Japan. It wanted to take what the Pacific from what Oceanian scholars Epeli
Hau'ofa (Tongan) and Lisa Kahaleole Hall (Kanaka Maoli) called "our Sea
of Islands" and establish an American empire of bases.[9]

The Pacific Ocean is best understood as not a single body of water, but as
"multiple seas, cultures, and peoples…a historical assemblage of smaller elements: interlocking navigations, migrations, and settlements within regions"
linked through the overlapping transits between them.[10] The United States
could no more contain the Pacific worlds or travels through them than it
could seize a wave in its fists. Still, by subduing islands and their peoples, and
by thrashing its fists, the Pacific became a "theater of America's sovereignty,
the site of its skirmishes and wars that settled its sovereign status among the
crumbling European states of the Atlantic world," and so was vital to the
United States rise as a global power.[11]

When the Deportation Special finally arrived at the station at Third and
Townsend in San Francisco, deportees clambered from the train and found
their bags. As the immigration agents went over their paperwork, John, the
Pullman car porter, along with the other full-time Southern Pacific staff,
would have begun the train's wind-down operations: sweeping the floors,
pulling the bedding, checking the bars that ran across the windows, emp-
tying the trash and detritus that had accumulated over the last nine days'
close living, and then stocking and prepping for the next round. When those
labors were through, perhaps John's wife, who saw him off when he left a
month earlier, returned to the station to welcome him home.

The terminal in Hoboken was designed to quarantine unfree passengers
from their surroundings; there is no indication that the Southern Pacific
Station at Third and Townsend in San Francisco was similarly contained.
Immigration guards, likely joined by a contingent stationed at Angel Island,
would have to rely on shackles or the threat of violence as they loaded Luey
Mo, Tarashima Tokizo, Frederick Berger, and the others onto streetcars from
the train station to the waterfront at Pier 7. The ferry from San Francisco to
Angel Island ran a few times each day.[12]

The Immigration Station and detention center on Angel Island opened in
1910. It replaced the notorious detention shed on Pier 40 that Pacific Mail

FIGURE 12. Angel Island Immigration Station, 1915. *Source:* Henry DeYoung Collection, Korean American Digital Archive, USC Digital Library, University of Southern California.

Steamship operated for the prior thirty years as the primary site where Asian migrants were detained and interrogated. As one former prisoner put it, the detention shed was "another name for a 'Chinese jail.' I have visited quite a few jails and State prisons in this country, but have never seen any place half so bad.... We were treated like a group of animals, and we were fed on the floor. Kicking and swearing by the white man in charge was not a rare thing. I was not surprised when one morning, a friend pointed out to me the place where a heartbroken Chinaman had hanged himself after forth [*sic*] months' imprisonment in this dreadful dungeon, thus to end his agony and the shameful outrage."[13]

Until Angel Island opened, Pacific Mail Steamship Service had the material spaces, haphazard as they were, to detain immigrants: buildings on docks and hulks barely afloat, over which the state claimed no jurisdiction. This was convenient, because Pacific Mail's detention shed, like its ships, was legally held not to be on American soil. As one report put it, imprisoned Chinese were considered "to be constructively on board."[14] Migrants were kept in these liminal nonstate zones, whose ambiguous designation prevented them from making claims on the nation's spatially based law. Housed by private firms, guarded by private guards, and kept in private detention centers, the firms used their financial as well as coercive capacity to help police national borders.[15]

By 1910 officials believed it was in the state's best interest to assume control over the facilities and decided on Angel Island. The detention center on Angel Island sat within a ten-acre fenced enclosure on the island's north side. Its eighteen buildings sprawled up the hillside facing Raccoon Straits, a windy stretch of water that, along with an enclosing fence, enabled the facilities' doubled isolation—a prison on an island—keeping migrants separate from the soldiers stationed at the island's two other facilities.[16] Many had passed through Angel Island when they first arrived in North America. Sometimes called the Ellis Island of the West, Asian migrants were interrogated and incarcerated as officials tried to enforce the breadth of regulatory and exclusionary immigration laws. Even those who hadn't been to Angel Island were nonetheless affected by it. If they had taken circuitous routes to make a clandestine entry across arduous land borders, it was because they knew how difficult and degrading Angel Island's processes had become.

As the deportees arrived, officials in the administration building processed their paperwork, drawing on the methods that deportation agent Leo Russel had refined. It is unclear if staff at Angel Island used the same colored tags for bodies and baggage that their colleagues did at Ellis Island, but it would stand to reason that they did. Next, they would be directed to the quarters deemed appropriate to their race and sex. Unlike the constricted space of the Deportation Special, there was ample room in Angel Island's carceral facilities to permit strident segregation, reflecting what its administrators saw the irreducible differences among variously racialized peoples across the Pacific world, and also the collective racialization imposed by the US state under the category of "Asian."[17] So unless there was room in the hospital ward, Luey Mo would have been housed with Chinese travelers. Tarashima Tokizo and Kondo Johei would have bunked with Japanese travelers, and Salig Ram with others South Asian Indians. Sex also determined different locations, and ethnicity and class also influenced the quality of treatment people were afforded—though some elite women complained at being housed with prostitutes and other supposedly disreputable women.[18] Perhaps unsurprisingly, given the centrality of the Chinese in the US immigration apparatus, the "Chinese building" was the largest in the complex, and its dormitory could hold some three hundred men at a time. Chinese men and women were kept apart.[19]

Though it was rarer, Europeans were also detained on the island, either as part of the number of new arrivals fleeing the Russian Revolution or the European war. Others, like Frederick Berger, were imprisoned for their political radicalism—and European anarchists and communists, along with those deemed mad, were locked there before their own eastbound, overland journey to Ellis Island. So were Germans or Austro-Hungarians identified as enemy aliens during the war.[20] It is unclear how long people typically waited at Angel Island before they were deported. Available data does not distinguish between travelers who were investigated and deported (more accurately, debarred) upon arriving at Angel Island after a transpacific or coastal journey, and those residents, like Luey Mo, whose deportation from the US interior used Angel Island as a final way station in the removal journey.[21] It could be days, or it could be weeks. Given that many of the legal battles and much of the logistical work of arranging passage and such was completed before deportees were loaded on the westbound Deportation Special, it seems likely that their wait at Angel Island would have been somewhat shorter.

No matter how long they waited, Angel Island's detention facilities were "crowded, noisy, unsanitary, and sparsely furnished," worse for Chinese and other Asian prisoners than for Europeans. Days followed a "mundane routine of endless waiting that was occasionally interrupted by periods of anxiety, even terror."[22] There were modest recreation facilities (these too were racially segregated), but detainees spent much of their of time in their dormitories. Rough canvas bunks were stacked two or three tiers high, and the density of both vertical and horizontal space left little room for socializing. People might pass time in sitting rooms, but these might as easily be repurposed into guards' offices when the need arose.[23] When fully occupied, there was little room to move. "It was like being in prison," recalled Mock Ging Sing. "Everyone suffered great pain and mental anguish." Everyone was affected by the facility: "The living space was so small and so confining, it just made us feel more depressed."[24] Deportation was not legally understood to be a punishment, but it was hard to see confinement at Angel Island as anything else. Kamechiyo Takahashi, a young Japanese woman in 1917, was shocked: "I had never seen such a prison-like place as Angel Island." She wondered at the indignity of why she "had to be kept in a prison?" In 1921 a French woman was reported to protest "Oh, they put me in pree-zohn," and threatened suicide: "give me a rope, I will kheel myself!"[25]

Meals gave shape to largely formless days. Records from 1917 explain that breakfast was served at 7:15 a.m., lunch at 1:00 p.m., and dinner at 4:45 p.m.

Between six hundred and seven hundred people ate at each meal. When it was crowded, detainees had only thirty minutes before the next shift of diners would arrive. Meals were also racially segregated.[26] Detainees killed time playing dominoes, reading, mulling over their cases and, in some cases, carving poems into the wooden walls of the building.[27] One man named Mr. Lowe explained: "I had nothing to do there. During the day, we stared at the scenery beyond the barbed wire—the sea and the clouds that were separated from us."[28]

New arrivals who had just crossed the Pacific were apprehensive about their pending investigations and whether the answers they gave to the inspectors' many and confusing questions would permit them to enter the United States.[29] The anxieties of people in the midst of removal were different, but no less real. In 1917, Mary Bamford worried that many Chinese women would be sold into sexual slavery on return to Hong Kong, and the women themselves surely had few illusions about the prospects that awaited them, whatever they might hold.[30] Chinese men and boys would have their own concerns; most had left China for a reason and feared an ignominious return. Some preferred death—the French woman's despair, her dialect's caricature notwithstanding, was no exaggeration. In 1931, Lester Tom Lee witnessed the suicide of a man who "knew that he was going to be deported...and... would have been seen as a failure" by his family and community. As we have seen, Chinese men often cut their queues and donned collared shirts and such to demonstrate their Westernization and suitability for American life.[31] At Angel Island, Gerald Won saw one man, despondent, hang himself with a necktie.[32]

However long they may have waited, once arrangements with the shipping firms were finalized and their ship arrived, their time at Angel Island was up. If procedures were similar to those at Ellis Island, a guard would enter the holding rooms with a batch of cards and read out the names of the people who would be removed. As Theodore Irwin put it, it ended "the long tedium of waiting for the complex machine to get into gear, pick them up and hoist them out."[33] They would bid farewell to the others who remained and walk down the pathways from the main building and onto the Angel Island ferry. They would cross the choppy bay to San Francisco's waterfront, and be forced aboard the ships that would carry them across the Pacific. Yet leaving detention at Angel Island hardly meant an end to imprisonment; boarding the transpacific steamships simply signaled a new phase of their mobile unfreedom, one more leg in what now became a globe-crossing carceral journey. Even as they traversed the vast Pacific, the ships they boarded became new sites of confinement. And for many, arrival in the lands of their birth signaled not freedom and the benefits of citizenship—the unmet promise of the nation-state system—but new regimes of state containment and imperial control.

The ships were different, of course, with varying characteristics, designs, speed, tonnage, and so forth. But all the unfree passengers could expect to stay in the ships' worst and cheapest steerage quarters. This was the case if they were being deported at the US Immigration Bureau's expense, which would spend as little as possible. And it was the same if the shipping firms, having been found liable for bringing a supposedly unfit passenger in the first place, were paying for the trip.[34]

Kondo Johei, Tarashima Tokizo, and Hirakawa Kizo were among the thirteen Japanese people who were taken off of Angel Island and loaded aboard the *Tenyo Maru*, of the Toyo Kisen Kaisha Line. Choi Si, the young Korean man arrested in Nebraska for violating his student status by working for wages, would travel with them, bound for Japanese-occupied Korea. When Choi Si boarded the *Tenyo Maru*, he left the jurisdiction of the sprawling US prison and immigrant detention system. But as a Korean national, he immediately returned to conditions of Japanese colonial control. Six more Chinese people were being deported to Hong Kong. Another unfree passenger on the vessel was bound for Singapore.[35] When Angel Island's immigration agents oversaw the transfer of these men and women onto the TKK ships in San Francisco, they took part in the complex transimperial interactions taking shape in the Pacific world.[36] In 1908, TKK launched the *Tenyo Maru*. Built in Nagasaki's Mitsubishi shipyards, the 575-foot-long vessel could cross the Pacific twice as fast the older generation of steamers and signified new stakes in the struggle among the Pacific's imperial powers.[37] Its wealthier 275 first-class passengers and 54 second-class passengers might enjoy time in an opulently upholstered reading room, with a nursery, darkroom, barber shop, while the opium den harkened back to an earlier generation of transpacific ships.[38]

Though its name bespoke comfort (*Tenyo Maru* meant, roughly, Heavenly Ocean), it could hardly have felt that way when Kondo Johei, Tarashima Tokizo, Hirakawa Kizo, and Choi Si, with the others facing removal, descended into the ship's steerage quarters. It had room for 800 people, but return trips from the Americas tended to run below capacity, so they likely joined around 560 others.[39] The imbalance of passenger service between the Americas and Asia was one reason that TKK would gladly sell tickets to the US Immigration Bureau and support its deportation efforts. Profiting off of forced removal and assuring comity between imperial partners by regulating poor peoples' movement: this was something on which the imperial powers could agree.

Steerage accommodation on Pacific vessels would have been familiar to the passengers from the Deportation Special, though many, no doubt, would have preferred to forget. While they had been separated by race at Angel Island, class status kept steerage passengers together, and apart from the rest of the ship. The few authors who reflected on Pacific steerage of the era tended to discuss the journey to the Americas, but Maedakō Hiroichirō wrote of returning travelers' experience. He described a "sense of longing, retaining preconceptions about Japan, the trip, and returning to life in Japan." Hiroichirō's narrator continued:

> In each of the beds, the men and women with healthy bodies were tormented with loneliness, the weight of "time" that occupied their future prospects almost suffocated them, without a thought as to how they would pass it, while they were granted a short release from their instinct of manual labor, they just didn't know what to do and simply stared absent-mindedly at the stained ceiling or at the top sailcloth bed that was plump with the body of a human being.[40]

If passengers with healthy bodies experienced mental anguish on this crossing, we can speculate that people like Luey Mo, with cognitive ailments, suffered greatly. Luey Mo, like other unwell passengers, was supposed to be barred from taking part in shipboard leisure, or even in staying in the steerage cabin of the Pacific Mail's *SS Ecuador*. When deportation agents were arranging Luey Mo's transit, a Pacific Mail employee explained how mentally ill passengers taxed the conditions of steerage-class deportation. Steerage aboard the *Ecuador* consisted of "one large room forward containing one hundred berths; large room aft containing forty seven berths; and a so-called women's room containing twelve berths, and," he continued, "for this reason it is indeed extremely difficult to take care of a violently insane person." Pacific Mail "cannot place [Luey Mo] in the hospital," which he said would be "contrary to law." But—still seeking the deportation business—the agent said Pacific Mail "should indeed like to help you in this case but if the passenger is violently insane [, the steamship company] can hardly see our way clear to do so."[41] It would cost Pacific Mail more than it was worth.

As a result, the Immigration Bureau had to hire the ship's surgeon, Vincent P. Mulligan, at a rate of three dollars per day, to attend to Luey Mo and another unwell passenger en route from San Francisco to Hong Kong.[42] Despite the Pacific Mail agent's warning, Luey Mo did indeed spend the forty-two-day voyage to Hong Kong in *Ecuador*'s steerage.[43] Mulligan likely administered heavily sedation for the voyage. As aboard the deportation train, the physician served the purpose of quelling the disruption that people with cognitive differences posed.

The transpacific journey was broken up by a stop in Hawai'i. Luey Mo departed San Francisco aboard the *Ecuador* on February 7. It arrived in Honolulu some eight days later. Hawai'i had been the literal center of US strategy in the Pacific since at least 1887, when a collective of US missionaries and sugar magnates forced Hawai'i's King Kalakaua at gunpoint to sign what became known as the "Bayonet Constitution," and radically diminished Native Hawaiian sovereignty—already transformed by generations of imperialist intervention and capitalist incursion—and placed power in the hands of settler plantation owners and businessmen. In 1893, after Queen Lili'uokalani and her supporters challenged the Bayonet Constitution's legitimacy, sugar magnates and US Marines militarily suppressed Hawaiian sovereignty movements, leading to annexation in 1898 and seizure as a formal US Territory in 1900.[44] Signs of this history might have been visible to the *Ecuador*'s passengers, in stretches of cane fields or pineapple plantations, as nearby ships took on new cargo, or in glimpses of the nearby and recently completed drydocks and naval facilities at Pearl Harbor.

The *Ecuador* left Honolulu and spent thirteen days traveling to Yokohama. Tarashima Tokizo, Kondo Johei, and Hirakawa Kizo, who had traveled on the *Tenyo Maru*, would disembark and meet with attending authorities in Yokohama, though records are silent about how they might have made their way from the ship to their home prefectures.[45] Japanese passengers aboard the *Ecuador* would have disembarked too, while others might have remained on the *Ecuador* for another day's sailing to Kobe. Their reception at home would have been ambivalent, at best. Some saw Japanese emigration within a national project to incorporate new skills and gain income through trade and remittances, but many Japanese viewed emigrants as unpatriotic cowards who fled conscription, or as "trash," who could not survive in Japanese culture.[46] For those who felt this way, Kondo, Tarashima, and Hirakawa's return after deportation—apparent failure at overseas ventures—would have been especially shameful.

For the previous nine months, Choi Si had been locked in multiple United States facilities. US immigration officials had not been able complete the logistical arrangement of passage from San Francisco to Busan, Korea, because this fell within what the United States accepted as Japan's regional sphere of influence. Instead, the immigration officials arranged for the TKK line to manage Choi Si's "maintenance...while awaiting trans-shipment."[47] Choi Si was returning to a maelstrom of anticolonial uprising and repression. He debarked from the *Tenyo Maru* in Kobe, and the housing conditions TKK provided for this Korean man were unlikely to be generous. In June 1919, Japanese forces were in the thick of crushing the Korean nationalist uprisings that began the previous March. Choi Si had not shown any of Chang Yill Lee's political sensibilities in Nebraska, but it would have been impossible to escape the turmoil after transshipment through Kobe, Busan, and then, when he returned to his home in the mountainous provinces of the country's far northeast. Whatever his political disposition, and however it may have changed, he must have looked forward to being reunited with his parents, his wife, and the daughter he hadn't seen since she was an infant. He could have only hoped that the conditions of life and everyday occupation by Japan had not destroyed his family, as it had many others.

The *Ecuador* continued on for another five days' voyage from Kobe to Shanghai, to unload and gather more cargo and passengers. Four days later, it arrived in Manila, where it would remain at dock for five more days. Luey Mo almost certainly would have been prohibited from departing the ship while docked. It would take two more days to reach Hong Kong.[48] And so, forty-two days after leaving San Francisco—and forty-eight days after leaving the Southwestern Insane Asylum in San Antonio—Luey Mo arrived in Hong Kong.

Vincent P. Mulligan had been instructed to deliver Luey Mo to his uncle, Luey Mee Moo, at the Sing Chong Lung company, on Wing Lock Street in Hong Kong's Sheung Wan neighborhood.[49] But instead, Mulligan signed Luey Mo over to the captain superintendent of police, who "took him into their custody and declined to allow him to be accompanied by any custodian of our selection, although we stood ready to furnish one." Mulligan informed the Hong Kong police that Luey Mo required special attention, and local authorities promised that he would be sent to the properly specified destination.[50]

Luey Mo dropped from the Immigration Bureau's paper trail at this point. We cannot know how the captain superintendent of police treated the returning thirty-three-year-old man. Neither can we know the extent to which his demons returned with him on the Deportation Special, and the transpacific voyage, back to Hong Kong, whence he had departed many years earlier. We can hope that Luey Mo might have found some comfort or familiarity in his return to Hong Kong. We can hope that his uncle would have the interest and the capacity to offer care. But given the stigma that attended to madness, and difficulties families faced looking after mentally unwell members, it seems likely that Luey Mo would have been sent to Hong Kong's woefully overcrowded asylum, or else to have been forcibly moved—again—to the Canton Refuge for the Insane in Fong Tsuen, opened by American missionaries.[51] And so, in some ways, being locked in mainland China's first mental institution, designed by an American, might have drawn familiar ghosts to Luey Mo.

Having attended to Luey Mo, Dr. Mulligan was also supposed to ensure that another passenger was transshipped on another Pacific Mail ship from Hong Kong to Calcutta.[52] The *Ecuador* would go no further, instead retracing its route to gather passengers and commodities before crossing from Hawai'i, to San Francisco once more. But other vessels would continue the westbound deportation journey and force South Asians' expulsion from North America and delivery to the lands they had left.

Sundar Singh and Salig Ram saw little in the way of welcome through their transpacific and Indian Ocean routes on their return to South Asia. Sikh migrants captured in the United States were fed into a transimperial carceral network that spanned from the Pacific Northwest, across the Pacific Ocean, and through British imperial nodes in the Far East and Indian Ocean worlds. Aided by both military and police forces, its reach extended into the Punjabi hinterlands, where migrants remained under colonial surveillance. The paths Sundar Singh, Surup Singh, and Salig Ram traveled were set through the empire's response to the Ghadrite revolutionaries and *Komagata Maru* radicals. During the Great War, officials adopted a counterinsurgent footing to inspect Sikhs returning from North America, or who were being transshipped through East Asian ports. They feared not only anticolonial working-class radicalism but also that German agents had returning Sikhs to rebel against British authority.[53]

Imperial officials differed over the degree to which returning Sikhs and Punjabis should be investigated and detained. But even relative moderates were concerned that "Sikhs who went to Canada as loyal subjects of the Raj" may have been radicalized by their time in North America and exposure to the "provocations of the 'Ghadr' party." Radical thought, one officer believed, threatened to "convert…them…into blood-thirsty fanatical revolutionaries."[54] Far from being dupes, however, many travelers were dedicated political actors in deliberative and increasingly direct action against a government whose legitimacy they doubted.[55] Returning Sikhs confronted an extensive and multifaceted carceral and surveillance network.[56] Punjabi officers stationed at Calcutta would offer support and better local knowledge of Punjabi anti-imperial movements.[57] Plainclothes and uniformed officers conducted interrogations and investigations, and particularly targeted working-class Punjabi Sikhs.[58]

Historian Suchetana Chattopadhyay described a ship's arrival in Calcutta in early 1915. The vessel held 175 Punjabi passengers from North America, some of whom were suspected of being radical anticolonial agents. A sizable contingent of armed officers met them at the dock; customs agents scrutinized their documents and rifled through their belongings for weapons or seditious literature. All Punjabi men's names were registered, and they were told to leave Calcutta within four days and report to an officer immediately on arrival in Ludhiana.[59] According to Chattopadhyay, particularly rebellious returnees were "forced to board the 'special' train to Punjab," which she called "a prison on wheels."[60] While the levels of scrutiny diminished somewhat after 1915, surveillance of Punjabis and Sikhs returning from North America remained in place through 1919.[61] After facing this kind of scrutiny, Surup Singh and the others returned to communities embroiled in counterinsurgent politics and repression. As migrants returning from North American revolutionary hotbeds, they surely felt the weight of suspicion. In March 1915 the governor of Punjab demanded support in rooting out any potential revolutionary factions, and conservative Sikh leaders cooperated. In April 1915 the government began conspiracy trials that would last for two years.[62]

Surup Singh and his traveling companions were among the approximately 3,200 returned migrants in Punjab at the time. We cannot know if they were among the 175 facing conspiracy trials and bore the weight resentfully or, perhaps more likely, if they were among the witnesses and shifted its burden by testifying against others. Twenty of the accused revolutionaries were hanged, seventy-six transported to the Andaman Islands Convict colony for life, and fifty-eight sentenced to shorter terms within India.[63] Hundreds were imprisoned without trial; many were restricted to their villages. For many, wartime confinement to their villages meant they were unable to work or farm—they could neither buy seeds nor conduct business in larger commercial centers. Those lucky enough to own a plot of land might lease it to someone else.[64] One hopes that they had been able to save some money from their itinerant North American labors, or the village arrest would have been exceedingly difficult. Surup Singh and the rest, like the other returning Sikh migrants, would have remained under varying degrees of surveillance and regimes of restricted movement in the villages where they had been born.

Back in San Francisco, the Deportation Special began to get under way once more. Clerks in Washington, DC, sent telegrams to regional offices and received word about new people who had been drawn into the deportation regime, and would be ready for the next time one of Leo Russel or Edwin Kline's "deportation parties" came through town.

Epilogue

IN JULY 1916 THE DEPORTATION SPECIAL left Chicago without Henry
Weiss. The polylingual deportation agent had been unwell when the train
stopped in Denver. He had worked through injuries before, but now his condition deteriorated. One of his first tasks in developing the deportation system had been to assess the medical services provided to deportees aboard
Hamburg American Line ships, and had a doctor been available now, Weiss
might have lived. Instead, he arrived in Chicago with a perforation in his
small intestine that led to general peritonitis. His wife left Seattle to be with
him, but her train was too slow. He died the day before she got there.

Seattle's Commissioner Sergeant, with whom Weiss had worked for many
years, lobbied for the Immigration Bureau to pay Weiss's medical costs and
for the return of his body to his family. The requests were denied. The Nickel
Plate Railroad's passenger agent was more generous. He extended professional courtesy to the man with whom his firm had worked over the past
two years, and gave Weiss's body free passage on this final journey west from
Chicago to San Francisco, where he would be buried.[1] The Weiss family was
distraught. Henry Weiss's eldest daughter, Dorothy, accused the bureau of
working her father to death. "There is not a doubt but what his premature
death at the age of fifty, was due to the fact of his continuous travelling for the
government," she fumed.[2] Despite his ailments, Weiss "insisted on remaining
with the car." According to his daughter, her father's "sense of duty…was so
omnipotent that he truly gave his life up for it."[3]

The family's mourning was compounded by financial desperation. Henry
Weiss's ongoing government service provided a salary that kept his family just one accident away from poverty—that accident had now come to
pass. Dorothy begged for the bureau's help. "Surely…the Bureau must feel
the urgency of our appeal. Our father's life can never be given back to us

again but cannot some reimbursement be made for the enormous expense incurred through his dying in the city of Chicago?" Her mother's travel to Chicago cost $300, embalming an additional $150, on top of $1,215 for funeral expenses.[4] Weiss's two youngest children were still in school. His wife was unwell. Dorothy, age twenty-two, was now the family's sole source of support. Dorothy Weiss, in essence, informed the Immigration Bureau that her father's death threatened to make them into public charges, like so many who rode her father's train. Her appeal for the government's support when a family's principal breadwinner was lost sounded a familiar refrain.

> What I desire to ask of you (realizing…that the "Government" is no individual who can feel a heart throb) is, can "specific authority" *be made* to help defray our great expense, now that our main means of support is cut off, in lieu of the fact that my father gave thirteen years of work—enthusiastic, conscientious, and splendid work, to his employer, the "Government."[5]

But no funds would be forthcoming. According to the acting commissioner general, no money had "been appropriated by Congress for defraying expenses of that kind." Much as he would like to, he regretted that he could make no changes "as a matter of sentiment."[6]

Dorothy Weiss asked for financial support based on the sacrifice that her father, and his family, had made to the Immigration Bureau and to the country. But sentiment was no match for institutional structure. Long rebuffed from promotions and the transfers he sought, but finally recognized for his work in expelling immigrants less fortunate than himself, Henry Weiss died as a cog in the machine he helped build. Still, since Dorothy Weiss was born on one side of an imaginary but increasingly important line—she was a citizen, understood as white—she could apply for to the government for relief. It would hardly have been enough, though, and whatever actions she may have taken, it is clear that three years after Weiss's death, the family remained in dire straits. In 1919, Dorothy still had her father's immigrant inspector badge. A sentimental person might have kept it as a memento of the career that meant so much to her father. But Dorothy, having seen the value of sentiment, asked to return the badge for some sort of cash refund. Once more, her request was denied. But she was told to return the badge as soon as possible.[7]

The early twentieth-century American deportation regime created a punitive governmental infrastructure that swept within and extended beyond the nation's borders. It outsourced inspection to shipping firms and overseas consular officials, sifted through the arriving population, and then scoured the nation's expansive range of prisons, jails, hospitals, and welfare institutions in search of people to cast out. Its history belies America's celebrated immigration tale. Instead of arriving in a new land, overcoming tribulations through hard work, and earning a place in the national mythos, deportees saw their options foreclosed. Once captured and marked by disciplinary institutions, they lost whatever version of American freedom they might have hoped to claim, including the settler-colonial goal of land ownership, or even more fundamentally, control over their own bodies and labors. It is a story of leg irons, not bootstraps. Loaded onto deportation trains, the wide-open spaces of the American renown rushed by through barred windows.

On the Deportation Special migrants from the United States' Pacific colonial spheres and undesirable Europeans and others from the Atlantic world had been deported along a looping east-west circuit. The Chinese Exclusion Acts set the federal legal template and Southern Pacific's prison cars provided the material foundation, but the deportation regime would continue to transform over the 1920s and across the rest of the century. The 1924 Johnson-Reed Act set finite and racially explicit national origins quotas and enabled the most restrictive immigration policy yet devised, and a 1929 act explicitly criminalized undocumented entry.

By the 1930s, deportation increasingly followed a southerly vector. Pinoys from the Philippines would be excluded, Mexicans were deported in massive numbers, and US racial politics came to newly value European migrants and their children. As white ethnic organizations mobilized and garnered political power within the New Deal order, deportable Europeans whose families might be torn apart by removal appealed to administrative pity and were increasingly allowed to remain, as they slowly shed ethnic identification for less differentiated whiteness.[8] People from Asia had fewer opportunities. When they arose, they were contingent on US geopolitical goals and were always retractable. Thanks to the US alliance with China in World War II, Chinese migrants were no longer considered ineligible for citizenship. At the same time, the anti-Japanese Gentlemen's Agreement remained in place, and in 1942 the Immigration Bureau offered its trains and personnel to transfer Japanese Americans into internment camps.

When World War II ended, immigration officials focused their attention on the US–Mexico border. Mexicans could cross the lengthy if still hazily defined land border at many places and fill the massive demands for their labor, but authorities applied new counterinsurgency doctrine to migrant policing, replete with roundups, checkpoints, and mobile task forces across the borderlands. Mexican "illegal aliens" became the most frequently deported peoples.[9] Much as they had with the innovation of the train car, immigration officers took advantage of new technologies for removal. The first internal deportation airlift took place aboard an Air Force B-25 bomber in late 1946. The deportation regime soon began contracting with private airlines, but military ties remained. In June 1951 the Flying Tiger Line, founded by ex–Air Force pilots, made nightly runs from Southern California to Guadalajara. In its first year Flying Tiger helped deport more than thirty-four thousand people.[10] The rail lines, of course, tried to regain the lost income. "We are very anxious to again participate in the handling of this Mexican deport business," railroad agents wrote. They dropped their rates and promised guards to entice the bureau back.[11] It was not to be. As the postwar highways system and air travel infrastructures took shape, the age of rail was passing. Deportation planes were joined by Pacific Greyhound buses and for a while by boatlifts aboard squalid cargo ships.[12]

Automotive deportation required less centralized administrative planning and allowed more local discretion among border patrol officers in removing Mexican nationals.[13] Moreover, the Immigration and Naturalization Service would develop its own transportation fleet, lessening its reliance on private firms. Still, in the 1950s some train lines maintained their coercive transport portfolio and, under the auspices of Termination and Relocation Acts, helped move Indigenous peoples from their reservations to impoverished urban neighborhoods and low-paying jobs.[14]

Over the next half century, immigration policy continued to be pulled between employers' desire for low-wage labor, restrictionists' calls for ethnonational protection, and geopolitical and imperial aims, as Operation Wetback in 1954, Operation Intercept in 1969, and Operation Gatekeeper in 1994, among others, reveal.[15] The Hart-Celler Act of 1965 was lauded as a civil rights victory for rescinding the racist national origins quotas set in 1924, and though its limits on Mexican migration effectively criminalized hundreds of thousands of people who came to work in the country each year, its family reunification component would eventually permit nonquota migrants to legally arrive.[16]

Even as migrants fleeing from US Cold War enemies were granted refugee status, American law tried to constrain migrants' political and religious lives.[17] Red Scares repressed domestic labor struggles and anticolonial insur-

FIGURE 13. Migrants facing deportation in the age of automobility, 1977. *Source: Los Angeles Times* Photographic Archive, Charles E. Young Research Library Special Collections, University of California at Los Angeles.

gencies; in the post–Cold War era, heightened Islamophobia helped to justify an endless and ill-defined War on Terror.[18] For all of the procedures that the US deportation regime refined, the administrative devices it developed, and the technologies it deployed to either prevent or facilitate mobility, it did nothing to remedy the structural conditions that drove migration to begin with. Global inequalities set in motion more than a century earlier persisted, and still produce a racialized world of haves and have-nots. Migrants who suffered expulsion, or their children, or their children's children, return to the US border with great frequency.

But in the neoliberal era, even the American beneficiaries of global capitalism cannot help but feel unsteady. Many Americans' livelihoods and securities were undermined by deindustrialization, outsourcing, and spirals of automation. They have tried to stabilize the political economic sands shifting beneath them by building fortified walls on national borders. But walls against human movement are relentlessly ineffective and do nothing to stem the more profoundly disruptive flows of capital. Rather than blaming neoliberalism for outsourcing work, mechanization for cutting jobs, or executives for seeking ever new tax shelters, and thus a dwindling tax base for services, some politicians find racial scapegoating an easier sell to explain their constituents' woes.

Twenty-first-century American politicians have sought to secure political legitimacy and to guarantee the United States as a settler nation through a late modern carceral system that conjoined the anti-Black tenets of mass incarceration and anti-immigrant border policing and detention.[19] Mass incarceration and mass deportation became bipartisan political efforts, driven by Republicans since the Nixon years but embraced by Democrats under Bill Clinton, even as those governments undermined the welfare state on which their citizens relied and which they jealously guarded from racialized "welfare queens" and migrants whom they accused of sapping government resources. Neoliberal calls for "small government" notwithstanding, the United States is a land with, by a recent count, 1,719 state prisons, 102 federal prisons, 2,259 detention centers for minors, 3,286 local jails, 79 jails on Native American reservations, and more than 200 immigrant detention facilities—all connected by a sprawling network of government and profit-driven transport fleets.

In order to rid the nation of those on whom this antistate state refuses to spend money, Republicans and Democrats have together built the most comprehensive deportation regime the world has ever known, expelling more than four hundred thousand people each year. The twenty-first-century infrastructures of capture and of forced mobility draw on enormously sophisticated and seemingly invisible algorithmic big-data analyses and logistical systems but are executed through very familiar forms of racism, violence, and chaos.[20] And though many twenty-first-century critics decry the public unaccountability of proliferating privately operated immigration detention facilities, for-profit detention preceded neoliberalism's generalized privatization. Its roots are in the early twentieth century, and they continue to sustain the modern national, and international, immigration infrastructure.[21]

Still, in 2016 many US voters perceived the deportation regime as insufficient. Donald Trump made border control and a militarized deportation force his signature campaign issue.[22] Trump's conjuration of Mexican rapists and criminal aliens, however, was a blatant falsehood. Very few people deported as criminals in recent years have been convicted of violent crimes: 2 percent for sexual assault, 2 percent for robbery, and 6 percent for assault. Those facing deportation have been largely vulnerable workers whose principal offense was "illegal entry," stemming from the criminalization of spatial status and lack of documentation. The next largest group of "criminal" deportees were convicted of traffic offenses. Fewer than half of the people deported from the United States in 2012 were convicted of any crime at all.[23] Still, Trump's racial xenophobia tapped into and amplified his supporters' sense of aggrieved white racial entitlement, which in January 2021 took shape in nothing less than insurrectionary attacks on the US Capitol and on the practice of democracy itself.[24]

Despite the modern deportation regime's fearsome effectiveness at intimidation, capture, and expulsion, its structural violence, while terrifying to migrant communities, had become relatively invisible to most white audiences. The catharsis that white mobs enjoyed a century earlier was nowhere to be found in Barack Obama's deportation regime. When Donald Trump championed a fearsome Deportation Force, and White House press secretary Sean Spicer promised to "take the shackles off" ICE and Border Patrol, they offered a characteristically Trumpian rhetorical inversion: Border Patrol and ICE agents, these men implied, were the real victims of the liberal state, not the children in cages or the refugees denied asylum.[25] Trumpist authoritarian populism invoked police action unencumbered by law, rejecting the putative softness of a feminine administrative state in favor of angrier, masculinist, expressive forms. Beyond the well-documented rise in racist hate crimes, the Trumpist "zero tolerance" immigration and deportation regime has combined the infliction of suffering—most famously, the intentional removal of children from their parents, including breastfeeding infants from their mothers—with the indifference that often characterizes large institutions. Despite widespread criticism, and two years after the policy publicly ended, at the time of this writing, more than five hundred children remain without their parents.[26]

Yet other people push back. Despite the tragedy of the global COVID-19 pandemic and the radical isolation it has prompted, and despite the worst death tolls among the United States working classes and people of color, massive social movements have taken to the streets in 2020 against police violence, the carceral state, and the inequalities they guarantee. Protestors have challenged the idea that the Democratic Party's progressive neoliberalism or the Republican Party's authoritarian racial nationalism are the only possibilities. Democratic politics expressing abiding faith in fragile norms and adherence to procedural civility through the administrative state's reports, investigations, and impeachment have been largely stymied by the Republican Party's pursuit of a rightist, sovereign, untrammeled "unitary executive" to enact its will.

FIGURE 14. Postcard from the American Committee for the Protection of the Foreign Born, 1932. *Source:* RG 85, Entry 9, 54809/General, National Archives and Records Administration, Washington, DC.

As a result, it has fallen to women of color, and often queer Black and Latinx and Indigenous women in and around the Movement for Black Lives and related movements, to show other Americans how to demand democracy in the face of authoritarianism. For women of color it is a struggle older than the country itself.[27] Protests against the police killings of George Floyd and Breonna Taylor, among the latest in a long line, have drawn on interrelated but not synonymous traditions of Black liberation, liberal and antiracist feminisms, queer rights struggles, Indigenous sovereignty and decolonization, religious freedom, workers' rights, environmental justice, amid calls to abolish the police, prisons, and to dismantle ICE. They have contributed to sanctuary movements that are both urgent and expansive.[28] They build upon earlier generations of mass struggle that made connections that many are only now coming to understand.

Indeed, in 1932—another era of mass movement and the age of the deportation train—the American Committee for the Protection of the Foreign Born issued this remarkable postcard.[29] The committee's supporters sent the cards to the Department of Labor, calling for "the release of all foreign born held for deportation." The image on the front of the card showed an octopus in a top hat—symbolizing the capitalism of what today might be called "the 1 percent"—with tentacles that stretch menacingly toward a multiethnic crowd of men, women, and children. The tentacles bear the words "Wage Cuts," "Frame Up," "Deportations," and, partially obscured, "Lynch," while signs, hanging around the necks of the crowds, indicate the locations to which they would be expelled: "To China," "To Hungary," and "To Italy." And at the edge of the image, the words: "Native and Foreign Born, Negro and White—Unite!"[30] The card offered a remarkable assessment of racial capitalism and the carceral state as a single organism in which state and corporate interests used economic exploitation, domestic racist terror, and nativist international deportation to control American life.[31]

Today's movements expand upon these traditions, and coalesce around an ethic of mutualism and care that transcend acceptance of vast wealth disparities, are bigger than the heteropatriarchal family, more expansive than race, and, most crucially, cannot be bound by the nation. They honor Indigenous sovereignties, insisting that there be no walls or bans on stolen lands.[32] Together, these movements celebrate interconnection and solidarities within the human and the more-than-human world, rather than the brittle infrastructures of extraction, externalization, foreclosure, expulsion, or exclusion. The octopus looming at the center of the postcard is with us still, and fierce. But we know it lashes out in fear, because it is surrounded by far vaster forces.

NOTES

INTRODUCTION

1. John Mone, "Deported Immigrants Get on "ICE Air," *Associated Press*, December 17, 2018, www.youtube.com/watch?v=O2AxkpM9Nsg; Nick Miroff, "ICE Air: Shackled Deportees, Air Freshener and Cheers. America's One-Way Trip Out," *Washington Post*, August 11, 2019; and Adam Goodman, "Bananas North, Deportees South: Punishment, Profits, and the Human Costs of the Business of Deportation," *Journal of American History* (March 2020): 949–974, 972.

2. Mone, "Deported Immigrants Get on 'ICE Air'"; Miroff, "ICE Air: Shackled Deportees, Air Freshener and Cheers"; Nancy Hiemstra, *Detain and Deport: The Chaotic U.S. Immigration Enforcement Regime* (Athens: University of Georgia Press, 2019), 114–116; William Walters, "Flight of the Deported: Aircraft, Deportation, and Politics," *Geopolitics* 21, no. 2 (2016): 435–458; and University of Washington Center for Human Rights, "Hidden in Plain Sight: ICE Air and the Machinery of Mass Deportation," UW Center for Human Rights Report, April 23, 2019, http://jsis.washington.edu/humanrights/2019/04/23/ice-air/, accessed February 21, 2020.

3. Joe Welsh, Bill Howes, and Kevin J. Holland, *The Cars of Pullman* (Minneapolis, MN: Voyageur Press, 2010), 9.

4. Amy G. Richter, *Home on the Rails: Women, the Railroad, and the Rise of Public Domesticity* (Chapel Hill: University of North Carolina Press, 2005).

5. Correspondence and blueprints from J. N. Haynes, Lehigh Valley Railroad Company, to P. S. Millspaugh, April 23, 1934, in 56193/283, RG 85, Entry 9, National Archives and Records Administration (NARA)–Washington, DC. The modifications included additional storage space for bedding.

6. Leo Stanley, "To Ellis Island and Back," 18–19, Leo L. Stanley Papers, Box 1, Vol. 2, SC 070, Stanford University Library Special Collections, Stanford, CA.

7. Stanley, "To Ellis Island and Back," 32–33.

8. Stanley, "To Ellis Island and Back," 39.

9. Theodore Irwin, *Strange Passage* (New York: Harrison Smith and Rob-

ert Hass, 1935), 11. Freelance journalist and author Theodore Irwin wrote books and articles in popular magazines on a wide array of topics. His wife, Rita, was a social worker, an author, and an advocate of birth control for women as a means of family planning and sexual freedom. Early in his professional career, and in the context of considerable anti-Semitism, he changed his surname from Isaacs to Irwin. *Strange Passage* is very much linked with the political vision that US communism promised in the 1930s, although in later life he disavowed membership in the Communist Party. The novel's most sympathetic characters attacked both the liberal integrationist and conservative exclusionary variants of American capitalism but also anarchism and proclaimed the Soviet Union as an ideal workers' state. The novel championed artistic expression as a means of politics and of contributing to the world, while conveying a kind of openness to ethnic difference. That said, *Strange Passage* offered regrettable, if predictable, portrayals of Black characters; and Asian and Mexican characters were nonexistent in the novel. See also Michael F. Scully, *The Never-Ending Revival: Rounder Records and the Folk Alliance* (Urbana: University of Illinois Press, 2008), 61–63.

10. Irwin, *Strange Passage*, 12.

11. My sense of assemblages is guided by Bruno Latour, *Aramis: Or, The Love of Technology*, trans. Catherine Porter (Cambridge, MA: Harvard University Press, 1994), and similar to Saskia Sassen's identification of complex systems that combine "persons, networks, and machines with no obvious center." Saskia Sassen, *Expulsions: Brutality and Complexity in the Global Economy* (Cambridge, MA: Harvard University Press, 2014), 10. Thanks to Mark Finnane's formulation of security in the lecture "Keeping Them Out and Keeping Them In: Enemies, Aliens and Criminals in Australian Security History," University of Western Australia, November 6, 2014.

12. Claudio Lomnitz, *Death and the Idea of Mexico* (New York: Zone Books, 2005), 58.

13. On deportation's legal precedents in forced Indian removal, see Daniel Kanstroom, *Deportation Nation: Outsiders in American History* (Cambridge, MA: Harvard University Press, 2007), 63–74. On links between forced Indian removal and Asian expulsion in Northern California, see Jean Pfaelzer, *Driven Out: The Forgotten War against Chinese Americans* (Berkeley: University of California Press, 2007), esp. 343–346; and on exclusion within the development of the modern state, see Erika Lee, *At America's Gates: Chinese Immigration during the Exclusion Era, 1882–1943* (Chapel Hill: University of North Carolina Press, 2003), 10.

14. Matthew Frye Jacobson, *Barbarian Virtues: The United States Encounters Foreign Peoples at Home and Abroad* (New York: Hill and Wang, 2000), 5, 17, 61. My usage of the term "governmental" draws on its common adjectival usage but also the broadly Foucauldian concept as "the ensemble constituted by the institutions, procedures, analyses, and reflections, the calculations and tactics that permit the exercise of this quite specific, albeit very complex form of power, which has, as its principle target, population; as its main form of knowledge, political economy; and, as its essential technical means, apparatuses of security." Michel

Foucault, *Securité, territoire, population: Cours au Collège de France, 1977–1978* (Paris: Seuil, 2004), 111, translated by and quoted in Bob Jessop, "From Micro-Powers to Governmentality: Foucault's Work on Statehood, State Formation, Statecraft, and State Power," *Political Geography* 26 (2007): 34–40, 37. My understanding of racial capitalism as a world racial economic system is inspired by Cedric J. Robinson, *Black Marxism: The Making of the Black Radical Tradition* (Chapel Hill: University of North Carolina Press, 2000).

15. *Annual Report of the Commissioner General of Immigration, United States Department of Labor, FY ending June 1919* (Washington, DC: Government Printing Office, 1919) (hereafter *AR-CGI* with relevant year), p. 17.

16. *AR-CGI 1931*, Table 106, pp. 256–257.

17. Calculated from *AR-CGI 1917*, Table XVIIa, p. 84; *AR-CGI 1918*, Table XVIIa, p. 150; *AR-CGI 1919*, Table XVIIa, pp. 181–182; *AR-CGI 1920*, Table XVIIa, pp. 196–198; and *AR-CGI 1931*, Table 106, pp. 256–257.

18. Deirdre M. Moloney, *National Insecurities: Immigrants and U.S. Deportation Policy since 1882* (Chapel Hill: University of North Carolina Press, 2012), Appendix B, 264. The Department of Homeland Security defines "removal" as "the compulsory and confirmed movement of an inadmissible or deportable alien out of the United States based on an order of removal. An alien who is removed has administrative or criminal consequences placed on subsequent reentry owing to the fact of the removal." The DHS defines "return" as "the confirmed movement of an inadmissible or deportable alien out of the United States not based on an order of removal." By this count, 646,751 were *removed* from 1914 to 1945, and 292,705 were *returned* between 1927 (when this was first recorded) and 1945. Department of Homeland Security, *2015 Yearbook of Immigration Statistics,* www.dhs.gov/immigration-statistics/yearbook/2015/table39; and Department of Homeland Security, "Table 39. Aliens Removed or Returned, FY1892-2018," in *Yearbook of Immigration Statistics 2018,* www.dhs.gov/immigration-statistics/yearbook/2018/table39.

19. Nancy Heimstra, "Deportation and Detention: Interdisciplinary Perspective, Multi-Scalar Approaches, and New Methodological Tools," *Migration Studies* 4, no. 3 (November 2016): 1–14; Cindy Hahamovitch, *No Man's Land: Jamaican Guestworkers in America and the Global History of Deportable Labor* (Princeton, NJ: Princeton University Press, 2011); Tanya Maria Golash-Boza, *Deported: Immigrant Policing, Disposable Labor, and Global Capitalism* (New York: New York University Press, 2015); Torrie Hester, "Deportability and the Carceral State," *Journal of American History* (2015): 141–151, and Torrie Hester, *Deportation: The Origins of U.S. Policy* (Philadelphia: University of Pennsylvania Press, 2017); David Manuel Hernández, "Pursuant to Deportation: Latinos and Immigrant Detention," *Latino Studies*, no. 6 (2008): 35–63, and "Surrogates and Subcontractors: Flexibility and Obscurity in U.S. Immigrant Detention," in Critical Ethnic Studies Collective, eds., *Critical Ethnic Studies: A Reader* (Durham, NC: Duke University Press, 2016); Mae M. Ngai, *Impossible Subjects: Illegal Aliens and the Making of Modern America* (Princeton, NJ: Princeton University

Press, 2004); Elliott Young, *Alien Nation: Chinese Migration in the Americas from the Coolie Era through World War II* (Chapel Hill: University of North Carolina Press, 2014); Kanstroom, *Deportation Nation*; Francisco E. Balderrama and Raymond Rodríguez, *Decade of Betrayal: Mexican Repatriation in the 1930s* (Albuquerque: University of New Mexico Press, 2006); Camille Guerin-Gonzales, *Mexican Workers and the American Dream: Immigration, Repatriation, and California Farm Labor, 1900–1939* (New Brunswick, NJ: Rutgers University Press, 1994); Kitty Calavita, *Inside the State: The Bracero Program, Immigration, and the I.N.S.* (New York: Routledge, 1992); and Adam Goodman, *Deportation Machine: America's Long History of Expelling Immigrants* (Princeton, NJ: Princeton University Press, 2020).

20. Department of Homeland Security, "Table 39: Aliens Removed or Returned, FY1892-2018," *Yearbook of Immigration Statistics 2018*, www.dhs .gov/immigration-statistics/yearbook/2018/table39; and Goodman, *Deportation Machine*, 1.

21. Total removals were lower in 2017 than 2016, largely due to fewer entries and a processing backlog. Interior arrests, detentions, and removal have increased. According to its 2017 report, "ICE removed 25 percent more aliens arrested during interior enforcement activities in FY2017 compared to the previous year." It also incarcerated 139,553 people in the interior, a 42 percent increase over in 2016. US Immigration and Customs Enforcement, *Fiscal Year 2017 ICE Enforcement and Removal Operations Report*, www.ice.gov/sites/default/files/documents/ Report/2017/iceEndOfYearFY2017.pdf.

22. Edwin E. Grant, "Scum from the Melting-Pot," *American Journal of Sociology* 30, no. 6 (May 1925): 641–651, esp. 641.

23. Harry H. Laughlin, *The Eugenical Aspects of Deportation, Hearings before the Committee on Immigration and Naturalization* (Washington, DC: Government Printing Office, 1928), 3.

24. Ruben Oppenheimer, National Commission on Law Observance and Enforcement, "Report on the Enforcement of the Deportation Laws of the United States" (Washington, DC: Government Printing Office, 1931), 4.

25. Within a substantial literature, see Immanuel Wallerstein, *The Modern World System*, vol. 1, *Capitalist Agriculture and the Origins of the European World-Economy in the Sixteenth Century* (New York: Academic Press, 1974); Christopher Chase-Dunn and Peter Grimes, "World-Systems Analysis," *Annual Review of Sociology* 21 (1995): 388–389, 398; and Chamsy el-Ojeili, "Reflections on Wallerstein: The Modern World System, Four Decades On," *Critical Sociology* 41, no. 5 (2015): 679–700.

26. Among other works, and hardly the most strident, see Christian Wolmar, *The Great Railroad Revolution: The History of Trains in America* (New York: Public Affairs, 2012), xix.

27. Quoted in Jeffrey Marcos Garcilazo, *Traqueros: Mexican Railroad Workers in the United States, 1870–1930* (Denton: University of North Texas Press, 2012), 15.

28. The literature on the history of rail is massive, but see Oscar Osburn Win-

ther, *The Transportation Frontier: Trans-Mississippi West, 1865–1890* (Albuquerque: University of New Mexico Press, 1964); Richard J. Orsi, *Sunset Limited: The Southern Pacific Railroad and the Development of the American West, 1850–1930* (Berkeley: University of California Press, 2005); Maury Klein, *Union Pacific: Vols. I and II, 1862–1893, and 1894–1969* (Minneapolis: University of Minnesota Press, 2006); William Cronon, *Nature's Metropolis: Chicago and the Great West* (New York: W. W. Norton, 1992); Richter, *Home on the Rails*; Richard White, *Railroaded: The Transcontinentals and the Making of Modern America* (New York: W. W. Norton, 2011); and Manu Karuka, *Empire's Tracks: Indigenous Nations, Chinese Workers, and the Transcontinental Railroad* (Oakland: University of California Press, 2019). Karuka in particular offers a vital definition of what he calls "railroad colonialism": "Territorial expansion through financial logics and corporate organization, using unfree imported laborers, blending the economic and military functions of the state, materializing in construction projects across the colonized world. Railroad colonialism was central to the co-constitutions of the modern imperial state and finance capitalism, in the latter half of the nineteenth-century" (Karuka, *Empire's Tracks*, xiv).

29. Ryan Dearinger, *The Filth of Progress: Immigrants, Americans, and the Building of Canals and Railroads in the West* (Oakland: University of California Press, 2016).

30. Zaragosa Vargas, *Proletarians of the North: A History of Mexican Industrial Workers in Detroit and the Midwest, 1917–1933* (Berkeley: University of California Press, 1993), 34–35; Barbara A. Driscoll, *The Tracks North: The Railroad Bracero Program of World War II* (Austin: University of Texas Press, 1999), 14–17; and Garcilazo, *Traqueros*, 36.

31. The image is reproduced in Grey Brechin, *Imperial San Francisco: Urban Power, Earthly Ruin* (Berkeley: University of California Press, 1999), 8.

32. Depicted in Kelly Lytle Hernández, *City of Inmates: Conquest, Rebellion, and the Rise of Human Caging in Los Angeles, 1771–1965* (Chapel Hill: University of North Carolina Press, 2017), 11.

33. John Ford, dir., *The Iron Horse* (William Fox, 1924). Literature on the historical production of whiteness is substantial, but see David R. Roediger, *The Wages of Whiteness: Race and the Making of the American Working Class* (New York: Verso, 1991); Noel Ignatiev, *How the Irish Became White* (New York: Routledge, 1995); Neil Foley, *The White Scourge: Mexican, Blacks, and Poor Whites in Texas Cotton Culture* (Berkeley: University of California Press, 1997); Matthew Frye Jacobson, *Whiteness of a Different Color: European Immigrants and the Alchemy of Race* (Cambridge, MA: Harvard University Press, 1998); Ian F. Haney López, *White by Law: The Legal Construction of Race* (New York: New York University Press, 1998); Grace Elizabeth Hale, *Making Whiteness: The Culture of Segregation in the South, 1890–1940* (New York: Vintage, 1998); and more broadly, Michael Omi and Howard Winant, *Racial Formation in the United States: From the 1960s to the 1990s*, 2nd edition (New York: Routledge, 1994).

34. Lorenzo Veracini differentiates between settlers (who carry their sover-

eignty with them) and migrants (who do not) in *The Settler Colonial Present* (New York: Palgrave Macmillan, 2015), 32–48. On the relationship between political economics of unemployment and anticriminal deportation over time, see Ryan D. King, Michael Massoglia, and Christopher Uggen, "Employment and Exile: U.S. Criminal Deportations, 1908–2005," *American Journal of Sociology* 117, no. 6 (2012): 1786–1825.

35. Ethan Blue, "Strange Passages: Carceral Mobility and the Liminal in the Catastrophic History of American Deportation," *National Identities* 17, no. 2 (2015): 175–194; and Hernández, *City of Inmates*, 7–9.

36. On the individual level, arrest was akin to the process that Allan Feldman identified as "individualizing disorder" rather than assessing its structurally driven, and governmentally imposed, components. Allan Feldman, *Formations of Violence: The Narrative of the Body and Political Terror in Northern Ireland* (Chicago: University of Chicago Press, 1991), 109.

37. Alexander G. Weheliye, *Habeas Viscus: Racializing Assemblages, Biopolitics, and Black Feminist Theories of the Human* (Durham, NC: Duke University Press, 2014), esp. 2–4, 11–13.

38. My thinking is inspired by Robinson, *Black Marxism*, as well as by Robin D. G. Kelley's 2000 foreword in Robinson, *Black Marxism*, xi–xxvi, and Walter Johnson's brief discussion with Adam McGee, "The Souls of White Folk," *Boston Review*, November 18, 2016. I use it as a means of critical dialogue with Immanuel Wallerstein's world-systems theory.

39. David Theo Goldberg, "'Polluting the Body Politic': Racist Discourse and Urban Location," in Malcolm Cross and David Keith, eds., *Racism, the City, and the State* (New York: Routledge, 1993), 45–60.

40. Patrick Wolfe developed and popularized the theoretical formulation that many others have since critically extended. Two key works are Patrick Wolfe, *Settler Colonialism and the Transformation of Anthropology: The Politics and Poetics of an Ethnographic Event* (London: Cassell, 1999); and Wolfe, "Settler Colonialism and the Elimination of the Native," *Journal of Genocide Research* 8, no. 4 (2006): 387–409.

41. Wendy Brown, *Walled States, Waning Sovereignty* (New York: Zone Books, 2014).

42. Kunal M. Parker, *Making Foreigners: Immigration and Citizenship Law in America, 1600–2000* (New York: Cambridge University Press, 2015), 5.

43. Veracini, *Settler Colonial Present*, 40–42.

44. Hernández, *City of Inmates*; Wolfe, *Settler Colonialism and the Transformation of Anthropology*; and Patrick Wolfe, "Land, Labor, and Difference: Elementary Structures of Race," *American Historical Review* 106, no. 3 (2001): 866–905. This is the distinction immigration authorities posed between desirable immigrants and undesirable aliens, or, as Jodi A. Byrd has put it, between welcomed immigrants and those arrivants displaced by the forces of global racial capitalism and empire. Jodi A. Byrd, *The Transit of Empire: Indigenous Critiques of Colonialism* (Minneapolis: University of Minnesota Press, 2011), xix; and Iyko

Day, *Alien Capital: Asian Racialization and the Logic of Settler Colonial Capitalism* (Durham, NC: Duke University Press, 2016), 20–21.

45. W.E.B. Du Bois, "The African Roots of War," *Atlantic* (1915): 707–714, esp. 712.

46. Populations, according to this analysis, are to be seen as "a sort of technical political object of management and government." Foucault, in *Security, Territory, Population*, 70, quoted in Patricia Ticineto Clough and Craig Willse, *Beyond Biopolitics: Essays on the Governance of Life and Death* (Durham, NC: Duke University Press, 2011), 5.

47. Key texts are Michel Foucault, *Society Must Be Defended: Lectures at the Collège de France, 1975–1976*, trans. David Macey (New York: Picador, 2003), esp. 239–264; Achille Mbembe, "Necropolitics," trans. Libby Meintjes, *Public Culture* 15 (2003): 11–40; and Weheliye, *Habeas Viscus*. On the attempted administrative annihilation of Jews, see Raul Hilberg, *The Destruction of the European Jews* (Chicago: Quadrangle Books,1961); and on Nazi deportation trains, see Simone Gigliotti, *The Train Journey: Transit, Captivity, and Witnessing in the Holocaust* (New York: Berghahn Books, 2009).

48. Between 1885 and 1925 the largest and most powerful imperial nations in the global North developed interconnected systems of immigrant restriction to counter the massive upswell of human migration in the late nineteenth century. These large and wealthy states did not typically act in direct concert (though imperial states did collaborate to control South Asian anticolonial insurgents), but they nevertheless knew what the others were doing. They acted in aggregate, and the dynamics involved were both national and international. Aristide R. Zolberg, "Global Movements, Global Walls: Responses to Migration, 1885—1925," in Wang Gungwu, ed., *Global History and Migrations* (Boulder, CO: Westview Press, 1997), 279–307. Also see Marilyn Lake and Henry Reynolds, *Drawing the Global Colour Line: White Men's Countries and the International Challenge of Racial Equality* (Cambridge, UK: Cambridge University Press, 2012).

49. Hahamovitch, *No Man's Land*, 12–13.

50. Linda Gordon, *Pitied but Not Entitled: Single Mothers and the History of Welfare, 1890–1935* (Cambridge, MA: Harvard University Press, 1994).

51. In Nikolas Rose's understanding: "The free citizen was one who was able and willing to conduct his or her own conduct according to the norms of civility; the delinquent, the criminal, the insane person, with their specialized institutions of reformation, were the obverse of this individualization and subjectivation of citizenship." Nikolas S. Rose, *Powers of Freedom: Reframing Political Thought* (Cambridge, UK: Cambridge University Press, 1999), 233. Also see Chandan Reddy, *Freedom with Violence: Race, Sexuality, and the US State* (Durham, NC: Duke University Press, 2011), 101; and Evelyn Nakano Glenn, *Unequal Citizenship: How Race and Gender Shaped American Citizenship and Labor* (Cambridge, MA: Harvard University Press, 2002), esp. 19–29.

52. Gordon, *Pitied but Not Entitled*, 9. See Dimitris Papadopoulos, Niamh Stephenson, and Vassilis Tsianos, *Escape Routes: Control and Subversion in the*

Twenty-First Century (London: Pluto, 2008), 14; and William Walters, "Deportation, Expulsion, and the International Police of Aliens," in Nicholas De Genova and Nathalie Peutz, eds., *The Deportation Regime: Sovereignty, Space, and the Freedom of Movement* (Durham, NC: Duke University Press, 2010), 69–100, esp. 91.

53. On similar processes but with less attention to noncitizen removal, see David Garland, *Punishment and Welfare: A History of Penal Strategies* (Aldershot, UK: Ashgate, 1985).

54. To understand the United States' attempt to deport as many people as it did (but always fewer than its advocates wanted), it is useful to asses deportation as an assemblage or a complex network with multiple actors, agents, forces, ideas, and based upon a material and informational infrastructure. The materiality of the prison railcar—a carceral vessel and object of capital traversing settler space on private rail networks—radically impacted the opportunities for human action and processes of subject formation. Scholars commonly use machinic metaphors for state practices—building the machinery for immigration control and so on—and I do too. But as we discuss trains, networks, and telegraphy, I also want to use ideas of technology and machinery not just as a metaphor for complex bureaucracies but as literal machines of state formation. To think about the deportation network in this way is to preface the inescapable depth of historical relationships, congealed in objects, channeled by new engineering practices, given motive power by human labor and by steam engines, powered by resources extracted with very real human and environmental consequences, and facilitated through the political struggles of state formation and class struggle, and the intersecting struggles across multiple forms of difference to allocate power inequalities. On logistics, see Deborah Cowen, *The Deadly Life of Logistics: Mapping Violence in Global Trade* (Minneapolis: University of Minnesota Press, 2014), 28–29. On infrastructures generally, see Brian Larkin, "The Politics and Poetics of Infrastructure," *Annual Review of Anthropology* 42 (2013): 327–343, esp. 330. More specifically, see William Walters, "Aviation as Deportation Infrastructure: Airports, Planes, and Expulsion," *Journal of Ethnic and Migration Studies* 44, no. 2 (2017): 1–22; and Torsten Feys, "Riding the Rails of Removal: The Impact of Railways on Border Controls and Expulsion Practices," *Journal of Transport History* 40, no. 2 (2019): 189–210.

55. William J. Novak has drawn on sociologist Michael Mann's distinction between despotic power and infrastructural power. Despotic power is domination by political elites, while infrastructural power "refers to the positive capacity of the state to 'penetrate civil society' and implement policies throughout a given territory." The history of deportation reveals the increasing cohesion of a power that was at once infrastructural and despotic. It was infrastructural in that it linked the many different horizontal forms of government—from municipal sheriffs and hospitals to state prisons and federal agencies, connected by private firms. It was despotic in that the people it policed were subjected to fundamental forms of domination and rule across each of these levels and institutions. William

J. Novak, "The Myth of the 'Weak' American State," *American Historical Review* 113, no. 3 (2008): 752–772, esp. 763.

56. Cowen, *Deadly Life of Logistics*, 28–29. In the twenty-first century the militarized border policing and attendant mass deportation have been enabled by a host of informational and other technical systems—Integrated Computer-aided Detention Systems, Secure Communities, Secure Border Initiative Network, Investigative Case Management Systems and databases, and even the local Neighborhood Watch. These have gone hand-in-hand with the proliferation of high-power weaponry, military-style training, and body armor for ICE agents. Daniel Gonzalez, "Logistical Borderlands: Latinx Migrant Labor in the Information Age," *Society+Space*, April 12, 2019.

57. It owes a debt to Todd Presner, who, based on his study of German railways, suggested that "if one takes space (rather than time) as the prerequisite of historical narrative, it becomes impossible to write unidirectional, developmental stories; instead, there is a nearly infinite proliferation of perspectives, stories, interactions, and possibilities. What would it mean to produce narratives that looked more like railway systems or webs, with a multiplicity of connecting segments, branches, nodes, and possible pathways to get from 'here' to 'there'?" Todd Presner, David Shepard, and Yoh Kawano, *HyperCities: Thick Mapping in the Digital Humanities* (Cambridge, MA: Harvard University Press, 2014), 64–65. John Berger's notes on the tendency against linear narration in modern novels serves us well here, too: "Instead of being aware of a point as an infinitely small part of a straight line, we are aware of it as an infinitely small part of an infinite number of lines, as the centre of a star of lines. Such awareness is the result of our constantly having to take into account the *simultaneity and extension* of events and possibilities." Quoted in Edward W. Soja, *Postmodern Geographies: The Reassertion of Space in Critical Social Theory* (New York: Verso, 1989), 22.

58. Throughout the book I employ a method that I call entangled microhistories. For a historiographical review of microhistory, see Sigurður Gylfi Magnússon, "The Singularization of History: Social History and Microhistory within the Postmodern State of Knowledge," *Journal of Social History* 36, no. 3 (2003): 701–735. I attempt to reconstruct these entangled microhistories through available historical sources. These are, in the largest measure, the case files that immigration agents gathered to prosecute a successful deportation case. The deck was stacked against the accused and, as contemporary critics noted, inspectors acted as investigators, prosecutor, and judges in most matters. Therefore they emphasize what agents believed were the unlovely aspects of a person's character or legal status. Nevertheless, they offer an account—partial and certainly positioned—but still, among best available accounts of the lives of people who were forcibly expelled from the United States. Note that I cite the full archival reference upon first mention in a chapter's notes: National Archive and Records Administration location (generally NARA–Washington, DC), record group (generally RG 85), Entry Number (typically Entry 9), and the file number (such as 54645/325). In subsequent notes, I refer only to the file number.

59. In addition to Guthrie's song, see Tim Z. Hernandez, *All They Will Call You: The Telling of the Plane Wreck at Los Gatos Canyon* (Tucson: University of Arizona Press, 2017).

60. Within a substantial literature, see Gabriela De Lima Grecco and Sven Schuster, "Decolonizing Global History? A Latin American Perspective," *Journal of World History* 31, no. 2 (2020): 425–446; and Jeremy Adelman, "What Is Global History Now?" *Aeon*, March 2, 2017, https://aeon.co/essays/is-global-history-still-possible-or-has-it-had-its-moment.

61. An empirical description of the trains' existence, and their passengers' forced coexistence, provides a unique synthesis in American scholarship. That many of the deportees' predecessors actually helped build the transcontinental railroads on which they rode—and many worked on the railroads themselves—is symbolic of the complex political economies of labor and migrant restriction. Richter, *Home on the Rails*; Linda Gordon, *The Great Arizona Orphan Abduction* (Cambridge, MA: Harvard University Press, 1999); Douglas C. Baynton, *Defectives in the Land: Disability and Immigration in the Age of Eugenics* (Chicago: University of Chicago Press, 2016); Rodgers M. Smith, *Civic Ideals: Conflicting Visions of Citizenship in US History* (New Haven, CT: Yale University Press, 1999); Alexandra Minna Stern, *Eugenic Nation: Faults and Frontiers of Better Breeding* (Berkeley: University of California Press, 2006); John Bodnar, *The Transplanted: A History of Immigrants in Urban America* (Bloomington: Indiana University Press, 1987); Dearinger, *The Filth of Progress*; and Rebecca McLennan, *The Crisis of Imprisonment: Protest, Politics, and the Making of the American Penal State, 1776–1941* (New York: Cambridge University Press, 2008).

62. To draw on Foucauldian terminology, the deportation train was an exemplary heterotopic space. It was an infrastructure that brought together people whose principle commonality was the disdain they met from the settler state. More specifically, Foucault (in "Of Other Spaces") called spaces like this "heterotopias of deviation...in which individuals whose behavior is deviant in relation to the required mean or norm are placed." Heterotopias, he wrote, juxtapose "in a single real place several spaces, several sites that are in themselves incompatible."

63. I draw inspiration from CLR James's insight about the centrality of Black studies to the understanding the United States, and indeed, the modern world, as a whole, transposed to the experience of migration denied. "Now talk to me about black studies as if it's something that concerned black people is an utter denial," James (quoted in Weheliye, *Habeas Viscus*, 17) wrote. "This is the history of Western Civilization. I can't see it otherwise. This is the history that black people and white people and all serious students of modern history and the history of the world have to know. To say it's some kind of ethnic problem is a lot of nonsense."

64. Cowen, *Deadly Life of Logistics*, 17–18.

65. Developing a concept of *migrant imaginaries*, Rachel Ida Buff refers ways of living that exceed, reorient, and reimagine ideas of national sovereignty or the

desires and demands of racial capitalism. Buff, *Against the Deportation Terror: Organizing for Immigrant Rights in the Twentieth Century* (Philadelphia: Temple University Press, 2018), 3. The deportation regime responded, fitfully, to these practices.

CHAPTER I. PLANNING THE JOURNEY

1. "Record of Chinese Deportations, Jan. 1902–June 1903," RG 85, Entry 142, Vol. 1, NARA–Washington, DC.

2. Lee, *At America's Gates*, 9, 10; Pfaelzer, *Driven Out*; Hidetaka Hirota, *Expelling the Poor: Atlantic Seaboard States and the Nineteenth-century Origins of American Immigration Policy* (New York: Oxford University Press, 2017); Ethan Blue, "Finding Margins on Borders: Shipping Firms and Immigration Control across Settler Space," *Occasion: Interdisciplinary Studies in the Humanities* 5 (2013): 1–20; Ethan Blue, "From Lynch Mobs to the Deportation State," *Law, Culture, and the Humanities* (October 12, 2017): 1–24, https://doi.org/10.1177/1743872117734168; and Ethan Blue, "Building the American Deportation Regime: Governmental Labor and the Infrastructure of Forced Removal in the Early Twentieth Century," *Journal of American Ethnic History* 38, no. 2 (2019): 36–64. Towns in the early republic based welfare and removal practices on English poor law traditions and were responsible for driving the poor beyond their own municipal boundaries to their places of birth. In the 1840s, for example, the constable from Albany, New York, had to spend his own money to house, feed, and transport the unwanted poor. With tight scrutiny and up to a year's wait before any likely reimbursement, Albany's overseer of the poor reported, the constable tried to "rid himself of [paupers] at the least possible expense." See Michael B. Katz, *In the Shadow of the Poorhouse: A Social History of Welfare in America* (New York: Basic Books, 1986), 21; and "Report of the Secretary of State [of New York] in 1824 on the Relief of the Poor," 967, 952, quoted in Katz, *In the Shadow of the Poorhouse*, 21.

3. Assistant Commissioner-General (CG), "MEMORANDUM FOR THE ACTING SECRETARY, In re arrangement for deportation parties from the Coast to New York and from the East to San Francisco," February 1, 1916, RG 85, Entry 9, File 53775/202d, NARA–Washington, DC; *AR-CGI 1921*, p. 15; and *AR-CGI 1931* Annual Report, p. 37. In 1932 there were eighteen transcontinental parties. *AR-CGI 1932*, p. 30.

4. Ruben Oppenheimer, National Commission on Law Observance and Enforcement, "Report on the Enforcement of the Deportation Laws of the United States" (Washington, DC: Government Printing Office, 1931), 23. Adam Goodman (in *Deportation Machine*, 1, 38) has argued that "voluntary departures" are very much coerced, and—akin to plea bargaining in the criminal justice system—offered accused but not formally tried people a choice among harsh

options. This allowed the deportation system to function and expand over the past century on the cheap.

5. All in 52903/60, RG 85, Entry 9, NARA–Washington, DC: F. H. Larned to B. N. Austin, B&O Railroad, April 20, 1905; Cable to San Francisco Commissioner of Immigration (CI), March 26, 2010; Crawford to the CG, March 23, 1910; correspondence between the San Francisco and the DC office, April 4, 1910; Keefe to Cable, April 6, 1910; Keefe to San Francisco office, March 23, 1911; and letter from Saint Louis to CGI, December 23, 1912.

6. George T. Díaz, *Border Contraband: A History of Smuggling across the Rio Grande* (Austin: University of Texas Press, 2015); and Peter Andreas, *Smuggler Nation: How Illicit Trade Made America* (New York: Oxford University Press, 2013), 215. Deirdre Moloney (*National Insecurities*, 14–16), among others, has stressed the continued importance of how the federal government tried to regulate the laboring population through immigration control, as exemplified in the long-standing administrative housing under the federal agencies that are responsible for labor. The incorporative, restrictive, and expulsive functions would be braided more tightly together again in 1933 under the Immigration and Naturalization Service. The shift in 1940, to the Department of Justice, signaled the ascendant model of immigration control as border and crime control, the fruition of an increasingly police-based model for population management. This shift was solidified and indeed crystalized in 2003 under the Department of Homeland Security, in which immigration is understood as a national security issue driven by inchoate fears of terrorism.

7. Mary Roberts Coolidge, *Chinese Immigration* (New York: Henry Holt, 1909), 312–313, quoted in Robert Eric Barde, *Immigration at the Golden Gate: Passenger Ships, Exclusion, and Angel Island* (Westport, CT: Praeger, 2008), 202; and Lauren D. Catterson, "The Case of the Waylaid Immigrant Inspector: Authority, Respectability, and Sexual Misconduct, 1921," *Journal of American Ethnic History* 38, no. 1 (2018): 36, 42.

8. Assessment of deportation agents' working lives offers a history of the state not from above (the politicians and policymakers of traditional political history) or from below (those targeted, subordinated, or constituted by policy as told through New Social Histories of the state) or from without (such as experts, interest groups, private firms, or professional associations—as in work in new political histories and American Political Development), but rather, from within the administrative state. For the first, see William E. Leuchtenberg, *Franklin D. Roosevelt and the New Deal* (New York: Harper and Row, 1963); for the second, see Moloney, *National Insecurities*; Margot Canaday, *The Straight State: Sexuality and Citizenship in Twentieth-Century America* (Princeton, NJ: Princeton University Press, 2009); for the third, see Louis Galambos, "The Emerging Organizational Synthesis in Modern American History," *Business History Review* 44, no. 3 (1970), 279–290; Brian Balogh, "Reorganizing the Organizational Synthesis: Federal-Professional Relations in Modern America," *Studies in American Political Development* 5 (1991): 119–172; and Novak, "Myth of the 'Weak' American State,"

752–772. On the rise of the administrative state, Stephen Skowronek, *Building a New American State: The Expansion of Administrative Capacities, 1877–1920* (New York: Cambridge University Press, 1982). Also, see Brian Balogh, "The State of the State among Historians," *Social Science History* 27, no. 3 (2003): 445–463.

9. W. O. Henderson, "German Economic Penetration in the Middle East, 1870–1914," *Economic History Review* 18, no. 1/2 (1948): 54–64, esp. 55–56.

10. Travel agents, according to historian Tony Judt, exemplified the "commercial energies released by the possibilities of rail travel." Thomas Cook, in Judt's words, "organized travel itself." Tony Judt, "The Glory of the Rails," *The New York Review of Books*, December 23, 2010, accessed online February 10, 2011, www.nybooks.com/articles/2010/12/23/glory-rails/; Weiss Personal Question tion Sheet, Parts 1 and 2, filed May 31, 1904, Department of Labor (DoL) files; December 4, 1906, F. H. Larned to Secretary of Commerce and Labor, both in NARA–Saint Louis.

11. A process, in Chandan Reddy's formulation, of securing freedom with violence. Chandan Reddy, *Freedom with Violence: Race, Sexuality, and the US State* (Durham, NC: Duke University Press, 2011); and Nikhil Pal Singh, *Race and America's Long War* (Berkeley: University of California Press, 2017), 28.

12. Marcus Braun, a multilingual Hungarian Jew, became renowned as a bureau special investigator, looking into so-called White Slavery rings in the United States and overseas with another Hungarian-born assistant, Andrew Tedesco. See Jessica R. Pliley, *Policing Sexuality: The Mann Act and the Making of the FBI* (Cambridge, MA: Harvard University Press, 2014), 36–37; also Mae M. Ngai, *Lucky Ones: One Family and the Extraordinary Invention of Chinese America* (Boston: Houghton Mifflin Harcourt, 2010); Vincent J. Cannato, *American Passage: The History of Ellis Island*, 1st edition (New York: Harper, 2009), 178–179; Barde, *Immigration at the Golden Gate*; Lisa Rose Mar, *Brokering Belonging: Chinese in Canada's Exclusion Era, 1885–1945* (New York: Oxford University Press, 2010); and Nancy J. Carnevale, "'No Italian Spoken for the Duration of the War': Language, Italian-American Identity, and Cultural Pluralism in the World War II Years," *Journal of American Ethnic History* 22, no. 3 (2003): 3–33, esp. 4.

13. Larned to Weiss, November 12, 1903, Department of Justice (DoJ) files, NARA–Saint Louis.

14. Estell to CGI, February 2, 1904, Washington, DC, DoJ files, NARA–Saint Louis.

15. Weiss to CGI, March 28, 1910, Washington, DC, DoJ files, NARA–Saint Louis.

16. All in DoJ files, NARA–Saint Louis: Estell to CGI, June 23, 1905, Washington, DC; Sargent to Estell, August 3, 1905; and December 1905 correspondence.

17. All in DoJ files, NARA–Saint Louis: Estell to CGI, June 23, 1905, Washington, DC; Sargent to Estell, August 3, 1905; and December 1905 correspondence.

18. All in DoJ files, NARA–Saint Louis: Weiss to Estell, March 30, 1906; Weiss to Estell, July 5, 1906; and Weiss to Sargent, December 9, 1907.

19. Secretary of Commerce and Labor to Kahn, April 4, 1908, DoL files, NARA–Saint Louis.

20. Larned to Inspector in Charge, October 6, 1908, Seattle, DoJ file, NARA–Saint Louis.

21. Portland Commissioner to CGI, March 13, 1912, Washington DC, DoJ file, NARA–Saint Louis.

22. For more theoretically inclined readers, this might be understood as a maturation and transfer point between the carceral-disciplinary mode, which targets individual bodies, and the more fully biopolitical mode of power, which seeks to control whole populations. As Michel Foucault suggested, "after a first seizure of power over the body in an individualizing mode, we have a second seizure of power that is not individualizing, but, if you like, massifying, that is directed not at man-as-body but at man-as-species." Populations, he wrote, are to be seen as "a sort of technical political object of management and government." Foucault, in *Society Must Be Defended*, 243, and Michel Foucault, *Security, Territory, Population: Lectures at the Collège de France, 1977–1978* (New York: Picador, 2009), 70. Both quoted in Patricia Ticineto Clough and Craig Willse, introduction to Clough and Willse, *Beyond Biopolitics: Essays on the Governance of Life and Death* (Durham, NC: Duke University Press, 2011), 5.

23. Kevin D. Haggerty and Richard V. Ericson, "The Surveillant Assemblage," *British Journal of Sociology* 52, no. 4 (2000): 605–622.

24. Hester, *Deportation*, 145–146, 177.

25. William Preston, *Aliens and Dissenters: The Federal Suppression of Radicals, 1903–1933*, 2nd edition (Urbana: University of Illinois Press, 1994), 14.

26. By 1932, the commissioner-general, Harry Hull, wanted to give district heads the legal power of arrest without consulting Washington: "It is not believed that such a power would be abused by the intelligent and experienced heads of immigration districts." He thought it a "logical extension of present powers in dealing with aliens." They would need to consult with Washington via telegraph for deportation warrants, however. Harry E. Hull, *AR-CGI 1932*, 30.

27. Lucy E. Salyer, *Laws Harsh as Tigers: Chinese Immigrants and the Shaping of Modern Immigration Law* (Chapel Hill: University of North Carolina Press, 1995), 232; Preston, *Aliens and Dissenters*, 14; and Abraham Hoffman, "Stimulus to Repatriation: The 1931 Federal Deportation Drive and the Los Angeles Mexican Community," *Pacific Historical Review* 42, no. 2 (1973): 205–291, 216.

28. State Dept. Solicitor (signature illegible) to Mr. MacMurray, January 24, 1925, 150.06/366, Box 26, RG 59, NARA–College Park.

29. *AR-CGI 1920*, 309. After the October Revolution the Soviets scarcely accepted anyone who had emigrated before 1917, because they were not Soviet citizens. The problem was little better a decade later. In late 1930 the State Department kept up considerable correspondence with Germany, as well as Brazil, Czechoslovakia, Lithuania, Norway, and Spain regarding their deportees and the length of time it took to receive passports from them. Although the Soviets had ideological reasons for denying many returned deportees, other nations

simply lacked the developed state administrative capacities or the breadth and depth of an internal apparatus for surveillance. It was not at all clear where some should be deported to when they country's borders had moved during or after the First World War, when older empires crumbled and new national territories and administrations were created. See US Department of State Records, RG 59, Box 26, file 150.06/339, NARA–College Park.

30. In addition to acts passed in 1645, 1655, and 1700, the 1756 act was intended to "Prevent Charges Arising by Sick, Lame or Otherwise Infirm Persons, not belonging to this Province, Being Landed and Left Within the Same." *Acts and Resolves of the Province of Massachusetts Bay* (Boston: Albert Wright, 1878), vol. 3, chapter 4, p. 982, in E. P. Hutchinson, *Legislative History of American Immigration Policy, 1798–1965* (Philadelphia: University of Pennsylvania Press, 1981), 391; Cybelle Fox, *Three Worlds of Relief: Race, Immigration, and the American Welfare State from the Progressive Era to the New Deal* (Princeton, NJ: Princeton University Press, 2012), 132–133; and Blue, "Finding Margins on Borders."

31. "In re Co-Operation Received from Officials of States, Cities, Municipalities, etc., in Connection with the Enforcement of the Immigration Laws," October 8, 1923, 54951/Gen, RG 85, Entry 9, NARA–Washington, DC.

32. Fox, *Three Worlds of Relief*, chapter 6, 7.

33. "In re Co-Operation Received...," October 8, 1923, p. 2.

34. Bonham to CGI, August 5, 1912, Washington, DC, DoJ file, NARA–Saint Louis.

35. Keefe to Immigration Service, October 17, 1912, Seattle, DoJ file, NARA–Saint Louis.

36. Acting CG to CI, October 18, 1912, Ellis Island, DoJ file, NARA–Saint Louis.

37. All in 52903/60, RG 85, Entry 9, NARA–Washington, DC: Cable's March 26, 1910, to SF CI; San Francisco's Crawford to CG in Washington, March 23, 1910; correspondence SF and DC offices, April 4, 1910; memo from Keefe to Benjamin Cable, April 6, 1910; Keefe to SF office, March 23, 1911; also, Saint Louis office to the CG, December 23, 1912. Also, Torrie Hester, "Deportation: The Origins of a National and International Power," PhD dissertation, University of Oregon, 2008, p. 123, documents similar correspondence in a July 1913 memo, Acting Immigration Inspector to IC, Immigration Service, LA, California, July 9, 1913, File 53678/21-33, INS.

38. Bernard Marinbach, *Galveston, Ellis Island of the West* (Albany: State University of New York Press, 1983), 63.

39. Cudihee as quoted in "Pullman Prison Car for Alien Criminals: Seattle Rushes Ten of Them East and Deports Them under the Mann Act," *New York Times*, June 6, 1913.

40. Joseph J. Kanna to CGI, June 21, 1913, 53659/2, RG 85, Entry 9, NARA–Washington, DC.

41. Andrew Urban, *Brokering Servitude: Migration and the Politics of Domestic*

Servitude during the Long Nineteenth Century (New York: New York University Press, 2018), 167–168; and Ngai, *Lucky Ones*, 137–139.

42. Hester, "Deportation," 79–81.

43. Report, Taylor to CGI, December 22, 1913, Washington, DC, 52903/60-A, RG 85, Entry 9, NARA–Washington, DC.

44. Calahan to Taylor, December 9, 1913, 52903/60-A.

45. Calahan to Gentlemen, April 6, 1914, 52903/60-B.

46. Orsi, *Sunset Limited*, 41.

47. Report, Taylor to CGI, Washington DC, December 22, 1913, 52903/60-A.

48. Report, Taylor to CGI, December 22, 1913, 52903/60-A; and Taylor to CGI, January 16, 1914, 52903/60-A.

49. Report, Taylor to CGI, December 22, 1913, 52903/60-A.

50. Uhl to CGI, Washington DC, January 22, 1914, 52903/60-A; Uhl to Combes Sanitarium, January 14, 1914; EJ Murray, Physician in Charge, to CI, January 17, 1914, 52903/60-A; and Contract with Combes Sanitarium, March 17, 1914, 52903/60-B.

51. Taylor to CI, Seattle, February 3, 1914, 52903/60-A.

52. Both in 52903/60-A: Taylor to CGI, Washington, DC, January 16, 1914; and Taylor to CI, Seattle, February 3, 1914.

53. Taylor to CI, Seattle, February 3, 1914, 52903/60-A.

54. Taylor to Fee, February 3, 1914, SP General traffic Manager, 52903/60-A; and Sargent to CGI, March 18, 1914, 52903/60-B.

55. White to Taylor, February 19, 1914, 52903/60-B.

56. Taylor to CI Seattle, February 3, 1914, 52903/60-A.

57. Backus to DC, February 20, 1914, 52903/60-A.

58. Keagy's thoughts were reported in Sargent to CGI, March 18, 1914, 52903/60-B.

59. Sargent to CGI, March 18, 1914, 52903/60-B.

60. Circular, March 6, 1914, 52903/60-B.

61. Circular, March 6, 1914, 52903/60-B.

62. Circular, March 6, 1914, 52903/60-B, emphasis in original.

63. Circular, March 6, 1914, 52903/60-A.

64. Yet for all of their instrumentalization and dehumanization, uncanny traces of meaning-making remained in the telegrams. The coded designations linguistically replicated the different quality of threat deportees were taken to pose. The words used in the code were remarkably if perhaps accidentally poetic, combining alliterative or sonic similarities to the words they represent as well as rich meanings in themselves. Without a better understanding of how governmental codes were developed, it is hard to interpret this with anything other than speculation. Nonetheless, the word choices are at least suggestive of either pathos or a bureaucratic sense of humor. According to the circular, "Devolution," followed by a date, train number, and number of people, was coded to mean that a deportation party would arrive on a certain date, on a certain track, and with the specified number of deportees. Its longer meaning derives from the Latin for "roll-

ing down," referring to the passing of authority from a greater to a lesser power, or, in a curiously eugenic sense, to a process of social degeneration. "Dauphine," followed by a number, indicated the number of mad deportees. Other than also beginning with the letter D, and the French word for a female dolphin, "Dauphine" refers to the wife of an heir apparent to France. Perhaps closer was Mark Twain's usage in *Huck Finn*, referring to a con artist claiming to be descended from French royalty. Or it might refer to a woman with delusions of grandeur, who claims that rather than being mad or impoverished, she is of royal blood. "Desperado" was a more straightforward designation of dangerousness, its root derived from the Spanish, for one who is reckless or dangerous from despair but taken up in the context of westward expansion and conflict with Mexicans and Mexican Americans. The number following that code referred to the number of dangerous deportees, of "violent cases requiring restraining." All deportees other than the mad and the dangerous—in other words, the merely pathetic but not especially disruptive—were referred to by the code "Despondent"—from the Latin for "to give up, to abandon," perhaps a perceptive impression of many in the midst of forced removal. The memo, however, eschewed this poesy and gave an example of the code in use: "Devolution February forth ten morning Pennsylvania train ten Dauphine five, Desperado Smolek Panayotis, Despondent Doe, Roe, Smith, Jones, Brown." Circular, March 6, 1914, 52903/60-A.

65. Gigliotti, *Train*, 41–42.

66. Circular, March 6, 1914, 52903/60-B.

67. Circular, March 6, 1914, 52903/60-B.

68. Backus to CGI, March 11, 1914, 52903/60-B.

69. Backus to CGI, March 11, 1914, 52903/60-B.

70. White to CGI Caminetti, April 29, 1914, 53775/202.

71. Minneapolis inspector in charge to CGI, March 18, 1914, 52903/60-B.

72. White to CGI Caminetti, April 29, 1914, 53775/202.

73. Backus to Immigration Bureau, March 27, 1914, 52903/60-B.

74. Backus to Immigration Bureau, March 27, 1914, 52903/60-B.

75. Backus to CI, Seattle, March 24, 1914, 52903/60-B.

76. Larned to SF office, March 31, 1914, 52903/60-B.

77. Acting CG to inspector in charge, Chicago, April 4, 1914, 52903/60-B.

78. Larned to Immigration Service, Chicago, April 7, 1914, 52903/60-B.

79. Larned to Chicago Inspector in Charge, April 16, 1914, 52903/60-B.

80. Prentis to CGI, Washington, DC, April 18, 1914, 52903/60-B.

81. Prentis to CGI, Washington, DC, April 18, 1914, 52903/60-B.

82. Prentis to CGI, Washington, DC, April 18, 1914, 52903/60-B.

83. Prentis to CGI, Washington, DC, April 18, 1914, 52903/60-B.

84. CG Caminetti to CIs, Seattle and San Francisco, April 22, 1914, 52903/60-B.

85. O'Donnell Memorandum for CG, April 17, 1914, 52903/60-B.

86. Caminetti to Weiss, April 22, 1914, DoJ file, NARA–Saint Louis.

87. Memorandum, February 16, 1916, File 53775/202d.

88. Richter, *Home on the Rails*, 81–83.

89. Southern Pacific began carrying contract Chinese laborers aboard barred cars from San Francisco to New Orleans, and then by sea to Cuba, to work in the island's booming sugar and molasses industries. Despite the exclusions against the Chinese and other groups, international law required that those otherwise denied entry would still be permitted the "privilege of transit" through US territory—a fact that many migrants used to evade immigration law. Yet Southern Pacific would do all that it could to prevent escapes—thus the bars and the guards. They were not always successful. Duvon C. Corbitt, "Chinese Immigrants in Cuba," *Far Eastern Survey* 13, no. 14 (1942): 130–132; Evelyn Hu-DeHart, "Chinese Coolie Labor in Cuba in the Nineteenth Century: Free Labor of Neoslavery," *Contributions in Black Studies* 12, no. 1 (1994): 38–54; Moon-Ho Jung, *Coolies and Cane: Race, Labor and Sugar in the Age of Emancipation* (Baltimore, MD: Johns Hopkins University Press, 2006); and Andrea Geiger, "Caught in the Gap: The Transit Privilege and North America's Ambiguous Borders," in *Bridging National Borders in North America: Transnational and Comparative Histories*, ed. Benjamin H. Johnson and Andrew R. Graybill (Durham, NC: Duke University Press, 2010), 199–222.

90. Michel de Certeau saw the ordinary passenger train car as "a bubble of panoptic and classifying power," with passengers arranged in the carriage "like a piece of printer's type on a page arranged in military order." This certainly matched deportation agents' desire. As de Certeau understood of urban walkers, if not rail travelers, even unfree passengers challenged this spatial arrangement. Michel de Certeau, *The Practice of Everyday Life*, trans. Steven Rendall (Berkeley: University of California Press, 1984), 111.

91. JT Ransom to Caminetti, March 10, 1919, 54645/325, RG 85, Entry 9, NARA–Washington, DC.

92. JT Ransom to Caminetti, March 10, 1919, 54645/325. The Immigration Bureau's *Lorenzo* contract was modeled on wartime "movements of United States hospital cars used for the transportation of wounded men." Pullman provided up to six attendants along with the car, for the wartime rate of $15 per day. Gerris Fort to CGI, O'Donnell, March 28, 1919, 54645/325.

93. Russell to CGI, June 24, 1919, 54645/325.

94. CG to Ransom, September 29, 1919, 54645/325.

95. Blueprint 6771 and 6771 Revised; Sleeping Car No. 1099 Blueprint, "Reconditioning Cars for Deportation parties," RG 85, Entry 9, 56193/283, NARA–Washington, DC; and Ethan Blue, "Capillary Power, Rail Vessels, and the Carceral Viapolitics of Early Twentieth-Century American Deportation," in *Viapolitics: Borders, Migration, and the Power of Locomotion*, ed. William Walters, Charles Heller, Lorenzo Pezzani (Durham, NC: Duke University Press, 2021).

96. Personal Question Sheet, filed January 23, 1907, Russell DoL, NARA–Saint Louis.

97. Both in NARA–Saint Louis: Labor Department Abstract of Official

Record of Employee, April 23, 1924, DoJ; and Personal Question Sheet, filed January 23, 1907, Russell DoL file.

98. All in NARA–Saint Louis: Letter from Russell to Secretary of the Department of Commerce and Labor, November 16, 1906; Certificate for Transfer, January 5, 1907; Russell Oath of Office, January 22, 1907, Russell DoL; and Efficiency Report, May 29, 1909, Russell DoJ file.

99. Adam McKeown, "Ritualization of Regulation: The Enforcement of Chinese Exclusion in the United States and China," *American Historical Review* 108, no. 2 (April 2003): 377–403, 384.

100. Novak, "Myth of the 'Weak' American State."

101. All from Russell DoJ, NARA–Saint Louis: Efficiency Report, undated, ca. 1911; December 21, 1912, General Appointment—Fixed Date; and Memorandum for the Assistant Secretary, January 15, 1912.

102. CG to Russell, December 5, 1911, Russell DoJ, NARA–Saint Louis.

103. From Russell DoJ, NARA–Saint Louis: CG to Russell, November 9, 1912; and Morton to Immigration Bureau, February 18, 1915.

104. From Russell DoJ, NARA–Saint Louis: Parker to Russell, July 27, 1916; and Acting CG to Russell, August 1, 1916.

105. From Russell DoJ, NARA–Saint Louis: Efficiency Rating [undated, est. mid-1917]; Memorandum for the Assistant Secretary, July 1, 1917; and General Appointment—Fixed Date, July 17, 1917.

106. On overseas antecedents to domestic policing, see Alfred W. McCoy, Francisco A. Scarano, and Courtney Johnson, "On the Tropic of Cancer: Transitions and Transformations in the U.S. Imperial State," in *Colonial Crucible: Empire in the Making of the Modern American State*, ed. Alfred W. McCoy and Francisco A. Scarano, 3–33 (Madison: University of Wisconsin Press, 2009), esp. 7–17. In a continuation of the domestic/international policing loop, the commissioner-general reported that some of the bureau's "most experienced investigators" joined other branches government handling "investigation of much larger proportions than anything they had theretofore been called upon to handle." Russell's expertise in managing large amounts of data, generated through immigrant policing at ports and borders (the threshold between of the foreign and domestic imperial projects), thus helped the US Navy expand its own informational systems, and for the United States to project military power across the seas. *AR-CGI 1917*, xi.

107. All in Russell DoJ, NARA–Saint Louis: Russell to CGI, November 22, 1918; Wells to CGI, December 16, 1918; and Memorandum to the Acting Secretary of Labor, December 28, 1918.

108. Wells to CGI, December 16, 1918, Russell DoJ, NARA–Saint Louis.

109. Russell, June 15, 1921, 54933/351, RG 85, Entry 9, NARA–Washington, DC.

110. Russell, June 15, 1921, 54933/351.

111. All from NARA–Saint Louis: CG to Russell, May 16, 1922; Russell to Stusband, May 21, 1922, Russell DoJ; Acting CG to Russell, April 25, 1924; July 1,

1924, General Appointment—Fixed Date, Russell DoJ; and New Appointment Classification Sheet, July 1, 1924, Russell DoL.

112. All in Russell DoJ, NARA–Saint Louis: CG to Secretary of Labor, November 15, 1924; Appointment Clerk to CGI, November 17, 1924; General Appointment—Fixed Date, November 18, 1924; CG to Secretary of Labor, December 16, 1924; and Memorandum for Bureau Officials Concerned, November 14, 1924.

113. Russell Career "Status" table, 1907–1925, Russell DoL, NARA–Saint Louis.

114. *AR-CGI 1931*, Table 106; and DHS, *2015 Yearbook of Immigration Statistics*, Table 39.

115. George C. Shaffer, Florist, Receipt, June 13, 1930, Russell DoJ, NARA–Saint Louis.

116. DHS, *2015 Yearbook of Immigration Statistics*, Table 39.

117. All in Kline DoJ, NARA–Saint Louis: CG Caminetti to SecLab, November 18, 1919; Oath of Office, November 18, 1919; Oath of Office, May 6, 1920; General Appointment—Fixed Term, April 22, 1920; General Appointment—Fixed Date, July 12, 1920; and General Appointment—Fixed Date, November 6, 1920.

118. Johnson to Secretary of Treasury, August 3, 1898, Kline DoC, NARA–Saint Louis.

119. Personal Question Sheet, March 12, 1906, Kline DoC, NARA–Saint Louis.

120. All in Kline DoC, NARA–Saint Louis: Director to Secretary of Treasury, October 27, 1899; Civil Service President to Secretary of Treasury, November 15, 1899; and Johnson to Secretary of Treasury, November 18, 1899.

121. Cortelyou to Kline, April 2, 1904, Kline DoC, NARA–Saint Louis; and John Cloud, "Extending Relief to the Nation: Director Raymond Stanton Patton (1929–1937)," in *Science on the Edge: The Story of the Coast and Geodetic Survey from 1867–1970*, www.lib.noaa.gov/noaainfo/heritage/coastandgeodeticsurvey/Pattonchapter.pdf, accessed June 1, 2015.

122. Andrews to McHarg, July 5, 1909, Kline DoC, NARA–Saint Louis.

123. Both in Kline DoC, NARA–Saint Louis: Kline to OH Tittmann, February 26, 1914; and Perkins to Kline, March 2, 1914.

124. See E. F. Sweet to various agencies, February 26, 1914, Kline DoC, NARA–Saint Louis.

125. Commissioner Bureau of Corporations to Assistant Secretary, March 16, 1914, Kline DoC, NARA–Saint Louis.

126. All in Kline DoC, NARA–Saint Louis: Thurman to "Gentlemen," April 16, 1914; and President, Civil Service Commission, to Secretary of Commerce, April 24, 1914.

127. *Annual Report of the Director of the Census*, FY June 30, 1914 (Washington, DC: Government Printing Office, 1914), 19–20.

128. Mullen to W. M. Stewart, May 25, 1915, Kline DoC, NARA–Saint Louis.

129. Chief Clerk to Farnum, May 8, 1916, Kline DoC, NARA–Saint Louis.

130. Erika Lee and Judy Yung, *Angel Island: Immigrant Gateway to America* (New York: Oxford University Press, 2010), 159–160.

131. Cannato, *American Passage*, 193.

132. If we look at three points of Kline's pre–Immigration Bureau governmental labor—the Census, the Coastal Survey, and remarkably, if briefly, preparing displays for the 1904 Louisiana Purchase Exposition—we can understand him as a minor and occasionally burdensome functionary in the bureaucratic production of knowledge about US territory, economy, and population. Kline may have been a man of middling talents, and boosted by nepotism and whiteness, but he contributed quite literally to the production of maps, censuses, and museums— which, as Benedict Anderson has argued, are all essential technologies in the making of modern nations. Efficiency Rating of Departmental Employee, January 15, 1917, DoJ, NARA–Saint Louis; and Benedict Anderson, *Imagined Communities: Reflections on the Origins and Spread of Nationalism*, revised and expanded edition (New York: Verso, 1991), 163–185.

133. General Appointment, DoL, July 28, 1917, Kline DoJ, NARA–Saint Louis.

134. All in Kline DoJ, NARA–Saint Louis: Chief Clerk to "Sir" [Kline], January 12, 1918; DoL Oath of Office, January 7, 1918; General Appointment—Fixed Date, March 2, 1918; Letter from Assistant Director General to Assistant Secretary of Labor, May 23, 1918; General Appointment—Fixed Date, June 1, 1918; Change of Status blank, September 10, 1918; Acting Director General, US Employment Service, to Secretary of Labor, September 16, 1918; and General Appointment— Fixed Date, September 26, 1918.

135. All in Kline DoJ, NARA–Saint Louis: General Appointment—Fixed Date, May 26, 1919; General Appointment—Fixed Date, July 11, 1919; General Appointment—Fixed Date, July 24, 1919; Director General, US Employment Service to Secretary of Labor, July 11, 1919; and Letter from Chief Clerk to "Sir" [Kline], October 18, 1919.

136. *AR-CGI, 1920* (Washington, DC: Government Printing Office, 1920), 310. All in Kline DoJ, NARA–Saint Louis: Caminetti to Secretary of Labor, November 18, 1919; Oath of Office, November 18, 1919; Oath of Office, May 6, 1920; General Appointment—Fixed Term, April 22, 1920; General Appointment—Fixed Date, July 12, 1920; and General Appointment—Fixed Date, November 6, 1920.

137. Leo Stanley, "To Ellis Island and Back," Box 1, Vol. 2, SC 070, Leo L. Stanley Papers, Stanford University Library Special Collections, Stanford, CA.

138. Oath of Office, November 19, 1925, Kline DoJ, NARA–Saint Louis.

139. Today, National Archives online records note that these "groups were dubbed 'Kline parties,' after Deporting Officer Edward M. Kline who was in charge of this procedure." An advanced search for "Kline Party" in the NARA's "Research our Records" field should yield this result; see https://catalog.archives .gov/search?q=Kline%20Party, accessed February 21, 2018.

140. New Appointment Classification Sheet, July 1, 1924, Kline DoJ, NARA– Saint Louis.

141. Hoffman, "Stimulus to Repatriation"; Balderrama and Rodríguez, *Decade of Betrayal*; and Guerin-Gonzales, *Mexican Workers and American Dreams*.

142. William D. Carrigan and Clive Webb, *Forgotten Dead: Mob Violence against Mexicans in the United States, 1848–1928* (Oxford, UK: Oxford University Press, 2013), 21–23; also, Timothy J. Dunn, *The Militarization of the US-Mexico Border, 1978–1992: Low-Intensity Conflict Doctrine Comes Home* (Austin, TX: CMAS Books, 1996).

143. Kelly Lytle Hernández, *MIGRA! A History of the U.S. Border Patrol* (Berkeley: University of California Press, 2010).

144. Balderrama and Rodríguez, *Decade of Betrayal*, 57–58.

145. Balderrama and Rodríguez, *Decade of Betrayal*, 99.

146. Balderrama and Rodríguez, *Decade of Betrayal*; and Guerin-Gonzales, *Mexican Workers and American Dreams*. Given the shift in eliminatory practice—from lynch mobs to the deportation state that La Placita demonstrated—LULAC's relative successes in limiting mob violence through inclusionist civil rights strategies would do little, even if it wanted to, for Mexican nationals who faced expulsion. See Carrigan and Webb, *Forgotten Dead*, 167; and Blue, "From Lynch Mobs to the Deportation State," esp. 14. This is not to suggest the federal government played no role at La Placita or in what followed or that local authorities were unimportant for the federal deportation apparatus via rail.

147. Balderrama and Rodríguez, *Decade of Betrayal*, 103.

148. Blue, "From Lynch Mobs to the Deportation State."

149. S. Deborah Kang, *INS on the Line: Making Immigration Law on the US-Mexico Border, 1917–1954* (New York: Oxford University Press, 2017), 62–86, 69. For similar comments on the Palmer Raids of 1919–1920, see Louis F. Post, *The Deportations Delirium of Nineteen-Twenty* (Chicago: Charles H. Kerr, 1923).

150. Marie Masumoto, "Griffith Park (detention facility)," *Densho Encyclopedia*, http://encyclopedia.densho.org, accessed October 1, 2014; Engin F. Isin and Kim Rygiel, "Abject Spaces: Frontiers, Zones, Camps," in *Logics of Biopower and the War on Terror*, ed. E. Dauphinee and C. Masters, 181–203 (Houndsmill, UK: Palgrave, 2007), esp. 189; and A. Naomi Paik, *Rightlessness: Testimony and Redress in U.S. Prison Camps since World War II* (Chapel Hill: University of North Carolina Press, 2016).

151. May 29, 1942, DoJ Personnel Recommendation (Civil Service); and Letter from Attorney General to Kline, May 29, 1942, Kline DoJ, NARA–Saint Louis.

152. Employee Service Record, Saint Louis, June 30, 1953, Kline DoJ, NARA–Saint Louis.

153. DHS, *2015 Yearbook of Immigration Statistics*, Table 39.

154. Department of Justice/INS, *Monthly Review* (October 1946), 50–51.

155. Willis Thornton, "Kline's Deportation Party Is a Grim Affair for Aliens," *Milwaukee Journal*, January 11, 1940, p. 1, col. 4–6.

156. *AR-CGI 1920*, 11.

157. "In re Co-Operation Received...," October 8, 1923; Torrie Hester, *Deportation: The Origins of US Policy* (Philadelphia: University of Pennsylvania Press,

2017), 36; and Emily Pope-Obeda, "'When in Doubt, Deport!': U.S. Deportation and the Local Policing of Global Migration during the 1920s," PhD dissertation, University of Illinois at Urbana-Champaign, 2016, pp. 47–49.

PART TWO

1. W.E.B. Du Bois, "The Souls of White Folk," in *Darkwater: Voices from Within the Veil* (1920; reprint, New York: Cosimo Classics, 2007), 18.

CHAPTER 2. SEATTLE

1. *AR-CGI 1914*, 21.

2. Kornel S. Chang, *Pacific Connections: The Making of the U.S.-Canadian Borderlands* (Berkeley: University of California Press, 2012), esp. 148–149; and Andrew R. Graybill, *Policing the Great Plains: Rangers, Mounties, and the North American Frontier, 1875–1910* (Lincoln: University of Nebraska Press, 2007).

3. Horwitz to Inspector in Charge, June 8, 1914, 53775/263, RG 85, Entry 9, NARA–Washington, DC.

4. Treasury Department statement, November 5, 1913, 53775/263.

5. Horwitz to Inspector in Charge, June 8, 1914, 53775/263.

6. Horwitz to Inspector in Charge, June 8, 1914; and Report, Vancouver Inspector in Charge Jenkins, June 8, 1914, 53775/263.

7. Report, Vancouver Inspector in Charge Jenkins, June 8, 1914, 53775/263.

8. Report, Vancouver Inspector in Charge Jenkins, June 8, 1914, 53775/263.

9. Correspondence from Inspector in Charge, Vancouver, to CI, Montreal, July 20, 1914, 53775/263.

10. Correspondence from Inspector in Charge, Vancouver, to CI, Montreal, July 24, 1914, 53775/263.

11. Massimo Costantini, "Economia, società e territorio nel lungo periodo," in *L'Abruzzo: Storia d'Italia Le regioni dall'Unità a oggi*, ed. Massimo Costantini and Costantino Felice, 99–101 (Turin: Giulio Einaudi, 2000). Thanks to Giuseppe Finaldi for help here.

12. Richard Bosworth, *Italy and the Wider World, 1860–1960* (London: Routledge, 1996), 128.

13. Carlo Levi, *Christ Stopped at Eboli*, trans. Frances Frenaye (New York: Farrar, Straus and Giroux, 1947), 59–60, quoted in Robert Anthony Orsi, *The Madonna of 115th Street: Faith and Community in Italian Harlem, 1880–1950* (New Haven, CT: Yale University Press, 1985), 150.

14. Weiss Hearing and Findings, no date, 53775/263.

15. Deportation Warrant, September 17, 1914, 53775/263.

16. Deidre M. Moloney, "Women, Sexual Morality, and Economic Depen-

dency in Early U.S. Deportation Policy," *Journal of Women's History* 18, no. 2 (2006): 95–122.

17. *AR-CGI 1914*, 9; and Pope-Obeda, "When in Doubt," 211.

18. Each of these is feasible but unverified. I have written about staff-structured carceral white supremacy and inmate cultures in Ethan Blue, *Doing Time in the Depression: Everyday Life in Texas and California Prisons* (New York: New York University Press, 2012).

19. Inspector in Charge Hines to John Clark, November 20, 1914, 53860/194, RG 85, Entry 9, NARA–Washington, DC.

20. John Sargent to CGI, Washington, DC, October 8, 1914, 53852/19, RG 85, Entry 9, NARA–Washington, DC. In the records Surup Singh's name was occasionally rendered as Sarup Singh.

21. Kornel Chang, quoting Sargent, in "Enforcing Transnational White Solidarity: Asian Migration and the Formation of the U.S.-Canadian Boundary," *American Quarterly* 60, no. 3 (2008): 671–696, 676.

22. J. Neilson Barry, "The Indians in Washington, Their Distribution by Languages," *Oregon Historical Quarterly* 28, no. 2 (1927): 147–162, esp. 153.

23. Coll-Peter Thrush and Robert H. Keller Jr., "'I See What I Have Done': The Life and Murder Trial of Xwelas, a S'Klallam Woman," *Western Historical Quarterly* 26, no. 2 (1995): 168–183, esp. 170–171.

24. Salag Ram Examination, September 24, 1914; and Attar Singh Examination, October 2, 1914, 53852/19. Records sometimes rendered Salig Ram as Salag Ram.

25. The first might be understood as waging what Antonio Gramsci called a war of maneuver, seeking to overthrow imperial political economic systems, while the second engaged in a war of position by subverting those systems. Antonio Gramsci, *Selections from the Prison Notebooks*, ed. and trans. Quintin Hoare and Geoffrey Nowell Smith (New York: International Publishers, 1971), 229–239.

26. Tony Ballantyne, *Between Colonialism and Diaspora: Sikh Cultural Formations in an Imperial World* (Durham, NC: Duke University Press, 2006), 31.

27. Ballantyne, *Between Colonialism and Diaspora*, 31.

28. Arunajeet Kaur, "*Komagata Maru* Sails from the Far East: Cartography of the Sikh Diaspora within the British Empire," *South Asian Diaspora* 8, no. 2 (July 2, 2016): 155–165, 158, 159.

29. Kaur, "*Komagata Maru* Sails from the Far East," 159.

30. Hugh Johnston, *Voyage of the Komagata Maru: The Sikh Challenge to Canada's Colour Bar* (Delhi: Oxford University Press, 1979), 2; and Ronald Takaki, *Strangers from a Different Shore: A History of Asian Americans* (New York: Penguin Books, 1989), 302.

31. Ballantyne, *Between Colonialism and Diaspora*, 76; and Kaur, "*Komagata Maru* Sails from the Far East," 159–160.

32. On the continuous passage act, see Chang, *Pacific Connections*; and Johnston, *Voyage of the Komagata Maru*, 4. On the evolution and global travel of ostensibly race neutral, but clearly racist restrictive legislation, see Jeremy Martens, "A Transnational History of Immigration Restriction: Natal and New South Wales,

1896–97," *Journal of Imperial and Commonwealth History* 34, no. 3 (2006): 323–344; and Lake and Reynolds, *Drawing the Global Colour Line*.

33. Johnston, *Voyage of the Komagata Maru*, 7.

34. Johnston, *Voyage of the Komagata Maru*, 10–16.

35. *El Paso Herald*, March 26, 1914, p. 1, col. 1.

36. *Arizona Republican*, March 27, 1914, p. 7, col. 2.

37. Johnston, *Voyage of the Komagata Maru*, 24, 25.

38. Quoted in Johnston, *Voyage of the Komagata Maru*, 30.

39. Johnston, *Voyage of the Komagata Maru*, 27–30.

40. Johnston, *Voyage of the Komagata Maru*, 32; and Chang, *Pacific Connections*, 169.

41. Johnston, *Voyage of the Komagata Maru*, 37. Twenty passengers, who had previously lived in Canada, were permitted to land.

42. Johnston, *Voyage of the Komagata Maru*, 1, 2; Chang, *Pacific Connections*, 166–170; and *Daily Missoulian*, October 22, 1914, p. 1, cols. 2 and 3.

43. Johnston, *Voyage of the Komagata Maru*, 61.

44. Johnston, *Voyage of the Komagata Maru*, 74–75.

45. "Restriction on Immigration," Hearings, House Immigration Committee, 63rd Congress, 2d session (Washington, DC: Government Printing Office, 1914), quoted in Chang, *Pacific Connections*, 173.

46. Inspector in Charge to CI, October 29, 1914, quoted in Chang, *Pacific Connections*, 173.

47. Johnston, *Voyage of the Komagata Maru*, 125.

48. Nayan Shah, *Stranger Intimacy: Contesting Race, Sexuality, and the Law in the North American West* (Berkeley: University of California Press, 2011), 219.

49. Shah, *Stranger Intimacy*, 219; and Johnston, *Voyage of the Komagata Maru*, 128, 129.

50. Ethan Blue, "Cognitive Maps and Spatial Narratives: US Deportation Hearings and the Imaginative Cartographies of Forced Removal," in *The Social Work of Narrative: Human Rights and the Literary Imaginary*, ed. Gareth Griffiths and Philip Mead, 263–278 (Stuttgart: Ibidem-Verlag, 2017).

51. William C. Van Vleck, *The Administrative Control of Aliens: A Study in Administrative Law and Procedure* (New York: The Commonwealth Fund, 1932; reprint, New York: Da Capo Press, 1971), esp. 91–92, 101–105.

52. Mar, *Brokering Belonging*; and Ngai, *Lucky Ones*.

53. Herman R. Landon, "Deportation Procedure and Practice," 1943 Lecture Series, US Citizenship and Immigrations Services Archives and Library, Washington, DC, pp. 17–18.

54. De Certeau, *Practice of Everyday Life*, 122–125. These spatial stories also provide the spatio-temporal material on which this book's maps are based.

55. Chandan Singh hearing; Surain (sometimes written as "Suren") Singh hearing, September 24, 1914, 53852/19.

56. Salag Ram Testimony, September 24, 1914, 53852/19.

57. Chandan Singh Hearing, September 24, 1914, 53852/19.

58. Chandan Singh Hearing, September 24, 1914, 53852/19.

59. In some ways the questions about Marysville echoed questions asked about the geography of villages from whence Chinese migrants came, the difference being that the inspector may have had lived experience in addition to a Cartesian map of Marysville, while, as Madeleine Hsu has shown, he would likely have been profoundly ignorant of village geography and only sought to test the migrant's representation against the Immigration Bureau's paper record. Madeline Y. Hsu, *Dreaming of Gold, Dreaming of Home: Transnationalism and Migration Between the United States and South China, 1882–1943* (Stanford, CA: Stanford University Press, 2000), 82, 84.

60. Quoted in Takaki, *Strangers from a Different Shore*, 295.

61. Chandan Singh Hearing, September 24, 1914, 53852/19.

62. Chandan Singh Hearing, September 24, 1914, 53852/19.

63. Chandan Singh Testimony, September 24, 1914, 53852/19.

64. Attar Singh Testimony, September 24, 1914, 53852/19.

65. Sundar Singh Hearing, September 24, 1914, 53852/19.

66. Santa Singh Hearing, September 24, 1914, 53852/19.

67. Fred L. Boalt, "Hindu Kills High Priest on Altar in Vancouver!" *Seattle Star*, September 11, 1914, p. 6, col. 3.

68. Supplemental Memorandum for the Acting Secretary, November 18, 1914, 53852/19.

69. Report by Senior Watchman Thomas Latham to CG, November 30, 1914, 53852/19.

70. Report of Watchman Louis H. Engels, November 29, 1914, 53852/19.

71. Report by Senior Watchman Thomas Latham to CG, November 30, 1914, 53852/19.

72. Report of Watchman Louis H. Engels, November 29, 1914, 53852/19.

73. Correspondence from Sargent to CGI, December 4, 1914; and Report by Senior Watchman Thomas Latham to CG, November 30, 1914, 53852/19.

74. Correspondence from Sargent to CGI, December 4, 1914, 53852/19.

75. Skinner to USCI, December 12, 1914, 53852/19.

76. Sargent to CGI, December 10, 1919, 53852/19.

77. Skinner to USCI, December 12, 1914, 53852/19.

78. CG to CI, Angel Island, June 20, 1933, 53852/19.

79. White to CGI, Washington, DC, January 14, 1915, 53860/194.

80. *Tacoma Times*, January 11, 1915, p. 1 col. 3.

81. *Seattle Star*, October 21, 1914, p. 2, col. 3; and Chang, *Pacific Connections*, 170.

82. White to CGI, January 16, 1915, 53775/263, RG 85, Entry 9, NARA–Washington, DC.

83. Irwin, *Strange Passage*, 42–43.

84. Richard White, *The Organic Machine: The Remaking of the Columbia River* (New York: Hill and Wang, 1995), 46.

85. Garcilazo, *Traqueros*, 25.

86. Peter Boag, *Same Sex-Affairs: Constructing Homosexuality in the Pacific Northwest* (Berkeley: University of California Press, 2003), 17.

CHAPTER 3. PORTLAND

1. Shah, *Stranger Intimacy.*

2. Eithne Luibhéid, *Entry Denied: Controlling Sexuality at the Border* (Minneapolis: University of Minnesota Press, 2002).

3. The law was expanded considerably in 1910, when not just noncitizen sex workers could be deported, but any noncitizen women who worked in places where prostitutes might be thought to gather, including a "music or dance hall or other place of amusement." Moreover, anyone who gave aid or assistance to a sex worker could also be deported. Act of March 26, 1910, 36 Stat. 263, in Hutchinson, *Legislative History of American Immigration Policy, 1798–1965*, 452.

4. *AR-CGI 1914*, 7.

5. Robert D. Johnston, *The Radical Middle Class: Populist Democracy and the Question of Capitalism in Progressive Era Portland, Oregon* (Princeton, NJ: Princeton University Press, 2003), 61.

6. Ruth Rosen, *The Lost Sisterhood: Prostitution in America, 1900–1918* (Baltimore, MD: Johns Hopkins University Press, 1982), xi.

7. Clifford G. Roe and B. S. Steadwell, eds., *The Great War on White Slavery; Or, Fighting for the Protection of Our Girls* (1911), esp. 16.

8. Bruller as quoted in Hester, *Deportation: The Origins of U.S. Policy*, 82.

9. *AR-CGI 1931*, Table 106, 255–256. The numbers drawn from records relating to prostitution or procuring.

10. Rosen, *Lost Sisterhood*, 48.

11. Rosen, *Lost Sisterhood*, 49.

12. Hester, *Deportation: The Origins of U.S. Policy*, 83.

13. Boag, *Same-Sex Affairs*, 65, 188.

14. *Oregonian*, November 6, 1907, p. 7, quoted in Boag, *Same-Sex Affairs*, 68.

15. Boag, *Same-Sex Affairs*, 68.

16. *Oregonian*, April 28, 1895, p. 20, quoted in Boag, *Same-Sex Affairs*, 68.

17. I discuss other elements of Monet's case in Blue, "Cognitive Maps and Spatial Narratives."

18. Telegraphic Warrant Application, November 14, 1914, and Response, November 16, 1914, 53835/245, RG 85, Entry 9, NARA–Washington, DC.

19. Van Vleck, *Administrative Control of Aliens*, 224.

20. Hearing before Inspector Robbins, November 14, 1914, 53835/245.

21. Heather Lee Miller, "Trick Identities: The Nexus of Sex and Work," *Journal of Women's History* 5, no. 4 (2004): 145–152; and Rosen, *Lost Sisterhood*, 92.

22. Hearing, November 14, 1914, 53835/245.

23. Interrogation, November 16, 1914, 53835/245.

24. Arrest Warrant, November 16, 1914, 53835/245; and B. S. Steadwell, "The Great Purity Movement," in Roe and Steadwell, *Great War on White Slavery*, 442–448.

25. Inspector in Charge to CGI, Washington, DC, November 19, 1914, 53835/245.

26. Hester, *Deportation: The Origins of U.S. Policy*, 87.

27. On the significance of charitable institutions in US state formation, see Elisabeth S. Clemens, "Lineages of the Rube Goldberg State: Building and Blurring Public Programs, 1900–1940," in *Rethinking Political Institutions: The Art of the State*, ed. Ian Shapiro, Stephen Skowroneck, and Daniel Galvin, 380–443 (New York: New York University Press, 2007).

28. Estelle B. Freedman, *Their Sisters' Keepers: Women's Prison Reform in America, 1830–1930* (Ann Arbor: University of Michigan Press, 1981), 131–132; Cheryl D. Hicks, *Talk with You Like a Woman: African American Women, Justice, and Reform in New York, 1890–1935* (Chapel Hill: University of North Carolina Press, 2010); Kali N. Gross, *Colored Amazons: Crime, Violence, and Black Women in the City of Brotherly Love, 1880–1910* (Durham, NC: Duke University Press, 2006); and Luana Ross, *Inventing the Savage: The Social Construction of Native American Criminality* (Austin: University of Texas Press, 1998). Southern women's convict systems were more radically racially and spatially segregated: Sarah Haley, *No Mercy Here: Gender, Punishment, and the Making of Jim Crow Modernity* (Chapel Hill: University of North Carolina Press, 2016); and Talitha L. LeFlouria, *Chained in Silence: Black Women and Convict Labor in the New South* (Chapel Hill: University of North Carolina Press, 2015).

29. Rosen, *Lost Sisterhood*, 21.

30. Densmore to Portland Office, December 12, 1914, 53835/245.

31. Bonham to Immigration Bureau, February 24, 1919, 53835/245.

32. Monet Statement, April 12, 1919, 53835/245.

33. Bonham to CG, April 15, 1919, 53835/245.

34. In contrast, Clemence Genty was arrested for prostitution in Los Angeles in October 1914 and was loaded about an eastbound Deportation Special and returned to France two months later. See 52835/204, RG 85, Entry 9, NARA–Washington, DC. Also, James McMillan, "War," in *Political Violence in Twentieth Century Europe,* ed. Donald Bloxham and Robert Gerwith, 40–86 (Cambridge, UK: Cambridge University Press, 2011), 60.

35. Deportation Warrant, issued May 2, 1919, 54616/21, RG 85, Entry 9, NARA–Washington, DC.

36. Rose Abbott to "Sir," July 22, 1919, 54616/21.

37. Shah, *Stranger Intimacy*, esp. 129–152.

38. A. J. Gillis Statement, p. 12, February 14, 1919, 54616/21.

39. Its population grew alongside its diversifying economy, from 4,709 residents in 1890 to 19,364 in 1910. Beyond the small industries that supported local agriculture, Walla Walla was home to two daily newspapers, Whitman College, a business school, and a small symphony. Boag, *Same-Sex-Affairs*, 179–184, 180.

40. Inmates from Walla Walla and elsewhere, accustomed to long years incarcerated, might make themselves comfortable on the trains. In his novel *Theodore Irwin* (*Strange Passage*, 14–15) described: "The big mule faced man from the Walla Walla pen stood in the middle of the car waiving [*sic*] his arms and yelling in a rasping voice: Here y'are, ladies and gentlemen, here's a chance for you to buy some real bargains, better'n you can get in any department store. Genuine horsehair belts. Took me two months to make one at the Big House.... It was an auction. The other Walla Walla man, stubby and pock-marked, showed the articles around while his partner speieled [*sic*] and took bids. A beaded bag, Bring back a souvenir [*sic*] to the old country, remember your girl-friend or your old lady. Wah tam I bid.... Rings, watch fobs and chains earrings. No one would bid high enough. The Walla Walla men abandoned their auctioneering, tore up slips of paper, numbered them, and sold them for five cents a chance."

41. Abbott Hearing, February 14, 1919; and Inspector's Findings, February 21, 1919, 54616/21.

42. Charles Abbott Testimony, February 14, 1919, 54616/21.

43. Isabella Abbott Testimony, March 19, 1919, 54616/21.

44. Isabella Abbott Testimony, March 19, 1919, 54616/21.

45. Isabella Abbott Testimony, March 19, 1919, 54616/21.

46. Isabella Abbott Testimony, March 19, 1919, 54616/21.

47. Abbott Hearing, February 14, 1919, 54616/21.

48. Whitman Dramatic Club Playbill, March 20, 1919, 54616/21.

49. Abbott Hearing, February 14, 1919, 54616/21.

50. Boag, *Same-Sex Affairs*, 162–163.

51. E. R. Liggett Testimony, 54616/21.

52. Edwin Smith Testimony, 54616/21.

53. Edwin Smith Testimony, 54616/21.

54. Edwin Smith Testimony, 54616/21.

55. Boag, *Same-Sex Affairs*, 203.

56. A. J. Gillis Testimony, 54616/21.

57. A. J. Gillis Testimony; and Applegate Testimony, 54616/21.

58. A. J. Gillis Testimony, 54616/21.

59. Abbott Hearing, February 14, 1919, 54616/21.

60. Boag, *Same-Sex Affairs*, 9.

61. Inspector's Findings, February 21, 1919, 54616/21.

62. Shah, *Stranger Intimacy*; and Boag, *Same-Sex Affairs*, esp. 89–153.

63. Quoted in Boag, *Same-Sex Affairs*, 181. Discussion of the Gibson case draws from Boag, *Same-Sex Affairs*, 179–184.

64. Boag, *Same-Sex Affairs*, 61.

65. Boag, *Same-Sex Affairs*, 59–60.

66. Canaday, *Straight State*; and Baynton, *Defectives in the Land*, 46.

67. Abbott Hearing, February 14, 1919, 54616/21.

68. Boag, *Same-Sex Affairs*, 28, 119–124.

69. Shah, *Stranger Intimacy*, 133.

70. Feris and Abbott, within Edwin Smith Testimony, 54616/21.

71. Abbott Hearing, February 14, 1919, 54616/21.

72. Boag, *Same-Sex Affairs*, 182.

73. Gillis Hearing Statements, pp. 10–12, February 14, 1919, relating discussion with the physicians, 54616/21.

74. Gillis Hearing Statements, pp. 10–12, February 14, 1919, relating discussion with the physicians, 54616/21. As the century progressed, social hygienists expressed fears over men known as "wolves" or "jockers" having insertive sex with younger males and thereby sexually exploiting and "feminizing" them. That was not the case with Abbott, but it hardly exonerated him. Instead, Abbott's vilification meshed with the sense that he offered himself to be the receptive partner in the proposed (but not consummated) sexual encounters—that he would play the feminine role, and the youth the insertive and thus masculine role. In different contexts—for older youths or men in prison, transient camps, or such urban centers as New York; or in the context of what was understood as situational homosexuality—the proposed insertive act might have validated (rather than undermined) their nascent manhood. But in Walla Walla, in the recent context of the YMCA scandals, and with the specifics of the youngsters reporting and of Abbott's case, it turned out differently. George Chauncey, *Gay New York: Gender, Urban Culture, and the Making of the Gay Male World, 1890–1940* (New York: Basic Books, 1994); Regina Kunzel, "Situating Sex: Prison Sexual Culture in the Mid-Twentieth-Century United States," *GLQ* 8, no. 3 (2002): 293–270; Regina G. Kunzel, *Criminal Intimacy: Prison and the Uneven History of Modern American Sexuality* (Chicago: University of Chicago Press, 2008); Blue, *Doing Time in the Depression*; and Todd DePastino, *Citizen Hobo: How a Century of Homelessness Shaped America* (Chicago: University of Chicago Press, 2003), 85–91.

75. On endocrine knowledges, see Ethan Blue, "The Strange Career of Leo Stanley: Remaking Manhood and Medicine at San Quentin State Penitentiary, 1913–1951," *Pacific Historical Review* 78, no. 2 (2009): 210–241; Michael Pettit, "Becoming Glandular: Endocrinology, Mass Culture, and Experimental Lives in the Interwar Age," *American Historical Review* 118, no. 4 (2013): 1052–1076; and David Serlin, *Replaceable You: Engineering the Body in Postwar America* (Chicago: University of Chicago Press, 2004), 118–123.

76. Boag, *Same-Sex Affairs*, 127, 129.

77. Gail Bederman, *Manliness and Civilization: A Cultural History of Gender and Race in the United States, 1880–1917* (Chicago: University of Chicago Press, 1995).

78. Gillis Statement, p. 12, February 14, 1919, 54616/21.

79. Inspector's Findings, February 21, 1919, 54616/21.

80. Deportation Warrant, issued May 2, 1919, 54616/21.

81. Deportation Warrant, issued May 2, 1919, 54616/21.

82. Boag, *Same-Sex Affairs*, 206–216.

83. Mrs. Abbott Testimony, March 19, 1919, 54616/21.

84. Blue, "Strange Career of Leo Stanley," 211.

85. Mrs. R. Abbott to "Sir," May 21, 1919, 54616/21.

86. Mrs. R. Abbott to "Sir," May 21, 1919, 54616/21.

87. Mrs. Abbott to "Sir," July 1, 1919; Rose Abbott to Sir, July 22, 1919; and Rose Abbott to English Consul, Portland, June 29, 1919, 54616/21.

88. Rose Abbott to English Consul, Portland, June 29, 1919, 54616/21.

89. Quoted in Boag, *Same-Sex Affairs*, 182.

90. Pfaelzer, *Driven Out*, 343–345.

CHAPTER 4. SAN FRANCISCO

1. Brechin, *Imperial San Francisco*, 19, 123, 126, 135.

2. Leo Stanley, "Five Weeks Leave," 1, 2, Leo L. Stanley Papers, Box 1, Vol. 4, SC 070, Stanford University Library Special Collections, Stanford, CA.

3. Susan M. Schweik, *The Ugly Laws: Disability in Public* (New York: New York University Press, 2009), 2. Schweik quotes the *San Francisco Call*.

4. Stanley, "Five Weeks Leave," 2.

5. Stanley, "Five Weeks Leave," 2.

6. Stanley, "Five Weeks Leave," 8.

7. Stanley, "Five Weeks Leave," 2–3, 6; Stanley, "Trot, Trot, Trot to Boston," 26–27, Leo L. Stanley Papers, Box 1, Vol. 3, SC 070, Stanford University Library Special Collections, Stanford, CA; Jack Santino, *Miles of Smiles, Years of Struggle: Stories of Black Pullman Porters* (Urbana: University of Illinois Press, 1991), 31, 50–51, 126; C. L. Dellums, who worked as a porter, said they worked twenty hours each day; and Albert S. Broussard, *Black San Francisco: The Struggle for Racial Equality in the West, 1900–1954* (Lawrence: University Press of Kansas, 1993), 51.

8. Blue, "Strange Career of Leo Stanley," 210–241; and Stern, *Eugenic Nation*.

9. Stanley, "To Ellis Island and Back," 2, Leo L. Stanley Papers, Box 1, Vol. 2, SC 070, Stanford University Library Special Collections, Stanford, CA.

10. Leo L. Stanley, with Evelyn Wells, *Men at Their Worst* (New York: D. Appleton-Century, 1940); Blue, "Strange Career of Leo Stanley"; and Ethan Blue, "Abject Correction and Penal Medical Photography in the Early Twentieth Century," in *The Punitive Turn: New Approaches to Race and Incarceration*, ed. Deborah E. McDowell, Claudrena N. Harold, and Juan Battle, 108–130 (Charlottesville: University of Virginia Press, 2013).

11. Stanley, "To Ellis Island and Back."

12. Stanley, "To Ellis Island and Back," 3.

13. Kelly Lytle Hernández, "Hobos in Heaven: Race, Incarceration, and the Rise of Los Angeles, 1880–1910," *Pacific Historical Review* 83, no. 3 (2014): 410–447.

14. Robert L. Santos, *Azoreans to California: A History of Migration and Settlement* (Denair, CA: Alley-Cass Publications, 1995), 8, 15, 19–20.

15. Santos, *Azoreans to California*, 15.

16. Between 1880 and 1920, some 14 percent of Azorean migrants traveled to

Brazil, while 84 percent traveled to the United States. Santos, *Azoreans to California*, 22–24, 43.

17. Andrade Examination, October 7, 1914, 53851/34, RG 85, Entry 9, NARA–Washington, DC.

18. Andrade Examination, October 7, 1914, 53851/34. San Leandro, in the East Bay, was the spatial heart of Azorean life in California, and its geography and economy allowed both small-scale shop ownership as well as intensive market or truck farming, akin to what many had done in the Azores. Santos, *Azoreans to California*, 43, 45.

19. Certificate of Admission, dated August 24, 1914, 53851/34.

20. Mark Twain, *The Innocents Abroad* (New York: P.F. Collier & Son, 1911), 39–40. Quoted in Santos, *Azoreans to California*, 16.

21. Santos, *Azoreans to California*, 17–18, 50, 53, 56.

22. Santos, *Azoreans to California*, 23–24.

23. Certificate of Admission, dated August 24, 1914, 53851/34.

24. Stockton State Hospital patient record, December 12, 1913, 53851/34.

25. Medical Certificate—Prior to Landing, September 1, 1914, 53851/34.

26. *Laws of the State of Delaware, 1700–1797*, vol. 1, 166–170, in Hutchinson, *Legislative History of American Immigration Policy, 1798–1965*, 392–393.

27. G. Alder Blumer, "Presidential Address," *American Journal of Insanity* 60 (1903): 1–18, quoted in Ian Robert Dowbiggin, *Keeping America Sane: Psychiatry and Eugenics in the United States and Canada, 1880–1940* (Ithaca, NY: Cornell University Press, 2003), 192.

28. Dowbiggin, *Keeping America Sane*, 191, 206, 215.

29. Richard Noll, *American Madness: The Rise and Fall of Dementia Praecox* (Cambridge, MA: Harvard University Press, 2011), 26–31, 34–35.

30. Edward J. Kempf, "The Unsane Treatment of our Insane Patients," in *Edward J: Kempf, Selected Papers*, ed. Dorothy Clarke Kempf and John C. Burnham (Bloomington: University of Indiana Press, 1974), 19, quoted in Noll, *American Madness*, 33.

31. Joel T. Braslow, *Mental Ills and Bodily Cures: Psychiatric Treatment in the First Half of the Twentieth Century* (Berkeley: University of California Press, 1997), 2, 9, 39, 48–50; and Sarah C. Sitton, *Life at the Texas State Lunatic Asylum, 1857–1997* (College Station: Texas A & M University Press, 1999), 69, 77.

32. Stockton State Hospital Patient Record, December 12, 1913, 53851/34.

33. Medical Certificate—Prior to Landing, September 1, 1914, 53851/34.

34. Inspector H. (illeg.) to CI, Angel Island, December 31, 1914, 53851/34.

35. Deportation Warrant, January 23, 1915; correspondence from Acting CG to CI, Ellis Island, January 23, 1915, 53851/34.

36. *AR-CGI 1921*, 14.

37. Executed Deportation Warrant, April 26, 1915, 53851/34.

38. Record of Ocean Voyage, May 4, 1915, 53851/34.

39. Santos, *Azoreans to California*, 14.

40. Record of Land Trip and Delivery at Final Destination, 53851/34.

41. Scott Lauria Morgensen, "Theorising Gender, Sexuality and Settler Colonialism: An Introduction," *Settler Colonial Studies* 2, no. 2 (2012): 2–22; Albert L. Hurtado, *Intimate Frontiers: Sex, Gender and Culture in Old California* (Albuquerque: University of New Mexico Press, 1999), xxii–xxiii; and Lindsey Schneider, "(Re)producing the Nation: Treaty Rights, Gay Marriage, and the Settler State," in *Critical Ethnic Studies: A Reader,* ed. Critical Ethnic Studies Collective, 92–105 (Durham, NC: Duke University Press, 2016), esp. 100–101. Elements of the following argument draw on Blue, "From Lynch Mobs to the Deportation State," 1–24.

42. Ned Blackhawk, *Violence over the Land: Indians and Empires in the Early American West* (Cambridge, MA: Harvard University Press, 2006); Jon Christensen, "The Silver Legacy: San Francisco and the Comstock Lode," in *Reclaiming San Francisco: History, Politics, Culture*, ed. James Brook, Chris Carlsson, and Nancy J. Peters, 89–99 (San Francisco: City Lights Books, 1998); and Brechin, *Imperial San Francisco*, 19, 39.

43. Urban, *Brokering Servitude*, 169–170.

44. Minnie Brundage also leveled accusations of what would today be called spousal rape against James Pepper, though in muted fashion. Inspectors noted rumors circulating in Fairview that Minnie told people in town that he was "too amorous" to her. Pepper insisted on his innocence. "We always had the most lenient understandings about that thing," he claimed, "and never in any way did she object to me or accuse me of being too amorous." It was a strange linguistic contortion, and one that the inspector and Pepper shared, in which spousal rape was explained as a man having an excess of love. James Pepper Hearing, August 18, 1914, 53835/61, RG 85, Entry 9, NARA–Washington, DC.

45. Peggy Pascoe, *Relations of Rescue: The Search for Female Moral Authority in the American West, 1874–1939* (New York: Oxford University Press, 1990).

46. Estelle B. Freedman, *Redefining Rape: Sexual Violence in the Era of Suffrage and Segregation* (Cambridge, MA: Harvard University Press, 2013), 11.

47. Moloney, "Women, Sexual Morality, and Economic Dependency in Early U.S. Deportation Policy," 98.

48. Backus to CGI Washington, October 23, 1914, 53835/61.

49. Lawler to CI, Angel Island, December 7, 1914, 53835/61.

50. Backus to CGI, Washington, December 10, 1914, 53835/61.

51. Irwin, *Strange Passage*, 20.

52. Catterson, "Case of the Waylaid Immigrant Inspector"; and Pope-Obeda, "When in Doubt, Deport!," 275–276.

53. Stanley, "Five Weeks Leave," 18.

54. Stanley, "To Ellis Island and Back."

55. Irwin, *Strange Passage*, 43.

56. Stanley, "To Ellis Island and Back," 8.

57. Stanley, "Five Weeks Leave," 17.

1. Wheeler as quoted in Katherine Benton-Cohen, *Borderline Americans: Racial Division and Labor War in the Arizona Borderlands* (Cambridge, MA: Harvard University Press, 2009), 1, 212–213.

2. Samuel Truett, *Fugitive Landscapes: The Forgotten History of the U.S.-Mexico Borderlands* (New Haven, CT: Yale University Press, 2006), 90.

3. Benton-Cohen, *Borderline Americans*, 211, 217–222.

4. Benton-Cohen, *Borderline Americans*, 3, 211, 222–223.

5. Benton-Cohen, *Borderline Americans*, 216.

6. Presidential Mediation Committee, "Report on the Bisbee Deportations," p. 6, as quoted in Benton-Cohen, *Borderline Americans*, 234.

7. *AR-CGI 1931*, Table 106, 255.

8. Stephen J. Leonard, "Denver, Colorado," in *The New Encyclopedia of the American West*, ed. Howard J. Lamar, 296–299 (New Haven: Yale University Press, 1998), esp. 297. Elizabeth Jameson, *All That Glitters: Class, Conflict, and Community in Cripple Creek* (Urbana: University of Illinois Press, 1998), 2–3.

9. Thomas J. Noel and Nicholas J. Wharton, *Denver Landmarks and Historic Districts* (Boulder: University Press of Colorado, 2016), 4–6.

10. Noel and Wharton, *Denver Landmarks and Historic Districts*, 43.

11. Carlos A. Schwantes, "The Concept of the Wageworkers Frontier: A Framework for Future Research" *Western Historical Quarterly* 18, no. 1 (1987): 39–55; Gunther Peck, "Padrones and Protest: 'Old' Radicals and 'New' Immigrants in Bingham, Utah, 1905–1912," *Western Historical Quarterly* 24, no. 2 (1993): 157–178; Jameson, *All That Glitters*; and Thomas G. Andrews, *Killing for Coal: America's Deadliest Labor War* (Cambridge, MA: Harvard University Press, 2008).

12. Joe Kennedy case file, undated image and document attached to March 13, 1924, correspondence from State Department to W. W. Husband, DoL, 54161/74, RG 85, Entry 9, NARA–Washington, DC.

13. Kennedy was similar to a great many immigrant anarchists; less a direct inheritor of European anarchist traditions than one who came to anarchist positions from lived experience. Kenyon Zimmer, *Immigrants against the State: Yiddish and Italian Anarchism in America* (Urbana: University of Illinois Press, 2015). On the broad basis of state and civil-society coercion in World War I, see Christopher Capozzola, *Uncle Sam Wants You: World War I and the Making of the Modern American Citizen* (New York: Oxford University Press, 2008).

14. Joe Kennedy interrogation, February 19, 1919, 54161/74; and David M. Emmons, *The Butte Irish: Class and Ethnicity in an American Mining Town* (Urbana: University of Illinois Press, 1989), 2.

15. Kevin Kenny, *The American Irish: A History* (New York: Longman, 2000), 134–136.

16. Emmons, *Butte Irish*, 2–3; and Kenny, *American Irish*.

17. Kenny, *American Irish*, 134.

18. Michael P. Malone, *The Battle for Butte: Mining and Politics on the Northern Frontier, 1864–1906* (Seattle: University of Washington Press, 2006), 3–4.

19. Emmons, *Butte Irish*, 19–21.

20. Emmons, *Butte Irish*, 20–21.

21. Malone, *Battle for Butte*, 61.

22. Production grew from $1.2 million in 1881 to more than $27 million in 1890. Emmons, *Butte Irish*, 23.

23. Emmons, *Butte Irish*, 24.

24. Malone, *Battle for Butte*, 33.

25. Malone, *Battle for Butte*, 61–65, 68.

26. Gertrude Atherton, quoted in Malone, *Battle for Butte*, 61.

27. March 19, 1919, testimony, 54161/74.

28. Average expenses in Butte outpaced other industrial cities by $400 per year. Emmons, *Butte Irish*, 367.

29. Emmons, *Butte Irish*, 367.

30. March 19, 1919, testimony, 54161/74.

31. Quoted in Emmons, *Butte Irish*, 370. "Some faint in the stope and some faint coming out of the stope," Kennedy reported. It was too hot to wear a shirt, so Kennedy and his fellow miners worked in coveralls and shoes. No water was available, so Kennedy had to lug his in a dinner bucket, and once the bucket was dry, he had to climb 150 feet for a drink. March 19, 1919, testimony, 54161/74.

32. Robert V. Hine and John Mack Faragher, *The American West: A New Interpretive History* (New Haven, CT: Yale University Press, 2000), 270.

33. March 19, 1919, testimony, 54161/74.

34. March 19, 1919, testimony, 54161/74.

35. Emmons, *Butte Irish*, 370.

36. Malone, *Battle for Butte*, 76.

37. March 19, 1919, testimony, 54161/74.

38. Arnon Gutfeld, "The Speculator Mine Disaster in 1917: Labor Resurgence at Butte, Montana," *Arizona and the West* 11, no. 1 (1969): 27–38, esp. 27–28.

39. Gutfeld, "Speculator Mine Disaster in 1917," 27–38, esp. 27–28.

40. Quoted in Gutfeld, "Speculator Mine Disaster," 28.

41. Melvyn Dubofsky, *We Shall Be All: A History of the Industrial Workers of the World* (Chicago: Quadrangle Books, 1969), 366.

42. Gutfeld, "Speculator Mine Disaster," 29.

43. Gutfeld, "Speculator Mine Disaster," 29.

44. March 19, 1919, testimony, 54161/74.

45. Dubofsky, *We Shall Be All*, 366. The Butte Miners Union was defunct, the Butte Mine Workers Union was tiny, the local affiliate of the American Federation of Labor had little purchase with miners, and the Western Federation of Miners and IWW locals remained relatively small.

46. March 19, 1919, testimony, 54161/74.

47. Dubofsky, *We Shall Be All*, 367.

48. Quoted in Emmons, *Butte Irish*, 349–350.

49. Emmons, *Butte Irish*, 359–360.

50. Tom Campbell and Joe Shannon were both Wobblies who played a considerable role in the MMWU leadership. Dubofsky, *We Shall Be All*, 367.

51. Kenyon Zimmer, "The Voyage of the *Buford*: Political Deportations and the Making and Unmaking of America's First Red Scare," in *Deportation in the Americas: Histories of Exclusion and Resistance*, ed. Kenyon Zimmer and Cristina Salinas, 132–163 (College Station: Texas A&M University Press, 2018), 135.

52. Dubofsky, *We Shall Be All*, 349–358.

53. Capozzola, *Uncle Sam Wants You*, 8–11.

54. Emmons, *Butte Irish*, 361–362.

55. Dubofsky, *We Shall Be All*, 376.

56. Dubofsky, *We Shall Be All*, 377–378.

57. Quoted in David Cole, *Enemy Aliens: Double Standards and Constitutional Freedoms in the War on Terrorism* (New York: Free Press, 2003), 117.

58. Dubofsky, *We Shall Be All*, 373.

59. Preston, *Aliens and Dissenters*, 105.

60. Preston, *Aliens and Dissenters*, 106.

61. Preston, *Aliens and Dissenters*, 106–108.

62. Quoted in Dubofsky, *We Shall Be All*, 433.

63. Dubofsky, *We Shall Be All*, 437.

64. Dubofsky, *We Shall Be All*, 380.

65. Jane Little Botkin, *Frank Little and the IWW: The Blood That Stained an American Family* (Norman: University of Oklahoma Press, 2017), 12–14.

66. Arnon Gutfeld, "The Murder of Frank Little: Radical Labor Agitation in Butte, Montana," *Labor History* 10, no. 2 (March 1969): 177–192, esp. 178.

67. Rebecca N. Hill, *Men, Mobs, and Law: Anti-Lynching and Labor Defense in U.S. Radical History* (Durham, NC: Duke University Press, 2008), 147.

68. Quoted in Gutfeld, "Murder of Frank Little," 183.

69. Michael Cohen, "'The Ku Klux Government': Vigilantism, Lynching, and the Repression of the IWW," *Journal for the Study of Radicalism* 1, no. 1 (2007): 31–56, esp. 41.

70. Quoted in Gutfeld, "Murder of Frank Little," 185, emphasis in original.

71. *Butte Daily Post*, July 28, 1917, quoted Gutfeld, "Murder of Frank Little," 186.

72. Gutfeld, "Murder of Frank Little," 186.

73. Gutfeld, "Murder of Frank Little," 177–178, 187.

74. Gutfeld, "Murder of Frank Little," 177–178, 187; and Botkin, *Frank Little and the IWW*, 5.

75. *Helena Independent*, August 2, 1917, quoted in Gutfeld, "Murder of Frank Little," 190.

76. Both quoted in Cohen, "Ku Klux Government," 42.

77. March 19, 1919, testimony, 54161/74.

78. Gutfeld, "Murder of Frank Little," 189.

79. They grew stronger when Anaconda smelter workers joined in. The International Union of Mine, Mill, and Smelter Workers had recently been remarkably conciliatory to Anaconda Copper, but after the Speculator disaster, eight hundred smelter workers joined the MMWU and voted to strike. The company was left with no one to refine the ore that strikebreakers brought up, and copper production fell from 17,000 tons per day to 1,600. Nevertheless, after receiving some concessions, most of the smelter workers returned to the job in late September, too reliant on smelter income to sustain a long strike and fearing losing their jobs to newcomer strikebreakers. Laurie Mercier, *Anaconda: Labor, Community, and Culture in Montana's Smelter City* (Urbana: University of Illinois Press, 2001), 19; and Emmons, *Butte Irish*, 372.

80. Emmons, *Butte Irish*, 368.

81. Melvin Dubofsky, *The State and Labor in Modern America* (Chapel Hill: University of North Carolina Press, 1994), 67. Preston, *Aliens and Dissenters*, 110.

82. Quotes and emphasis in Preston, *Aliens and Dissenters*, 111.

83. Joe Kennedy Interrogation Transcript, February 19, 1919, 54161/74.

84. March 19, 1919, testimony, 54161/74.

85. Dubofsky, *We Shall Be All*, 359.

86. Emmons, *Butte Irish*, 380.

87. Defense brief for Joe Kennedy, by attorneys Nolan + Donavan and H. A. Tyvand (last signature illegible), sent from the Helena immigration office to the CG, April 30, 1919, 54161/74.

88. E. W. Byrn to A. B. Bielaski, September 15, 1918, Department of Justice File 195397-1, and US Attorney Wheeler to Thomas W. Gregory, September 16, 1918, Department of Justice File 195397-2, quoted in Preston, *Aliens and Dissenters*, 114.

89. Dubofsky, *We Shall Be All*, 450–452.

90. Quoted in Dubofsky, *We Shall Be All*, 452.

91. Dubofsky, *We Shall Be All*, 451.

92. Dubofsky, *We Shall Be All*, 451.

93. On the strategy more broadly and particularly *Colyer v. Skeffington* (1919), see Moloney, *National Insecurities*, 180–182.

94. March 19, 1919, testimony: Questions from Tyvand, 54161/74.

95. Zimmer, "Voyage of the *Buford*," 143.

96. *AR-CGI 1919*, 34fn1.

97. The numbers refer to those recoded in *AR-CGI 1919*, 34.

98. Both in 54161/74: Arrest Warrant, February 20, 1919; and Deportation Warrant, May 1, 1919.

99. Zimmer, "Voyage of the *Buford*," 146.

100. Cannato, *American Passage*, 312.

101. Quoted in Cannato, *American Passage*, 312.

102. Zimmer, "Voyage of the *Buford*," 146–151.

103. Many thanks to Philip Chilton for insight into the legacies of the 1916 Easter Rising.

104. Correspondence from Second Assistant Secretary (name illegible, initials A.A.A.) to Secretary of State, June 28, 1919, 54161/74.

105. Undated image and document attached to March 13, 1924, correspondence from State Department to W. W. Husband, DoL, 54161/74.

106. In Zimmer, *Immigrants against the State*, 156–158, the author argues that deportation was relatively ineffective in suppressing anarchist movements in the United States due to anarchists' skillful legal maneuvering within federal bureaucratic complexity and inefficiencies. The total number of people deported for anarchism may have been small, but the symbolic violence and threat of removal was powerful repression. Zimmer ably documents this too, in his discussion of Ludovico Caminita's experience after a 1920 raid in Patterson, New Jersey, which undermined regional anarchist networks (see *Immigrants against the State*, 152–156).

107. *AR-CGI 1919*, 35, emphasis added.

108. Preston, *Aliens and Dissenters*, 232–233.

109. Preston, *Aliens and Dissenters*, 232–233.

110. Dubofsky, *State and Labor*, 69.

111. John Higham, *Strangers in the Land: Patterns of American Nativism* (New Brunswick, NJ: Rutgers University Press, 1955), 221–222.

112. Cole, *Enemy Aliens*, 105–128.

113. Preston, *Aliens and Dissenters*, 208–237; Louis F. Post, *The Deportation Delirium of 1920* (Chicago: Charles H. Kerr, 1923); and Cole, *Enemy Aliens*, 105–128.

CHAPTER 6. CHICAGO

1. Leo Stanley, "To Ellis Island and Back," 37, Leo L. Stanley Papers, Box 1, Vol. 2, SC 070, Stanford University Library Special Collections, Stanford, CA.

2. Upton Sinclair, *The Jungle* (New York: Grosset & Dunlop, 1906), chapter 2, www.gutenberg.org/files/140/140-h/140-h.htm.

3. Cronon, *Nature's Metropolis*.

4. Pliley, *Policing Sexuality*, 61.

5. Leo Stanley, "Trot, Trot, Trot to Boston," 25, 28, Leo L. Stanley Papers, Box 1, Vol. 3, SC 070, Stanford University Library Special Collections, Stanford, CA.

6. Irwin, *Strange Passage*, 95.

7. Stanley, "Trot, Trot, Trot to Boston," 24.

8. Stanley, "Trot, Trot, Trot to Boston," 25–26.

9. Spiros Olebos Case File, 53835/252, RG 85, Entry 9, NARA–Washington, DC.

10. Henry Pratt Fairchild, *Greek Immigration to the United States* (New Haven, CT: Yale University Press, 1911), 29, 24.

11. Numbers calculated reflect 1916–1931 (but not 1915), as per *AR-CGI 1931*, Table 106, 225–226.

12. Mitcho M. Pappas, "The Greek Immigrant in the United States since 1910," MA thesis, Montana State University, 1949, p. 4; and Theodore Saloutos, *The Greeks in the United States* (Cambridge, MA: Harvard University Press, 1964), 45.

13. "Greeks," *Encyclopedia of Chicago*, www.encyclopedia.chicagohistory.org/pages/548.html.

14. Manuel Borutta and Sakis Gekas, "A Colonial Sea: The Mediterranean, 1798–1956," *European Review of History* 19, no. 1 (2012): 2–3.

15. Richard Clogg, "The Greek Diaspora: The Historical Context," in *The Greek Diaspora in the Twentieth Century*, ed. Richard Clogg, 1–23 (Houndsmills: Macmillan Press, 1999), 12.

16. Nicos P. Mouzelis, *Modern Greece: Facets of Underdevelopment* (London: Macmillan, 1978), 12–15, 18–19, 29; and Sakis Gekas, "Colonial Migrants and the Making of a British Mediterranean," *European Review of History* 19, no. 1 (2012): 75–92, esp. 77–80.

17. Gunther Peck, *Reinventing Free Labor: Padrones and Immigrant Workers in the North American West, 1880–1930* (New York: Cambridge University Press, 2000), 127.

18. Saloutos, *Greeks in the United States*, 29; and Mouzelis, *Modern Greece*, 19–21.

19. Peck, *Reinventing Free Labor*, 127.

20. Clogg, "Greek Diaspora," 6–7.

21. On family, masculinity, and honor in Greek villages—treated as timeless in midcentury anthropological literature and eschewing regional variation—see J. K. Campbell, *Honour, Family and Patronage: A Study Institutions and Moral Values in a Greek Mountain Village* (Oxford, UK: Oxford University Press, 1964); and Juliet du Boulay, *Portrait of a Greek Mountain Village* (Oxford, UK: Oxford University Press, 1974). For well-placed criticisms, see Peck, *Reinventing Free Labor*.

22. Saloutos, *Greeks in the United States*, 31, 34–35, 39.

23. Isaac James Quillen, "Industrial City: A History of Gary, Indiana to 1929," PhD dissertation, Yale University, 1942, p. 161.

24. Hearing, December 12, 1914; and copy of Certificate of Admission, dated November 24, 1914, 53835/252.

25. Saloutos, *Greeks in the United States*, 46–48.

26. "Chicago, 1900–1914," University of Chicago Library, www.lib.uchicago.edu/e/collections/maps/chi1900/; and Walter Nugent, "Demography: Chicago as a Modern World City," *Encyclopedia of Chicago*, www.encyclopedia.chicagohistory.org/pages/962.html.

27. Raymond A. Mohl and Neil Betten, *Steel City: Urban and Ethnic Patterns in Gary, Indiana, 1906–1950* (New York: Holmes & Meier, 1986), 11.

28. Quillen, "Industrial City," 11–18.

29. Quillen, "Industrial City," 34.

30. In its first year US Steel was responsible for more than 60 percent of all national ore output. By 1907 it controlled some 80 percent of ore around the Lake Superior region, from the Menominee, Marquette, Geobic, Vermillion, and Mesabi Ranges. It maintained its own railroads and shipping fleets to get that ore to production plants in Chicago and Gary. It controlled some of the most extensive and most sophisticated coal mining, coking, and transport facilities in the world. By 1913, US pig iron production was three times greater and finished steel more than four times greater than the United Kingdom's output. R. Boeckel, "The Iron and Steel Industry," *Editorial Research Reports 1930*, vol. 2 (Washington, DC: CQ Press, 1930); and Quillen, "Industrial City," 31–33.

31. Carol D. Griskavich, "From Mill Gates to Magic City: U.S. Steel and Welfare Capitalism in Gary, Indiana, 1906–1930," MS thesis, Michigan Technical University, 2014, p. 11.

32. Griskavich, "From Mill Gates to Magic City," 11, 16.

33. Quoted in Mohl and Betten, *Steel City*, 14.

34. Steve McShane, "The Magic City of Steel," U.S. Steel Gary Works Photograph Collection, 1906–1971, Indiana University, http://webapp1.dlib.indiana .edu/ussteel/context/essay.jsp, accessed November 28, 2018; see also Quillen, "Industrial City," 197–200.

35. Mohl and Betten, *Steel City*, 14.

36. Another booster proclaimed that "never before in the history of the material development of the American continent, or its people . . . has an industrial enterprise of such gigantic proportions been conceived and put into execution, and carried out, as the marvelous enterprise now building at Gary, Indiana" (in Mohl and Betten, *Steel City*, 14).

37. McShane, "Magic City of Steel," 197–200.

38. Certificate of Admission, dated November 24, 1914; and Hearing, December 12, 1914, 53835/252. Jim and Gust's address in the author's copy of December 1914 hearing is difficult to read but appears to be 1751 Pearson Street. I can find no Pearson Street in Gary; this may have been a mistranscription of Pierce Street.

39. Fairchild, *Greek Immigration to the United States*, 239.

40. Quoted in Saloutos, *Greeks in the United States*, 66.

41. Quoted in Saloutos, *Greeks in the United States*, 66.

42. Saloutos, *Greeks in the United States*, 67.

43. Saloutos, *Greeks in the United States*, 68.

44. Evelyn Brooks Higginbotham, *Righteous Discontent: The Women's Movement in the Black Baptist Church, 1880–1920* (Cambridge, MA: Harvard University Press, 1994).

45. Saloutos, *Greeks in the United States*, 63.

46. Andonis Piperoglou, "Vagrant 'Gypsies' and Respectable Greeks: A Defining Moment in Early-Colonial Melbourne, 1897–1900," in *Reading, Interpreting, Experiencing: An Inter-Cultural Journey into Greek Letters,* ed. M. Tsianikas, G. Couvalis, and M. Palaktsoglou, 140–151 (Modern Greek Studies Association of Australia and New Zealand, 2015); and Andonis Piperoglou, "'Border

Barbarisms,' Albury 1902: Greeks and the Ambiguity of Whiteness," *Australian Journal of Politics and History,* vol. 64, no. 4 (2018): 1–15.

47. Saloutos, *Greeks in the United States,* 63, 232–237.

48. Hearing, December 12, 1914, 53835/252.

49. David Montgomery, *The Fall of the House of Labor: The Workplace, the State, and American Labor Activism, 1865–1925* (New York: Cambridge University Press, 1987), 29, 45–46, 258.

50. Montgomery, *Fall of the House of Labor,* 24–25.

51. Quillen, "Industrial City," 219.

52. Quillen, "Industrial City," 219; and Juan R. García, *Mexicans in the Midwest, 1900–1932* (Tucson: University of Arizona Press, 1996), 72.

53. Mohl and Betten, *Steel City,* 28.

54. Arundel Cotter, *The Authentic History of the U.S. Steel Corporation* (New York: Moody Magazine and Book Co., 1916), 4, quoted in Quillen, "Industrial City," 4.

55. Griskavich, "From Mill Gates to Magic City," 91–92.

56. Griskavich, , "From Mill Gates to Magic City," 92–93.

57. US Steel wanted to avoid the charges of autocratic paternalism that the Pullman company faced in the nearby eponymous town. Griskavich, "From Mill Gates to Magic City," 6.

58. Quillen, "Industrial City," 162.

59. Mohl and Betten, *Steel City,* 28.

60. Quillen, "Industrial City," 218.

61. Mohl and Betten, *Steel City,* 18–19.

62. James B. Lane, *City of the Century: A History of Gary, Indiana* (Bloomington: Indiana University Press, 1978), 34.

63. Lane, *City of the Century,* 35.

64. Lane, *City of the Century,* 36.

65. Quillen, "Industrial City," 130.

66. Quillen, "Industrial City," 146.

67. Quillen, "Industrial City," 232.

68. Quillen, "Industrial City," 146.

69. Quillen, "Industrial City," 175.

70. Quillen, "Industrial City," 220.

71. Saloutos, *Greeks in the United States,* 82.

72. Gust Olebos testimony, December12, 1914, Hearing, 53835/252.

73. November 22, 1914, Statement, Mary Olimbos [*sic*], 53835/252.

74. November 22, 1914, Statement, Mary Olimbos [*sic*], 53835/252.

75. November 22, 1914, Statement, Mary Olimbos [*sic*], 53835/252.

76. December 12, 1914, Hearing, 53835/252.

77. December 12, 1914, Hearing, 53835/252.

78. December 12, 1914, Hearing, 53835/252.

79. Peck, *Reinventing Free Labor,* 124–125, 129; and Saloutos, *Greeks in the United States,* 87.

80. Peck, *Reinventing Free Labor*, 125n14; and Margaret Alexiou, "Sons, Wives, and Mothers: Reality and Fantasy in Some Modern Greek Ballads," *Journal of Modern Greek Studies*1, no. (1983): 73–111, esp. 86–87.

81. Quillen, "Industrial City," 259–262.

82. December 12, 1914, Hearing, 53835/252.

83. December 12, 1914, Hearing, 53835/252.

84. Sarah F. Rose, *No Right to Be Idle: The Invention of Disability, 1840s–1930s* (Chapel Hill: University of North Carolina Press, 2017), 125–126, 165.

85. Rosen, *Lost Sisterhood*, 139, 148, 150.

86. Quillen, "Industrial City," 204, 207–215.

87. Quillen, "Industrial City," 210.

88. December 12, 1914, Hearing, 53835/252.

89. Pliley, *Policing Sexuality*, 138.

90. December 12, 1914, Hearing, 53835/252.

91. Mary Olimbos Statement, November 22, 1914, 53835/252; and Pliley, *Policing Sexuality*, 203.

92. Mary Olimbos Correspondence, US Immigration Office, Chicago, November 24, 1914, 53835/252.

93. Pliley, *Policing Sexuality*, 131–132, 147–148.

94. December 12, 1914, Hearing, 53835/252.

95. December 12, 1914, Hearing, 53835/252. Of course, it isn't impossible that Mary herself would threaten Spiros, or that she had faced circumstances in which violence was necessary for self–protection. It is difficult to interpret from a distance, but it appears that affection, violence, and threats of violence can coexist among psychological dynamics of intimate family violence situations.

96. December 12, 1914, Hearing, 53835/252.

97. Prentis to CGI, December 14, 1914, 53835/252.

98. Memorandum for Acting Secretary, December 12, 1914; and Deportation Warrant, December 23, 1914, 53835/252.

99. Itinerary in Stanley, "To Ellis Island and Back."

CHAPTER 7. BUFFALO

1. Irwin, *Strange Passage*,108.

2. Stanley, "To Ellis Island and Back," 41.

3. Irwin, *Strange Passage*, 108.

4. Pope-Obeda, "When in Doubt, Deport," 105. On Canada's deportation regime, see Barbara Roberts, *Whence They Came: Deportation from Canada, 1900–1935* (Ottawa: University of Ottawa Press, 1988).

5. Clemens, "Lineages of the Rube Goldberg State"; Fox, *Three Worlds of Relief*; Gordon, *Pitied but Not Entitled*; Hiroshi Motomura, *Americans in Wait-*

ing: The Lost Story of Immigration and Citizenship in the United States (New York: Oxford University Press, 2006); and Baynton, *Defectives in the Land.*

6. Between 1916 and 1931 some 11,668 people were deported from the interior on the bases of mental or physical "defectiveness," or illness. Calculated from "public charges from causes existing prior to entry" and "mentally or physically defective at time of entry," in *AR-CGI 1931*, Table 106, 225.

7. It isn't clear what sort of work Minnie Lester's parents might have done, or if their livelihoods were hurt by the increasing competition from cheap US-made goods and which led in part to the depression. The address Minnie would later use, on Portchester Street, north of Birmingham's city center, was near both the jewelry- and gun-making districts, two important features of the city's political economy. By the 1890s, Birmingham's manufacturers had undergone increasing horizontal consolidation, but despite greater oversight of their work by employers, members of the privileged working classes saw relatively little industrial strife. Eric Hopkins, "Industrial Change and Life at Work in Birmingham, 1850–1914," *Midland History* 27, no. 1 (2002): 130–145, esp. 115, 119. Minnie and John Lester's file is at 53845/202, RG 85, Entry 9, NARA–Washington, DC.

8. Asa Briggs, *Victorian Cities* (London: Odhams Press, 1963), 197, 203, quote on 234.

9. Briggs, *Victorian Cities*, 228.

10. Quoted in Briggs, *Victorian Cities*, 229.

11. Briggs, *Victorian Cities*, 229. Briggs does not address whether or not prior residents of the newly cleansed areas would be welcome in the surely dearer accommodation.

12. Briggs, *Victorian Cities*, 219.

13. Report of Hearing, December 29, 1914, 53845/202.

14. Walter Nugent, *Crossings: The Great Transatlantic Migrations, 1870–1914* (Bloomington: Indiana University Press, 1992), Table 10, 46.

15. Urban, *Brokering Servitude*, 139; and Moloney, "Women, Sexual Morality, and Economic Dependency in Early U.S. Deportation Policy," 95–122.

16. Alice Kessler-Harris has referred to the ability to make a sustainable living as economic citizenship, defined as "the independent status that provides the possibility of full participation in the polity." I draw on Kessler-Harris's insight but am wary of reliance on the notion of *citizenship* as a just measure of social inclusion, when the citizenship is continually produced through the disavowal of those marked by alienage. Kessler-Harris, *In Pursuit of Equity: Women, Men, and the Quest for Economic Citizenship in 20th-century America* (New York: Oxford University Press, 2001), 5.

17. Kristin Szczepzniec, *Indigenous People of Western New York* (Cornell University ILR Digital Commons, February 2018), 1–4, https://digitalcommons .ilr.cornell.edu/cgi/viewcontent.cgi?article=1376&context=buffalocommons, accessed April 2, 2019.

18. Blake McKelvey, *Rochester on the Genesee: The Growth of a City*, 2nd edition (Syracuse, NY: Syracuse University Press, 1993), 1–3.

19. McKelvey, *Rochester on the Genesee,* 24–25.

20. McKelvey, *Rochester on the Genesee,* 71.

21. Blake McKelvey, "Historic Origins of Rochester's Social Welfare Agencies," *Rochester History* 9, nos. 2–3 (1947): 13.

22. McKelvey, *Rochester on the Genesee,* 122–23.

23. McKelvey, *Rochester on the Genesee,* xiv.

24. McKelvey, "Historic Origins of Rochester's Social Welfare Agencies," 19.

25. McKelvey, *Rochester on the Genesee,* 138.

26. McKelvey, *Rochester on the Genesee,* 138–140, 163.

27. In 1900, 77 percent of single mothers were widows. A Philadelphia study found that more than 20 percent of working mothers had lost husbands. Gordon, *Pitied but Not Entitled,* 19, 22.

28. Laura Briggs, *How All Politics Became Reproductive Politics: From Welfare Reform to Foreclosure to Trump* (Berkeley: University of California Press, 2017), 2.

29. Mary V. Robinson, *Domestic Workers and Their Employment Relations: A Study Based on the Records of the Domestic Efficiency Association of Baltimore, Maryland* (Washington, DC: Government Printing Office, 1924), p. 4, https:// catalog.hathitrust.org/Record/003263016, accessed March 1, 2019.

30. C. E. Persons, "Women's Work and Wages in the United States," *Quarterly Journal of Economics* 29, no. 2 (1915): 201–234, esp. 202.

31. Rosen, *Lost Sisterhood,* 155.

32. Gordon, *Pitied but Not Entitled,* 22.

33. Urban, *Brokering Servitude.*

34. W.A.K. Koren, *Benevolent Institutions, 1904,* US Census Bureau (Washington, DC: Government Printing Office, 1905), p. 102, https://books.google .com.au/books?id=NqlZPl1qj4EC&pg=PA102&lpg=PA102&dq=Rochester+ind ustrial+school+exchange+street&source=bl&ots=S_HeF6zCGC&sig=BB8D11 4K4wJWoCf6xU1rQKR5WoQ&hl=en&sa=X&ved=0ahUKEwj8_ffPmfPRAh VKv48KHdcBAQwQ6AEIJTAC#v=onepage&q=Rochester%20industrial%20 school%20exchange%20street&f=false, accessed February 3, 2017.

35. Ruth Rosenberg-Naparsteck, "A Brief History of Rochester Childfirst Network," *Rochester History* (Fall 2006), 4.

36. McKelvey, "Historic Origins of Rochester's Social Welfare Agencies," 6.

37. *Union & Advertiser,* January 10, 1868, p. 2, col. 5; and *First Annual Report,* January 2, 1858, quoted in Rosenberg–Naparsteck, "Brief History of Rochester Childfirst Network," 6.

38. *Times-Union,* January 21, 1984, quoted in Rosenberg-Naparsteck, "Brief History of Rochester Childfirst Network," 15.

39. Urban, *Brokering Servitude.*

40. *Times-Union,* January 21, 1984, quoted in Rosenberg-Naparsteck, "Brief History of Rochester Childfirst Network," 16.

41. Report of Hearing, December 29, 1914, RG 85, Entry 9, 53845/202.

42. Rose, *No Right to Be Idle,* 223–224.

43. Rose, *No Right to Be Idle,* 224.

44. A Massachusetts study from 1912 found that 57 percent of children who did not live with their widowed mothers had been separated from them due to the family's poverty, rather than due to a lack of maternal affection. Gordon, *Pitied but Not Entitled*, 23.

45. Gordon, *Pitied but Not Entitled*, 24.

46. Bridges to Martin, November 30, 1914, 53845/202.

47. Fox, *Three Worlds of Relief*, 55–56.

48. Report of Hearing, December 29, 1914, 53845/202.

49. Natalia Molina, "Deportable Citizens: The Decoupling of Race and Citizenship in the Construction of the 'Anchor Baby,'" in *Deportation in the Americas: Histories of Exclusion and Resistance*, ed. Kenyon Zimmer and Cristina Salinas, 164–191 (College Station: Texas A&M University Press, 2018).

50. Fox, *Three Worlds of Relief*, 113.

51. Fox, *Three Worlds of Relief*, 143, 156.

52. Report of Hearing, December 29, 1914. 53845/202.

53. Howard Knox, "Tests for Mental Defects: How the Public Health Service Prevents Contamination of Our Racial Stock by Turning Back Feeble-Minded Immigrants—General Characteristics Noted and Progressive Series of Tests Applied to Determine Exact Mentality," *Journal of Heredity* 5, no. 3 (1914): 122–130, esp. 125. Quoted in Jay Dolmage, "Disabled upon Arrival: The Rhetorical Construction of Disability and Race at Ellis Island," *Cultural Critique* 77 (Winter 2011): 24–69, esp. 45.

54. Report of Hearing, December 29, 1914, 53845/202.

55. Clark to CGI, Washington DC, January 5, 1915, 53845/202.

56. Rose, *No Right to Be Idle*, esp. 221–224.

57. County Physician to "whom it may concern," December 31, 1914; and Memorandum For Acting Secretary, January 11, 1915, 53845/202.

58. Linda Reeder, "When the Men Left Sutera: Sicilian Women and Mass Migration, 1880–1920," in *Women, Gender, and Transnational Lives: Italian Workers of the World*, ed. Donna Gabaccia and Franca Iacovetta, 45–75 (Toronto: University of Toronto Press, 2002), 45, 50–51.

59. Donna R. Gabaccia and Franca Iacovetta, introduction to *Women, Gender, and Transnational Lives: Italian Workers of the World*, ed. Donna Gabaccia and Franca Iacovetta, 3–42 (Toronto: University of Toronto Press, 2002), 10.

60. Angela Ferrer, Certificate of Admission, copy dated February 4, 1915; Salvatore Piazza, Certificate of Admission, copy dated February 4, 1915; and Report of Hearing, plus Hearing, February 25, 1915, 53934/39, RG 85, Entry 9, NARA–Washington, DC.

61. The numbers of Italian-born Rochester residents grew from 51 in 1880, to 1,287 in 1900, to 10,639 in 1910, and nearly 20,000 in 1920. By 1920, Rochester had the third-highest proportion of Italian-born residents in the nation. Boris H. Mikolji, "Ethnic Groups in America: The Italians of Rochester," *Il Politico* 36, no. 4 (December 1971): 660–682, esp. Table 1, 664.

62. Mikolji, "Italians of Rochester," esp. 662, 667.

63. Mikolji, "Italians of Rochester," esp. 662.

64. The earliest Italian settlement was known as Sleepy Hollow, north of the downtown center, squeezed between Andrews Street, St. Paul Street, and the Genesee River. A decade later, with population increase, Italians expanded westward to live in the still-depressed slums on the west side of the Genesee, around State, Mill, and Platt Streets. Mikolji, "Italians of Rochester," 665.

65. Mikolji, "Italians of Rochester," 669.

66. Mikolji, "Italians of Rochester," 668.

67. Mikolji, "Italians of Rochester," 670.

68. Edgar P. Reed, "Rochester and the Shoe Industry," *Quarterly Journal of the New York State Historical Association* 1, no. 5 (1920): 241–243.

69. McKelvey, *Rochester on the Genesee*, 101–103.

70. McKelvey, *Rochester on the Genesee*, 153.

71. Reed, "Rochester and the Shoe Industry," 242.

72. Salvatore Piazza Report of Hearing, plus Hearing, February 25, 1915, 53934/39.

73. Proof that Alien has become a public charge from causes existing prior to landing, November 18, 1914, 53934/39.

74. Report of Hearing, plus Hearing, February 25, 1915; and Proof that Alien has become a public charge from causes existing prior to landing, November 18, 1914, 53934/39.

75. Angelina Piazza Report of Hearing, plus Hearing, February 25, 1915, 53934/39.

76. January 26, 1915, correspondence from Monroe County Superintendent of the Poor, T. J. Bridges to US Immigrant Inspector George Clark, 53934/39.

77. Howk, in Proof that Alien has become a public charge from causes existing prior to landing, November 18, 1914, 53934/39.

78. January 26, 1915, correspondence from Monroe County Superintendent of the Poor, T. J. Bridges to US Immigrant Inspector George Clark, 53934/39.

79. Ronald H. Bayor, *Encountering Ellis Island: How European Immigrants Entered America* (Baltimore, MD: John Hopkins University Press, 2014), 44–47.

80. Salvatore Piazza Report of Hearing, plus Hearing, February 25, 1915, 53934/39.

81. Angelina Piazza Report of Hearing, plus Hearing, February 25, 1915, 53934/39.

82. McKelvey, *Rochester on the Genesee*, 130–141.

83. Salvatore Piazza Report of Hearing, plus Hearing, February 25, 1915, 53934/39.

84. Angelina Piazza Report of Hearing, plus Hearing, February 25, 1915, 53934/39.

85. Deportation Warrant, filed March 22, 1915, 53934/39.

86. Physician's Note, February 28, 1915, 53934/39.

1. Stanley, "Trot, Trot, Trot to Boston," 14–15.

2. Stanley, "Trot, Trot, Trot to Boston," 19–20.

3. Stanley, "Trot, Trot, Trot to Boston," 13.

4. Stanley, "To Ellis Island and Back," 36.

5. Stanley, "To Ellis Island and Back," 38–39, 43–44.

6. Irwin, *Strange Passage*, 108, 112–114, 216.

7. Irwin, *Strange Passage*, 93.

8. Russell to CGI, June 23, 1919, 54519–3, University Publications, INS Series a supplement to Part 1, Reel 9, frames 106–193, NARA–San Bruno.

9. Stanley, "Five Weeks Leave," 69.

10. Both in RG 85, Entry 9, NARA–Washington, DC: Uhl to CGI, Washington, DC, January 22, 1914, 52903/60-A; and Prentis to CGI, Washington DC, April 18, 1914, 52903/60-B.

11. On US removal being forced to work within bilateral (if asymmetrical) relations, see Pope-Obeda, "When in Doubt, Deport!" 61, 306; and Hester, *Deportation*, chapter 2.

12. DL&W RR Depot and Ferry House postcard, ca. 1920, copy in author's possession; and US Department of Interior, "National Register of Historic Places Inventory—Nomination Form, Erie-Lackawanna Railroad Terminal at Hoboken," July 24, 1973, esp. pp 2–3, 9–10.

13. Assistant Commissioner-General, Memorandum for the Acting Secretary, February 1, 1916 53775-202d, RG 85, Entry 9, NARA–Washington, DC.

14. See photograph "Figure 5, Application of Area in Need of Redevelopment Criteria," p. 39, in Phillips Preiss Shapiro Associates, Inc., "Redevelopment Study for the Hoboken Terminal & Yard of the City of Hoboken," prepared for the City of Hoboken Planning Board, 2006, www.hobokennj.org/pdf/mplan/Redevelopment_Plans/Hoboken_Rail_Yards/HobokenRailYards.pdf, accessed April 5, 2013.

15. Stanley, "To Ellis Island and Back," 46–47.

16. Stanley, "Trot, Trot, Trot to Boston," 32–33.

17. Edward Corsi, *In the Shadow of Liberty: The Chronicle of Ellis Island* (New York: MacMillan, 1935), 5, quoted in Bayor, *Encountering Ellis Island*, 30.

18. Stanley, "Five Weeks Leave," 72.

19. Irwin, *Strange Passage*, 112.

20. Bayor, *Encountering Ellis Island*, 31–34.

21. Bayor, *Encountering Ellis Island*, 4.

22. Edward A. Steiner, *On the Trail of the Immigrant* (New York: Flemming H. Revell, 1906), 72, quoted in Bayor, *Encountering Ellis Island*, 38.

23. Katherine Reed, "'The Prison, By God, Where I Have Found Myself': Graffiti at Ellis Island Immigration Station, New York, c. 1900–1923," *Journal of American Ethnic History* 38, no. 3 (2019): 5–35, esp. 18.

24. Quoted in Bayor, *Encountering Ellis Island*, 88.

25. Irwin, *Strange Passage*, 218.

26. Stanley, "Trot, Trot, Trot to Boston," 33–34.

27. Stanley, "Trot, Trot, Trot to Boston," 33–34.

28. William Williams, "Ellis Island: Its Organization and Some of Its Work" (1912), Appendix 1 in Barry Moreno, *Encyclopedia of Ellis Island* (Westport, CT: Greenwood Press, 2004), 283–304, esp. 299.

29. Williams, "Ellis Island: Its Organization and Some of Its Work," 259–276, esp. 271. On green cards, see Irwin, *Strange Passage*, 219.

30. Frank Martocci, quoted in Bayor, *Encountering Ellis Island*, 42–43.

31. Quoted in Bayor, *Encountering Ellis Island*, 43.

32. Quoted in Bayor, *Encountering Ellis Island*, 43.

33. Quoted in Bayor, *Encountering Ellis Island*, 106.

34. Williams quoted in Bayor, *Encountering Ellis Island*, 271.

35. American Committee for the Protection of the Foreign Born (ACPFB) files, Folder: Ellis Island Complaints, Joseph A. Labadie Collection, University of Michigan.

36. Barry Moreno, *Encyclopedia of Ellis Island* (Westport, CT: Greenwood Press, 2004), 195.

37. Quoted in Reed, "The Prison, By God, Where I Have Found Myself," 24.

38. Both quoted in Bayor, *Encountering Ellis Island*, 84–85.

39. Quoted in Bayor, *Encountering Ellis Island*, 41.

40. Quoted in Bayor, *Encountering Ellis Island*, 86.

41. Quoted in Bayor, *Encountering Ellis Island*, 88.

42. William C. White, "Ellis Island Altered by Immigration Trends," *New York Times*, October 8, 1933.

43. Reed, "The Prison, By God, Where I Have Found Myself," 9–18.

44. The eastbound itinerary for May–June 1919 listed the prospective deportees to be collected by the deportation party, many names are paired with the modifying statement "If passports obtained" or "If sailing dates received from Ellis Island." If passports or tickets were not yet available, these deportees would not be put on the train and would wait until arrangements were finalized. 54519–3, University Publications, INS Series A Supplement to Part 1, Reel 9, frames 106–193, NARA–San Bruno.

45. Ellis Island's Commissioner Howe, a liberal humanist and political progressive, was concerned with the conditions of arrival and immigrant rights. Though his predecessor William Williams was more concerned with efficiency in sifting through large numbers of immigrants—many of whom he felt were resolutely undesirable—Howe was concerned with maintaining their dignity and well-being. After receiving the Red Special deportees, he slowed the process of the radicals' removal. See Cannato, *American Passage*, 298–301, 314. Howe was less generous with ordinary deportees.

46. Both in 53934/39, RG 85, Entry 9, NARA I–Washington, DC: Landis to CI, Montreal, March 26, 1915; and Deportation Warrant filed March 22, 1915.

47. For Sullivan, Kennedy, and Lester Case Files, see 54257/8; 54161/74; and 53845/202, all in RG 85, Entry 9, NARA–Washington, DC.

48. Hirsch to Wilson, Secretary of Labor, June 30, 1919, 53678/170, RG 85, Entry 9, NARA–Washington, DC (spelling as in original).

49. Hoffman, "Stimulus to Repatriation"; and Balderrama and Rodríguez, *Decade of Betrayal.*

50. Pope-Obeda, "When in Doubt, Deport!" 276, 289–290.

51. Irwin, *Strange Passage,* 221–222.

52. Irwin, *Strange Passage,* 220.

53. Pope-Obeda, "When in Doubt, Deport!" 289.

54. Zimmer, "Voyage of the *Buford.*

55. See Baer's correspondence from February 8, February 21, and March 16, 1936, as examples. ACPFB, Baer Case File, Folder 2. Baer's records are held with the papers of the American Committee for the Protection of the Foreign Born, Joseph A. Labadie Collection, at the University of Michigan.

56. Baer to ACPFB, May 1, 1936, Ellis Island, Room 211, ACPFB records, Baer Case File, Folder 2, Labadie Collection.

57. Baer to "Sprad and friends," February 24, 1936, ABPFB records, Baer Case File, Folder 2, Labadie Collection.

58. Baer to "Sprad et al.," March 16, 1936, ACPFB, Baer Case File, Folder 2, Labadie Collection.

59. Irwin, *Strange Passage,* 261–262.

60. Irwin, *Strange Passage,* 265.

61. Irwin, *Strange Passage,* 265.

62. Irwin, *Strange Passage,* 254.

63. Irwin, *Strange Passage,* 264.

64. Irwin, *Strange Passage,* 231.

65. White, "Ellis Island Altered by Immigration Trends."

66. Hisham Matar, "The Return," *The New Yorker,* April 8, 2013, p. 47.

67. Irwin, *Strange Passage,* 215.

68. Williams, "Ellis Island: Its Organization and Some of Its Work," 271.

69. Bayor, *Encountering Ellis Island,* 20.

70. Quoted in Bayor, *Encountering Ellis Island,* 21.

71. Quoted in Bayor, *Encountering Ellis Island,* 21.

72. Quoted in Bayor, *Encountering Ellis Island,* 21.

73. Bayor, *Encountering Ellis Island,* 21.

74. Mary Zuk, quoted in Bayor, *Encountering Ellis Island,* 21.

75. Quoted in Bayor, *Encountering Ellis Island,* 22.

76. Zimmer, "Voyage of the *Buford.*"

77. Carlson to Comrades, July 13, 1935, Ray Carlson Case File, Box 26, ACPFB records, Labadie Collection.

78. Carlson to ACPFB, July 16, 1935, Ray Carlson Case File, Box 26, ACPFB records, Labadie Collection.

79. Carlson to ACPFB, August 12, 1935, Ray Carlson Case File, Box 26, ACPFB records, Labadie Collection.

PART THREE

1. Matthew Frye Jacobson, *Roots Too: White Ethnic Revival in Post–Civil Rights America* (Cambridge, MA: Harvard University Press, 2008).

CHAPTER 9. CARBONDALE

1. Postcard image at http://stationcarbondale.org, accessed October 10, 2019.

2. Tom Redmond and Vickie Devenport, "US Department of the Interior, Illinois Central Railroad Passenger Depot, National Register of Historic Places Registration," December 4, 2001, p. 2, http://gis.hpa.state.il.us/pdfs/219007.pdf, accessed August 27, 2019.

3. This chapter relies on the Genero Huerto Case File 54646/229; the Yndalecio Huerto Case File 54626/122; and the extended Vallejo Family Case File 56464/231, all RG 85, Entry 9, NARA–Washington, DC.

4. For a more recent elaboration, see Lauren Martin, "Governing through the Family: Struggles over US Non-citizen Family Detention Policy," *Environment and Planning A* 44 (2012): 866–888.

5. Amtrak, "Carbondale, Il," Great American Stations Project, www.great americanstations.com/stations/carbondale-il-cdl/, accessed August 27, 2019.

6. "A History of Carbondale's Railroads," Station Carbondale website (2018), http://stationcarbondale.org/history/, accessed August 27, 2019.

7. Amtrak, "Carbondale, Il."

8. Redmond and Devenport, "US Department of the Interior, Illinois Central Railroad Passenger Depot, National Register of Historic Places Registration," 8.

9. Redmond and Devenport, "US Department of the Interior, Illinois Central Railroad Passenger Depot, National Register of Historic Places Registration," 8.

10. "History of Carbondale's Railroads."

11. Redmond and Devenport, "US Department of the Interior, Illinois Central Railroad Passenger Depot, National Register of Historic Places Registration," 10, 13.

12. Genealogy Trails History Group listings for Jackson County Il, and Carbondale Census of 1910 do not offer definitive census data, but it is suggestive; see http://genealogytrails.com/ill/jackson/index_census.htm, accessed October 10, 2019.

13. "Blacksnake Hills," "Robidoux Landing" and "St. Joseph," in State Historical Association of Missouri, *Buchanan County Place Names*, drawing on Martha K. Ewing, "Place Names in the Northwest Counties of Missouri," MA the-

sis, University of Missouri-Columbia, 1929, http://shsmo.org/collections/man
uscripts/ramsay/buchanan, accessed October 23, 2019.

14. The website of the Pony Express Museum describes the significance and
mythology of the system developed; see http://ponyexpress.org/, accessed October 1, 2019.

15. Quoted in David P. Thelen, *Paths of Resistance: Tradition and Dignity in
Industrializing Missouri* (New York: Oxford University Press, 1986), 30.

16. Thelen, *Paths of Resistance*, 31.

17. Thelen, *Paths of Resistance*, 33.

18. Thelen, *Paths of Resistance*, 70–77.

19. Thelen, *Paths of Resistance*, 79–84.

20. Thelen, *Paths of Resistance*, 244–246, 263–264. They won meager victories,
but rail companies passed every new cost levied against them on to consumers.

21. Thelen, *Paths of Resistance*, 255–258.

22. George J. Sánchez, *Becoming Mexican American: Ethnicity, Culture, and
Identity in Chicano Los Angeles, 1900–1945* (New York: Oxford University Press,
1993), 39; and Carey McWilliams, *Factories in the Field: The Story of Migratory
Farm Labor in California* (Berkeley: University of California Press, 1939).

23. José E. Limón, "*Al Norte* toward Home: Texas, the Midwest, and Mexi-
can American Critical Regionalism," in *The Latina/o Midwest Reader*, ed. Omar
Valerio-Jímenez, Santiago Vaquera-Vásquez, and Claire F. Fox, 40–56 (Urbana:
University of Illinois Press, 2017), 44–45, 55–56.

24. Michael M. Smith, "Beyond the Borderlands: Mexican Labor in the Central Plains, 1900–1930," *Great Plains Quarterly* (1981): 239–251, 240.

25. Genero Huerto Hearing March 8, 1919, 54646/229.

26. Yndalecio Huerto Hearing, March 7, 1919, conducted at State Hospital
#2 in Saint Joseph, Missouri, 54626/122; and Genero Huerto Hearing, March 8,
1919, 54646/229.

27. García, *Mexicans in the Midwest*, 5; and Rodolpho Acuña, *Occupied America: A History of Chicanos*, 4th edition (New York: Longman, 2000), 159.

28. Acuña, *Occupied America*, 185.

29. Genero Huerto was far from the first man from Mexico's central plateau
to help construct rail lines across the United States. In the last quarter of the nineteenth century, Mexican workers from the region built railroads in the northern
Mexican borderlands as part of the Porfirian project of capitalist modernization.
In the decades around the turn of the twentieth century, more entered the still
hazily policed southwestern United States and built railroads for the Southern
Pacific. By the 1890s, Southern Pacific had largely replaced Chinese workers along
the rails across the West with Mexican workers. The Southern Pacific counted
some 4,500 ethnic Mexicans on its payroll in 1900. Indeed, Mexican workers
had laid as much as half of the railroad track in the US West by 1900. They also
helped build roads in the Midwest in the 1880s and 1890s, but their numbers
grew substantially early in the new century. The US Census, which notoriously
undercounted migratory workers, identified some 103,000 Mexican-born peoples

in 1900. The number more than doubled to 224,275 in 1910, and nearly doubled again by 1920, when the Mexican-born population was listed at 651,596. Garcilazo, *Traqueros*, 31; Vicki L. Ruiz, foreword to Jeffrey Marcos Garcilazo, *Traqueros: Mexican Railroad Workers in the United States, 1870–1930* (Denton: University of North Texas Press, 2012); 1; Driscoll, *Tracks North*, 18, 21; Smith, "Beyond the Borderlands," 243; and Acuña, *Occupied America*, 185.

30. Dearinger, *The Filth of Progress*.

31. García, *Mexicans in the Midwest*, 28.

32. Driscoll, *Tracks North*, 42.

33. Quoted in Nathaniel Otjen, "Creating a Barrio in Iowa City, 1916–1936: Mexican Section Laborers and the Chicago, Rock Island and Pacific Railroad Company," *Annals of Iowa* 76, no. 4 (2017): 406–432, 411. The expanding work was necessary in the war years because the tracks were facing serious disrepair. Railroads spent lavishly on building roads in the decade before the United States entered the war but not on track maintenance. Larger, heavier wartime loads brought more wear on the lines, and so demanded more work. When the federal government took control of the rail lines during the war, they also set track workers' rates of pay, which made the jobs more regular and more appealing to Mexican workers. Otjen, "Creating a Barrio in Iowa City," 417; and Driscoll, *Tracks North*, 6, 16.

34. David Montejano, *Anglos and Mexicans in the Making of Texas, 1836–1986* (Austin: University of Texas Press, 1987), 201.

35. Vargas, *Proletarians of the North*, 7.

36. Smith, "Beyond the Borderlands," 241.

37. David Dorado Romo, "To Understand the El Paso Shooter, Look to the Long Legacy of Anti-Mexican Violence at the Border," *Texas Observer*, August 9, 2019, www.texasobserver.org/to-understand-the-el-paso-massacre-look-to-the-long-legacy-of-anti-mexican-violence-at-the-border/, accessed August 13, 2019.

38. Natalia Molina, *Fit to Be Citizens? Public Health and Race in Los Angeles, 1879–1939* (Berkeley: University of California Press, 2006), 55–60; and Stern, *Eugenic Nation*, 59–72.

39. García, *Mexicans in the Midwest*, 5; and Garcilazo, *Traqueros*, 37, 45.

40. Genero Huerto Hearing, March 8, 1919, 54646/229.

41. Genero Huerto Hearing, March 8, 1919, 54646/229.

42. Genero Huerto Hearing, March 8, 1919, 54646/229.

43. García, *Mexicans in the Midwest*, 33.

44. In 1905 the fifty-two Mexican track workers in the Santa Fe's Kansas City Division comprised 6.5 percent of total track workforce. Between 1905 and 1927, Mexican laborers climbed from being 6.5 percent to more than 90 percent of the Santa Fe's track workers in Kansas City. Garcilazo, *Traqueros*, Table 2.2, p. 51.

45. Cited in Garcilazo, *Traqueros*, 53.

46. Genero Huerto Hearing conducted March 8, 1919, 54646/229.

47. Garcilazo, *Traqueros*, 56, Paul Michel Taillon, *Good, Reliable, White Men: Railroad Brotherhoods, 1877–1917* (Urbana: University of Illinois Press, 2009).

48. Even though they were disdained as "common" and unskilled laborers, gang work was difficult. Timing the maul blows on the spikes required remarkable precision—if they missed the spike, they could hurt themselves, their fellow workers, or damage the rails, which would cost them wages and pride. Neophytes marveled at older hands' skill and strength. Garcilazo, *Traqueros*, 62–63.

49. Mexican track laborers most often worked in crushing summer heat, but they often had to work in freezing cold too. Some track workers for the Burlington Northern in Minnesota had to work in conditions that were -20 below zero. They warmed themselves by burning meager supplies of coal, or toxic creosote-soaked ties. According to two more privileged contemporaries rail workers, the *traqueros* also worked when more privileged workers "are sleeping, mush around in the water in big rains. . . . When a wreck occurs, they are the first to get there though it be, as it usually is, at night." His colleague asked, in response, "what kind of chance have they to enjoy their work? They are doing work that the average American would not and cannot think of doing. Last week . . . in the desert the heat killed three Mexicans and prostrated a score more. The temperature was up to 120 degrees." For many, fortitude was a point of masculine pride. A flipside of this valorized physical masculinity, however, was a likelihood to denigrate men they thought were too frail or weak to keep up. Vargas, *Proletarians of the North*, 38, quote on 35; and Garcilazo, *Traqueros*, 74.

50. Garcilazo, *Traqueros*, 61–62; and Thelen, *Paths of Resistance*, 50.

51. Quoted in Garcilazo, *Traqueros*, 75.

52. Garcilazo, *Traqueros*, 36.

53. The single men in extra gangs lived jammed in boxcar bunkhouses that could be rolled along the track and deposited wherever their work was needed. More than a dozen men bunked in each car. Each was supposed to have 170 cubic feet of airspace, which was half of what government guidelines suggested. As one observer reported: "The stench on the inside from grease and filth is almost unbearable. The [boxcar] dwellers work, eat and sleep in the same wearing apparel, and apparently never change a garment until it is worn out and another secured." Had their wages allowed the disposable income, of course, and if their working conditions permitted accumulating many materials possessions, they would surely have enjoyed a more varied wardrobe and additional opportunities to do laundry. Garcilazo, *Traqueros*, 78, quote on 79.

54. Genero Huerto Hearing conducted on March 8, 1919, 54646/229.

55. Thelen, *Paths of Resistance*, 43.

56. Department of the Interior, Census Office, *Twelfth Census of the United States: Census Reports*, vol. 9, *Manufactures*, part 3 (Washington, DC: US Census Office, 1902), 393; and "Descriptive of St. Joseph's Wonderful Industrial Progress, Special Illustrated Number," *St. Joseph Journal of Commerce*, July 1900, both in US Department of the Interior, "National Register of Historic Places Registration Form—St. Joseph Mo, Livestock Exchange Building," filed March 4, 2004, pp. 20, 21.

57. Smith, "Beyond the Borderlands," 246.

58. It grew somewhat in the next decade, from 77,403 to just under 78,000 in 1920. Bureau of Commerce and Labor, *Thirteenth Census: Statistics for Missouri, 1910* (Washington, DC: Government Printing Office, date illegible), 568; and Bureau of Commerce and Labor, *Fourteenth Census: 1920* (Washington, DC: Government Printing Office), 8.

59. García, *Mexicans in the Midwest*, vii.

60. Melisa Nobles, *Shades of Citizenship: Race and the Census in Modern Politics* (Stanford, CA: Stanford University Press, 2000), 72–74.

61. Bureau of Commerce and Labor, *Thirteenth Census: 1910*, Table 5, p. 631; and Bureau of Commerce and Labor, *Fourteenth Census: 1920*, Table 10, p. 46.

62. Bureau of Commerce and Labor, *Thirteenth Census: 1910*, p. 599; and *Fourteenth Census: 1920*, Table 12, p. 49.

63. Bureau of Commerce and Labor, *Thirteenth Census: 1910*, Table 1, p. 606.

64. Bureau of Commerce and Labor, *Thirteenth Census: 1910*, Table 2, p. 626.

65. Bureau of Commerce and Labor, *Fourteenth Census: 1920*, Table 12, p. 50.

66. Thelen, *Paths of Resistance*, 54–55.

67. Rick Halpern, *Down on the Killing Floor: Black and White Workers in Chicago's Packinghouses, 1904–54* (Chicago: University of Illinois Press, 1997), 81.

68. Quoted in Vargas, *Proletarians of the North*, 49.

69. Vargas, *Proletarians of the North*, 49–50.

70. Yndalecio Huerto Hearing, March 7, 1919, 54626/122, RG 85, Entry 9, NARA–Washington, DC; Mickey Parish, "How Do Salt and Sugar Prevent Microbial Spoilage?" *Scientific American*, February 21, 2006, www.scientificam erican.com/article/how-do-salt-and-sugar-pre/, accessed October 10, 2019; and Interstate Commerce Commission, *Vol. 55: Decisions of the Interstate Commerce Commission of the United States, June–December 1919* (Washington, DC: Government Printing Office, 1920), 434–435.

71. Bureau of Commerce and Labor, *Thirteenth Census: 1910*, Table 5, p. 631; and Bureau of Commerce and Labor, *Fourteenth Census: 1920*, Table 13, p. 52.

72. Bureau of Commerce and Labor, *Fourteenth Census: 1920*, Table 13, p. 52.

73. García, *Mexicans in the Midwest*, 53.

74. García, *Mexicans in the Midwest*, 53–55.

75. Aristide R. Zolberg, *A Nation by Design: Immigration Policy in the Fashioning of America* (Cambridge, MA: Harvard University Press, 2008), 241.

76. Yndalecio Huerto Hearing, January 25, 1919, 54626/122.

77. Yndalecio Huerto Hearing, January 25, 1919, 54626/122.

78. Otjen, "Creating a Barrio in Iowa City," 415–421.

79. Drawn from and quoted in Thelen, *Paths of Resistance*, 108.

80. Drawn from and quoted García, *Mexicans in the Midwest*, 116–117.

81. Greenman to Long, January 24, 1919, 54626/122.

82. "A Walking Haberdashery," *Kansas City Journal*, February 7, 1910, www .vintagekansascity.com/100yearsago/labels/mental%20health.html, accessed October 24, 2019; and "Jack Gallagher in the Workhouse," *Kansas City Jour-*

nal, July 17, 1908, www.vintagekansascity.com/100yearsago/labels/Col.%20J.%20 C.%20Greenman.html, accessed October 24, 2019.

83. "Men Who Made Kansas City," adapted from George Kreel and John Slavens, *Men Who Are Making Kansas City* (1902), http://vintagekansascity.com/ menwhomadekc/greenman_james_c.html, accessed October 24, 2019.

84. "Believes He's Roosevelt," *Kansas City Journal*, December 15, 1908; and "Cunning Shown by Gallagher," *Kansas City Journal*, June 16, 1908, both from www.vintagekansascity.com/100yearsago/labels/Col.%20J.%20C.%20Greenman .html, accessed October 24, 2019.

85. "Workhouse Not Fit Place for Insane," *Kansas City Journal*, July 14, 1909, www.vintagekansascity.com/100yearsago/labels/Col.%20J.%20C.%20Greenman .html, accessed October 24, 2019.

86. Greenman to Long, January 24, 1919, 54626/122.

87. Fox, *Three Worlds of Relief*, 13.

88. Greenman to Long, January 24, 1919, 54626/122. Much of the consuls' time was spent trying help Mexican nationals when railroad companies or labor contractors failed to deliver on the promises they made, but they also worked on Mexican migrants' behalf when they ran afoul of the US legal system. Consuls tended to come from the ranks of Mexico's elite and frequently held themselves above the migrant workers, but, on occasion, advocated on their behalf. They found that police brutality was rife, that state appointed defenders did little for Mexican clients, and the conditions behind bars were grim. As one consul reflected: "Because of the lack of adequate legal counsel, the jails and penitentiaries of the United States . . . are full of Mexicans. . . . I could cite specific cases of Mexicans who were condemned to life imprisonment who were perfectly innocent." García, *Mexicans in the Midwest*, 111, 114–118.

89. Arrest Warrant Application, January 27, 1919, 54626/122.

90. *AR-CGI 1931*, Table 106, p. 255.

91. Quoted at Glore Psychiatric Museum website, www.stjosephmuseum.org/ glore-psychiatric-museum, accessed October 23, 2019.

92. On Kirkbride buildings and Moral Treatment, see Ethan McElroy, www .kirkbridebuildings.com/, accessed October 23, 2019; on unfree labor in asylums, see Rose, *No Right to be Idle*, 84–88.

93. Scott Clark interview in Taylor Chase, "Insane Asylums: Mental Retreat or Living Hell," https://83681755.weebly.com/state-lunatic-asylum-no-2.html, accessed October 23, 2019. Clark also in Ron Davis, "In Minnesota, A Museum of Madness," *Washington Post*, April 4, 1999.

94. Long to St. Louis, March 10, 1919, 54626/122.

95. Yndalecio Huerto Hearing, March 7, 1919, 54626/122.

96. Braslow, *Mental Ills and Bodily Cures*, 2, 39, 48–50.

97. Sarah C. Sitton, *Life at the Texas State Lunatic Asylum, 1857–1997* (College Station: Texas A&M University Press, 1999), 92.

98. Sitton, *Life at the Texas State Lunatic Asylum*, 88, 119–120.

99. Yndalecio Huerto Hearing, March 7, 1919, 54626/122.

100. Yndalecio Huerto Hearing, March 7, 1919, 54626/122.

101. Genero Huerto Warrant of Arrest, March 8, 1919, 54646/229.

102. Correspondence from Long to Inspector-in-Charge, Saint Louis, March 10, 1919, 54646/229.

103. Genero Huerto Warrant of Arrest, March 8, 1919, 54646/229.

104. M. Patricia Holmes, "Buchanan County Courthouse Nomination to National Registry of Historic Places," June 20, 1972, https://dnr.mo.gov/shpo/nps-nr/72001563.pdf, accessed October 25, 2019.

105. Hearing, March 10, 1919, 54646/229.

106. The records give the name "Veyejo," which I offer here as Vallejo. Gumiciendo Vallejo, March 8, 1919; José Vallejo Hearing, March 8, 1919; Concepcion Ranjel and Children Hearing, March 8, 1919; and José Pérez Hearing, March 8, 1919; all in 56464/231.

107. In order to counteract the workers' agency and departures railway firms developed new ways to prevent *solos* from leaving their work. Unlike the quasi-legal and violent means that south Texas farmers used, these more commonly involved subtler controls. One involved only paying once a month, which guaranteed a labor force for that period, unless someone was willing to lose the money they had already earned. This method satisfied one engineer who thought that "whenever [Mexican workers] get a dollar or two ahead they seem to want to go somewhere else." Payment at the end of the month also meant that workers accrued debts to the company commissary that supplied them with bad food, at inflated prices. But that wasn't enough. Garcilazo, *Traqueros*, 117, 76.

108. Smith, "Beyond the Borderlands," 244.

109. Garcilazo, *Traqueros*, 44, 117.

110. Gumiciendo Vallejo, March 8, 1919, 56464/231.

111. Gumiciendo Vallejo, March 8, 1919; and José Vallejo Hearing, March 8, 1919, 56464/231.

112. Gumiciendo Vallejo, March 8, 1919, 56464/231.

113. Garcilazo, *Traqueros*, 26.

114. Garcilazo, *Traqueros*, 35; and Otjen, "Creating a Barrio in Iowa City," 430.

115. Otjen, "Creating a Barrio in Iowa City," 412.

116. Garcilazo, *Traqueros*, 129.

117. Vargas, *Proletarians of the North*, 39.

118. Garcilazo, *Traqueros*, 125.

119. Boxcar barrios and section gang housing quite literally took their shape from the Rock Island's needs. Early iterations of trackworker housing were made from materials cast off from the shops; literally constructed from the rail companies' waste. Decrepit boxcars were durable capital investments with no productive purpose, and reused as cheap workers' housing. A Kansas engineer proposed that rather than boxcars, they might slap together old bridge ties, sewage pipes, scrap boards; old rails could be roof rafters, discarded ties for the walls, concrete could be stabilized with secondhand barbed wire. The homes were set in empty corners or otherwise unproductive spaces in the railyards. Some settlements had

only a few boxcars, others held up to a dozen, arranged in rows or a courtyard pattern, as space permitted. Families preferred being as far as possible from the main yards, where it was safer for their children to play. There was less soot from the roundhouse to soil clean clothes drying on the line, and less smoke to make the children cough. Garcilazo, *Traqueros*, 122, 127.

120. Quoted in Otjen, "Creating a Barrio in Iowa City," 425.

121. Quoted in Otjen, "Creating a Barrio in Iowa City," 418.

122. A general manager for one firm wrote that Mexican families had low expectations for housing. "As a rule, the average Mexican laborer and family are satisfied with the most primitive arrangements as far as comfort goes.... He makes no demand for conveniences, facilities, or arrangements for his well-being, accepting a box car with wooden bunks and no windows with the same readiness that he would...a new section house fitted up with the latest pattern in steel bunks." Railroad firms justified the poor housing through the predictably racist supposition that Mexicans did not want or need anything else. "Their manner of living is very crude," one official stated. "Tortitas [*sic*], chille [*sic*], and beans, potatoes, eggs and coffee constitute their principal articles of diet. Camp facilities for them do not require very much, consisting principally of bunk cars, stoves for heating purposes in the winter, and water." Garcilazo, *Traqueros*, 117–118, 67.

123. Garcilazo, *Traqueros*, 120.

124. Otjen, "Creating a Barrio in Iowa City," 421.

125. Quoted in and from Garcilazo, *Traqueros*, 124–125, 128.

126. Michael Innis-Jímenez, "Mexican Workers and Life in South Chicago," in *The Latina/o Midwest Reader*, ed. Omar Valerio-Jímenez, Santiago Vaquera-Vásquez, and Claire F. Fox, 71–84 (Urbana: University of Illinois Press, 2017), 74–75; and Vargas, *Proletarians of the North*, 39.

127. Garcilazo, *Traqueros*, 45.

128. Garcilazo, *Traqueros*, 126.

129. Garcilazo, *Traqueros*, 119.

130. Garcilazo, *Traqueros*, 127.

131. Quoted in Garcilazo, *Traqueros*, 128.

132. Garcilazo, *Traqueros*, 61–62.

133. Garcilazo, *Traqueros*, 127–128.

134. Caran Amber Crawford Howard, "'I've always been for education': Mexicana/o Participation in Formal, Non–Formal, and Informal Education in the Midwest, 1910–1955," PhD dissertation, University of Iowa, 2015.

135. Garcilazo, *Traqueros*, 143–144.

136. Garcilazo, *Traqueros*, 141.

137. García, *Mexicans in the Midwest*, 92–93.

138. Mexican women also began to work in packing houses, garment industries, and laundries. They earned income for themselves and their families as well as some distance from broader patriarchal control over family income. They tended to be hired on an ad hoc basis and were typically paid half the wages of men. In rail yards, women might be hostler helpers, engine watchers, coach clean-

ers, wipers, car men, boiler washers, firebuilders, pitmen, cinder laborers, carpenters, and shop laborers. García, *Mexicans in the Midwest*, 89–90.

139. Innis-Jímenez, "Mexican Workers and Life in South Chicago," 77.

140. García, *Mexicans in the Midwest*, 83.

141. García, *Mexicans in the Midwest*, 135.

142. Thelen, *Paths of Resistance*, 157.

143. Quoted in García, *Mexicans in the Midwest*, 56.

144. Quoted in García, *Mexicans in the Midwest*, 57.

145. García, *Mexicans in the Midwest*, 135.

146. García, *Mexicans in the Midwest*, 38–40.

147. Vargas, introduction to *Proletarians of the North*.

148. Quoted in Otjen, "Creating a Barrio in Iowa City," 420, 421.

149. Otjen, "Creating a Barrio in Iowa City," 420, 421.

150. Otjen, "Creating a Barrio in Iowa City," 415–416.

151. Fox, *Three Worlds of Relief*, 90.

152. Bryan Winston, "Mexican Migrants in Urban Missouri: Social Welfare Institutions and Racial Boundaries in Kansas City and St. Louis, 1915–1940," *Missouri Historical Review* 113, no. 4 (2019): 269–283, 268.

153. Winston, "Mexican Migrants in Urban Missouri," 206.

154. Fox, *Three Wolds of Relief*, 103–113, 74.

155. Sánchez, *Becoming Mexican American*, 97–104; quotes in and drawn from Winston, "Mexican Migrants in Urban Missouri," 264–267.

156. *AR-CGI 1919*, 13.

157. *AR-CGI 1920*, 8, 10.

158. Fox, *Three Worlds of Relief*, 88; and Goodman, *Deportation Machine*, 33.

159. Arrest Warrant, dated March 5, 1919, 56464/231.

160. See hearings for Jose Perez, Jose Vallejo, Conception Ranjel, Gumiciendo Veyejo, Angel Ramirez, all March 8, 1919, 56464/231.

161. Gumiciendo Vallejo Hearing, March 8, 1919, 56464/231.

CHAPTER 10. NEW ORLEANS

1. See Andrea Armstrong, "The Impact of 300 Years of Jail Conditions," *The New Orleans Prosperity Index: Tricentennial Collection* (New Orleans: The Data Center, March 2018), www.datacenterresearch.org/reports_analysis/300-years-of-jail-conditions/.

2. Huiping Ling, "A History of Chinese Female Students in the United States, 1880s–1990s," *Journal of American Ethnic History* 16, no. 3 (1997): 82–88; and Weili Ye, *Seeking Modernity in China's Name: Chinese Students in the United States, 1900–1927* (Stanford, CA: Stanford University Press, 2001).

3. Quoted in Michael H. Hunt, "The American Remission of the Boxer Indemnity: A Reappraisal," *Journal of Asian Studies* 31, no. 3 (1972): 539–559, esp. 450; Mad-

eline H. Hsu, *The Good Immigrants: How the Yellow Peril Became the Model Minority* (Princeton, NJ: Princeton University Press, 2015), 23–54; and Paul A. Kramer, "Is the World Our Campus? International Students and U.S. Global Power in the Long Twentieth Century," *Diplomatic History* 33, no. 5 (2009): 775–806.

4. Hsu, *Good Immigrants*, 44; and Kitty Calavita, "The Paradoxes of Race, Class, Identity, and 'Passing': Enforcing the Chinese Exclusion Acts, 1882–1910," *Law & Social Inquiry* 25, no. 1 (Winter 2000): 1–40, 26.

5. For more on Choi Si, see 54555/18, RG 85, Entry 9, NARA–Washington, DC.

6. Bong Youn Choy, *Koreans in America* (Chicago: Nelson-Hall, 1979), 77–78.

7. Preliminary examination, Council Bluffs, Iowa, September 21, 1918, 54555/18.

8. Kyung Moon Hwang, *A History of Korea: An Episodic Narrative* (New York: Palgrave Macmillan, 2010), 118–125.

9. Hwang, *History of Korea*, 132.

10. Hwang, *History of Korea*, 132–134.

11. Bruce Cumings, *Korea's Place in the Sun: A Modern History*, updated edition (New York: W. W. Norton, 2005), 147–151.

12. Jun Uchida, *Brokers of Empire: Japanese Settler Colonialism in Korea, 1876–1945* (Cambridge, MA: Harvard University Press, 2011), 79–85.

13. Uchida, *Brokers of Empire*, 7, 14.

14. Cumings, *Korea's Place in the Sun*, 152–153.

15. Cumings, *Korea's Place in the Sun*, 141.

16. Linda Shin, "Koreans in America, 1903–1945," *Amerasia Journal* 1, no. 3 (1971): 32–39, 34.

17. Cumings, *Korea's Place in the Sun*, 145–146.

18. Shin, "Koreans in America," 32; and Choy, *Koreans in America*, 73–76.

19. Choy, *Koreans in America*, 76.

20. Shin, "Koreans in America," 32–33.

21. A sizable number but a small portion of a larger and historically lengthier Korean diaspora. Between the 1860s and 1930s some six hundred thousand Koreans traveled to Manchuria and two hundred thousand more traveled to Siberia. Richard S. Kim, "Inaugurating the American Century: The 1919 Philadelphia Korean Congress, Korean Diasporic Nationalism, and American Protestant Missionaries," *Journal of American Ethnic History* 26, no. 1 (Fall 2006): 50–76, esp. 73n6.

22. Adam M. McKeown, *Melancholy Order: Asian Migration and the Globalization of Borders* (New York: Columbia University Press, 2008), 142, 258; and Hsu, *Good Immigrants*, 36.

23. Chang Yill Lee's family appears to have followed Western naming conventions, with the family name coming last, due perhaps to his brother's longer tenure in the United States, and I am treating Lee as his family name. In contrast, according to traditional Korean naming conventions (with family name coming first), I emphasize Choi as Choi Si's family name.

24. Uhl to CGI, February 27, 1914, in Chang Yill Lee's file, 53710/606, RG 85, Entry 9, NARA–Washington, DC.

25. Uhl to CGI, February 27, 1914; and February 16, 1918, Hearing plus February 18 comments and correspondence, 53710/606.

26. Board of Special Inquiry, February 25, 1914; and Fred Song Testimony, Ellis Island, 53710/606.

27. Seek Hun Kimm to the President, March 6, 1914, 53710/606.

28. Special Inspectress Helen M. Bullis Report, March 12, 1914, 53710/606.

29. Given the ethnoracial basis of the white slavery mythology on which Bullis but her career, her anti-immigrant racism was unsurprising. See especially Pliley, *Policing Sexuality*, esp. 35.

30. Nayan Shah, *Contagious Divides: Epidemics and Race in San Francisco's Chinatown* (Berkeley: University of California Press, 2001).

31. The racist sensibility accorded to the belief, fairly widely held among white Americans, that Koreans were more racially backward and thus simpler than the Japanese, akin to African Americans in the US South. See Chris Suh, "What Yun Ch'i-ho Knew: U.S.-Japan Relations and Imperial Race Making in Korea and the American South, 1904–1919," *Journal of American History* 104, no. 1 (2017): 73–81.

32. Bullis Report, March 12, 1914, 53710/606.

33. "Facts about Hastings College," Hastings College, www.hastings.edu/about-hastings-college/facts-about-hastings, accessed September 18, 2018.

34. Bullis Report, March 12, 1914, 53710/606.

35. Takaki, *Strangers from a Different Shore*, 272.

36. Supplemental Memorandum for the Acting Secretary, March 17, 1914, 53710/606.

37. Correspondence to Attorney General, July 7, 1922, 53710/606.

38. February 16, 1918, Hearing and February 18 comments and correspondence, 53710/606.

39. For example, Takaki, *Strangers from a Different Shore*.

40. Syngman Rhee, with whom Pak had been close, led the other principal tendency, which tended toward liberal and diplomatic rather than military challenges to Japanese occupation. Choy, *Koreans in America*, 79.

41. Margaret Stines Nielsen, "The Korean Connection," *Buffalo Tales: Buffalo County Historical Society* 20, no. 3 (1997), www.bchs.us/BTales_199705.html, accessed January 11, 2017.

42. *Kearney Daily Hub*, August 30, 1909, quoted in Nielsen, "Korean Connection."

43. Nielsen, "Korean Connection."

44. Shin, "Koreans in America," 36.

45. Kingsley K. Liu, "Korean Nationalist Activities in Hawaii and the Continental United States, 1900–1945, Part I: 1900–1919," *Amerasia Journal* 4, no. 1 (1977): 66–68, 71–73.

46. Choy, *Koreans in America*, 85.

47. Richard S. Kim, *The Quest for Statehood: Korean Immigrant Nationalism and U.S. Sovereignty, 1905–1945* (New York: Oxford University Press, 2011), 23.

48. Choy, *Koreans in America*, 82.

49. February 16, 1918, Hearing plus February 18 comments and correspondence, 53710/606.

50. Assistant Commissioner to CGI Washington, October 28, 1916; and Assistant Commissioner to CGI Washington, July 3, 1916, 53710/606.

51. Coykendall to CI, Ellis Island, October 8, 1917, 53710/606.

52. Dunn to CI, Ellis Island, January 24, 1918, 53710/606.

53. Anthony Caminetti, Second Supplemental Memorandum, February 8, 1918, 53710/606.

54. Quoted in McKeown, *Melancholy Order*, 258.

55. Chang Yill Lee to Sir, February 6, 1918, 53710/606.

56. CG to Saint Louis, February 13, 1918, 53710/606.

57. February 16, 1918, Hearing plus February 18 comments and correspondence, 53710/606.

58. February 16, 1918, Hearing plus February 18 comments and correspondence, 53710/606.

59. February 16, 1918, Hearing plus February 18 comments and correspondence , 53710/606.

60. February 16, 1918, Hearing plus February 18 comments and correspondence (emphasis added), 53710/606.

61. February 16, 1918, Hearing plus February 18 comments and correspondence, 53710/606.

62. Third Supplemental Memorandum, April 2, 1918; and April 5, 1918, CGI to Saint Louis Inspector in Charge, 53710/606.

63. Holton to Dunn, December 24, 1918, 53710/606.

64. Kyoung Chas. Lee to Commissioner, Ellis Island, January 24, 1919, 53710/606.

65. Holton to Dunn, December 24, 1918, 53710/606.

66. Deportation Warrant signed January 27, 1919, 53710/606.

67. Telegram, January 27, 1919, 53710/606.

68. Telegram Chang Yill Lee to Immigration Bureau, February 6, 1919; and Fifth Memorandum for the Acting Secretary, February 7, 1919, 53710/606.

69. Shin, "Koreans in America," 36.

70. Cumings, *Korea's Place in the Sun*, 140–143.

71. Kim, "Inaugurating the American Century," 68, 75n57. American positions softened somewhat after the Korean Congress in late 1919, as white, US-based Protestant missionaries advocated on Koreans' behalf against Japan, and as Korean nationalists incorporated US-based liberal imperialist rhetoric.

72. Suh, "What Yun Ch'i-ho Knew," 68–96.

73. Cumings, *Korea's Place in the Sun*, 154–155; and Uchida, *Brokers of Empire*, 143–144.

74. Travis Workman, *Imperial Genus: The Formation and Limits of the Human in Modern Korea and Japan* (Berkeley: University of California Press, 2016), 8.

75. Chang Yill Lee to Immigration Bureau, April 28, 1919, 53710/606.

76. Chang Yill Lee to Immigration Bureau, April 28, 1919, 53710/606.

77. Acting Secretary to Saint Louis office, May 10, 1919, 53710/606.

78. Dunn to CGI, July 21, 1919, 53710/606.

79. Nielsen, "Korean Connection."

80. Kim, "Inaugurating the American Century," 50–76.

81. Preliminary examination, September 21, 1918, 54555/18.

82. Built in 1885 and only closed in 1969, it was one of eighteen "rotary" style jails. Jailers operated a crank that rotated the cells within the building's towering cylindrical cage, so that only the cells aligned with the door could be opened at any time. It was modeled loosely on Jeremy Bentham's panopticon, designed to minimize contact between inmates and guards. The front of the building held offices for jailkeepers, a kitchen, and cells for trustees or women prisoners, and it was surely in one of these rooms that immigration authorities interviewed Choi. The rest of the building—three stories tall—consisted of wedge-shaped cells. One can imagine that it would be terrifying to be locked within this three-story machine, to know that if the rotating mechanism failed, there was literally no way out of your cell. In the most literal sense, too, it was unstable. The cells would jitter and shake, the gears screech and whine, and any belongings rattle whenever the keepers rotated the cells. Its designers proclaimed that "the object of our invention is to produce a jail in which prisoners can be controlled without the necessity of personal contact between them and the jailer." It would, they believed, allow "maximum security with minimum jailer attention." According to one officer, "If a jailer could count...and he had a trusty he could trust...he could control the jail." From "Historic Pottawattamie County Squirrel Cage Jail," Historical Society of Pottawattamie County, https://web.archive.org/web/20110308112949/http://thehistoricalsociety.org/jail.htm, accessed August 22, 2018. Also, "Pottawattamie County Jail," Wikipedia, https://en.wikipedia.org/wiki/Pottawattamie_County_Jail#cite_note-pottcounty-2, accessed August 22, 2018.

83. Saint Louis Inspector in Charge to CGI, December 7, 1918, 54555/18.

84. Stanley, "Five Weeks Leave," 40.

85. Stanley, "Five Weeks Leave," 40.

86. Stanley, "Five Weeks Leave," 42–43.

CHAPTER 11. SAN ANTONIO

1. Julian Lim, *Porous Borders: Multiracial Migrations and the Law in the U.S.-Mexico Borderlands* (Chapel Hill: University of North Carolina Press, 2017), 58.

2. Stanley, "Five Weeks Leave." Page illegible in author's copy.

3. For a postcard image of Southern Pacific's Sunset Station, see www.txtrans portationmuseum.org/history-rr-overview.php, accessed March 28, 2018.

4. Richard Flores, *Remembering the Alamo: Memory, Modernity, and the Master Symbol* (Austin: University of Texas Press, 2002), esp. xvii–xviii.

5. William Knox, 1927, 3–4, quoted in Flores, *Remembering the Alamo*, 3.

6. Montejano, *Anglos and Mexicans in the Making of Texas*; and Truett, *Fugitive Landscapes*.

7. Berkshire to CGI, July 11, 1919, Yndalecio Huerto records, 54626/122, NARA–Washington, DC.

8. R. B. Sims, an Arizona state prison officer wanted deportees to be sent to "some other far interior point," otherwise, he thought, the process was "an absolute farce." Quoted in Goodman, *Deportation Machine*, 78.

9. The mass deportation and repatriation drives of the 1930s saw a binational deportation regime deliver people deeper into Mexico on trains, but fares provided were often insufficient and left people stranded far from natal communities. After April 1945 the Mexican federal government and the US government collaborated further to deliver deportees deep into the Mexican hinterland and far from the border. Laura D. Gutiérrez, "'Trains of Misery': Repatriate Voices and Responses in Northern Mexico during the Great Depression," *Journal of American Ethnic History* 39, no. 4 (2020): 13–26; and Hernández, *MIGRA!*, 127.

10. Luey Mo's story is drawn from 54646/170, RG 85, Entry 9, NARA–Washington, DC. Principal biographical documents for his early life are Luey Moo [*sic*] Patient History, Southwestern Insane Asylum, January 29, 1919, Listed as Exhibit B; and Luey Mo Warrant Hearing, conducted March 14, 1919, Southwestern Insane Asylum, San Antonio, C. K. Schafer, Examining Officer, William Sims, Interpreter.

11. Robert Eric Barde, *Immigration at the Golden Gate: Passenger Ships, Exclusion, and Angel Island* (Westport, CT: Praeger, 2008), 83.

12. Tatsuzō Ishikawa, quoted in Barde, *Immigration at the Golden Gate*, 113–114.

13. Quoted in Barde, *Immigration at the Golden Gate*, 115.

14. Tokuji Hoshino, from "Guest in a Strange Land," 1903, quoted in Barde, *Immigration at the Golden Gate*, 113.

15. Heitaro Hikida, quoted in Barde, *Immigration at the Golden Gate*, 115–116.

16. Barde, *Immigration at the Golden Gate*, 117, 119.

17. Barde, *Immigration at the Golden Gate*, 90, 91.

18. Lee, *At America's Gates*, 157.

19. Robert Chao Romero, *The Chinese in Mexico, 1882–1940* (Tucson: University of Arizona Press, 2010), 1.

20. Romero, *Chinese in Mexico*, 192.

21. Romero, *Chinese in Mexico*, 4, 58, 61–62, 192.

22. Romero, *Chinese in Mexico*, 61–62.

23. Romero, *Chinese in Mexico*, esp. 97–118.

24. Romero, *Chinese in Mexico*, 117.

25. Luey Mo Warrant Hearing, March 14, 1919, Southwestern Insane Asylum, San Antonio, 54646/170.

26. Grace Peña Delgado, *Making the Chinese Mexican: Global Migration, Localism, and Exclusion in the U.S.-Mexico Borderlands* (Stanford, CA: Stanford University Press, 2012), 101–103; Molina, *Fit to Be Citizens*; and Shah, *Contagious Divides*.

27. These cultural representations similarly attacked Mexican women who had amorous relations with Chinese men as not only greedy, but shameless, dirty, and even traitorous to an emergent Mexican national project. Romero, *Chinese in Mexico*, esp. 81; and Delgado, *Making the Chinese Mexican*, 10.

28. John Mason Hart, *Anarchism and the Mexican Working Class, 1860–1931* (Austin: University of Texas Press, 1987), 102–103.

29. Romero, *Chinese in Mexico*, esp. 149–150.

30. Delgado, *Making the Chinese Mexican*, 105–125.

31. Justin Leroy, "Black History in Occupied Territory: On the Entanglements of Slavery and Settler Colonialism," *Theory & Event* 19, no. 4 (2016), muse.jhu.edu/article/633276.

32. "John J. Pershing Biography," www.biography.com/people/john-j-pershing, accessed March 23, 2018.

33. Emilio Zamora, *The World of the Mexican Worker in Texas* (College Station: Texas A&M University Press, 1993), 81–84; and Rachel St. John, *Line in the Sand: A History of the Western U.S.-Mexico Border* (Princeton, NJ: Princeton University Press, 2011), 129.

34. Miguel Antonio Levario, *Militarizing the Border: When Mexicans Became the Enemy* (College Station: Texas A&M University Press, 2012), 67; and William D. Carrigan and Clive Webb, *Forgotten Dead: Mob Violence against Mexicans in the United States, 1848–1928* (New York: Oxford University Press, 2013), esp. 22–33, 84–88.

35. Levario, *Militarizing the Border*, 69, 70; and Frederich Katz, "Pancho Villa and the Attack on Columbus, New Mexico," *American Historical Review* 83, no. 1 (1978): 101–130.

36. Delgado, *Making the Chinese Mexican*, 131; and Julian Lim, "Immigration, Asylum, and Citizenship: A More Holistic Approach," *California Law Review* 101 (2013): 1013–1077, esp. 1034.

37. "Chinese on Army's Hands: 300 with Pershing Fear Mexicans If Americans Withdraw," *New York Times*, July 18, 1916.

38. Lim, "Immigration, Asylum, and Citizenship," esp. 1034, 1035.

39. Andrew Urban, "Asylum in the Midst of Chinese Exclusion: Pershing's Punitive Expedition and the Columbus Refugees from Mexico, 1916–1921," *Journal of Policy History* 32, no. 2 (2011): 204–229, 208.

40. For images of the expedition's return, see "Camp Furlong and Columbus, New Mexico, 1916," http://demingnewmexico.genealogyvillage.com/CampFurlong/menu.htm, accessed March 27, 2018.

41. Urban, "Asylum in the Midst of Chinese Exclusion," 204.

42. For images of Camp Furlong, see "Camp Furlong and Columbus, New Mexico, 1916."

43. Horace Daniel Nash, "Town and Sword: Black Soldiers in Columbus, New Mexico, in the Early Twentieth Century," PhD dissertation, Mississippi State University, 1996, pp. 29–30.

44. Moloney, *National Insecurities*, 138–146.

45. Urban, "Asylum in the Midst of Chinese Exclusion," 209.

46. Edward Eugene Briscoe, "Pershing's Chinese Refugees in Texas," *Southwestern Historical Quarterly* 62, no. 4 (1959): 467–488, 470; and Urban, "Asylum in the Midst of Chinese Exclusion," 206.

47. A hard lesson, as many Iraqi translators for the US military have learned since the invasion of Iraq in 2003 and have been denied entry to the United States, despite promises from US allies. Consider the program "Taking Names," *This American Life*, no. 499, June 28, 2013; also from the twenty-first century for Afghan contractors with the US military, "Special Immigrant Visa Holders Still Face Questioning Upon Reaching U.S.," National Public Radio, *Morning Edition*, March 27, 2017.

48. Urban, "Asylum in the Midst of Chinese Exclusion," 211.

49. Immigration Serial No, 101–138, Consular No. 486, 54646/170.

50. Urban, "Asylum in the Midst of Chinese Exclusion," 212.

51. Quoted in Urban, "Asylum in the Midst of Chinese Exclusion," 211.

52. Urban, "Asylum in the Midst of Chinese Exclusion," 212.

53. Urban, "Asylum in the Midst of Chinese Exclusion," 213, 214.

54. The support for their special legal status was aided by wartime labor shortages and skepticism over other possible low-wage/unfree workers, notably fears of Mexican and Mexican American laborers in context of Zimmerman Telegram and the Plan de San Diego. Pershing's reliance on Chinese at the outset and their use here anticipates later imperial reliance on "third country nationals" as a US military infrastructural strategy.

55. Blue, *Doing Time in the Depression*; Glen A. Gildemeister, *Prison Labor and Convict Competition with Free Workers in Industrializing America, 1840–1890* (New York: Garland Publishing, 1987); and McLennan, *The Crisis of Imprisonment*.

56. Urban, "Asylum in the Midst of Chinese Exclusion," 215.

57. Briscoe, "Pershing's Chinese Refugees in Texas," 470.

58. Urban, "Asylum in the Midst of Chinese Exclusion," 209.

59. Nash, "Town and Sword," 29–30.

60. Gerris Fort to CGI, ATTN Roger O'Donnell, March 28, 1919, 54645/325, RG 85, Entry 9, NARA–Washington, DC.

61. Briscoe, "Pershing's Chinese Refugees in Texas," 471.

62. Briscoe, "Pershing's Chinese Refugees in Texas," 472.

63. Edward Briscoe offered a prototype Asian American model minority story and went to great lengths to paint the refugees' happiness—and, in a move appropriate to Cold War liberalism, their American assimilability. Urban, "Asylum in

the Midst of Chinese Exclusion," 217; Briscoe, "Pershing's Chinese Refugees in Texas," 474–477; and Lim, "Immigration, Asylum, and Citizenship," 1037.

64. In Urban, "Asylum in the Midst of Chinese Exclusion," 217–218.

65. Briscoe, "Pershing's Chinese Refugees in Texas," 476.

66. *San Antonio Express*, June 17, 1917, quoted in Briscoe, "Pershing's Chinese Refugees in Texas," 474.

67. Mel Brown, *The Chinese Heart of Texas: The San Antonio Community, 1875–1975,* www.home.earthlink.net/~melbjr/chineseheartoftexas/id12.html, accessed June 15, 2016.

68. Urban, "Asylum in the Midst of Chinese Exclusion," 216.

69. Memorandum by C. K. Schafer, February 3, 1919, 54646/170.

70. Page quoted in Lim, "Immigration, Asylum, and Citizenship," 1065.

71. Memorandum by C. K. Schafer, February 3, 1919; Correspondence from Mr. Tracy Page, "in Charge of the Chinese Refugees" to San Antonio Immigration Services (Exhibit A), January 24, 1919, 54646/170.

72. Allred Box, 1985/024-95, Folder 2: Texas Prison System: General Correspondence and Proclamations, May 1935, Texas State Library and Archives Commission, Austin, TX.

73. California State Board of Charities and Corrections, Seventh Biennial Report, July 1, 1914, to June 30, 1916 (Sacramento: California State Printing Office, 1916), 42, quoted in Braslow, *Mental Ills and Bodily Cures*, 17.

74. He would have been sent to the Southwestern Insane Asylum sooner, but the asylum was in the grip an influenza outbreak. By December the outbreak had abated. Page to San Antonio Immigration Services (Exhibit A), January 24, 1919, 54646/170. Reference to the use of leather restraints in transfer from jail to hospital in Braslow, *Mental Ills and Bodily Cures*, 18.

75. Noll, *American Madness*, 7.

76. William R. Geise and James W. Markham, "San Antonio State Hospital," *Handbook of Texas Online*, accessed July 6, 2016.

77. Sitton, *Life at the Texas State Lunatic Asylum*, 88, 119–120.

78. From Clifford Whittingham Beers, "A Mind That Found Itself: An Autobiography," Project Gutenberg, 2008 [1908]) chapter 21, www.gutenberg.org/files/11962/11962-h/11962-h.htm, accessed March 19, 2021. Also in Sitton, *Life at the Texas State Lunatic Asylum,* 69.

79. Sitton, *Life at the Texas State Lunatic Asylum*, 77.

80. *The Snake Pit*, 17, quoted in Sitton, *Life at the Texas State Lunatic Asylum*, 92.

81. On therapeutic control, see Braslow, *Mental Ills and Bodily Cures*, 9.

82. Allan M. Brandt, *No Magic Bullet: A Social History of Venereal Disease in the United States since 1880* (New York: Oxford University Press, 1987), 12, quoted in Sitton, *Life at the Texas State Lunatic Asylum*, 97.

83. Braslow, *Mental Ills and Bodily Cures*, 2, 39, 48–50.

84. Luey Mo Warrant Hearing, March 14, 1919, 54646/170.

85. As Geoffrey Raume has argued, ignoring the complex testimonies of those

whom he calls "mad" is a sign of political and intellectual failure: "Ignoring this history constitutes a form of historical disempowerment of a group of people who were, and many of whom still are, disempowered in their own lives." Reaume, "Mad People's History," *Radical History Review* 94 (2006): 170–182, esp. 171.

86. Luey Moo [*sic*] Patient History, Southwestern Insane Asylum, January 29, 1919, 54646/170.

87. Page quote in Luey Moo [*sic*] Patient History, Southwestern Insane Asylum, January 29, 1919, 54646/170.

88. Luey Moo [*sic*] Patient History, January 29, 1919, 54646/170.

89. Memorandum by C. K. Schafer, San Antonio office, re: Luey Mo, February 3, 1919, 54646/170.

90. Luey Moo [*sic*] Warrant Hearing, March 14, 1919, 54646/170.

91. Luey Moo [*sic*] Patient History, January 29, 1919, 54646/170.

92. "Proof that Alien has become a Public Charge from Causes Existing Prior to Landing" January 30, 1919; and Luey Moo [*sic*] Patient History, January 29, 1919, 54646/170.

93. Secretary of State, January 8, 1914, Secretary of State to Secretary of Commerce and Labor, 52516/10, RG 85, Entry 9, NARA–Washington, DC.

94. Luey Moo [*sic*] Patient History, January 29, 1919, 54646/170.

95. The refugees' unfree labor on US military bases anticipated the twenty-first century military in Afghanistan, Iraq, and beyond, in which the United States uses so-called "Third Country Nationals." They are cheaper than US-based contractors, are thought to be unlikely to be ideologically sympathetic to local insurgents, and can be deported if they are at all unsatisfactory. These workers are essentially unfree, or are at the very least, marginally coerced workers, akin to the so-called coolies of a century ago. Darryl Li, "Migrant Workers and the US Military in the Middle East," *Middle East Research and Information Project* 275, no. 45 (2015), www.merip.org/mer/mer275/migrant-workers-us-military-middle-east#_2.

CHAPTER 12. EL PASO

1. Lim, *Porous Borders*, 74–75, 90–94; and El Paso Sanborne Map, 1908, Key, http://legacy.lib.utexas.edu/maps/sanborn/d-f/txu-sanborn-el_paso-1908-1k.jpg, accessed January 22, 2019.

2. Mario T. García, *Desert Immigrants: The Mexicans of El Paso, 1880–1920* (New Haven, CT: Yale University Press, 1981), 11.

3. Lim, *Porous Borders*, 24–25; and Carlos G. Vélez-Ibáñez, *Border Visions: Mexican Cultures of the Southwest United States* (Tucson: University of Arizona Press, 1996), 20–56.

4. Lim, *Porous Borders*, 23, 35–36.

5. As historian Julian Lim has put it, the borderlands were a "treasure trove of rich copper, gold, silver, mercury, lead, zinc, and azurite deposits" that also soon

yielded "coal, iron, brick, clay, cement, and many other raw materials" beneath miners' hands, hammers, and bent backs. Lim, *Porous Borders*, 38–39.

6. The numbers of residents grew from 736 in 1880 to nearly 16,000 in 1900, and almost 40,000 in 1910. In 1916, El Paso was home to some 1,526 Black residents, 243 Chinese, 32,724 ethnic Mexicans, and 27,405 residents designated as White or Other. Lim, *Porous Borders*, Table 1, pp. 43, 49.

7. This chapter, along with the discussion of the Huerto brothers and the Vallejo family in a previous chapter, demonstrates the differential elements of the border/interior-policing-deportation-regime as (1) an extended infrastructure and (2) a hard barrier. The Vallejo family's experience demonstrates the first: the differential and selective porosity of the border/interior-policing-deportation-regime, in which selected workers (such as rail workers in wartime) might gain tenuous admission on the condition of deportability for any host of noncompliant behaviors, or when their labor was no longer deemed necessary. In this chapter we see the formation of the border as a hardening, militarized barrier, guaranteed by violence, preventing some people's movement—and particularly Asians deemed racially ineligible to citizenship.

8. Their documents are gathered in case file 54646/192, RG 85, Entry 9, NARA–Washington, DC.

9. McClatchy testimony in *Japanese Immigration: Hearings before the Committee on Immigration and Naturalization*, Sixty-sixth Congress, 2d session, 1920, Part 1 (Washington, DC: Government Printing Office, 1921), esp. 235–240.

10. "Rejoices at the Fall of Schmitz in 'Frisco," *Boston Sunday Herald*, June 16, 1907, www.sfmuseum.org/conflag/phelan.html; and more broadly, Roger Daniels, *The Politics of Prejudice: The Anti-Japanese Movement in California and the Struggle for Japanese Exclusion* (Berkeley: University of California Press, 1977), esp. 81–84.

11. "California and the Oriental—Japanese, Chinese, and Hindus—Report of the State Board of Control of California," in *Japanese Immigration: Hearings before the Committee on Immigration and Naturalization*, 72, 75.

12. Japan's rulers in the Tokugawa period, seeking to maintain isolation from Western powers, had prohibited emigration from Japan from the 1600s until the middle of the nineteenth century, after Commodore Matthew Perry's black ships arrived and forced open the Kingdom's markets to Western influence. Takaki, *Strangers from a Different Shore*, 43.

13. Tamar Diana Wilson, introduction to *Latin American Perspectives: East Asian Migrations to Latin America* 31, no. 3 (2004): 3–17, esp. 4; Zolberg, "Global Movements, Global Walls, 292. It also sought to dismantle the Tokugawa-era caste categories. Known as *mibun*, the caste system separated samurai, farmers, and merchants from the untouchable castes of leatherworkers, butchers, blacksmiths, coal miners, and others whom the higher castes considered polluted. Meiji modernizers thought *mibun* was anachronistic and unhelpful to their modernization project, but its legacies persisted. Andrea Geiger, *Subverting Exclusion:*

Transpacific Encounters with Race, Caste, and Borders, 1885–1928 (New Haven, CT: Yale University Press, 2011).

14. By 1879, Japan annexed Okinawa, which had been a sovereign kingdom with ties to China. Japan turned Okinawa into a huge sugar-exporting region and subject the already poor farmers to withering taxes. This was the background of Okinawan migration, initially to Japanese cities and later, Korea and across the Pacific. Rapid agricultural modernization and industrialization, coupled with a monetary policy failure in 1881, led to a surplus of unemployed and underemployed farmers. New tax policies forced farmers and peasants to sell their land, which concentrated agricultural holdings pulled the landless into cities. Military conscription led to major grievances, partially because of coercion involved but also because farmers resented being forced into proximity with people in previously outcaste *mibun* categories. And when fishing economies collapsed in the late nineteenth century, more people were cast adrift. Wilson, introduction to *Latin American Perspectives*, 4; Geiger, *Subverting Exclusion*, 26–27, 29; and Ayumi Takenaka, "The Japanese in Peru: History of Immigration, Settlement, and Racialization," *Latin American Perspectives* 31, no. 3 (May 2004): 77–98, 79.

15. Remittances reached up to 10 percent of total annual trade surpluses in the interwar period. Takenaka, "Japanese in Peru," 79.

16. Takenaka, "Japanese in Peru," 78; and Sidney Xu Lu, "Japan's Asian–Pacific Migrations and the Making of the Japanese Empire, 1868–1945," PhD dissertation, University of Pennsylvania, 2013, p. 212.

17. Takaki, *Strangers from a Different Shore*, 45, 49; and Takenaka, "Japanese in Peru," 80.

18. Takenaka, "Japanese in Peru," 80.

19. Kondo Johei Hearing, February 20, 1919, 54646/192.

20. Tarashima Tokizo Hearing, February 20, 1919, 54646/192.

21. Hirakawa Kizo Hearing, February 20, 1919, 54646/192. Though caste distinctions were no longer officially recognized, it is possible that Hirakawa, unlike Tarashima or Kondo, had been among the *buraku jūmin*, or the untouchable castes. In some regions blacksmiths were considered untouchable, and Hiroshima was among the prefectures with the largest number of outcaste villages. Estimates of the so-called untouchables among Japanese emigrants vary from 1 percent to 30 percent. Geiger, *Subverting Exclusion*, 17, 33–35, 38, 70–71.

22. Kim, "Inaugurating the American Century," 68, 75n57.

23. Many elite Japanese officials accommodated US racism and explained it as actually *merited* by unworthy Japanese, a sensibility that accorded to persistent (if unofficial) disdain of the historical caste categories. As one Japanese politician reflected: "Only the lowest section of the Japanese are being discriminated against.... The more respectable classes of Japanese are well treated and respected by the Americans.... In California and other Pacific coast states only has unfriendliness been shown toward our people. This is because many Japanese in those regions are unworthy." Quoted in Geiger, *Subverting Exclusion*, 56–57.

24. Takaki, *Strangers from a Different Shore*, 203–207.

25. McClatchy testimony in *Japanese Immigration: Hearings before the Committee on Immigration and Naturalization*, 235, 237.

26. Chang, *Pacific Connections*, 153–154.

27. Japanese migrants had traveled to Latin America since the last years of the nineteenth century. They arrived in Mexico in 1892, in Peru in 1898, in Chile in 1903, in Argentina in 1907, in Brazil in 1908, in Panama in 1915, in Bolivia in 1916, in Columbia in 1921, in Uruguay and Paraguay in 1930, and in Venezuela in 1931. Wilson, introduction to *Latin American Perspectives*, 8.

28. On examinations when leaving Japan, see Geiger, *Subverting Exclusion*, 109.

29. By the 1890s, Peru's rulers were the inheritors of the Spanish empire's South American reaches, with its own attendant histories of conquest over the Inca empire in the sixteenth century and the development of a brutal *encomienda* system of forced labor in agriculture and mining.

30. Wilson, introduction to *Latin American Perspectives*, 5.

31. The could not lure many European migrants because *latifundistas* generally refused to cede land to newcomers. Takenaka, "Japanese in Peru," 83–84.

32. They were promised 25-yen per month over the term of their four-year contracts. Japanese emigration companies, with ties to Peruvian businesses, led migrants to believe that Peru was a "land full of gold." Takenaka, "Japanese in Peru," 77.

33. Takenaka, "Japanese in Peru," 84.

34. Concerted racism, Takenaka argues (in "Japanese in Peru," 85, 89), led to relative insularity and the development of an internally facing market. Many became barbers, and smaller numbers became shopkeepers, restaurant owners, or merchants that served their ethnic communities. A handful managed to acquire land and began growing cotton.

35. Takenaka, "Japanese in Peru," 88. A 1910 decree prohibited Japanese from owning land in Sierra regions, with anti-Asian movement gathering steam and ferocity in the following decades. An Anti-Asian Association formed in 1917 to prohibit Asian migration, and successfully prohibited contract labor in 1923. National quota systems prohibited further Japanese arrivals, save for any direct family members. New national citizenship laws also worked to restrict or to withdraw the birthright citizenship of Japanese Peruvians. On the economic front, by the 1930s Peru passed laws that required all businesses to employ 80 percent Peruvians. See Takenaka, "Japanese in Peru," 84–87.

36. Kondo Johei Hearing, February 20, 1919, 54646/192.

37. Takenaka, "Japanese in Peru," 88.

38. Jonathan Hyslop, "Steamship Empire: Asian, African and British Sailors in the Merchant Marine, c. 1880–1945," *Journal of Asian and African Studies* 44, no. 1 (2009): 49–67.

39. Hirakawa Hearing, February 20, 1919, 54646/192.

40. Hirakawa Hearing, February 20, 1919, 54646/192. The British-owned

West Coast of America Telegraph Company operated a single-boiler steam-driven cable ship called *Retriever* between 1909 and 1939. This was likely his ship (see "SS Retreiver," *Wreck Site*, at www.wrecksite.eu/wreck.aspx?98835, accessed December 8, 2016).

41. Kondo Johei Hearing, February 20, 1919, 54646/192.

42. Anna Pegler-Gordon, "Shanghaied on the Streets of Hoboken: Chinese Exclusion and Maritime Regulation at Ellis Island," *Journal for Maritime Research* 16, no. 2 (July 3, 2014): 229–245, 236.

43. Keiko Itoh, *The Japanese Community in Pre-war Britain: From Integration to Disintegration* (Richmond, Surrey, UK: Curzon, 2001), 25.

44. Quoted in Itoh, *Japanese Community in Pre-war Britain*, 25.

45. Andrew Urban, "Restricted Cargo: Chinese Sailors, Shore Leave, and the Evolution of U.S. Immigration Policies, 1882–1942," in *People-Works: The Labor of Transport*, ed. Kate McDonald (2018), https://t2m.org/restricted-cargo-chinese -sailors-shore-leave-and-the-evolution-of-u-s-immigration-policies-1882-1942/, accessed August 23, 2019.

46. Quoted in Itoh, *Japanese Community in Pre-war Britain*, 25.

47. Hirakawa Hearing, February 20, 1919; and Kondo Hearing, February 20, 1919, both in 54646/192.

48. Jonathan C. Brown, *Oil and Revolution in Mexico* (Berkeley: University of California Press, 1993), 324.

49. Jonathan C. Brown, "Jersey Standard and the Politics of Latin American Oil Production, 1911–30," in *The Oil Business in Latin America: The Early Years*, ed. John D. Wirth, 1–50 (Lincoln: University of Nebraska Press, 1985), 19.

50. Brown, *Oil and Revolution in Mexico*, 16–17, 27–30, 55.

51. Mexico became the world's second largest oil producer (after the United States), and by 1927, Jersey Standard won $36.5 million worth of stock dividends for Jersey's shareholders from Mexican holdings. By 1930s, Standard was the largest oil producer in the Southern Hemisphere. Brown, *Oil and Revolution in Mexico*, 70, 77; also, Brown, "Jersey Standard and the Politics of Latin American Oil Production, 1911–30," 1–50, but esp. 1–2, 23–26.

52. Brown, *Oil and Revolution in Mexico*, 309.

53. In 1900 most of Tampico's 17,500 residents had been born in the region. They were joined in smaller numbers by Mexicans from other parts of the country, and around 1,000 people from overseas. The vast majority were farmers and field laborers, some 855 in commerce of some sort, and just 49 registered as industrial workers. In 1915, Chinese (2,000), Spaniards (1,000), Americans (750), Britons (300), Germans (129), Dutch (57), and others (379) lived in Tampico. Brown, *Oil and Revolution in Mexico*, 71, 310.

54. Brown, *Oil and Revolution in Mexico*, 310.

55. Others lived amid the oozing runoff, haze, and smoke along the riverbanks near refineries. Still, they built churches, markets, and plazas. Native itinerant Mexican workers, predominantly Indigenous peasants who did many of the worst paid jobs, typically faced the worst living conditions. Mortality rates in Tampico

increased by more than 50 percent between in the boom years between 1910 and 1917, and, predictably, hit the poorest workers the hardest. Brown, *Oil and Revolution in Mexico*, 310–311.

56. Brown, *Oil and Revolution in Mexico*, 311.

57. Brown, *Oil and Revolution in Mexico*, 84.

58. Brown, *Oil and Revolution in Mexico*, 320–321, 332–333.

59. Brown, "Jersey Standard and the Politics of Latin American Oil Production, 1911–30," esp. 1–2, 23–26.

60. Brown, *Oil and Revolution in Mexico*, 309.

61. Brown, *Oil and Revolution in Mexico*, 317, 335, 344.

62. Tarashima Tokizo Interview, February 24, 1919, 54646/192.

63. Brown, *Oil and Revolution in Mexico*, 317, 335, 344.

64. Kondo Hearing, February 20, 1919, 54646/192.

65. Hirakawa Kizo Interrogation, February 20, 1919, 54646/192.

66. Geiger, *Subverting Exclusion*, 129.

67. Young, *Alien Nation*, 161–162, 182.

68. And more recently, see Gilberto Rosas, *Barrio Libre: Criminalizing States and Delinquent Refusals of the New Frontier* (Durham, NC: Duke University Press, 2012).

69. Young, *Alien Nation*, 268–270; Lee, *At America's Gates*; and Truett, *Fugitive Landscapes*, 124–125.

70. Tokizo Interview, February 24, 1919; and Hirakawa Interrogation, February 20, 1919, 54646/192.

71. Pegler–Gordon, "Shanghaied on the Streets of Hoboken," 235, 238.

72. February 24, 1919, Hirakawa Kizo, Interrogation conducted February 20, 1919, by Inspector Wm. A. Brand, 54646/192.

73. Kondo Hearing, February 20, 1919, 54646/192.

74. Correspondence from Berkshire to CGI, February 28, 1919, 54646/192.

75. There is a considerable scholarship on the early creation and militarization of the US-Mexico border, but I have drawn on Hernández, *MIGRA!*; Gloria Anzaldúa, *Borderlands/La Frontera: The New Mestiza* (San Francisco: Aunt Lute, 2007); St. John, *Line in the Sand*; Vélez-Ibáñez, *Border Visions*; Dunn, *Militarization of the US-Mexico Border*; Kang, *INS on the Line*; Jeremy Adelman and Stephen Aron, "From Borderlands to Borders: Empires, Nation-States, and the Peoples in between in North American History," *American Historical Review* 104, no. 3 (June 1999): 814–841; and Levario, *Militarizing the Border*.

76. Reviel Netz, *Barbed Wire: An Ecology of Modernity* (Middletown, CT: Wesleyan University Press, 2004).

77. Quoted in St. John, *Line in the Sand*, 104.

78. Micol Seigel, *Violence Work: State Power and the Limits of Police* (Durham, NC: Duke University Press, 2018).

79. Quoted in Levario, *Militarizing the Border*, 95.

80. Hernández, *MIGRA!*, 19–22; and David Manuel Hernández, "Carceral Shadows: Entangled Lineages and Technologies of Migrant Detention," in *Cag-*

ing Borders and Carceral States: Incarcerations, Immigration Detentions, and Resistance, ed. Robert T. Chase, 57–92 (Chapel Hill: University of North Carolina Press, 2019), 69.

81. Carrigan and Webb, *Forgotten Dead*, 21.

82. Kang, *INS on the Line*.

83. Kang, *INS on the Line*, 53, 61, 148.

84. Chang, *Pacific Connections*, 148–149; Rutvica Andrijasevic, "From Exception to Excess: Detention and Deportations across the Mediterranean Space," in *The Deportation Regime: Sovereignty, Space, and the Freedom of Movement*, ed. Nicholas De Genova and Nathalie Peutz, 147–165 (Durham, NC: Duke University Press, 2010); and Walters, "Deportation, Expulsion, and the International Police of Aliens," 82.

85. Hernández, "Surrogates and Subcontractors"; and Pope-Obeda, "When in Doubt, Deport!," 280.

86. Arrest Warrant, February 25, 1919; and Warrant Application, February 24, 1919, 54646/192.

87. Kondo Johei Warrant Hearing, February 27, 1919, 54646/192.

88. Levario, *Militarizing the Border*, 57–66.

89. Levario briefly mentions the trustee system, in *Militarizing the Border*, 59–61.

90. Berkshire to CGI, February 28, 1919, 54646/192.

91. Tarashima Tokizo Interview, February 24, 1919, 54646/192.

92. Warrant Hearing, Tarashima Tokizo, February 27, 1919, 54646/192.

93. Berkshire to CGI, April 17 and 23, 1919, 54646/192.

CHAPTER 13. ANGEL ISLAND

1. Stanley, "Five Weeks Leave," 19.

2. 54519-3, University Publications, INS Series A Supplement to Part 1, Reel 9, frames 106–193, NARA–San Bruno.

3. Maria Sakovich, "When the 'Enemy' Landed at Angel Island," *Prologue* 41, no. 2 (2009), www.archives.gov/publications/prologue/2009/summer/angel.html, accessed April 22, 2013.

4. See also Muwekma Ohlone Tribe, "Historical Overview," www.muwekma .org/tribalhistory/historicaloverview.html, accessed December 2, 2019; Alan Leventhal, Les Fields, Hank Alvarez, and Rosemary Cambra, "The Ohlone Back from Extinction," in *The Ohlone Past and Present: Native Americans of the San Francisco Bay Region*, ed. Lowell John Bean, 301–336 (Ballena Press Anthropological Papers 42, 1994); and Monica V. Arellano et al. "An Ethnohistory of Santa Clara Valley and Adjacent Regions; Historic Ties of the Muwekma Ohlone Tribe of the San Francisco Bay Area and Tribal Stewardship over the Tupiun Táareštak [Place of the Fox Man] Site: Ca-Scl-894," www.muwekma.org/images/Ethnohis

tory_Section_from_Muwekma_Ohlone_Burial_Site_CA-SCL-894_San_Jose_Chapter_9_April_15,_2014.pdf, accessed January 9, 2020.

5. Matt K. Matsuda, *Pacific Worlds: A History of Seas, Peoples, and Cultures* (New York: Cambridge University Press, 2012), 244.

6. Chris Carlsson, "The Railroad Comes to SF?" *FoundSF*, www.foundsf.org/index.php?title=THE_RAILROAD_COMES_TO_SF%3F, accessed November 20, 2019.

7. "Southern Pacific Announces Plans for Depot," *San Francisco Chronicle*, November 25, 1912, www.sfmuseum.net/hist7/spdepot.html, accessed November 20, 2019.

8. Chang, *Pacific Connections*, 10–11.

9. Epeli Hau'ofa, "Our Sea of Islands," *Contemporary Pacific* 6, no. 1 (1994): 148–161; Lisa Kahaleole Hall, "Navigating Our Own 'Sea of Islands': Remapping a Theoretical Space for Hawaiian Women and Indigenous Feminism," *Wicazo Sa Review* 24, no. 2 (2009): 15–38; and Chalmers Johnson, "America's Empire of Bases," TomDispatch.com, January 2004.

10. Matsuda, *Pacific Worlds*, 2; also, Katrina Gulliver, "Finding the Pacific World," *Journal of World History* 22, no. 1 (2011): 83–100.

11. Reddy, *Freedom with Violence*, 96.

12. Barde, *Immigration at the Golden Gate*, 201.

13. Quoted in Goodman, *Deportation Machine*, 76.

14. Wheeler, "Memorandum for the Secretary," January 28, 1909, file 52270/21, RG 85, Entry 9, 14/14/02, box 468, NARA, quoted in Barde, *Immigration at the Golden Gate*, 75.

15. Blue, "Finding Margins on Borders," 2.

16. Mary Bamford, *Angel Island: Ellis Island of the West* (Chicago: Women's American Baptist Home Mission Society, 1917), 12, 15; and Lee and Yung, *Angel Island*.

17. Bamford, *Angel Island*; and Lee and Yung, *Angel Island*, 24.

18. Lee and Yung, *Angel Island*, 58–59.

19. Lee and Yung, *Angel Island*, 24.

20. Sakovich, "When the 'Enemy' Landed at Angel Island."

21. Nevertheless, the Pacific Mail Steamship Service, one among a handful of transpacific firms that handled deportation traffic, recorded 757 people listed as deportees at Angel Island between 1913 and 1919. Of this group, only eighteen spent no nights at Angel Island. The rest spent a mean number of thirty-four days and a median number of twenty-four days in detention while their cases were being investigated or their removal finalized. Robert Barde and Gustavo J. Bobonis, "Detention at Angel Island: First Empirical Evidence," *Social Science History* 30, no. 1 (2006): 103–136, esp. Table 3, p. 116.

22. Lee and Yung, *Angel Island*, 95, 59.

23. Lee and Yung, *Angel Island*, 57.

24. Mock Ging Sing quoted in Lee and Yung, *Angel Island*, 59.

25. Both women quoted in Lee and Yung, *Angel Island,* 58.

26. Lee and Yung, *Angel Island,* 60–61.

27. Bamford, *Angel Island,* 16. On carved poetry, see Him Mark Lai, Genny Lim, and Judy Yung, eds., *Island: Poetry and History of Chinese Immigrants on Angel Island, 1910–1940* (Seattle: University of Washington Press, 1980).

28. Quoted in Lee and Yung, *Angel Island,* 99.

29. McKeown, "Ritualization of Regulation"; Lee, *At America's Gates*; and Blue, "Cognitive Maps and Spatial Narratives."

30. Bamford, *Angel Island,* 19.

31. Anna Pegler-Gordon, *In Sight of America: Photography and the Development of U.S. Immigration Policy* (Berkeley: University of California Press, 2009).

32. In Lee and Yung, *Angel Island,* 101.

33. Irwin, *Strange Passage,* 261–262.

34. Blue, "Finding Margins on Borders."

35. White to CGI Washington, June 17, 1919; and Executed Deportation Warrant, 54646/192, RG 85, Entry 9, NARA I–Washington, DC.

36. Founded in the 1890s, the TKK Line initially bought older ships from US and British firms to develop Japan's position as a Pacific power. In its early days the TKK cooperated with the SP-linked Pacific Mail, dividing up passenger, cargo, and other areas, and using Pacific Mail's infrastructure and docking facilities. Tension grew as Pacific Mail introduced new ships to compete with TKKs' passenger traffic and when TKK ships were sent to the Russo-Japanese War, signaling Japan's increasing strength and ambition. E. Mowbray Tate, *Transpacific Steam: The Story of Steam Navigation from the Pacific Coast of North America to the Far East and the Antipodes, 1867—1941* (New York: Cornwall Books, 1986), 62, 64; and Barde, *Immigration at the Golden Gate,* 182.

37. Tate, *Transpacific Steam,* 64; and "Ship/Pacific Liners," *Encyclopedia Britannica,* 1911, p. 887, https://en.wikisource.org/wiki/1911_Encyclop%C3%A6dia_Britannica/Ship#PacificLiners, accessed November 25, 2019; and Christopher Howe, *The Origins of Japanese Trade Supremacy: Development Technology in Asia from 1540 to the Pacific War* (London: Hurst and Company, 1996), 291.

38. Howe, *Origins of Japanese Trade Supremacy,* 291n50; "*Tenyo Maru* Reading Room" postcard, *The Daily Postcard,* http://postcardparadise.blogspot.com/2011/09/ss-tenyo-maru.html, accessed November 25, 2019; Barde, *Immigration at the Golden Gate,* 128; and "Ship/Pacific Liners," 887.

39. Asia-bound passenger traffic was about 70 percent of North America–bound traffic in the era. "Ship/Pacific Liners," 887; and Barde, *Immigration at the Golden Gate,* 133.

40. Maedakō Hiroichirō, *Santo senkyaku, Gendai Nihon bungaku taikei* 59 (Tokyo: Chikuma shobo, 1973), 12, quoted in Barde, *Immigration at the Golden Gate,* 133.

41. White to CG, October 3, 1919, 54646/170, RG 85, Entry 9, NARA–Washington, DC.

42. Angel Island to CG, June 15, 1920; and White to Terrill, February 6, 1920, 54646/170.

43. Record of Ocean Voyage, Sheet B, March 19, 1920, 54646/170.

44. Matsuda, *Pacific Worlds*, 249–250; and Noenoe K. Silva, *Aloha Betrayed: Native Hawaiian Resistance to American Colonialism* (Durham, NC: Duke University Press, 2004), 122–203.

45. White to CGI, Washington, June 17, 1919, 54646/192.

46. Geiger, *Subverting Exclusion*, 47.

47. White to CGI, Washington, June 17, 1919, 54646/192.

48. Pacific Mail Steamship Company, "Transpacific Service Schedule No. 8, 1919–1921," image made from the collection of Björn Larsson, http://timetables.com/maritime/images/pml19.htm.

49. White to C. L. Terrill, February 6, 1920, 54646/170.

50. Record of Land Trip and Delivery at Final Destination, Sheet C, 54646/170.

51. Zhai Hailong and Gao Yan, "Early Psychiatric Services in Hong Kong from 1841 to 1947," *Mental Health in Family Medicine* 13 (2017): 435–437.

52. White to C. L. Terrill, February 6, 1920, 54646/170.

53. Suchetana Chattopadhyay, "Closely Observed Ships," *South Asian Diaspora* 8, no. 2 (July 2, 2016): 203–222, 218; and Johnston, *Voyage of the Komagata Maru*, 112.

54. Chattopadhyay, "Closely Observed Ships," 207.

55. G. Balachandran, "Indefinite Transits: Mobility and Confinement in the Age of Steam," *Journal of Global History* 11, no. 2 (July 2016): 187–208, 194–195.

56. It was orchestrated by Calcutta's commissioner of police and the Intelligence Branch but drew on the expertise and manpower of the Central Intelligence Department in Delhi and Simla, the provincial governments of Punjab and Bengal, and a host of military and police agencies as well as shipping agents and port authorities to share intelligence. Moreover, "Creative interpretation of the Ingress into India Ordinance" (V of 1914) justified the examination of all returning Sikhs. Relevant portions of the ordinance were intended for those defined as foreigners, even though Punjabi Sikhs were hardly that; see Chattopadhyay, "Closely Observed Ships," 211, 205.

57. Chattopadhyay, "Closely Observed Ships," 209–210.

58. Chattopadhyay, "Closely Observed Ships," 204, 205.

59. Chattopadhyay, "Closely Observed Ships," 217.

60. Chattopadhyay, "Closely Observed Ships," 204.

61. Chattopadhyay, "Closely Observed Ships," 209, 211.

62. Johnston, *Voyage of the Komagata Maru*, 114.

63. Johnston, *Voyage of the Komagata Maru*, 114.

64. Johnston, *Voyage of the Komagata Maru*, 114.

1. All from DoJ file, NARA–Saint Louis: Ebey to CGI Washington, July 25, 1916; July 12, 1916, telegram Caminetti to Chicago office; July 14, 1916, correspondence from Acting Commissioner Sargent to CGI Washington, DC; July 15, 1916, telegram from Prentis to CGI Washington, DC; July 21, 1916, correspondence from Sargent to CGI Washington, DC; and Ebey to CGI Washington, July 25, 1916.

2. Dorothy Weiss to CGI, September 9, 1916, Weiss DoJ file.

3. Dorothy Weiss to CGI, September 9, 1916, Weiss DoJ file.

4. Dorothy Weiss to CGI, September 9, 1916, Weiss DoJ file.

5. Dorothy Weiss to CGI, September 9, 1916, Weiss DoJ file.

6. Acting CG to Dorothy Weiss, September 22, 1916, Weiss DoJ file.

7. Both from Weiss DoJ file: Dorothy Weiss to DoL, October 13, 1919; and reply Acting CG to Weiss, October 16, 1919.

8. Mae M. Ngai, "The Strange Career of the Illegal Alien: Immigration Restriction and Deportation Policy in the United States, 1921–1965," *Law and History Review* 21, no. 1 (2003): 69–107, 101–103; and Jacobson, *Whiteness of a Different Color.*

9. Kang, *INS on the Line*; Buff, *Against the Deportation Terror*; Dunn, *Militarization of the U.S.-Mexico Border*; Hernández, "Carceral Shadows"; and Hernández, *MIGRA!*

10. Goodman, *Deportation Machine*, 79–80.

11. Quoted in Goodman, *Deportation Machine*, 88.

12. Goodman, *Deportation Machine*, 81–106; and Hernández, *MIGRA!*, esp. 149, 184, 185.

13. Hernández, *MIGRA!*, 77.

14. Charles F. Wilkinson and Eric R. Biggs, "The Evolution of Termination Policy," *American Indian Law Review* 5, no. 139 (1977): 139–184; Simon J. Ortiz, "Indigenous Activism, Our Resistance, Our Revitalization, Our Indigenous Native Studies: And Our Healing Within Our Indigenous Context (or From Alcatraz 1969 to Standing Rock 2017. Or Perhaps-truth be told—Liars, Killers, Thieves Invade Sacred Stone Camp," American Indian Studies Association Conference Keynote Address, *Wicazo Sa Review* 32, no. 2 (Fall 2017): 108; Roxanne Dunbar-Ortiz, *An Indigenous Peoples' History of the United States* (Boston: Beacon Press, 2014), 173–174, 190–191; and Donald Lee Fixico, *Termination and Relocation: Federal Indian Policy, 1945–1960* (Albuquerque: University of New Mexico Press, 1990). For an important study of American Indian survivance through movement, see Douglas K. Miller, *Indians on the Move: Native American Mobility and Urbanization in the Twentieth Century* (Chapel Hill: University of North Carolina Press, 2019).

15. Hernández, *MIGRA!*; and Patrick Timmons, "Trump's Wall at Nixon's Border," *NACLA Report on the Americas* 49 (March 2017): 15–24; and Rosas, *Barrio Libre.*

16. Mae M. Ngai, "Hart-Celler at Fifty: Lessons for Immigration Reform in Our Time," *Labor* 12, no. 3 (2015): 19–22; and Geraldo L. Cadava, "How Should Historians Remember the 1965 Immigration and Nationality Act?" *American Historian* (October 3, 2015), www.oah.org/tah/issues/2015/august/how-should-historians-remember-the-1965-immigration-and-nationality-act/, accessed November 5, 2020.

17. Carl J. Bon Tempo, *Americans at the Gate: The United States and Refugees during the Cold War* (Princeton, NJ: Princeton University Press, 2008).

18. Buff, *Against the Deportation Terror.*

19. For a sample from a substantial recent literature, see Jenna M. Loyd, Matt Mitchelson, and Andrew Burridge, eds., *Beyond Walls and Cages: Prisons, Borders, and Global Crisis* (Athens: University of Georgia Press, 2012); and Robert T. Chase, ed *Caging Borders and Carceral States: Incarcerations, Immigration Detentions, and Resistance* (Chapel Hill: University of North Carolina Press, 2019).

20. Robert T. Chase, "Carceral Networks: Rethinking Region and Connecting Carceral Borders," in *Caging Borders and Carceral States*, ed. Robert T. Chase, 1–54 (Chapel Hill: University of North Carolina Press, 2019), 6; Eli Hager and Alysia Santo, "Inside the Deadly World of Private Prisoner Transport," *The Marshall Project*, July 6, 2016; Hiemstra, *Detain and Deport*; Golash-Boza, *Deported*; William Walters, "Aviation as Deportation Infrastructure," 1–22; Peter Waldman, Lizette Chapman, and Jordan Robertson, "Palantir Knows Everything about You," *Bloomberg Businessweek*, April 19, 2018; and Gonzalez, "Logistical Borderlands." On the antistate state, see Ruth Wilson Gilmore, *Golden Gulag: Prisons, Surplus, Crisis, and Opposition in Globalizing California* (Berkeley: University of California Press, 2007), 245.

21. In the United States, see Mark Dow, *American Gulag: Inside U.S. Immigration Prisons* (Berkeley: University of California Press, 2004); and globally, see Michael Flynn and Cecilia Cannon, "The Privatization of Immigration Detention: Towards a Global View," Global Detention Project Working Paper, September 2009, www.globaldetentionproject.org/fileadmin/docs/GDP_PrivatizationPaper_Final5.pdf; and Blue, "Finding Margins on Borders."

22. Donald J. Trump, "Transcript of Donald Trump's Immigration Speech," *New York Times*, September 1, 2016.

23. Golash-Boza, *Deported*, 8–11.

24. Michael D. Shear and Ron Nixon, "New Trump Deportation Rules Allow Far More Expulsions," *New York Times*, February 21, 2017; and Brown, *Walled States, Waning Sovereignty*, esp. 107–133; Luke Mogelson, "The Storm," *The New Yorker* (January 25, 2021), 32—53.

25. Shear and Nixon, "New Trump Deportation Rules Allow Far More Deportations."

26. Michael D. Shear, Katie Benner, and Michael S. Schmidt, "'We Need to Take Away Children,' No Matter How Young, Justice Dept. Officials Said," *New York Times*, October 6, 2020; Caitlin Dickerson, "Parents of 545 Children Separated at the Border Cannot Be Found," *New York Times*, October 21, 2020;

and Heidi Beirich, "The Year in Hate: Rage against Change," *Intelligence Report*, February 20, 1919.

27. Consider leaders from Harriet Tubman to Ida B. Wells; from Emma Tenayuca and Ella Baker to Sylvia Rivera, Angela Y. Davis, Grace Lee Boggs and the Combahee River Collective; from Alicia Garza, Patrisse Cullors, and Opal Tometi to Freda Hudson and LaDonna Bravebull Allard. Keeanga-Yamahtta Taylor, *From #BlackLivesMatter to Black Liberation* (Chicago: Haymarket Books, 2016); Keeanga-Yamahtta Taylor, ed., *How We Get Free: Black Feminism and the Combahee River Collective* (New York: Haymarket Books, 2017); Barbara Ransby, *Making All Black Lives Matter: Reimagining Freedom in the Twenty-first Century* (Oakland: University of California Press, 2018); Movement for Black Lives, "Vision for Black Lives," https://m4bl.org/policy-platforms/, accessed March 22, 2021; and Nick Estes and Jaskiran Dhillon, eds., *Standing with Standing Rock: Voices form the #NoDAPL Movement* (Minneapolis: University of Minnesota Press, 2019).

28. A. Naomi Paik, *Bans, Walls, Raids, Sanctuary: Understanding U.S. Immigration for the Twenty-first Century* (Oakland: University of California Press, 2020).

29. 54809/General, recorded as "54809/General to 54809/General No 2," Folder 3, RG 85, Entry 9, NARA–Washington, DC.

30. Committee for the Protection of the Foreign Born and the International Labor Defense, 54809/General. On the longer history of the American Committee for the Protection of the Foreign Born, see Buff, *Against the Deportation Terror*.

31. The image recalled Frank Norris's critique of the Southern Pacific Railroad's vast monopolistic power in his 1901 novel *The Octopus: A Story of California* (Garden City, NY: Doubleday, 1901). It also compliments Theodore Irwin's depiction of the deportation train as a monster, writhing across the land, consuming and excreting migrants. The image of train as monster resonates with more recent depictions of another train, known as La Bestia, that carries migrants from Central America and through Mexico, who cling to its back atop swaying freight cars, on a perilous journey toward the US border. Riding La Bestia is a brutal journey, but clearly for its passengers it is less dangerous than remaining at home. Valeria Luiselli, *Tell Me How It Ends: An Essay in Forty Questions* (Minneapolis, MN: Coffee House Press, 2017).

32. Marisa Franco, "A Radical Expansion of Sanctuary: Steps in Defiance of Trump's Executive Order, *Truthout*, January 25, 2017; Paik, *Bans, Walls, Raids, Sanctuary*, 112–114; and Lenard Monkman, "'No Ban on Stolen Land,' Say Indigenous Activists in U.S.," *CBC News*, February 2, 2017.

BIBLIOGRAPHY

ARCHIVES

Calumet Regional Archives, Indiana University Northwest, Gary, Indiana.

Henry DeYoung Collection, Korean American Digital Archive, USC Digital Library, University of Southern California.

General Photograph Collection, University of Texas at San Antonio.

J. B. Sawyer Papers, Bancroft Library, University of California at Berkeley.

Joseph A. Labadie Collection, University of Michigan.

Leo L. Stanley Papers, Stanford University Library Special Collections.

Los Angeles Times and *Los Angeles Daily News* Photographic Archives, Charles E. Young Library Special Collections, University of California at Los Angeles.

National Archives and Records Administration, Saint Louis, MO (NARA–Saint Louis).

NARA, San Bruno, CA (NARA–San Bruno).

NARA, Seattle, WA (NARA–Seattle).

NARA, Washington, DC (NARA–Washington, DC).

NARA, College Park, MD (NARA–College Park).

Texas State Library and Archives Commission, Austin, Texas.

US Citizenship and Immigrations Services Archives and Library, Washington, DC.

Walter P. Reuther Library, Archives of Labor and Urban Affairs, Wayne State University Digital Collections.

SOURCES

Acuña, Rodolfo. *Occupied America: A History of Chicanos.* 4th ed. New York: Longman, 2000.

Adelman, Jeremy. "What Is Global History Now?" *Aeon*, March 2, 2017. https://aeon.co/essays/is-global-history-still-possible-or-has-it-had-its-moment.

Adelman, Jeremy, and Stephen Aron. "From Borderlands to Borders: Empires, Nation-States, and the Peoples in between in North American History." *American Historical Review* 104, no. 3 (June 1999): 814–841.

Alexiou, Margaret. "Sons, Wives, and Mothers: Reality and Fantasy in Some Modern Greek Ballads." *Journal of Modern Greek Studies* 1, no. 1 (1983): 73–111.

Amtrak. "Carbondale, Il." Great American Stations Project. www.great americanstations.com/stations/carbondale-il-cdl/, accessed August 27, 2019.

Anderson, Benedict. *Imagined Communities: Reflections on the Origin and Spread of Nationalism.* Revised and extended edition. New York: Verso, 1991.

Andreas, Peter. *Smuggler Nation: How Illicit Trade Made America.* New York: Oxford University Press, 2013.

Andrews, Thomas G. *Killing for Coal: America's Deadliest Labor War.* Cambridge, MA: Harvard University Press, 2008.

Andrijasevic, Rutvica. "From Exception to Excess: Detention and Deportations across the Mediterranean Space." In *The Deportation Regime: Sovereignty, Space, and the Freedom of Movement.* Edited by Nicholas De Genova and Nathalie Peutz, 147–165. Durham, NC: Duke University Press, 2010.

Annual Report of the Commissioner General of Immigration (AR-CGI), United States Department of Labor, FY ending June 1909–1932. Washington, DC: Government Printing Office.

Anzaldúa, Gloria. *Borderlands/La Frontera: The New Mestiza.* San Francisco: Aunt Lute, 2007.

Arellano, Monica V., Alan Leventhal, Rosemary Cambra, Shelia Guzman Schmidt, and Gloria Arellano Gomez. "An Ethnology of Santa Clara Valley and Adjacent Regions; Historic Ties of the Muwekma Ohlone Tribe of the San Francisco Bay Area and Tribal Stewardship over the Tupiun Táareštak [Place of the Fox Man] Site: CA-SCL-894." www.muwekma.org/images/Ethnohistory _Section_from_Muwekma_Ohlone_Burial_Site_CA-SCL-894_San_Jose _Chapter_9_April_15,_2014.pdf, accessed January 9, 2020.

Armstrong, Andrea. "The Impact of 300 Years of Jail Conditions." *The New Orleans Prosperity Index: Tricentennial Collection.* New Orleans: The Data Center, March 2018. www.datacenterresearch.org/reports_analysis/300-years -of-jail-conditions/.

Balachandran, G. "Indefinite Transits: Mobility and Confinement in the Age of Steam." *Journal of Global History* 11, no. 2 (July 2016): 187–208.

Balderrama, Francisco E., and Raymond Rodríguez. *Decade of Betrayal: Mexican Repatriation in the 1930s.* Albuquerque: University of New Mexico Press, 2006.

Ballantyne, Tony. *Between Colonialism and Diaspora: Sikh Cultural Formations in an Imperial World.* Durham, NC: Duke University Press, 2006.

Balogh, Brian. "Reorganizing the Organizational Synthesis: Federal-Professional Relations in Modern America." *Studies in American Political Development* 5 (1991): 119–172.

———. "The State of the State among Historians." *Social Science History* 27, no. 3 (2003): 445–463.

Bamford, Mary. *Angel Island: Ellis Island of the West*. Chicago: Women's American Baptist Home Mission Society, 1917.

Barde, Robert, and Gustavo J. Bobonis. "Detention at Angel Island: First Empirical Evidence." *Social Science History* 30, no. 1 (2006): 103–136.

Barde, Robert Eric. *Immigration at the Golden Gate: Passenger Ships, Exclusion, and Angel Island*. Westport, CT: Praeger, 2008.

Barry, J. Neilson. "The Indians in Washington, Their Distribution by Languages." *Oregon Historical Quarterly* 28, no. 2 (1927): 147–162.

Baynton, Douglas C. *Defectives in the Land: Disability and Immigration in the Age of Eugenics*. Chicago: University of Chicago Press, 2016.

Bayor, Ronald H. *Encountering Ellis Island: How European Immigrants Entered America*. Baltimore, MD: John Hopkins University Press, 2014.

Bederman, Gail. *Manliness and Civilization: A Cultural History of Gender and Race in the United States, 1880–1917*. Chicago: University of Chicago Press, 1995.

Beers, Clifford Whittingham. *A Mind That Found Itself: An Autobiography*. Project Gutenberg, 2008 [1908]. www.gutenberg.org/files/11962/11962-h/11962-h.htm, accessed March 19, 2021.

Beirich, Heidi. "The Year in Hate: Rage against Change." *Intelligence Report* (February 20, 1919).

"Believes He's Roosevelt." *Kansas City Journal*, December 15, 1908. www.vintagekansascity.com/100yearsago/labels/Col.%20J.%20C.%20Greenman.html, accessed October 24, 2019.

Benton-Cohen, Katherine. *Borderline Americans: Racial Division and Labor War in the Arizona Borderlands*. Cambridge, MA: Harvard University Press, 2009.

Blackhawk, Ned. *Violence over the Land: Indians and Empires in the Early American West*. Cambridge, MA: Harvard University Press, 2006.

Blue, Ethan. "Abject Correction and Penal Medical Photography in the Early Twentieth Century." In *The Punitive Turn: New Approaches to Race and Incarceration*. Edited by Deborah E. McDowell, Claudrena N. Harold, and Juan Battle, 108–130. Charlottesville: University of Virginia Press, 2013.

———. "Building the American Deportation Regime: Governmental Labor and the Infrastructure of Forced Removal in the Early Twentieth Century." *Journal of American Ethnic History* 38, no. 2 (2019): 36–64.

———. "Capillary Power, Rail Vessels, and the Carceral Viapolitics of Early Twentieth-Century American Deportation." In *Viapolitics: Borders, Migration, and the Power of Locomotion*. Edited by William Walters, Charles Heller, and Lorenzo Pezzani. Durham, NC: Duke University Press, 2021.

———. "Cognitive Maps and Spatial Narratives: US Deportation Hearings and the Imaginative Cartographies of Forced Removal." In *The Social Work of Narrative: Human Rights and the Literary Imaginary*. Edited by Gareth Griffiths and Philip Mead, 263–278. Stuttgart: Ibidem-Verlag, 2017.

———. *Doing Time in the Depression: Everyday Life in Texas and California Prisons*. New York: New York University Press, 2012.

———. "Finding Margins on Borders: Shipping Firms and Immigration Control across Settler Space." *Occasion: Interdisciplinary Studies in the Humanities* 5 (2013): 1–20.

———. "From Lynch Mobs to the Deportation State." *Law, Culture, and the Humanities* (October 12, 2017): 1–24. https://doi.org/10.1177/1743872117734168.

———. "The Strange Career of Leo Stanley: Remaking Manhood and Medicine at San Quentin State Penitentiary, 1913–1951." *Pacific Historical Review* 78, no. 2 (2009): 210–241.

———. "Strange Passages: Carceral Mobility and the Liminal in the Catastrophic History of American Deportation." *National Identities* 17, no. 2 (2015): 175–194.

Blumer, G. Alder. "Presidential Address." *American Journal of Insanity* 60 (1903): 1–18.

Boag, Peter. *Same-Sex Affairs: Constructing Homosexuality in the Pacific Northwest.* Berkeley: University of California Press, 2003.

Boalt, Fred L. "Hindu Kills High Priest on Altar in Vancouver!" *Seattle Star,* September 11, 1914.

Bodnar, John E. *The Transplanted: A History of Immigrants in Urban America.* Bloomington: Indiana University Press, 1987.

Boeckel, R. "The Iron and Steel Industry." *Editorial Research Reports 1930.* Volume 2. Washington, DC: CQ Press, 1930.

Bon Tempo, Carl J. *Americans at the Gate: The United States and Refugees during the Cold War.* Princeton, NJ: Princeton University Press, 2008.

Borutta, Manuel, and Sakis Gekas. "A Colonial Sea: The Mediterranean, 1798–1956." *European Review of History* 19, no. 1 (2012): 1–13.

Bosworth, Richard. *Italy and the Wider World, 1860–1960.* New York: Routledge, 1996.

Botkin, Jane Little. *Frank Little and the IWW: The Blood That Stained an American Family.* Norman: University of Oklahoma Press, 2017.

Brandt, Allan M. *No Magic Bullet: A Social History of Venereal Disease in the United States since 1880.* New York: Oxford University Press, 1987.

Braslow, Joel T. *Mental Ills and Bodily Cures: Psychiatric Treatment in the First Half of the Twentieth Century.* Berkeley: University of California Press, 1997.

Brechin, Gray A. *Imperial San Francisco: Urban Power, Earthly Ruin.* Berkeley: University of California Press, 1999.

Briggs, Asa. *Victorian Cities.* London: Odhams Press, 1963.

Briggs, Laura. *How All Politics Became Reproductive Politics: From Welfare Reform to Foreclosure to Trump.* Berkeley: University of California Press, 2017.

Briscoe, Edward Eugene. "Pershing's Chinese Refugees in Texas." *Southwestern Historical Quarterly* 62, no. 4 (1959): 467–488.

Broussard, Albert S. *Black San Francisco: The Struggle for Racial Equality in the West, 1900–1954.* Lawrence: University Press of Kansas, 1993.

Brown, Jonathan C. "Jersey Standard and the Politics of Latin American Oil Production, 1911–30." In *The Oil Business in Latin America: The Early Years.* Edited by John D. Wirth, 1–50. Lincoln: University of Nebraska Press, 1985.

———. *Oil and Revolution in Mexico.* Berkeley: University of California Press, 1993.

Brown, Mel. *The Chinese Heart of Texas: The San Antonio Community, 1875–1975.* www.home.earthlink.net/~melbjr/chineseheartoftexas/id12.html, accessed June 15, 2016 (no longer available) .

Brown, Wendy. *Walled States, Waning Sovereignty.* New York: Zone Books, 2014.

Buff, Rachel Ida. *Against the Deportation Terror: Organizing for Immigrant Rights in the Twentieth Century.* Philadelphia: Temple University Press, 2018.

Bureau of Commerce and Labor. *Fourteenth Census: 1920.* Washington, DC: Government Printing Office. www2.census.gov/prod2/decennial/documents /06229686v20-25ch4.pdf, accessed March 22 2021.

———. *Thirteenth Census: Statistics for Missouri, 1910.* Washington, DC: Government Printing Office, date illegible.

———. *Twelfth Census of the United States: Census Reports.* Volume 9. Department of the Interior. Washington, DC: Government Printing Office.

Byrd, Jodi A. *The Transit of Empire: Indigenous Critiques of Colonialism.* Minneapolis: University of Minnesota Press, 2011.

Cadava, Geraldo L. "How Should Historians Remember the 1965 Immigration and Nationality Act?" *American Historian* (October 3, 2015), www.oah.org/tah /issues/2015/august/how-should-historians-remember-the-1965-immigration -and-nationality-act/, accessed November 5, 2020.

Calavita, Kitty. *Inside the State: The Bracero Program, Immigration, and the I.N.S.* New York: Routledge, 1992.

———. "The Paradoxes of Race, Class, Identity, and 'Passing': Enforcing the Chinese Exclusion Acts,1882–1910." *Law & Social Inquiry* 25, no. 1 (Winter 2000): 1–40.

California State Board of Charities and Corrections. *Seventh Biennial Report July 1, 1914 to June 30, 1916.* Sacramento: California State Printing Office, 1916.

Campbell, J. K. *Honour, Family and Patronage: A Study Institutions and Moral Values in a Greek Mountain Village.* Oxford, UK: Oxford University Press, 1964.

"Camp Furlong and Columbus, New Mexico, 1916." http://demingnewmexico .genealogyvillage.com/CampFurlong/menu.htm, accessed March 27, 2018.

Canaday, Margot. *The Straight State: Sexuality and Citizenship in Twentieth-Century America.* Princeton, NJ: Princeton University Press, 2009.

Cannato, Vincent J. *American Passage: The History of Ellis Island.* 1st edition. New York: Harper, 2009.

Capozzola, Christopher. *Uncle Sam Wants You: World War I and the Making of the Modern American Citizen.* New York: Oxford University Press, 2008.

Carlsson, Chris. "The Railroad Comes to SF?" *FoundSF.* www.foundsf.org/index .php?title=THE_RAILROAD_COMES_TO_SF%3F, accessed November 20, 2019.

Carnevale, Nancy J. "'No Italian Spoken for the Duration of the War': Language,

Italian-American Identity, and Cultural Pluralism in the World War II Years." *Journal of American Ethnic History* 22, no. 3 (2003): 3–33.

Carrigan, William D., and Clive Webb. *Forgotten Dead: Mob Violence against Mexicans in the United States, 1848–1928*. Oxford, UK: Oxford University Press, 2013.

Catterson, Lauren D. "The Case of the Waylaid Immigrant Inspector: Authority, Respectability, and Sexual Misconduct, 1921." *Journal of American Ethnic History* 38, no. 1 (2018): 43–61.

Chang, Kornel S. "Enforcing Transnational White Solidarity: Asian Migration and the Formation of the U.S.-Canadian Boundary." *American Quarterly* 60, no. 3 (2008): 671–696.

———. *Pacific Connections: The Making of the U.S.-Canadian Borderlands.* Berkeley: University of California Press, 2012.

Chase, Robert T. "Carceral Networks: Rethinking Region and Connecting Carceral Borders." In *Caging Borders and Carceral States: Incarcerations, Immigration Detentions, and Resistance.* Edited by Robert T. Chase, 1–54. Chapel Hill: University of North Carolina Press, 2019.

Chase, Robert T., ed. *Caging Borders and Carceral States: Incarcerations, Immigration Detentions, and Resistance.* Chapel Hill: University of North Carolina Press, 2019.

Chase-Dunn, Christopher, and Peter Grimes. "World-Systems Analysis." *Annual Review of Sociology* 21 (1995): 387–417.

Chattopadhyay, Suchetana. "Closely Observed Ships." *South Asian Diaspora* 8, no. 2 (July 2, 2016): 203–222.

Chauncey, George. *Gay New York: Gender, Urban Culture, and the Making of the Gay Male World, 1890–1940*. New York: Basic Books, 1994.

"Chinese on Army's Hands: 300 with Pershing Fear Mexicans If Americans Withdraw." *New York Times*, July 18, 1916.

Choy, Bong Youn. *Koreans in America.* Chicago: Nelson-Hall, 1979.

Christensen, Jon. "The Silver Legacy: San Francisco and the Comstock Lode." In *Reclaiming San Francisco: History, Politics, Culture.* Edited by James Brook, Chris Carlsson, and Nancy J. Peters, 89–99. San Francisco: City Lights Books, 1998.

Clemens, Elisabeth S. "Lineages of the Rube Goldberg State: Building and Blurring Public Programs, 1900–1940." In *Rethinking Political Institutions: The Art of the State.* Edited by Ian Shapiro, Stephen Skowroneck, and Daniel Galvin, 380–443. New York: New York University Press, 2007.

Clogg, Richard. "The Greek Diaspora: The Historical Context." In *The Greek Diaspora in the Twentieth Century.* Edited by Richard Clogg, 1–23. Houndsmills, UK: Macmillan Press, 1999.

Cloud, John. "Extending Relief to the Nation: Director Raymond Stanton Patton (1929–1937)." In *Science on the Edge: The Story of the Coast and Geodetic Survey from 1867–1970.* www.lib.noaa.gov/noaainfo/heritage/coastandgeodeticsurvey /Pattonchapter.pdf, accessed June 1, 2015.

Clough, Patricia Ticineto, and Craig Willse. Introduction to *Beyond Biopolitics: Essays on the Governance of Life and Death*. Edited by Patricia Ticineto Clough and Craig Willse, 1–16. Durham, NC: Duke University Press, 2011.

Clough, Patricia Ticineto, and Craig Willse, eds. *Beyond Biopolitics: Essays on the Governance of Life and Death*. Durham, NC: Duke University Press, 2011. doi:10.2307/j.ctv11smsp0, accessed November 2, 2020.

Cohen, Michael. "'The Ku Klux Government': Vigilantism, Lynching, and the Repression of the IWW." *Journal for the Study of Radicalism* 1, no. 1 (2007): 31–56.

Cole, David. *Enemy Aliens: Double Standards and Constitutional Freedoms in the War on Terrorism*. New York: New Press, 2003.

Coolidge, Mary Roberts. *Chinese Immigration*. New York: Henry Holt, 1909.

Corbitt, Duvon C. "Chinese Immigrants in Cuba." *Far Eastern Survey* 13, no. 14 (1942): 130–132.

Corsi, Edward. *In the Shadow of Liberty: The Chronicle of Ellis Island*. New York: MacMillan, 1935.

Costantini, Massimo. "Economia, società e territorio nel lungo periodo." In *L'Abruzzo: Storia d'Italia Le regioni dall'Unità a oggi*. Edited by Massimo Costantini and Costantino Felice, 99–101. Turin: Giulio Einaudi, 2000.

Cotter, Arundel. *The Authentic History of the U.S. Steel Corporation*. New York: Moody Magazine and Book Co., 1916.

Cowen, Deborah. *The Deadly Life of Logistics: Mapping Violence in Global Trade*. Minneapolis: University of Minnesota Press, 2014.

Cronon, William. *Nature's Metropolis: Chicago and the Great West*. New York: W. W. Norton, 1992.

Cumings, Bruce. *Korea's Place in the Sun: A Modern History*. Updated edition. New York: W. W. Norton, 2005.

"Cunning Shown by Gallagher." *Kansas City Journal*, June 16, 1908. www.vintagekansascity.com/100yearsago/labels/Col.%20J.%20C.%20Greenman.html, accessed October 24, 2019.

Daniels, Roger. *The Politics of Prejudice: The Anti-Japanese Movement in California and the Struggle for Japanese Exclusion*. Berkeley: University of California Press, 1977.

Davis, Ron. "In Minnesota, A Museum of Madness." *Washington Post*, April 4, 1999.

Day, Iyko. *Alien Capital: Asian Racialization and the Logic of Settler Colonial Capital*. Durham, NC: Duke University Press, 2016

Dearinger, Ryan. *The Filth of Progress: Immigrants, Americans, and the Building of Canals and Railroads in the West*. Oakland: University of California Press, 2016.

De Certeau, Michel. *The Practice of Everyday Life*. Translated by Steven Rendall. Berkeley: University of California Press, 1984.

Delgado, Grace Peña. *Making the Chinese Mexican: Global Migration, Localism, and Exclusion in the U.S.–Mexico Borderlands.* Stanford, CA: Stanford University Press, 2012.

Department of Homeland Security (DHS). "Table 39: Aliens Removed or Returned, FY1892-2018." In *Yearbook of Immigration Statistics 2018.* www.dhs .gov/immigration-statistics/yearbook/2018/table39.

———. *2015 Yearbook of Immigration Statistics.* www.dhs.gov/immigration -statistics/yearbook/2015/table39, accessed April 25, 2017.

Department of Justice/Immigration and Naturalization Service (INS). *Monthly Review* (October 1946).

DePastino, Todd. *Citizen Hobo: How a Century of Homelessness Shaped America.* Chicago: University of Chicago Press, 2003.

Díaz, George T. *Border Contraband: A History of Smuggling across the Rio Grande.* Austin: University of Texas Press, 2015.

Dickerson Caitlin. "Parents of 545 Children Separated at the Border Cannot Be Found." *New York Times,* October 21, 2020.

Dolmage, Jay. "Disabled upon Arrival: The Rhetorical Construction of Disability and Race at Ellis Island." *Cultural Critique* 77 (Winter 2011): 24–69.

Dow, Mark. *American Gulag: Inside U.S. Immigration Prisons.* Berkeley: University of California Press, 2004.

Dowbiggin, Ian Robert. *Keeping America Sane: Psychiatry and Eugenics in the United States and Canada, 1880–1940.* Ithaca, NY: Cornell University Press, 2003.

Driscoll, Barbara A. *The Tracks North: The Railroad Bracero Program of World War II.* Austin: CMAS Books, University of Texas Press, 1999.

Du Bois, W.E.B. "The African Roots of War." *Atlantic* (1915): 707–714.

———. "The Souls of White Folk." *Darkwater: Voices from Within the Veil.* 1920; reprint, New York: Cosimo Classics, 2007.

Du Boulay, Juliet. *Portrait of a Greek Mountain Village.* Oxford, UK: Oxford University Press, 1974.

Dubofsky, Melvyn. *The State & Labor in Modern America.* Chapel Hill: University of North Carolina Press, 1994.

———. *We Shall Be All: A History of the Industrial Workers of the World.* Chicago: Quadrangle Books, 1969.

Dunbar-Ortiz, Roxanne. *An Indigenous Peoples' History of the United States.* Boston: Beacon Press, 2014.

Dunn, Timothy J. *The Militarization of the U.S.-Mexico Border, 1978–1992: Low-Intensity Conflict Doctrine Comes Home.* Austin: CMAS Books, University of Texas Press, 1996.

el-Ojeili, Chamsy. "Reflections on Wallerstein: The Modern World System, Four Decades On." *Critical Sociology* 41, no. 5 (2015): 679–700.

Emmons, David M. *The Butte Irish: Class and Ethnicity in an American Mining Town: 1875–1925.* Urbana: University of Illinois Press, 1990.

Estes, Nick, and Jaskiran Dhillon, eds. *Standing with Standing Rock: Voices from the #NoDAPL Movement.* Minneapolis: University of Minnesota Press, 2019.

Ewing, Martha K. "Place Names in the Northwest Counties of Missouri." MA thesis, University of Missouri-Columbia, 1929. https://collections.shsmo.org /manuscripts/columbia/C2366, accessed October 23, 2019.

Fairchild, Henry Pratt. *Greek Immigration to the United States.* New Haven, CT: Yale University Press, 1911.

Feldman, Allen. *Formations of Violence: The Narrative of the Body and Political Terror in Northern Ireland.* Chicago: University of Chicago Press, 1991.

Feys, Torsten. "Riding the Rails of Removal: The Impact of Railways on Border Controls and Expulsion Practices." *Journal of Transport History* 40, no. 2 (2019): 189–210.

Finnane, Mark. "Keeping Them Out and Keeping Them In: Enemies, Aliens and Criminals in Australian Security History." Lecture, University of Western Australia, November 6, 2014.

Fixico, Donald Lee. *Termination and Relocation: Federal Indian Policy, 1945–1960.* Albuquerque: University of New Mexico Press, 1986.

Flores, Richard R. *Remembering the Alamo: Memory, Modernity, and the Master Symbol.* Austin: University of Texas Press, 2002.

Flynn, Michael, and Cecilia Cannon. "The Privatization of Immigration Detention: Towards a Global View." Global Detention Project Working Paper, September 2009. www.globaldetentionproject.org/fileadmin/docs/GDP _PrivatizationPaper_Final5.pdf.

Foley, Neil. *The White Scourge: Mexicans, Blacks, and Poor Whites in Texas Cotton Culture.* Berkeley: University of California Press, 1997.

Ford, John, dir. *The Iron Horse.* William Fox, 1924.

Foucault, Michel. "Of Other Spaces: Utopias and Heterotopias." Translated by Jay Miskowiec. In *Architecture/Mouvement/Continuité* (October, 1984); also in *Diacritics* 16, no. (1986): 22—27.

———. *Society Must Be Defended: Lectures at the Collège De France, 1975–76.* Translated by David Macey. New York: Picador, 2003.

———. *Security, Territory, Population: Lectures at the Collège de France, 1977–1978.* New York: Picador, 2009.

Fox, Cybelle. *Three Worlds of Relief: Race, Immigration, and the American Welfare State from the Progressive Era to the New Deal.* Princeton, NJ: Princeton University Press, 2012.

Franco, Marisa. "A Radical Expansion of Sanctuary: Steps in Defiance of Trump's Executive Order." *Truthout* (January 25, 2017).

Freedman, Estelle B. *Redefining Rape: Sexual Violence in the Era of Suffrage and Segregation.* Cambridge, MA: Harvard University Press, 2013.

———. *Their Sisters' Keepers: Women's Prison Reform in America: 1830–1930.* Ann Arbor: University of Michigan Press, 1981.

Gabaccia, Donna R., and Franca Iacovetta. Introduction to *Women, Gender, and Transnational Lives: Italian Workers of the World.* Edited by Donna Gabaccia and Franca Iacovetta, 3–42. Toronto: University of Toronto Press, 2002.

Galambos, Louis. "The Emerging Organizational Synthesis in Modern American History." *Business History Review* 44, no. 3 (1970): 279–290.

Garland, David. *Punishment and Welfare: A History of Penal Strategies*. Aldershot, UK: Ashgate, 1985.

García, Juan Ramon. *Mexicans in the Midwest, 1900–1932*. Tucson: University of Arizona Press, 1996.

García, Mario T. *Desert Immigrants: The Mexicans of El Paso, 1880–1920*. New Haven, CT: Yale University Press, 1981.

Garcilazo, Jeffrey Marcos. *Traqueros: Mexican Railroad Workers in the United States, 1870 to 1930*. Denton: University of North Texas Press, 2012.

Geiger, Andrea. "Caught in the Gap: The Transit Privilege and North America's Ambiguous Borders." In *Bridging National Borders in North America: Transnational and Comparative Histories*. Edited by Benjamin H. Johnson and Andrew R. Graybill, 199–222. Durham, NC: Duke University Press, 2010.

———. *Subverting Exclusion: Transpacific Encounters with Race, Caste, and Borders, 1885–1928*. New Haven, CT: Yale University Press, 2011.

Geise, William R., and James W. Markham. "San Antonio State Hospital." *Handbook of Texas Online*. www.tshaonline.org/handbook/entries/san-antonio-state-hospital, accessed July 6, 2016.

Gekas, Sakis. "Colonial Migrants and the Making of a British Mediterranean." *European Review of History* 19, no. 1 (2012): 75–92.

Genealogy Trails History Group. "Jackson County Il" and "Carbondale Census" of 1910. http://genealogytrails.com/ill/jackson/index_census.htm, accessed October 10, 2019.

Gigliotti, Simone. *The Train Journey: Transit, Captivity, and Witnessing in the Holocaust*. New York: Berghahn Books, 2009.

Gildemeister, Glen A. *Prison Labor and Convict Competition with Free Workers in Industrializing America, 1840–1890*. New York: Garland Publishing, 1987.

Gilmore, Ruth Wilson. *Golden Gulag: Prisons, Surplus, Crisis, and Opposition in Globalizing California*. Berkeley: University of California Press, 2007.

Glenn, Evelyn Nakano. *Unequal Freedom: How Race and Gender Shaped American Citizenship and Labor*. Cambridge, MA: Harvard University Press, 2002.

Glore Psychiatric Museum. www.stjosephmuseum.org/glore-psychiatric-museum, accessed October 23, 2019.

Golash-Boza, Tanya Maria. *Deported: Immigrant Policing, Disposable Labor, and Global Capitalism*. New York: New York University Press, 2015.

Goldberg, David Theo. "'Polluting the Body Politic': Racist Discourse and Urban Location." In *Racism, the City, and the State*. Edited by Malcolm Cross and David Keith, 45–60. New York: Routledge, 1993.

Gonzalez, Daniel. "Logistical Borderlands: Latinx Migrant Labor in the Information Age." *Society+Space* (April 12, 2019), www.societyandspace.org/articles/logistical-borderlands-latinx-migrant-labor-in-the-information-age, accessed May 15, 2019.

Goodman, Adam. "Bananas North, Deportees South: Punishment, Profits, and the Human Costs of the Business of Deportation." *Journal of American History* (March 2020): 949–974.

———. *The Deportation Machine: America's Long History of Expelling Immigrants.* Princeton, NJ: Princeton University Press, 2020.

Gordon, Linda. *The Great Arizona Orphan Abduction.* Cambridge, MA: Harvard University Press, 1999.

———. *Pitied but Not Entitled: Single Mothers and the History of Welfare,1890–1935.* Cambridge, MA: Harvard University Press, 1994.

Gramsci, Antonio. *Selections from the Prison Notebooks.* Edited and translated by Quintin Hoare and Geoffrey Nowell Smith. New York: International Publishers, 1971.

Grant, Edwin E. "Scum from the Melting-Pot." *American Journal of Sociology* 30, no. 6 (May 1925): 641–651.

Graybill, Andrew R. *Policing the Great Plains: Rangers, Mounties, and the North American Frontier, 1875–1910.* Lincoln: University of Nebraska Press, 2007.

Grecco, Gabriela De Lima, and Sven Schuster. "Decolonizing Global History? A Latin American Perspective." *Journal of World History* 31, no. 2 (2020): 425–446.

Griskavich, Carol D. "From Mill Gates to Magic City: U.S. Steel and Welfare Capitalism in Gary, Indiana, 1906–1930." MS thesis, Michigan Technical University, 2014.

Gross, Kali N. *Colored Amazons: Crime, Violence, and Black Women in the City of Brotherly Love, 1880–1910.* Durham, NC: Duke University Press, 2006.

Guerin-Gonzales, Camille. *Mexican Workers and American Dreams: Immigration, Repatriation, and California Farm Labor, 1900–1939.* New Brunswick, NJ: Rutgers University Press, 1994.

Gulliver, Katrina. "Finding the Pacific World." *Journal of World History* 22, no. 1 (2011): 83–100.

Gutfeld, Arnon. "The Murder of Frank Little: Radical Labor Agitation in Butte, Montana, 1917." *Labor History* 10, no. 2 (March 1969): 177–192.

———. "The Speculator Mine Disaster in 1917: Labor Resurgence at Butte, Montana." *Arizona and the West* 11, no. 1 (1969): 27–38.

Gutiérrez, Laura D. "'Trains of Misery': Repatriate Voices and Responses in Northern Mexico during the Great Depression." *Journal of American Ethnic History* 39, no. 4 (2020): 13–26.

Hager, Eli, and Alysia Santo. "Inside the Deadly World of Private Prisoner Transport." *The Marshall Project*, July 6, 2016.

Haggerty, Kevin D., and Richard V. Ericson. "The Surveillant Assemblage." *British Journal of Sociology* 52, no. 4 (2000): 605–622.

Hahamovitch, Cindy. *No Man's Land: Jamaican Guestworkers in America and the Global History of Deportable Labor.* Princeton, NJ: Princeton University Press, 2011.

Hailong, Zhai, and Gao Yan. "Early Psychiatric Services in Hong Kong from 1841 to 1947." *Mental Health in Family Medicine* 13 (2017): 435–438.

Hale, Grace Elizabeth. *Making Whiteness: The Culture of Segregation in the South,1890–1940*. New York: Vintage Books, 1998.

Haley, Sarah. *No Mercy Here: Gender, Punishment, and the Making of Jim Crow Modernity*. Chapel Hill: University of North Carolina Press, 2016.

Hall, Lisa Kahaleole. "Navigating Our Own 'Sea of Islands': Remapping a Theoretical Space for Hawaiian Women and Indigenous Feminism." *Wicazo Sa Review* 24, no. 2 (2009): 15–38.

Halpern, Rick. *Down on the Killing Floor: Black and White Workers in Chicago's Packinghouses, 1904–54*. Urbana: University of Illinois Press, 1997.

Hart, John Mason. *Anarchism and the Mexican Working Class, 1860–1931*. Austin: University of Texas Press, 1987.

Hastings College. "Facts about Hastings College," www.hastings.edu/about-hastings-college/facts-about-hastings, accessed September 18, 2018.

Hau'ofa, Epeli. "Our Sea of Islands." *Contemporary Pacific* 6, no. 1 (1994): 148–161.

Henderson, W. O. "German Economic Penetration in the Middle East, 1870–1914." *Economic History Review* 18, no. 1/2 (1948): 54–64.

Hernández, David M. "Carceral Shadows: Entangled Lineages and Technologies of Migrant Detention." In *Caging Borders and Carceral States: Incarcerations, Immigration Detentions, and Resistance*. Edited by Robert T. Chase, 57–92. Chapel Hill: University of North Carolina Press, 2019.

———. "Pursuant to Deportation: Latinos and Immigrant Detention." *Latino Studies*, no. 6 (2008): 35–63.

———. "Surrogates and Subcontractors: Flexibility and Obscurity in Immigrant Detention." In *Critical Ethnic Studies: A Reader*. Edited by the Critical Ethnic Studies Collective. Durham, NC: Duke University Press, 2016.

Hernández, Kelly Lytle. *City of Inmates: Conquest, Rebellion, and the Rise of Human Caging in Los Angeles, 1771–1965*. Chapel Hill: University of North Carolina Press, 2017.

———. "Hobos in Heaven: Race, Incarceration, and the Rise of Los Angeles, 1880–1910." *Pacific Historical Review* 83, no. 3 (2014): 410–447.

———. *MIGRA! A History of the U.S. Border Patrol*. Berkeley: University of California Press, 2010.

Hernandez, Tim Z. *All They Will Call You: The Telling of the Plane Wreck at Los Gatos Canyon*. Tucson: University of Arizona Press, 2017.

Hester, Torrie. "Deportability and the Carceral State." *Journal of American History* 102, no. 1 (2015): 141–151.

———. "Deportation: The Origins of a National and International Power." PhD dissertation, University of Oregon, 2008.

———. *Deportation: The Origins of U.S. Policy*. Philadelphia: University of Pennsylvania Press, 2017.

Hicks, Cheryl D. *Talk with You Like a Woman: African American Women, Justice, and Reform in New York, 1890–1935*. Chapel Hill: University of North Carolina Press, 2010.

Hiemstra, Nancy. "Deportation and Detention: Interdisciplinary Perspective,

Multi-Scalar Approaches, and New Methodological Tools." *Migration Studies* 4, no. 3 (November 2016): 433–446.

———. *Detain and Deport: The Chaotic U.S. Immigration Enforcement Regime.* Athens: University of Georgia Press, 2019.

Higginbotham, Evelyn Brooks. *Righteous Discontent: The Women's Movement in the Black Baptist Church, 1880–1920.* Cambridge, MA: Harvard University Press, 1993.

Higham, John. *Strangers in the Land: Patterns of American Nativism, 1860–1925.* New Brunswick, NJ: Rutgers University Press, 1955.

Hilberg, Raul. *The Destruction of the European Jews.* Chicago: Quadrangle Books, 1961.

Hill, Rebecca Nell. *Men, Mobs, and Law: Anti-Lynching and Labor Defense in U.S. Radical History.* Durham, NC: Duke University Press, 2008.

Hine, Robert V., and John Mack Faragher. *The American West: A New Interpretive History.* New Haven, CT: Yale University Press, 2000.

Hirota, Hidetaka. *Expelling the Poor: Atlantic Seaboard States and the Nineteenth-century Origins of American Immigration Policy.* New York: Oxford University Press, 2017.

Historical Society of Pottawattamie County. "Historic Pottawattamie County Squirrel Cage Jail." https://web.archive.org/web/20110308112949/http://thehistoricalsociety.org/jail.htm, accessed August 22, 2018.

"A History of Carbondale's Railroads." Station Carbondale website (2018). http://stationcarbondale.org/history/, accessed August 27, 2019.

Hoffman, Abraham. "Stimulus to Repatriation: The 1931 Federal Deportation Drive and the Los Angeles Mexican Community." *Pacific Historical Review* 42, no. 2 (1973): 205–219.

Holmes, M. Patricia. "Buchanan County Courthouse Nomination to National Registry of Historic Places." June 20, 1972. https://dnr.mo.gov/shpo/nps-nr/72001563.pdf, accessed October 25, 2019.

Hopkins, Eric. "Industrial Change and Life at Work in Birmingham, 1850–1914." *Midland History* 27, no. 1 (2002): 130–145.

Howard, Caran Amber Crawford. "'I've always been for education': Mexicana/o Participation in Formal, Non-Formal, and Informal Education in the Midwest, 1910–1955." PhD dissertation, University of Iowa, 2015.

Howe, Christopher. *The Origins of Japanese Trade Supremacy: Development and Technology in Asia from 1540 to the Pacific War.* Chicago: University of Chicago Press, 1996.

Hsu, Madeline Y. *Dreaming of Gold, Dreaming of Home: Transnationalism and Migration between the United States and South China, 1882–1943.* Stanford, CA: Stanford University Press, 2000.

———. *The Good Immigrants: How the Yellow Peril Became the Model Minority.* Princeton, NJ: Princeton University Press, 2015.

Hu-DeHart, Evelyn. "Chinese Coolie Labor in Cuba in the Nineteenth Century: Free Labor of Neoslavery." *Contributions in Black Studies* 12, no. 1 (1994): 38–54.

Hunt, Michael H. "The American Remission of the Boxer Indemnity: A Reappraisal." *Journal of Asian Studies* 31, no. 3 (1972): 539–559.

Hurtado, Albert L. *Intimate Frontiers: Sex, Gender, and Culture in Old California*. Albuquerque: University of New Mexico Press, 1999.

Hutchinson, Edward P. *Legislative History of American Immigration Policy, 1798–1965*. Philadelphia: University of Pennsylvania Press, 1981.

Hwang, Kyung Moon. *A History of Korea: An Episodic Narrative*. New York: Palgrave Macmillan, 2010.

Hyslop, Jonathan. "Steamship Empire: Asian, African and British Sailors in the Merchant Marine, c. 1880–1945." *Journal of Asian and African Studies* 44, no. 1 (2009): 49–67.

Ignatiev, Noel. *How the Irish Became White*. New York: Routledge, 1995.

Innis-Jímenez, Michael. "Mexican Workers and Life in South Chicago." In *The Latina/o Midwest Reader*. Edited by Omar Valerio-Jímenez, Santiago Vaquera-Vásquez, and Claire F. Fox, 71–84. Urbana: University of Illinois Press, 2017.

Interstate Commerce Commission. *Vol 55: Decisions of the Interstate Commerce Commission of the United States, June–December 1919*. Washington, DC: Government Printing Office, 1920.

Irwin, Theodore. *Strange Passage*. New York: Harrison Smith and Robert Hass, 1935.

Isin, Engin F., and Kim Rygiel. "Abject Spaces: Frontiers, Zones, Camps." In *Logics of Biopower and the War on Terror*. Edited by E. Dauphinee and C. Masters, 181–203. Houndsmill, UK: Palgrave, 2007.

Itoh, Keiko. *The Japanese Community in Pre-war Britain: From Integration to Disintegration*. Richmond, Surrey, UK: Curzon, 2001.

"Jack Gallagher in the Workhouse." *Kansas City Journal*, July 17, 1908. www.vintagekansascity.com/100yearsago/labels/Col.%20J.%20C.%20Greenman.html, accessed October 24, 2019.

Jacobson, Matthew Frye. *Barbarian Virtues: The United States Encounters Foreign Peoples at Home and Abroad*. New York: Hill and Wang, 2000.

———. *Roots Too: White Ethnic Revival in Post–Civil Rights America* (Cambridge, MA: Harvard University Press, 2008).

———. *Whiteness of a Different Color: European Immigrants and the Alchemy of Race*. Cambridge, MA: Harvard University Press, 1998.

Jameson, Elizabeth. *All That Glitters: Class, Conflict, and Community in Cripple Creek*. Urbana: University of Illinois Press, 1998.

Jessop, Bob. "From Micro-Powers to Governmentality: Foucault's Work on Statehood, State Formation, Statecraft, and State Power." *Political Geography* 26 (2007): 34–40.

"John J. Pershing Biography." www.biography.com/people/john-j-pershing, accessed March 23, 2018.

Johnson, Chalmers. "America's Empire of Bases." TomDispatch.com, January 2004.

Johnson, Walter, with Adam McGee. "The Souls of White Folk." *Boston Review*, November 18, 2016.

Johnston, Hugh. *Voyage of the Komagata Maru: The Sikh Challenge to Canada's Colour Bar*. Delhi: Oxford University Press, 1979.

Johnston, Robert D. *The Radical Middle Class: Populist Democracy and the Question of Capitalism in Progressive Era Portland, Oregon*. Princeton, NJ: Princeton University Press, 2003.

Judt, Tony. "The Glory of the Rails." *The New York Review of Books*, December 23, 2010. www.nybooks.com/articles/2010/12/23/glory-rails/, accessed February 10, 2011.

Jung, Moon-Ho. *Coolies and Cane: Race, Labor, and Sugar in the Age of Emancipation*. Baltimore, MD: Johns Hopkins University Press, 2006.

Kang, S. Deborah. *The INS on the Line: Making Immigration Law on the US-Mexico Border, 1917–1954*. New York: Oxford University Press, 2017.

Kanstroom, Daniel. *Deportation Nation: Outsiders in American History*. Cambridge, MA: Harvard University Press, 2007.

Karuka, Manu. *Empire's Tracks: Indigenous Nations, Chinese Workers, and the Transcontinental Railroad*. Oakland: University of California Press, 2019.

Katz, Frederich. "Pancho Villa and the Attack on Columbus, New Mexico." *American Historical Review* 83, no. 1 (1978): 101–130.

Katz, Michael B. *In the Shadow of the Poorhouse: A Social History of Welfare in America*. New York: BasicBooks, 1986.

Kaur, Arunajeet. "*Komagata Maru* Sails from the Far East: Cartography of the Sikh Diaspora within the British Empire." *South Asian Diaspora* 8, no. 2 (July 2, 2016): 155–165.

Kelley, Robin D. G. Foreword to Cedric J. Robinson, *Black Marxism: The Making of the Black Radical Tradition*, xi–xxvi. Chapel Hill: University of North Carolina Press, 2000.

Kenny, Kevin. *The American Irish*. New York: Longman, 2000.

Kessler-Harris, Alice. *In Pursuit of Equity: Women, Men, and the Quest for Economic Citizenship in 20th-century America*. New York: Oxford University Press, 2001.

Kim, Richard S. "Inaugurating the American Century: The 1919 Philadelphia Korean Congress, Korean Diasporic Nationalism, and American Protestant Missionaries." *Journal of American Ethnic History* 26, no. 1 (Fall 2006): 50–76.

———. *The Quest for Statehood: Korean Immigrant Nationalism and U.S. Sovereignty, 1905–1945*. New York: Oxford University Press, 2011.

King, Ryan D., Michael Massoglia, and Christopher Uggen. "Employment and Exile: U.S. Criminal Deportations, 1908–2005." *American Journal of Sociology* 117, no. 6 (2012): 1786–1825.

Klein, Maury. *Union Pacific: Vols. I and II, 1862–1893, and 1894–1969*. Minneapolis: University of Minnesota Press, 2006.

Knox, Howard. "Tests for Mental Defects: How the Public Health Service Prevents Contamination of Our Racial Stock by Turning Back Feeble-Minded Immigrants—General Characteristics Noted and Progressive Series of Tests Applied to Determine Exact Mentality." *Journal of Heredity* 5, no. 3 (1914): 122–130.

Koren, W.A.K. *Benevolent Institutions, 1904.* US Census Bureau. Washington, DC: Government Printing Office, 1905. https://books.google.com.au/books?id=NqlZPl1qj4EC&pg=PA102&lpg=PA102&dq=Rochester+industrial+school+exchange+street&source=bl&ots=S_HeF6zCGC&sig=BB8D114K4wJWoCf6xU1rQKR5WoQ&hl=en&sa=X&ved=0ahUKEwj8_ffPmfPRAhVKv48KHdcBAQwQ6AEIJTAC#v=onepage&q=Rochester%20industrial%20school%20exchange%20street&f=false, accessed February 3, 2017.

Kramer, Paul A. "Is the World Our Campus? International Students and U.S. Global Power in the Long Twentieth Century." *Diplomatic History* 33, no. 5 (2009): 775–806.

Kreel, George, and John Slavens. "Men Who Are Making Kansas City" (1902). http://vintagekansascity.com/menwhomadekc/greenman_james_c.html, accessed October 24, 2019.

Kunzel, Regina. *Criminal Intimacy: Prison and the Uneven History of Modern American Sexuality.* Chicago: University of Chicago Press, 2008.

———. "Situating Sex: Prison Sexual Culture in the Mid-Twentieth-Century United States." *GLQ* 8, no. 3 (2002): 253–270.

Lai, Him Mark, Genny Lim, and Judy Yung, eds. *Island: Poetry and History of Chinese Immigrants on Angel Island, 1910–1940.* Seattle: University of Washington Press, 1980.

Lake, Marilyn, and Henry Reynolds. *Drawing the Global Colour Line: White Men's Countries and the International Challenge of Racial Equality.* Cambridge, UK: Cambridge University Press, 2012.

Landon, Herman R. "Deportation Procedure and Practice." 1943 Lecture Series, US Customs and Immigration Services Archives, Washington, DC.

Lane, James B. *City of the Century: A History of Gary, Indiana.* Bloomington: Indiana University Press, 1978.

Larkin, Brian. "The Politics and Poetics of Infrastructure." *Annual Review of Anthropology* 42 (2013): 327–343.

Latour, Bruno. *Aramis: Or, The Love of Technology.* Translated by Catherine Porter. Cambridge, MA: Harvard University Press, 1994.

Laughlin, Harry H. *The Eugenical Aspects of Deportation, Hearings before the Committee on Immigration and Naturalization.* Washington, DC: Government Printing Office, 1928.

Lee, Erika. *At America's Gates: Chinese Immigration during the Exclusion Era, 1882–1943.* Chapel Hill: University of North Carolina Press, 2003.

Lee, Erika, and Judy Yung. *Angel Island: Immigrant Gateway to America.* New York: Oxford University Press, 2010.

LeFlouria, Talitha L. *Chained in Silence: Black Women and Convict Labor in the New South.* Chapel Hill: University of North Carolina Press, 2015.

Leonard, Stephen J. "Denver, Colorado." In *The New Encyclopedia of the American*

West. Edited by Howard J. Lamar, 296–299. New Haven, CT: Yale University Press, 1998.

Leroy, Justin. "Black History in Occupied Territory: On the Entanglements of Slavery and Settler Colonialism." *Theory & Event* 19, no. 4 (2016).

Leuchtenberg, William E. *Franklin D. Roosevelt and the New Deal*. New York: Harper and Row, 1963.

Levario, Miguel Antonio. *Militarizing the Border: When Mexicans Became the Enemy*. College Station: Texas A&M University Press, 2012.

Leventhal, Alan, Les Fields, Hank Alvarez, and Rosemary Cambra. "The Ohlone Back from Extinction." In *The Ohlone Past and Present: Native Americans of the San Francisco Bay Region*. Edited by Lowell John Bean, 301–336. Ballena Press Anthropological Papers 42. 1994.

Levi, Carlo. *Christ Stopped at Eboli*. Translated by Frances Frenaye. New York: Farrar, Straus and Giroux, 1947.

Li, Darryl. "Migrant Workers and the US Military in the Middle East." *Middle East Research and Information Project* 275, no. 45 (2015). www.merip.org/mer/mer275/migrant-workers-us-military-middle-east#_2_.

Lim, Julian. "Immigration, Asylum, and Citizenship: A More Holistic Approach." *California Law Review* 101 (2013): 1013–1077.

———. *Porous Borders: Multiracial Migrations and the Law in the U.S.-Mexico Borderlands*. Chapel Hill: University of North Carolina Press, 2017.

Limón, José E. "*Al Norte* toward Home: Texas, the Midwest, and Mexican American Critical Regionalism." In *The Latina/o Midwest Reader*. Edited by Omar Valerio-Jímenez, Santiago Vaquera-Vásquez, and Claire F. Fox, 40–56. Urbana: University of Illinois Press, 2017.

Ling, Huiping. "A History of Chinese Female Students in the United States, 1880s–1990s." *Journal of American Ethnic History* 16, no. 3 (1997): 82–88.

Lomnitz, Claudio. *Death and the Idea of Mexico*. New York: Zone, 2005.

López, Ian F. Haney. *White by Law: The Legal Construction of Race*. New York: New York University Press, 1998.

Loyd, Jenna M., Matt Mitchelson, and Andrew Burridge, eds. *Beyond Walls and Cages: Prisons, Borders, and Global Crisis*. Athens: University of Georgia Press, 2012.

Lu, Sidney Xu. "Japan's Asian-Pacific Migrations and the Making of the Japanese Empire, 1868–1945." PhD dissertation, University of Pennsylvania, 2013.

Luibhéid, Eithne. *Entry Denied: Controlling Sexuality at the Border*. Minneapolis: University of Minnesota Press, 2002.

Luiselli, Valeria. *Tell Me How It Ends: An Essay in Forty Questions*. Minneapolis, MN: Coffee House Press, 2017.

Lyu, Kingsley K. "Korean Nationalist Activities in Hawaii and the Continental United States, 1900–1945, Part I: 1900–1919." *Amerasia Journal* 4, no. 1 (1977): 23–90.

Magnússon, Sigurður Gylfi. "The Singularization of History: Social History and

Microhistory within the Postmodern State of Knowledge." *Journal of Social History* 36, no. 3 (2003): 701–735.

Malone, Michael P. *The Battle for Butte: Mining and Politics on the Northern Frontier, 1864–1906.* Seattle: University of Washington Press, 2006.

Mar, Lisa Rose. *Brokering Belonging: Chinese in Canada's Exclusion Era, 1885–1945.* New York: Oxford University Press, 2010.

Marinbach, Bernard. *Galveston, Ellis Island of the West.* Albany: State University of New York Press, 1983.

Martens, Jeremy. "A Transnational History of Immigration Restriction: Natal and New South Wales, 1896–97." *Journal of Imperial and Commonwealth History* 34, no. 3 (2006): 323–344.

Martin, Lauren. "Governing through the Family: Struggles over US Noncitizen Family Detention Policy." *Environment and Planning A*, 44 (2012): 866–888.

Masumoto, Marie. "Griffith Park (Detention Facility)." *Densho Encyclopedia.* http://encyclopedia.densho.org, accessed October 1, 2014.

Matar, Hisham. "The Return." *The New Yorker*, April 8, 2013.

Matsuda, Matt K. *Pacific Worlds: A History of Seas, Peoples, and Cultures.* New York: Cambridge University Press, 2012.

Mbembe, Achille. "Necropolitics." Translated by Libby Meintje. *Public Culture* 15 (2003): 11–40.

McCoy, Alfred W., Francisco A. Scarano, and Courtney Johnson. "On the Tropic of Cancer: Transitions and Transformations in the U.S. Imperial State." In *Colonial Crucible: Empire in the Making of the Modern American State.* Edited by Alfred W. McCoy and Francisco A. Scarano, 3–33. Madison: University of Wisconsin Press, 2009.

McElroy, Ethan. "Kirkbride Buildings." www.kirkbridebuildings.com/, accessed October 23, 2019.

McKelvey, Blake. "Historic Origins of Rochester's Social Welfare Agencies." *Rochester History* 9, nos. 2–3 (1947): 1–36.

———. *Rochester on the Genessee: The Growth of a City.* 2nd edition. Syracuse, NY: Syracuse University Press, 1993.

McKeown, Adam. *Melancholy Order: Asian Migration and the Globalization of Borders.* New York: Columbia University Press, 2008.

———. "Ritualization of Regulation: The Enforcement of Chinese Exclusion in the United States and China." *American Historical Review* 108, no. 2 (April 2003): 377–403.

McLennan, Rebecca M. *The Crisis of Imprisonment: Protest, Politics, and the Making of the American Penal State, 1776–1941.* New York: Cambridge University Press, 2008.

McMillan, James. "War." In *Political Violence in Twentieth Century Europe.* Edited by Donald Bloxham and Robert Gerwith, 40–86. Cambridge, UK: Cambridge University Press, 2011.

McShane, Steve. "The Magic City of Steel." U.S. Steel Gary Works Photograph

Collection, 1906–1971. Indiana University. http://webapp1.dlib.indiana.edu/ussteel/context/essay.jsp, accessed November 28, 2018.

McWilliams, Carey. *Factories in the Field: The Story of Migratory Farm Labor in California*. Berkeley: University of California Press, 1939.

Mercier, Laurie. *Anaconda: Labor, Community, and Culture in Montana's Smelter City*. Urbana: University of Illinois Press, 2001.

Mikolji, Boris H. "Ethnic Groups in America: The Italians of Rochester." *Il Politico* 36, no. 4 (December 1971): 660–682.

Miller, Douglas K. *Indians on the Move: Native American Mobility and Urbanization in the Twentieth Century*. Chapel Hill: University of North Carolina Press, 2019.

Miller, Heather Lee. "Trick Identities: The Nexus of Sex and Work." *Journal of Women's History* 5, no. 4 (2004): 145–152.

Miroff, Nick. "ICE Air: Shackled Deportees, Air Freshener and Cheers. America's One-Way Trip Out." *Washington Post*, August 11, 2019.

Mogelson, Luke. "The Storm," *The New Yorker* (January 25, 2021): 32–53.

Mohl, Raymond A., and Neil Betten. *Steel City: Urban and Ethnic Patterns in Gary, Indiana, 1906–1950*. New York: Holmes & Meier, 1986.

Molina, Natalia. "Deportable Citizens: The Decoupling of Race and Citizenship in the Construction of the 'Anchor Baby.'" In *Deportation in the Americas: Histories of Exclusion and Resistance*. Edited by Kenyon Zimmer and Cristina Salinas, 164–191. College Station: Texas A&M University Press, 2018.

———. *Fit to Be Citizens? Public Health and Race in Los Angeles, 1879–1939*. Berkeley: University of California Press, 2006.

Moloney, Deirdre M. *National Insecurities: Immigrants and U.S. Deportation Policy since 1882*. Chapel Hill: University of North Carolina Press, 2012.

———. "Women, Sexual Morality, and Economic Dependency in Early U.S. Deportation Policy." *Journal of Women's History* 18, no. 2 (2006): 95–122.

Mone, John. "Deported Immigrants Get on 'ICE Air.'" *Associated Press*, December 17, 2018. www.youtube.com/watch?v=O2AxkpM9Nsg, accessed August 17, 2020.

Monkman, Lenard. "'No Ban on Stolen Land,' Say Indigenous Activists in U.S." *CBC News*, February 2, 2017.

Montejano, David. *Anglos and Mexicans in the Making of Texas*. Austin: University of Texas Press, 1987.

Montgomery, David. *The Fall of the House of Labor: The Workplace, the State, and American Labor Activism, 1865–1925*. New York: Cambridge University Press, 1987.

Moreno, Barry. *Encyclopedia of Ellis Island*. Westport, CT: Greenwood Press, 2004.

Morgensen, Scott Lauria. "Theorising Gender, Sexuality and Settler Colonialism: An Introduction." *Settler Colonial Studies* 2, no. 2 (2012): 2–22.

Motomura, Hiroshi. *Americans in Waiting: The Lost Story of Immigration and Citizenship in the United States*. New York: Oxford University Press, 2006.

Mouzelis, Nicos P. *Modern Greece: Facets of Underdevelopment*. London: Macmillan, 1978.

Movement for Black Lives. "Vision for Black Lives." https://m4bl.org/policy-platforms/, accessed March 22, 2021.

Muwekma Ohlone Tribe. "Historical Overview." www.muwekma.org/tribal history/historicaloverview.html, accessed December 2, 2019.

Nash, Horace Daniel. "Town and Sword: Black Soldiers in Columbus, New Mexico, in the Early Twentieth Century." PhD dissertation, Mississippi State University, 1996.

Netz, Reviel. *Barbed Wire: An Ecology of Modernity*. Middletown, CT: Wesleyan University Press, 2004.

Ngai, Mae M. "Hart-Celler at Fifty: Lessons for Immigration Reform in Our Time." *Labor* 12, no. 3 (2015): 19–22.

———. *Impossible Subjects: Illegal Aliens and the Making of Modern America*. Princeton, NJ: Princeton University Press, 2004.

———. *The Lucky Ones: One Family and the Extraordinary Invention of Chinese America*. Boston: Houghton Mifflin Harcourt, 2010.

———. "The Strange Career of the Illegal Alien: Immigration Restriction and Deportation Policy in the United States, 1921–1965." *Law and History Review* 21, no. 1 (2003): 69–107.

Nielsen, Margaret Stines. "The Korean Connection." *Buffalo Tales: Buffalo County Historical Society* 20, no. 3 (1997). www.bchs.us/BTales_199705.html, accessed January 11, 2017.

Nobles, Melissa. *Shades of Citizenship: Race and the Census in Modern Politics*. Stanford, CA: Stanford University Press, 2000.

Noel, Thomas J., and Nicholas Wharton. *Denver Landmarks & Historic Districts*. Boulder, CO: University Press of Colorado, 2016.

Noll, Richard. *American Madness: The Rise and Fall of Dementia Praecox*. Cambridge, MA: Harvard University Press, 2011.

Norris, Frank. *The Octopus: A Story of California*. Garden City, NY: Doubleday, 1901.

Novak, William J. "The Myth of the 'Weak' American State." *American Historical Review* 113, no. 3 (2008): 752–772.

Nugent, Walter. *Crossings: The Great Transatlantic Migrations, 1870–1914*. Bloomington: Indiana University Press, 1992.

———. "Demography: Chicago as a Modern World City." *Encyclopedia of Chicago*, www.encyclopedia.chicagohistory.org/pages/962.html, accessed March 15, 2021.

Omi, Michael, and Howard Winant. *Racial Formation in the United States: From the 1960s to the 1990s*. 2nd edition. New York: Routledge, 1994.

Oppenheimer, Ruben. National Commission on Law Observance and Enforcement. "Report on the Enforcement of the Deportation Laws of the United States." Washington, DC: Government Printing Office, 1931.

Orsi, Richard J. *Sunset Limited: The Southern Pacific Railroad and the Development of the American West, 1850–1930*. Berkeley: University of California Press, 2005.

Orsi, Robert Anthony. *The Madonna of 115th Street: Faith and Community in Italian Harlem, 1880–1950*. New Haven, CT: Yale University Press, 1985.

Ortiz, Simon J. "Indigenous Activism: Our Resistance, Our Revitalization, Our Indigenous Native Studies: And Our Healing within Our Indigenous Context (or From Alcatraz 1969 to Standing Rock 2017. Or Perhaps—Truth Be Bold—Liars, Killers, Thieves Invade Sacred Stone Camp)." American Indian Studies Association Conference Keynote Address. *Wicazo Sa Review* 32, no. 2 (Fall 2017): 106–114.

Otjen, Nathaniel. "Creating a Barrio in Iowa City, 1916–1936: Mexican Section Laborers and the Chicago, Rock Island and Pacific Railroad Company." *Annals of Iowa* 76, no. 4 (2017): 406–432.

Paik, A. Naomi. *Bans, Walls, Raids, Sanctuary: Understanding U.S. Immigration in the Twenty-first Century*. Oakland: University of California Press, 2020.

———. *Rightlessness: Testimony and Redress in U.S. Prison Camps since World War II*. Chapel Hill: University of North Carolina Press, 2016.

Papadopoulos, Dimitris, Niamh Stephenson, and Vassilis Tsianos. *Escape Routes: Control and Subversion in the Twenty-First Century*. London: Pluto, 2008.

Pappas, Mitcho M. "The Greek Immigrant in the United States since 1910." MA thesis, Montana State University, 1949.

Parish, Mickey. "How Do Salt and Sugar Prevent Microbial Spoilage?" *Scientific American* (February 21, 2006). www.scientificamerican.com/article/how-do -salt-and-sugar-pre/, accessed October 10, 2019.

Parker, Kunal M. *Making Foreigners: Immigration and Citizenship Law in America, 1600–2000*. New York: Cambridge University Press, 2015.

Pascoe, Peggy. *Relations of Rescue: The Search for Female Moral Authority in the American West, 1874–1939*. New York: Oxford University Press, 1990.

Peck, Gunther. "Padrones and Protest: 'Old' Radicals and 'New' Immigrants in Bingham, Utah, 1905–1912." *Western Historical Quarterly* 24, no. 2 (1993): 157–178.

———. *Reinventing Free Labor: Padrones and Immigrant Workers in the North American West, 1880–1930*. New York: Cambridge University Press, 2000.

Pegler-Gordon, Anna. *In Sight of America: Photography and the Development of U.S. Immigration Policy*. Berkeley: University of California Press, 2009.

———. "Shanghaied on the Streets of Hoboken: Chinese Exclusion and Maritime Regulation at Ellis Island." *Journal for Maritime Research* 16, no. 2 (July 3, 2014): 229–245.

Persons, C. E. "Women's Work and Wages in the United States." *Quarterly Journal of Economics* 29, no. 2 (1915): 201–234.

Pettit, Michael. "Becoming Glandular: Endocrinology, Mass Culture, and Experimental Lives in the Interwar Age." *American Historical Review* 118, no. 4 (2013): 1052–1076.

Pfaelzer, Jean. *Driven Out: The Forgotten War against Chinese Americans*. Berkeley: University of California Press, 2007.

Phillips Preiss Shapiro Associates, Inc., "Redevelopment Study for the Hoboken Terminal & Yard of the City of Hoboken." Prepared for the City of Hoboken Planning Board, 2006. www.hobokennj.org/pdf/mplan/Redevelopment_Plans /Hoboken_Rail_Yards/HobokenRailYards.pdf, accessed April 5, 2013.

Piperoglou, Andonis. "'Border Barbarisms,' Albury 1902: Greeks and the Ambiguity of Whiteness." *Australian Journal of Politics and History* 64, no. 4 (2018): 529–534.

———. "Vagrant 'Gypsies' and Respectable Greeks: A Defining Moment in Early–Colonial Melbourne, 1897–1900." In *Reading, Interpreting, Experiencing: An Inter-Cultural Journey into Greek Letters*. Edited by M. Tsianikas, G. Couvalis, and M. Palaktsoglou, 140–151. Modern Greek Studies Association of New Zealand, 2015.

Pliley, Jessica R. *Policing Sexuality: The Mann Act and the Making of the FBI*. Cambridge, MA: Harvard University Press, 2014.

Pony Express Museum. http://ponyexpress.org/, accessed October 1, 2019.

Pope-Obeda, Emily. "'When in Doubt, Deport!': U.S. Deportation and the Local Policing of Global Migration during the 1920s." PhD dissertation, University of Illinois at Urbana-Champaign, 2016.

Post, Louis F. *The Deportations Delirium of Nineteen-Twenty*. Chicago: Charles H. Kerr, 1923.

Presner, Todd Samuel, David Shepard, and Yoh Kawano. *HyperCities: Thick Mapping in the Digital Humanities*. Cambridge, MA: Harvard University Press, 2014.

Preston, William. *Aliens and Dissenters: Federal Suppression of Radicals, 1903–1933*. 2nd edition. Urbana: University of Illinois Press, 1994.

"Pullman Prison Car for Alien Criminals: Seattle Rushes Ten of Them East and Deports Them under the Mann Act." *New York Times*, June 6, 1913.

Quillen, Isaac James. "Industrial City: A History of Gary, Indiana to 1929." PhD dissertation, Yale University, 1942.

Ransby, Barbara. *Making All Black Lives Matter: Reimagining Freedom in the Twenty-first Century*. Oakland: University of California Press, 2018.

Reaume, Geoffrey. "Mad People's History." *Radical History Review* 94 (2006): 170–182.

Reddy, Chandan. *Freedom with Violence: Race, Sexuality, and the US State*. Durham, NC: Duke University Press, 2011.

Redmond, Tom, and Vickie Devenport. "US Department of the Interior, Illinois Central Railroad Passenger Depot, National Register of Historic Places Registration." December 4, 2001. http://gis.hpa.state.il.us/pdfs/219007.pdf, accessed August 27, 2019.

Reed, Edgar P. "Rochester and the Shoe Industry." *Quarterly Journal of the New York State Historical Association* 1, no. 5 (1920): 241–243.

Reed, Katherine. "'The Prison, By God, Where I Have Found Myself': Graffiti at

Ellis Island Immigration Station, New York, c. 1900–1923." *Journal of American Ethnic History* 38, no. 3 (2019): 5–35.

Reeder, Linda. "When the Men Left Sutera: Sicilian Women and Mass Migration, 1880–1920." In *Women, Gender, and Transnational Lives: Italian Workers of the World*. Edited by Donna Gabaccia and Franca Iacovetta, 45–75. Toronto: University of Toronto Press, 2002.

"Rejoices at the Fall of Schmitz in 'Frisco." *Boston Sunday Herald*. June 16, 1907. www.sfmuseum.org/conflag/phelan.html.

Richter, Amy G. *Home on the Rails: Women, the Railroad, and the Rise of Public Domesticity*. Chapel Hill: University of North Carolina Press, 2005.

Roberts, Barbara Ann. *Whence They Came: Deportation from Canada, 1900–1935*. Ottawa: University of Ottawa Press, 1988.

Robinson, Cedric J. *Black Marxism: The Making of the Black Radical Tradition*. Chapel Hill: University of North Carolina Press, 2000.

Robinson, Mary V. *Domestic Workers and Their Employment Relations: A Study Based on the Records of the Domestic Efficiency Association of Baltimore, Maryland*. Washington, DC: Government Printing Office, 1924. https://catalog .hathitrust.org/Record/003263016, accessed March 1, 2019.

Roe, Clifford G., and B. S. Steadwell, eds. *The Great War on White Slavery; Or, Fighting for the Protection of Our Girls*. N.p., 1911.

Roediger, David R. *The Wages of Whiteness: Race and the Making of the American Working Class*. New York: Verso, 1991.

Romero, Robert Chao. *The Chinese in Mexico, 1882–1940*. Tucson: University of Arizona Press, 2010.

Romo, David Dorado. "To Understand the El Paso Shooter, Look to the Long Legacy of Anti-Mexican Violence at the Border." *Texas Observer*, August 9, 2019. www.texasobserver.org/to-understand-the-el-paso-massacre-look-to-the -long-legacy-of-anti-mexican-violence-at-the-border/, accessed August 13, 2019.

Rosas, Gilberto. *Barrio Libre: Criminalizing States and Delinquent Refusals of the New Frontier*. Durham, NC: Duke University Press, 2012.

Rose, Nikolas S. *Powers of Freedom: Reframing Political Thought*. Cambridge, UK: Cambridge University Press, 1999.

Rose, Sarah F. *No Right to Be Idle: The Invention of Disability, 1840s–1930s*. Chapel Hill: University of North Carolina Press, 2017.

Rosen, Ruth. *The Lost Sisterhood: Prostitution in America, 1900–1918*. Baltimore, MD: Johns Hopkins University Press, 1982.

Rosenberg-Naparsteck, Ruth. "A Brief History of Rochester Childfirst Network." *Rochester History* (Fall 2006): 3–23.

Ross, Luana. *Inventing the Savage: The Social Construction of Native American Criminality*. Austin: University of Texas Press, 1998.

Ruiz, Vicki L. Foreword to *Traqueros: Mexican Railroad Workers in the United States, 1870–1930*, by Jeffrey Marcos Garcilazo. Denton: University of North Texas Press, 2012.

Sakovich, Maria. "When the 'Enemy' Landed at Angel Island." *Prologue* 41, no.

2 (2009). www.archives.gov/publications/prologue/2009/summer/angel.html, accessed April 22, 2013.

Saloutos, Theodore. *The Greeks in the United States*. Cambridge, MA: Harvard University Press, 1975.

Salyer, Lucy E. *Laws Harsh as Tigers: Chinese Immigrants and the Shaping of Modern Immigration Law*. Chapel Hill: University of North Carolina Press, 1995.

Sanborne Map, El Paso. 1908. Key, http://legacy.lib.utexas.edu/maps/sanborn /d-f/txu-sanborn-el_paso-1908-1k.jpg, accessed January 22, 2019.

Sánchez, George J. *Becoming Mexican American: Ethnicity, Culture, and Identity in Chicano Los Angeles, 1900–1945*. New York: Oxford University Press, 1993.

Santino, Jack. *Miles of Smiles, Years of Struggle: Stories of Black Pullman Porters*. Urbana: University of Illinois Press, 1991.

Santos, Robert L. *Azoreans to California: A History of Migration and Settlement*. Denair, CA: Alley-Cass Publications, 1995.

Sassen, Saskia. *Expulsions: Brutality and Complexity in the Global Economy*. Cambridge, MA: Harvard University Press, 2014.

Schneider, Lindsey. "(Re)producing the Nation: Treaty Rights, Gay Marriage, and the Settler State." In *Critical Ethnic Studies: A Reader*. Edited by the Critical Ethnic Studies Collective, 92–105. Durham, NC: Duke University Press, 2016.

Schwantes, Carlos A. "The Concept of the Wageworkers Frontier: A Framework for Future Research." *Western Historical Quarterly* 18, no. 1 (1987): 39–55.

Schweik, Susan M. *The Ugly Laws: Disability in Public*. New York: New York University, 2009.

Scott Clark interview. In "Insane Asylums: Mental Retreat or Living Hell," by Taylor Chase. https://83681755.weebly.com/state-lunatic-asylum-no-2.html, accessed October 23, 2019.

Scully, Michael F. *The Never-Ending Revival: Rounder Records and the Folk Alliance*. Chicago: University of Illinois Press, 2008.

Seigel, Micol. *Violence Work: State Power and the Limits of Police*. Durham, NC: Duke University Press, 2018.

Serlin, David. *Replaceable You: Engineering the Body in Postwar America*. Chicago: University of Chicago Press, 2004.

Shah, Nayan. *Contagious Divides: Epidemics and Race in San Francisco's Chinatown*. Berkeley: University of California Press, 2001.

———. *Stranger Intimacy: Contesting Race, Sexuality, and the Law in the North American West*. Berkeley: University of California Press, 2011.

Shear, Michael D., and Ron Nixon. "New Trump Deportation Rules Allow Far More Expulsions." *New York Times*, February 21, 2017.

Shear, Michael D., Katie Benner, and Michael S. Schmidt. "'We Need to Take Away Children,' No Matter How Young, Justice Dept. Officials Said." *New York Times*, October 6, 2020.

Shin, Linda. "Koreans in America, 1903–1945." *Amerasia Journal* 1, no. 3 (1971): 32–39.

"Ship/Pacific Liners." *Encyclopedia Britannica*, 1911. https://en.wikisource.org /wiki/1911_Encyclop%C3%A6dia_Britannica/Ship#PacificLiners, accessed November 25, 2019.

Silva, Noenoe K. *Aloha Betrayed: Native Hawaiian Resistance to American Colonialism*. Durham, NC: Duke University Press, 2004.

Sinclair, Upton. *The Jungle*. New York: Grosset & Dunlop, 1906, www.gutenberg .org/files/140/140-h/140-h.htm.

Singh, Nikhil Pal. *Race and America's Long War*. Berkeley: University of California Press, 2017.

Sitton, Sarah C. *Life at the Texas State Lunatic Asylum, 1857–1997*. College Station: Texas A & M University Press, 1999.

Skowronek, Stephen. *Building a New American State: The Expansion of National Administrative Capacities, 1877–1920*. New York: Cambridge University Press, 1982.

Smith, Michael M. "Beyond the Borderlands: Mexican Labor in the Central Plains, 1900–1930." *Great Plains Quarterly* (1981): 239–251.

Smith, Rodgers M. *Civic Ideals: Conflicting Visions of Citizenship in US History*. New Haven, CT: Yale University Press, 1999.

Sohi, Seema. *Echoes of Mutiny: Race, Surveillance, and Indian Anti-Colonialism in North America*. New York: Oxford University Press, 2014.

Soja, Edward W. *Postmodern Geographies: The Reassertion of Space in Critical Social Theory*. New York: Verso, 1989.

"Southern Pacific Announces Plans for Depot." *San Francisco Chronicle*, November 25, 1912. www.sfmuseum.net/hist7/spdepot.html, accessed 20 November 20, 2019.

"Special Immigrant Visa Holders Still Face Questioning Upon Reaching U.S." *National Public Radio*, Morning Edition, March 27, 2017.

"SS Retriever." *Wreck Site*. www.wrecksite.eu/wreck.aspx?98835, accessed December 8, 2016.

St. John, Rachel. *Line in the Sand: A History of the Western U.S.-Mexico Border*. Princeton, NJ: Princeton University Press, 2011.

Stanley, Leo L., with Evelyn Wells. *Men at Their Worst*. New York: D. Appleton-Century, 1940.

Steadwell, B. S. "The Great Purity Movement." In *The Great War on White Slavery*. Edited by Clifford G. Roe and B. S. Steadwell, 442–448. N.p., 1911.

Steiner, Edward A. *On the Trail of the Immigrant*. New York: Flemming H. Revell, 1906.

Stern, Alexandra Minna. *Eugenic Nation: Faults and Frontiers of Better Breeding in Modern America*. Berkeley: University of California Press, 2005.

Suh, Chris. "What Yun Ch'i-ho Knew: U.S.-Japan Relations and Imperial Race Making in Korea and the American South, 1904–1919." *Journal of American History* 104, no. 1 (2017): 73–81.

Szczepzniec, Kristin. *Indigenous People of Western New York*. Cornell University ILR Digital Commons, February 2018. https://digitalcommons.ilr.cornell.edu

/cgi/viewcontent.cgi?article=1376&context=buffalocommons, accessed April 2, 2019.

Takaki, Ronald T. *Strangers from a Different Shore: A History of Asian Americans.* New York: Penguin Books, 1989.

Takenaka, Ayumi. "The Japanese in Peru: History of Immigration, Settlement, and Racialization." *Latin American Perspectives* 31, no. 3 (May 2004): 77–98.

"Taking Names." *This American Life*, no. 499, June 28, 2013.

Taillon, Paul Michel. *Good, Reliable, White Men: Railroad Brotherhoods, 1877–1917.* Urbana: University of Illinois Press, 2009.

Tate, E. Mowbray. *Transpacific Steam: The Story of Steam Navigation from the Pacific Coast of North America to the Far East and the Antipodes, 1867–1941.* New York: Cornwall Books, 1986.

Taylor, Keeanga-Yamahtta. *From #BlackLivesMatter to Black Liberation.* Chicago: Haymarket Books, 2016.

———, ed. *How We Get Free: Black Feminism and the Combahee River Collective.* New York: Haymarket Books, 2017.

"*Tenyo Maru* Reading Room" postcard. *The Daily Postcard.* http://postcardparadise .blogspot.com/2011/09/ss-tenyo-maru.html, accessed November 25, 2019.

Thelen, David P. *Paths of Resistance: Tradition and Dignity in Industrializing Missouri.* New York: Oxford University Press, 1986.

Thornton, Willis. "Kline's Deportation Party Is a Grim Affair for Aliens." *Milwaukee Journal*, January 11, 1940.

Thrush, Coll-Peter, and Robert H. Keller Jr. "'I See What I Have Done': The Life and Murder Trial of Xwelas, a S'Klallam Woman." *Western Historical Quarterly* 26, no. 2 (1995): 168–183.

Timmons, Patrick. "Trump's Wall at Nixon's Border." *NACLA Report on the Americas* 49 (March 2017): 15–24.

Truett, Samuel. *Fugitive Landscapes: The Forgotten History of the U.S.-Mexico Borderlands.* New Haven, CT: Yale University Press, 2006.

Trump, Donald J. "Transcript of Donald Trump's Immigration Speech." *New York Times*, September 1, 2016.

Twain, Mark. *The Innocents Abroad.* New York: P. F. Collier & Son, 1911.

Uchida, Jun. *Brokers of Empire: Japanese Settler Colonialism in Korea, 1876–1945.* Cambridge, MA: Harvard University Press, 2011.

University of Washington Center for Human Rights. "Hidden in Plain Sight: ICE Air and the Machinery of Mass Deportation." UW Center for Human Rights Report, April 23, 2019. http://jsis.washington.edu/humanrights/2019/04 /23/ice-air/, accessed February 21, 2020.

Urban, Andrew. "Asylum in the Midst of Chinese Exclusion: Pershing's Punitive Expedition and the Columbus Refugees from Mexico, 1916–1921." *Journal of Policy History* 23, no. 2 (April 2011): 204–229.

———. *Brokering Servitude: Migration and the Politics of Domestic Servitude during the Long Nineteenth Century.* New York: New York University Press, 2018.

———. "Restricted Cargo: Chinese Sailors, Shore Leave, and the Evolution of

U.S. Immigration Policies, 1882–1942." In *People-Works: The Labor of Transport*. Edited by Kate McDonald (2018). https://t2m.org/restricted-cargo-chinese -sailors-shore-leave-and-the-evolution-of-u-s-immigration-policies-1882-1942/, accessed August 23, 2019.

US Department of Interior. "National Register of Historic Places Inventory— Nomination Form, Erie-Lackawanna Railroad Terminal at Hoboken," filed July 24, 1973.

———. "National Register of Historic Places Registration Form—St. Joseph Mo, Livestock Exchange Building," filed March 4, 2004.

US Congress. "California and the Oriental—Japanese, Chinese, and Hindus— Report of the State Board of Control of California." In *Japanese Immigration: Hearings before the Committee on Immigration and Naturalization*. Sixty-sixth Congress, 2d session, 1920, Part 1. Washington, DC: Government Printing Office, 1921.

US Immigration and Customs Enforcement. *Fiscal Year 2017 ICE Enforcement and Removal Operations Report*. www.ice.gov/sites/default/files/documents /Report/2017/iceEndOfYearFY2017.pdf.

Van Vleck, William C. *The Administrative Control of Aliens: A Study in Administrative Law and Procedure*. New York: The Commonwealth Fund, 1932. Reprint, New York: Da Capo Press, 1971.

Vargas, Zaragosa. *Proletarians of the North: A History of Mexican Industrial Workers in Detroit and the Midwest, 1917–1933*. Berkeley: University of California Press, 1993.

Vélez-Ibáñez, Carlos G. *Border Visions: Mexican Cultures of the Southwest United States*. Tucson: University of Arizona Press, 1996.

Veracini, Lorenzo. *The Settler Colonial Present*. New York: Palgrave Macmillan, 2015.

Waldman, Peter, Lizette Chapman, and Jordan Robertson. "Palantir Knows Everything about You." *Bloomberg Businessweek*, April 19, 2018.

Wallerstein, Immanuel. *The Modern World System*. Vol. 1, *Capitalist Agriculture and the Origins of the European World-Economy in the Sixteenth Century*. New York: Academic Press, 1974.

"A Walking Haberdashery." *Kansas City Journal*, February 7, 1910. www .vintagekansascity.com/100yearsago/labels/mental%20health.html, accessed October 24, 2019.

Walters, William. "Aviation as Deportation Infrastructure: Airports, Planes, and Expulsion." *Journal of Ethnic and Migration Studies* 44, no. 2 (2017): 1–22.

———. "Deportation, Expulsion, and the International Police of Aliens." In *The Deportation Regime: Sovereignty, Space, and the Freedom of Movement*. Edited by Nicholas De Genova and Nathalie Peutz, 69–100. Durham, NC: Duke University Press, 2010.

———. "Flight of the Deported: Aircraft, Deportation, and Politics." *Geopolitics* 21, no. 2 (2016): 435–458.

Weheliye, Alexander G. *Habeas Viscus: Racializing Assemblages, Biopolitics, and*

Black Feminist Theories of the Human. Durham, NC: Duke University Press, 2014.

Welsh, Joe, Bill Howes, and Kevin J. Holland. *The Cars of Pullman*. Minneapolis, MN: Voyageur Press, 2010.

White, Richard. *The Organic Machine: The Remaking of the Columbia River*. New York: Hill and Wang, 1995.

———. *Railroaded: The Transcontinentals and the Making of Modern America*. New York: W. W. Norton & Co., 2011.

White, William C. "Ellis Island Altered by Immigration Trends." *New York Times*, October 8, 1933.

Wilkinson, Charles F., and Eric R. Biggs. "The Evolution of Termination Policy." *American Indian Law Review* 5, no. 139 (1977): 139–184.

Williams, William. "Ellis Island: Its Organization and Some of Its Work" (1912). Appendix 1 in Barry Moreno, *Encyclopedia of Ellis Island*. Westport, CT: Greenwood Press, 2004.

Wilson, Tamar Diana. Introduction to *Latin American Perspectives* 31, no. 3, East Asian Migration to Latin America (2004): 3–17.

Winston, Bryan. "Mexican Migrants in Urban Missouri: Social Welfare Institutions and Racial Boundaries in Kansas City and St. Louis, 1915–1940." *Missouri Historical Review* 113, no. 4 (2019): 269–283.

Winther, Oscar Osburn. *The Transportation Frontier: Trans-Mississippi West, 1865–1890*. Albuquerque: University of New Mexico Press, 1964.

Wolfe, Patrick. "Land, Labor, and Difference: Elementary Structures of Race." *American Historical Review* 106, no. 3 (2001): 866–905.

———. "Settler Colonialism and the Elimination of the Native." *Journal of Genocide Research* 8, no. 4 (2006): 387–409.

———. *Settler Colonialism and the Transformation of Anthropology: The Politics and Poetics of an Ethnographic Event*. London: Cassell, 1999.

Wolmar, Christian. *The Great Railroad Revolution: The History of Trains in America*. 1st US edition. New York: Public Affairs, 2012.

"Workhouse Not Fit Place for Insane." *Kansas City Journal*, July 14, 1909. www.vintagekansascity.com/100yearsago/labels/Col.%20J.%20C.%20Greenman.html, accessed October 24, 2019.

Workman, Travis. *Imperial Genus: The Formation and Limits of the Human in Modern Korea and Japan*. Oakland: University of California Press, 2016.

Ye, Weili. *Seeking Modernity in China's Name: Chinese Students in the United States, 1900–1927*. Stanford, CA: Stanford University Press, 2001.

Young, Elliott. *Alien Nation: Chinese Migration in the Americas from the Coolie Era through World War II*. Chapel Hill: University of North Carolina Press, 2014.

Zamora, Emilio. *The World of the Mexican Worker in Texas*. College Station: Texas A&M University Press, 1993.

Zimmer, Kenyon. *Immigrants against the State: Yiddish and Italian Anarchism in America*. Urbana: University of Illinois Press, 2015.

————. "The Voyage of the *Buford*: Political Deportations and the Making and Unmaking of America's First Red Scare." In *Deportation in the Americas: Histories of Exclusion and Resistance.* Edited by Kenyon Zimmer and Cristina Salinas, 132–163. College Station: Texas A&M University Press, 2018.

Zolberg, Aristide R. "Global Movements, Global Walls: Responses to Migration, 1885–1925." In *Global History and Migrations.* Edited by Wang Gungwu, 297–307. Boulder, CO: Westview Press, 2008.

————. *A Nation by Design: Immigration Policy in the Fashioning of America.* Cambridge, MA: Harvard University Press, 2006.

304–5n44; networks within, 69, 91; relation to colonial modernity, 89, 217

racisms: anti-Asian, 41, 102–3, 221, 239–40, 245, 250, 262–63, 268, 274, 358n29, 367n23, 368n34; anti-Black, 103, 139, 156, 173, 183, 194, 197, 199, 234, 247, 250, 263, 272, 294, 299–300n9, 326n28; anti-Greek, 134, 139; anti-Indigenous, 8–10, 12–13, 63, 77, 96, 102, 138, 189, 239, 242, 247, 263, 266, 292; anti-Mexican, 187, 196–97, 199, 209–10, 212; and mobility, 12, 294; scientific, 6, 134, 153, 160. *See also* nativism

radicalism, 4, 102, 129–31, 177–78, 181–82, 183, 280, 287. *See also* anarchism; communism; Ghadr Movement; Industrial Workers of the World

railroads: colonial conquest, 7–9, 112–13, 137–38, 234–35, 302–3n28; deportation infrastructure, 4–5, 13, 17, 23, 33, 170; labor (*see also* Mexicans: *traqueros*), 7–8, 71, 137, 140, 188, 191–95, 198, 205–8, 257, 349–50n29, 351n48, 351n49, 351n53, 353n88, 354n107; mythology of, 7, 9–11; political economy, 8, 79, 110, 112–13, 116, 135, 137–38, 188–90, 257–59, 350n33

Ram, Salig, 69, 71, 73, 75–77, 279, 286, 322n24

Ramírez, Angel, 204, 206, 208, 211–12, 235

Ranjel, Concepcíon, 187, 204, 208, 211, 235

Raume, Geoffrey, 364–65n85

Red Scare, 43, 292

Reed, Edgar, 163

Rhee, Syngman, 229, 358n40

Rio Grande, 205, 257–58

Mr. Roak (immigration inspector), 147–48, 150

Robert Emmet Literary Association, 120, 127

Robidoux, Joseph, 189

Robinson, Cedric J., 300–301n14, 304n38

Rochester, New York: demography, 154–55; geography, 154–55, 188; Haudenosaunee worlds, 155; Industrial School, 156–57; migration to, 154–55, 162; police department, 162; political economy, 156–57, 160, 162–65; shoe industry, 162–63

Rock Island Lines, 33, 40, 190, 192, 195, 206–7, 212, 350n33

Rock Island Magazine, 206

Rocky Mountains, 112–13

Romania, 176; authorities of, 31; migrants from, 144, 206

Roosevelt, Theodore, 33, 228

Rose, Nikolas, 305n51

Mr. Rowe (immigration inspector), 166

Russell, Leo, 43–46, 48–50, 52, 168–69, 317n106

Russia, 135, 217–18; migrants from, 142, 174, 196, 198

Sacramento, California, 103–4, 224, 231*m*

Saint Joseph, Missouri, 187, 189, 195–97, 199, 202, 204–6, 208–9, 213*m*; ethnic Mexican boxcar communities, 206–10; State Hospital at, 200

Saint Louis, Missouri, 38, 133, 195–96, 204, 225, 227–28, 230, 258

Salt Lake City, Utah, 35, 220, 232*m*

Samish people, 64

San Antonio, Texas, 1, 18*m*, 21, 184*m*, 203*m*, 213*m*, 232*m*, 234–36, 246–49, 252, 255*m*, 256–57; County Jail of, 249; Sunset Station, 234, 256

San Antonio Express, 247

San Francisco, California: geography, 96–97, 276; immigration office, 33, 36, 38, 41, 51, 288; migration to/through, 28, 71, 96–98, 101–2, 115, 135, 168, 220, 238, 245, 261, 262; Ohlone peoples, 276; political economy, 96–98, 258, 276, 286; radicalism, 67–68, 224; as removal site, 34–35, 37, 40, 77, 96–97, 228, 276, 282, 284–85; Southern Pacific Station, 99, 276–77

San Quentin: State Penitentiary, 33, 52, 101–2, 132, 175; village, 98

Santa Fe, New Mexico, 193–94, 198, 258, 272

Santos, Robert, 106

São Bento (Azores), 102, 105

Sargent, Frank, 47

Sargent, John H., 29, 37, 64

Sassen, Saskia, 300n11

Mr. Schafer (inspector), 252–54

Soviet Union, 300n9, 312–13n29
space: as analytic, 10, 16–17, 70, 164, 191, 294, 306n54, 307n57, 316n90; carceral, 1, 4, 15, 20, 23, 29, 43–45, 170, 173–79, 181, 233, 244, 249–51, 269, 272, 275, 277–81, 286–87, 294, 299n5, 306n54; domestic, 140, 142–44, 207–8, 354n119; heterotopic, 308n62
Spofford Junction, Texas, 257, 259
Stanley, Leo L., 52, 98–101, 110, 132–34, 150–52, 167, 169–72, 231–34, 248, 276
Steadwell, B. S., 81
Steen, Emanuel, 172
steerage class, 62, 66, 180–81, 233, 236; "Asiatic," 236–38, 282–84, 289
Steiner, Edward, 180
Stephanie (character in *Strange Passage*), 109–10, 178–79
Stephens, Durham, 219
Stephens, William, 260
Stockton, California, 66, 71, 101; State Asylum, 99, 102, 104–5
Stoddard, Lothrop, 6
Strange Passage (1935), 4, 109, 168, 177, 299–300n9, 327n40
Strauss, New Mexico, 268, 273m
Sullivan, Hannah, 175
Sumas, Washington, 60–62
Sweden, 31, 142; migrants from, 3, 116, 142, 170, 181
Swift Airlines, 1–2

Takahashi, Kamechiyo, 280
Taldihari (India), 71
Tampico (Mexico), 265–68, 273m, 274, 369nn53, 55
Tarashima Tokizo, 257, 259, 261, 263–74, 273m, 277, 279, 282, 284–85, 367n21
Tatsuzō Ishikawa, 237
Taylor, James, 89
Taylor, Richard H., 33–37, 51–52
technology, 4–5, 27, 45, 189, 293, 306n54
Tejanx, 234, 244
telegraphy, 16, 30, 38–39, 113, 169, 258, 264, 368n40; codes, 39, 314–15n64; warrants, 30, 272, 312n26
Terceira (Azores), 102
Texas, 1, 53, 175, 190–94, 198, 216, 234, 241,

246–50, 252, 257, 271–72, 354n107; Pacific Railroad, 205; Rangers, 53, 241, 270
Mr. Thomas (officer), 269–72, 274
Thornton, Willis, 54–55
timber industry, 79–81, 190
Tohono O'odham people, 269
Tokuji Hoshino, 237
Topeka, Kansas, 195, 210
Torreón massacre, 240
Toyo Kisen Kaisha Line, 217, 236, 282–83, 285, 373n36
Trump, Donald, 6, 294–95
Tucson, Arizona, 36, 232m, 276
Turks, 3, 42, 136
Twain, Mark, 103, 314–15n64

Union of Russian Workers, 129
Union Pacific Railroad, 9, 96, 112, 116; station at Denver, 112–13
United States Line, 182
US Border Patrol, 53, 235, 270–71, 292, 295
US Coast and Geodetic Survey (USCGS), 50
US Congress, 6, 25, 262, 290; Pacific Railway Commission of, 7
US Department of Homeland Security, 5–6, 301n18, 310n6
US Department of Immigration, 49, 54, 130, 163
US Department of Justice, 121, 127, 131, 230, 310n6; Alien Enemy Bureau of, 121
US Department of Labor, 2, 30, 33, 50–51, 103, 130, 245, 296; predecessor and successor agencies in immigration, 26–27. *See also* Immigration Bureau
US Employment Service, 52
US-Mexico War (1846–1848), 53, 190
US State Department, 30, 312n29
US Steel, 136–38, 140–42, 145, 210, 338n30, 339n57
US Treasury Department, 26, 50, 60

Vallejo, Gumeciendo, 187–90, 204–6, 209, 211–12, 213m, 235, 267, 272, 276, 366n7
Vallejo family, 204–5, 211–12, 213m
Vancouver (Canada), 62, 64, 66, 68, 71, 73–74, 78m, 84, 87m